Issues for Debate in American Foreign Policy

**SECOND
EDITION**

⑤SAGE | **CQPRESS**

Los Angeles | London | New Delhi
Singapore | Washington DC

SELECTIONS FROM **CQ RESEARCHER**

CQ Press
2300 N Street, NW, Suite 800
Washington, DC 20037

Phone: 202-729-1900; toll-free, 1-866-4CQ-PRESS (1-866-427-7737)

Web: www.cqpress.com

Cover design: Cynthia Richardson
Cover photo: Getty Images

♾ The paper used in this publication exceeds the requirements of the American National Standard for Information Sciences—Permanence of Paper for Printed Library Materials, ANSI Z39.48-1992.

Printed and bound in the United States of America

15   13   12   11   10   1   2   3   4   5

A CQ Press College Division Publication

Executive director	Brenda Carter
Editorial director	Charisse Kiino
Acquisitions editor	Elise Frasier
Development editor	Dwain Smith
Marketing manager	Christopher O'Brien
Composition	C&M Digitals (P) Ltd.
Managing editor	Catherine Forrest Getzie
Production editor	Mirna Araklian
Production manager	Paul Pressau

The Library of Congress cataloged the first issue of this title as follows:

Library of Congress Cataloging-in-Publication Data

Issues for debate in American foreign policy : selections from CQ Researcher.
    p. cm.
  Includes bibliographical references.
  ISBN 978-1-60871-000-3 (pbk. : alk. paper) 1. United States—Foreign relations—2009- 2. United States—Foreign relations—2001-2009. 3. National security—United States. 4. United States—Military policy.
I. Congressional Quarterly, inc. II. CQ researcher

JZ1480.I87 2009
327.73—dc22

                                                                                    2009043857

Contents

Annotated Contents

The sixteen *CQ Researcher* reports reprinted in this book have been reproduced essentially as they appeared when first published. In the few cases in which important developments have since occurred, updates are provided in the overviews highlighting the principal issues examined.

SECURITY ISSUES

Attacking Piracy

After centuries of inactivity, piracy has returned with a vengeance. Maritime marauders now operate across the globe from Peru to the Philippines, but they pose the biggest threat off the coast of Somalia — a failed state in the Horn of Africa. In the first six months of 2009, attacks by Somali pirates jumped sixfold over the same period in the previous year. Piracy costs global shippers $10 billion to $50 billion a year in ransoms, lost cargoes, higher insurance premiums and disrupted shipping schedules — costs that are passed on to consumers. The world's largest navies have sent warships to the Horn of Africa in recent months and have captured more than 100 pirates. But it may be too costly to maintain the naval patrols over the long term. In addition, murky anti-piracy laws and jurisdictional issues are hampering prosecutions. Moreover, some security experts fear pirates may be exposing vulnerabilities that terrorists could exploit to disrupt global trade, raising the stakes in the fight to solve a growing international problem.

Confronting Rape as a War Crime

Rape has been a consequence of military defeat for millennia. But in the last 20 years — from Bosnia to Rwanda, from Colombia to the Democratic Republic of Congo — sexual violence against women, and sometimes even against men, has become a strategic military tactic designed to humiliate victims and shatter enemy societies. And increasingly, governments presiding over peaceful countries are using mass rape in deliberate and targeted campaigns to spread terror and humiliation among political dissenters, often during election seasons. The strategic use of rape has been recognized by international courts as an act of genocide and ethnic cleansing. The United Nations is working to change the mindset that wartime rape is inevitable, urging governments to end the violence and prosecute perpetrators. But silence and shame shroud the issue, and some governments that deny wartime rape occurs in their countries have banned international aid groups that treat their citizens who have been victimized. In the spring of 2010, the United Nations' first special representative for sexual violence began a two-year campaign to help curb the crime. But experts say strategic rape won't be easy to eradicate.

Dangerous War Debris

Long after the guns of war have gone silent, people around the world are killed or maimed every day by the "silent killers" of warfare — the tens of millions of landmines, cluster bombs and other unexploded ordnance that litter abandoned battlefields, farmland and urban areas. Most of the victims are civilians, and many are children. Besides claiming more than 5,000 victims each year, dangerous war debris also prevents war refugees from returning to their homelands, stifles fragile economies and prevents farmers from planting crops or developers from investing in a nation's future. Many nations and organizations help the victims and work to ban, remove and disarm landmines and other "explosive remnants of war" (ERW). But questions are being asked about how best to help victims and whether enough is being done to destroy ERWs and stockpiles of banned chemical weapons.

Terrorism and the Internet

A decade ago, terrorist organizations operated or controlled only about a dozen Web sites. Today there are more than 7,000. Terrorist groups use the Internet for many activities, ranging from raising funds to explaining how to build a suicide bomb. They find the Internet appealing for the same reasons everyone else does: It's cheap, easily accessible, unregulated and reaches a potentially enormous audience. As terrorist content spreads to chat rooms, blogs, user groups, social networking sites and virtual worlds, many experts, politicians and law enforcement officials are debating how government and industry should respond. Some want Internet companies to stop terrorists from using the Web, while others say that is not the role of Internet service providers. As governments enact laws based on the belief that the Internet plays a significant role in promoting terrorism, critics say the new measures often overstep free-speech and privacy rights.

Drone Warfare

Unmanned "drone" aircraft controlled from remote video consoles are being used in increasing numbers by the U.S. military in Afghanistan and by the CIA in Pakistan and other places outside of recognized war zones. Some scholars argue the CIA strikes in Pakistan are illegal, while others say they comply with the laws of war. The spread of armed drones, along with resulting civilian deaths, is raising ethical concerns as well as questions about drones' effectiveness. The U.S. military now possesses some 7,000 drones, and more than 40 nations, including Iran and China, have drone technology. Unmanned aircraft are being used for everything from border control and environmental monitoring to drug interdiction and building inspections. Some policy experts worry that as drones expand worldwide, they not only could make the United States a more potent military force but also put it at greater risk of attack from enemies possessing the technology.

Prosecuting Terrorists

The Obama administration has reluctantly decided to prosecute Khalid Sheik Mohammed, the self-described mastermind of the September 11 attacks, in a military commission at Guantanamo Bay, Cuba, instead of in a civilian federal court in the United States. In announcing the decision, Attorney General Eric Holder continued to defend federal court trials for accused terrorists, but bowed to restrictions approved by Congress against bringing any Guantanamo prisoners to U.S. soil. The move focuses renewed attention on the military commission system, which the administration has changed to accord defendants more procedural rights but which civil liberties and human- rights advocates continue to criticize as second-class justice. Despite the reforms, the system has been stalled, but now will be put to use not only for Khalid Sheik Mohammed but also for the trial of a key suspect in the October 2000 bombing of the *USS Cole*. Meanwhile, the government continues to prosecute and win convictions in federal courts of accused terrorists apprehended within the United States.

ECONOMIC ISSUES

Future of Globalization

Global trade has plummeted in recent months by rates not seen since the Great Depression. The World Trade Organization announced that trade tumbled by 12 percent in 2009 alone, the biggest contraction since World War II. While countries so far have avoided the kind of disastrous trade wars that marked the 1930s, protectionist measures and nationalist sentiments are rising across the globe, reflected in the original "Buy American" provision of the U.S. government's economic stimulus package. Clearly, globalization, so recently hailed in books like Thomas Friedman's best-selling *The World Is Flat*, has stalled. Some economic historians even believe the world is entering an era of "deglobalization," with nations turning inward economically and culturally, which could lead to a dangerous increase in international tensions. Other analysts say the economic, technological and social ties that bind nations to each other have grown so strong that globalization is an irreversible phenomenon that will help the global economy recover.

Future of the Euro

Portugal has become the third eurozone government to seek a bailout loan from the European Union, which is struggling to prevent a debt crisis from crippling its poorest members and spreading to richer euro countries. Historically impoverished nations such as Ireland, Portugal and Greece experienced a surge of wealth in the 1990s after adopting the euro. But in the wake of the worldwide economic crash and recession, that wealth proved to be an illusion based on cheap credit from Germany and other stronger economies. The euro's defenders say the crisis has created a new determination to fix the eurozone's defects, particularly its lack of strong centralized governance. But the rise of nationalist parties in richer countries opposed to bailouts could hamper a solution. And despite years of rhetoric about European unity, critics say individual nations will never give up enough of their sovereignty — especially their right to tax and spend on liberal social programs — to become part of a United States of Europe.

Climate Change

Delegates from around the globe arrived in Copenhagen, Denmark, for the U.N. Climate Change Conference in December 2009 hoping to forge a significant agreement to reduce greenhouse gas emissions and temper climate change. But despite years of diplomatic preparation, two weeks of intense negotiations and the clamor for action from thousands of protesters outside the meeting, the conferees adopted no official treaty. Instead, a three-page accord — cobbled together on the final night by President Barack Obama and the leaders of China, India, Brazil and South Africa — established only broad, nonbinding goals and postponed tough decisions. Yet defenders of the accord praised it for requiring greater accountability from emerging economies such as China, protecting forests and committing billions in aid to help poorer nations. But the key question remains: Will the accord help U.N. efforts to forge a legally binding climate change treaty for the world's nations?

REGIONAL ISSUES

Sub-Saharan Democracy

Despite a recent economic renaissance, some say much of sub-Saharan Africa is drifting toward a new age of authoritarianism. After the Cold War — when the superpowers propped up African dictators as proxy pawns in a global ideological chess match — the seeds of democracy rapidly spread across the continent. By 2000, nearly half of sub-Saharan Africa's 48 countries were considered electoral democracies. But democratic progress stalled and even regressed in the 2000s. By one measure, freedom in the region has retreated to about the same level it was in 1992–1993. Human rights are eroding in influential countries like Nigeria, South Africa, Zimbabwe and Ivory Coast. Experts blame Africa's continuing ethnic tensions and the emergence of China as a major trading partner. Western governments are skittish about pressing for democratic reforms now that they must compete for Africa's natural resources with China, which ignores such issues in its business dealings.

Europe's Immigration Turmoil

Recent gains by European right-wing political parties advocating halts in immigration from Muslim countries signal a growing resentment against foreigners as Europe faces an economy with fewer jobs to go around. Anti-immigrant parties have received unprecedented shares of the vote in famously tolerant Sweden and the Netherlands. Mainstream politicians in France, Germany and Britain have vowed to cut immigration, complaining that many immigrants — especially conservative Muslims — fail to integrate into mainstream society. Ironically, anti-immigrant fervor is rising just as the economic downturn is slowing immigration to many countries. Some economists argue that aging Europe needs young immigrants to fill its work force and support its growing pension costs. Other experts say governments need to do more to integrate Muslims, many of whom are native-born. As governments pass laws to ban burqas, headscarves and minarets, many are asking how much cultural conformity Europe can demand in an increasingly globalized world. Immigrant advocates say language requirements and citizenship tests discriminate against Muslim immigrants and, together with immigration caps, send a hostile message to the skilled workers Europe needs to attract from abroad.

Crime in Latin America

Fed by the drug trade with the United States, crime and corruption threaten Latin America as never before, reaching from the highest levels of government to the most-impoverished slums. Once largely focused on illegal drugs, crime cartels have now expanded into a complex range of activities from money laundering to human trafficking. The crisis is prompting both U.S. and Latino experts and policy makers to ask how governments and citizens can fight criminal groups, reduce social inequality and create new opportunities for unemployed young people tempted by a life of crime. At the same time, the United States, which has long been involved with Colombia's fight against crime and drug trafficking, is

increasingly concerned about the lawlessness and horrific violence in Mexico, now threatening to spill over into the U.S. While experts say the situation is likely to get worse before it gets better, there are some bright spots, including criminal justice reforms that have reduced crime and corruption in several Latin American countries.

Democracy in Southeast Asia

Indonesia is the world's third-largest democracy and one of its newest. But while Indonesia is consolidating its democratic institutions and slowly making progress against endemic corruption, democracy elsewhere in Southeast Asia is in distress. High-level corruption and politically motivated murders are obstructing democracy in the Philippines. In Thailand, 14 years of turbulent democracy ended with a military coup in 2006. Elections eventually resumed, but after anti-government protesters camped in Bangkok's commercial center for months in the spring of 2010 demanding new elections, the government finally broke up the demonstrations and began shooting and arresting protesters. True democracy is largely a fiction in Cambodia, Singapore and Malaysia, and Myanmar (Burma) is run by a brutal authoritarian regime. Against this backdrop, opposition politicians, scholars and human rights activists debate how best to encourage democracy in Southeast Asia.

Turmoil in the Arab World

Massive, largely peaceful demonstrations in January and February 2011 forced longtime autocrats in Tunisia and Egypt from power, including Hosni Mubarak, who had dominated Egypt for more than 30 years. Subsequently, protests erupted in at least a dozen other countries across the Arab world, several of which continue. Using social media to organize, young demonstrators have called for the removal of long-entrenched corrupt regimes, greater freedom and more jobs. They have been met with violent government crackdowns in Syria, Yemen and Bahrain, while in Libya strongman Moammar Gadhafi is battling a ragtag rebel force backed by NATO. As the region reverberates with calls for change, scholars say some key questions must be answered: Will the region become more democratic or will Islamic fundamentalists take control? And will relations with the West and Israel suffer? Then, a few months later on May 1, al Qaida chief Osama bin Laden was killed in a U.S. raid in Pakistan. Once, such news might have triggered anti-U.S. protests across the region. Now, it seemed, those bin Laden had tried to radicalize were more interested in jobs and freedom than in bin Laden's dream of a vast, new Muslin caliphate.

U.S.-China Relations

Disputes that have bedeviled relations between the United States and China for decades flared up again following President Obama's decision to sell weapons to Taiwan and receive Tibet's revered Dalai Lama. From the U.S. perspective, China's refusal to raise the value of its currency is undermining America's — and Europe's — economic recovery. Beijing also rebuffed Obama's proposal of "a partnership on the big global issues of our time." In addition, the Chinese insist on tackling their pollution problems in their own way, and have been reluctant to support U.S. diplomatic efforts to impose tough sanctions on nuclear-minded Iran. With the central bank of China holding more than $800 billion of the U.S. national debt in the form of Treasury notes in 2010, and their economy speeding along at a 9 percent growth rate, the Chinese are in no mood to be accommodating.

Afghanistan Dilemma

Nearly ten years ago, U.S. forces first entered Afghanistan to pursue the al Qaeda terrorists who plotted the Sept. 11 terror attacks. American troops are still there today, along with thousands of NATO forces. Under a strategy crafted by the Obama administration, military leaders are trying to deny terrorists a permanent foothold in the impoverished Central Asian country and in neighboring, nuclear-armed Pakistan, whose western border region has become a sanctuary for Taliban and al Qaeda forces. The Afghanistan-Pakistan conflict — "Af-Pak" in diplomatic parlance — poses huge challenges ranging from rampant corruption within Afghanistan's police forces to a multibillion-dollar opium economy that funds the insurgency. But those problems pale in comparison with the ultimate nightmare scenario: Pakistan's nuclear weapons falling into the hands of terrorists, which foreign-policy experts say has become a real possibility.

Preface

Can Western-style democracy take root in Arab countries? Do drone strikes comply with international law? Is the Eurozone a workable idea? These questions—and many more—are at the heart of American foreign policy. Students must first understand the facts and contexts of these and other foreign policy issues if they are to analyze and articulate well-reasoned positions.

The second edition of *Issues for Debate in American Foreign Policy* includes sixteen up-to-date reports by *CQ Researcher,* an award-winning weekly policy brief that explains difficult concepts and provides balanced coverage of competing perspectives. Each article analyzes past, present and possible political maneuvering and is designed to promote in-depth discussion and further research to help readers formulate their own positions on crucial international issues.

This collection is organized into three subject areas—security issues, economic issues and regional issues—to cover a range of topics found in most American foreign policy courses. Citizens, journalists and business and government leaders also can turn to the collected articles to become better informed on key issues, actors and policy positions.

CQ RESEARCHER

CQ Researcher was founded in 1923 as *Editorial Research Reports* and was sold primarily to newspapers as a research tool. The magazine was renamed and redesigned in 1991 as *CQ Researcher.* Today, students are its primary audience. While still used by hundreds of journalists and newspapers, many of which reprint portions of the reports, *Researcher*'s main subscribers are now high school, college and public libraries. In 2002, *Researcher* won the American Bar Association's coveted Silver Gavel Award for magazine excellence for a series of nine reports on civil liberties and other legal issues.

Researcher staff writers — all highly experienced journalists — sometimes compare the experience of writing a *Researcher* report to drafting a college term paper. Indeed, there are many similarities. Each report is as long as many term papers — about 11,000 words — and is written by one person without any significant outside help. One of the key differences is that the writers interview leading experts, scholars and government officials for each issue.

Like students, staff writers begin the creative process by choosing a topic. Working with *Researcher*'s editors, the writer identifies a controversial subject that has important public policy implications. After a topic is selected, the writer embarks on one to two weeks of intense research. Newspaper and magazine articles are clipped or downloaded, books are ordered and information is gathered from a wide variety of sources, including interest groups, universities and the government. Once the writers are well informed, they develop a detailed outline and begin the interview process. Each report requires a minimum of ten to fifteen interviews with academics, officials, lobbyists and people working in the field. Only after all interviews are completed does the writing begin.

CHAPTER FORMAT

Each issue of *CQ Researcher*, and therefore each selection in this book, is structured in the same way. A selection begins with an introductory overview, which is briefly explored in greater detail in the rest of the report.

The second section chronicles the most important and current debates in the field. It is structured around a number of key issues questions, such as "Can Singapore and Malaysia become liberal democracies?" and "Is enough being done to destroy banned toxic weapons? " This section is the core of each selection. The questions raised are often highly controversial and usually the object of much argument among scholars

and practitioners. Hence, the answers provided are never conclusive, but rather detail the range of opinion within the field.

Following those issue questions is the "Background" section, which provides a history of the issue being examined. This retrospective includes important legislative and executive actions and court decisions to inform readers on how current policy evolved.

Next, the "Current Situation" section examines important contemporary policy issues, legislation under consideration and action being taken. Each selection ends with an "Outlook" section that gives a sense of what new regulations, court rulings and possible policy initiatives might be put into place in the next five to ten years.

Each report contains features that augment the main text: sidebars that examine issues related to the topic, a pro/con debate by two outside experts, a chronology of key dates and events and an annotated bibliography that details the major sources used by the writer.

CUSTOM OPTIONS

Interested in building your ideal CQ Press Issues book, customized to your personal teaching needs and interests? Browse by course or date, or search for specific topics or issues from our online catalog of *CQ Researcher* issues at http://custom.cqpress.com.

ACKNOWLEDGMENTS

We wish to thank many people for helping to make this collection a reality. Thomas J. Billitteri, managing editor of *CQ Researcher,* gave us his enthusiastic support and cooperation as we developed this edition. He and his talented staff of editors and writers have amassed a first-class collection of *Researcher* articles, and we are fortunate to have access to this rich cache. We also thankfully acknowledge the advice and feedback from current readers and are gratified by their satisfaction with the book.

Some readers may be learning about *CQ Researcher* for the first time. We expect that many readers will want regular access to this excellent weekly research tool. For subscription information or a no-obligation free trial of *Researcher,* please contact CQ Press at www.cqpress.com or toll-free at 1-866-4CQ-PRESS (1-866-427-7737).

We hope that you will be pleased by the second edition of *Issues for Debate in American Foreign Policy.* We welcome your feedback and suggestions for future editions. Please direct comments to Elise Frasier, Acquisitions Editor for International Relations and Comparative Politics, College Publishing Group, CQ Press, 2300 N Street, NW, Suite 800, Washington, DC 20037; or send e-mail to *efrasier@cqpress.com.*

—*The Editors of CQ Press*

Contributors

Eliza Barclay is a web producer/reporter for the science desk at National Public Radio in Washington, D.C., who was based in Mexico City for three years. She has reported from Latin America, Africa and Asia, and her writing has appeared in *The Atlantic*, *The New York Times*, *The Washington Post* and other publications. She has received fellowships from the International Reporting Project and the Metcalf Institute for Marine and Environmental Reporting. She graduated with a B.S. from the University of California at Berkeley and is working on an M.A. in science writing from Johns Hopkins University.

Thomas J. Billitteri is managing editor of the *CQ Researcher*. He has more than 30 years' experience covering business, nonprofit institutions and public policy for newspapers and other publications. He holds a BA in English and an MA in journalism from Indiana University.

Roland Flamini is a Washington-based correspondent who writes on foreign-affairs for *The New Republic* and other publications. Fluent in six languages, he served as *Time* bureau chief in Rome, Bonn, Beirut, Jerusalem and the European Common Market and later served as international editor at United Press International. His previous reports for *CQ Researcher* were on Afghanistan, NATO, Latin America, Nuclear Proliferation and U.S.-Russia Relations. His most recent reporting trip to China was in November-December 2009.

Sarah Glazer, a London-based freelancer, is a regular contributor to *CQ Global Researcher*. Her articles on health, education and social-policy issues also have appeared in *The New York Times* and *The Washington Post*. Her recent *CQ Global Researcher* reports include "Radical Islam in Europe" and "Social Welfare in Europe." She graduated from the University of Chicago with a B.A. in American history.

Alan Greenblatt covers foreign affairs for National Public Radio. He was previously a staff writer at *Governing* magazine and *CQ Weekly*, where he won the National Press Club's Sandy Hume Award for political journalism. He graduated from San Francisco State University in 1986 and received a master's degree in English literature from the University of Virginia in 1988. For the *CQ Researcher*, his reports include "Confronting Warming," "Future of the GOP" and "Immigration Debate." His most recent *CQ Global Researcher* reports were "Attacking Piracy" and "Rewriting History."

Associate Editor **Kenneth Jost** graduated from Harvard College and Georgetown University Law Center. He is the author of the *Supreme Court Yearbook* and editor of *The Supreme Court from A to Z* (both *CQ Press*). He was a member of the *CQ Researcher* team that won the American Bar Association's 2002 Silver Gavel Award. His previous reports include "States and Federalism" and "Campaign Finance Debates." He is also author of the blog *Jost on Justice* (http://jostonjustice.blogspot.com).

Reed Karaim, a freelance writer living in Tucson, Arizona, has written for *The Washington Post, U.S. News & World Report, Smithsonian, American Scholar, USA Weekend* and other publications. He is the author of the novel, *If Men Were Angels*, which was selected for the Barnes & Noble Discover Great New Writers series. He is also the winner of the Robin Goldstein Award for Outstanding Regional Reporting and other journalism awards. Karaim is a graduate of North Dakota State University in Fargo.

Robert Kiener is an award-winning writer whose work has appeared in the *London Sunday Times, The Christian Science Monitor, The Washington Post, Reader's Digest, Time Life Books, Asia Inc.*, and other publications. For more than two decades he lived and worked as an editor and correspondent in Guam, Hong Kong and England and is now based in the United States. He frequently travels to Asia and Europe to report on international issues. He holds an M.A. in Asian Studies from Hong

Kong University and an M.Phil. in International Relations from Cambridge University.

Alex Kingsbury has written about national security and the intelligence community for *U.S. News & World Report*. He made several trips to Iraq in 2007 and 2008 to cover the Iraq War. He holds a B.A. in history from George Washington University and an M.S. in journalism from Columbia University.

Barbara Mantel is a freelance writer in New York City whose work has appeared in *The New York Times*, the *Journal of Child and Adolescent Psychopharmacology* and *Mamm Magazine*. She is a former correspondent and senior producer for National Public Radio and has won several journalism awards, including the National Press Club's Best Consumer Journalism Award and the Front Page Award from the Newswomen's Club of New York for her April 18, 2008, *CQ Researcher* report "Public Defenders." She holds a B.A. in history and economics from the University of Virginia and an M.A. in economics from Northwestern University.

Jason McLure has been an Africa correspondent since 2007, reporting for publications including Bloomberg News, *Newsweek* and *The New York Times*. Currently based in Ghana, he previously worked for *Legal Times* in Washington, D.C., and in *Newsweek*'s Boston bureau. His writing has appeared in *The Economist, Business Week*, the *British Journalism Review* and *National Law Journal*. His last *CQ Global Researcher* was "The Troubled Horn of Africa." His work has been honored by the Washington, D.C., chapter of the Society for Professional Journalists, the Maryland-Delaware-District of Columbia Press Association and the Overseas Press Club of America Foundation.

Jina Moore is a multimedia journalist who covers science, human rights and foreign affairs from the United States and Africa. Her work has appeared in *The Christian Science Monitor, Newsweek, The Boston Globe, Foreign Policy* and *Best American Science Writing*, among others. She was a 2009 Ochberg Fellow with the Dart Society for Journalism and Trauma. Her May 2010 story for the *CQ Global Researcher*, "Confronting Rape as a War Crime," won honorable mention in the 2011 American Society of Journalists and Authors awards, in the Reporting on a Significant Topic category.

1

Attacking Piracy

Alan Greenblatt

A Chinese destroyer escorts two Chinese freighters in the pirate-infested waters off the coast of Somalia. Warships from dozens of nations, including the United States, the European Union, China, India and Russia now patrol the region against a sudden upsurge in piracy, which costs the global shipping industry up to $50 billion a year. Despite the show of force, many experts argue that given Somalia's grinding poverty, eradicating piracy requires more than a naval solution.

From *CQ Researcher*,
August 8, 2009.

Hassan Abdalla was on his way to deliver rice to starving Somalis when his freighter, the *Semlow*, was surrounded by small boats manned by pirates with AK-47 assault rifles and rocket-propelled grenades (RPGs).

Claiming to belong to the so-called Somali Marines — the largest of the many pirate gangs operating off the Somali coast — the hijackerstook over the *Semlow* and began using it as a "mother" ship — for launching smaller, faster boats to attack other ships. Four months later Abdalla and his fellow mariners were released, after more than $500,000 in ransom was paid to the pirates.

"I knew they would hijack again, because ransom money is sweet," Abdalla told Daniel Sekulich, a reporter with *The Globe and Mail* in Toronto and author of a new book about piracy, *Terror on the Seas*. "Once you've tasted it, you want more."[1]

Indeed, the lure of easy money has turned the seas around the Horn of Africa into danger zones for commercial ships. Some 30,000 vessels per year use the region's shipping lanes to deliver oil and other goods between Europe, the Middle East and Asia.[2] In the first half of this year, armed Somali pirates attacked at least 150 oceangoing vessels in the area, a sixfold jump in attacks in that region over the same period in 2008.[3]

More than 250 years since the end of the so-called Golden Age of Piracy — the days of Blackbeard, Captain Kidd and other legendary figures — pirates have returned to the high seas, threatening maritime security, commerce and, some terrorism experts say, global security. "Piracy, the scourge of the 17th and 18th centuries, has emerged from

Piracy Spans the Globe

Piracy occurs in most of the world's tropical oceans — including the Pacific waters off Peru, the east and west coasts of Africa and the seas of Southeast Asia. More than 60 percent of the 240 attacks in the first half of 2009 were attributed to heavily armed Somalis attacking ships in the Gulf of Aden and off the coast of Somalia. The second-largest number of pirate attacks this year occurred in the Southeast Asia/Far East region.

Successful and Attempted Pirate Attacks
(January-June, 2009)

Source: International Maritime Bureau

the history books and has returned with deadly, terrifying results," writes John Burnett, a London-based maritime security consultant and former reporter, in his 2002 book *Dangerous Waters*.[4]

A record 889 crew members were taken hostage in 2008 — a 207 percent increase over 2007, according to Peter Chalk, a maritime security analyst with the RAND Corporation think tank. Although ransom negotiations are kept confidential, pirates collected an estimated $30 million to $150 million in booty last year. Many worry that such big — and rapidly growing — sums will only encourage, and fund, further attacks. Currently, Somali pirates are holding 10 foreign vessels hostage, awaiting ransom payments.[5]

Piracy costs the shipping industry overall — in ransoms, lost cargoes, higher insurance premiums and interrupted shipping schedules — from $10 billion to $50 billion a year, according to Sekulich. "Even the lowball estimates," he notes, are "well above the gross domestic product of numerous nations [and] virtually unprecedented in our global economic history."[6]

And, while no direct link has been established between the Somali pirates and terrorists, some worry the weaknesses in maritime security exploited by pirates will prove useful to those seeking to spread terror. Martin N. Murphy, a senior research fellow at the Center for Strategic and Budgetary Assessments in Washington and author of a 2009 book on piracy and marine terrorism, says Web traffic and intelligence intercepts clearly indicate that Islamic extremist groups "are watching what's happening off Somalia. It reveals a clear weakness, and terrorists can exploit this."

While most pirate attacks today occur near Somalia, pirates also operate off the coasts of other countries, including Peru, Brazil and Nigeria. Private yachts in the Caribbean and Gulf of Mexico also have been attacked. For decades, pirates plagued Southeast Asia, especially the

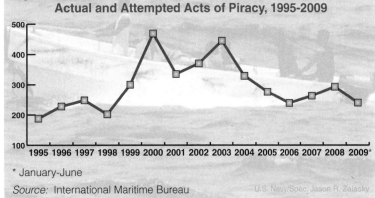

Piracy Could Set New Record This Year

In the first half of 2009 there were 240 attempted and successful pirate attacks worldwide — twice the number in the same period last year. The increase is due largely to attacks by Somali pirates in the Gulf of Aden and off the coast of Somalia. At the current rate, global piracy this year will surpass its modern peak of 469 attacks in 2000. Most of those attacks occurred in Southeast Asia and the Malacca Strait between Malaysia, Indonesia and Singapore. After those governments jointly cracked down, piracy declined dramatically in the region.

Actual and Attempted Acts of Piracy, 1995-2009

* January-June

Source: International Maritime Bureau

U.S. Navy/Spec. Jason R. Zalasky

Malacca Strait — the strategic waterway that runs between Singapore, Indonesia and Malaysia and links northeast Asia with the Indian Ocean. But a tough, new, regional anti-piracy campaign has helped to control the attacks in recent years.

Recent pirate attacks have been concentrated off Somalia and in the Gulf of Aden/Red Sea area: Attacks by Somalis in the first six months of this year accounted for more than 60 percent of the world's 240 pirate incidents. At that rate, total attacks in 2009 could surpass the modern-day record of 469 incidents in 2000, when most piracy was occurring in Southeast Asia. But experts say shipowners only report about a third of actual attacks, because they don't want their voyages delayed further by criminal or insurance investigations.

One of the most dramatic attacks occurred in April, when Somali pirates boarded the *Maersk Alabama* — the first such incident against a U.S. vessel manned by an American crew. The captain, Richard Phillips, gave himself up as a hostage in exchange for the release of his crew and ship. Several days later he was dramatically rescued

Piracy Shifts From Asia to East Africa

The world's piracy hot spot has shifted dramatically from Southeast Asia to East Africa over the last decade. In 2000, nearly half of the 469 pirate attacks occurred in Southeast Asia, and only 5 percent in East Africa. But since Singapore, Malaysia and Indonesia jointly adopted a strong anti-piracy program in 2004, pirate attacks in the region have plummeted. In the first half of 2009, Southeast Asia experienced only 10 percent of the world's pirate attacks, and 60 percent occurred in Somalia, the Gulf of Aden and the Red Sea.

Location of Piracy Incidents, 2000 and 2009*

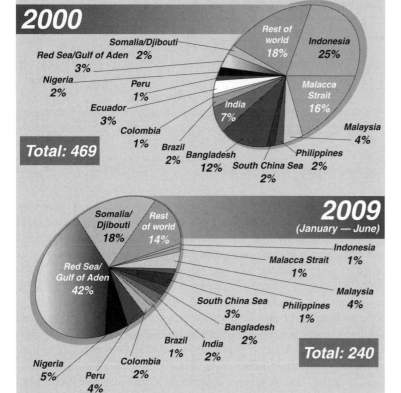

2000

Red Sea/Gulf of Aden 3%
Somalia/Djibouti 2%
Rest of world 18%
Indonesia 25%
Nigeria 2%
Peru 1%
Malacca Strait 16%
Ecuador 3%
India 7%
Malaysia 4%
Colombia 1%
Brazil 2%
Bangladesh 12%
South China Sea 2%
Philippines 2%

Total: 469

2009
(January — June)

Somalia/Djibouti 18%
Rest of world 14%
Indonesia 1%
Malacca Strait 1%
Red Sea/Gulf of Aden 42%
South China Sea 3%
Philippines 1%
Malaysia 4%
Bangladesh 2%
Brazil 1%
India 2%
Nigeria 5%
Colombia 2%
Peru 4%

Total: 240

* January to June

Source: International Maritime Bureau

The debate about the use of force reflected a larger point: Navies are uncertain how to handle the problem. They don't engage with pirates until after an attack has occurred, and, even when they do capture pirates, it's not always clear what they should do with them or who has jurisdiction over crimes committed in international waters. Because many Western nations lack clear anti-piracy statutes, dozens of captured pirates have been disarmed and released. Some have been taken to neighboring countries, especially Kenya, for prosecution.

In the past year the ranks of Somali pirates have burgeoned, as more and more citizens of the failed state — lucky to earn $2 a day and attracted by the lucrative spoils — have joined their ranks. Today there are at least 3,000 Somali pirates, up significantly from the roughly 200 that were operating in early 2008, according to Burnett. Russian Vice Admiral Oleg Burtsev puts the number at 5,000 or more.[8]

"If you're young and able-bodied, what else can you do but join the pirates?" asks Peter Lehr, a terrorism-studies lecturer at the University of St. Andrews in Scotland. "It's like the California Gold Rush."

Regardless of the exact number, Somali pirates have grown bolder in recent months, targeting large container ships and even supertankers like the *Sirius Star*, which was carrying $100 million worth of oil and eventually was ransomed for an estimated $3 million.

Up to 90 percent of the world's goods travel by boat, making ships at sea the weak link in the global trading system. Given the threat, warships from nearly two-dozen countries, part of a "combined task force" set up by the United States in January, are now patrolling the area. The European Union is running a separate escort

when three Navy SEAL snipers shot and killed his three captors.

Some in the shipping industry complained afterwards that killing pirates might endanger future hostages, who until now have mainly been unharmed. Some Somali pirates at the time boasted they would now target and kill American sailors, but that hasn't happened.[7]

and patrol operation to protect food aid shipments like the one carried by the *Semlow*. It is the EU's first naval mission and the first time Britain's Royal Navy has been on an anti-piracy mission in nearly 200 years.[9] In addition, France, China, India, South Korea and Russia have sent their own vessels.

Despite the show of force, naval officials concede it's not enough. Patrolling more than half a million square miles of water would take hundreds of warships, not a couple dozen. "The weird thing is, piracy has increased while we have the heaviest presence of naval warships in that region that's ever been seen," says author Sekulich.

Many argue that ending piracy requires more than a naval solution. Piracy, particularly the Somali brand, reflects that country's poverty, limited opportunities and lack of a functioning central government. Since the fall of a dictatorial regime in 1991, Somalia has had a new government about once every 14 months, on average.[10] It's also awash in arms, after decades of civil war and Cold War efforts to play the Soviets off against the Americans.

But while Somalia has devolved into a failed state, its pirate gangs have become increasingly sophisticated, Sekulich points out. "Somalia has transformed itself, or rather the pirates have transformed themselves, into the most advanced and effective type of pirates we've seen in centuries."

The pirates often turn a portion of the ransom money over to their backers — sophisticated organized crime figures — who reinvest much of it in high-powered weaponry, faster boats, global positioning systems (GPS) and satellite phones. And the pirates now are apparently sharing intelligence about the movement of merchant ships.

"The most recent evidence shows that the mother vessels are telling each other about potential targets," British Rear Adm. Philip Jones, commander of the EU naval task force, said in May. "They are exchanging positional information, . . . information about ships they have seen or may have tried to attack. Obviously, that is a significant development."[11]

Given the enormous profits Somalis are pulling in, some analysts worry that the piracy problem will spread.

As the global community struggles to combat piracy, here are some of the questions people are debating:

Can navies defeat piracy?

Piracy has been a menace since ancient times. Cicilian pirates from what is now Turkey disrupted commerce between cities and kidnapped important officials until 67 B.C., when a Roman commander, Gnaeus Pompeius Magnus ("Pompey the Great"), shut down the pirate operation in less than two months with a massive naval and land campaign.

Pompey divided his massive fleet into 13 naval squadrons responsible for various sections of the Mediterranean. He kept 60 ships under his direct command, using them to harass pirates into the areas patrolled by his commanders. Within 40 days, he cleared the western Mediterranean of pirates and chased them inland using tens of thousands of soldiers, attacking pirate strongholds in Turkey.

Similarly, the rise of modern-day piracy off Somalia has attracted the attention of the world's great navies, and their warships are having an effect. The United Nations had stopped sending food aid to Somalia for nearly three years due to pirate raids on the shipments. But since the EU launched its "Operation Atalanta" mission in December, not a single escorted U.N. shipment has been stopped, and 1.6 million Somalis are being fed by the U.N.'s World Food Programme (WFP) every day. In addition to protecting food shipments, Atalanta's ships and helicopters escort commercial vessels and provide aerial surveillance and other measures to deter piracy in the region.

"We hope very much that with this anti-piracy operation in the Horn of Africa — one of the busiest transit routes in the world — we can bring these piracy activities down," says Cristina Gallach, spokeswoman for the European Union's high Representative for the Common Foreign and Security Policy.

Although the EU recently extended the Atalanta mission for another year, Gallach says it's not a panacea. Pirates who can't hit ships along their accustomed corridors now attack ships as far south as the Seychelles. "It's just like any other criminal activity," says RAND's Chalk. "They'll exploit some other area where there isn't so much law enforcement."

Shippers want navies to disrupt piracy before attacks occur, says Pottengal Mukundan, director of the International Chamber of Commerce's International Maritime Bureau. Capturing or sinking the mother ships would be particularly helpful, he says.

Reuters/Crack Palinggi

Indonesian naval personnel guard pirates suspected of hijacking the palm oil tanker MT Kraton in the Strait of Singapore. Although the pirates changed the ship's name, a joint anti-piracy campaign by Indonesia, Malaysia and Singapore used a new international database to uncover the name change and apprehend the pirates in September 2007.

The Indian navy sank a mother ship last November, 325 miles southwest of Oman's port of Salalah. And in April, a French frigate sailing under the EU banner intercepted a mother ship in the Gulf of Aden, detaining 11 pirates.

"Navies have to increase their deterrent efforts — before pirates get on board," says Lee Willett, head of the maritime studies program at the Royal United Services Institute for Defence and Security Studies in London. "Stop them on shore, create exclusion zones bigger than the current corridors, stop any vessel out there with small engines, which are obviously out there for no good reason."

But aside from the "balloon effect" of pushing pirates out to new, unguarded areas, the battle against piracy

ultimately must be won on land, says Gallach. "The problem of piracy is on land, not on the high seas."

Many observers agree the problem is "land-based," the result of Somalia's 18 years without a functioning government. Without law enforcement or any sense of order, Somali gangs and warlords have become increasingly sophisticated in their sponsorship of crimes extending out to the high seas. "Piracy is the maritime ripple effect of anarchy on land," wrote foreign policy journalist Robert D. Kaplan.[12]

Piracy has prospered because pirates have safe havens back home, and the ruined economy is not producing legitimate jobs for young Somalis. Since Somalia's 2,000-mile-long coastline sits near a key transit corridor — the Gulf of Aden — the country's problems have filtered far out to sea.

"You've got the most powerful naval armada assembled in recent history to fight the scourge of pirates who are really lightly armed in some puny boats, and they still can't stop them," says Burnett.

Historical battles against piracy have generally required action on land, from Pompey's use of 120,000 infantry to clemency deals cut with Chinese and Caribbean pirates. More recently, piracy in the Strait of Malacca and the surrounding region dropped from 187 attacks in 2003 to 65 in 2008 after Singapore, Indonesia, Malaysia and Thailand — with Japanese prodding and funding — launched a coordinated anti-piracy campaign.[13]

But without a functioning government in Somalia, "there's no way of controlling pirates internally," Burnett says. "There are efforts to build a coast guard there, but that's so far down the road."*

Chris Trelawny — head of maritime security for the U.N.'s London-based International Maritime Organization (IMO) — is more hopeful. He points out that 17 countries in the region drafted a code of conduct in January vowing to seize pirate ships and cooperate in the arrest and prosecutions of pirates.

---

* The Transitional Federal Government, formed in 2004, is the latest in a string of efforts to establish a central government in Somalia in the last 18 years. President Sheikh Sharif Sheikh Ahmed, elected in January, has not yet been able to provide essential services or maintain security. The externally funded, ultra-conservative jihadist al-Shabaab group controls much of the southern part of the country and some parts of the capital.

Until a land-based solution can be instituted in Somalia, Trelawny says, "We welcome the work of the navies in carrying out what are essentially constabulary efforts."

The International Maritime Bureau's Mukundan disagrees. "It is a naval problem," he says. "In today's world, navies have the responsibility to protect maritime trade routes. They have stepped up to the mark splendidly." But he concedes that naval efforts are only a "temporary measure."

Willett concurs, saying naval action is needed to buy time for Somalia and other regional countries to get a handle on the problem. "While navies are a short-term element in the process," he says, "navies need to be there to keep a lid on it."

Despite the recent EU extension of its convoy program, some wonder whether the great powers will sustain their presence in the region for the years it undoubtedly will take for the Somali government to get its house in order enough to start prosecuting piracy.

The relatively low incidence of pirate attacks — only 240 so far this year on the tens of thousands of ships plying the world's oceans — has implications for how military resources are allocated, Michèle Flournoy, undersecretary of Defense for policy, told the Senate Armed Services Committee in May. She noted that merchant ship crews had thwarted 78 percent of the unsuccessful attacks, while military or law enforcement interventions had blocked only 22 percent.[14]

The millions being spent on naval patrols might even be counterproductive, suggests RAND's Chalk. "We're investing too much in naval solutions, to the detriment of long-term solutions."

"Navies cannot defeat piracy," insists EU spokeswoman Gallach. "Navies can . . . give protection to those who are in transit — the merchants, the ships that are transporting humanitarian aid."

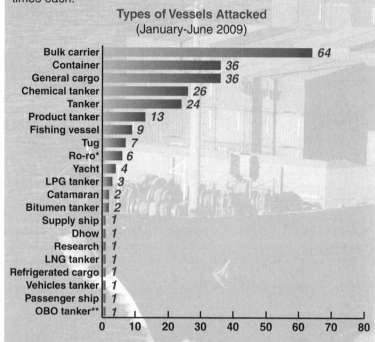

Bulk Carriers Are Main Pirate Target

More than a quarter of the 240 pirate attacks in the first half of 2009 were on bulk carriers that transport commodities like grain. Container ships and general cargo vessels were attacked 36 times each.

Types of Vessels Attacked
(January-June 2009)

Bulk carrier	64
Container	36
General cargo	36
Chemical tanker	26
Tanker	24
Product tanker	13
Fishing vessel	9
Tug	7
Ro-ro*	6
Yacht	4
LPG tanker	3
Catamaran	2
Bitumen tanker	2
Supply ship	1
Dhow	1
Research	1
LNG tanker	1
Refrigerated cargo	1
Vehicles tanker	1
Passenger ship	1
OBO tanker**	1

* For "roll-on-roll-off" vessels used to transport vehicles

** For oil, bulk commodities or ore

Source: "Piracy and Armed Robbery Against Ships," International Maritime Bureau, January-June 2009

Besides, as Flournoy and others suggest, chasing down pirates would divert their resources and attention from their fundamental strategic defense missions. "Prosecuting detained pirates . . . is simply not our business," said Cmdr. Achim Winkler, who heads an EU flotilla in the Gulf of Aden.[15]

Should shipping crews be armed?

A growing chorus of voices — including *Maersk Alabama* Capt. Phillips — are now convinced that maritime crews should be armed and trained to defend their ships.

"Arming the crew as part of an overall strategy could provide an effective deterrent under certain circumstances," Phillips told the Senate Foreign Relations Committee on

No Link Seen Between Pirates and Terrorists

But some fear terrorists could adopt pirates' tactics.

Given the logistical difficulties involved, it's not surprising that terrorists have struck on land much more often than they've tried to strike at sea. Since the 1960s, there have been fewer than 200 maritime terror attacks worldwide, compared with over 10,000 terrorist incidents overall.[1]

But there is now some concern among defense analysts that the rapid growth of piracy might lead to more terror at sea. "Similar forces allow piracy and maritime terrorism to flourish," says Peter Chalk, a policy analyst with the RAND Corporation think tank. "The model of piracy could be mimicked by terrorists, including ransom demands."

Chalk notes that piracy can weaken political systems by encouraging corruption among public officials. And it's clear that piracy has been used as a fundraising tool by some terrorists, including the Free Aceh Movement in Indonesia and the Tamil Tigers in Sri Lanka. The two-decade-long Tiger insurgency was defeated by the Sri Lankan government in May.

"In the last year, we have seen structures related to al Qaeda that are taking advantage of the lawlessness that exists in Somalia," says Christina Gallach, a spokeswoman for the European Union.[2]

As Gallach and others point out, however, there appears to be no credible evidence of a direct link between pirates off the Somali coast and terrorists. "We are working very firmly in the belief that there is no proven link between piracy and al Qaeda-type terrorism," says Chris Trelawny, security chief of the International Maritime Organization. "What makes Somali piracy unique is that they are purely taking ships for kidnap and ransom."

In fact, pirates and terrorists work at cross-purposes, suggests Daniel Sekulich, author of the 2009 book, *Terror on the Seas: True Tales of Modern-Day Pirates.* Pirates' tools are subterfuge and anonymity, while terrorists want, more than anything else, to attract attention for their deeds.

"Pirates and terrorists have diametrically opposed goals," Sekulich says. "Pirates are seeking economic gain that comes from a steady supply of the world's shipping. They love all those container ships. Terrorists want to slow [or disrupt] shipping . . . for their own nefarious means."

Still, both piracy and terror are dangers because of the vulnerable nature of ocean-going trade. Piracy is a reflection of the fact that the weakest link in world trade is the lone vessel at sea, which could also be hit by politically motivated attackers.

April 30, just weeks after his spectacular rescue by Navy sharpshooters. But he doesn't think it would be "the best or ultimate solution to the problem."[16]

Vice Admiral James Winnefeld, director of strategic plans and policy for the Joint Chiefs of Staff, agrees. "It's a capacity issue," he told the Senate Armed Services Committee. "We believe this is something private industry needs to do for themselves."

The idea that shipowners should arm and train crew members — or hire private security forces to accompany ships or their escorts — appears to be gaining currency with U.S. defense officials. "It may be useful for Congress to consider developing incentives to encourage merchant ships to invest in security measures," Defense undersecretary Flournoy told the Armed Service Committee. "These could range from tax credits to reduced insurance rates for ships with enhanced security."

In other countries, however, proposals to arm crewmen or hire mercenaries remain highly controversial. Shipowners, insurers and seafarers all cite increased risks and legal and logistical complications posed by having firearms aboard merchant ships.

"Arming seafarers — that is totally out of the question," says Arild Wegener, chief of security for the Norwegian Shipowners Association.

Arming crews would trigger an arms race between the pirates and the crews and could increase the risk of serious harm and death onboard, even without a pirate attack, he says. So far, Somali pirates have shown little interest in harming their hostages, because they want to be able to collect ransom payments for them. But arming ship crews could change the equation.

"Arming merchant sailors may result in the acquisition of even more lethal weapons and tactics by the

"We believe the division between piracy and terrorism is much more blurred than some people seek to argue," says Andrew Linington, spokesman for the Nautilus International seafarers' union. "Certainly, our big worry is that a dozen guys in a fiberglass boat can take command of a ship like the *Sirius Star*, a massive vessel with millions of dollars of oil on board.

"We think that's an intolerable situation and should be sending huge warning signals out to governments about the fragility of safety at sea," he continues.

The deadliest terror attack at sea occurred in 2004, when 116 people were killed in the bombing of the Philippine *SuperFerry 14*. The ferry was blown up by 16 sticks of dynamite hidden in a hollowed out television set by members of the Abu Sayyaf Islamist separatist group. Such attacks worry security officials because they areso cheap and easy to carry out. Planning for the bombing took only a couple of months and cost no more than $400t.[3]

Marine terrorism is not new in the region of the world where piracy now dogs the shipping industry. In 2002, two suicide bombers attacked the oil tanker *Limburg* off Yemen, killing themselves and one crew member. The attack triggered a rise in the price of oil and area shipping insurance rates, causing a 93 percent drop in the container business at the Port of Aden.[4]

The disproportionate impact of such terrorist attacks is why some worry about the potential for piracy to lead to increases in maritime terrorism. Some experts worry, for example, that a liquefied natural gas tanker could be hijacked and turned into a massive bomb.

"No matter how well-protected, every ship afloat — and this includes those that carry enough reactor fuel to build a few nuclear devices — is physically highly vulnerable," writes maritime security consultant John Burnett.[5]

A more likely scenario, though, is that terrorists could take over or blow up a ship along one of the major shipping chokepoints, such as the Strait of Hormuz or the Suez Canal, disrupting the flow of oil or other crucial cargo. "With deliberate preparation and the occasional well-placed attack, a few men with small boats can keep the navies churning for years," writes journalist William Langewiesche in his 2004 book *The Outlaw Sea*.[6]

"If terrorists like al Qaeda want to keep Western powers tied up, would it not be logical for them to open another front to get attention off Afghanistan and Pakistan?" asks Lee Willett, a British naval security expert.

---

[1] Martin N. Murphy, *Small Boats, Weak States, Dirty Money* (2009), p. 185.

[2] For background, see Jason McLure, "The Troubled Horn of Africa," *CQ Global Researcher*, June 2009, pp. 149-176.

[3] Peter Chalk, "The Maritime Dimension of International Security: Terrorism, Piracy and Challenges for the United States," RAND Corporation, 2008, p. 26.

[4] *Ibid.*, p. 24.

[5] John S. Burnett, *Dangerous Waters* (2002), p. 288.

[6] William Langewiesche, *The Outlaw Sea* (2004), p. 39.

pirates, a race that merchant sailors cannot win," John Clancey — chairman of the energy and shipping company Maersk Inc., which owns the *Maersk Alabama* — said during congressional testimony on April 30.[17]

"It has been our very strong policy that seafarers should not be armed," echoes Andrew Linington, a spokesman for Nautilus International, a British and Dutch seafarers' union. "It would be counterproductive and actually make things worse, partially because of the fear that in the wrong hands guns could actually inflame the situation."

For example, in a commonly cited case, New Zealander Sir Peter Blake, who had twice won the America's Cup, was anchored in the Amazon in 2001, when his ship was attacked by several armed men. Although Blake had a rifle and fired it in defense, he was shot and killed.[18]

Besides crew members being shot, Linington adds, gunfire could ignite a shipboard fire or cause other serious damage. Moreover, further problems would crop up when ships want to dock. Merchant ships are allowed to sail freely through territorial waters and come into port if they are not a threat to the security of the coastal state. That right of "innocent passage" could be forfeited if they were armed. The U.S. Coast Guard, for instance, considers armed vessels within U.S. territorial waters a threat.

"In many jurisdictions, a crew member could be arrested for possessing weapons," says John Bainbridge, who represents the International Transport Workers' Federation before the IMO on piracy issues. Most sailors also opppose having to undergo training and be responsible for protecting their workplaces along with their many other duties. "When asked, the

Sailors from the guided-missile cruiser USS Gettysburg stop suspected pirates in the Gulf of Aden as part of the multinational task force conducting anti-piracy operations throughout the region. Since patrols began earlier this year, more than three times as many pirates have been interdicted as in all of 2008.

overwhelming majority of seafarers have rejected this option," Bainbridge says.

"The shipping industry is entirely against arming crews," says Neil Roberts, senior technical executive with Lloyd's Market Association, a London-based insurer.

But private security companies are anxious to offer their services. Blackwater Worldwide, a U.S. security firm, has offered dozens of shipping and insurance companies various options, such as a 181-foot long escort ship and certified mariners with small-arms training.

"The pirates are going after soft targets," said Jeff Gibson, vice president for international training and operations at Blackwater. "If a ship is being escorted by another boat, or some small boats or even a helicopter overhead, [the pirates] are going to decide, let's not make the effort."[19]

But hiring private security companies would be expensive — viable only for ships carrying the most valuable cargoes. And using private security companies "is fraught with difficulties," Roberts says, "not least because owners are unable to gauge the quality of various companies," since they are unregulated. If security guards kill someone, the shipping company could also be held liable.

And, many worry that hiring private security forces would ratchet up the potential for violence. Hiring armed security guards just escalates the situation "on both sides,"

says David M. Crane, a Syracuse University law professor. "Then you have a type of combat situation."

Despite such concerns, however, the rapid growth of piracy has led at least some analysts to rethink the longstanding prohibition against arming merchant ships. "Today's personnel, in signing up for a maritime career, do not wish to take upon themselves the responsibility and risk of providing for their own security in this way," says Graham Gerard Ong-Webb, a research fellow at the Centre for Defence and International Security Studies in London. "But I think these added responsibilities are inescapable today."

"We simply have to pay them more to do so," he continues. "I believe all maritime seafarers either have to undergo the requisite training to perform the basic defensive measures in deterring or staving off a pirate attack, or their employers should contract private security companies to do the job for them."

Those who argue that arming merchant ships will deter attackers rather than escalate the violence point out that Israeli and Russian merchant ships — which are assumed to be armed — are generally not attacked. For instance, in 2001, Burnett notes, no Russian or Israeli ships were attacked by pirates, compared to 27 attacks on U.S. and British ships.[20]

"It's very difficult to create a defense against armed pirates with unarmed ships," author Burnett says.

Nevertheless, he prefers that unarmed crew members use defenses such as water cannon, barbed wire around the decks or long-range acoustic devices that can destroy the eardrums of attackers — along with evasive maneuvers and general vigilance. "Guns aboard ships, unless they're military, just don't belong," he says.

Recalling the time when his own ship was boarded by pirates, Burnett says, "If I had been armed, if I had had my 12-gauge on board when I was attacked, I'd be dead today."

"If weapons are on board, they will get used," says Willett, of the Royal United Services Institute for Defence and Security Studies.

Should shipowners pay ransom?

Early pirate history is full of tales of extreme violence and even torture being used against captives. And earlier in this decade, when the greatest area of concern was in the Strait of Malacca, pirates generally stole the ships and cargo and killed crew members or set them adrift.

But Somali pirates are not out to kill: They need the crew alive for ransom from shipowners and insurance companies. The IMO's Trelawny points out that only two hostages have died in recent years while in pirate hands — one killed by a ricocheting bullet, another a heart attack.[21]

"They were never nice to us and treated us the whole time as a potential threat," said Leszek Adler, an officer on the *Sirius Star*, the Saudi oil tanker taken by Somali pirates last November. But, "other than a few minor episodes, they weren't hostile toward us all, although there were a few of them that had a hotter temper."[22]

"Crew members are lots of money on two legs," says Lehr, the lecturer in terrorism studies at the University of St. Andrews.

A Congressional Research Service report points out that "while individual ransom payments can be significant," the payment of ransoms has kept Somali piracy violence "relatively low."[23] And because only a small percentage of ships in the area are successfully attacked and captured, some commercial entities view the overall risk of paying ransoms as low.

"What's the practical alternative?" asks Linington of Nautilus, the seafarers' union. "What are you going to do if you're not going to pay? Nobody seems to have a proper answer to that."

Indeed, once pirates control a ship, few alternatives remain. Navies can attempt rescues, but the casualty risk is high. French special forces storming a yacht taken by pirates in April may have killed its skipper during the firefight to rescue him and other hostages.[24]

But even the successful rescue of Capt. Phillips sparked criticism that it could lead pirates to greater violence. "Paying ransom certainly does encourage piracy, but they really don't have much alternative," says RAND's Chalk. "The amount of money paid for ransom is insignificant compared to the value of the ship.

"Shipowners remain concerned that should pressure be brought against them to not pay ransom, it will increase the danger that pirates might kill off a couple of crew members to establish the seriousness of their demands," he continues.

"The last people who want to pay a ransom are the industry," says the International Maritime Bureau's Mukundan. "They don't want to have to pay millions of dollars to get their ships and crews back. But . . . they don't have a choice. Inside Somali waters, no one else can

help them. They have to do whatever they can. Today it means paying a ransom."

Governments don't pay ransoms. "We as a government do not condone the paying of ransom," said U.S. Defense undersecretary Flournoy. "We seek to end the paying of ransom."

But private shipping companies view paying ransom — or having their insurance companies pay — as the cheapest alternative and the most compassionate for the crew. "There is a concern that it sets a precedent, but ransoms do get paid," says Willett, of the Royal United Services Institute for Defence and Security Studies. "The amount tends to be only a small percentage of the value of the ship."

But even if paying ransoms is the more prudent course, is it the wisest? Trelawny feels it only exacerbates the situation. "Five years ago, the ransoms were in the tens of thousands, now they're in the millions," he says.

Though final payments are generally kept confidential, estimates of the total amount of ransoms paid to Somali pirates in 2008 range from $30 million up to $150 million.[25]

"At the moment, we seem to be approaching the worst of all possible worlds," wrote Bloomberg columnist Matthew Lynn. "Shipping companies either avoid the African coastline or . . . agree to pay what amounts to protection money for safe passage. Neither is satisfactory in the long term. Over time, the pirates will just grow stronger, the attacks will cover a wider area, and the ransom demands will get bigger."[26]

Little of the money stays with the pirates who carried out the crime. Usually, most of it goes to their backers — organized-crime syndicates or warlords. "In a typical ransom payment, 70 percent of that money is not returned to the pirates that undertake the operation. That goes to businessmen on land," Chalk writes.[27]

"To make matters worse, we know pirates use much of the ransom money paid to them to buy heavier and larger caliber weapons and bigger engines for their skiffs to make it even easier to overtake larger vessels," Senate Foreign Relations Committee Chairman John F. Kerry, D-Mass., said at the April 30 hearing. "They also use ransom money to arm and equip private militias. This is a dangerous and a vicious cycle, and it needs to be addressed."

Inevitably, the pirates' price comes down as negotiations drag on, sometimes for months. The pirates who took the *Sirius Star*, for instance, initially demanded $25 million but settled for an estimated $3 million after nearly two months of talks.

"What we want for this ship is only $25 million, because we always charge according to the quality of the ship and the value of the product," one of the hijackers told a reporter during the standoff.[28]

Delivering the ransoms has become another big business. Lawyers in London often handle the negotiations on behalf of shipowners, and private companies charge up to $1 million to deliver the ransoms, which are always paid in cash to avoid computer tracking. Bundled bills might be parachuted directly on board captured ships or delivered in suitcases to middlemen in cities such as Nairobi and Djibouti or to villages along the coast.

Recently, pirates have become more sophisticated, demanding only $50 and $100 bills and refusing easily traceable years of issue. The *Sirius Star*'s hijackers even brought a counting machine and a counterfeit-money detector on board with them.

However, the $3 million ransom they collected apparently was too much to carry away. The small getaway boat some of them took capsized. Five of the pirates drowned along with their shares, with one reportedly washing ashore with $153,000 in his pockets.[29] "The small boat was overloaded and going too fast," pirate leader Mohammed Said told the Agence France-Presse news agency. "The survivors told us they were afraid some foreign navies would attempt to catch them."[30]

Ong-Webb, of the Centre for Defence and International Security Studies, says it's perfectly understandable that shipping companies pay ransoms for their crews, but "it is not sustainable in the long term." Too much depends on global shipping to make payments to criminals a normal cost of doing business, he says.

Some countries, such as the United Kingdom, want to discourage private industry from paying ransom. But it will be difficult to come up with an alternative, since the decision about paying ransoms is made among shipping companies, insurers, national governments and captured crew members' families.

"Payment does encourage further attacks, and each one raises the bar, but unless shipowners pay ransoms they will be faced with a total loss of their ships," says Roberts, of Lloyd's Market Association.

But, he says, "While ships trade through such waters, there is no practical alternative to ransoms."

BACKGROUND

Piracy's 'Golden Age'

The poet Homer recorded an act of piracy in *The Odyssey*, written around 800 B.C., and in 75 B.C. the imperial barge carrying Roman Emperor Julius Caesar was apparently hijacked during a Mediterranean crossing.[31]

But piracy was tolerated — and even encouraged — by some rulers, who gave "letters of marque," or licenses, to privateers, legalizing their plundering so long as the ruler received a cut. "Piracy has always benefited from the support of unscrupulous great men only too happy to receive bribes and cheap pirated goods at no risk to themselves," writes British historian Peter Earle.[32]

Perhaps the most famous privateer was Francis Drake, who plundered gold and jewels from Spanish ships in the 1570s in support of Britain's Elizabeth I. Investors in Drake's voyage, including Elizabeth, received 47 British pounds for every pound they'd invested.[33]

"Elizabeth was not a weak monarch," writes Murphy of the Center for Strategic and Budgetary Assessments, "but she depended for the defense of her realm upon the sea power she could not afford."[34]

The most infamous pirates of all — Blackbeard, Captain Kidd and Henry Morgan — sacked towns in the Caribbean and North America and attacked ships during the so-called Golden Age of Piracy from the 1650s until the 1720s. Many were based in the lawless British colony of the Bahamas.

The pirates successfully eluded the British navy for years. Even when they were caught, the legal procedure for dealing with them, which dated from 1536, required them to be tried by an admiralty court in London. In 1700, Parliament passed the Act for the More Effectual Suppression of Piracy, which allowed trials outside England and authorized the death penalty outside of Great Britain.[35]

The new law allowed the British Navy to more aggressively dispatch armadas to drive pirates from their lairs and bring them to justice. Between 1716 and 1726 more than 400 men were hanged for piracy, effectively eliminating most of the leaders and decimating the general ranks.[36] "The Golden Age of Piracy . . . was conducted by a clique of 20 to 30 pirate commodores and a few thousand crewmen," writes journalist and author Colin Woodard.[37] Their trials and executions were highly public, with Captain

CHRONOLOGY

1700s-1800s *Rampant piracy in the Caribbean, Mediterranean and South China Sea is crushed.*

1700 Britain updates its piracy laws, enabling prosecution of pirates and use of the death penalty overseas. More than 400 men are hanged for piracy in the Atlantic and Caribbean.

Late 1700s U.S. builds a navy to fight state-sponsored piracy in North Africa. Two Barbary Wars ensue (1801-1805 and 1815-1816).

1810 China asks Western powers to help combat piracy in the South China Sea. Female pirate leader Cheng I Sao accepts amnesty deal, leading to surrender of hundreds of ships and more than 17,000 pirates.

1980s *Maritime piracy reemerges, especially in Southeast Asia.*

1985 Palestinian terrorists attack the Italian cruise ship *Achille Lauro*, prompting an international convention on maritime terrorism.

1988 Rome Convention makes seizing or endangering ships illegal.

1990s-2000s *Piracy and maritime terrorism grow in Asia and Africa.*

1990 In early example of "phantom ship" piracy, the *Marta* is hijacked en route to Korea, with pirates knowing all the details in advance about its whereabouts and cargo.

1991 *MV Naviluck* is attacked, ransacked and burned and the crew killed or thrown overboard on Jan. 12 — the first recorded modern piracy incident off Somalia. . . . Gen. Mohamed Siad Barre's dictatorship later collapses, triggering Somalia's "failed state" status and widespread piracy in the region.

1992 Oil tanker *Valiant Carrier* is attacked, sparking creation of the International Maritime Bureau's Piracy Reporting Centre. . . . Indonesia, Malaysia and Singapore begin anti-pirate patrols in Strait of Malacca; program is dropped due to cost.

1999 India captures and prosecutes hijackers of Japanese freighter *Alondra Rainbow*.

2000 Suicide bombers attack the *USS Cole* in Yemen, killing 17 sailors.

2002 In a post-9/11 security measure, President George W. Bush allows Navy to intercept merchant ships on high seas. . . . Al Qaeda suicide bombers damage the oil tanker *Limburg*, temporarily interrupting Gulf of Aden shipping.

2004 Terrorists bomb Philippine ferry, killing 116. . . . Singapore, Malaysia and Indonesia adopt coordinated anti-piracy policy.

2005 International Maritime Organization calls for action against piracy.

2006 Congress allows Pentagon to help other countries improve maritime security.

2008 Somali pirates seize French yacht *Le Ponant* and release the hostages; French commandos capture six of the pirates in the Djibouti desert (April 4). . . . Separatist attack forces Royal Dutch Shell to close its largest Nigerian offshore oil well (June 19). . . . Supertanker *Sirius Star* is hijacked near Kenya (Nov. 15). . . . Indian frigate destroys Somali pirate "mother ship" (Nov. 18). . . . U.N. authorizes all necessary measures to suppress Somali piracy (Dec. 16).

2009 International task force begins patrolling Gulf of Aden (Jan. 8), and capture more than 100 pirates in the first few months. . . . 17 nations adopt anti-piracy Code of Conduct (Jan. 29). . . . Capt. Richard Phillips of American freighter *Maersk Alabama* is taken hostage, freed by Navy sharpshooters off the Somali coast, (April 8). . . . Pirate survivor of *Maersk Alabama* incident is indicted in New York (May 19). . . . International Maritime Bureau says pirates struck 240 times during first half of 2009 — more than double the rate in the same period of 2008 — with Somali pirates responsible for more than 60 percent of the attacks and 86 percent of the 561 hostages taken in 2009 (July 15). . . . Trials scheduled to resume in Yemen for more than 20 Somali pirates captured by Indian and Russian forces (October).

Countries Outsource Piracy Prosecutions

Western nations try pirates in Kenyan courts.

Francis Kadima has suddenly gotten very busy. The Kenyan defense attorney is taking on new clients by the dozen, brought to him by a variety of countries asking that Kenya become the venue of choice for Western countries wanting to bring captured pirates to trial.

Yemen has 30 alleged pirates awaiting trial in its courts, and Seychelles has 20, according to the International Maritime Organization. But Kenya has some 250 suspected pirates awaiting trial, sent there by the United Kingdom, United States and European Union. Those nations all signed memorandums of understanding offering Kenya — as one of Somalia's closest neighbors with a functioning judicial system — funding, computers and legal assistance if it would prosecute pirates.

Justice is being outsourced to Kenya largely because of the murkiness of the laws regarding piracy. According to maritime -law experts, under international law — including the U.N. Convention on the Law of the Sea — piracy is a universal crime and can be prosecuted by any country. However, because piracy had abated for centuries, few Western countries still have specific anti-piracy statutes on their books.

"In the majority of European Union states, piracy is not a crime," says Christina Gallach, an EU spokeswoman. "It's not in the criminal code anymore. It's something that happened many years ago."

Another obstacle: Pirates are jurisdictional orphans. Because of the multinational nature of global shipping, it is unclear who has jurisdiction to prosecute a pirate. For instance, if Somali pirates are captured in international waters by an Indian warship after they attacked a Panamanian-registered ship owned by a Japanese company and crewed by Filipinos, which country prosecutes the pirates?

Under current practice, the capturing country does the prosecuting. That's what India did in the scenario described above, when it caught pirates who had stolen goods from the *Alondra Rainbow* in 1999. But it's still a logistical and linguistic nightmare to bring foreign witnesses in to testify against foreign offenders. That's why several nations prefer to try the alleged pirates as close to the point of capture as possible, especially if the captor's home country has no anti-piracy statute.

Because of the legal limbo and logistical issues, many captured pirates are merely disarmed and released. Canadian and Dutch warships have caught pirates this year only to let them go, in what critics have mocked as "catch and release." "They can't stop us," Jama Ali, a pirate aboard a hijacked Ukrainian freighter, told *The New York Times* last December. "We know international law."[1]

"While nobody would advocate the ancient naval tradition of just making them walk the gangplank, equipment like GPS [receivers], weapons (and) ladders are often just tossed overboard and the pirates let go," said a Kenya-based diplomat.[2]

In fact, naval powers making up the combined international task force on piracy in the Gulf of Aden and Somalia have disarmed and released 121 pirates since it was established in January and turned 117 others over to Kenya for prosecution, U.S. Navy officials told Congress in March.

At one point the U.S. Navy held a piracy suspect for seven months because of confusion over where he would be prosecuted.[3]

And in the only modern piracy case being tried in the United States, an 18-year-old Somalians captured during the April attack on the *Maersk Alabama* was indicted in New York in May for piracy and conspiracy to seize a ship and take hostages. U.S. piracy laws are still on the books

Kidd's tarred body left to hang in a gibbet — an iron cage — over the Thames for years as a warning.

Barbary Piracy

About the same time, North Africa's Barbary corsairs — Muslim pirates and privateers who had long plagued the southern Mediterranean Sea — earned a special place in early U.S. naval history. In the late 1700s the pirates thought they had found easy pickings in merchant ships from the newly independent United States, which had lost the protection of the British Royal Navy. For years the Barbary pirates captured American ships and held the crews for ransoms and annual "tribute" payments from the U.S. government — just as they had traditionally extracted money from European governments. Signing treaties to buy off the pirates' state but haven't been used in 100 years. Once punishable by death, piracy has carried a mandatory life sentence in the United States since 1819.[4]

"It is a workable model," Pottengal Mukundan, director of the International Maritime Bureau, a London-based office of the International Chamber of Commerce, says of the Kenya prosecution contracts. He hopes to see more international arrangements to bring pirates to trial within the region, noting that countries such as China are not party to the agreements with Kenya.

utsourcing piracy justice to Kenya, however, presents a major obstacle: Kenya's judicial system already has a backlog of 800,000 cases of all kinds in its courts. Suspects often spend a year or more in jail just waiting for a hearing.[5]

"What we would like to see is some measures coming from the International Maritime Organization or from the U.N., which allows for . . . all the countries with naval vessels in the region to hand over pirates for prosecutions to countries in the area," Munkundan says. "If the [navies] can't prosecute, then they might let them go or not pursue them with full vigor."

But Daniel Sekulich, a Canadian journalist and author of *Terror on the Seas*, says it's a mistake to outsource pirate justice. He prefers that nations update their laws and set up an international court.

"It is not going to result in the conviction of every captured suspect, but it is a reflection of the resolve of nations to not only dispatch warships but also prosecute suspects to the full extent of the law," he says.

The idea of an international court for piracy has received a fair amount of attention, but it remains controversial and would take years to implement.

In the interim, there are concerns that Kenya won't be able to handle the load. Aside from the heavy case backlog, there have been allegations that Kenya's courts are prone to corruption and questions about whether the country can provide western standards of due process.

"The problem is that Kenya itself cannot handle hundreds of pirate cases," Mukundan says, arguing for more

Suspected Somali pirates appear in court in Mombasa, Kenya, on April 23, 2009, after being apprehended by the French navy, which is part of Operation Atalanta, the EU anti-piracy effort.

international support. "It may grind down their own legal system." The critical question, then, is how much money and support rich nations will pour in to build judicial capacity there.

The fact that Kenya's parliament itself hasn't fully signed off on the international agreements is an issue Kadima has raised on behalf of his clients. "You can't just go around making up laws, you know," he said. "There is a process."[6]

---

[1] Jeffrey Gettleman, "Pirates in Skiffs Still Outmaneuvering Warships Off Somalia," *The New York Times*, Dec. 16, 2008, p. A6, www.nytimes.com/2008/12/16/world/africa/16pirate.html.

[2] Katharine Houreld and Mike Corder, "Navies ask: What do you do with a captured pirate?" The Associated Press, ABC News, April 17, 2009, http://abcnews.go.com/US/wireStory?id=7365467.

[3] Mike Corder, "Nations Look to Kenya as Venue for Piracy Trials," The Associated Press, April 17, 2009.

[4] Houreld and Corder, *op. cit.*

[5] *Ibid.*

[6] Jeffrey Gettleman, "Rounding Up Suspects, the West Turns to Kenya as Piracy Criminal Court," *The New York Times*, April 24, 2009, p. A8, www.nytimes.com/2009/04/24/world/africa/24kenya.html.

---

sponsors — Tripoli, Tunis, Morocco and Algiers — was considered cheaper for the new country, still in debt from its Revolutionary War, than building its own navy.[38]

The ransoms and tributes prompted a debate that echoed today's controversy over whether paying ransom only encourages more piracy. Then-Ambassador to France Thomas Jefferson felt that paying ransom only invited more

demands, so he tried to organize an international naval coalition to battle the pirates and their state sponsors.

"The states must see the rod," Jefferson wrote in an Aug. 18, 1786, letter to future president James Monroe, then a member of Congress. And in a letter to Yale College president Ezra Stiles, Jefferson wrote, "It will be more easy to raise ships and men to fight these pirates into reason, than money to bribe them."[39]

Crew members of the French tourist yacht Le Ponant prepare to board a French frigate after Somali pirates released them on April 11, 2008. The ship had been hijacked a week earlier in the Gulf of Aden. French commandos captured six of the pirates after the hostages were released.

Although Jefferson was unable to establish a coalition, the payoffs were a blow to national pride. And in 1794, in response to Algerian seizures of American ships and crews, Congress appropriated $688,888 to build six frigates "adequate for the protection of the commerce of the United States against Algerian corsairs."[40]

After becoming president in 1801, Jefferson refused Tripoli's demands for $225,000, followed by annual payments of $25,000. Tripoli declared war, and the two Barbary Wars (1801-1805 and 1815-1816) ensued.

The first war involved a series of daring raids and bombardment of Tripoli. The turning point came in 1805, when a handful of U.S. Marines led 500 Greek, Arab and Berber mercenaries on a dramatic overland march across the desert from Alexandria, Egypt, to capture the Tripolitan city of Derna. When they raised the American flag in Derna, it was the first time the flag was raised in victory on foreign soil — an act memorialized in the "shores of Tripoli" line in the Marines' Hymn.

The Barbary nations were emboldened by the War of 1812, when the British chased U.S. ships from the Mediterranean. But eventually the Americans captured some Algerian ships, leading Algeria to foreswear further demands for tribute. In 1816, a massive bombardment of Algiers by an Anglo-Dutch fleet helped to end piracy in the Mediterranean.

Following their heyday, pirates were seen by some people as folk heroes. "Reason tells us that pirates were no more than common criminals, but we still see them as figures of romance," writes David Cordingly in *Under the Black Flag*.[41]

Part of that heroic image — at least to some — may have stemmed from the democratic way they ran their ships, unlike the navies of the time. Pirates elected their own captains and shared their booty according to set terms. "A hundred years before the French Revolution, the pirate companies were run on the lines in which liberty, equality and brotherhood were the rule rather than the exception," Cordingly writes.[42]

As piracy declined, the image of pirates as romantic buccaneers began to grow. In 1814, Lord Byron's poem "The Corsair" sold out seven editions in its first month of publication.[43] Pirates were further romanticized by novelists such as Walter Scott and Robert Louis Stevenson, whose *Treasure Island* in 1883 created the template for much pirate lore. In the 20th century, Hollywood also portrayed pirates as heroes — played by such romantic leading men as Errol Flynn, Douglas Fairbanks and Johnny Depp — whose playful portrayal of pirate Jack Sparrow in the "Pirates of the Caribbean" film series has grossed $2.7 billion worldwide for the Disney company.

Cold War's End

But portraying violent thieves as romantic or comedic characters was fundamentally misleading, argues author Murphy. It was "as if the period that began at the end of the 19th century, when piracy became a nursery story and later was thrown up on the silver screen, formed an impervious barrier through which the reality of maritime depredation could not seep into the modern era," he writes.[44]

In addition, he notes, the rise of sea power and the vast reach of Britain's Royal Navy led Westerners to believe by the early 20th century that piracy was obsolete.[45] "Piracy was seen as a problem out of history," with little relevance to the modern world, wrote Murphy.[46]

However, when the fall of the Soviet Union ended the Cold War, the super powers were no longer routinely patrolling the world's oceans. And merchant ships became more vulnerable as automation allowed shipowners to hire skeleton crews and rising fuel costs led to slower cruising speeds.

Meanwhile, modern pirates were gaining high-tech advantages, including satellite phones, GPS devices and faster fiberglass boats.

Romantic Pirate Lore Is Mostly Fiction

Aarrgh, but they did have parrots and peg legs.

By the early 19th century, piracy had been largely eliminated from the Atlantic and Mediterranean seas, but pirates lived on in the Western imagination as glamorous outlaws.

Like cowboys, pirates starred as highly romanticized heroes in movies and novels, such as Robert Louis Stevenson's 1883 classic, and heavily embroidered, *Treasure Island*. And as a result, much of what most people believe today about pirates isn't actually true.

"The effect of *Treasure Island* on our perception of pirates cannot be overestimated," writes David Cordingly, a former curator at England's National Maritime Museum. "Stevenson linked pirates forever with maps, black schooners, tropical islands and peg-legged seamen with parrots on their shoulders."[1]

Here's a brief guide to sorting out pirate fact and fiction:

- **Walking the plank — Myth.** Captain Hook may have planned to make the "Lost Boys" of J. M. Barrie's *Peter Pan* walk the plank, but real pirates rarely made time for such dastardly deeds. There is no mention of pirates making anyone walk the plank during the so-called Golden Age of Piracy, although an account from a later era survives. "However," writes Canadian journalist and author of a book about pirates Daniel Sekulich, "throwing individuals overboard is another thing altogether and a common enough occurrence in the annals of piracy."[2]
- **Treasure chests and maps — Myth.** Although 18th-century pirates certainly stole doubloons and pieces of eight when they could get them, their typical booty consisted of bales of silk and cotton, barrels of tobacco, spare sails, carpenters' tools and the occasional slave. And maps with an X marking the location of buried treasure were the invention of the illustrator of *Treasure Island*. Pirates usually spent their money in port on gambling, prostitutes and alcohol before they could bury it. The legend grew largely out of reports that Captain Kidd had buried gold and silver from a plundered ship near his home before he was arrested.

- **Peg legs, earrings and parrots — Fact.** "Pirates really did tie scarves or large handkerchiefs around their heads, and they did walk around armed to the teeth with pistols and cutlasses," Cordingly writes.[3] They also wore frock coats, which were typical of the Stuart period, when the Caribbean buccaneers were most active. Tricorn hats were also typical of the period, but skull-and-crossbones emblems were an embellishment added by Barrie in *Peter Pan*.

The common depiction of pirates wearing earrings is accurate. Many people at the time believed that wearing gold or silver in the earlobe improved eyesight or offered protection from drowning.[4] Expressions such as "Aarrgh," "avast" and "shiver me timbers" were part of the seafarers' vocabulary of the day.

As for the wooden legs and parrots, pirates were vulnerable to serious injury, and historical accounts describe several pirates who had lost limbs having replacements fitted by ship's carpenters. And seamen traveling in the tropics often picked up birds and animals as souvenirs. Parrots were popular because they commanded a good price in the London bird markets and were easier to keep on board than monkeys and other wild animals.

---

[1] David Cordingly, *Under the Black Flag* (1995), p. 7.

[2] Daniel Sekulich, *Terror on the Seas* (2009), p. 285.

[3] Cordingly, *op. cit.*, p. xiv.

[4] David Pickering, *Pirates* (2006), p. 160.

And, while piracy largely disappeared from the Atlantic and Mediterranean, it continued almost without interruption in Asia.

Asian Straits

Shih Fa-Hsien, a Buddhist monk from Sri Lanka, recorded cases of piracy in the Malacca Strait and South China Sea in 414 A.D. And 14th-century Moroccan traveler Ibn Battuta described being victimized by pirates off western India and commercial ships crossing the Indian Ocean in armed convoys for protection.[47]

"Slightly earlier," writes journalist Kaplan, "Marco Polo described many dozens of pirate vessels off Gujarat, India, where the pirates would spend the whole summer at sea with their women and children, even as they plundered merchant vessels."[48]

Should an international piracy court be established?

YES
Peter Lehr
Lecturer, Terrorism Studies
University of St. Andrews, Scotland

Written for *CQ Researcher*, August 2009

Let's face it: Responding to piracy off the coast of Somalia took us quite a while. Now, relatively effective anti-piracy patrols have been established, acts of piracy foiled and scores of pirates arrested. But what should be done with them?

Most nations cannot legally try foreign nationals attacking crews and ships of another foreign country at a foreign location. In the absence of such laws, many pirates simply were disarmed and sent back to their own shores, in their own skiffs.

Since such a response to a serious crime is quite underwhelming, an agreement with Kenya was hastily cobbled together envisioning that pirates would have to stand trial in Mombasa and serve a prison sentence in a Kenyan prison — at least until the Somalian government could establish its own court. So, mission accomplished?

Legal experts in Germany and the Netherlands beg to differ. Since the 2007 post-election riots in Kenya, they point out, the Kenyan judiciary system has been overstretched, and, in any case, it does not meet Western standards. Thus, dumping Somali pirates on the already creaking Kenyan judicial system is hardly a long-term solution. And the Somalis do not have a monopoly on piracy — so an agreement with Kenya addresses only one part of global piracy.

Creating an international piracy tribunal would speed up proceedings and guarantee a fair and efficient trial matching Western standards. It would also solve jurisdictional problems that have marred too many piracy cases in the past.

The Netherlands and Russia are exploring the details of such a tribunal, and some German politicians suggest extending the brief of the Hamburg-based International Tribunal for the Law of the Sea (ITLOS). Hamburg has the facilities and experts for such trials and would thus be a good place.

Sentenced pirates could then serve their terms in states that have adopted the U.N. Convention on the Law of the Sea (which don't include the United States, by the way).

Setting up an international piracy tribunal will cost money, of course, but it's a better solution to a problem that won't go away any time soon. It is politically viable at the moment, and it most definitely is a much fairer solution in the long run than yet another quick fix in the shape of a kangaroo court.

NO
John Knott
Consultant
Holman Fenwick Willan LLP*
London, England

Written for *CQ Researcher*, July 9, 2009

Amid continuing pirate attacks off the coasts of Somalia and legal difficulties in prosecuting captured pirates, it is not surprising that an international piracy tribunal — similar to the International Criminal Court (ICC) at The Hague — has been proposed. While there are some superficial attractions in such a plan, an examination reveals it to be impractical.

Such tribunals take a long time to set up, are very expensive to run and their trials often last for years. The ICC was created by the Rome Statute of 1998 and took four years to become effective, when 60 states ratified it in 2002. That followed the many years it took to draft and negotiate the statute. Even so, the ICC does not include China, India, Russia or the United States. A solution is needed for dealing with Somali pirates that can be implemented much sooner.

A rather vague, hybrid proposal to establish a "regional tribunal" and "an international tribunal" in an unnamed country in the region was considered at a July 7 meeting at The Hague. But more focused, practical and simpler solutions are available.

For instance, the catchment area could be expanded for trials among the African and Arab nations that in January signed a regional Code of Conduct for repressing piracy. Early signatories were Djibouti, Ethiopia (the only non-coastal state), Kenya, Madagascar, the Maldives, the Seychelles, Somalia, Tanzania and Yemen. The code called for participating nations to review their legislation to ensure that adequate laws were in place to criminalize piracy and related crimes and that captured pirates would be treated with a degree of uniformity in the region.

To simplify prosecutions, law enforcement detachments from these countries could be stationed aboard warships operating in the region (under the auspices of NATO, the Combined Task Force 151 and Operation Atalanta) to serve as arresting officers and to ensure that a single legal system is applied throughout a pirate's captivity.

Another possibility: A Somali-constituted court could sit in another country (as did a Scottish court when dealing with the Lockerbie air disaster), and convicted pirates could be housed in special U.N.-funded piracy jails in Puntland and Somaliland. There would be clear advantages in encouraging Somalia to help solve its own problems in this way, while avoiding the need for an international court in any guise.

In the early 19th century, about 40,000 pirates on hundreds of junks dominated the South China Sea coastal waters. From 1807, they were led by Cheng I Sao — known as "Mrs. Cheng" — a former prostitute from Canton, who took command after her husband died. She enforced a stricter code than the West Indies pirates, with punishments including beheading for disobeying orders or stealing from the common treasury.

By 1809, she had amassed a fleet larger than most navies. The following year, the Chinese enlisted the help of Portuguese and British warships in their battle against the pirates. As it became clear that an all-out attack on piracy was imminent, Mrs. Cheng reportedly showed up unannounced at the governor-general's mansion in Canton — surrounded by women and children — to negotiate a peace settlement. The government allowed her to keep her plunder but executed some of her pirates while allowing others to join the Chinese army. Two days later, 17,382 pirates formally surrendered, and 226 junks were handed over to authorities.[49]

Although the large-scale threat was eliminated, local attacks remained a constant. In recent years, Chinese provincial officials were accused of being complicit in smuggling and theft, until the country's growing role in world trade led to an official crackdown in the 1990s.

But piracy remained acute in the strategic Strait of Malacca, where some 70,000 vessels each year transport half the world's oil and more than a third of its commerce, including supply ships heading to and from China and Japan.[50] Batam, an Indonesian island just across the Singapore Strait from Singapore, became a haven for criminals, including pirates.

In 1992, Indonesia, Malaysia and Singapore began aggressively patrolling the region, virtually eliminating piracy for a while. But due to the high cost, including air support and surveillance, they dropped the strategy after six months.[51]

By the early 2000s, the Malacca Strait was the world's piracy hot spot, giving rise to the brutal phenomenon of "phantom ship" piracy. Pirates would board vessels and kill or cast off the crews, stealing not just the cargo but the ships themselves. They would then repaint the ships and change their names and registries — creating "phantoms" that they used as mother ships.

A Singaporean Navy ship patrols Singapore harbor, which faces the busy Strait of Malacca. Half the world's oil supplies pass through the narrow strait, which until recently was a popular target of pirates. Officials fear the strategic waterway could become a target of terrorists seeking to cripple world shipping.

United States Navy/SFC Eric L. Beauregard

By 2006, piracy in the region was so bad that many fishermen simply stayed home. Roughly half the 300 locals who fished off the coast of the Malaysian city of Melaka, for instance, refused to go out.[52]

To address the problem, the International Maritime Organization (IMO) instituted a unique ship-numbering system. Pirates also lost their markets for phantom ship cargo when the Chinese government and customs agents began cracking down on the illicit trade. Equally important, smaller neighboring countries renewed their efforts at aggressive patrols after receiving prodding and funding from outside powers such as Japan and the United States.

Besides conducting joint patrols, the littoral states share data. Pirates who hijacked the tanker *MT Kraton* in September 2007 thought they could hide their deed by changing the ship's name to *Ratu*. But a new international database allowed Malaysian authorities to inform other countries about the name change. Using additional information from Singapore, the Indonesian navy intercepted the tanker off southern Johor and nabbed all 13 hijackers.[53]

According to the latest IMB annual report, there were only two pirate incidents in the Malacca Strait in 2008, down from 34 in 2004. And only 65 attacks occurred within all of Southeast Asia, compared with 187 in 2003. "If pirates here were to try a copycat attack like in Somalia, it won't be easy for them because the governments in this region won't hesitate to take action," said Noel Choong, head of the bureau's Malaysia-based Piracy Reporting Centre.[54]

Growth in Somalia

Most piracy experts agree that getting regional powers together to combat piracy around the Horn of Africa like they have in Southeast Asia won't happen anytime soon. The IMO has been leading talks in the area for years, resulting in January in the adoption of a "code of conduct" by 17 nations regarding interdiction, investigation and prosecution of pirates, as well as the establishment of information and training centers.

But the lack of a functioning Somali government makes the country a "black hole," author Murphy says. Coastal waters were already lawless before dictator Mohamed Siad Barre's regime collapsed in 1991. Reportedly the Somali National Movement — which eventually overthrew Barre — seized three ships as early as 1989.[55]

The first officially recorded modern Somali piracy incident, however, took place on Jan. 12, 1991, when three boatloads of pirates attacked the Russian ship *MV Nauviluck*, killing three crew members and forcing the rest overboard. They were later rescued by a trawler.[56]

Somali piracy initially appealed to fishermen "fed up with the depletion of their fisheries" by big, foreign factory ships, says maritime security consultant Burnett, who served as a United Nations official in Somalia, in the 1990s. "The foreign fishing fleets were basically raping the Somali fishing grounds." Fishing within another country's territorial waters is illegal under international law but is a common problem off Africa's coasts.

"The foreign vessels gave no consideration to the welfare and future growth of the marine life," says Abdulkareem Jama, chief of staff for the newly elected Somali president, Sheikh Sharif Sheikh Ahmed.

The Somalis say Europeans were not only destroying their fishing grounds but were dumping a variety of toxic materials, including radioactive uranium, lead, cadmium and mercury and industrial, hospital and chemical wastes.

Somali regional administrators eventually authorized small groups of fishermen to capture and fine vessels caught illegally fishing or dumping wastes in Somali waters. "What started as law enforcement effort became a lucrative business for individuals and groups," says Jama. Soon, every ship that came near Somali waters was a target for ransom.

Some Somali pirates still fancy themselves as eco-warriors, guarding the coast for local fishermen and protecting it against international toxic-waste dumping. But it's clear the area is now plagued by maritime criminals who are not above attacking ships bringing humanitarian food shipments to Somalia's starving millions.

The attacks — on everything from cruise ships and oil tankers to fishing vessels and container ships — began drawing serious attention from the world's great powers last year. Media attention and shipowners' pleas eventually triggered formation of an impressive armada — warships from NATO, the European Union, France, the United States, China, Russia, India and two-dozen other countries.

"All these powers are showing up for these guys with AK-47s and flip-flops," says Abukar Arman, a Somali journalist and activist based in Ohio.

CURRENT SITUATION

Organized Gangs

In the first six months of 2009, Somali pirates have been responsible for more than 60 percent of the world's attacks, 86 percent of the world's maritime hostage-takings and virtually all of the growth in piracy.[57]

The pirate gangs come alongside trawlers and merchant ships in fast-moving skiffs and scamper on board using ladders or grappling hooks. They are typically armed with rocket-propelled grenades and AK-47s. "All you need is three guys and a little boat, and the next day you're millionaires," said Adullahi Omar Qawden, a former captain in Somalia's long-defunct navy.[58]

Several pirate gangs operate in Somalia, undoubtedly with connections to politicians and organized criminal gangs. "Believe me, a lot of our money has gone straight into the government's pockets," Farah Ismail Eid, a captured pirate, told *The New York Times*.

He said his team typically gave 20 percent to their bosses and 30 percent to government officials, allocating 20 percent for future missions and keeping 30 percent for themselves.[59] Abdi Waheed Johar, director general of Puntland's fisheries and ports ministry, acknowledges that some government officials are working with the pirates.

When Somali pirates attacked the *MV Faina*, a Ukrainian ship carrying tanks and ammunition to

Mombasa last September, "they knew the number of crew on board and even some names," says Somali journalist Arman. "These are illiterate people — they're being given information."

"Without any form of domestic law and order within Somalia, organized militia groups and pirate gangs have managed to fill this vacuum," says Sekulich, the Canadian journalist and author. "They have it all — command-and-control structures, logistics people, armories, financiers."

In a country with an average annual income of $600, pirates now drive the biggest cars, run many businesses and throw the best parties, sometimes with foreign bands brought in for the occasion. "Entire clans and coastal villages now survive off piracy," *The New York Times* reported in December, "with women baking bread for pirates, men and boys guarding hostages and others serving as scouts, gunmen, mechanics, accountants and skiff builders."[60]

Pirates are also the best customers for retailers. "They pay $20 for a $5 bottle of perfume," Leyla Ahmen, a shopkeeper in Xarardheere, a coastal Somali pirate hangout, told the *Times.*

The huge amounts of cash flooding northeastern Somalia have created serious inflation in the region and corrupts the morals of youths and women in the conservative Muslim society, says Somali presidential chief of staff Jama. "Young men started paying $100 for a cup of tea and telling the waiter to 'Keep the change,'" he explained. And some women have left their husbands for rich, young pirates. "These ill-gotten fast riches . . . are as damaging to the very fabric of the society onshore as it is damaging to international trade offshore."

While the pirates may move freely on land, their movements at sea are now being curtailed. The massive new international armada has captured dozens of pirates and deterred attacks on vessels carrying food aid. Stephen Mull, U.S. acting assistant secretary of State for political and military affairs, says nearly three times as many pirates were interdicted in the first four months of the year as in all of 2008. Under the new international agreements, many of the prisoners are now being sent to Kenya and other area countries for trial.

But Burnett, author of *Dangerous Waters,* attributes the southwest monsoon season — which makes the water too rough for small boats — to a temporary reduction in piracy attacks this summer. The pirates will be back in force by October, he predicts.

A U.S. Navy SEAL trains Indonesian marines during joint anti-piracy exercises in 2006. Since Southeast Asian governments began coordinating their efforts in 2004, piracy has declined dramatically in the region.

AFP/Getty Images/Bay Ismoyo

Meanwhile, the United States recently sent 40 tons of weapons and ammunition to shore up Somalia's Transitional Federal Government (TFG) against the Islamist al-Shabaab rebels who control much of southern Somalia. And the European Union is considering helping to train Somali police and create courts and other legal infrastructures.[61]

"We are not being utilized as much as we could be," Somali Prime Minister Omar Abdirashid Ali Sharmarke told the *Los Angeles Times* in April. "We need to fight pirates on land. We have information about how they function and who they are. The long-term objective should be to build institutions that will deal with pirates from inside the country."[62]

"The solution is easy if the will-power is there," says Jama. "If a team of 500 Somali soldiers are given special advanced training in, say, Djibouti or Uganda for three months and are given swift boats equipped with good firepower, GPS tracking and 10 helicopters, piracy can be eliminated or severely curtailed in 6 months.

Two dozen crew members were taken hostage when this Norwegian chemical tanker was hijacked off the Somali coast on March 26, 2009. Both the ship and crew were released on April 10 after a $2.6 million ransom was paid. Somali pirates are still holding 10 cargo ships.

"Only Somalis can deny pirates the land to use their ill-gotten loot," he continues. "The international community would be wise to try this solution with little to lose and much to gain. Insurance companies in the UK have offered to help fund a local solution. Other governments would be wise to join."

However, at the moment Sheikh Ahmed's fledgling government is fighting for its survival against foreign-funded extremists, Jama acknowledged.

The administration of President Sheikh Ahmed is the 16th government that has tried to control the country since the fall of Barre in 1991. And while the moderate cleric is regarded by many as one of the few men whose clan base and political skills might bring peace to the war-ravaged country, many foreign observers are skeptical about the TFG's chances of restoring law and order. Currently, the TFG only controls part of Mogadishu, the capital, and fighting breaks out there frequently.

Moreover, suggests terrorism lecturer Lehr of the University of St. Andrews, the summer lull in piracy due to the monsoon season has stalled momentum toward devising a regional anti-piracy strategy, which had garnered particular interest in nearby countries such as Oman and Saudi Arabia.

A better idea, Lehr says, would be to aid stable provincial governments in Puntland, a semi-autonomous region in northeastern Somalia — home to much of the piracy problem — and neighboring Somaliland, a stable,

democratically run state in northwestern Somalia that declared its independence in 1991. Although neither "republic" has received international recognition, they may be more capable of imposing law and order than the fragile central government in Mogadishu.

Puntland President Abdirahman Mohamed Farole may have been complicit in piracy at one time, says piracy author Murphy, of the Center for Strategic and Budgetary Assessments, but he now wants it stopped because the lawlessness and corruption could undermine his regime and make it more vulnerable to insurgencies such as al-Shabaab.

"The piracy is happening in Puntland, not Mogadishu," Murphy says. "We can't address it in Mogadishu." Puntland has already begun imposing 15- to 30-year prison sentences for piracy.

Supporting provincial efforts, Lehr says, "would be a much better option in the long run" and "would take the thunder out" of the Islamist movements, which denounce the presence of foreign navies offshore as Western militarism, he says.

"It would be cheaper and would regionalize the issue," he continues. "They should have a bigger interest in securing their own waters than we have."

Defensive Maneuvers

Although Somali pirates have garnered the most attention, piracy is a problem across the globe, from the Philippines to Peru. In West Africa, Nigerian rebel activity has spilled out of the Niger Delta into the Gulf of Guinea, where violent attacks on mariners occur almost weekly. Seaborne assaults on offshore oil facilities have cut Nigeria's oil exports by more than a quarter since 2006.[63]

In the Indian Ocean, pirates prey on Bangladeshi fishermen in the Ganges Delta and international ships anchored in Chittagong port in Bangladesh. And Somali pirates have extended their reach south along the East African coast to Kenya, Tanzania and the Seychelles.

Although worldwide piracy declined between 2003 and 2006, after Southeast Asian countries cracked down on regional piracy, it's been on the upswing since then, as pirates began ramping up activity in the Horn of Africa.[64] Maritime crimes largely stem from the inability of poor coastal nations to police their territorial waters.

As Murphy writes, "common piracy can be suppressed, or at least contained, by onshore police work supported by vigorous maritime patrolling."[65] But, he notes, the 1982 U.N. Law of the Sea Treaty gave countries greater jurisdiction over their territorial waters — extending jurisdiction 200 nautical miles out to sea, without regard to their ability to exercise authority over that expanded area. Shortly after the law was adopted, a Nigerian official said it "imposes on coastal states, regardless of their resources, an undue burden for providing security in long stretches of sea."[66]

While weak coastal states have allowed piracy to fester, the extent of the Somali piracy problem has forced larger nations to flex their naval muscles. Great Power politics are at work in the anti-piracy armada — a sort of dress rehearsal for further influence or combat in the Indian Ocean.

Japan, for instance, wants to escape the post-World War II constitutional constraints that limit its military posture to self-defense. On June 19, Japan's House of Representatives approved a bill authorizing the Self-Defense Forces to protect any commercial ships, regardless of nationality. Other countries, including China, are trying to determine which waters they may need to patrol to ensure oil shipments.

"They're learning the long-distance deployment ropes," says Murphy.

And the shipping industry is learning how better to defend itself. The International Maritime Organization now recommends ships stay at least 600 nautical miles off the coast of Somalia.

The U.S. Coast Guard issued new rules in May requiring U.S. ships plying pirate-infested waters to post lookouts and be ready to fend off pirates with water hoses and high-speed maneuvers. [67] "Anything over 14 or 15 knots tends to be fast, as far as the pirates are concerned," said Marcus Baker, managing director of the global marine practice at Marsh Ltd., an insurance broker in London.[68]

Many companies are fitting their ships with barbed wire and high-decibel long range acoustic devices — which are louder than standing behind a 747 jet during take-off and can be pointed at pirates up to 1,000 feet away. Some are stationing security guards on board for the most dangerous stretches of water.

"There's a bit of everything" being tried, says Wegener, the Norwegian Shipowners Association's security chief. "It does cost more, and so much more management time must be put into finding preventive measures."

Most of the world's shippers — predominantly those with larger ships — are following "best practice" security

A Somali fisherman hauls his catch to market in Mogadishu. Environmentalists and Somali officials say that after the government collapsed in 1991, foreign vessels illegally entered the country's territorial waters to exploit the rich fishing grounds or dump toxic wastes. Initially, the government encouraged Somali fishermen to collect fines from the foreign vessels, but those efforts soon morphed into full-blown piracy, the government says.

AP Photo/Mohamed Sheikh Nor

guidelines, but smaller ships that account for two-thirds of the Somali attacks remain more vulnerable. "Shipping companies are also hit very hard by the economic downturn," says Lehr. "You can't make much money right now with cargo ships, so they're not very keen at throwing more money at security."

OUTLOOK
No Quick Fix

Although the recent surge in piracy has momentarily captured the world's attention, most maritime experts say sustained, concerted effort is needed over the long term.

"Piracy off the Horn of Africa is not a problem we will cure overnight, nor is there a single solution," Vice Admiral Winnefeld told the Senate Armed Services Committee in May.

Criminal activity that has long occurred on land in Somalia — kidnapping, roadblocks and violence — has migrated out to sea, so "something has to be done on land in Somalia," says Wegener. "They operate safe havens, and it's totally risk-free on the part of the pirates."

Although the Europeans and Americans recently have stepped up aid to Somalia, it remains to be seen whether external assistance will have much impact, given the long history of unsuccessful attempts to establish a functioning government.

Most observers expect it to take years for stability to come to Somalia. "That's a long-term endeavor, and a costly one," says RAND's Chalk.

"In Somalia, let us hope that in 10 years there is the beginning of some kind of solution ashore," says the International Maritime Bureau's Mukundan.

Somalia's internal problems create a particularly fertile breeding ground for maritime piracy, says Mukundan. So he doubts similar problems will arise elsewhere. But others aren't so sure.

"There is a risk of this being contagious, when criminals in other parts of the world see how profitable this can be," Wegener says.

For their part, the Somalis say if the international community were serious about halting piracy, foreign in the region would try to halt the illegal fishing or toxic dumping that triggered the upsurge in piracy in the first place. But that's not happening.

"It would be much cheaper to prevent these illegal activities and provide some basic support for the fishing villages and central government so they could deny the pirates land to operate from," says Somali presidential aide Jama.

It's also unclear how long the world's major powers will maintain their naval presence in the region. Historically, says Murphy — the author and Center for Strategic and Budgetary Assessments research fellow — it has taken decades to defeat piracy, using both political and economic measures.

Western nations must decide what level of piracy is tolerable. "None of the people I spoke to — shipping insiders, government officials, naval people — ever said that piracy could be completely eradicated," says author Sekulich. "The best you can do is to suppress and contain it. What's different now is a greater awareness of the economic impact that maritime piracy can have on the global community."

But if piracy is seen as mostly a nuisance, rich nations may decide it's not worth the expense to aggressively patrol for pirates. "Like most other crimes, piracy will not go away," says Ong-Webb, of the Centre for Defence and International Security Studies. "The question we need to answer is what levels of piracy we are prepared to live with."

It's important that the great powers continue to combat the problem, suggests Bainbridge of the International Transport Workers' Federation. "Piracy always has and always will be around," he says. "The trick is not to let the message out that it is easy and safe to do and highly profitable."

NOTES

1. Daniel Sekulich, *Terror on the Seas* (2009), p. 6.

2. www.eaglespeak.us/2009/04/somali-pirates-convoys-could-work.html.

3. "ICC-IMB Piracy and Armed Robbery Against Ships Report — Second Quarter 2009," ICC International Maritime Bureau, July 2009, pp. 5-6.

4. John S. Burnett, *Dangerous Waters* (2002), p. 9.

5. Sahal Abdulle and Rob Crilly, "Rich pickings for pirates hook fishermen," *The Times* (London), April 7, 2009, p. 33, www.timesonline.co.uk/tol/news/world/africa/article6045092.ece.

6. Sekulich, *op. cit.*, p. 80.

7. Elizabeth A. Kennedy, "Pirates Target, Vow to Kill U.S. Crews," The Associated Press, April 16, 2009, www.boston.com/news/world/africa/articles/2009/04/16/pirates_target_vow_to_kill_us_crews/.

8. "Over 5,000 pirates operate off Somali coast: Russian Navy," *Hindustan Times*, July 19, 2009, www.hindustantimes.com/StoryPage/StoryPage.aspx?sectionName=HomePage&id=adf76ecd-a7be-41ca-a08f-072def60b7e0&Headline='Over+5K+pirates+operate+off+Somali+coast.

9. Andy Crick, "Pirates," *The Sun* (England), June 8, 2009, p. 1, www.thesun.co.uk/sol/homepage/showbiz/tv/2468907/Ross-Kemps-yo-ho-no-go.html.

10. For background, see Jason McLure, "The Troubled Horn of Africa," *CQ Global Researcher*, June 2009, pp. 149-176.

11. "ICC-IMB Piracy and Armed Robbery Against Ships Report — Second Quarter 2009," *op. cit.*, p. 34.

12. Robert D. Kaplan, "Anarchy on Lands Means Piracy at Sea," *The New York Times*, April 12, 2009, p. WK9,

www.nytimes.com/2009/04/12/opinion/12kaplan.html.

13. Ian Storey, "What's Behind Dramatic Drop in S-E Asian Piracy?" *The Straits Times* (Singapore), Jan. 19, 2009, http://app.mfa.gov.sg/pr/read_content.asp?View,11946,.

14. "Statement for the Record, Ms. Michèle Flournoy. Undersecretary of Defense (Policy) and Vice Admiral James A. Winnefeld, Director for Strategic Plans and Policy, Joint Chiefs of Staff," Senate Armed Services Committee, May 5, 2009, www.marad.dot.gov/documents/Flournoy-Winnefeld_05-05-09.pdf.

15. Katharine Houreld, "Navies ask: What do you do with a captured pirate?" The Associated Press, April 18, 2009, http://abcnews.go.com/US/wireStory?id=7365467.

16. His testimony is at http://foreign.senate.gov/testimony/2009/PhillipsTestimony090430p.pdf.

17. His testimony is at http://foreign.senate.gov/testimony/2009/ClanceyTestimony090430p.pdf.

18. Burnett, *op. cit.*, p. 85.

19. Peter Spiegel and Henry Chu, "Grappling With a Forgotten Scourge," *Los Angeles Times*, Nov. 20, 2008, p. A1, http://8.12.42.31/2008/nov/20/world/fg-highseas20.

20. Burnett, *op. cit.*, p. 88.

21. Lauren Ploch, *et al.*, "Piracy off the Horn of Africa," Congressional Research Service, April 21, 2009, p. 8, www.fas.org/sgp/crs/row/R40528.pdf.

22. Paul Alexander, "Boredom, Hunger and Fear for Pirates' Hostages," The Associated Press, April 19, 2009, http://abcnews.go.com/International/wireStory?id=7373830.

23. Ploch, *et al.*, *op. cit.*

24. Henry Samuel, "Pirates' Hostage 'Shot by French Rescuers,'" *The Daily Telegraph*, May 5, 2009, p. 15, www.telegraph.co.uk/news/worldnews/europe/france/5272730/French-skipper-held-hostage-by-pirates-shot-dead-by-special-forces.html.

25. "Trial of Somali pirates opens in Yemen," *RIA Novosti*, July 2, 2009, www.globalsecurity.org/military/library/news/2009/07/mil-090702-rianovosti05.htm.

26. Matthew Lynn, "Ignoring Piracy Poses Risk for World Economy," *Sydney Morning Herald*, Dec. 8, 2008, p. 45, www.bloomberg.com/apps/news?pid=newsarchive&sid=aRgDvDy5TQpU.

27. David Osler, "Preventing Piracy," *Lloyd's List*, May 28, 2009, p. 7.

28. Sharon Otterman, "Pirates Said to Ask for $25 Million Ransom," *The New York Times*, Nov. 20, 2008, www.nytimes.com/2008/11/21/world/africa/21pirates.html.

29. Mohamed Olad Hassan, "Five Pirates Drown With Share of $3 Million Ransom a Day After Freeing Saudi Tanker," The Associated Press, Jan. 10, 2009, www.cbsnews.com/stories/2009/01/10/world/main4711893.shtml.

30. Jean-Marc Mojon, "Ransom Payments: The Hole in Somali Pirates' Net," Agence France-Presse, Jan. 12, 2009, www.google.com/hostednews/afp/article/ALeqM5gGilBVHvFJS-ae2dlsyDb84aDiKg.

31. Burnett, *op. cit.*, p. 75.

32. Peter Earle, *The Pirate Wars* (2004), p. 20.

33. Sekulich, *op. cit.*, p. 33.

34. Martin P. Murphy, *Small Boats, Weak States, Dirty Money* (2009), p. 11.

35. David Cordingly, *Under the Black Flag* (1995), p. 203.

36. *Ibid.*, p. 277.

37. Colin Woodard, *The Republic of Pirates* (2007), p. 1.

38. Bill Weinberg, "Book Review: Jefferson's War: America's First War on Terror, 1801-1805," *Journal, Middle East Policy Council*, fall 2006, www.mepc.org/journal_vol13/0609_Weinberg2.asp.

39. Gerard W. Gawalt, "America and the Barbary Pirates: An International Battle Against an Unconventional Foe," The Thomas Jefferson Papers, Library of Congress, http://memory.loc.gov/ammem/collections/jefferson_papers/mtjprece.html.

40. Michael B. Oren, *Power, Faith and Fantasy* (2007), p. 35. Also see "Barbary Wars," U.S. Department of State, www.state.gov/r/pa/ho/time/jd/92068.htm.

41. Cordingly, *op. cit.*, p. xiii.

42. *Ibid.*, p. 96.

43. *Ibid.*, p. xx.

44. Murphy, p. 1.

45. *Ibid.*, p. 9.

46. *Ibid.*, p. 13.

47. *Ibid.*, p. 10.

48. Kaplan, *op. cit.*

49. Cordingly, *op. cit.*, p. 77.

50. Sean Yoong, "Pirate Abduction in Malacca Strait After Long Quiet," The Associated Press, Feb. 21, 2009, www.thejakartapost.com/news/2009/02/21/pirate-abduction-malacca-strait-after-long-quiet.html.

51. Murphy, *op. cit.*, p. 32.

52. Sekulich, *op. cit.*, p. 46.

53. K. C. Vijayan, "Data-Sharing System Boost for Malacca Strait Security," *The Straits Times* (Singapore), March 29, 2008, http://app.mfa.gov.sg/pr/read_content.asp?View,9678,.

54. Storey, *op. cit.*

55. See McLure, *op. cit.*

56. Murphy, *op. cit.*, p. 31.

57. "ICC-IMB Piracy and Armed Robbery Against Ships Report — Second Quarter 2009," *op. cit.*, p. 11.

58. Jeffrey Gettleman, "Somali's Pirates Flourish in a Lawless Nation," *The New York Times*, Oct. 31, 2008, p. A1, www.nytimes.com/2008/10/31/world/africa/31pirates.html.

59. *Ibid.*

60. Jeffrey Gettleman, "Pirates in Skiffs Still Outmaneuvering Warships Off Somalia," *The New York Times*, Dec. 16, 2008, p. A6, www.nytimes.com/2008/12/16/world/africa/16pirate.html.

61. Mary Beth Sheridan, "U.S. Has Sent 40 Tons of Munitions to Aid Somali Government," *The Washington Post*, June 27, 2009, p. A5, www.washingtonpost.com/wp-dyn/content/article/2009/06/26/AR2009062604261.html.

62. Edmund Sanders, "Let Us Handle Pirates, Somalis Say," *Los Angeles Times*, April 15, 2009, p. A22, http://articles.latimes.com/2009/apr/15/world/fg-somalia-pirates15.

63. "A Clear and Present Danger," *The Economist*, April 18, 2009, www.economist.com/displaystory.cfm?story_id=13496711.

64. Peter Chalk, "The Maritime Dimension of International Security: Terrorism, Piracy and Challenges for the United States," RAND Corporation, 2008.

65. Murphy, *op. cit.*, p. 161.

66. *Ibid.*, p. 32.

67. "US Beefs Up Anti-Piracy Action for Ships," Agence France-Presse, May 13, 2009, www.blnz.com/news/2009/05/13/beefs_anti-piracy_action_ships_9407.html.

68. "Nigerian Pirates Blamed for Hike in Marine Premium," *Africa News*, June 30, 2009, http://allafrica.com/stories/200907010274.html.

BIBLIOGRAPHY

Books

Burnett, John S., *Dangerous Waters: Modern Piracy and Terror on the High Seas*, **Dutton, 2002.**
After being robbed at sea, a former UPI reporter — now a marine security consultant — investigates the rise of modern piracy, talking with leading authorities and riding on board an oil tanker crossing the Indian Ocean.

Cordingly, David, *Under the Black Flag: The Romance and the Reality of Life Among the Pirates*, **Random House, 1995.**
The former head of exhibitions at England's National Maritime Museum recounts the history of 17th- and 18th-century pirates and the legends they inspired.

Langewiesche, William, *The Outlaw Sea: A World of Freedom, Chaos, and Crime*, **North Point Press, 2004.**
A writer for *The Atlantic* and *Vanity Fair* looks at the oceans post-9/11, finding that piracy and terror are

symptomatic of the stateless, "inherently disorderly" nature of the seas, which are largely beyond the reach of nations and their laws.

Murphy, Martin N., *Small Boats, Weak States, Dirty Money: Piracy and Maritime Terrorism in the Modern World*, **Columbia University Press, 2009.**
A research fellow at King's College, London, thoroughly assesses piracy and terrorism, drawing careful distinctions between them but explaining how the two problems may overlap.

Sekulich, Daniel, *Terror on the Seas: True Tales of Modern-Day Pirates*, **Thomas Dunne Books, 2009.**
A Canadian journalist travels around the Indian Ocean, tracing the origins of contemporary piracy through interviews with experts and personal experiences.

Woodard, Colin, *The Republic of Pirates: Being the True and Surprising Story of the Caribbean Pirates and the Man Who Brought Them Down*, **Houghton Mifflin Harcourt, 2007.**
A journalist and author tells the story of the Caribbean pirates of the 18th century and the colonial governors and the former privateer who brought them to justice.

Articles

Alexander, Paul, "Boredom, Hunger and Fear for Pirates' Hostages," The Associated Press, April 19, 2009.
Hostages released by Somali pirates share accounts of fear and deprivation.

Bradsher, Keith, "Captain's Rescue Revives Debate Over Arming Crews," *The New York Times*, **April 12, 2009, p. A8.**
Amid growing calls for arming merchant ship crews against pirates, questions persist about whether it would escalate the level of violence.

Carney, Scott, "Cutthroat Capitalism," *Wired*, **July 2009, www.wired.com/images/multimedia/magazine/1707/Wired1707_Cutthroat_Capitalism.pdf.**
A graphics-heavy "economic analysis of the Somali pirate business model" examines the ratio of risk vs. rewards of attacking multiple ships when only a few pay off big. The package includes interviews with a pirate, a security contractor and a former hostage.

Gettleman, Jeffrey, "Rounding Up Suspects, the West Turns to Kenya as Piracy Criminal Court," *The New York Times*, **April 24, 2009, p. A8.**
Kenya will prosecute Somali pirates captured by the European Union, the United Kingdom and the United States.

Kaplan, Robert D., "Anarchy on Land Means Piracy at Sea," *The New York Times*, **April 12, 2009, p. WK9.**
Maritime piracy is a ripple effect of anarchy on land and could potentially serve as a platform for terrorism.

Storey, Ian, "What's Behind Dramatic Drop in S-E Asian Piracy," *The* [Singapore] *Straits Times*, **Jan. 19, 2009.**
Although worldwide piracy reached record levels in 2008, the number of regional incidents in Southeast Asia has dropped by two-thirds since 2003, thanks to improved security cooperation among Singapore, Indonesia and Malaysia.

Sudderuddin, Shuli, and Debbie Yong, "It's a Terrible Time to be a Seaman," *The* [Singapore] *Straits Times*, **Nov. 23, 2008.**
Seafarers describe being hijacked and held hostage by pirates.

Reports and Studies

Chalk, Peter, "The Maritime Dimension of International Security: Terrorism, Piracy and Challenges for the United States," RAND Corporation, 2008; available at www.rand.org/pubs/monographs/2008/RAND_MG697.pdf.
A policy analyst with the California think tank finds no nexus between maritime piracy and terrorism in the early years of this decade. Chalk does suggest, however, that the vulnerabilities that have encouraged piracy also apply to terrorism.

Ploch, Lauren, et al., "Piracy off the Horn of Africa," Congressional Research Service, April 24, 2009, www.fas.org/sgp/crs/row/R40528.pdf.
The United Nations allows international ships to combat piracy in Somali waters, but anarchy in Somalia feeds the problem. U.S. officials pledge a more robust response.

For More Information

Congressional Research Service, 101 Independence Ave., S.E., Washington, DC 20540; (202) 707-7640; www.loc.gov. The research arm of the U.S. Congress that has produced detailed reports about maritime piracy and its effects on insurance.

International Maritime Bureau, 26 Wapping High Street, London E1W 1NG, United Kingdom; (44) 0 20 7423 6960; www.icc-ccs.org. A division of the International Chamber of Commerce that aims to identify and investigate fraud and other threats; manages the Piracy Reporting Centre in Kuala Lumpur, which issues warnings to shippers and reports pirate attacks to local law enforcement.

International Maritime Organization, 4, Albert Embankment, London SE1 7SR, United Kingdom; (44) 20 7735 7611; www.imo.org. A U.N. agency responsible for helping to improve the safety and security of international shipping.

International Shipping Federation, 12 Carthusian Street, London EC1M 6EZ, United Kingdom; (44) 20 7417 8844; www.marisec.org. The principal international shipowners organization.

International Transport Workers' Federation, 49-60 Borough Road, London, SE1 1DR, United Kingdom; (44) 20 7403 2733; www.itf.org.uk. A federation of 654 transport workers' unions, representing 4.5 million workers in 148 countries.

International Union of Marine Insurance, c/o Swiss Insurance Association, C.F. Meyer-Strasse 14, Postfach 4288, CH-8022 Zurich, Switzerland; (41) (44) 208-2870; www.iumi.com. A professional association that provides a forum for exchanging information on issues of importance to the marine shipping and insurance sectors.

Nautilus International, 750-760 High Road, Leytonstone, London E11 3BB, United Kingdom; (44) 20 8989 6677; www.nautilusint.org. A union representing 25,000 seafarers and other workers employed by British and Dutch shipping companies.

RAND Corporation, 1776 Main Street, Santa Monica, CA 90401 USA; (310) 393-0411; www.rand.org. A think tank that has produced reports about piracy and maintains a comprehensive database of terrorism incidents worldwide.

Voices From Abroad:

CYRUS MODY

Manager, International Maritime Bureau, England

Economic conditions cause piracy
"Socioeconomic status in Somalia is very bad right now, as we know, and this is one of the reasons pirates have turned to hijacking. There are a few people who are gaining a lot."

Kuwait Times, December 2008

PETER LEHR

Lecturer in Terrorism Studies, University of St. Andrews, Scotland

Consequences for pirates are not grave
"It's quite encouraging for them. The threat to your life is quite low, and the chance you get arrested and sent to a not-so-nice Kenyan prison is quite low as well."

Birmingham Post (England), April 2009

AHMED ABDULLAH MUSA

Suspected pirate, Somalia

Defending the fish
"We are not pirates, but we are defending our country. There are a lot of ships that throw poisonous rubbish into our territorial waters and go back loaded with our fish."

Saba news agency (Yemen), April 2009

NOEL CHOONG

Chief, Piracy Reporting Centre, Malaysia

Who will be the leader?
"If there's a will, I'm sure governments can find a solution to stop these pirates. But who's going to lead the way? That's the big question. Any answer costs a lot of money."

Chicago Tribune, September 2008

The International Herald Tribunel/Patrick Chappatte

MOHAMED OSMAN ADEN

Somali diplomat, Kenya

Circumstances don't justify piracy
"It's true that the pirates started to defend the fishing business. And illegal fishing is a real problem for us. But this does not justify these boys to now act like guardians. They are criminals. The world must help us crack down on them."

The New York Times, October 2008

BAN KI-MOON

Secretary General, United Nations

A threat to global security
"Piracy is a symptom of the state of anarchy which has persisted in that country (Somalia) for over 17 years. This lawlessness constitutes a serious threat to regional stability and to international peace and security."

The New York Times, December 2008

MARGARET ORAKWUSI

President, Nigerian Trawler Owners Association

A new pirate republic

"Only 19 fishing companies are now operating with just 170 vessels. The issue of piracy and sea robberies has contributed immensely to this drastic reduction and, if allowed to continue, will lead to total collapse of the fishing industry in the country. . . . The pirates have constituted themselves into republics where settlements and clearance have to be made. . . . This is a republic within a Republic of Nigeria."

This Day (Nigeria), December 2008

ROGER MIDDLETON

Researcher, Chatham House (NGO), England

Piracy is easy to understand

"It is a serious business going on here. People are making a lot of money, and they are investing in equipment, in boats, in men and in weapons. They live in the poorest part of the poorest country in Africa, and it is easy to understand why they would resort to crime, but that makes them no less scary for people who are captured and threatened."

Independent on Sunday (England), October 2008

LIAM MORRISSEY

Partner, BGN Risk England

No better option

"Five warships can't guarantee complete safety. Logistics in the area are difficult, and the ongoing regional instability creates challenges for private security firms. The alternative option of traveling the long way around Africa in safer waters adds a minimum of 20 days transit time, bringing associated increased costs in fuel, payroll and lost delivery time."

The Scotsman, November 2008

2

Confronting Rape as a War Crime

Jina Moore

AP Photo/Ben Curtis

Kula, a 47-year-old victim of the mass rapes that occurred during Liberia's civil war, covers her face in shame as she tells counselors at a treatment center about her wartime trauma. While some experts say more men are needed in the fight for justice for war rape victims, women's advocates say local and international courts must prosecute rapists.

From *CQ Global Researcher*,
May 2010.

Last fall in Guinea, soldiers killed 157 pro-democracy protestors in the capital city of Conakry. The horrific violence in and around the city's sports stadium was tragic but not unprecedented in West Africa. But then reports emerged that the soldiers also had raped at least 109 women in broad daylight. The conservative Muslim country — and the international community — were shocked by both the public nature and the sheer viciousness of the attacks.

In a deliberate attempt to engender public humiliation, the victims were often stripped on the streets and gang-raped in front of onlookers, some of whom recorded the attacks with cell phone cameras. Eyewitnesses and survivors told of women being raped with guns and then shot; of soldiers using knives to slice off women's clothing and then to sexually assault them. Some women reportedly were dragged into houses where they were held captive and gang-raped for days.

"It is simply horrifying. Women were raped, gang-raped in the open, in and around the stadium, in the cold light of day," one woman said. "I have never seen such violence in my life. I swear that this is the first time in Guinea that we have witnessed women's bodies being treated as if they were battlefields. It goes against our culture and traditions. . . . We're all horrified."[1]

Guinea's mass rapes were only the latest example of the strategic use of rape, a common wartime tactic that is now also increasingly used to spread terror and humiliation among political opponents. "A woman's place is in the home. If you want political rallies, we'll show you political rallies. We'll show you who's in command in this country," one Guinean woman remembered her attacker saying.[2]

Africa Hit Hardest by Wartime Sexual Violence

More than two dozen countries around the world suffered widespread or numerous rapes during civil wars between 1980 and 1999. Ten nations experienced widespread sexual violence during conflicts, including five in Africa.

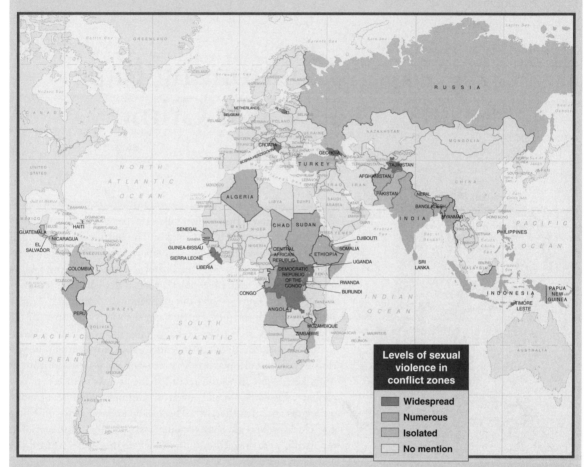

Levels of sexual violence in conflict zones

- Widespread
- Numerous
- Isolated
- No mention

Source: Dara Kay Cohen, "The Causes of Sexual Violence by Insurgents During Civil War: Cross-National Evidence," University of Minnesota, 2009

The U.N. Security Council dispatched a commission of inquiry to Guinea to investigate the incidents. In December the panel reported that the rapes and massacre were ordered by the then-leader of Guinea's military, Moussa Dadis Camara, who had taken over the government in a coup d'etat nine months before the stadium massacre. Camara's government had tried to cover up the September massacre, the panel said, by denying victims medical treatment, sabotaging evidence and intimidating witnesses — actions not uncommon by governments after their soldiers commit mass rape.[3]

Rape in conflict zones is not new. As long as there has been war and conflict between men, soldiers have raped women. And wartime rape is not limited by time or geography. From World War II to the 1971 war in Bangladesh, from Latin America to the disputed

Kashmir region claimed by India and Pakistan — rape as a war strategy exploded in the 20th century and continues today.

But as the mass rapes in Guinea exemplified, today's rape is often different — in its brutality, scope and goals. Women are no longer simply part of the spoils of war — "booty and beauty," as Gen. Andrew Jackson reportedly quipped, protesting the barbarity of the British during the War of 1812.[4] Neither is modern wartime rape an isolated occurrence perpetrated by rogue soldiers. In many conflicts, as in Guinea, mass rape has become an official strategy — a tactic premeditated at the highest levels of military and civilian leadership.

"In modern conflicts, rape is the front line of conflict. It is not a side effect," says Margot Wallström, appointed in February as the first special representative to the U.N. secretary-general for sexual violence. No one knows how many women are raped in conflicts each year; the number of rapes reported is believed to be low because many go unreported due to the stigma associated with rape. Survivors often don't speak up because they believe they will be ostracized for bringing shame to their families and communities.

Guinea is not the only place where mass rape has been used to spread terror among dissidents. More than 2,000 women and girls — allegedly associated with the opposition party — were raped leading up to and immediately after the disputed 2008 presidential elections in Zimbabwe.[5] Agents of President Robert Mugabe's ZANU-PF party fanned out across the country in a deliberate campaign of rape as political retribution against opposition supporters, according to an investigation by AIDS-Free World.[6] And in Kenya, up to 3,000 women were raped

Rape: A Weapon Used in War and Peace

Hundreds of thousands of women have been raped during modern conflicts — both military and political. The victims range from hundreds of thousands of Eastern Europeans raped by Soviet troops after World War II to the thousands raped in Zimbabwe, Kenya and Guinea during recent election or political violence.

Number of Victims in Selected Mass Rapes

Up to 80,000 — By Japanese occupiers in the Chinese city of Nanking during World War II (1937-38).

Up to 110,000 — By the Soviet Army in Berlin plus hundreds of thousands — some say as many as 2 million — across Eastern Europe at the end of the World War II (1945).

200,000-400,000 — During Bangladesh's "war of liberation" (1971).

20,000-50,000 — By Serbs during the war in Bosnia and Herzegovina (early 1990s).

250,000-500,000 — Tutsi women raped by Hutus over the three-month period of the Rwandan genocide (1994).

50,000-64,000 — Women and girls living in internal displaced persons camps during the civil war in Sierra Leone (1990s).

Up to 3,000 — Women attacked during post-election violence in Kenya (2008).

More than 2,000—Females associated with the political opposition raped before and after the disputed presidential election in Zimbabwe (2008).

109 — Raped by government soldiers in Guinea in premeditated effort to terrorize dissidents (2009).

12,000-15,000 per year — Raped during the ongoing conflict in eastern Democratic Republic of the Congo (2000-present).

Sources: "Security Council Resolution 1820: Women, Peace and Security," U.N. Development Fund for Women; Iris Chang and Laura Flanders, in Anne L. Barstow, ed., War's Dirty Secret (2000); Conway W. Henderson, "The Political Repression of Women," Human Rights Quarterly, November 2004; Susanne Beyer, "German Woman Writes Ground-Breaking Account of WW2 Rape," Der Spiegel, Feb. 26, 2010

in the ethnic violence that erupted after the 2007 presidential elections.[7] Mass rape has also been used as a tool of ethnic cleansing or genocide in Bosnia and Herzegovina, Rwanda, Bangladesh and Darfur in western Sudan.

During the war in the Balkans in the early 1990s, an estimated 20,000 Muslim women were raped by Serb soldiers, some in "rape camps" set up expressly for that purpose.[8] The conflict led the United Nations to recognize rape as a tool of ethnic cleansing[9] and the International Criminal Tribunal for the former Yugoslavia to rule, for the first time in history, that rape is a crime against humanity.[10]

The International Criminal Tribunal for Rwanda in 1998 recognized rape as an act of genocide as committed during the 1994 Rwandan genocide, when machete-wielding extremist Hutu militias murdered up to 800,000 minority Tutsis and moderate Hutus and also raped 250,000-500,000 Tutsi women and girls. Their goal was to punish the women for their ethnic identity or to infect them with HIV/AIDS.[11]

More recently, roving *janjaweed* militias, mostly of Arab descent, have raped black Sudanese women in Darfur in what many say is a genocidal campaign. "They grabbed my donkey and my straw and said, 'Black girl, you are too dark. You are like a dog. We want to make a light baby,' " recalled 22-year-old Sawela Suliman. " 'You get out of this area and leave the child when it is made.' "[12]

And while the Guinean population was shocked by the sheer brutality of the mass rapes in Conakry, the level of violence was not uncommon, according to physicians and aid workers who minister to the victims. "A stick was pushed through the private parts of an 18-year-old pregnant girl and it appeared [through her abdomen]. She was torn apart," a Colombian woman told Amnesty International of a crime she had witnessed.[13]

Similarly horrific rapes have occurred during the ongoing conflict in eastern Democratic Republic of Congo (DRC). Denis Mukwege, a physician who specializes in treating rape victims at the Panzi Hospital in DRC, said, "When you talk about rape in New York or Paris everyone can always say, 'Yes we have rape here, too.' But it's not the same thing when a woman is raped by four or five people at the same time, when a woman is raped in front of her husband and children, when a woman is not just raped but then . . . her genitals are attacked with a gun, a stick, a torch or a bayonet. That's not what you see in New York. That's not what you see in Paris."[14]

On a recent trip to the DRC, Secretary of State Hillary Rodham Clinton — the first person in her post to visit since the fighting erupted there nearly 10 years ago — demanded accountability for the Congo rapes. "We state to the world that those who attack civilian populations using systematic rape are guilty of crimes against humanity," she said.[15] Her comment reflects a new understanding that rape in conflict areas is about more than opportunity, or testosterone gone wild or the notion of spoils in war. Wartime rape is about terror, about targeting and about threatening whole communities by violating their women.

Another type of wartime rape has emerged: rape against men, which aid workers say has increased in the past year in eastern Congo.[16] Researchers also have documented rape against men in conflicts in Peru and El Salvador, among others. No one knows how many such crimes have occurred, however, because men and boys — facing perhaps even greater difficulty telling their stories than female rape victims — report the crime in far fewer numbers. And when they do, it often is not recorded as sexual violence.

Women's advocates say rape against men is too easily sensationalized and detracts attention from the much more pervasive problem of rape against women. But Yale University political science professor Elisabeth Jean Wood says to "really understand the different forms and settings where sexual violence occurs . . . we need to understand the patterns of sexual violence against men and boys as well."

Whether committed as an act of terror or genocide or as a crime of opportunity, wartime rape of women serves a unique function: It destroys communities. "This is certainly used as a way to intimidate women, as a way to break the backs of communities, to bring shames to communities," says Maryam Elahi, director of the International Women's Program at the Open Society Institute, a democracy-promoting organization financed by the George Soros Foundation in New York.

Desiree Zwanck agrees. She is a German expert on violence against women with the HEAL Africa hospital in Goma, in eastern DRC, where UNICEF has reported that more than 1,000 women are raped each month. [17] "They've been rejected by their husbands, by their families, even by entire communities, which basically don't want to be close to them or associated with them any more," she says.

Mukesh Kapila, a Sri Lankan physician, has worked in Rwanda, DRC and Darfur, where he was considered a "whistleblower" on rape and genocide. He points out that rape is also "a cheap way to prosecute a war," because it doesn't require guns or munitions to devastate the "morale . . . the very integrity of the society."

Nearly everyone agrees impunity contributes to the proliferation of the problem. Both international and domestic courts have been slow to prosecute wartime rapists. The Rome Statute, which delineates the crimes under the International Criminal Court's (ICC) jurisdiction, defines rape as both a crime against humanity and a war crime.[18] Established in 2002 to prosecute war crimes and crimes against humanity, the ICC has confirmed charges against only two defendants for rape or sexual violence charges, even though it has filed charges against 13 people for alleged war crimes in Sudan, the Central African Republic, the DRC and Uganda.[19] The court is investigating the political rapes in Guinea and Kenya, but no charges have been filed yet.[20] In eastern Congo, the government has prosecuted 27 soldiers — none of them high-level officers — for sexual violence in 2008, even though the United Nations documented nearly 8,000 new cases of rape committed by Congolese soldiers or by rebel or militia groups in the region.[21]

Still, some new precedents have been established. The Special Court for Sierra Leone, created in 2002 to prosecute atrocities committed during the country's civil war, ruled in 2008 that taking a woman as a "bush wife" — a kind of forced marriage of the battlefield — was a crime against humanity.[22] In the last two years, the Security Council passed two resolutions aimed at better protecting women in war zones. Resolution 1888, adopted in September 2009, established Wallström's post. A U.N. resolution in 2008 demanded an end to both sexual violence and impunity for perpetrators.

But Kapila says it will take generations to curb wartime rape and its legacy. "The atmosphere, the feeling it leaves behind, the degradation of society as a whole, the relationships of men and women, the effect on children — it will be at least a couple of generations" before the crime is overcome, he says. "Violent societies beget violent societies."

As international organizations and governments around the world strive to end wartime rape and cope with the aftermath, here are some of the questions being asked:

Is rape an inevitable consequence of war?

For millennia, war and rape were thought to go hand in hand, and political and military leaders alike have long claimed it is impossible to rein in troops. A veteran journalist described the reaction as a "worldwide shrug, in effect saying rape is an unavoidable part of the battlefield."[23]

Some have argued that war gives men cover to commit violence against women, others that war whips men into a frenzy from which sex is a release. Often, wartime rape has been construed as an unfortunate consequence of circumstantial celibacy; both Japanese Gen. Matsui Iwane and American Gen. George S. Patton thought during World War II that men without wives or girlfriends needed prostitutes, and that the availability of sex workers might keep soldiers from raping civilians in the theater. Japan even went so far as to forcibly conscript up to 200,000 "comfort women" from among the populations of countries they occupied, primarily China, Korea and the Philippines.[24]

In his book examining biological explanations for war, British historian David Livingstone Smith argues that rape is necessarily intertwined with battle. "Warriors have a twofold sexual advantage," he writes. "They are especially attractive to women in their own communities . . . [and] they can also sexually coerce the wives and daughters of defeated enemies." Smith thinks this gave warriors a reproductive edge, resulting in successive generations inheriting "the war-like temperament" — and, presumably, instinct for rape —"of their fathers."[25]

Maurizia Tovo, a social protection specialist for Africa at the World Bank, thinks an element of mass psychology is at work. Particularly in Côte d'Ivoire (Ivory Coast), where rebels and government forces alike have used rape in an armed conflict dating back to 2002, rape is sometimes committed by "men who individually wouldn't do that," she says. "In a group, it becomes sort of a frenzy, or at least an acceptable thing to do. Inevitable may be a strong word, but it's close to it."[26]

But the Open Society Institute's Elahi says rape does not necessarily have to be the norm in conflict situations. "It's taken for granted that soldiers kill, loot and rape," she says. "That's a myth we have to start fighting against."

Indeed, in some conflicts at least one side has abstained from rape. For instance, very little rape occurred during ethnic and political violence in Indonesia from 1999 to 2002, in part because militia members'

Secretary of State Hillary Rodham Clinton speaks with U.N. peacekeepers during a trip to Goma in the Democratic Republic of Congo in August 2009. She demanded accountability for the thousands of rapes in the war-ravaged eastern part of the country, calling them "crimes against humanity."

communal traditions generally forbade the sexual assault of women.[27] In Guatemala, where the government violence against Mayans has been described as genocide, guerrilla fighters generally abstained from the use of rape.[28] So, too, did insurgents during the separatist conflict in Sri Lanka and in El Salvador's civil struggle in the 1970s and 1980s.[29]

Yale's Wood studies conflicts in which rape is not used as a tool of war. She attributes the abstention, in part, to the norms of behavior that govern the fighters. "Recruits come into an armed group with certain cultural norms about what kind of violence is appropriate against whom," she says. Leaders "build training camps and develop internal regulations to transform those cultural norms . . . into . . . norms that support the kinds of violence the armed group wants to engage in." In other words, the use of rape is a deliberate choice, often of the military elite who set the standards for acceptable behavior on and off the battlefield.

Sometimes, researchers say, rape is used asymmetrically. Michele Leiby, a researcher at the University of New Mexico, found that insurgents in Guatemala and El Salvador abstained from rape. In Sierra Leone, on the other hand, the rebel Revolutionary United Front engaged in widespread rape, and some of the perpetrators were women, either as accomplices in gang rape or as direct participants, using guns, bottles or both.[30]

Wood says the war experience may change the warriors, including those predisposed not to engage in rape. "Once in combat, wielding violence and seeing violence wielded and suffering violence, many combatants undergo some very profound psychological processes," she says. "Some become desensitized to violence; they tend to dehumanize those associated with the enemy and to [blame] . . . the civilians they're shooting at," individually or collectively. All of that can change the idea of acceptable behavior, she says.

Financial considerations may also motivate some officers to direct their troops to rape, since rape is a low-cost way to destroy an enemy society. "I don't think it is a consequence of a lack of discipline. These are acts of commission," says Kapila. "Very definitely, it appears orchestrated, that officers and those in command are using [rape] strategically."

If rape is a choice, say Kapila and others, it is not inevitable, and the key to its prevention may be changing that cost-benefit analysis: Making sexual violence an unappealing, costly option.

Can the global community stop strategic rape?

The international community has taken several steps recently to address the problem of wartime rape.

In February the U.N. appointed Wallström as special representative on sexual violence to report to U.N. Secretary-General Ban Ki-moon and the U.N. Security Council. Two earlier resolutions in 2000 and 2008 demanded the cessation of rape, promised punishment for perpetrators and encouraged women to get involved in negotiating peace and rebuilding nations and communities.[31]

But few feel resolutions alone can prevent strategic rape. "We need those expressions," says Kapila of the formal resolutions, if only to acknowledge that the rapes are occurring. "One of the things I remember from my own Darfur experience is that [women] felt that they were not [there]; there was a complicity of silence. But," he continues, "as always with such resolutions, it is the enforcement . . . that is necessary."

U.N. special representative Wallström took a similar point of view four months before her appointment. The resolutions "are excellent, they are very good texts," she said, "but the problem is implementation and enforcement, so very little has happened. I would say almost nothing."[32]

Today, she interprets her appointment as a call for implementation and enforcement, and she is optimistic about the U.N.'s ability to help prevent the ongoing use of rape. "There is a window of political opportunity at the moment, especially with me reporting directly to the Security Council," she says. "There is this chance of creating a political accountability, and I would say this is what I would have to use to the full."

Creating accountability is one solution, but the path to combating rape depends on the cause. If rape is a crime of opportunity, says Wallström, then opportunity must be eliminated. For instance, refugee camps can be designed in ways that minimize rape risk factors, such as reducing the distance women must travel to fetch firewood, a trip that can leave women and girls isolated, exposed and vulnerable to rapists. A U.N. peacekeeper in DRC suggested that governments could pay soldiers on time, eliminating the need for them to loot houses for food.

But where rape is used as a weapon, the calculus of the perpetrators must be changed, experts say. "Armed groups that are good at extracting resources, carrying out offensives and retreating should be able to apply those same military hierarchies to prohibiting sexual violence and other forms of violence against civilians if they have the right incentives to do so," says Yale's Wood.

Punishment, or at least legal accountability, should be the top priority among those incentives, many say. If perpetrators are never tried, in either local or international courts, then the crime is cost-free. Tovo, at the World Bank, says even one well-publicized trial could be helpful. "It would be good to have some symbolic [judicial] processes," she says. "If . . . the culprit is actually condemned, with a lot of publicity around it, it will send the message that

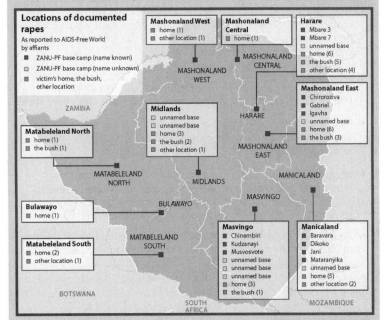

Rapists Targeted Opponents in Zimbabwe Election

During the disputed 2008 presidential election in Zimbabwe, more than 2,000 women and girls were raped by agents of President Robert Mugabe's ZANU-PF party, according to AIDS-Free World. Some of the victims reportedly opposed Mugabe; others were married to opposition supporters. In some cases, the victims were taken to ZANU-PF camps in eastern Zimbabwe, the organization said.

Locations Where Rapes Were Documented in Zimbabwe, 2008

Locations of documented rapes
As reported to AIDS-Free World by affiants
■ ZANU-PF base camp (name known)
□ ZANU-PF base camp (name unknown)
▪ victim's home, the bush, other location

Mashonaland West
■ home (1)
■ other location (1)

Mashonaland Central
■ home (1)

Harare
■ Mbare 3
■ Mbare 7
□ unnamed base
■ home (6)
■ the bush (5)
■ other location (4)

Mashonaland East
■ Chiroroziva
■ Gabriel
■ Igavha
□ unnamed base
■ home (6)
■ the bush (3)

Midlands
□ unnamed base
□ unnamed base
■ home (3)
■ the bush (2)
■ other location (1)

Matabeleland North
■ home (1)
■ the bush (1)

Bulawayo
■ home (1)

Matabeleland South
■ home (2)
■ other location (1)

Masvingo
■ Chinembiri
■ Kudzanayi
■ Musvosvote
□ unnamed base
□ unnamed base
□ unnamed base
■ home (3)
■ the bush (1)

Manicaland
■ Baravara
■ Dikoko
■ Jani
■ Mataranyika
□ unnamed base
■ home (5)
■ other location (2)

Source: "Electing to Rape: Sexual Terror in Mugabe's Zimbabwe," AIDS-Free World, December 2009

'This is not acceptable; it is not right; and if you do it you will be punished.'"

On the other hand, she says, making the cost of rape too high could have unintended consequences. "If you make a huge deal out of rape, and you put the person in prison for life, at this point the person may think he's better off after he rapes the woman to also kill her. He then limits the risk of being condemned, because there's no witness," she says.

Trials aren't the only way to send a signal to armed groups that rape has consequences. Dara Kay Cohen, an

U.N. Recognizes Rape as War Tactic

The U.N. Security Council adopted Resolution 1820 in 2008, explicitly recognizing sexual violence as a tactic of war and giving the council authority to intervene when necessary to provide security to victims. It also demands that conflicting parties train troops and enforce military discipline in an effort to end sexual violence.

Key Elements of Resolution 1820

- Explicitly links sexual violence as a tactic of war with the maintenance of international peace and security. It will no longer be possible to portray rape in war as an issue that does not warrant the council's attention.

- Recognizes sexual violence as a security issue, thus justifying a security response. The council thus has a clear mandate to intervene, including through sanctions and empowering field staff.

- Requests a comprehensive report from the secretary-general on strategies for improving providing the council with better data to inform better responses.

- Demands that parties in armed conflicts adopt concrete protection/ prevention measures to end sexual violence, including training troops, enforcing military discipline, upholding command responsibility and investigating past perpetrators.

- Asserts the importance of women's participation in all processes related to ending sexual violence in conflict, including peace talks.

Source: "Security Council Resolution 1820," U.N. Action Against Sexual Violence in Conflict

assistant professor at the University of Minnesota's Hubert H. Humphrey Institute of Public Affairs, has done extensive fieldwork talking to Sierra Leonean ex-combatants, including rapists, many of whom said they contracted sexually transmitted diseases after participating in gang rape. "It was not only unpleasant and uncomfortable but directly affected the ability of combatants to fight, to walk, to run, to urinate," Cohen says. That, in turn, led to concern about engaging in rape.

Sending signals from the international community may be less important than ensuring protection on the ground, says Doris Mpoumou, director of the International Coalition for the Responsibility to Protect, a New York based organization that advocates protection for civilians in conflict zones. She wants the U.N. to better prepare peacekeepers to protect women by including

rape prevention in the formal rules of engagement approved by the Security Council that set the scope of a peace-keeping mission.

"We've heard directly from the women in Bunia or in the Kivus [in eastern DRC] that some women can be raped in front of the blue berets [U.N. peacekeepers] and they don't even act, because it's not in their mandate, which is just ridiculous," Mpoumou says. "The mandate is key."

The U.N. mandate in the DRC does require its soldiers to "protect civilians under imminent threat of physical violence," but critics often charge that civilian protection clauses are vague, and unless they are translated into direct marching orders by commanders, soldiers often do not know when they should or shouldn't intervene.

Meanwhile, the U.N. itself has a spotty record when it comes to troop behavior. In 2009, the world body received more than 100 reports of sexual abuse or exploitation committed by its peacekeepers, the vast majority of them in the DRC. But only about a dozen reports received follow-up by the U.N. member states whose troops allegedly were involved.[33]

Does speaking out about strategic rape do more harm than good?

In March 2005, the Dutch branch of Médecins Sans Frontières, or Doctors Without Borders, published a report about rape in Darfur. The Sudanese government responded by arresting two of the organization's doctors and charging them with espionage. In 2006, the government effectively evicted the Norwegian Refugee Council for its report on gender-based violence in Darfur.[34]

"You can't even talk about" rape in Sudan, says Susanna Sirkin, deputy director of Physicians for Human Rights. Organizations have opted for euphemisms like "protection," but even those are becoming problematic. "The word 'protection' is dangerous because that implies people need to be protected," which might anger a government intent on denying the severity of the conflict. "So then it becomes 'services for support to women.' Those are necessary code words to talk about women who have been raped in war."

In both Sudan and the DRC, Sirkin says, perpetrators have begun creating obstacles to prevent women from accessing health services after they've been raped. In Sudan, President Omar al-Bashir evicted 13 aid organizations after the International Criminal Court indicted him for genocide. With their departure, services for survivors of rape and other gender-based violence (GBV) were cut back dramatically. As one aid worker put it, "After the expulsions, the message was clear — work on GBV, and you'll be kicked out."[35]

The chilling effect knows no borders. In Chad, Sudan's western neighbor, humanitarian organizations are reluctant to offer services to rape victims. And in Burma (also known as Myanmar), activists see the same hesitancy. "The international organizations I met with very informally in Burma are very fearful of doing anything, because they're afraid they'll be thrown out," says Jody Williams, the Nobel Peace Prize laureate for her work to ban land mines and chair of the Nobel Women's Initiative, an Ontario-based association of women Nobel laureates promoting gender rights and accountability for sexual violence around the world. "Sometimes we think, 'Do something. Be thrown out. You're not making any change!'"

Burmese women's activist Phyu Phyu Sann agrees. "I worked inside Burma. International organizations . . . fear. They become like the Burmese people," says Sann, now a researcher with the Center for Global Justice in New York. "They don't want to lose their projects. They don't want to lose their jobs."

Though the trade-off can be risky, not everyone agrees that silence is worth the price. Sann insists that speaking out in Burma is an obligation. "If you see it's injustice, that it's not right, at least we can put it in a report," she says.

Rape survivors also face the trade-off between speaking out and keeping silent. In many countries, women are blamed for the attack. "In some cases if a woman speaks up she is kicked out. She becomes ostracized, sometimes she is kicked out by the family, and sometimes by the whole village," says Tovo of the World Bank.

In many cases, women try to keep rape a secret. In Nepal, victims often are silenced by their husbands. "Sometimes the wife wants to talk about it, but the husband shuts her up, saying 'You better not talk about it or go any place to report about it, because I also feel ashamed that you've been raped,'" says Bandana Rana, president of the Kathmandu-based women's organization Saathi-Nepal.

Some rape victims may even be formally punished. "When I was eight months pregnant from the rape, the police came to my hut and forced me with their guns to go to the police station. They asked me questions, so I told them that I had been raped. They told me that as I was not married, I will deliver this baby illegally," a rape survivor in Sudan told Doctors Without Borders. She was beaten and imprisoned with other women who were also carrying children from rape. She was released after 10 days, but she had to pay a $65 fine for her "crime."[36]

On the other hand, in some countries the widespread nature of the crime can actually encourage women to speak out. "When rape is something so commonly experienced by victims, at least some of the stigma seems to be mitigated," as in Sierra Leone, says Cohen, of the University of Minnesota.

Indeed, after the war that created Bangladesh — in which 3 million people died and an estimated 200,000 women were raped — authorities declared rape victims national heroines, hoping to break through the stigma and urge husbands to take back their wives, no longer sinners but patriots.[37]

Tovo says getting survivors' stories into public discussion is the only way to change the status quo on both the individual and collective levels. The more women speak freely, she says, the less likely their communities will reject them. Meanwhile, growing public attention to the problem has resulted in better interventions. "It became more acceptable to talk about it, and therefore there are more . . . resources to help survivors, as they should be called," she says.

Tovo also thinks a healthy public discourse about rape may help prevent its recurrence. "I'm the mother of a boy, for example. I would hope my boy, the way he has been brought up, would never, ever dream of doing something like that," Tovo says. "If there is enough discussed in the culture, I would hope that at least in some cases, the discussion would act as a brake."

Helping Survivors Heal After War Rape

'Women have had enough of these things happening. They want this to end.'

The use of rape as a weapon of war may be global, but today the Democratic Republic of Congo (DRC) is often called the epicenter of the crisis. The eastern part of one of Africa's biggest countries has been the site of on-and-off fighting for the last 10 years. As peace talks come and go, violence ebbs and flows.

"We say the war has ended," said Denis Mukwege, a physician who treats rape victims in eastern Congo's South Kivu province. "But really it has not ended."[1]

The consequences of rape are many — physical, psychological, spiritual and social — and they linger. But intervention specialists, from doctors to gender advisers to lawyers, are trying to improve the situation for rape survivors in eastern Congo.

Their primary concern is the physical effect of rape. Eastern DRC has become infamous for the particularly traumatic physical consequences of some rapes there. The condition, known as fistula, occurs when the wall between the vagina and the rectum tears; it can happen in childbirth, as well, but it has lately been a consequence of rape in which foreign objects are used. Women who suffer from fistula can't control their excretions, and they are often isolated by their communities, left to suffer alone. They are, as one survivor described it, "not women anymore."[2]

Fistula can be fixed with surgery. And after recent international and national publicity about the dire situation for eastern Congo's rape victims, survivors have begun turning up to ask for the surgery. Doctors also are being trained in how to perform it.

HEAL Africa hospital in Goma, capital of DRC's North Kivu province, takes a more holistic and communal approach to rape and its consequences. It treats the physical and psychological needs of survivors and creates community outreach programs. "We try to help these women by having counselors on the ground," says Desiree Zwanck, the group's gender advisor, "When a woman comes back [from the hospital] to her community, we try to discuss it with the husbands and with the families and start a mediation process."

Zwanck has also found that giving returning survivors access to microcredit can improve their chances for acceptance in their homes and communities — and improve their own sense of self-respect.[3] "A lot of families here are in such dire need that they are actually more inclined to accept the woman back into the household when there is an economic incentive for it," she says. "When they are able to manage their own funds, their own livestock, their own little boutique, the family respects them more, and so does the community."

But HEAL Africa is also home to professionals who don't usually walk the hospital halls: legal advisors.

The American Bar Association (ABA) has a one-room office at the hospital. Flanked by offices for psychological and spiritual counseling, the offices are a "one-stop shop" for survivor services. The ABA helps women who want to press charges against the men who raped them. The choice is becoming more and more popular, says Mirielle Amani Kahatwa, an ABA program officer at the hospital. "Women have had enough of these things happening. They want this to end."

BACKGROUND

Spoils of War

There has always been rape during wartime. But today's strategic rape — in which rape becomes a weapon of war — is fundamentally different from the sexual assault perpetrated by an individual soldier against a vulnerable woman. Strategic rape is committed with a specific political intent.

It is "rape unto death, rape as massacre, rape to kill and to make the victims wish they were dead," wrote American human rights lawyer Catherine A. MacKinnon. "It is rape as an instrument of forced exile, rape to make you leave your home and never want to go back. It is rape to be seen and heard and watched and told to others: rape as spectacle. It is rape to drive a wedge through a community, to shatter a society, to destroy a people. It is rape as genocide."[38]

While there have been isolated examples of such intentional use of rape throughout history, the practice — on today's broad scale — is relatively new. In the 1975 book *Against Our Will*, the first comprehensive look at rape,

So they turn to the courts to fight against impunity, hoping that punishing some rapists might deter others. Since last September, the ABA has helped move 226 cases through local Congolese courts, resulting in 20 convictions.

Kahatwa says the process can be difficult: Not all perpetrators are known, and those who are can't always be found. And in some cases, like that of Marie Chantal Murakamanzi, the rapists are in positions of authority themselves.

Murakamanzi wears the brightly patterned *kitenge* fabric popular among Congolese women; a baby suckles at her breast. She has two other children, but she left them alone, without even a word, fleeing, as she tells it, for her life after a local police commander raped her.

The policeman controls her part of Masisi, in rural eastern Congo. He accused her and her brother of orchestrating a cattle theft the night before; her brother was tortured. She, too, was abused. "Then he said, 'If you don't agree to have sex with me, I will torture you more than your brother,'" she recalls, explaining that she knew she would not survive the torture. "I was obliged to agree."

She fled to Goma after the rape, hoping that if she reported it to the authorities they might free her brother and prosecute the commander. She was treated at HEAL Africa and reported the rape, but the ABA legal clinic hasn't been able to get the commander arrested: No one is willing to serve him with the papers. Murakamanzi, meanwhile, is afraid to go home. "I may be killed by him," she says.

That makes the risk of pursuing prosecution worth it, she says. "If he isn't arrested, his family could do its best to kill me" to make the allegation disappear, she says. "If he is arrested, I will feel secure. Everyone will see the greatness of the crime that he has done, and that will bring my family security."

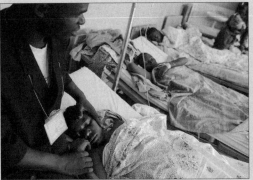

Father Samuel prays with a Congolese rape victim on Aug. 11, 2009, before she undergoes surgery at the Heal Africa clinic in Goma to repair severe physical damage caused to her internal organs by her brutal rape.

As Murakamanzi's story suggests, despite much progress in treating eastern Congo's rape victims, impunity is still widespread.

Kahatwa sees this, too. In fact, she says, impunity is an even bigger problem than war rape. "Before, it was like a gun in war. Today, things have cooled down," she says. "But the mind remains in people, especially in soldiers . . . and the perpetrators know they may rape with impunity."

— Jina Moore

[1] "Surgeon describes horrors that ensue when rape is a 'weapon of war,'" *Harvard Gazette*, April 17, 2008, http://news.harvard.edu/gazette/story/2008/04/surgeon-describes-horrors-that-ensue-when-rape-is-a-'weapon-of-war'/.

[2] Stephanie Nolen, "Congo's Rape Survivors," *Ms. Magazine*, Spring 2005, www.msmagazine.com/spring2005/congo.asp.

[3] For background, see Sarah Glazer, "Evaluating Microfinance," *CQ Global Researcher*, April 2010, pp. 79-104.

American feminist author Susan Brownmiller finds evidence of rape from the Homeric epics to the Crusades, from the American Revolution to Vietnam — but not always en masse or as a tactical tool of warfare.

"In the name of victory and the power of the gun, war provides men with a tacit license to rape," Brownmiller writes.[39] For instance, she concludes, the action in the first of Homer's two epic poems, *The Iliad*, is driven as much by warriors' "rights" to women as by battle necessity. It was, after all, the capture — and presumed rape — of Helen of Troy that proverbially launched a thousand ships.[40] In

Geoffrey Chaucer's *Canterbury Tales*, a knight — a symbol of the warrior class — rapes an elderly woman.

But sanctions against wartime rape also stretch back through time. In one of the earliest behavioral codes for soldiers in battle, Richard the II of England decreed in 1385 that no English soldier should "force any woman" — under penalty of death.[41]

Nevertheless, authorities historically have responded to rape by soldiers with the attitude that "boys will be boys."[42] Jonathan Gottschall — an English professor at Washington and Jefferson College in Washington, Pa., and author of *The*

Japan forced up to 200,000 "comfort women" in occupied countries — primarily Korea, China, and the Philippines — to serve as sex slaves for Japanese soldiers. Aging survivors periodically hold protest rallies — like this one in front of the Japanese Embassy in Manila in 2007 — demanding that Japan apologize and pay them restitution.

Rape of Troy: Evolution, Violence, and the World of Homer — has crafted a list of wartime rape, often done en masse. In the 20th century alone, he finds rape committed by armed forces in 43 countries, in Europe, Asia, Latin and South America and Africa, but he insists the list is incomplete.[43] Such a list, though, obscures other relevant details — the scale or intensity of the rape, the perpetrating groups and the purpose.

Rape, both ancient and modern, also has been used as a collective punishment for the vanquished. The Old Testament book of Isaiah tells of a coming war with Babylon; Isaiah, the narrator, describes a vision of the battle in which, "Their infants will be dashed to pieces before their eyes; their houses will be looted and their wives ravished."[44]

Rape as punishment was practiced on an especially brutal scale during the Second World War. In the Asian theater, when the Japanese army invaded China, its horrific violence against civilians in Nanking became known as "the rape of Nanking." In the eight weeks following the city's surrender in 1937, the Japanese murdered an estimated 300,000 people, both military and civilian, and raped some 20,000-80,000 women.[45]

In her book *The Rape of Nanking*, the first to bring serious attention to Japan's wartime sexual violence,

journalist Iris Chang documented the stories of thousands of survivors — and some perpetrators. A former Japanese soldier told Chang, "No matter how young or old, [women] could not escape the fate of being raped." While rape technically violated Japan's military code of conduct, Chang's research convinced her that rape was an integral part of Japanese military culture.

Thus not only did the code not protect women from being raped, it gave soldiers an incentive to kill them. One confessed to Chang, "It would be all right if we only raped them. I shouldn't say alright. But we also stabbed and killed them. Because dead bodies don't talk."[46]

Ironically, the mass rape in Nanking led directly to the Japanese military's institution of "comfort women." Hundreds of thousands of women, mainly Korean, were captured and taken to Japanese military bases throughout the theater, where they were forced to become sex slaves for soldiers. The idea was to prevent a repetition of mass rape in conquered cities — and in part to protect soldiers from sexually transmitted diseases. The practice today is recognized as a crime against humanity.

Perhaps the most infamous mass rape in the European theater of World War II occurred in Berlin. When the German capital and its surroundings fell, victorious Soviet soldiers literally hunted down their female victims. Gabrielle Köpp, the first German woman to write a memoir about wartime rape under her own name, remembers Russians searching with flashlights for girls. In a single three-day span, Köpp, then 15, was raped five times, and later, "relentlessly, for two weeks."[47]

A Polish woman who experienced the brutality of the Soviets before they rolled into Berlin later described her encounter. "They beat on the door with their rifle butts until it was opened. Without any consideration for my mother and aunt, who had to get out of bed, we were raped by the Russians, who always held a machine pistol in one hand," she said. "They lay in bed with their dirty boots on, until the next lot came."[48]

These circumstances are not confined to World War II, nor to Asian or Eurasian perpetrators. During the so-called Winter Soldier Investigation, conducted by the Vietnam Veterans of America in 1971, U.S. veterans testified on atrocities they witnessed in Vietnam, telling repeated stories of rape, mass rape and other sexual violence by American soldiers. In her research, Brownmiller uncovered U.S. Army records showing that 86 soldiers were tried for rape or

CHRONOLOGY

1930s-1940s *Rape occurs on a massive scale during World War II.*

1937-1938 From 20,000-80,000 women are raped by Japanese soldiers in Nanking, China, in the infamous "rape of Nanking," which is virtually ignored for 50 years.

1945 Soviet army sweeps through Nazi-controlled Eastern Europe to Berlin; soldiers rape thousands of German women. . . . U.S.-backed courts in Nuremberg, Germany, and Tokyo, Japan, try Nazi and Japanese soldiers for war crimes. Despite mass rapes by both armies, no one is charged with sexual violence.

1970s-1980s *Rape is used during conflicts and civil wars from Indonesia to Guatemala.*

1971 About 200,000 women are raped in the war that establishes Bangladesh as a sovereign country.

1975 Indonesia annexes newly independent East Timor, beginning two decades of military rule that included civilian massacres and widespread rape.

1982 Guatemalan soldiers slaughter most inhabitants of the Mayan village of Rio Negro, raping many women before killing them. Such government-sponsored violence occurred throughout the country's 36-year civil war, in which an estimated 200,000 Mayans were killed.

1990s-2000s *Rape is used a tool of ethnic warfare in Bosnia and Rwanda; international tribunals determine that mass rape is a crime against humanity.*

1991 Indian soldiers gang-rape 23 women in Kunan, Kashmir, in a incident that became the symbol of the military's willingness to use rape to intimidate citizens in the disputed border region claimed by India and Pakistan.

1991-1993 Serb forces commit mass rape against Bosnian Muslims.

1993 International Criminal Tribunal for the former Yugoslavia enumerates rape as a crime against humanity, paving the way for landmark prosecutions against perpetrators.

1994 An estimated half-million minority Tutsi women are raped during the Rwandan genocide.

1998 International Criminal Tribunal for Rwanda recognizes rape as an act of genocide. . . . Burma's junta forcibly relocates its ethnic minorities, raping many women in the process.

2001 International Tribunal for the former Yugoslavia secures its first conviction for rape as a crime against humanity.

2004 Initial reports emerge from Darfur about the use of rape as a tool of ethnic cleansing; Amnesty International's earliest report finds evidence of at least 500 rapes.

2008 In February, the Special Court for Sierra Leone finds that the use of "bush wives" — women forced to marry and have sexual intercourse with a soldier — is a crime against humanity. . . . Rape becomes notorious as a tool of warfare in the Democratic Republic of Congo (DRC). . . . U.N. Security Council passes Resolution 1820, demanding all armed groups cease using rape and other forms of sexual violence. Mass rapes occur in connection with elections in Kenya and Zimbabwe.

2009 In August, U.S. Secretary of State Hillary Rodham Clinton visits the DRC, and announces $17 million in U.S. funding to train female police officers and local doctors. . . . On Sept. 28, an estimated 107 women are raped in public by Guinean soldiers seeking to quell pro-democracy protests. . . . U.N. Security Council appoints a special representative on sexual violence. . . . U.N. task force on the Guinea violence says orders to kill protestors and rape women may have come from top military and government officials.

2010 Nobel Women's Initiative holds a proxy international tribunal in March about sexual assaults committed against Burmese women. . . . In April, U.N. Special Representative for Sexual Violence Margot Wallström visits the DRC, speaking with government leaders, peacekeepers and rape survivors.

U.N. Anti-Rape Czar: 'Mission Irresistible'

Rape is a security issue, not a gender issue, says Margot Wallström.

Margot Wallström was appointed the United Nations' Special Representative for Sexual Violence in February. Her assignment: to help reduce wartime rape worldwide. The week before her first trip to the Democratic Republic of Congo, she talked by phone with CQ Global Researcher *reporter Jina Moore about her trip, which she called "not a mission impossible but a mission irresistible."*

CQGR: You said that right now, you think there is a window of political opportunity for dealing with rape in war. What is unique about this moment?

MW: We have never before acknowledged this as a security problem to the extent that the most recent [U.N.] resolutions [have] expressed. So it has come to the very top of the economic development and security agenda, and I think that's what is different. Now it is acknowledged as an international crime.

Also, the agenda for fighting sexual violence is made more concrete. Everybody focuses on, of course, ending impunity, but also at the same time empowering women — protecting women but also empowering women.

CQGR: If we've only recently seen rape as a security problem, how were we looking at it before? What's changed?

MW: It was on the gender agenda. You can see that most men are not that interested, unfortunately, in the gender agenda. . . . It's easier to brush aside if they think this is feminism or something that only women care for. They say, 'It's a women's issue.' But this is a human rights issue; it's a criminal issue. I have often quoted Madeline Albright, who says that [rape] 'is not cultural, it's criminal.' They have to realize that it is at the core of security policy, so that it comes to the attention of both men and women.

CQGR: How can the international community better protect women from rape?

MW: We have learned that from how you design setting up refugee camps to the daily patrolling or the way you define protection of civilians affects this problem. We had a few good examples where firewood patrols and the fact that they have constructed these fuel-efficient stoves has reduced the number of rapes.

If we can have more peacekeepers that are women that will also . . . help us. [These] can seem like very simple things, but they reflect this understanding of the problem. It has to be thought of from the very beginning.

CQGR: What about protecting women from rape as a deliberate strategy of armed groups?

MW: That is . . . very much linked to impunity. If the perpetrators go unpunished . . . then this will only get worse. I've been saying in my speeches that in modern conflicts, rape is the front line. It is not a side effect. That means that it requires also a security response. . . . It also has to be part of the peace negotiations. Amnesty is not an option.

CQGR: There is concern among Africans that their continent is singled out by the International Criminal Court, all of whose open cases are in Africa. And, of

attempted rape and related crimes in Vietnam; 50 were convicted. But she warned, "As an indicator of the actual number of rapes committed by the American military in Vietnam, [the numbers] are practically worthless," as few are likely to have been reported to senior officers, let alone carried through to court-martial.[49]

Equally universal was the silence that fell on the victims and their stories after the conflicts had ended. The "Rape of Nanking" was among the charges brought forward at the Tokyo War Crimes Trial, a U.S.-backed tribunal held after the war. But the full scope of the crime did not emerge, and the story gradually faded from view. By the time Chang published her book in 1997, Japan had omitted references to the violence in Nanking from its history textbooks.[50]

In Germany, talking about the Soviet rapes was taboo for more than half a century. One woman anonymously published her diary in Germany in the 1950s (it was reissued, still anonymously, in 2006). Then in March Köpp published her *Why Was I Born a Girl* — the first memoir about the Soviet rapes with a name and a face attached to it.

course, we hear a great deal about rape in Congo. What other regions might you be dealing with?

MW: I'm very clear about my team having to prioritize. . . . I think we will have to choose not only Africa but probably also choose one or two other places where we have rape in conflict or post-conflict [situations]. Of course a lot of people say Afghanistan; we will have to see what can realistically be done. . . . It is true that this is not only an African problem, although Congo is very much described as being the epicenter of sexual violence, but I think it's so important to recognize that this is unfortunately a global problem.

CQGR: There are also reports of sexual exploitation or abuse by U.N. peacekeepers. How will your office advocate for women in the face of those accusations?

MW: This is the first thing I hear very often: 'How can you be credible, if your own peacekeepers sexually exploit women on the ground, if they rape women as well?' This is extremely important, that we have the credibility of implementing the policy that has been introduced and we show that there is no impunity in our system. . . .

A lot has been done over the past couple of years, but it's a constant struggle. We have to do even more. . . . I will travel definitely to some of the big troop-contributing countries. I can go and talk to India, Pakistan or Bangladesh and make sure I engage with their governments.

CQGR: What might your position allow you to accomplish that hasn't happened before?

MW: For example, we have finalized a team of legal experts, we are recruiting the people to this team of legal experts. We think we will have six to eight, maximum, people on that team. The head of that team will be located with me, and I will be able, in my political context . . . to hopefully offer to governments [the team's] expertise to

AFP/Getty Images/Mychele Daniau

Margot Wallström, the U.N.'s first special representative for sexual violence, says rape is the front line, not a side effect, of modern warfare.

modernize and upgrade their legal frameworks for addressing all the problems that have to do with sexual violence.

It's very important to meet at the highest political levels to address this . . . but also to be interested in how it works operationally on the ground. And never to forget who you're working for. They are both the victims and the most important actors in society; as I say, what is an African village without the women?

— Jina Moore

Rape and Ethnic Cleansing

The final decade of the 20th century saw a brutal refinement of the use of rape in warfare. During the war in the Balkans in the early 1990s, the Serb army explicitly wielded rape as a tool of ethnic cleansing. Not only was rape widespread and systematic, experts say. It was also clearly Serb policy.

The policy took several forms, including the establishment of "rape camps" similar to the concentration camps of World War II. Muslim women were herded into the camps with the express intent of impregnating them with

"Serb babies." Only about 20 percent of the women survived their detention.[51]

The imprisoned women were raped day and night by men, usually in groups. "The degradation and molestation of women was central to the conquest" in Bosnia, writes Roy Gutman, an American journalist who won a Pulitzer Prize for his reporting on the Balkan conflict.[52] In particular, he said, Serbs targeted single women, whom Muslim custom obliged to remain chaste until marriage.

A United Nations investigation in 1992 found that "sexual assault and rape have been carried out by some of

AP Photo/Pavel Rahman

AP Photo/Hidajet Delic

Demanding Long-Delayed Justice

"We demand punishment for war criminals" says a poster with a caricature of a blood-thirsty war criminal held by activists at a Bangladesh Independence Day celebration in Dhaka on March 26 (top). Bangladesh recently established a war crimes tribunal for the long-delayed trials of people accused of war crimes during the country's 1971 war of independence with Pakistan, when 200,000-400,000 women were reportedly raped. At the U.N. office in Sarajevo on July 18, 2008, Bosnian women protest a decision by a U.N. war crimes tribunal in the Netherlands not to prosecute two Bosnian Serb military leaders for organizing mass rapes of hundreds of Muslim women held in "rape camps" during the 1992-95 Bosnian war. The two men — Milan and Sredoje Lukic — were being prosecuted for other war crimes.

the parties so systematically that they strongly appear to be the product of policy;" a follow-up report clarified that it was indeed a policy of ethnic cleansing practiced by the Serbs.[53] The clarification was important. Local television in the Balkans was airing reports about rape — but in

those reports the victims were said to be Serbs, the perpetrators Muslim. In fact, the Serbian propaganda campaign used footage of its own soldiers raping Muslim women but lied about the identities of victim and perpetrator.[54]

After the conflict, the International Criminal Tribunal for the former Yugoslavia (ICTY) — the U.N.-backed court established to try the war's most heinous crimes — for the first time recognized mass rape as a crime against humanity.

Shortly after the world was horrified by the images from the Balkans, attention shifted to the ongoing genocide in Rwanda, where the Hutu ethnic group set upon the Tutsis. In 100 days in the spring of 1994, Hutu soldiers and militiamen murdered some 800,000 Tutsis (and moderate Hutus) and raped thousands of Tutsi women.

The seeds of sexual violence were wrapped up in the nature of the genocide. Ever since Belgian colonists brought their notions of beauty and eugenics to Rwanda, the Tutsis, tall and slender with big eyes and narrow noses, were thought to be "superior" Africans. They looked more like the Belgians than did the Hutu, whom colonial literature describes as short and stout. A missionary described the Tutsi as "European[s] under black skin."[55]

Thus, explained a woman who survived the genocide, "Tutsi women have always been viewed as enemies of the state."[56] In the run-up to the genocide, Rwandan radio programs broadcast gender-based slanders about Tutsi women designed to incite the Hutu to hatred and violence.[57]

During the 100-day killing spree, Hutu men raped up to half a million Tutsi women and girls. The attacks were "part of a pattern in which Tutsi women were raped after they had witnessed the torture and killings of their relatives and the destruction and looting of their homes."[58] The pattern of rape was recognized by the International Criminal Tribunal for Rwanda (ICTR) in 1998 as an act of genocide.[59]

Political Rape

Rape is also used to spread terror during elections. Both before and during presidential elections in 2008, the party of Zimbabwe's President Mugabe reportedly used violence against his opponents and rape to intimidate opposition communities, according to the international organization AIDS-Free World. It investigated the use of rape in the lead-up and aftermath of the controversial election and found evidence of a coordinated rape campaign by the ZANU-PF, Mugabe's political party, to terrorize his opponents.

"Unless you love ZANU-PF, we are going to kill you because you don't listen. That is what we are raping you for," a survivor recalled her perpetrator as saying.[60]

Some of the women targeted, the organization found, were politically active. Others were simply married to activists and were raped to punish and terrorize their husbands for supporting the opposition. Sometimes, the rapes occurred in the women's villages; sometimes, the victims were taken to ZANU-PF camps in five provinces in the eastern part of the country.[61]

Similarly, rape was used after Kenya's controversial 2007 election. Kenyan police recorded 876 reports of rape, but since rape victims rarely report the crime, observers think the actual number is higher. Kenyan health clinics reported treating far more victims than the official number reported by police.[62] And most recently, rape was used for retribution against dissidents in the Guinean military junta's crackdown on democracy protesters in 2009. According to some reports, it was the first time rape had been used as a tactic of military oppression in Guinea.[63]

All Talk, No Action?

In the last 10 years, the U.N. Security Council has passed increasingly stringent resolutions about the treatment of women in war zones. The first, UNSC Resolution 1325, called for greater participation of women in peace negotiations and post-war peace building. Although largely focused on broad-based gender issues, the resolution also recognized that civilians generally — and women and children in particular — suffer the most from armed warfare and, increasingly, are targets of militants.[64]

The resolution helped pave the way for a tougher measure, passed by the Security Council in 2008, demanding that armed groups immediately stop using rape in conflict zones. Last September, three days after the Guinea rapes, the council passed a third resolution, establishing a special representative to help oversee and integrate U.N. resolutions and other efforts to prevent and punish rape in warfare.

"Really, the problem is the international community comes in almost when it's too late," says Mpoumou, of the International Coalition for the Responsibility to Protect. "It took the international community five years" to

A billboard in Monrovia, Liberia, encourages women who have been raped to seek treatment. The country's brutal civil war left hundreds of rape victims suffering in silent shame. But some are coming forward now to seek treatment for their physical, psychological and emotional wounds, which experts say can last a lifetime.

recognize the problem of sexual violence in the DRC, she points out.

But the world seems to have finally had enough of the rapes in Congo. In the lead-up to last September's resolution, U.S. Secretary of State Clinton visited the DRC, promising funds for, among other things, medical and legal aid for rape victims.

"We are raising this issue at the highest levels of [the Congolese] government," she told a group of civil society and public health organizations in Goma. "[T]hese crimes, no matter who commits them, must be prosecuted and punished. That is particularly important when those who commit such acts are in position of authority, including members of the Congolese military."[65]

CURRENT SITUATION
Demanding Accountability

Although recent international attention has focused on strategic rape in the DRC, some observers hope the publicity will catalyze awareness of other, lesser-known rape crises. They also hope attention from powerful political players will translate into better judicial accountability.

Will recent U.N. resolutions help protect women?

YES
Kudakwashe Chitsike
Programme Manager
Women's Programme Research and
Advocacy Unit (RAU) Zimbabwe

Written for *CQ Researcher*, May 2010

The adoption of U.N. Resolutions 1820 and 1880 was welcomed. Finally the international community was recognizing the treatment of women during war and conflict. Women all over the world felt a sense of relief, albeit with a little apprehension.

The relief came from the fact that the world now realizes women suffer differently in wars than men. Women frequently are raped to dehumanize them and to punish the men to whom they are related. Often the women are even forced to bear the children of their violators. So they suffer not only for their own actions, but also for those of their men. The long-awaited resolutions also show that the international community now views sexual violence as a security issue that needs urgent attention.

The apprehension arises from concerns that the international community may not be prepared to respond to the issue. The world will have to look at the problems caused by sexual violence, including the fear instilled by the perpetrators, the stigma associated with reporting sexual violence and the cultural beliefs where the issue is reported. Resolutions are easy, but implementation can be enormously difficult, especially since protecting women's rights must inevitably confront patriarchal structures of society.

The international community has taken steps before to afford women necessary and special protection, such as setting up institutions to address gender-based violence. Because these instruments have not taken into consideration the situation on the ground, they have failed to make an impact on the very people they were attempting to serve.

Protection for women will only be achieved if there is no impunity for past offenders; if command responsibility is enforced and if there is training not only for troops but also for communities, including men and women, on the dangers and consequences of sexual violence. It is critical to remember that once violence is embedded in a culture it always makes women vulnerable, especially during periods of tension, and it constitutes a major obstacle to development, peace and security. It must be guaranteed that women are consulted and centrally involved in all processes that aim to end sexual violence. For the resolutions to offer protection there has to be zero tolerance for sexual violence by the U.N. as this will encourage more women to speak out where it occurs.

NO
Rosebell Kagumire
Ugandan human rights journalist and blogger

Written for *CQ Global Researcher*, May 2010

In 2008, Major Gen. Patrick Cammaert — former U.N. force commander in eastern Democratic Republic of Congo (DRC) — told a U.N. Security Council meeting: "It is now more dangerous to be a woman than to be a soldier in modern conflict."

As the 20th century ended, wars had changed. Civil wars trapped civilians on undefined frontlines, and sexual violence was embraced as part of a military strategy to inflict fear and subjugate the "other."

Women in my country have not escaped mass sexual violence. For two decades the Lord's Resistance Army (LRA) has wreaked havoc in northern Uganda, DRC and Central African Republic, killing civilians and abducting women and girls as sex slaves. Most of the rapes are committed by "rebels" — young men abducted as children and forced into rebellion. The International Criminal Court has indicted LRA leaders for rape — but this has yet to stop them.

Thus, it seems unlikely that recent U.N. resolutions will translate into accountability and prevention of sexual violence. While the resolutions show the world is finally paying attention, ensuring protection for women in wartime still has a long way to go.

While such resolutions help build cases against leaders who perpetrate mass rape, they don't help to prevent sexual violations in areas where the security situation has disintegrated. To do that, governments must be held accountable for women's security. Countries must improve their judicial infrastructure. In Uganda, most rape victims cannot seek justice because of lengthy court procedures and expensive access to lawyers.

The political will to enforce accountability is also critical. The Ugandan government remains opposed to civil trials for soldiers in relation to the war in northern Uganda. While several reports indicate government soldiers have raped women, the army insists such cases have been tried in military courts, but there is no record of such trials.

Finally, sexual violence is not just a wartime problem. Even in peaceful regions of Uganda, women often must pay a police surgeon to get a medical check after a sexual offense. And women are still blamed for being raped. If we cannot protect vulnerable women in peacetime, how can we do it once countries have fallen into such lawlessness?

That could start in The Hague, where ICC Prosecutor Luis Moreno-Ocampo is pursuing sexual violence charges against eight of 14 defendants facing trial, including Sudanese President al-Bashir.[66] Among other charges, he has been indicted for genocide based on his support of alleged rape and sexual assault — the first time the ICC has used the precedent set by the tribunal for Rwanda.

Moreno-Ocampo also is investigating the post-election violence in Kenya in 2008, where, he said, rape allegations "will be central to the investigation."[67] Local human rights groups, meanwhile, say neither justice nor support services are forthcoming for the women, including those who testified at a Kenyan national commission that investigated the violence. "There is no support absolutely," said Kenyan human rights advocate Maina Kiai.[68]

In Guinea, progress in bringing perpetrators of last fall's mass rapes to justice has been slow. Although Secretary Clinton has called for the rapists to face justice, and ICC investigations are ongoing, but no indictments have been filed.[69]

Victims' Voices

In the DRC, radio journalist Chouchou Namegabe Dubuisson has co-founded, with three other women, the South Kivu Women's Media Association, known by its French acronym "AFEM." They collect rape survivors' stories and broadcast them for women in rural eastern Congo, along with information about women's health and human rights.

When the broadcasts began, the radio program faced "many cultural restrictions," Dubuisson recalls. "You couldn't talk about sex on the radio. We had to borrow a word from Tanzanian Swahili, *ubakaji*. . . . There are many local languages, but they didn't have a word to talk about it. They talked around it."

The journalists who work for AFEM began in 2003 as self-taught volunteers; four years later, they had a small studio and were broadcasting on six radio stations. At first, their work wasn't exactly welcome. "It was a scandal," she remembers. "People were saying, 'How can they talk widely about sex?!' " But as the programs continued, and humanitarian organizations in the region began their own outreach to combat the stigma associated with rape, the outrage abated.

Congolese gynecologist Denis Mukwege won the Olof Palme Prize for his aid to women victims of rape and war crimes in the Democratic Republic of Congo. One reason the world doesn't end wartime rape is that men are not the victims, he says. "Do we need men to start being killed so that other men will react?" he asks.

AFP/Getty Images/Fredrik Sandberg

Now, the community reacts differently to rape cases, Dubuisson says. "Before it was a shame. Victims were rejected," she remembers. "After we began, it changed. Victims say it's a first step to heal their internal wounds — to talk, to confide what happened to them."

In Burma (Myanmar), anti-rape activists have taken a different grassroots approach. In a country ruled by a notoriously cruel military junta that uses sexual violence to repress ethnic groups, rape is not discussed. "You can't talk about it," says Hseng Noung, a Burmese journalist and an advisory board member of the Women's League of Burma, an association of local organizations that operates clandestinely inside Burma. "There's nowhere for women, or anyone, to go and get justice."

So the league, along with the Nobel Women's Initiative — a network of female Nobel Peace Prize laureates, including Burmese democracy activist Aung San Suu Kyi — launched an international "tribunal" for Burma in

Two young rape victims being treated at Panzi hospital in Bukavu, Democratic Republic of the Congo, walk with their lawyer (center). Women's rights advocates say the problem of mass rape in wartime will only be solved when more perpetrators are brought to justice.

New York in March. The mock court process included testimony by Burmese women, some in person, some by video and some read aloud by proxy witnesses. Each account represented dozens more like it. "The testifiers are just one [person] — but there are so many, so many people like them," says Burmese refugee Phyu Phyu Sann, a researcher at the Center for Global Justice in New York.

Raising awareness about rape was only part of the goal, Sann says. She and other activists want Burma's case referred to the International Criminal Court for prosecution. But because Burma has not signed the treaty that established the court, the U.N. Security Council would have to vote to make the referral.

Williams, the 1997 Nobel Peace laureate for her work to ban land mines,[70] says the groups hope to shame the Security Council into making the referral. "The international community seems a little lame, if you will, on actual action," she says. "We decided if they couldn't do it, we'd do it and use that as an organizing tool."

Burma has been the subject of other Security Council resolutions recognizing the use of rape or sexual violence against women, but unless a case is sent to the ICC for prosecution, critics say the junta will continue to enjoy impunity.

Whatever the outcome of the campaign to pressure the Security Council, Sann says the people's tribunal brought Burmese women a different kind of relief. "My whole life, I saw everything, all the atrocities, and even me, I have held my tears," she says. "Here, I can speak up. Now we are hopeful. Here, the world is at least listening to us."

OUTLOOK

No End in Sight

Although the fight against rape as a weapon of war has made major strides — especially in the last two years — few observers think the problem will disappear anytime soon.

For all the recent publicity about rape in war zones, little is understood about "the context and conditions under which armed groups engage in sexual violence . . . and do not," says Wood of Yale. Experts lack evidence — both qualitative and quantitative — about why perpetrators engage in wartime rape. Researchers hope scholarly attention to the topic in the future will make "policy interventions," in Wood's words, "more sophisticated."

Special Representative Wallström is already thinking about how to make current humanitarian responses more sophisticated. Two innovations have helped reduce rape in Darfur, she says: fuel-efficient stoves, which allow female refugees and internally displaced persons to make fewer trips outside of the camps in search of firewood, and peacekeepers assigned to "firewood patrols," accompanying women as they forage for wood.

On her trip to Congo, Secretary Clinton expressed hope that other technological advances could help curb rape. She introduced a plan to give women in Congo video cameras, so they can document assaults. Critics responded that a lack of evidence wasn't the problem, and that the money could be better spent on other interventions.

Physician Mukwege at Panzi Hospital in DRC says one reason the world doesn't put an end to wartime rape is that men are not usually the victims. Although he has been working for more than a decade to bring attention to the plight of rape victims in Congo, "sometimes it seems that ears are closed. So we've been wondering: . . . Do we need men to start being killed so that other men will react?"[71]

Men are, however, getting involved in prevention. The organization Women for Women International has hired local men to reach out to other Congolese men, teaching them not to rape and not to blame their wives who become victims. As program director Cyprien Walupakah put it, "If men are not involved, it will not change."[72]

In fact, Sri Lankan physician Kapila thinks "men should be in leadership positions" in the effort to prevent wartime rape. "All these gender advisors are being appointed, and they're all women," he points out. "Women talking about women's problems to other women is only going to go so far. This is one area where we need reverse gender discrimination." He suggests that perhaps the next special representative should be a man or that powerful men should advocate more vocally for an end to sexual violence.

Female advocates, however, say having men in powerful positions has been part of the problem. In fact, women say they have spent years seeking support from powerful men in the international community. In Colombia, for example, women's groups, human rights organizations and female lawmakers say they have been demanding attention to the problem of sexual violence for the past 20 years. But their demands have fallen on deaf ears.[73]

In the end, it may take the passionate determination of women to end the practice of wartime rape. As a female doctor in Guinea insisted after last fall's attacks, "With the last breath in my body, I will fight to restore the dignity of our women. The soldiers may have beaten us, they may have raped us, but we will win the battle for decency, democracy and respect in Guinea."[74]

NOTES

1. Ofeibea Quist-Arcton, "Guinea Shaken By Wave Of Rapes During Crackdown," "All Things Considered," National Public Radio, Oct. 20, 2009, www.npr .org/templates/story/story.php?storyId=113966999.

2. *Ibid.*

3. Neil MacFarquhar, "U.N. Panel Calls for Prosecution of Guinea's Military Leaders Over Massacre," *The New York Times*, Dec. 22, 2009, p. A6, www.nytimes .com/2009/12/22/world/africa/22guinea.html.

4. Quoted in Susan Brownmiller, *Against Our Will: Men, Women and Rape* (1975), p. 37.

5. "Hear Us," May 2009, a video production of the Zimbabwean Research and Advocacy Unit and WITNESS, http://hub.witness.org/en/HearUs-ViolenceAgainstWomeninZimbabwe.

6. "Electing to Rape: Sexual Terror in Mugabe's Zimbabwe," AIDS-Free World, December 2009, p. 19, www.swradioafrica.com/Documents/23919945-Electing-to-Rape-Final.pdf.

7. Zoe Alsop, "Kenya's Rape Probe Falters after Lawyers Drop Out," Women's eNews, Dec. 14, 2008, www .womensenews.org/story/rape/081214/kenyas-rape-probe-falters-after-lawyers-drop-out.

8. "International Justice Failing Rape Victims," Institute for War and Peace Reporting, Feb. 15, 2010, www.iwpr.net/report-news/international-justice-failing-rape-victims.

9. Angela M. Banks, "Sexual Violence and International Criminal Law," Women's Initiatives for Gender Justice, September 2005, p. 21.

10. Barnaby Mason, "Rape: A crime against humanity," BBC, Feb. 22, 2001, http://news.bbc.co.uk/2/hi/europe/1184763.stm.

11. Judgment in *The Prosecutor vs. Jean Paul Akayesu*, International Criminal Tribunal for Rwanda, Case No. ICTR-96-4-T, Sept. 2, 1998.

12. Emily Wax, " 'We want to make a light baby': Arab militiamen in Sudan said to use rape as a weapon of ethnic conflict," *The Washington Post*, June 30, 2004, p. A1, www.washingtonpost.com/wp-dyn/articles/A16001-2004Jun29.html.

13. "Colombia: Scarred Bodies, Hidden Crimes," Amnesty International, p. 3 www.amnesty.org/en/library/asset/AMR23/040/2004/en/ec8e59b4-d598-11dd-bb24-1fb85fe8fa05/amr230402004en .pdf.

14. Jeb Sharp, "Healing the victims," Public Radio International, Jan. 8, 2008, www.pri.org/theworld/?q=node/15166.

15. "Secretary Clinton Tours Refugee Camp," U.S. Department of State press release, Aug. 11, 2009, www.state.gov/secretary/rm/2009a/08/127181.htm.

16. Jeffrey Gettleman, "Symbol of Unhealed Congo: Male rape victims," *The New York Times*, Aug. 5, 2009, www.nytimes.com/2009/08/05/world/africa/05congo.html.

17. Tanya Turkovich, "As DR Congo crisis persists, UN classifies rape as a weapon of war," UNICEF, June 24, 2008, www.unicef.org/infobycountry/drcongo_44598.html.

18. Rome Statute of the International Criminal Court, 1998, www2.ohchr.org/english/law/criminalcourt.htm.

19. Charges were also confirmed against a third defendant, who was ultimately released by the court. Brigid Inder, "Making a Statement: A Review of Charges and Prosecutions for Gender-based Crimes before the International Criminal Court," Women's Initiatives for Gender Justice, February 2010, pp. 10-13.

20. "Situations and Cases," International Criminal Court, www.icc-cpi.int/Menus/ICC/Situations+and+Cases/.

21. Sarah Childress, "Clinton Addresses War Crimes in Congo," *The Wall Street Journal*, Aug. 11, 2009, http://online.wsj.com/article/SB124993248728220321.html.

22. Jina Moore, "In Africa, justice for bush wives," *The Christian Science Monitor*, June 10, 2008, www.csmonitor.com/World/Africa/2008/0610/p06s01-woaf.html.

23. Thom Shanker, "Sexual Violence," in Crimes of War, www.crimesofwar.org/thebook/sexual-violence.html.

24. For background, see "Comfort Women: World War II Sex Slavery — Survivors continue to call for justice, compensation, apology from Japanese government," Women's U.N. Report Network, March 8, 2010, www.wunrn.com/news/2010/03_10/03_15_10/031510_comfort.htm.

25. David Livingstone Smith, *The Most Dangerous Animal: Human nature and the origins of war* (2007), p. 90.

26. "My Heart is Cut: Sexual Violence by Rebels and Pro-Government Forces in Côte d'Ivoire," Human Rights Watch, August 2007, p. 3, www.hrw.org/en/reports/2007/08/01/my-heart-cut.

27. Christopher Wilson, "Overcoming Violent Conflict, Volume 5: Peace and Development Analysis in Indonesia," United Nations Development Program, 2005, pp. 2, 50, www.internal-displacement.org/8025708F004CE90B/(httpDocuments)/AF478B69BD73D815C125724400378515/$file/Overcoming+violent+conflict+Vol5+Indonesia.pdf.

28. Michele Leiby, "Wartime Sexual Violence in Guatemala and Peru," *International Studies Quarterly*, vol. 43, 2009, p. 454.

29. Elisabeth Jean Wood, "Armed Groups and Sexual Violence: When is wartime rape rare?" *Politics and Society*, vol. 37, 2009, pp. 146.

30. Dara Kay Cohen, "Female Combatants and Violence in Armed Groups: Women and Wartime Rape in Sierra Leone (1991-2002)" Jan. 26, 2010.

31. Resolutions 1882 (2009), 1820 (2008) and 1325 (2000), U.N. Security Council.

32. Michele Keleman, "In war zones, rape is a powerful weapon," National Public Radio, Oct. 21, 2009, www.npr.org/templates/story/story.php?storyId=114001201.

33. Thalif Deen, "U.N. envoy to crack down on sexual violence," Inter Press Service, Feb. 2, 2010, http://ipsnews.net/news.asp?idnews=50198.

34. "Agency ends Darfur aid after obstruction," Reuters, Nov. 10, 2006, www.abc.net.au/news/newsitems/200611/s1786169.htm.

35. Rebecca Hamilton, "Left Behind," *The New Republic*, Oct. 14, 2009, www.tnr.com/article/world/left-behind.

36. "The Crushing Burden of Rape: Sexual Violence in Darfur," *Médecins Sans Frontiéres*, 2005, p. 5, www.doctorswithoutborders.org/publications/reports/2005/sudan03.pdf.

37. Brownmiller, *op. cit.*, pp. 78-80.

38. Quoted in "Rape as Genocide: Bangladesh, the Former Yugoslavia, and Rwanda," *New Political Science*, vol. 22, Issue 1, March 2000, p. 89.

39. Brownmiller, *op. cit.*, p. 33.

40. *Ibid.*, pp. 33-36.

41. *Ibid.*, p. 34.

42. See Myriam Miedzian, *Boys Will Be Boys: Breaking the Link Between Masculinity and Violence* (2002).

43. Jonathan Gottschall, *The Rape of Troy: Evolution, Violence and the World of Homer* (2008), p. 76.

44. Holy Bible, Isaiah 13:16.

45. Iris Chang, "The Rape of Nanking," in Anne Llewellyn Barstow, ed., *War's Dirty Secret: Rape, Prostitution and Other Crimes Against Women* (2001), p. 46.

46. *Ibid.*, pp. 46-49.

47. Susanne Beyer, "Harrowing Memoir: German Woman Writes Ground-breaking Account of WW2 Rape," Feb. 26, 2010," www.spiegel.de/international/germany/0,1518,680354,00.html.

48. Quoted in Brownmiller, *op cit.*, p. 69.

49. *Ibid.*, pp. 99-101.

50. Barstow, *op. cit.*, p. 46.

51. Todd Salzman, "Rape Camps, Forced Impregnation and Ethnic Cleansing," in Barstow, *ibid.*, p. 75; Kelly Dawn Askin, in "Rape: Weapon of Terror," *Aware*, 2001, p. 37.

52. Roy Gutman, "Foreward," in Alexandra Stiglmayer, ed., *Mass Rape: The War Against Women in Bosnia-Herzegovina* (1994), p. x.

53. Quoted in Salzman, *op. cit.*, p. 70.

54. *Ibid.*, p. 68.

55. Jina Moore, "From noses to hips, Rwandans redefine beauty," *The Christian Science Monitor*, July 18, 2008, www.csmonitor.com/World/Africa/2008/0718/p01s05-woaf.html.

56. Binaifer Nowrojee, "Shattered Lives: Sexual Violence During the Rwandan Genocide and its Aftermath," Human Rights Watch, 1996.

57. *Ibid.*

58. Nowrojee, *op. cit.*

59. Judgment in *The Prosecutor vs. Jean Paul Akayesu, op. cit.* Also see Laura Flanders, "Rwanda's Living Casualties," in *War's Dirty Secret, op. cit.*, p. 96.

60. "Electing to Rape: Sexual Terror in Mugabe's Zimbabwe," *op. cit.*

61. *Ibid.*, p. 25.

62. "Kenya: Post-election violence not spontaneous," *Daily Nation*, April 2, 2010, http://allafrica.com/stories/201004020934.html.

63. Adam Nossiter, "In a Guinea Seized by Violence, Women are Prey," *The New York Times*, Oct. 5, 2009, www.nytimes.com/2009/10/06/world/africa/06guinea.html.

64. U.N. Security Council Resolution 1325 (2000), Oct. 31, 2000, www.un.org/events/res_1325e.pdf.

65. U.S. Department of State release of remarks at HEAL Africa, Goma, DRC, Aug. 11, 2009, www.state.gov/secretary/rm/2009a/08/127171.htm.

66. Inder, *op cit.*

67. "ICC to probe Kenya post-election violence," The Associated Press, April 1, 2010, www.cbc.ca/world/story/2010/04/01/icc-kenya-investigation.html.

68. Caroline Wafula, "Rape victims awaiting justice," *Daily Nation*, March 8, 2010, http://multimedia.marsgroupkenya.org/?StoryID=283546&p=Gender+Commission.

69. Adam Nossiter, "US Envoy protests rape in Guinea," *The New York Times*, Oct. 9, 2009, www.nytimes.com/2009/10/07/world/africa/07guinea.html.

70. For background on land mines, see Robert Kiener, "Dangerous War Debris," *CQ Global Researcher*, March 2010, pp. 51-78.

71. Nergui Manalsuren, "How Many More Will Be Raped?" Inter Press Service, Feb. 12, 2009, http://ipsnews.net/africa/nota.asp?idnews=45751.

72. Matthew Clark, "Congo: Confronting rape as a weapon of war," *The Christian Science Monitor*, Aug. 4, 2009, www.csmonitor.com/World/Africa/2009/0804/p17s01-woaf.html.

73. Helda Martinez, "Colombia: Sexual violence as a weapon of war," Inter Press Service, Oct. 21, 2009, http://ipsnews.net/news.asp?idnews=48942.

74. Quist-Arcton, *op. cit.*

BIBLIOGRAPHY

Books

A Woman in Berlin: Eight Weeks in the Conquered City, translated by Philip Boehm, *Picador,* 2006.
This anonymous diary broke the silence about the rapes of German women by Soviet soldiers after the fall of Berlin in 1945.

Barstow, Anne Llewelyn, ed., *War's Dirty Secret: Rape, Prostitution and Other Crimes Against Women, Pilgrim Press,* 2000.
A former State University of New York professor of history has assembled expert essays about the use of rape in conflicts worldwide.

Shannon, Lisa, *A Thousand Sisters: My Journey Into the Worst Place on Earth to Be a Woman, Seal Press,* 2010.
A former Portland, Ore., photographer who founded Run for Congo Women, an awareness and fundraising initiative for Congolese rape survivors, describes her year living in eastern Congo, helping and learning from the country's rape survivors.

Soh, C. Sarah, *The Comfort Women, University of Chicago Press,* 2009.
A San Francisco State University professor of anthropology interviews surviving Korean "comfort women," who were forced into sexual slavery by the Japanese military in World War II.

Articles and Broadcasts

"Hear Us: Women Affected by Political Violence in Zimbabwe Speak Out," *WITNESS,* 2009.
A human rights video organization presents the voices of opposition women raped by members of Zimbabwean President Robert Mugabe's ZANU-PF political party in what has been called an orchestrated campaign to intimidate voters through rape.

Hamilton, Rebecca, "Left Behind," *The New Republic,* Oct. 14, 2009, www.tnr.com/article/world/left-behind.
A former assistant to International Criminal Court Prosecutor Luis Moreno-Ocampo visits Darfur and finds that after the court indicted Sudanese president Omar al-Bashir for genocide, aid to rape survivors has been halted.

Hochschild, Adam, "Rape of the Congo," *The New York Review of Books,* Aug. 13, 2009, www.nybooks.com/articles/archives/2009/aug/13/rape-of-the-congo/.
The best-selling author of *King Leopold's Ghost,* a history of Belgian brutality in colonized Congo, visits the women of eastern Congo and tries to understand the circumstances that have victimized them.

Jackson, Lisa F., "The Greatest Silence," *Jackson Films with Fledgling Films and HBO Documentary Films,* 2008.
An Emmy-Award-winning producer spends a year in eastern Congo talking to women, aid workers and peacekeepers about the rape epidemic.

Sharp, Jeb, "Congo Rape," *Public Radio International,* January 2008.

An award-winning two-part series about rape and its aftermath in Democratic Republic of Congo.

Reports and Studies

"Bloody Monday: The September 28 Massacre and Rapes by Security Forces in Guinea," *Human Rights Watch,* Dec. 17, 2009, www.hrw.org/node/87190.
This 108-page report describes the preplanned murders and sexual assaults at an opposition rally in and around a stadium in Conakry last September by Guinea's elite Presidential Guard.

"Characterizing Sexual Violence in the Democratic Republic of the Congo: Profiles of Violence, Community Responses, and Implications for the Protection of Women," *Harvard Humanitarian Initiative,* August 2009.
A team of doctors and public health specialists surveys women — and rapists — in Congo about the frequency and character of rape attacks.

"Making a Statement: Gender-based Crimes before the International Criminal Court," *Second Edition, Women's Initiatives for Gender Justice,* February 2010.
A Netherlands-based ICC watchdog summarizes the court's action on rape and related charges and suggests how the court can strengthen its investigations into sexual violence.

"My Heart Is Cut: Sexual Violence by Rebels and Pro-Government Forces in Côte d'Ivoire," *Human Rights Watch,* Aug. 2, 2007, www.hrw.org/en/reports/2007/08/01/my-heart-cut.
A 135-page report based on interviews with more than 180 victims and witnesses documents women and girls being subjected to individual and gang rape, sexual slavery, forced incest and other sexual assaults during the five-year military-political crisis in the West African country.

Wood, Elisabeth Jean, "Armed Groups and Sexual Violence: When Is Wartime Rape Rare?" *Politics and Society,* Vol. 37, 2009, pp. 131-161.
A Yale University political scientist examines data from wars in which rape is not used as a weapon and suggests that military norms and enforcement prevent fighters from assaulting women.

For More Information

American Bar Association, 740 15th St., N.W., Washington, DC 20005-1019; (202) 662-1000; www.abanet.org/rol/africa/democratic_republic_congo.html. Sponsors a Rule of Law Initiative in the Democratic Republic of Congo that gives rape survivors access to lawyers and the ability to press charges against their perpetrators.

Avega Agahozo, P.O. Box 1535, Kigali, Rwanda; +250 516125; www.avega.org.rw/English.html. An association founded by 50 women widowed during the Rwandan genocide; provides fellowship, health support and trauma counseling for other female genocide survivors of all ages.

Friends of the Congo, 1629 K St., N.W., Suite 300, Washington, DC 20006; (202) 584-6512; www.friendsofthecongo.org. Led by the Congolese diaspora; tries to address the country's problems, including wartime rape, with special attention to solutions that involve and empower Congolese citizens.

HEAL Africa, Goma, Democratic Republic of Congo, and P.O. Box 147, Monroe WA 98272; www.healafrica.org. The primary hospital in North Kivu, epicenter of the rape epidemic in eastern Congo, which specializes in surgery and other medical services for rape survivors.

International Women's Program, Open Society Institute, 400 West 59th St., New York, NY 10019; (212) 548-0600; www.soros.org/initiatives/women?a. George Soros-funded initiative that focuses on reducing gender violence and discrimination, strengthening women's access to justice and increasing the number of women in leadership and decision-making roles.

Nobel Women's Initiative, 430-1 Nicholas St., Ottawa, Ontario K1N 7B7, Canada; +1 613 569 8400; www.nobelwomensinitiative.org. A partnership of female Nobel Peace Prize laureates dedicated to advancing women's rights worldwide; co-hosted the International Gender Justice Dialogue in Mexico in April.

Raise Hope for Congo, 1225 Eye St., N.W., Suite 307, Washington, DC 20005; (202) 682-1611; www.raisehopeforcongo.org. A campaign by the ENOUGH Project, which fights against genocide and mass atrocities, that uses social media, college networks and other outreach efforts to bring attention to the plight of Congo's rape victims and unite voices across America in a demand for the end to sexual violence.

Saathi, Kathmandu, Nepal; www.saathi.org.np/. A Nepali nongovernmental organization working to end violence against women and train more women as negotiators and decision-makers in post-conflict governance.

UNIFEM, 304 East 45th St., New York, NY 10017; (212) 906-6400; www.unifem.org. The U.N. Development Fund for Women; has been a leading advocate of ending violence against women in both wartime and times of peace; seeks prevent violence against women by tackling the problem of gender inequality worldwide.

Women's Initiatives for Gender Justice, Anna Paulownastraat 103, 2518 BC, The Hague, Netherlands; +31 (70) 302 9911; www.iccwomen.org. International organization that monitors action by the International Criminal Court on gender-related crimes and partners with women's organizations worldwide to advocate against impunity for rape and sexual violence in war zones.

Women's League of Burma, www.womenofburma.org. An association of grassroots women's and human rights organizations working clandestinely in Burma to unite and protect women suffering under the junta's repressive dictatorship.

Voices From Abroad:

DEWEH GRAY

President, Association of Female Lawyers in Liberia

A difficult quest for justice
"The changing attitude we see is the increased reporting of these cases by people who want to access the system. . . . We realize everyone is anxious to see cases being tried but . . . the dynamics of a rape trial are not easy."

Africa News (Kenya), November 2009

VABAH GAYFLOR

Minister for Gender, Liberia

Using rape to wage war on children
"To tell you the truth, the situation is very bad. They are waging a war on children — it is pathetic. . . . I don't know if the violence has to do with the impunity people experienced during the war. Domestic violence was always a problem here, but rape was never part of our society."

The Observer (England) August 2009

HONORE BISIMWA

Member of the nonprofit Olame Center, a Congolese organization with a focus on women's issues Democratic Republic of the Congo

Women as the property of soldiers
"After reaching an area, the soldiers are taking everything there as the spoils of war, including the women. They take them like property."

The Washington Post August 2009

International Herald Tribune/Patrick Chappatte

EUGIDE MUGABO

Kigali Independent University student and genocide survivor, Rwanda

Rape is as brutal as the machete
"In Rwanda, rape was a weapon of genocide and it was as brutal as the machete. Tens of thousands of women were gang-raped by Hutu soldiers or members of the Interahamwe militias. . . . There are thousands of children who have lost their fathers to the machete and their mothers to AIDS."

The New Times (Rwanda) April 2010

CHOUCHOU NAMEGABE

Radio journalist Democratic Republic of the Congo

The destruction of communities
"[Rape is] a tactic to destroy communities. Women are being raped in front of their families, in front of their

children, in public. . . . To break the silence helps first the victims; it's the first step to heal their internal wounds. . . . It helps those still hiding. They come to us, thinking that they were the only ones. . . . It helps the community."

Africa News (Democratic Republic of the Congo)
November 2009

MELANNE VERVEER

U.S. Ambassador-At-Large for Global Women's Issues

Women as vessels for carrying out war strategy
"The victims of these [war rape] crimes are stripped of every shred of their humanity. To the perpetrators, they are nothing more than vessels for carrying out a war strategy — a war these women do not perpetrate and in which they play no voluntary military role."

Africa News (Democratic Republic of the Congo), August 2009

ELLEN JOHNSON SIRLEAF

President, Liberia

Wars bring rape into traditional societies
"[Long years of war] introduced into our national psyche a culture of violence. . . . Rape was never a problem for us in our traditional society. Today it is a serious problem, and it is young children who are being abused. . . . During these wars people's own private desires became paramount, and there is no consideration of the victim. The conflicts went on so long that now these things have become part of our cultural habits."

The Observer (England) August 2009

BAN KI-MOON

Secretary General United Nations

A goal to end gender-based violence
"In every country, women and girls continue to be plagued by violence, causing tremendous suffering. . . . Our goal is clear: to end these inexcusable crimes — whether it is the use of rape as a weapon of war, domestic violence, sex-trafficking, so-called 'honour' crimes or female genital mutilation."

BuaNews (South Africa) November 2009

3

Dangerous War Debris

Robert Kiener

Hussein Ahmed lost his hands in a landmine explosion in Mogadishu, Somalia. Experts say more than 250,000 landmines and other unexploded artillery shells, hand grenades, mortars, cluster bombs and rockets are scattered throughout war-torn Somalia. Tens of millions of live munitions threaten people in more than 70 nations around the world, and some 5,200 people worldwide were killed or maimed by landmines and other explosive war debris in 2008.

From *CQ Global Researcher*, March 2010.

AP Photo/Mohamed Sheikh Nor

Martine Niafouna, a rice farmer in Senegal, was walking down a path near her village when she stepped on a landmine. The explosion threw her into the air, blew off the lower part of her right leg and horrifically burned her left leg.

Unable to work, she wonders how she will ever support her two children and 10 siblings. "It's ruined my life," she said recently, sitting in her one-room hut, her eyes filling with tears. "I can't do anything anymore. Anything at all."[1]

Niafouna, 36, is one of 748 people killed or seriously injured by landmines left over from a 27-year conflict in the Casamance region of southern Senegal, home to rice fields and beautiful beaches.[2]

But the West African nation is only one of more than 70 countries endangered by tens of millions of antipersonnel landmines covering nearly 750,000 acres — an area the size of Rhode Island.[3] Left behind by warring armies and insurgents, landmines are often called "silent killers," because they lie in wait to kill or maim, often years after a conflict ends. After more than a decade of conflict, the Iraqi government claims that at least 25 million landmines have already been left in Iraq by warring factions.[4]

Worldwide, about 5,200 people were wounded or killed by landmines during 2008 — or about 14 people per day.[5] Adding to the misery they cause, landmines also hamper economic development by keeping large tracts of land off limits for agriculture or other uses.

Across the continent from Niafouna, on Africa's East Coast, Mohamed Olhaye Nour, 60, is a typical subsistence farmer in the war-torn Horn of Africa who can't earn a living due to landmines.

War Debris Affects 70 Nations

Civilians in some 70 countries — mainly in Africa, Asia and the Middle East — were killed or injured in 2008 by land mines or unexploded grenades and other explosive remnants of war (ERW) left over from conflicts.

Countries with Casualties from Dangerous War Debris, 2008

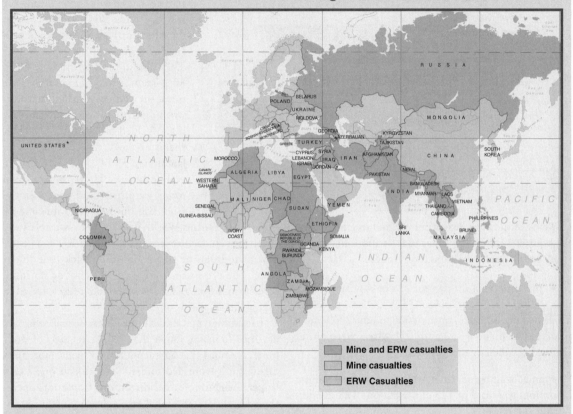

Legend:
- Mine and ERW casualties
- Mine casualties
- ERW Casualties

* U.S. casualties occurred when two men were fatally wounded after ordnance exploded at a metal recycling plant in Raleigh, N.C., and a man died while restoring a Civil War-era cannonball he had found.

Source: "Mines and Explosive Remnants of War (ERW) Casualties in 2008," Landmine Monitor, 2009

His village of Abuda — 15 miles southwest of Somaliland's capital, Hargeisa — was mined during both the 1977-1978 war between Somalia and Ethiopia and the decade-long war between the Somali National Movement and the Somali National Army that ended in 1991.[6]

"Before the war, our life was good; we did not worry about making ends meet," he said recently. Since the wars ended, Nour and others have been too terrified to return to their land. Two people who did return paid heavily: Both were injured by landmines; one lost both arms. Nour, who now ekes out a living keeping livestock, has lost 36 of his animals to the mines. Nour's story is not unusual; experts say more than 250,000 landmines and other unexploded ordnance (UXO) — artillery shells, hand grenades, mortars, cluster bombs and rockets — lie in wait throughout Somalia.[7]

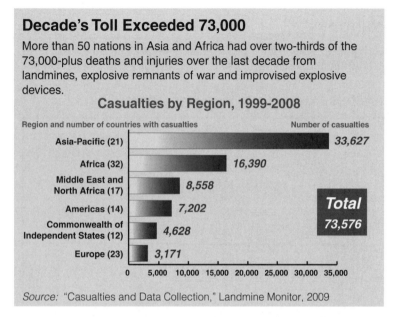

Decade's Toll Exceeded 73,000

More than 50 nations in Asia and Africa had over two-thirds of the 73,000-plus deaths and injuries over the last decade from landmines, explosive remnants of war and improvised explosive devices.

Casualties by Region, 1999-2008

Region and number of countries with casualties · Number of casualties

Region	Number of casualties
Asia-Pacific (21)	33,627
Africa (32)	16,390
Middle East and North Africa (17)	8,558
Americas (14)	7,202
Commonwealth of Independent States (12)	4,628
Europe (23)	3,171

Total 73,576

0   5,000   10,000   15,000   20,000   25,000   30,000   35,000

Source: "Casualties and Data Collection," Landmine Monitor, 2009

Many of the most heavily mined countries are among the poorest on the globe and can least afford to lose territory to the deadly weapons. For instance:

• In Cambodia, 40 percent of the population lives near explosive remnants of war (ERW). Over a three and a half year period from January 2006 to June 2009, more than 1,200 men, women and children were either maimed or killed by the weapons.[8]

• In Mozambique, from 500,000 to several million landmines were laid in 123 of the nation's 128 districts during the country's 25 years of revolution and civil war. Although more than 173,000 mines (plus 133,000 other items of unexploded ordnance) were removed between 1993 and 2006, today 9 percent of the population still lives in mine-affected areas. Removing them costs about $4.2 million per year — a sum the impoverished nation can ill afford and must get from foreign donations.[9]

• In Sri Lanka, although the civil war has recently ended, more than 1 million landmines contaminate about 100,000 acres in the northern part of the country, preventing thousands of displaced residents from returning to their homes and livelihoods.[10]

"Landmines are insidious," says Richard Moyes, director of policy and research at Action on Armed Violence, formerly called Landmine Action — a London-based nongovernmental organization working to reduce armed violence around the world. "They can lay dormant for decades until an innocent person treads on one with horrific results." They also are indiscriminate: 60 to 80 percent of landmine victims are innocent civilians, usually farmers working in fields or children playing.[11] Valued farm animals, such as sheep or cows, also fall victim to landmines.[12]

Landmines as we know them today were first used widely in the Civil War but were used much more extensively during World War II. They are relatively cheap to manufacture (costing as little as $3) and generally range from the size of a hockey puck to a dinner plate. The pressure-sensitive devices contain an inner core of explosives and a detonator and a fuse encased in rubber, metal, plastic or even wood.[13]

Landmines are especially insidious because they are designed to maim, rather than kill. "Designers of landmines reasoned that an enemy had to spend more time caring for a wounded soldier than a dead one," says Rupert Leighton, former director of Cambodia operations for the international mine-clearing organization Mines Advisory Group (MAG).

They are also designed to spread fear throughout the enemy's ranks. It's easy to imagine how terrifying it is to watch a fellow soldier lose a leg to a landmine just yards away. Because they can be planted ahead of time and explode on contact, they also free up soldiers for fighting elsewhere.

As British officer Col. J. M. Lambert wrote in 1952, "Mine warfare is an unpleasant business. It is foreign to our character to set traps cold-bloodedly, or to kill a man a fortnight in arrears so to speak, when you yourself are out of harm's way; and most British soldiers who have experienced it will own a rooted dislike of mine warfare in principle and in practice."[14] American Civil War General William Tecumseh Sherman called the use of landmines "Not war, but murder."[15]

While landmines remain widely used, their civilian toll helped to spawn a coordinated, international anti-mine campaign in the late 1980s, spurred by the Soviet Union's planting of mines throughout Afghanistan. The campaign was led largely by non-governmental organizations (NGOs) such as the International Red Cross, the Vietnam Veterans of America and the International Campaign to Ban Landmines (ICBL). In 1997 the late Princess Diana helped generate publicity for the cause by visiting land-mine victims in Angola.

Eventually, on Dec. 3, 1997, 122 nations signed the Ottawa Convention, also known as the Mine Ban Treaty (MBT), a landmark agreement banning the use, manufacture and sale of landmines. Since then 34 more countries have signed the treaty, but 39 states — including the United States, Russia, China and Pakistan — have not ratified it.

The United States, however, abides by many of the treaty's provisions. For example, it retains its stockpiles of landmines but has not used them since the 1991 Persian Gulf War and has not exported them since 1992, according to the ICBL. And no American company has manufactured landmines since 1997.[16] However, India, Pakistan and Burma (also called Myanmar) and some insurgent groups still build landmines. But there is no identifiable international trade in landmines.

The United States has not joined the treaty despite persistent lobbying by anti-landmine activists, largely because the U.S. military says landmines can be important weapons and officials don't want to be prohibited from ever using them again.

Rebuffed by the George W. Bush administration, many treaty advocates felt fortunes would change with the election of Democrat Barack Obama. However, just days before last November's MBT meeting in Cartagena,

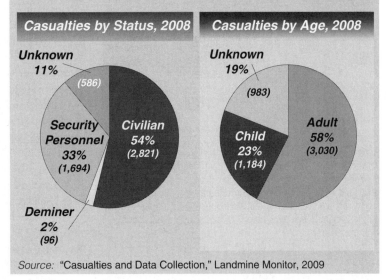

Most Landmine Casualties Are Civilian Adults

Of the nearly 5,200 landmine casualties worldwide in 2008, slightl more than half were civilians (left), and nearly a quarter were children (right).

Casualties by Status, 2008

Unknown 11% (586)

Security Personnel 33% (1,694)

Civilian 54% (2,821)

Deminer 2% (96)

Casualties by Age, 2008

Unknown 19% (983)

Child 23% (1,184)

Adult 58% (3,030)

Source: "Casualties and Data Collection," Landmine Monitor, 2009

Colombia, the U.S. State Department announced that the Obama administration had decided not to change the Bush-era policy and sign the treaty.[17]

That decision was "a default of U.S. leadership and a detour from the clear path of history," said an angry Sen. Patrick Leahy, D-Vt., a longtime proponent of the treaty. "The United States took some of the earliest and most effective steps to restrict the use of landmines. We should be leading this effort, not sitting on the sidelines."[18]

Jeff Abramson, deputy director of the Arms Control Association, a nonpartisan arms control policy group in Washington, also was amazed when the Obama administration affirmed the Bush administration's policy. "It seemed like a no-brainer for the new administration," he says. Human rights groups and NGOs echoed their comments. A day later the administration said it would review the decision, a process that is still ongoing.

While landmine activists continue to pressure other nations to ratify the MBT, few believe any of them will do so until the United States reconsiders. When confronted, non-signatories such as China, Israel, Russia and Pakistan point in their defense to the U.S. government's reluctance to sign the treaty. China has repeatedly

Bomb expert Frank Masche, technical field manager from the Mine Advisory Group, studies a cluster bomblet found in southern Lebanon after the 2006 war with Israel. Israel dropped an estimated 4 million cluster bombs during the brief war, generating a wave of negative publicity that helped to reignite a three-decade-old movement to ban the weapons, which scatter lethal debris over a wide area.

said it opposes a total ban on landmines, and it — like Russia and Israel — prefers to deal with the landmine issue within the framework of the Convention on Certain Conventional Weapons (CCW). That 1980 treaty, eventually signed by 109 countries, regulated the use and transfer of landmines but fell short of banning them outright.

While landmines may be the best-known and most notorious Explosive Remnants of War, there is a growing concern about other dangerous war debris like cluster bombs and other types of unexploded ordnance. "Large numbers of civilians are killed or injured each year by ERW," said the ICRC. These are the unexploded artillery shells, hand grenades, mortars, cluster bomblets, rockets and other explosive ordnance that remain after the end of an armed conflict. Like antipersonnel mines, the presence of these weapons has serious consequences for civilians and their communities."[19]

Cluster munitions are deployed either by aerial bombs or artillery shells that can release hundreds of smaller explosive devices, or bomblets, which can blanket an area as large as several football fields. Although most bomblets explode on impact, up to 10 percent don't. Like landmines, the bomblets can explode years later, maiming and killing indiscriminately. (For a Human

Rights Watch video demonstration of a cluster bomb, go to www.youtube.com/watch?v=TpGMiAlVM6g.)

NATO estimates that 10 percent of the cluster bombs dropped in Kosovo in the late 1990s did not explode, leaving some 30,000 unexploded "submunitions," as they are called, on the ground.[20] Civilians, especially inquisitive children, are often the unintended victims. According to Brussels-based Handicap International, 85 percent of the victims of landmines and unexploded ordnance are civilians and 23 percent children.[21]

Cluster munitions have been used since World War II, and by some estimates unexploded cluster bombs have caused up to 100,000 civilian casualties over the last 40 years.[22] However, after Israel dropped some 4 million cluster bombs over southern Lebanon during the 2006 Israel-Hezbollah war, the negative publicity it generated helped to re-ignite a three-decade-old movement to ban cluster bombs.[23]

After the MBT, activists and concerned governments began to campaign against cluster bombs, and in December 2008 more than 90 countries signed the Convention on Cluster Munitions (CCM), which bans cluster bombs and provides assistance to affected communities to help with removal and victim assistance. But as with the MBT, some of the world's major military powers and biggest users of cluster bombs have not signed the treaty, including the United States, Russia, Pakistan, Israel, India and China.

Many military experts describe cluster bombs as valuable weapons against entrenched forces. "With cluster bombs, they can take out a lot of your enemy at once," said Lawrence Freedman, a professor of war studies at King's College London. "And they can . . . make it hard for your enemy ground forces to operate."[24]

The United States last used cluster bombs in 2003 in Iraq. Although President Obama joined 29 other U.S. senators in voting in 2006 to restrict the sale and use of cluster munitions, his administration has not yet decided whether to sign the CCM. "From a humanitarian point of view it is completely unacceptable that the USA continues to opt out of the cluster bomb treaty," says Stephen Goose, director of the arms division of the New York City-based Human Rights Watch.

But the armed forces of the United States and other nonsignatory nations see cluster bombs as useful, effective weapons. Russia, for example, has repeatedly described cluster bombs as legitimate weapons of war if targeted correctly.

Meanwhile, other remnants of war — including more than 70,000 tons of stockpiled chemical weapons of which 95 percent belong to Russia and the United States — must be destroyed or decommissioned. And debate surrounds the question of what effects, if any, using depleted uranium in armor-piercing tank rounds may have on military troops and civilians.[25] While only the United States and the U.K. have admitted using depleted uranium weapons, up to 20 other countries are thought to have them. The Defense Department claims the depleted uranium weapons "pose no known" health risk, but many question those findings.[26]

As officials continue to debate what to do about toxic and dangerous war debris, here are some of the questions being asked:

Should the United States join the landmine and cluster bomb treaties?

Just two weeks before President Obama accepted the Nobel Peace Prize in Oslo, Norway, for his commitment to "disarmament and arms control" last year, his administration shocked activists around the world when it announced it would continue with the Bush administration's stance on landmines and not sign the international treaty banning them.

"It was painful that President Obama chose to reject this treaty just before he was to join the ranks of Nobel Peace laureates, a group that includes the International Campaign to Ban Landmines," says Human Rights Watch's Goose. "This decision lacks vision, compassion and basic common sense and contradicts the administration's professed emphasis on multilateralism, disarmament and humanitarian affairs."

Furthermore, said Jody Williams, the founding coordinator of the International Campaign to Ban Landmines (ICBL) and co-winner (with the ICBL itself) of the Nobel Peace Prize for her role in banning landmines, "This decision is a slap in the face to landmine survivors, their families and affected communities everywhere."[27]

Many argue that the United States should sign the treaty both for tactical reasons and on humanitarian and moral grounds. "Every member of NATO has joined the treaty," says Tim Rieser, an aide to Sen. Leahy. "They recognize that mines pose unacceptable risks to innocent civilians and to their own troops. The U.S. should follow their example. By joining, we would strengthen the treaty and eliminate the excuse that some countries use for not doing so: 'The U.S. hasn't, why should we?' "

Yet opponents of the treaty argue the global status of the United States requires it to reject the treaty. "Because of our unique role in the world, the United States needs to have certain strategic and tactical weapons available to it," says Steven Groves, a fellow at the conservative Heritage Foundation. "It is very easy for countries like Norway to pressure us to sign this treaty and the cluster bomb ban. However, when it comes time to bring armed force into a situation, it's not going to be the Norwegian Special Forces that are called upon; it will be U.S. forces. And if they need landmines to protect them from incursion or cluster munitions for protection or assault, these weapons need to be available."

The treaty's proponents point out that the United States has not used landmines in nearly 20 years. "Simply put, landmines aren't very good weapons, and the military is aware of how stigmatized they have become," says Goose. "Politically, it's poison to use them."

Moreover, says Rieser, "It would be a serious mistake to use landmines in Afghanistan, where the U.S. military is doing its utmost to reduce civilian casualties. Afghanistan has joined the treaty, as have our coalition partners. How would it look if innocent civilians, or United States soldiers, were blown up by a U.S. landmine in Afghanistan, the world's most heavily mined country, where the United States, the U.N. and others have spent hundreds of millions of dollars to remove the mines and help the injured?"

Groves counters: "War is terrible. Any civilian death is tragic. But anti-personnel mines and cluster munitions have legitimate purposes, and when used responsibly by the United States they can be effective on the battlefield. Signing these treaties would limit our strategic options."

Richard Garwin, a fellow at the Council on Foreign Relations think tank in New York, agreed, arguing that signing the MBT would "gravely increase the risk to our ground forces during combat, and to those civilians they may be sent to protect."[28]

Opponents of both landmines and cluster bombs point to their "indiscriminate" effects as reason enough to ban them. "Neither weapon can discriminate between a

2-year-old kid and an enemy combatant," says Rieser. "Besides, if landmines were so important strategically, why haven't we used them in two decades, and why have our allies banned them?"

Historically, the Pentagon has described antipersonnel landmines (APLs) as an "essential capability." As a Pentagon spokesman noted, "Should an operational commander determine that APLs are required to support operations or to protect U.S. men and women in uniform, he can request authority to use them in accordance with pre-established rules."[29]

Many landmine and cluster bomb opponents compare them to poison gas, which also does not differentiate between friend, foe or civilian. And, they remind landmine advocates, it took a U.S. president agreeing to outlaw poison gas before the Defense Department agreed to stop using it.

What about the so-called "smart" cluster bombs, which are designed to self-destruct after a set period of time? Could they justify the U.S. refusal to sign the CCM?

Human rights activists say some smart bombs fail to self-destruct up to 16 percent of the time. Moyes, at London's Action on Armed Violence, says, "With high failure rates and the inability to discriminate between combatant and civilian, these bomblets could never be termed 'smart.' "

"These are not the laser guided weapons the Pentagon showed destroying their targets during the invasion of Baghdad," says Sen. Leahy. "The cluster munitions that fail to explode as designed . . . remain as active duds, like landmines, until they are triggered by whoever comes into contact with them. Often it is an unsuspecting child or a farmer."

Leahy, a champion of assistance for landmine victims, is adamant the United States should ratify both treaties: "Victim-operated weapons should be a thing of the past. Period."

Is enough being done to destroy banned toxic weapons?

Amid much fanfare last May, Russia opened a new facility in Shchuchye, Siberia, dedicated specifically to neutralizing chemical weapons. Tons of deadly nerve agents, a single drop of which could kill a person, sat locked tightly behind a sturdy barbed-wire fence. Russia's chemical weapons

arsenal — the world's largest — includes the nerve agents sarin, mustard gas, phosgene and soman.[30]

Although long delayed, the facility's opening was welcome news to activists, who had been frustrated by Russia's tardiness in destroying its chemical weapons. Russia, like the United States and 188 other states, had signed the 1997 Chemical Weapons Convention (CWC), which bans chemical weapons and requires their destruction within a specified period of time.

Under the treaty, chemical stockpiles and production facilities were to have been destroyed by 2007. But so far, the seven treaty signatories known to have chemical weapons — the United States, Russia, India, Albania, South Korea, Iraq and Libya — have only destroyed 43 percent of their 70,000 metric tons of munitions.

Several years ago Russia and the United States — which has destroyed 70 percent of its 31,500-ton chemical arsenal — were given until April 29, 2012, to finish neutralizing their weapons. The United States now claims it needs another decade.

"Some of the delay in the U.S. can be attributed to bungling by the military," noted Jonathan B. Tucker, a senior fellow at the James Martin Center for Nonproliferation Studies in Washington. In addition, residents near the new disposal sites were worried about possible harmful effects from the incineration activities. Added Tucker: "The army was not prepared for the resistance from communities located near several of the . . . sites." Tucker is also skeptical that Russia will meet its new 2012 deadline.[31]

The U.S. disposal process has been hampered by delays, work stoppages, environmental issues and shortages of funds.[32] "During the Bush administration funds earmarked for chemical weapons disposal were often shifted over to the Iraq and Afghanistan war budgets," notes Tucker.

Craig Williams, executive director for the Kentucky-based Chemical Weapons Working Group, a coalition of citizen groups who live near stockpile sites, said: "To intentionally put tens of thousands of Americans at an unnecessary risk by continuing to store these weapons is reprehensible. Not only are they ignoring our international treaty obligations, they are undermining the military's obligation . . . to protect U.S. citizens."[33]

In April 2008 Iran rebuked the United States and Russia for insufficient progress in destroying the banned weapons, claiming the delay "is a matter of serious concern" because it indicates a state's intention to retain chemical weapons for military purposes.[34]

The Army claims it is working as fast as it can. The disposal program "is a tremendous success story," said Carmen Spencer, deputy assistant secretary of the Army for elimination of chemical weapons. "Not only is the U.S. doing all it can to meet its international commitments, but, more importantly, the [agency responsible for disposal] is contributing to the national security of the United States in the process. These weapons in the wrong hands can do harm. They are safely and securely storing and destroying them while providing maximum protection to the public and environment."[35]

Admittedly, disposal is a complex and costly exercise. U.S. costs alone will top $20 billion. "The dismantlement challenge is enormous," said Rogelio Pfirter, head of the U.N.'s Organization for the Prohibition of Chemical Weapons. "The financial crisis certainly doesn't help."[36]

Some experts criticize the CWC itself, saying it should include "non-lethal" chemical agents such as riot control and incapacitating agents. Others claim the treaty does not set up a suitable framework to allow on-site inspections of stockpiled chemical weapons.[37]

Until all nations sign the CWC treaty, chemical weapons continue to be a threat, say some critics. They note that of the seven nonsignatory nations — Angola, Egypt, Israel, Myanmar, North Korea, Somalia and Syria — Egypt is known to have used chemical weapons in conflict, while North Korea and Syria are suspected of maintaining chemical weapon stockpiles.

Libya, a treaty signatory that admitted having more than 25 metric tons of mustard gas in 2004, has not destroyed any of its stockpiles. It pulled out of an agreement for the United States to help build an incinerator for the weapons, citing environmental complaints from nearby residents, a claim few experts believe. Libyan leader "Quaddafi is mercurial, and we just don't know if

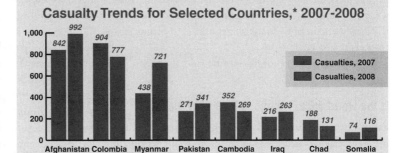

Casualties Rise in Some Countries, Fall in Others

Among countries with high rates of casualties from landmines and other unexploded ordnance, five countries — Afghanistan, Myanmar (Burma), Pakistan, Iraq and Somalia — saw casualties increase from 2007 to 2008. Casualties declined in Cambodia, Chad and Colombia.

Casualty Trends for Selected Countries,* 2007-2008

Casualties, 2007
Casualties, 2008

Country	2007	2008
Afghanistan	842	992
Colombia	904	777
Myanmar	438	721
Pakistan	271	341
Cambodia	352	269
Iraq	216	263
Chad	188	131
Somalia	74	116

* Countries with more than 100 landmine casualties in 2008.

Source: "Casualties and Data Collection," Landmine Monitor, 2009

he is serious about destroying his chemical weapons," says Tucker. "The jury is still out."

In addition to the chemical agents being destroyed under the CWC, another even more ominous source of chemical weapons exists: older, non-stockpiled arms that were abandoned — often dumped — after earlier wars. For example, after World War II, the U.S. Army secretly dumped 64 million pounds of nerve and mustard agents off the coasts of 11 states, along with 400,000 chemical-filled bombs, land mines and rockets.[38] According to some estimates more than 300 tons of chemical weapons were dumped into the world's oceans by the United States and other nations between 1946 and 1972.[39] And according to the Chinese government, Japan left some 2 million chemical weapons — including shells, bombs and barrels of mustard gas, phosgene and hydrogen cyanide — in China after they were defeated in 1945.[40]

There are countless other chemical weapons rotting away in fields or hidden in long-forgotten stockpiles, some from as long ago as World War I. Accidental discoveries are common. About 500 chemical weapons are found in Belgium every year. Danish fishermen have pulled up more than 200 mustard gas shells in their nets since the end of World War II. In 2006 the U.S. Army found 15 million pounds of chemical weapons dumped off the shores of Hawaii.[41] And in the affluent Spring

Valley section of Washington, D.C., crews have been excavating caches of World War I nerve gas from neighborhood yards for several years.

While the CCW treaty dictates that signatories work to recover these long-forgotten weapons, no one is pressuring governments to identify and collect "inaccessible" disposed chemical weapons. As one U.S.-based chemical weapons removal expert recently noted, these non-stockpiled chemical weapons will continue to plague generations to come.

"Our kids and grandkids will be finding them," he said.[42]

Is the world doing enough to help ERW victims?

Landmine and cluster bomb treaty activists agree that over the last decade much progress has been made to rid the world of these two "silent killers." Since 1999 a total area twice the size of London has been cleared in more than 90 countries. More than 2.23 million landmines and 17 million ERW have been destroyed, and annual casualties have dropped from around 20,000 a year to 5,200.[43]

International funds for mine clearing and victim assistance totaled $4.27 billion between 1992 and 2008.[44] As impressive at those numbers are, however, activists say much more must be done, particularly in the area of victim assistance.

"Despite this high level of overall funding, over the past decade victim assistance has made the least progress of all the major sectors of mine action, with funding and action falling far short of what was needed," said the International Campaign to Ban Landmines. "Most efforts remained focused on medical care and physical rehabilitation, often only when supported by international organizations and funding, rather than on promoting economic self-reliance for survivors, their families and communities."[45]

Brussels-based Handicap International recently reported that two-thirds of the 1,645 ERW victims surveyed in 25 countries said "their needs are not taken into account by national victim assistance plans."[46] Unemployment among the hundreds of thousands of survivors is high — 70 percent in Afghanistan — and fully 90 percent of those surveyed said they had little chance of getting a job.[47]

In addition to their often horrific injuries and the loss of income, ERW victims can also suffer from depression,

psychological trauma and social ostracism. Among the HI survey's respondents was Rosa Jose Njango, from Mozambique's Maputo province. She was 13 when she stepped on a landmine in 1981 and lost both her legs. She eventually married and had two children. However, when her husband died her relatives took her children, claiming she is unable to care for them. "She now lives alone in a humble hut," said the report.

Like many landmine and ERW victims, Rosa never received any psychological, economic reintegration or financial assistance. When asked what she would like to tell potential donors, she replied, "Enough words, now let's move to concrete actions."[48]

Only about 5 percent of the more than $4 billion spent on mine action over the last decade has gone to victim assistance. Dismayed by funding shortfalls at last year's Cartagena Convention, Christine Beerli, vice president of the Swiss-based ICRC, said: "Despite our efforts, the hopes that most landmine survivors had for this convention have not yet been fulfilled."[49]

Paul Vermeulen, director of Handicap International, was blunter about the need for change. "The first thought of landmine victims is suicide," he noted.[50]

More countries must increase their aid to ERW victims, say many activists. "I'm proud of the fact that the U.S. is the largest contributor to demining programs and assistance for landmine survivors," says Sen. Leahy. "But other countries could and should do more."

Some say countries are doing enough for landmine victims but that the manufacturers should offer more aid. "The focus ought to be to bind armament manufacturers to develop cleanup programs for their products that fail during military deployment," says James Shikwati, the Kenya-based founder and director of the Inter Region Economic Network, an African think tank. "More money devoid of tying responsibility to weapon manufacturers and suppliers will not prevent an increase in people falling victim to armaments left over from wars."

Marc Joolen, director general of Handicap International, said, "It is not enough for countries to destroy stockpiles and clear the land; they must also help the people who survived the explosions." Most survivors still have to fall back on their friends and families for support. Jobs and educational opportunities are the biggest needs.[51]

America's 'Secret War' Still Kills and Maims

Laos, the world's most bombed nation, still suffers from war debris

Even from the air the decades-old destruction in Laos is obvious. Flying into the Southeast Asian nation, visitors often marvel at the pockmarked moonscape below. The countryside is dotted with countless craters, many filled with water and resembling small, serene ponds or reservoirs. But their origin is far from peaceful.

The craters were formed during the 1960s and '70s, when U.S. aircraft unleashed planeload after planeload of bombs onto the lush, landlocked nation. The aim was to stop the North Vietnamese troops who were using Laos to infiltrate South Vietnam. Between 1966 and 1975 American forces flew some 80,000 missions over all but two of Laos' 17 provinces, dropping a staggering 2 million tons of bombs — the equivalent of one B-52 bomb load every eight minutes, around the clock, for nearly a decade.[1]

More ordnance was dropped on tiny Laos during what came to be known as the "Secret War," than was dropped on all of Europe by all combatants during World War II — giving Laos the dubious distinction of being the most bombed nation on Earth.[2] The U.S. bombings of Laos were called the "Secret War" because Laos was officially neutral, so the bombings were covered up by the U.S. government.

Up to a third of the tens of millions of bombs dropped on Laos failed to explode, turning the country into a vast minefield. Most of those 84 million unexploded weapons are cluster bomblets, or "bombies" as Laotians call them. Many failed to detonate either because they malfunctioned or were cushioned by lush trees or rice fields. Whatever the reason, Laos cannot afford the massive unexploded ordnance (UXO) cleanup operation it faces.

The bomblets lying in wait have left fully one-third of the country lethally contaminated.[3] Numerous mine-clearing groups such as the British group MAG (Mine Advisory Group), UXO Lao and others have been clearing mines, bomblets and other ordnance in Laos for decades.

But using present resources, experts say, it will take nearly a century to complete the cleanup. In the 15 years of demining operations ending in 2007, only 131 of the 87,000 square kilometers of contaminated land had been cleared.[4]

With so much live ordnance lying in wait, Laotians — 80 percent of whom are farmers — are at great risk. Between 1964 and 2008 more than 30,000 Laotians died from UXO and 20,000 were injured.[5] UXO-contaminated land stifles the economy and forces many farmers to risk clearing their lands themselves.

"In the end Lao people regard lack of food as much greater threat than unexploded bombs," said David Hayter, the Laos country director of the Mines Advisory Group. "Each UXO death is marked by a big bang, but deaths from lack of food or poor water are less noticeable."[6]

The link between unexploded ordnance and the economy is well documented. "UXO contamination continues to be an obstacle to agriculture production, thus reducing the potential livelihood outcomes," said a World Food Programme report. The study showed that 17 percent of households in UXO-affected villages have poor or borderline food consumption compared with 12 percent in other villages.[7]

In a nation where many live on less than $1 a day, the temptation to gather unexploded weapons for their scrap metal value is hard to resist. Adults and children in the risky business sell the high-end steel, aluminum and copper they gather to dealers from Vietnam and China. With prices of up to 35 cents a kilogram (about two pounds), it is tempting to those earning as little as $5 a month.[8]

Although rarely a day goes by without a serious UXO casualty in Laos, some good news is on the horizon. With the Convention on Cluster Munitions entering into force on Aug. 1, Laos will the host the treaty's first meeting of participating nations this November, the first time the country has taken such a leading international role in the cluster munitions treaty.

"For such a heavily bombed — and too-long ignored — nation to be hosting this event is momentous," says Richard Moyes, policy and research director of Action on Armed Violence, a London-based advocacy group. "The world is sure to take notice."

— Robert Kiener

---

[1] "Wartime cluster bombs still reap deadly harvest in Laos," Agence France-Presse, April 27, 2008. For a video about the Laos bombing aftermath, see "Bombies," Parts 1 and 2, at www.youtube.com/watch?v=Vru9c_ffQ5A and www.youtube.com/watch?v=NPdRpFZIBBQ&NR=1.

[2] Ian MacKinnon, "Forty years on, Laos reaps bitter harvest of the secret war," *The Guardian*, Dec. 3, 2008.

[3] "Laos: deadly cost of unexploded cluster munitions," IRIN, May 29, 2008.

[4] *Ibid.*

[5] "Survey reveals 50,000 victims of unexploded ordnance in Laos," *Korea Herald*, Feb. 6, 2010, www.koreaherald.co.kr/NEWKHSITE/data/html_dir/2010/02/06/201002060002.asp.

[6] Mackinnon, *op. cit.*

[7] Marwaan Macan-Markar, "Unexploded cluster bombs hold up farming," IPS, Feb. 5, 2010.

[8] "Laos: scrap metal income courts UXO danger," IRIN, Nov. 12, 2009.

Demining teams in 2008 cleared a record 62 square miles of landmines and other unexploded ordnance, including cluster bomblets (above). Since 1999 more than 2.2 million antipersonnel mines have been found and neutralized, and more than 44 million stockpiled landmines have been destroyed. Eleven nations have cleared all their known mine areas.

After reaching a peak in 2008, funding for mine neutralization has dropped off. Although 27 countries and 95 agencies last year submitted proposals to the United Nations for 227 projects costing $589 million, only $24 million had been secured as of December 2009.[52] The global recession has affected funding. Canada, for instance, recently announced it would slash funds for demining in Afghanistan from $77 million to $40 million for the next four years.[53]

In some cases, aid has been criticized as "too little and too late." For instance, the U.S. military sprayed about 12 million gallons of the toxic defoliant dioxin (known as Agent Orange) over nearly 10 percent of the Vietnamese countryside in the 1960s and 1970s to expose enemy hideouts during the Vietnam War.

"One scientific study estimated that between 2.1 million and 4.8 million Vietnamese were directly exposed to Agent Orange," noted a recent U.S. congressional study. And Vietnamese advocacy groups claim there are more than 3 million Vietnamese "suffering from serious health problems caused by exposure to the dioxin in Agent Orange."[54]

Those health problems, which range from multiple cancers to birth defects to diabetes, are similar to the health problems suffered by American Vietnam War veterans. For decades the U.S. government denied that the illnesses were caused by dioxin exposure but in 2009 allowed Vietnam veterans to claim disability and receive healthcare from the Veteran's Administration for more than a dozen diseases, ranging from Parkinson's disease to hairy-cell leukemia to ischemic heart disease.[55]

However, while the U.S. government has funded cleanup of dioxin-contaminated sites in Vietnam, it has not admitted responsibility for alleged dioxin-caused illnesses among the Vietnamese population, despite consistent lobbying by nations and activist groups. Between 2007 and 2009 the U.S. Congress allocated only $6 million to clean up dioxin-contaminated sites in Vietnam. Hardly any of this will help Vietnamese suffering from what they claim are dioxin-related illnesses.[56]

"It's appreciated that the U.S. Congress has twice agreed to allocate [money] for the [cleanup] work," said Ngo Quang Xuan, vice chair of the foreign relations committee of the Vietnamese National Assembly. But the money does not reach those who have suffered from dioxin-related illnesses, he complained.[57]

As for landmine cleanup, says Human Rights Watch's Goose, unless the aid money is spent wisely, increasing assistance won't solve victims' problems. "Lots of money was wasted on things in the past like general surveys of lands that produced incorrect results," he says. Money also was wasted on "supercostly, high-tech landmine clearing machines that didn't work. Much of that $4 billion [allocated so far] could have been better spent."

Finally, noted Dennis Barlow, director of the Mine Action Information Center at James Madison University in Harrisonburg, Va., the victims must be treated like human beings and not just casualty statistics.

"The solution — easy to state, hard to implement — is to use what we know now about landmine victims to individually design programs for each victim [and] to apply them locally, realistically and cost effectively," he said.[58]

BACKGROUND

Ancient 'Landmines'

Among the oldest form of arms, mines have their origins in such early weapons as spikes and stakes used 2,500 years. And some military experts link the mine to the

CHRONOLOGY

1910s-1920s *World War I combatants use chemical weapons, landmines.*

1914 French use tear gas; Germans retaliate.

1918 British Royal Engineers design and deploy anti-tank landmines; Germans attack U.S. forces with toxic gases phosgene and chloropicrin; United States begins chemical weapons program.

1930s-1940s *Widespread use of landmines by all forces turns them into "new form of warfare;" cluster bombs are developed.*

1939 Germans begin widespread use of landmines, planting more than 8 million a year by 1944. Allies also use mines widely.

1942 Nazis begin using Zyklon B in concentration camp gas chambers for mass murders of prisoners.

1943 Soviet Union uses air-dropped cluster munitions against Germany; Germans drop more than 1,000 butterfly bombs on the British port of Grimsby.

1960s-1970s *United States uses landmines and cluster bombs in Southeast Asia; Israel and others use cluster bombs in the Middle East.*

1960s United States drops millions of cluster bombs during Vietnam War. Landmines widely used by U.S. and Viet Cong forces; United States sprays "Agent Orange" defoliant in Vietnam.

1978 Israel drops cluster bombs in southern Lebanon.

1980s *Soviets use cluster munitions and landmines in Afghanistan, sparking campaign to ban their use; international treaty restricts landmine use. Iraq uses chemical weapons.*

1980 Convention on Certain Conventional Weapons (CCW) (Protocol II) restricts the use of landmines but doesn't ban them.

1987 Iraq attacks Kurds with mustard gas, hydrogen cyanide and other chemicals, killing thousands.

1990s *United States and its allies drop cluster munitions in first Persian Gulf War. International movement to ban landmines gathers strength.*

1991 United States, France, Great Britain and Saudi Arabia drop 61,000 cluster bombs during Gulf War.

1992 Activists establish International Campaign to Ban Landmines. . . . U.N. adopts Chemical Weapons Convention (CWC) banning chemical weapons.

1994 Russia uses cluster bombs against insurgents in Chechnya; President Bill Clinton calls for "eventual elimination" of landmines.

1996 CCW is amended to ban nondetectable antipersonnel mines and require some mines to have self-destruct devices.

1997 Mine Ban Treaty (MBT) is signed by 122 nations, excluding the Unites States, Russia, China and others.

2000s *Thirty more nations sign MBT. Pressure mounts to ban cluster bombs.*

2001-2002 United States drops 1,228 cluster bombs in Afghanistan.

2003 United States and U.K. use nearly 13,000 cluster munitions during Iraq War. Anti-cluster bomb activists form Cluster Munitions Coalition.

2006 Israel drops more than 4 million cluster bomblets against Hezbollah in Lebanon, according to U.N.

2008 Nearly 100 nations sign Convention on Cluster Munitions (CCM).

2009 Chemical Weapons Convention Coalition forms to press for a ban.

2010 CCM enters into force in August after ratification by 30 countries; Laos plans to host first meeting of participating nations in November.

Women Help Rid the World of Deadly Mines

All-female teams excel at formerly all-male job.

It is just before noon on a blistering hot day in western Cambodia, and Poy Ing is lying on the hard-baked ground, perspiring under 11 pounds of protective body armor and a blast-proof helmet. The sparse bamboo and mango tree forest is alive with the buzz of cicadas, mosquitos and biting black flies.

Like a surgeon probing a wound, the veteran deminer gingerly slips a 10-inch blade into the rich red soil in front of her as she hunts for a deadly landmine. Again and again she pushes the razor-sharp knife into the ground, carefully keeping the blade at a 30-degree angle, away from the sensitive top of any powerful landmine.

One wrong move, one slip, and she could be killed or seriously maimed.

Inch by inch, Ing, 54, explores the ground in an ever-widening arc. Suddenly, she feels the blade hit something. It could be a stone, a root or a discarded scrap of metal. Beads of sweat drip down her forehead as she begins to peel back the thick, dry grass around the object. Her body tenses as she uses the knife to carve away more earth.

There, lying just a few feet in front of her, and only inches below the surface, she sees the green, circular outline of a long-buried K5 landmine, packed with enough explosive to rip her body in half. Instinctively, she recoils and blows a loud blast on her whistle; a signal to the rest of the team that she has found a landmine, which could have been planted by any of the Khmer Rouge, Cambodian or Vietnam forces that have fought in the area over the last three decades.

As a member of an all-female demining team, Ing is part of a growing trend from Sudan to Lebanon to Laos. It's an idea that has caught on, for several reasons.

"Demining statistics throughout the world have shown that, while female deminers may be slower than their male counterparts, their work is more thorough," noted Stephen Bryant, a demining manager in Jordan.[1]

"Men are stronger and sometimes quicker than women deminers," echoed Seng Somla, another female Cambodian deminer, "but women are more patient, and they try harder so they easily make up."[2]

Other experts describe woman as "more reliable" and more effective than men. "They don't get drunk as the men often do," said a demining program manager in Sudan. "Over the past two years they are the teams that have found the most mines."[3]

Women also have proven to be more "team-oriented" than men. As one report noted, "There are no 'Rambos' amongst women deminers."[4]

Women team members also find it easier to talk with local women to get information about landmine locations, while all-male teams usually speak just to the men in a community about their knowledge of the mine threat in the area.[5]

ancient caltrop, which resembles a larger version of a child's jack. Made of four iron spikes (the earliest were made of bone) joined at the center, the caltrop was designed so that when thrown on the ground, one of the spikes would always be pointing upwards.

"One may imagine the efficiency of concealed caltrops," wrote Mike Croll, author of *The History of Landmines.* "Massed ranks of soldiers rushing towards an enemy, skewering their feet on unseen spikes . . . while the enemy launches spears at the wounded and prostrate bodies. An attack would rapidly turn into disarray, the front ranks being pressed forward by the rear, who would not see what was happening ahead of them."[59]

China's Song Dynasty used explosive landmines in 1277 A.D. to stop invading Mongol warriors. A 14th-century Chinese text, the Huolongjing, describes "self-trespassing" landmines, one of the first references to pressure-activated explosive devices. Europe's first landmine was created in the 16th century in Sicily and Southern Italy. Called a fougasse, the device resembled a cannon placed underground and showered rocks upon invaders when detonated.

By the 18th century Europe was using improvised mines: bombs buried under scrap metal or other hard objects that served as shrapnel. The word "mine" comes from the Latin word *mina*, which means "vein of ore."

David Hayter, director of the Laos office of the MAG (Mine Advisory Group), points out that women are more likely to focus on clearing mines in forests and along paths to water sources, because they are usually the ones collecting firewood and water. "Men and women have different roles in Laos, [so] their UXO clearance needs might be different. For example, women and children usually collect water, but men undertake construction tasks," he said.[6]

By working in what has long been a traditionally male-only position, female deminers are not just breaking down gender barriers. They're also bringing much-needed income to their families. In Cambodia, for example, some women deminers earn almost 10 times the national average wage.[7]

How does Cambodia deminer Somala feel about breaking into a previously male-only career? "This is a real example of what women in Cambodia can achieve," she said. "It will improve the profile of women and promote our position in society."[8]

— Robert Kiener

Female deminers, like this predominantly female team in Cambodia, are valued as more careful and effective workers than their male counterparts.

[1] "Jordan: First all-female demining team in Middle East," IRIN, Dec. 1, 2008, www.irinnews.org/Report.aspx?ReportId=81741.

[2] Sean Sutton, "Cambodian women clear mines," *Alert Net*, Dec. 19, 2003, www.alertnet.org/thenews/photogallery/KHmag.htm.

[3] "Demining not just a man's job," IRIN, June 23, 2009, www.reliefweb.int/rw/rwb.nsf/db900SID/MYAI-7VF9YD?OpenDocument.

[4] "The Hidden Impact of Landmines: Points of Enquiry for a Research into the Significance of Gender in the Impact of Mines and of Mine Action," Swiss Campaign to Ban Landmines, January 2007, www

.wilpf.int.ch/PDF/DisarmamentPDF/ClusterMunitions/WILPF-Women-and-Cluster-Munitions.pdf.

[5] Leah Young, "NPA's All-female Demining Team in Sudan," *The Journal of ERW and Mine Action*, Issue 12.2, Winter 2008/2009, http://maic.jmu.edu/journal/12.2/focus/young/young.htm.

[6] Fran Yeoman, "Women at the deadly end of the cluster-bomb debate," *The* [London] *Times*, Feb. 23, 2003, www.women.timesonline.co.uk/tol/life_and_style/women/article7036794.ece.

[7] Sutton, *op. cit.*

[8] *Ibid.*

This refers to the early military tactic of tunneling into an enemy's territory, filling the tunnel with explosives and detonating them from a distance.[60]

Mechanically fused antipersonnel mines were used during the Civil War in the Battle of Yorktown, after being invented and first used by Confederate Army Brigadier-Gen. Gabriel J. Rains. He used the devices to blow up a horse and its rider on May 4, 1862 — an act his commanding officer condemned as neither "a proper nor effective method of war."

Union Gen. George B. McClellan called the Confederates' use of the mines "murderous and barbarous conduct."[61]

Although only a few dozen men were killed or injured, the mines had a lasting effect on the troops. "The psychological damage was sufficient," Croll noted. "Soldiers would have imagined every conceivable place to be booby-trapped. An atmosphere of fear would have pervaded the abandoned Yorktown."[62] A century later, five live Confederate landmines were discovered in Alabama.[63]

Although landmines were used in some 19th-century colonial campaigns and the Russo-Japanese War (1902-1906), they weren't widely used until World War I. Anti-tank mines were developed to combat tanks, and antipersonnel mines were widely deployed to prevent the removal of those anti-tank mines. The Germans also developed pipe bombs, among the first mines designed to maim rather than kill. Reportedly, South Africans fighting the Germans in Africa were so outraged by such devices that many soldiers had to be restrained from killing prisoners for using them.[64]

New Warfare

The "golden age" of landmines occurred during World War II, when most of the mines we know today were developed. Mines were used extensively in battle theaters in dozens of countries as "force multipliers" or "silent soldiers," to deter the advancing enemy and free soldiers for combat.

During the war the Germans went from having only two types of anti-tank mines and one type of antipersonnel mine to 16 and 10, respectively. One of the most-feared antipersonnel mines was the "bouncing Betty." When stepped on, an initial charge would send it about three feet into the air; a second charge then would scatter up to 350 steel balls over more than 100 yards.

The Germans favored smaller anti-personnel mines because they used fewer explosives and were easier to lay than larger mines. But there were other, more horrific reasons. As historian Croll noted, "For attacking forces, small mines are more difficult to locate, and the wounded are a greater burden on medical and transport resources than the dead, [and] the sight of a limbless soldier in agony is more demoralizing to his comrades than a dead one, thus inhibiting aggressiveness."[65]

Landmines played a vital role in North Africa and on the Eastern front, where the Soviet Union used them to block the German advance. The Soviets deployed an estimated 222 million landmines in Europe during the war.[66] By the end of the war, the U.S. Army reported that landmines had caused 2.5 percent of combat fatalities and 20.7 percent of tank losses.

Cluster bombs were also used widely during World War II. German forces dropped so-called "butterfly bombs" that could detonate on impact or be set to explode later. During the Korean War about 4 percent of U.S. causalities were caused by landmines, some of which had been deployed by the United States. Landmines were used by both sides and many were deployed to prevent entry into the south from northern forces. Since

the fighting stopped in 1953, U.S. and South Korean forces have maintained a minefield along the demilitarized zone separating North and South Korea. (The United States officially transferred ownership of the landmines to South Korea.)

Landmines also featured heavily in the Vietnam War. Up to 30 percent of the American ground soldiers killed in battle in Vietnam were landmine victims. The Viet Cong used them against both civilian and military targets, the South Vietnamese used them to protect bases and villages and the United States laid them as perimeter defenses and to deter infiltration. The Viet Cong were adept at both stealing U.S.-laid mines and fabricating their own. About 90 percent of the mines that killed American forces were U.S. made or contained American components.[67]

The United States also dropped millions of cluster bombs on Vietnam, Laos and Cambodia during the 1960s and '70s, and many of the bomblets never exploded.

In the mid-1980s the U.S. Air Force replaced the Vietnam-era cluster bomb with the 1,000-pound CBU 87, which holds more than 200 bomblets that can blanket an area the size of several football fields with hundreds of small but deadly explosions.

The weapon uses an intricate delivery method. "As the CBU-87's soda can-sized bomblets fall, a 'spider' cup is stripped off the body, releasing a spring which pushes out a nylon 'parachute' (called the decelerator)," says a Human Rights Watch description of the weapon. "[That] inflates and then stabilizes and arms the bomblet. The bomblets orient perpendicular to the ground for optimal top attack, and the descent is slowed to approximately 125 feet per second. On impact the primary firing mechanism detonates the bomblet. A secondary firing system [detonates] if the bomblet impacts other than straight on, or if the bomblet lands in soft terrain or water."[68]

Cluster bombs also were dropped during the first Gulf War, in Kosovo in 1999, in Afghanistan in 2001 and Iraq in 2003. Of the more than 13 million bomblets dropped during the first Gulf War, 400,000 failed to explode. Weather was a common cause of failure.

NATO forces used cluster bombs during the air campaign in the former Yugoslavia from March to June 1999. U.S., British and Dutch aircraft dropped more than 1,765 cluster bombs containing more than 295,000 bomblets.

After the war more than 20,000 unexploded bomblets littered the area.

Up to 150 civilians died during these cluster bombings. On May 7, 1999, NATO forces dropped cluster bombs on the Nis Airfield, killing 14 civilians and injuring 28.[69] The casualties led to the United States restricting their use by American forces, which reduced civilian deaths.

Banning 'Silent Killers'

Nations have been encouraged over the last half-century to ban landmines. Protocol II of the 1980 Convention on Certain Conventional Weapons regulated the use and transfer of landmines. That section of the convention, which entered into force in December 1998, prohibited non-detectable mines but fell short of banning landmine use outright.

The CCW is seen as a "minimum international norm" for parties that have not agreed to ban landmines. It prohibits the use of "dumb" antipersonnel mines — those without self-destructing and self-deactivating mechanisms. It also restricts placement of mines, requires mines to be detectable, prohibits transfers of non-detectable mines and obliges parties to clear landmines after hostilities have ended. The United States, while not a party to the Ottawa Treaty, adheres to the CCW.

Present-day successes at banning landmines are attributed to the birth in 1992 of the International Campaign to Ban Landmines (ICBL). Worried that the 1980 conventional weapons treaty did not go far enough, six NGOs came together to work for a total ban on the use, production, stockpiling, sale, transfer and export of landmines. *They also lobbied for more victims' assistance and landmine awareness programs.

Within a year, the European Parliament had passed a five-year moratorium on the trade in antipersonnel mines, and Sen. Leahy had co-sponsored a bill calling for a one-year moratorium on U.S. landmine use and establishing a victims' aid program. After a conference to review the CCW in 1995 failed to produce any further changes,

Life After Landmines

Landmine victims warm up for volleyball practice at a rehabilitation center in Phnom Penh, Cambodia (top). Although deminers have destroyed some 2.7 million landmines and unexploded ordnance over the last two decades, there are still an estimated four to six million explosives in almost half of the nation's villages. Landmine victims eat lunch at a prosthetic rehabilitation program in Kabul, Afghanistan, run by the International Committee of the Red Cross (bottom). In recent decades, thousands of Afghans have been injured by mines and other war debris left behind by various conflicts. Recently, a new danger has appeared — improvised explosive devices, or IEDs, used by the Taliban in their fight with coalition forces.

campaigners decided that a total ban, via a completely separate treaty, was the only solution.

In October 1996 Canada hosted an international conference to devise a global ban on antipersonnel mines, supported by 50 governments, the United Nations, the

---

* The six groups were the Mines Advisory Group, the Vietnam Veterans of America Foundation, Human Rights Watch, Handicap International, Medico International and Physicians for Human Rights.

ICBL, the ICRC and other organizations. Nobel Peace Prize winner Williams, a treaty proponent, remembers that Canada's foreign minister, Lloyd Axworthy, "challenged the world to return to Canada in a year to sign an international treaty banning antipersonnel landmines. Members of the International Campaign to Ban Landmines erupted in cheers. . . . It was really breathtaking."[70]

The U.N. General Assembly then passed a resolution calling on all countries to agree to prohibit landmines "as soon as possible," and a draft text was drawn up. In September the final text of the treaty was negotiated and adopted. It defined antipersonnel mines as devices that are placed under, on or near the ground and detonated by the presence, proximity or contact of a person. Excluded from the treaty were anti-vehicle or anti-tank mines, including those with "anti-handling devices" that detonate when it's tampered with or otherwise intentionally disturbed.

The resultant Convention on the Prohibition of Anti-Personnel Mines, also known as the Ottawa Convention, required signatories to:

- Ban the use, production, transfer and stockpiling of landmines;
- Destroy existing stockpiles within four years of signing;
- Clear minefields under its jurisdiction within 10 years (unless they can justify an extension);
- Cooperate with a compliance regime; and
- Support mine clearance and victim assistance.

On Dec. 2, 1997, a month after Williams and the ICBL had been awarded the Nobel Peace Prize, delegates from 125 governments came to Ottawa for a treaty-signing conference.

The treaty was remarkable on several counts: It was the first time nations agreed to completely ban a weapon already widely used; it was drafted and signed within a few years and it was the first time such a wide-ranging treaty was negotiated outside of the United Nations process.

"The final treaty emerged from the negotiating process stronger than when negotiations started," said Williams. That would have been "essentially impossible inside the U.N. process, where reaching consensus, and therefore generally the lowest common denominator, is the rule."[71]

By going outside the U.N., the MBT activists did not need the support of the major powers, such as the United States or Russia, to achieve their ends. "The success of the Mine Ban Treaty shows that ordinary citizens can change the world without the support of superpowers," says Moyes, of London's Action on Armed Violence.

The movement to ban cluster munitions took its cue from the success of the landmine activists and worked outside of the United Nations to campaign for a similar ban. Like landmines, the 1980 conventional weapons treaty had restricted the use of cluster munitions, but activists felt the treaty's restrictions were inconsequential. In 2003, Protocol V — the Protocol on Explosive Remnants of War — was adopted, regulating the clearance of cluster munitions but not regulating or banning their use. So in November 2003, more than 200 organizations joined together to establish the Cluster Munition Coalition (CMC) at The Hague in the Netherlands.

Israel's 2006 war with Hezbollah, in which both sides were accused of dropping huge amounts of cluster munitions, further galvanized support for a cluster bomb ban. According to some estimates, Israel dropped so many cluster bombs in the last 72 hours of the war that a million unexploded bomblets lay scattered across southern Lebanon.[72]

"When hundreds of thousands of civilians displaced by the fighting began to return to the area, they found thousands of cluster bomblets in gardens, houses and streets, orange orchards, banana plantations and olive groves, often hanging from the branches," *Time* reported. At least 30 civilian deaths and 180 injuries were blamed on the bomblets.[73]

Alarmed by the Lebanese casualties and frustrated by the CCW's ineffectiveness, Norway announced an alternative effort to negotiate a cluster bomb treaty. At a meeting in Oslo in 2007 attended by 49 governments, the "Oslo Declaration" was hashed out. It aimed to "prohibit the use, production, transfer and stockpiling of cluster munitions that cause unacceptable harm to civilians."

After the Oslo meeting, 140 countries and members of the anti-cluster bomb coalition met repeatedly to discuss terms of a treaty. In May 2008 more than 100 countries met in Dublin and approved the final wording, which banned cluster weapons. The United States, Russia, China, Israel and Pakistan did not participate.

"While the United States shares the humanitarian concerns of those in Dublin, cluster bombs have demonstrated military utility, and their elimination from U.S. stockpiles would put the lives of our soldiers and those

U.S. Dumped Thousands of Tons of Chemicals

Following World War II, thousands of tons of toxic chemical weapons were dumped in oceans around the world, most of it by the U.S. military.

1, 2, 3 — Thousands of tons of mustard agent, Lewisite, hydrogen cyanide, nerve gas and other chemicals were dumped at numerous sites off Alaska, Hawaii, the West and East Coasts and the Gulf of Mexico.

4 North Sea — U.S. dumps about 4,500 tons of German chemical munitions (1948).

5 Norway/Denmark — U.S. and Britain dump about 170,000 tons of German mustard and nerve gas in Skagerrak area of North Sea (1945-1947). About 150 fishermen have been killed or seriously burned after accidentally pulling up gas containers.

6 Italy — U.S. dumps unknown quantities of chemical bombs and mustard gas off the coast (1945-1946).

7 France — About 3,400 chemical bombs are dumped into Mediterranean Sea off French Riviera by U.S. (1946).

8 Pakistan — Unknown quantities of mustard gas bombs are dumped in only 250 feet of water off coast of Karachi (1943).

9 Bay of Bengal — U.S. dumps about 16,000 chemical bombs off the coasts of India, Pakistan and Bangladesh (1945). Mustard gas, phosgene gas and cyanogene chloride bombs also are dumped.

10 Philippines — U.S. dumps unknown number of mustard gas bombs in Manila Bay (1941) and near Asunción (1945). About 1,000 pounds of white phosphorous shells and six tons of chlorine are dumped in Marveles Bay near oyster beds (1942).

11 Japan — U.S. dumps American and Japanese chemical weapons off coast after war. During the past 50 years, 52 people have been injured in 11 incidents at one of eight dumpsites alone.

12 Australia — U.S. dumps 30,400 tons of chemical weapons off Cape Moreton (1945). Since then fishing trawlers have pulled up two one-ton containers of mustard gas and another washed ashore.

13 New Caledonia — More than 4,200 tons of unidentified "toxic artillery ammunition" from Guadalcanal is dumped offshore (1945).

Sources: U.S. and Australian government data compiled by John M. R. Bull, "The Deadliness Below," *Daily Press* (Newport News, Va.), Oct. 31, 2005.

of our coalition partners at risk," explained a Pentagon spokesman.[74]

The United States has also argued that the proper forum to discuss cluster munitions is within the Convention on Certain Conventional Weapons framework. While the United States has not used cluster bombs since the 2003 invasion of Iraq, it wants to keep them in its arsenal for defensive use. It also says new cluster bombs with a failure rate of less than 1 percent are being developed.

In 2008 Congress limited the sale of cluster munitions to those with a 1 percent or lower failure rate and said other nations could use them only against military targets where no civilians are present.

The Convention on Cluster Munitions was signed by 94 states in Oslo in December 2008. So far, 104 parties have signed and 30 have ratified the treaty.

CURRENT SITUATION

Global Success

Demining work continues successfully worldwide today, changing lives for the better in communities around the globe.

For instance, in northwest Cambodia's Battambang province, the Mines Advisory Group recently removed or neutralized 3,000 antipersonnel mines and about 80 unexploded shells in the village of Ou Chamlong. Today the former minefields are rich with tapioca, beans and sweet corn. Farmers do a brisk trade selling their produce to nearby Thailand, and the standard of living for the village's 225 households has soared.

Should the United States sign the Mine Ban Treaty?

YES
Richard Moyes
Policy and Research Director
Landmine Action

NO
Steven Groves
Bernard and Barbara Lomas Fellow
The Margaret Thatcher Center for Freedom, The
Heritage Foundation

Written for *CQ Global Researcher*, March 2010

Written for *CQ Global Researcher*, March 2010

The Obama administration's review of U.S. policies on landmines represents a significant opportunity for the United States on the international stage. It is a chance to show strong commitment to protecting civilians from the effects of war — which is a fundamental strategic challenge in Afghanistan. Yet narrow thinking may cause the chance to be missed.

In 1997, as a response to the suffering of civilian men, women and children in many war-ravaged countries, an international agreement was reached prohibiting the use, production, stockpiling and sale of antipersonnel landmines. So far 156 countries have signed onto the agreement — 80 percent of the world's states — including all NATO members except Poland.

These nations joined not because they could imagine no circumstances in which antipersonnel mines might be useful weapons but because the limited military utility of these weapons was far outweighed by the suffering they caused.

Rather than joining the treaty, the United States has been keeping company with Russia, China, India, Pakistan, Israel and Iran — major powers whose military postures and actions will have a great influence on world affairs over the decades ahead.

It is in our common interest that these states develop a commitment to restraint in the use of force, and the United States should be pushing that commitment forward. If the United States were to join the Mine Ban Treaty, it would signal that self-imposed constraints, however small, have a role to play in achieving our greater security.

That signal also might strengthen U.S. forces, particularly in places such as Afghanistan, where they struggle to convince local populations that civilian protection is a priority.

The United States has not used antipersonnel mines since the treaty was established more that a decade ago, apparently constrained by its moral force yet unwilling to stand in support of it. In our globalized international society, it is a posture expressive of uncertainty about how to convert massive military power into positive political effects.

Accepting limitations on military capacity, even if of little or no operational significance now, is a serious matter and requires detailed analysis. Such analysis should look not only at whether a few hypothetical circumstances exist when antipersonnel mines would protect U.S. troops. It should also consider how commitment to civilian protection will also strengthen U.S. political and military authority — and which option will save more lives in the long run?

It is all well and good for most nations of the world to be party to the Ottawa Convention [the Mine Ban Treaty] and champion the absolute prohibition of antipersonnel landmines (APL). The United States, however, must balance its desire to promote humanitarianism with real-world military necessity.

The American military holds a unique position in the world: It is often called upon by U.S. national interests as well as the needs of the international community to engage in armed conflict. Unlike Ottawa Convention champions such as Norway, Switzerland and Belgium, the United States must retain the ability to deploy APL in ongoing and future conflicts. Properly deployed and responsibly removed at the end of hostilities, APL are essential to force protection, especially exposed positions and forward bases operating outnumbered in hostile territory.

Moreover, U.S. accession to the Ottawa Convention would undermine the existing international framework on landmines and other conventional weapons — the Convention on Certain Conventional Weapons (CCW) and Protocol II to the convention. Protocol II prohibits any use of nondetectable APL as well as the use of non-self-destructing and non-selfdeactivating mines outside fenced, monitored and marked areas. But the framework — which entered into force in 1983 — did not go far enough for landmine activist groups. Nothing short of an outright ban on APL of any kind was acceptable.

Stymied by an inability to ban APL outright, a group of 1,200 nongovernmental organizations (NGOs) calling itself the International Campaign to Ban Landmines convened its own treaty conference in 1996. One activist called the process "gently pushing aside the central feature of state sovereignty as the guide for all international relations."

And it is that lack of a multilateral process based on the consensus of sovereign nations that represents the fatal flaw of the Ottawa Convention. The CCW and Protocol II — whose members include China, India, Russia and the United States — have greater legitimacy than the Ottawa Convention, which counts none of those major nations among its members. The United States should not reward the transnationalist NGOs who birthed the "Ottawa Process" by ratifying its progeny.

The current U.S. policy on APL and other landmines — recently confirmed by the Obama administration and bolstered by the legitimacy of the CCW and Protocol II — strikes the proper balance between U.S. military needs and the threat of unexploded munitions.

"Development here has doubled," said village chief Kim Chin, noting that every bit of the land is now being used. "People's living conditions are now a lot better."[75]

In 2008 alone, demining teams cleared almost 62 square miles — the highest-ever annual total. Since 1999 more than 2.2 million antipersonnel mines have been found and destroyed, and more than 44 million stockpiled landmines have been destroyed. In fact, 11 nations have cleared all their known mine areas.[76]

But at least 70 states are still "mine affected," and more than 1,200 square miles need to be cleared.[77]

The task is massive. But at the Mine Ban Treaty's second five-year conference in Colombia late last year, attended by representatives from the more than 120 countries that signed the treaty, the mood was optimistic. In a little over a decade the effect of the MBT has been dramatic.

"Vast areas of previously contaminated land are now feeding some of the poorest communities on Earth instead of sowing fear in them," noted the ICRC's Beerli.[78]

Attendees learned that the number of countries that admit to still planting landmines has dropped from 15 in 1999 to just two today — Russia and Burma. In addition, three countries — India, Pakistan and Burma — produced the banned weapons in 2008, according to the ICBL, and 10 more countries have not yet renounced their right to produce them.[79] The MBT "has brought about a near halt to use of the weapons globally, the destruction of tens of millions of stockpiled mines and a huge expansion in mine clearance," said Human Rights Watch's Goose.[80]

Nongovernmental groups such as Taliban insurgents in Afghanistan and Pakistan, however, are planting new mines — known today as improvised explosive devices, or IEDs — with devastating results.[81] Recent figures from Afghanistan point to an increase in IED use by the Taliban. This January, 32 U.S. and allied troops were killed by IEDs, and 137 were wounded, compared with 14 killed and 64 injured last January.[82]

According to an Associated Press count, 40 percent of the U.S. fatalities in 2009 were caused by IEDs, and about three-quarters of all American deaths and injuries in Afghanistan are believed to have been caused by IEDs.[83] IEDs also were responsible for at least 40 percent of all coalition deaths in Iraq.

Nearly 60 insurgent groups — from Somalia to the Philippines — have stopped using landmines and, although the United States has not joined the treaty, the Obama administration is reviewing it.[84] The United States attended the 2009 MBT conference for the first time and participated as an observer state, seen by treaty proponents as a positive sign. They also welcomed comments by James Lawrence, head of the U.S. delegation and director of the State Department's Office of Weapons Removal and Abatement: "The administration's decision to attend this conference is the result of an ongoing review of U.S. landmine policy initiated at the direction of President Obama."[85]

Nonsignatories China and Russia also attended the meeting as observers. Along with the United States, these nations hold some 145 million stockpiled antipersonnel landmines. The Chinese delegation leader repeated Beijing's commitment to forbid their export. So far, all three nations favor following Protocol II of the Convention on Certain Conventional Weapons rather than joining the MBT or, for that matter, the cluster bomb treaty.

Banning Cluster Bombs

Although supporters hope the cluster bomb treaty will garner as much international support as the 1997 Mine Ban Treaty, that hasn't happened yet. A total of 104 countries, including most NATO members, have signed the convention, and many have begun destroying their stockpiles, but major military powers like the United States, China, Russia, Israel, India and Pakistan haven't joined the treaty.

Nonetheless, advocates hope the use of cluster bombs will generate the same stigma attached to landmines. "The moral stigma is going to be so powerful we think cluster bombs will also become a thing of the past," said Thomas Nash, coordinator of the Cluster Munition Coalition.[86]

Pentagon spokesmen, however, repeatedly have described cluster munitions as "legitimate weapons when employed properly and in accordance with existing international law." The Bush administration viewed the cluster bomb treaty as superfluous and restrictive. Instead of an outright ban, the military prefers to use only cluster bombs with a failure rate of less than 1 percent.

In March 2009, Obama signed legislation banning the sale of cluster bombs if they are suspected of being used where civilians are present.[87] This effectively bans

AFP/Getty Images/Georges Gobet

A female deminer checks a site in southern Senegal for the French organization Handicap International on May 10, 2008. Landmines planted during an armed insurrection that began in the region in the early 1980s still cause death and injury to the local population.

exports of the weapons because it is virtually impossible to guarantee they will be used in civilian-free zones.

In 2008, the Pentagon had asked to be allowed to export cluster bombs for another 10 years. Thus, the new legislation represents a "major turnaround in U.S. policy," said Human Rights Watch's Goose. "The passage of this measure is yet another indication the president should initiate a thorough review of U.S. policy with respect to cluster munitions. If it is unacceptable for foreign militaries to use these weapons, why would it be acceptable for the U.S. military to use them?"[88]

Few observers expect Obama to recommend joining either treaty in the immediate future. "With two wars raging, it's not likely he is about to antagonize the Pentagon

and ask them to give up a weapon they claim they need," explains Goose.

Although it hasn't signed either treaty, the United States still ranks as a world leader in aiding ERW victims and weapons cleanup operations. In 2008 international funding for mine action from 23 countries and the European Union totaled $518 million, the highest ever total.[89] Of that, the United States allocated nearly $85 million for mine clearance and victim assistance.[90]

To focus more attention on chemical weapons and convince even more countries to join the chemical weapon treaty, dozens of the world's NGOs in December formed the Chemical Weapons Convention Coalition. The group hopes to persuade Libya, the United States and Russia to conduct safe, sound and timely destruction of chemical weapons.[91]

Yet, while many treaty members are eliminating their banned chemical weapons, they are largely ignoring the massive amounts of weapons that were dumped at sea, many of which may now be slowly leaking toxins. While research is underway to locate — and map — the abandoned chemicals and check on their condition, more needs to be done to examine the harmful effects they may be having on the environment. As a recent report for the U.S. Congress noted, "Incomplete historical records significantly limit the ability to identify and assess the condition of these weapons, particularly to determine whether chemical agents may have leaked, or are likely to do so."[92]

Just this year activists in Sweden accused the Russian military of dumping radioactive waste into the Baltic Sea in the early 1990s.[93] Although Russians deny the claim, environmentalists point out that the world can no longer delay addressing the long-term effects of using the oceans as a waste disposal site. As some say, the clock is ticking.

OUTLOOK

Winning the War?

Attendees at last year's landmine conference in Cartagena had reason to celebrate. Landmines are well on their way to being confined to the dustbin of history. "Looking back, it's amazing to see how far we have come," says Leahy aide Rieser.

In the past decade, more than 2 million mines have been cleared, 156 nations have signed the Mine Ban Treaty and landmine use has been stigmatized. "There has been a growing acceptance that landmines are unacceptable," says Moyes, of London's Action on Armed Violence. "The world is winning the landmine war," the U.K.'s *Independent* recently trumpeted.[94]

The war is not over yet, however. Thirty-nine countries haven't signed the treaty, and massive stockpiles still exist. But many experts think time will change that.

"Ten years from now we will see more nations join the treaty," says the Human Rights Watch's Goose. "I think the Obama administration will do the right thing and come down on the humanitarian side of this issue."

"It is not a matter of if, but when, the United States joins the overwhelming majority of countries that have banned landmines," says Sen. Leahy. "We have by far the world's most powerful military. Landmines and cluster bombs — indiscriminate weapons that cause so many innocent casualties — have no place in our arsenal."

Once the United States signs the treaty, other nations will be under increasing pressure to join, say many landmine activists. "Twenty years ago there were dozens of nations using landmines; today almost no one does," explains Goose. He and others think landmines will largely disappear within decades.

Cluster bombs are another story. Efforts to ban them face more resistance. The U.S. military, for example, prefers developing higher-tech versions rather than banning them.

Few expect President Obama to pressure the Pentagon to change its mind anytime soon. "I think we are decades away from seeing similar progress," says Moyes.

But the Heritage Foundation's Groves sees "no reason for the USA to ban cluster munitions, now or 10 years down the road."

Both sides agree, however, that ERW victims will receive more help in the future. Treatment will improve as advancements, such as high-tech prostheses, become more widely available. And as ERW clearance operations wind down, more money can be available to help victims with psychological, social and economic problems.

Banned chemical weapons are being destroyed but more needs to be done to monitor those programs and convince countries such as Libya to speed up their disposal programs. Also, more research has to be done on possible side effects of depleted uranium when used on the battlefield.

Sadly, few expect wars and armed conflicts to cease in the near future. Remnants of war are the lethal legacy of armed conflict. Although a conflict may last only a few weeks, it can take years, even decades, to clean up and free civilians from the risk of death or injury. And although weapons will undoubtedly become more high-tech in the future, there will always be a risk to innocent civilians.

Landmines, cluster bombs, ERW and long-abandoned chemical weapons all share one characteristic in common: They all can take innocent lives and maim, long after peace has been made.

"The landmine cannot tell the difference between a soldier or a civilian — a woman, a child, a grandmother going out to collect firewood to make the family meal," said Nobel Prize winner Williams. "Once peace is declared the landmine does not recognize that peace. The landmine is eternally prepared to take victims."[95]

NOTES

1. "Senegal: Casamance still mined, still dangerous," International Committee of the Red Cross, Dec.12, 2009, www.icrc.org/web/eng/siteeng0.nsf/html/senegal-feature-231209.

2. *Ibid.*

3. "Landmine Monitor Report," (Executive Summary), International Campaign to Ban Landmines, 2009, http://lm.icbl.org/index.php/publications/display?url=lm/2009/es/toc.html.

4. "Local NGOs welcome cluster bomb ban," IRIN, Feb. 18, 2010, www.irinnews.org/Report.aspx?ReportId=88146; "Landmines in Afghanistan: a decades old danger," *Defense Industry Daily*, Feb. 1, 2009, www.defenseindustrydaily.com/Landmines-in-Afghanistan-A-Decades-Old-Danger-06143/.

5. "Casualties and Data Collection," *Landmine Monitor*, http://lm.icbl.org/index.php/publications/display?url=lm/2009/es/mine_casualties.html#1999-2009_overview.

6. For background, see Jason McLure, "Troubled Horn of Africa," *CQ Global Researcher*, June 2009.

7. "Somalia: "My land is full of mines," IRIN, Feb, 2, 2010, www.irinnews.org/report.aspx?Reportid=87953

8. David Randall, "The World is Winning the Landmine war," *The Independent*, Dec. 6, 2009, www.indepen dent.co.uk/news/world/politics/the-world-is-win ning-the-landmine-war-1835050.html.

9. "Mozambique: Demining is not a never ending story," IRIN, Oct, 27, 2009, www.irinnews.org/ Report.aspx?ReportId=86758.

10. "Sri Lanka: landmines, unexploded ordnance a bar rier to return," IRIN , Nov. 9, 2009 www.irinnews .org/Report.aspx?ReportId=86944.

11. "Landmine Monitor Report," *op. cit.*

12. *Ibid.*

13. "Explosive remnants of war and international humanitarian law," International Committee of the Red Cross, www.icrc.org/Web/eng/siteeng0.nsf/ htmlall/section_ihl_explosive_remnants_of_war.

14. Quoted in Mike Croll, *The History of Landmines* (1998), p. x.

15. *Ibid.*

16. Randall, *op. cit.*

17. David Alexander, "U.S. will not join treaty banning landmines," Reuters, Nov. 24, 2009 www.reuters .com/article/idUSN24329250.

18. "Leahy hits US refusal to join landmine treaty," Office of Senator Leahy, Nov. 25, 2009. www.earth-times.org/articles/show/leahy-hits-us-refusal-to-join-landmine-treaty,1062487.shtml.

19. International Committee of the Red Cross, *op. cit.*

20. "Explosive Remnants of War," International Committee of the Red Cross, July 2004, p. 9, www .icrc.org/Web/Eng/siteeng0.nsf/htmlall/p0828/ $FILE/ICRC_002_0828.pdf.

21. "Cluster bomb treaty reaches 30th milestone," Handicap International, www.handicap-interna tional.us/en/our-fight-against-landmines-and-clus ter-bombs/cluster-bombs/.

22. "Cluster Munitions at a Glance," Arms Control Association, www.armscontrol.org/node/3125.

23. "Landmines and Explosives," *Alert Net*, Jan. 12, 2009, www.alertnet.org/db/topics/landmines.htm.

24. Kim Murphy, "Britain deals a setback to US," *Los Angeles Times*, May 29, 2008, http://articles.latimes .com/2008/may/29/world/fg-cluster29.

25. "Iraq: war remnants, pollution behind rise in cancer deaths?" IRIN, Oct. 14, 2009, www.irinnews.org/ report.aspx?ReportId=86572. Also see "Current Issues: Depleted uranium weapons," Wise Uranium Project, December 2009, www.wise-uranium.org/diss.html.

26. *Ibid.*

27. Matthew Bolton, "Obama follows Bush on land-mines," *The Guardian*, Nov. 26, 2009, www.guard ian.co.uk/commentisfree/cifamerica/2009/nov/26/ obama-landmine-ban-treaty.

28. Richard Garwin, "Bush sets the right course in con-trol of land mines," *Los Angeles Times*, March 8, 2004, www.cfr.org/publication/6844/bush_sets_ the_right_course_in_control_of_land_mines.html.

29. John Stanton, "Uncertainty remains about US land-mine policy," *National Defense*, January 2004, www .nationaldefensemagazine.org/ARCHIVE/2004/ JANUARY/Pages/Uncertainty3678.aspx.

30. Amanda Walker, "Russia to destroy 6,000 tons of nerve gas," *Sky News*, June 10, 2009, http://news. sky.com/skynews/Home/World-News/Chemical-Weapons-Russia-To-Destroy-6000-Tons-Of-Nerve-Gas/Article/200906215299439?lpos=World_ News_Top_Stories_Header_4&lid= ARTI CLE_15299439_Chemical_Weapons:_Russia_To_ Destroy_6,000_Tons_Of_Nerve_Gas.

31. Rachel A. Weise, "Russia, U.S. lag on chemical arms deadline," Arms Control Association, July/August 2009, www.armscontrol.org/act/2009_07-08/chem ical_weapons.

32. Breanne Wagner, "Buried poison: abandoned chem-ical weapons pose continual threat," *National Defense*, Aug. 1, 2007, www.thefreelibrary.com/Buri ed+poison:+abandoned+chemical+weapons+pose+ continual+threat.-a0167430175.

33. Peter Eisler, "Chemical weapons' disposal delayed," *USA Today*, Nov. 20, 2006, www.usatoday.com/ news/washington/2006-11-20-chemical-weapons_ x.htm.

34. Weise, *op. cit.*

35. Kris Osborn, "US gains momentum destroying chemical weapons stockpiles," *AR News*, Feb. 4, 2010, www.globalsecurity.org/wmd/library/news/ usa/2010/usa-100204-arnews01.htm.

36. Jonathan Tirone, "US, Russia plans to destroy chemical arms imperiled by crisis," Bloomberg, Feb. 24, 2009, www.bloomberg.com/apps/news?pid=20601087&sid=aghJzZXxi_FQ&refer=home.

37. Chris Schneidmiller, "New Coalition Aims to Promote Chemical Weapons Disarmament, Nonproliferation," Global Security Newswire, Jan. 22, 2010, www.globalsecuritynewswire.org/gsn/nw_20100122_8824.php.

38. John M. R. Bull, "Special Report, Part 1: The deadliness below," *Daily Press*, Oct. 30, 2005, www.dailypress.com/news/dp-02761sy0oct30,0,2199000.story.

39. "Dumped chemical weapons missing at sea," *New Scientist*, March 23, 2008, www.newscientist.com/article/mg19726482.800-dumped-chemical-weapons-missing-at-sea.html?haasFormId=f9768f0e-e55c-439a-b647-e3a56f64a4f7&haasPage=0.

40. Andrew Monahan, "Japan's China weapons cleanup hits a snag," *Time*, March 31, 2008, www.time.com/time/world/article/0,8599,1726529,00.html.

41. Wagner, *op. cit.*

42. *Ibid.*

43. "Landmine Monitor Report 2009," *op. cit.*

44. *Ibid.*

45. *Ibid.*

46. "Voices from the Ground," *Handicap International*, September 2009, www.handicap-international.us/our-fight-against-landmines-and-cluster-bombs/in-brief/?dechi_actus%5Bid%5D=68&cHash=5a6b6d36d8.

47. "Countries do little to help landmine victims: report," Reuters, Sept. 2, 2009, www.reuters.com/article/idUSTRE5814XZ20090902.

48. "Voices from the ground," *op. cit.*, p. 150.

49. Anastasia Moloney, "Governments plan to improve help for landmine victims," Reuters, Nov. 12, 2009, www.alertnet.org/db/an_art/59877/2009/11/4-113151-1.htm.

50. "Focus on victims at Mine Ban Treaty meeting," IRIN, Dec. 4, 2009, www.irinnews.org/Report.aspx?ReportId=87323.

51. *Ibid.*

52. "Money for mine action is hard to come by," IRIN, Dec. 4, 2009, www.irinnews.org/Report.aspx?ReportId=87325.

53. Rosie DiManno, "Canada bails on Afghanistan land mine duty," *The Star*, Feb. 3, 2010, www.thestar.com/news/canada/afghanmission/article/759735-dimanno-canada-bails-on-afghanistan-land-mine-duty.

54. James Dao, "Door opens to health claims tied to Agent Orange," *The New York Times*, Oct. 13, 2009, www.nytimes.com/2009/10/13/us/politics/13vets.html.

55. *Ibid.*

56. Martha Ann Overland, "Agent Orange Poisons New Generations in Vietnam," *Time*, Dec. 19, 2009, www.time.com/time/world/article/0,8599,1948084,00.html.

57. Jane Zhou, "Agent Orange War Legacy Attracts Aid," World Watch Institute, July 2009, www.worldwatch.org/node/6208.

58. Dennis Barlow, "Seven common myths about landmine victim assistance," *Journal of Mine Action*, December 2002, www.maic.jmu.edu/journal/6.3/editorial/editorial.htm.

59. Croll, *op. cit.*, p. 5.

60. "Laying landmines to rest? Humanitarian Mine Action," IRIN, Feb. 22, 2009, www.irinnews.org/InDepthMain.aspx?InDepthId=19&ReportId=62881.

61. Croll, *op cit.*, p. 17.

62. *Ibid.*

63. "Laying landmines to rest? Humanitarian Mine Action," IRIN, Feb. 22, 2009, www.irinnews.org/InDepthMain.aspx?InDepthId=19&ReportId=62881.

64. "The History of Landmines," http://members.iinet.net.au/~pictim/mines/history/history.html.

65. Croll, *op. cit.*, p. 43.

66. Mary H. Cooper, "Banning Landmines," *CQ Researcher*, Aug. 8, 1997, pp. 697-720.

67. *Ibid.*

68. "Cluster bombs in Afghanistan," Human Rights Watch, October 2001, www.hrw.org/legacy/backgrounder/arms/cluster-bck1031.htm#CBU-87.

69. Julie Hyland, "Human Rights Watch says NATO killed over 500 civilians in air war over Yugoslavia," *World Socialist*, Feb. 14, 2000, www.wsws.org/articles/2000/feb2000/nato-f14.shtml.

70. "Ban History," International Campaign to Ban Landmines, www.icbl.org/index.php/icbl/Treaties/MBT/Ban-History.

71. "A Nobel laureate looks back on the first 10 years of the Mine Ban Treaty," IRIN, Nov. 26, 2009, www.irinnews.org/Report.aspx?ReportId=87200.

72. "Cluster munitions at a glance," Arms Control Association, undated, www.armscontrol.org/node/3125.

73. Nicholas Blanford, "The 'toys' that kill in Lebanon," *Time*, Feb. 2, 2007, www.time.com/time/world/article/0,8599,1585565,00.html.

74. Kevin Sullivan and Josh White, "111 nations, minus the US, agree to cluster-bomb ban," *The Washington Post*, May 29, 2008, www.washingtonpost.com/wp-dyn/content/story/2008/05/28/ST2008052803176.html.

75. "Cambodia: development doubles after MAG clears land," Mines Advisory Group, Nov. 23, 2009, www.maginternational.org/news/cambodia-development-doubles-after-mag-clears-land/.

76. "Landmine Monitor Report," 2009, *op. cit.*

77. *Ibid.*

78. Randall, *op. cit.*

79. "Ban Policy: Overview 1998-2009," *Landmine Monitor*, International Campaign to Ban Landmines, http://lm.icbl.org/index.php/publications/display?url=lm/2009/es/ban.html.

80. *Ibid.*

81. C. J. Chivers, "Counterinsurgency: one stuck truck at a time," *The New York Times*, Feb. 1, 2010, www.atwar.blogs.nytimes.com/2010/02/01/counterinsurgency-one-stuck-truck-at-a-time/.

82. Tom Vanden Brook, "Roadside bombs taking bigger toll in Afghanistan," *USA Today*, Feb. 14, 2010, www.usatoday.com/news/military/2010-02-14-ieds-afghanistan_N.htm.

83. "US Troop surge combats top threat: IEDs," Associated Press, Feb. 2, 2010, www.foxnews.com/story/0,2933,584514,00.html.

84. Randall, *op. cit.*

85. Jeff Abramson, "In a first, US attends landmine meeting," Arms Control Association, Jan/Feb 2010, www.armscontrol.org/act/2010_01-02/Landmines.

86. Liz Sly, "Can the cluster bomb treaty be more than a symbol?" *Chicago Tribune*, Dec. 3, 2008, http://archives.chicagotribune.com/2008/dec/03/nation/chi-lebanon-cluster_slydec03.

87. Frida Berrigan, "Progress on cluster bombs," *Foreign Policy in Focus*, March 25, 2009, www.fpif.org/articles/progress_on_cluster_bombs.

88. Peter Beaumont, "Obama takes US closer to a total ban on cluster bombs," *The Guardian*, March 13, 2009, www.guardian.co.uk/world/2009/mar/13/us-national-security-obama-administration.

89. "Landmine Monitor Report," International Campaign to Ban Landmines, 2009, p. 2.

90. "Victim Assistance," *ibid.*, http://lm.icbl.org/index.php/publications/display?act=submit&pqs_year=2009&pqs_type=lm&pqs_report=usa&pqs_section=%23victim_assistance#victim_assistance.

91. Chris Schneidmiller, "New coalition aims to promote chemical weapons disarmament, nonproliferation," Global Security Newswire, Jan. 22, 2010, www.globalsecuritynewswire.org/gsn/nw_20100122_8824.php.

92. "U.S. Disposal of Chemical Weapons in the Ocean: Background and Issues for Congress," Congressional Research Service, Jan. 3, 2007, www.fas.org/sgp/crs/natsec/RL33432.pdf.

93. Damien McGuinness, "Sweden wants explanation on Baltic nuclear 'dumping,' " BBC News, Feb. 4, 2010, http://news.bbc.co.uk/2/hi/europe/8499762.stm.

94. Randall, *op. cit.*

95. "Landmine quotes," www.betterworld.net/quotes/landmines-quotes.htm.

BIBLIOGRAPHY

Books

Croll, Mike, *Landmines in War and Peace: From Their Origin to the Present Day*, Pen and Sword, 2009.
Updating his earlier history of landmines, a former British military bomb disposal officer provides a comprehensive history of landmines as they evolved from basic weapons in ancient times to today's modern weapons.

Sigal, Leon, *Negotiating Minefields: The Landmines Ban in American Politics*, Routledge, 2006.
The director of the Northeast Asia Cooperative Security Project at the Social Science Research Council in New York presents a detailed, absorbing history of efforts to ban landmines.

Tucker, Jonathan, *War of Nerves: Chemical Warfare From World War I to Al-Qaeda*, Anchor, 2007.
An arms control expert and a senior researcher at the Monterey Institute's Center for Non-proliferation Studies provides a detailed historical review of chemical warfare.

Williams, Jody, *et al.*, (eds.), *Banning Landmines: Disarmament, Citizen Diplomacy, and Human Security*, Rowman and Littlefield, 2008.
Nobel Peace Prize laureate Williams and other activists edited these essays by diplomatic negotiators, mine survivors, arms experts and human rights defenders, who describe progress since the 1997 landmine ban went into effect.

Articles

Bohaty, Rochelle F. H., "Lying In Wait: Researchers help U.S. Army search for chemical munitions dumped at sea," *Chemical & Engineering News*, March 30, 2009, http://pubs.acs.org/cen/government/87/8713gov1.html.
Authorities are investigating abandoned chemical weapons dumped off the coast of Hawaii by the U.S. military after World War II.

Bull, John M. R., "Special Report: The Deadliness Below," *Newport News Daily Press*, Oct. 30, 2005, www.dailypress.com/news/dp-2761sy0oct30,0,2199000.story.
This four-part series details the dumping of chemical weapons and unexploded ordnance in the world's oceans.

Eisler, Peter, "Chemical weapons disposal on fast track," *USA Today*, May 6, 2009, www.usatoday.com/news/military/2009-05-05-chemicalweapons_N.htm.
The Pentagon hopes to speed up destruction of its stockpile of banned chemical weapons.

Hart, John, "Looking Back: The Continuing Legacy of Old and Abandoned Chemical Weapons," *Arms Control Association*, March 2008, www.armscontrol.org/act/2008_03/Lookingback.
The writer examines the state of old and abandoned chemical weapons and the effectiveness of the Chemical Weapons Convention.

MacKinnon, Ian, "Forty years on, Laos reaps bitter harvest of the secret war," *The Guardian*, Dec. 3, 2008, www.guardian.co.uk/world/2008/dec/03/laos-cluster-bombs-uxo-deaths.
Landmines and unexploded ordnance have had a crippling effect on the Laotian people and countryside.

Randall, David, "The world is winning the landmine war," *The Independent*, Dec. 6, 2009, www.independent.co.uk/news/world/politics/the-world-is-winning-the-landmine-war-1835050.html.
As the Cartagena landmine conference wraps up, the author examines the state of the landmine treaty and progress on mine clearance and aid.

Reports and Studies

"Landmine Monitor Report," *International Committee to Ban Landmines*, 2009.
This annual survey takes a comprehensive look at developments in landmine-ban policy and provides current statistics on clearance, victim assistance and casualties.

"Voices from the Ground: Landmine and Explosive Remnants of War Survivors Speak Out on Victim Assistance," *Handicap International*, September 2009.
An organization dedicated to raising awareness about disability and landmine issues describes the effects of

explosive remnants of war from the victims' viewpoint.

"Weapon Contamination Manual," *International Committee of the Red Cross*, **2007.**
This comprehensive manual introduces the issues the ICRC thinks are needed to reduce the impact of ERW and landmines through field activities.

Bearden, David M., "U.S. Disposal of Chemical Weapons in the Ocean: Background and Issues for Congress," *Congressional Research Service*, **2007.**
This detailed yet concise backgrounder provides the history and ramifications of chemical weapons dumped into the oceans.

For More Information

Action on Armed Violence (formerly Landmine Action), 2nd Floor, 89 Albert Enbankment, London, SE1 7TP, U.K.; +44 (0)20 7820 0222; www.landmineaction.org. Nongovernmental organization working to reduce the incidence and impact of armed violence around the world.

Arms Control Association, 1313 L St., N.W., Suite 130, Washington, DC 20005; (202) 463-8270; www.armscontrol .org. National nonpartisan organization dedicated to promoting public understanding and support for effective arms control policies.

Cluster Munitions Coalition, www.stopclustermunitions .org. A global network of organizations campaigning to ban cluster munitions.

Halo Trust, Carronfoot, Thornhill, Dumfries DG3 5BF, U.K.; +44 (0) 1848 331100; www.halotrust.org. International organization dedicated to clearing landmines and unexploded ordnance.

Handicap International, 67 Rue de Spastraat, B-1000 Brussels, Belgium; +32 2 280 16 01; www.handicap-international.be. International organization that offers help to those with disabilities.

Human Rights Watch, 350 Fifth Ave., 34th Floor, New York, NY 10118-3299; (212) 290-4700; www.hrw.org. Independent organization dedicated to defending and protecting human rights.

International Campaign to Ban Landmines, 9 Rue de Cornavin, CH-1201 Geneva, Switzerland; +41 (0)22 920 03 25; www.icbl.org. Nobel-prize winning group seeking complete ban on landmines; publishes *Landmine Monitor.*

International Committee of the Red Cross, Mine Action Sector, 19 Avenue de la Paix, 1202 Geneva, Switzerland; +41 22 734 60 01; www.icrc.org. Nonpartisan, independent humanitarian organization that provides assistance to victims of landmines and other unexploded ordnance.

Landmine Survivors Network, 2100 M St., N.W., Suite 302, Washington, DC 20037; (202) 464 0007; www.landminesurvivors.org. Helps mine victims and their families recover through peer counseling, sports and social and economic integration into their communities.

Mines Advisory Group, 47 Newton St., Manchester M1 1FT, U.K.; +44-161 236 4311; www.maginternational.org. Works to aid landmine-affected communities.

Voices From Abroad:

MARGARET MATHEW MATHIANG

Deputy Chair South Sudan Demining Authority

Landmines hinder recovery
"The existence of landmines . . . continues to hamper the delivery of humanitarian aid and the return of refugees and internally displaced peoples. . . . The implementation of humanitarian and development projects in this crucial post-war period is also affected. . . . Three bulldozers were blown up . . . [while] on a road expansion mission."

BBC (England), February 2010

ASHA-ROSE MIGIRO

U.N. Deputy Secretary-General

Steps toward eradication are necessary
"Cluster munitions have caused unacceptable harm to civilians in more than 20 countries and territories since they were first introduced in the Second World War. . . . We need to consign cluster munitions to the pages of history. . . . We must step up our efforts so that women, men and children can walk free of fear of the terrible injuries these munitions inflict."

The Independent (England), April 2009

CONOR FORTUNE

Spokesman Cluster Munition Coalition
United Kingdom

Nations move to ban cluster munitions
"The use of the [cluster bomb] weapon has become so stigmatized states fear using it, because the levels of international condemnation are so high. . . . Since the very beginning of the [cluster ban] negotiations, people affected have been involved in the process to ensure the treaty would provide assistance to them."

Africa News (Netherlands), February 2010

JACQUELINE HANSEN

Coordinator, Landmine Monitor, Canada

Setting a high standard
"A year ago in Dublin, 107 countries adopted the treaty text [to ban cluster munitions], and that was a huge victory. . . . What we've learned from the landmine campaign is to set a high standard and others will follow. It takes some time for this norm to take hold, but it's better to have an ambitious goal."

Straits Times (Singapore), June 2009

LUIS SILVESTRE WAMUSSE

National Coordinator and Co-Founder,
RAVIM Mozambique

Unexploded ordnance and healing
"If you compare someone who was born disabled, they had no choice but to adjust to their situation. It is more difficult for someone who lived a first life as a normal person and then, from one day to another, suddenly sees their dreams broken. They have to first accept their new condition and then start their second life. . . . The main

priorities for victims are psychological rehabilitation, the healing of the wound, and getting a prosthesis — but that first need is already not covered."

Africa News (Netherlands), November 2009

GEORGINA TE HEUHEU

Minister for Disarmament and Arms Control
New Zealand

Mine treaty should be universal
"The Mine Ban Treaty has been one of the success stories of international disarmament. . . . Even though very few countries would today consider the use of antipersonnel landmines, it is still important to continue to push towards universalisation of the treaty."

New Zealand Press Association, November 2009

MAMADY GASSAMA

Member, Association of Mine Victims, Senegal

More than just handouts
"It is not about just giving handouts to mine victims. Help him or her to become self-reliant. Outside assistance is not forever."

U.N. Integrated Regional Information Network (Kenya), September 2009

BAN KI-MOON

U.N. Secretary-General

Ratification ensures rights
"Only through the widest possible [treaty] ratification and full compliance will the international community succeed in preventing new injuries and fatalities while ensuring that victims and their families fully realize their rights."

New Vision (Uganda), April 2008

4

Terrorism and the Internet

Barbara Mantel

AP Photo/Ellis County Sheriff's Department

Hosam Maher Husein Smadi, a Jordanian teenager in the United States illegally, pleaded not guilty on Oct. 26 of trying to blow up a 60-story Dallas skyscraper. Smadi reportedly parked a vehicle in the building's garage on Sept. 24 hoping to detonate explosives with a cellphone. FBI agents, posing as al-Qaeda operatives, had been keeping tabs on Smadi after discovering him on an extremist Web site earlier this year where he stood out for "his vehement intention to actually conduct terror attacks in the United States."

From *CQ Researcher*, November 2009.

I n March 2008 a participant on the pro al-Qaeda online forum ek-Is.org posted six training sessions for aspiring terrorists. The first was entitled: "Do you want to form a terror cell?" Using the name Shamil al-Baghdadi, the instructor described how to choose a leader, recruit members and select initial assassination targets. The second lesson outlined assassination techniques.[1]

"Although the first two training lessons often contain very basic instructions that may be less significant for experienced jihadis, they provide essential training for novices," said Abdul Hameed Bakier, a Jordanian terrorism expert who translated and summarized the training manual.[2]

The sessions then progressed to more sophisticated topics. Lesson three explained in more detail how to carry out assassinations, including: suicide attacks using booby-trapped vehicles or explosive belts; sniper attacks using Russian, Austrian and American rifles and direct attacks through strangling, poison and booby-trapped cellular phones.[3] Lesson four explained how to steal funds, and the final two lessons gave detailed instructions on how to conduct "quality terror attacks," including strikes against U.S. embassies.[4]

While this particular forum can no longer be accessed under its original domain name, Web sites controlled or operated by terrorist groups have multiplied dramatically over the past decade.

"We started 11 years ago and were monitoring 12 terrorist Web sites," says Gabriel Weimann, a professor of communication at Haifa University in Israel and a terrorism researcher. "Today we are monitoring more than 7,000."

Analysts say nearly every group designated as a foreign terrorist organization by the U.S. State Department now has an online presence, including Spain's Basque ETA movement, Peru's Shining Path, al Qaeda, the Real Irish Republican Army and others.[5]

The Internet appeals to terrorists for the same reasons it attracts everyone else: It's inexpensive, easily accessible, has little or no regulation, is interactive, allows for multimedia content and the potential audience is huge.[6] And it's anonymous.

"You can walk into an Internet café, enter a chat room or Web site, download instructions to make a bomb, and no one can find you," says Weimann. "They can trace you all the way down to the computer terminal, but by then you'll already be gone."

Terrorism on the Internet extends far beyond Web sites directly operated or controlled by terrorist organizations. Their supporters and sympathizers are increasingly taking advantage of all the tools available on the Web. "The proliferation of blogs has been exponential," says Sulastri Bte Osman, an analyst with the Civil and Internal Conflict Programme at Nanyang Technological University in Singapore. Just two years ago, Osman could find no extremist blogs in the two predominant languages of Indonesia and Malaysia; today she is monitoring 150.

The University of Arizona's "Dark Web" project, which tracks terrorist and extremist content in cyberspace, estimates there are roughly 50,000 such Web sites, discussion forums, chat rooms, blogs, Yahoo user groups, video-sharing sites, social networking sites and virtual worlds.[7] They help to distribute content — such as videos of beheadings and suicide attacks, speeches by terrorist leaders and training manuals — that may originate on just a few hundred sites.

Security experts say terrorist groups use the Internet for five general purposes:

- **Research and communication:** The Sept. 11, 2001, terrorists who attacked the World Trade Center and the Pentagon used the Internet to research flight schools, coordinate their actions through e-mail and gather flight information.[8]
- **Training:** Global Islamic Media Front, a propaganda arm of al Qaeda, issued a series of 19 training lessons in 2003 covering topics like security, physical training, weapons and explosives. The document was later found on a computer belonging to the terrorist cell responsible for the 2004 train bombings

in Madrid, Spain, that killed 191 people. But most material is posted by individuals who use the Internet as a training library.[9]
- **Fundraising:** In 1997 the rebel Tamil Tigers in Sri Lanka stole user IDs and passwords from faculty at Britain's Sheffield University and used the e-mail accounts to send out messages asking for donations.[10]
- **Media operations:** Before his death in 2006, Abu Musab al Zarqawi, the mastermind behind hundreds of bombings, kidnappings and killings in Iraq, posted gruesome videos of terrorist operations, tributes immortalizing suicide bombers and an Internet magazine offering religious justifications for his actions.[11]
- **Radicalization and recruitment:** In 2006, Illinois resident Derrick Shareef pleaded guilty to attempting to acquire explosives to blow up a mall in Rockford, Ill. Although not part of a terrorist organization, he was inspired in part by violent videos downloaded from a Web site linked to al Qaeda.[12]

The use of the Internet for recruitment and radicalization particularly worries some authorities. But experts disagree over the extent to which cyber content can radicalize and convert young men and women into homegrown supporters of — or participants in — terrorism.

The Internet is where "the gas meets the flame," says Evan F. Kohlmann, a senior investigator with the NEFA Foundation, a New York-based terrorism research organization.* "It provides the medium where would-be megalomaniacs can try and recruit deluded and angry young men . . . and magnify that anger to convince them to carry out acts of violence." The Internet replaces and broadens the traditional social networks of mosques and Arabic community centers, which have come under intense government scrutiny since 9/11, says Kohlmann.

A frequent expert witness in terrorism cases, Kohlmann says the Internet comes up in nearly every prosecution. For instance, Hamaad Munshi — a British national convicted in 2008 of possessing materials likely to be used for terrorism — participated in an online British extremist group that shared terrorist videos and used chat rooms to discuss its plans to fight overseas.[13] He was arrested at age 16.

The group's ringleader, then 22-year-old Aabid Khan, another Briton, used the chat rooms to incite Munshi to fight, Kohlmann says; the youth's grandfather also

---

*NEFA stands for "Nine Eleven Finding Answers."

Internet Offers Vast Potential for Spreading Terror

The Internet has opened global communication channels to anyone with computer access, creating a simple and cheap venue for spreading terrorist ideology. Interestingly, the regions with the largest concentrations of terrorist groups — the Middle East and Asia — have some of the lowest Internet usage rates. The highest rates are in developed countries, such as the United States, Canada, Australia and New Zealand.

World Internet Usage Rates, by Region

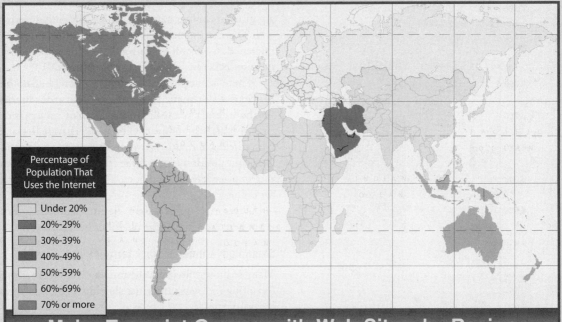

Percentage of Population That Uses the Internet

☐ Under 20%
■ 20%-29%
☐ 30%-39%
■ 40%-49%
☐ 50%-59%
■ 60%-69%
■ 70% or more

Major Terrorist Groups with Web Sites, by Region

Middle East: Hamas, Lebanese Hezbollah, al-Aqsa Martyrs Brigades, Fatah Tanzim, Popular Front for the Liberation of Palestine, Palestinian Islamic Jihad, Kahane Lives Movement, People's Mujahidin of Iran, Kurdish Workers' Party, Popular Democratic Liberation Front Party, Great East Islamic Raiders Front

Europe: Basque Euskadi Ta Askatasuna, Armata Corsa, Real Irish Republican Army

Latin America: Tupac-Amaru, Shining Path, Colombian National Liberation Army, Armed Revolutionary Forces of Colombia, Zapatista National Liberation Army

Asia: Al Qaeda, Japanese Supreme Truth, Ansar al Islam, Japanese Red Army, Hizb-ul Mujahidin, Liberation Tigers of Tamil Eelam, Islamic Movement of Uzbekistan, Moro Islamic Liberation Front, Lashkar-e-Taiba, Chechnyan rebel movement

Sources: "World Internet Penetration Rates by Geographic Region," Internet World Stats, June 30, 2009, www.internetworldststs.com/stats.htm; Gabriel Weimann, "Terror on the Internet," 2006

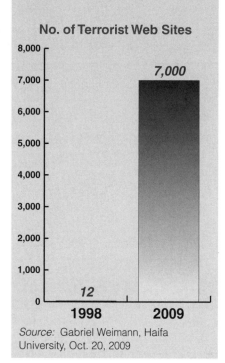

Terrorist Web Sites Have Proliferated

The number of Web sites run by terrorists or their supporters has grown since 1998 from a dozen to more than 7,000, with pro-jihad sites predominating, according to researcher Gabriel Weimann of Israel's Haifa University.

No. of Terrorist Web Sites

Source: Gabriel Weimann, Haifa University, Oct. 20, 2009

International Centre for the Study of Radicalisation and Political Violence at King's College in London. "In most cases, radicalization requires would-be terrorists to come in contact with social groups of people in the real world."

For instance, he pointed out, while much of Munshi's extremist activism took place online, "his radicalisation had been initiated in the 'real world.' " Through a friend at a local mosque, Munshi had met Khan, who spotted Munshi's computer expertise and groomed him to become a part of his online network. "It was the early meetings with Khan and some of his friends that helped turn a boy interested in religion into a young man dedicated to killing 'non-believers,' " according to Neumann.[15]

"There is anecdotal evidence out there, but no one has done a systematic study to show that radicalization via the Internet is a reality," says Maura Conway, a terrorism expert at Dublin City University in Ireland. Nevertheless, she adds, "governments are certainly acting as if radicalization through the Internet is possible, putting in place legislation that curbs how people can interact online."

As terrorists' presence on the Internet continues to grow, here are some of the questions being asked:

Should governments block terrorist Web sites?

Many of those who think the Internet is a major terrorist recruiting tool say authorities should simply shut down terrorists' sites.

Often the call comes from politicians. "It is shocking the government has failed to shut down a single Web site, even though Parliament gave them that power," Britain's opposition security minister, Baroness Pauline Neville-Jones, said last March. "This smacks of dangerous complacency and incompetence."[16]

In France, a minister for security said she wanted to stop terrorist propaganda on the Internet.[17] And a European Commission official called for a Europe-wide prohibition on Web sites that post bomb-making instructions.[18]

Although governments have shut down terrorist Web sites when they felt the information posted was too great a threat, some critics say such a move is legally complicated, logistically difficult and unwise.

Last year, three of the most important discussion forums used by Islamist terrorist groups disappeared from the Internet, including ek-Is.org, which had posted the six-part training manual. Jordanian terrorism expert

blamed the Internet. "This case demonstrates how a young, impressionable teenager can be groomed so easily through the Internet to associate with those whose views run contrary to true Muslim beliefs and values," Yakub Munshi said after the teen's conviction.[14]

But other researchers say online terrorism sites are largely about preaching to the choir and have limited influence on non-terrorists. "There has been very little evidence that the Internet has been the main or sole driver in radicalization," says Peter Neumann, director of the

Bakier says counterterrorism officials were so worried about the site that he "used to get requests from concerned agencies to translate the exact texts posted on ek-Is.org that were referenced in my articles. It was that serious."

"It is widely assumed that Western intelligence agencies were responsible for removing the three sites," and probably without the cooperation of the Internet service providers (ISPs) that host the sites, says Neumann, of King's College. "It would have required the cooperation of all the ISPs in the world," because those Web sites were not accessible at all, he explains. Instead, he thinks intelligence agencies may have launched so-called denial-of-service attacks against the sites, bombarding them with so many requests that they crashed. This September, one of the sites resurfaced; however, many experts believe it is a hoax.[19]

But government takedowns of terrorist sites — by whatever method — are not common, say many researchers. First, there are concerns about free speech.

"Who is going to decide who is a terrorist, who should be silenced and why?" asks Haifa University's Weimann. "Who is going to decide what kind of Web site should be removed? It can lead to political censorship."

Concern about free speech may be more acute in the United States than elsewhere. Current U.S. statutes make it a crime to provide "material support" — including expert advice or assistance — to organizations designated as terrorist groups by the State Department.[20] However, the First Amendment guarantee of free speech may trump the material support provisions.

"Exceptions to the First Amendment are fairly narrow" says Ian Ballon, an expert on Internet law practicing in California. "Child pornography is one, libelous or defamatory content another. There is no terrorism exception per se." Words that would incite violence are clearly an exception to the First Amendment, he says, "but there is a concept of immediacy, and most terrorism sites would not necessarily meet that requirement." A 1969 Supreme Court case, *Brandenburg v. Ohio*, held that the government cannot punish inflammatory speech unless it is inciting or likely to incite imminent lawless action.[21]

In Europe, where free-speech rights are more circumscribed than in the United States, the legal landscape varies. Spain, for instance, outlaws as incitement "the act of performing public ennoblement, praise and/or justification of a terrorist group, operative or act," explains

Tunisian Moez Garsallaoui, right, and his wife Malika El Aroud, the widow of an al-Qaeda suicide bomber, were convicted in Switzerland's first Internet terrorism trial of running pro-al-Qaeda Web sites that showed executions. Garsallaoui served three weeks in prison; El Aroud received no jail time. They are continuing their online work from Belgium, where El Aroud is described by Belgian State Security chief Alain Winants as a "leading" Internet jihadist.

Raphael Perl, head of the Action Against Terrorism Unit at the Organization for Security and Co-operation in Europe, a regional security organization with 56 member nations, based in Vienna, Austria. And the U.K. passed the Terrorism Acts of 2000 and 2006, which make it an offense to collect, make or possess material that could be used in a terrorist act, such as bomb-making manuals and information about potential targets. The 2006 act also outlaws the encouragement or glorification of terrorism.[22] Human Rights Watch says the measure is unnecessary, overly broad and potentially chilling of free speech.[23]

Yet, it does not appear that governments are using their legal powers to shut down Web sites. "I haven't heard from any ISP in Europe so far that they have been asked by the police to take down terrorist pages," says Michael Rotert, vice president of the European Internet Service Providers Association (EuroISPA).

For one thing, says Rotert, there is no common, legal, Europe-wide definition of terrorism. "We are requesting a common definition," he says, "and then I think notice and takedown procedures could be discussed. But right now, such procedures only exist for child pornography."

British officials, including Prime Minister Gordon Brown, center right, visit a London cyber security firm on June 25 during the launch of a new government campaign to counter cyber criminals and terrorists.

But even if a European consensus existed on what constitutes terrorism, the Internet has no borders. If an ISP shuts down a site, it can migrate to another hosting service and even register under a new domain name.

Instead of shutting down sites, some governments are considering filtering them. Germany recently passed a filtering law aimed at blocking child pornography, which it says could be expanded to block sites that promote terrorist acts. And Australia is testing a filtering system for both child pornography and material that advocates terrorism.

The outcry in both countries, however, has been tremendous, both on technical grounds — filtering can slow down Internet speed — and civil liberties grounds. "Other countries using similar systems to monitor Internet traffic have blacklisted political critics," wrote an Australian newspaper columnist. "Is this really the direction we want our country to be heading? Communist China anyone? Burma? How about North Korea?"[24]

Ultimately, filtering just may not be that effective. Determined Internet users can easily circumvent a national filter and access banned material that is legal elsewhere. And filtering cannot capture the dynamic parts of the Internet: the chat rooms, video sharing sites and blogs, for instance.

Even some governments with established filtering laws seem reluctant to remove terrorist sites. The government owns Singapore's Internet providers and screens all

Web sites for content viewed as " 'objectionable' or a potential threat to national security."[25] Yet Osman, of the Nanyang Technological University, says the government is not blocking Web sites that support terrorism. "I can still get access to many of them," she says, "so a lot of other people can, too."

In fact, counterterrorism officials around the world often prefer to monitor and infiltrate blogs, chat rooms, discussion forums and other Web sites where terrorists and sympathizers converse. If the sites remain active, they can be mined for intelligence.

"One reason [for not shutting down sites] is to take the temperature, to see whether the level of conversation is going up or down in terms of triggering an alert among security agencies," says Anthony Bergin, director of research at the Australian Strategic Policy Institute.

Another purpose is to disrupt terrorist attacks, says Bergin. Just recently, the violent postings of Texas resident Hosan Maher Husein Smadi to an extremist chat room attracted the attention of the FBI, which was monitoring the site. Agents set up a sting operation and arrested the 19-year-old Jordanian in late September after he allegedly tried to detonate what he thought was a bomb, provided by an undercover agent, in the parking garage beneath a Dallas skyscraper.[26]

Should Internet companies do more to stop terrorists' use of the Web?

Between 100 and 200 Web sites are the core "fountains of venom," says Yigal Carmon, president of the Middle East Media Research Institute, headquartered in Washington, D.C., with branch offices in Europe, Asia and the Middle East. "All the rest, are replication and duplication. You need to fight a few hundred sites, not thousands."

And many of these sites, he says, are hosted in the West. American hosting services, for instance, are often cheaper, have sufficient bandwidth to accommodate large video files and enjoy free-speech protection. But the companies often don't know they are hosting a site that, if not illegal, is perhaps violating their terms-of-service agreements.

Most Internet Service Providers, Web hosting companies, file-sharing sites and social networking sites have terms-of-service agreements that prohibit certain content. For instance, the Yahoo! Small Business Web hosting service states that users will not knowingly upload, post, e-mail, transmit or otherwise distribute any content that is "unlawful, harmful, threatening, abusive, harassing, tortious, defamatory, vulgar, obscene, libelous, invasive of another's privacy, hateful or racially, ethnically or otherwise objectionable."

It also specifically forbids users from utilizing the service to "provide material support or resources . . . to any organization(s) designated by the United States government as a foreign terrorist organization."

But Yahoo! also makes clear that it does not pre-screen content and that "You, and not Yahoo!, are entirely responsible for all Content that you upload, post, transmit, or otherwise make available."[27]

Some policy makers want Internet companies to begin screening the sites they host. Last year in the U.K., for instance, the House of Commons's Culture, Media and Sport Select Committee recommended that the "proactive review of content should be standard practice for sites hosting user-generated content."[28]

Internet companies, as well as civil libertarians and privacy advocates, disagree. "We do not think that ISPs should monitor anything since they are just in the business of transferring bits and bytes," says Rotert of EuroISPA. "We still believe in privacy laws."

David McClure, president and CEO of the U.S. Internet Industry Association, concurs. "If I'm a Web hoster, it is not my job to go snooping through the files and pages that people put on those Web sites," says McClure. "It's my job to keep the servers and the hosting service running." And, according to McClure, no U.S. law compels them to do more. Under the Telecommunications Act of 1996, McClure says, companies that host Web sites are not legally responsible for their content.

Still, ISPs and Web hosting companies do remove sites that violate their terms-of-service agreements, once

Southeast Asian Sites Now Espouse Violence

Extremist Web sites using the two main languages in Indonesia and Malaysia have evolved since 2006 from mostly propagandizing to providing firearm and bomb-making manuals and encouraging armed violence.

How the Sites Evolved

2006-July 2007	Posted al-Qaeda and Jemaah Islamiyah propaganda (videos, photographs, statements, etc.); articles about how Muslims are victimized and the necessity to fight back; celebrations of mujahidin victories; conspiracy theories; anger directed at the West; local grievances linked to global jihad; endorsements of highly selective Islamic doctrines
August 2007	First posting of manual on how to hack Web sites
February 2008	First posting of bomb-making manual and bomb-making video compilation in Arabic; emergence of a password-protected forum
April 2008	First posting of a firearm manual
Present	All of the above posted/available

Source: "Contents of Bahasa and Malay Language Radical and Extremist Web Sites, 2006 to 2009," in "Countering Internet Radicalisation in Southeast Asia," S. Rajaratnam School of International Studies, Singapore, and Australian Strategic Policy Institute, 2009

they are aware of them. Since 9/11 a variety of private watchdog groups — like the SITE Intelligence Group and Internet Haganah — have made it their business to track jihadi Web sites.

Some anti-jihadist activists, like Aaron Weisburd — who created and runs Internet Haganah — have even contacted ISPs in an effort to shame them into taking down sites. Perhaps hundreds of sites have been removed with his help. "It is rare to find an Internet company that does not care or that actively supports the terrorist cause," he says.

Weisburd says some sites should be left online because they are good sources of intelligence, "while many other sites can — and arguably should — be taken down." He says the main reason to remove them is not to get them off the Internet permanently — which is extremely difficult to do — but to track individuals as they open new accounts in order to gather evidence and prosecute them.

Members of the Peruvian revolutionary movement Tupac Amaru flash victory signs after seizing the Japanese ambassador's residence in Lima in December 1996, along with hundreds of hostages. The morning after the seizure, the rebels launched a new era in terrorist media operations by posting a 100-page Web site, based in Germany. As the four-month siege dragged on, the group updated the site periodically, using a laptop and a satellite telephone. The hostages were eventually rescued in a raid by the Peruvian military.

But ISPs don't always follow through. "Even when you get a complaint about a Web site that may be violating the terms of service, many Web hosting services may be unlikely to pursue it," says McClure. Investigating complaints is time-consuming and expensive, he says, and "once you start pursuing each complaint, you are actively involved in monitoring, and the complaints will skyrocket."

To monitor how the big Internet platforms respond to user complaints, Neumann, of King's College, suggests forming an Internet Users Panel, which could name and shame companies that don't take users' complaints seriously. "We don't want the panel to be a government body," says Neumann. "We are proposing a body that consists of Internet users, Internet companies and experts." It could publicize best practices, he says, and act as an ombudsman of last resort. ISPs would fund the panel.

But Neumann's proposal does not sit well with the ISPs. "A lot of people propose that ISPs do a lot of things," says McClure, "and what they want is for ISPs to do a lot of work for nothing."

Carmon also objects to relying on ISPs and Web hosting companies to respond to user complaints. "It's a totally untrustworthy system because you don't know who is making the complaint and why," Carmon says. "I issue a complaint against your Web site, but I may be settling an account against you, I may be your competitor in business." So ISPs must be very careful in evaluating complaints, which takes time, he says; ISPs don't want to be sued.

Instead, Carmon proposes creating what he calls a Civic Action Committee, based at an accredited research organization, which would monitor the Web and recommend sites that ISPs should consider closing. The committee would be made up of "intellectuals, writers, authors, people known for their moral standing, activists and legislators from different political parties," says Carmon.

Rotert is doubtful. "The ISPs in Europe would follow only government requests for notice and takedown procedures," he says, "because the ISPs know they cannot be held liable for destroying a business by taking down a site if the order came from the police."

Conway, of Dublin City University, has another objection to private policing of the Internet. "The capacity of private, political and economic actors to bypass the democratic process and to have materials they find politically objectionable erased from the Internet is a matter of concern," she said. Governments might want to consider legislation not just to regulate the Internet — "perhaps, for example, outlawing the posting and dissemination of beheading videos — but also writing into law more robust protections for radical political speech."[29]

Does cyberterrorism pose a serious threat?

Last year Pakistani President Asif Ali Zardari issued the following decree: "Whoever commits the offence of cyberterrorism and causes death of any person shall be punishable with death or imprisonment for life."[30]

In March India's cabinet secretary warned an international conference that cyber attacks and cyberterrorism are looming threats. "There could be attacks on critical infrastructure such as telecommunications, power distribution, transportation, financial services, essential public utility services and others," said K. M. Chandrasekhar. "The damage can range from a simple shutdown of a computer system to a complete paralysis of a significant portion of critical infrastructure in a specific region or even the control nerve centre of the entire infrastructure."[31]

Politicians, counterterrorism officials and security experts have made similarly gloomy predictions about cyberterrorism since 9/11 — and even before. But to date there have been no such attacks, although an ex-employee of a wastewater treatment plant in Australia used a computer and a radio transmitter to release sewage into parks and resort grounds in 2000.

Cyberterrorism is generally defined as highly damaging computer attacks by private individuals designed to generate terror and fear to achieve political or social goals. Thus, criminal hacking — no matter how damaging — conducted to extort money or for bragging rights is not considered cyberterrorism. (Criminal hacking is common. A year ago, for instance, criminals stole personal credit-card information from the computers of RBS WorldPay and then used the data to steal $9 million from 130 ATMs in 49 cities around the world.[32]) Likewise, the relatively minor denial-of-service attacks and Web defacements typically conducted by hackers aligned with terrorist groups also are not considered cyberterrorism.[33]

Skeptics say cyberterrorism poses only a slim threat, in part because it would lack the drama of a suicide attack or an airplane crash. "Let's say terrorists cause the lights to go out in New York City or Los Angeles, something that has already happened from weather conditions or human error," says Conway, of Dublin City University. "That is not going to create terror," she says, because those systems have been shown they can rapidly recover. Besides, she adds, terrorist groups tend to stick with what they know, which are physical attacks. "There is evolution but not sea changes in their tactics."

Even if terrorists wanted to launch a truly destructive and frightening cyber attack, their capabilities are very limited, says Irving Lachow, a senior research professor at the National Defense University in Washington, D.C. "They would need a multidisciplinary team of people to pull off a cyberterrorism attack," he says.

"A lot of these critical facilities are very complicated, and they have hundreds of systems," he continues. To blow up a power plant, for instance, a terrorist group would need an insider who knows which key computer systems are vulnerable, a team of experienced hackers to break into these systems, engineers who understand how the plant works so real damage can be done, a computer simulation lab to practice and lots of time, money and secrecy.

"At the end of the day, it's a lot easier just to blow something up," Lachow says.

But others fear that as governments continue to foil physical attacks, terrorists will expand their tactics to include cyberterrorism. Some analysts warn that terrorists could purchase the necessary expertise from cyber criminals. That, said Steven Bucci, IBM's lead researcher for cyber security, would be "a marriage made in Hell."[34]

According to Bucci, cybercrime is "a huge (and still expanding) industry that steals, cheats and extorts the equivalent of many billions of dollars every year." The most insidious threat, he said, comes from criminal syndicates that control huge botnets: worldwide networks of unwitting personal computers used for denial-of-service attacks, e-mail scams and distributing malicious software.[35]

The syndicates often rent their botnets to other criminals. Some analysts fear it's only a matter of time before a cash-rich terrorist group hires a botnet for its own use. "The cyber capabilities that the criminals could provide would in short order make any terrorist organization infinitely more dangerous and effective," said Bucci, and the permutations are "as endless as one's imagination." For example, terrorists could "open the valves at a chemical plant near a population center," replicating the deadly 1984 chemical accident in Bhopal, India.[36]

And a full-fledged cyberterrorism attack is not the only disturbing possibility, say Bucci and others. Perl at the Organization for Security and Co-operation believes terrorists are much more likely to use a cyber attack to amplify the destructive power of a physical attack. "One of the goals of terrorism is to create fear and panic," says Perl, "and not having full access to the Internet could greatly hamper governments' response to a series of massive, coordinated terrorist incidents." For example, terrorists might try to disable the emergency 911 system while blowing up embassies.

Some experts are particularly concerned that al Qaeda could launch a coordinated attack on key ports while simultaneously disabling their emergency-response systems, in order to immobilize the trade-dependant global economy. Al-Qaeda leaders have made it clear that destroying the industrialized world's economy is one of the group's goals.

But Dorothy Denning, a professor of conflict and cyberspace at the Naval Postgraduate School in Monterey, Calif., said, "Terrorists do not normally integrate

Governments Now Prosecute Suspected Online Terrorists

New laws apply to online activities.

Governments around the world have prosecuted suspected terrorists before they carry out acts of violence, but not many have been prosecuted solely for their alleged online activities in support of terrorism.

Those cases have been hampered by concerns about restricting free speech, the desire to monitor terrorist-linked sites for intelligence and the difficulty of identifying individuals online. Here are some examples of such cases:

Sami Al-Hussayen — A 34-year-old graduate student in computer science at the University of Idaho, Al-Hussayen was arrested in February 2003 and accused of designing, creating and maintaining Web sites that provided material support for terrorism. It was the U.S. government's first attempt at using statutes prohibiting material support for terrorism to prosecute activity that occurred exclusively online. The definition of "material support" used by the prosecutors had been expanded under the Patriot Act of 2001 to include "expert advice or assistance."

Al-Hussayen had volunteered to run Web sites for two Muslim charities and two Muslim clerics. But prosecutors alleged that messages and religious fatwas on the sites encouraged jihad, recruited terrorists and raised money for foreign terrorist groups. It didn't matter that Al-Hussayen had never committed a terrorist act or that he hadn't written the material. Prosecutors said it was enough to prove that he ran the Web sites and knew the messages existed.

Jurors were not convinced, however. They acquitted Al-Hussayen in June 2004. "There was no direct connection in the evidence they gave us — and we had boxes and boxes to go through — between Sami and terrorism," said one juror.[1]

The case attracted national attention, and according to University of Idaho law professor Alan Williams, "triggered a heated debate focused mainly on a key question: Were Al-Hussayen's Internet activities constitutionally protected free speech or did they cross the line into criminal and material support to terrorism?"[2]

The U.S. Supreme Court is scheduled to hear challenges to the material support statute — which critics complain is too vague — in two related cases this session.[3]

Younis Tsouli — In late 2005, British police arrested 22-year-old Tsouli, a Moroccan immigrant and student who prosecutors alleged was known online as "Irhaby 007" — or Terrorist 007. The government linked Tsouli and his accomplices Waseem Mughal and Tariq al-Daour to "the purchase, construction and maintenance of a large number of Web sites and Internet chat forums on which material was published which incited acts of terrorist murder, primarily in Iraq."[4]

Tsouli had been in active contact with al Qaeda in Iraq and was part of an online network that extended to Canada, the United States and Eastern Europe. In July 2007, Tsouli, Mughal and Al-Daour "became the first men to plead guilty to inciting murder for terrorist purposes" under the U.K.'s Terrorism Act of 2000.[5]

Samina Malik — In November 2007 the 23-year-old shop assistant became the first woman convicted of terrorism in the United Kingdom when she was found guilty of "possessing information of a kind likely to be useful to a person committing or preparing an act of terrorism."[6]

Malik had downloaded and saved on her hard drive *The Terrorist's Handbook*, *The Mujahideen Poisons Handbook* and

multiple modes of attack." If coordinating cyber and physical attacks did become their goal, Denning would expect to see evidence of failed attempts, training, discussions and planning. "Given terrorists' capabilities today in the cyber domain, this seems no more imminent than other acts of cyberterror," she said. "At least in the near future, bombs remain a much larger threat than bytes."[37]

But that doesn't mean critical infrastructure is secure from cyber criminal syndicates or nation-states, which do have the technical know-how, funds and personnel to launch a damaging attack, Denning said. "Even if our critical infrastructures are not under imminent threat by terrorists seeking political and social objectives," she said, "they must be protected from harmful attacks conducted for other reasons, such as money, revenge, youthful curiosity and war."[38]

other documents that appeared to support violent jihad. She had also written violent poems about killing non-believers. Her defense portrayed her as a confused young woman assuming a persona she thought was "cool."

Her conviction sparked public outrage. Muhammed Abdul Bari, secretary general of the Muslim Council of Britain, said, "Many young people download objectionable material from the Internet, but it seems if you are Muslim then this could lead to criminal charges, even if you have absolutely no intention to do harm to anyone else." An appeals court later overturned her conviction and clarified a new requirement that suspects must have a clear intent to engage in terrorism.[7]

Ibrahim Rashid — In 2007 German prosecutors charged the Iraqi Kurdish immigrant with waging a "virtual jihad" on the Internet. They argued that by posting al-Qaeda propaganda on chat rooms, Rashid was trying to recruit individuals to join al Qaeda and participate in jihad. It was Germany's first prosecution of an Islamic militant for circulating propaganda online.[8]

"This case underscores how thin the line is that Germany is walking in its efforts to aggressively target Islamic radicals," wrote Shawn Marie Boyne, a professor at Indiana University's law school. "While active membership in a terrorist organization is a crime . . . it is no longer a crime to merely sympathize with terrorist groups or to distribute propaganda."[9] Thus, the prosecution had to prove that Rashid's postings went beyond expressing sympathy and extended to recruiting. The court found him guilty in June 2008.

Saïd Namouh — On Oct. 1, the 36-year-old Moroccan resident of Quebec was convicted under Canada's Anti-Terrorism Act of four charges largely related to his online activities. In March 2007 he had helped publicize a video warning Germany and Austria that they would suffer a bomb attack if they didn't withdraw their troops from Afghanistan. He also distributed violent videos on behalf of Global Islamic Media Front, a propaganda arm of al Qaeda. Intercepted Internet chats revealed Namouh's plans to explode a truck bomb and die a martyr. "Terrorism is in

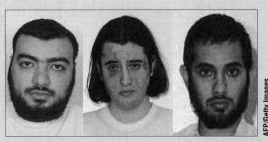

AFP/Getty Images

Tariq al-Daour, Younis Tsouli and Waseem Mughal (left to right), in 2007 became the first to plead guilty to inciting murder for terrorist purposes online under the U.K.'s Terrorism Act of 2000.

our blood, and with it we will drown the unjust," Namouh said online.[10]

— *Barbara Mantel*

[1] Maureen O'Hagan, "A terrorism case that went awry," seattletimes.com, Nov. 22, 2004, http://seattletimes.nwsource.com/html/local-news/2002097570_sami22m.html.

[2] Alan Williams, "Prosecuting Website Development Under the Material Support in Terrorism Statutes: Time to Fix What's Broken," *NYU Journal of Legislation & Public Policy*, 2008, p. 366.

[3] The cases are *Holder v. Humanitarian Law Project*; *Humanitarian Law Project v. Holder*, 08-1498; 09-89. See http://onthedocket.org/cases/2009.

[4] Elizabeth Renieris, "Combating Incitement to Terrorism on the Internet: Comparative Approaches in the United States and United Kingdom and the Need for an International Solution," *Vanderbilt Journal of Entertainment and Technology Law*, vol. 11:3:673, p. 698, 2009.

[5] *Ibid.*

[6] *Ibid.*

[7] *Ibid.*, pp. 699-700.

[8] Shawn Marie Boyne, "The Criminalization of Speech in an Age of Terror," working paper, June 12, 2009, p. 7, http://ssrn.com/abstract=1418496.

[9] *Ibid.*

[10] Graeme Hamilton, "Quebec terror plotter undone by online activities," *National Post*, Oct. 1, 2009, www.nationalpost.com/news/story.html?id=2054720.

BACKGROUND

Growth and Evolution

After seizing the Japanese embassy in Lima, Peru, on Dec. 17, 1996, the Tupac Amaru communist rebels "launched a new era in terrorist media operations," wrote Denning. The next morning the group had a Web site with more than 100 pages up and running out of

Germany, which it updated using a laptop and a satellite telephone.[39]

"For the first time, terrorists could bring their message to a world audience without mediation by the established press or interference by the government," Denning said. They could offer the first news accounts to the media, and they could use the Web site to communicate directly with their members and supporters. "The advantage the

CHRONOLOGY

1990s *Terrorist groups discover the Internet's usefulness for fundraising and publicity.*

1996 After seizing the Japanese embassy in Lima, Peruvian revolutionary movement Tupac Amaru creates a Web site to publicize its actions.

1997 Sri Lanka's Tamil Tigers use stolen Sheffield University faculty members' computer IDs and passwords to solicit donations.

1998 Researchers looking for online terrorism sites discover al Qaeda's Web site, www.alneda.com.

1999 Nearly all 30 U.S.-designated foreign terrorist organizations have an Internet presence.

2000-2005 *Extremist Web sites and discussion forums multiply; first prosecution of man accused of providing material online in support of terrorists fails.*

July 20, 2000 Terrorism Act of 2000 makes it illegal in the U.K. to collect, make or possess information likely to be used in terrorism.

2001 The 9/11 attackers use the Internet to research flight schools and flights and to coordinate their actions. On Oct. 26, 2001, President George W. Bush signs the USA Patriot Act, which prohibits "material support" for terrorists.

2003 Abdelaziz al-Muqrin, leader of al Qaeda in Saudi Arabia, pioneers several digital magazines, including *Sawt al-Jihad* (*The Voice of Jihad*).

2004 Video of the decapitation of kidnapped U.S. businessman Nicholas Berg is released on a Malaysian Web site. . . . University of Idaho graduate student Sami Omar al-Hussayen is acquitted of fostering terrorism online after his lawyers raise freedom of expression issues. Autobiography of Imam Samudra, mastermind of the 2002 Bali nightclub bombings that killed 202, promotes online credit-card fraud to raise funds. . . . Saudi Arabia launches the Sakinah Campaign, in which Islamic scholars steer religious questioners away from online extremists.

2005 YouTube, launched in February, quickly becomes repository for jihadist video content and commentary.

More than 4,000 Web sites connected to terrorist groups are on the Internet.

2006-Present *Governments reauthorize and expand antiterrorism laws; U.K. begins prosecuting those who use the Internet to "incite" others to commit terrorist acts.*

2006 President Bush reauthorizes Patriot Act. . . . U.K. passes Terrorism Act of 2006, outlawing encouragement or glorification of terrorism; civil libertarians raise concerns about free speech. . . . U.S. State Department creates Digital Outreach Team with two Arabic-speaking employees who converse online with critics of U.S. policies.

2007 EU police agency Europol begins "Check the Web" program, in which member states share in monitoring and evaluating terrorists' Web sites. . . . In July, U.K. resident Younis Tsouli pleads guilty to inciting terrorism after he and two associates used stolen credit cards to register Web site domains that promote terrorisim. . . . Samina Malik becomes the first woman convicted of terrorism in the U.K. for having documents that support violent jihad on her computer. A court of appeals later overturns her conviction, questioning her intent to engage in terrorism.

2008 Three important Islamist terrorist discussion forums disappear from the Internet; analysts assume counterterrorism agencies bombarded the sites with denial-of-service attacks. . . . On Nov. 6, Pakistan's president makes cyberterrorism punishable with death or life imprisonment. . . . In its first prosecution for promoting terrorism online, a German court finds Iraqi Kurdish immigrant Ibrahim Rashid guilty of waging a "virtual jihad" for attempting to recruit individuals online to join al Qaeda and participate in jihad.

2009 Canadian resident Saïd Namouh is convicted on Oct. 1 of planning terrorist acts and distributing jihadist propaganda via the Internet. . . . On Oct. 26 Jordanian teenager Hosam Maher Husein Smadi pleads not guilty of plotting to blow up a Dallas skyscraper on Sept. 24. FBI agents had been keeping tabs on Smadi after discovering him on an extremist Web site earlier this year. . . . Researchers are tracking more than 7,000 Web sites connected to terrorist groups and their supporters.

Web offered was immeasurable and recognized by terrorist groups worldwide."[40]

By the end of 1999, nearly all of the 30 organizations designated by the U.S. State Department as foreign terrorist organizations had a presence on the Internet. By 2005, there were more than 40 designated terrorist groups and more than 4,300 Web sites serving them and their supporters. Today, the number of such Web sites exceeds 7,000, according to Weimann, of Haifa University.[41]

Of these groups, Islamic terrorists have perhaps made the most use of the Internet. When al Qaeda suffered defeat in Afghanistan directly after 9/11, its recruiters in Europe "who had previously encouraged others to travel to mujahidin training camps in Afghanistan, Bosnia-Herzegovina and Chechnya began radically changing their message," wrote Kohlmann, of the NEFA Foundation. "Their new philosophy emphasized the individual nature and responsibility of jihad."[42] Recruits did not necessarily have to travel abroad; they could learn what they needed online.

Thus the Internet became a vital means for communication amid a global law enforcement clampdown on suspected terrorists.

Al Qaeda's first official Web site was the brainchild of a senior Saudi operative — and one-time Osama bin Laden bodyguard — Shaykh Youssef al-Ayyiri. The site contained audio and video clips of the al-Qaeda leader, justification for the 9/11 attacks and poetry glorifying the attackers and — on its English version — a message to the American people.[43]

After al-Ayyiri's 2003 death during a clash with Saudi security forces, his top lieutenant, Abdelaziz al-Muqrin, took control. He was a "firm believer in using the Web to disseminate everything from firsthand accounts of terrorist operations to detailed instructions on how to capture or kill Western tourists and diplomats," according to Kohlmann. Before he was killed by Saudi forces in 2004, al-Muqrin created several digital magazines, including *Sawt al-Jihad*, or *The Voice of Jihad*. The author of an article in its inaugural issue told readers, "The blood [of the infidels] is like the blood of a dog and nothing more."[44]

While al Qaeda's Saudi Arabian network pioneered the use of online publications, Kohlmann said, "The modern revolution in the terrorist video market has occurred in the context of the war in Iraq and under the watchful eye of Jordanian national Abu Musab al-Zarqawi." Until his death in 2006, Zarqawi led al Qaeda in Iraq and was known for "his penchant for and glorification of extreme violence

— particularly hostage beheadings and suicide bombings," many of them captured on video, including the murder of American civilian contractor Nicholas Berg.[45]

"Images of orange-clad hostages became a headline-news staple around the world — and the full, raw videos of their murders spread rapidly around the Web."[46]

Content on militant Islamist Web sites in Southeast Asia tends to "mimic the contents and features of their Arabic and Middle Eastern online counterparts," according to a study from the Australian Strategic Policy Institute. "Although they aren't yet on par in operational coordination and tradecraft, they are catching up."[47]

Between 2006 and July 2007, extremist content on radical Bahasa Indonesia (the official language of Indonesia) and Malay language Web sites consisted of propaganda from al Qaeda and the Indonesian jihadist group Jemaah Islamiyah. The sites celebrated mujahidin victories, aired local grievances linked to the global jihad and posted highly selective Koranic verses used to justify acts of terror. In August 2007, one of the first postings of instructions on computer hacking appeared, and in the first four months of 2008 the first bomb-making manual, bomb-making video and a password-protected forum emerged.[48]

Not all terrorist organizations use the Internet to showcase violence. Many, such as FARC (Revolutionary Armed Forces of Colombia), focus on human rights and peace. "In contrast to al Qaeda's shadowy, dynamic, versatile and often vicious Web sites," wrote Weimann, "the FARC sites are more 'transparent,' stable and mainly focused on information and publicity."

Established in 1964 as the military wing of the Colombian Communist Party, FARC has been responsible for kidnappings, bombings and hijackings and funds its operations through narcotics trafficking.[49] Yet there are no violent videos of these attacks. Instead, FARC Web sites offer information on the organization's history and laws, its reasons for resistance, offenses perpetrated by the Colombian and U.S. governments, life as a FARC member and women and culture. Weimann called the sophisticated FARC Web sites "an impressive example of media-savvy Internet use by a terrorist group."[50]

From Web 1.0 to 2.0

Terrorist content can now be found on all parts of the Internet, not just on official sites of groups like FARC and al Qaeda and their proxies. Chat rooms, blogs, social

'Terrorists Are Trying to Attract Young Recruits'

An interview with the director of the Dark Web project.

The University of Arizona's Dark Web project, funded by the National Science Foundation, studies international terrorism using automated computer programs. The project has amassed one of the world's largest databases on extremist/ terrorist-generated Internet content. Author Barbara Mantel recently interviewed Hsinchun Chen, the project's director.

CQ: What is the purpose of Dark Web?

HC: We examine who terrorists talk to, what kind of information they disseminate, what kind of new violent ideas they have, what kind of illegal activities they plan to conduct. We're looking at Web sites, forums, chat rooms, blogs, social networking sites, videos and virtual worlds.

CQ: How difficult is it to find terrorist content on the Web?

HC: From Google you can find some, but you won't be able to get into the sites that are more relevant, more intense and more violent.

CQ: So how do sympathizers find these sites?

HC: Typically people are introduced by word of mouth, offline. And there are different degrees of openness on these sites.

CQ: For example?

HC: There are many sites that require an introduction; they may require a password; moderators may also ask a series of questions to see if you are from the region, if you are real and if you are in their targeted audience.

CQ: How does the Dark Web project find these sites?

HC: We have been collaborating for six or seven years with many terrorism study centers all around the world, and they have been monitoring these sites for some time. So they know how to access these Web sites and whether they are legitimate forums. But most of them do not have the ability to collect all the content; they can do manual review and analysis.

So these researchers will give us the URLs of these sites, and they'll give us the user names and passwords they've been using to gain access. Once we get this information, we load it into our computer program, and the computers will spit out every single page of that site and download that into our database.

CQ: How much material are we talking about?

HC: The researchers we work with can analyze maybe hundreds or thousands of pages or messages, but we collect and analyze maybe half a million to 10 million pages easily.

CQ: How do you know that a site is actually linked to a terrorist group or supporter?

HC: Remember we start off with the URLs that terrorism researchers think are important. We also do "crawling" to find new sites. Any Web site will have links to other sites, and by triangulating those links from legitimate sites, we can locate other legitimate sites.

CQ: After finding the content, do you analyze it?

HC: Our claim to fame is analysis. We have techniques that look at social network linkages, that categorize the content into propaganda, training, recruiting, etc., and techniques that determine the sophistication of Web sites. We have a technique that looks at the extent of the violent sentiment in these sites and techniques that can determine authorship.

networking sites and user groups allow conversation and debate among a wide variety of participants.

"Yahoo! has become one of al Qaeda's most significant ideological bases of operations," wrote researchers Rita Katz and Josh Devon in 2003. "Creating a Yahoo! Group is free, quick and extremely easy. . . . Very often, the groups contain the latest links to jihadist Web sites, serving as a jihadist directory."[51] A Yahoo! user group is a hybrid between an electronic mailing list and a discussion forum. Members can receive posted messages and photos through e-mail or view the posts at the group's Web site.

While much of the original content on the terrorist-linked sites was text-based, videos began to play a much larger role after 2003, especially for militant Islamist organizations and their supporters. "Nevertheless, much of this video content remained quite difficult to access for Westerners and others, as it was located on Arabic-only Web sites" that were often frequently changing domain names and were therefore used "only by those who were strongly committed to gaining access," according to a study co-authored by Conway, of Dublin City University.[52]

CQ: None of this is done manually?

HC: Everything I talk about — almost 90 percent — is entirely automated.

CQ: What trends you are noticing?

HC: I'm not a terrorism researcher, but there are trends that we observe on the technology end. Terrorists are trying to attract young recruits, so they like to use discussion forums and YouTube, where the content is more multimedia and more of a two-way conversation. We also see many home-grown groups cropping up all over the world.

CQ: Do you share this information with government agencies?

HC: Many agencies — I cannot name them — and researchers from many countries are using the Dark Web forum portal.

CQ: How does the portal work?

HC: There is a consensus among terrorism researchers that discussion forums are the richest source of content, especially the forums that attract sometimes 50,000 members to 100,000 members. So we have created this portal that contains the contents from close to 20 different, important forums. And these are in English, Arabic and French. The French ones are found in North Africa.

We also embedded a lot of search, translation and analysis mechanisms in the portal. So now any analyst can use the content to see trends. For example, they can see what are the discussions about improvised explosive devices in Afghanistan, or they can look at who are the members that are interested in weapons of mass destruction.

CQ: Are these forums mostly extremist jihadi forums?

HC: Yes, they are. That's what analysts are primarily interested in. We are also creating another portal for multimedia content that will be available in another month or two. That would contain material from YouTube, for instance.

Hsinchun Chen oversees the University of Arizona's Dark Web project, which analyzes terrorists' online activities.

CQ: Do you collect information from U.S. extremist sites?

HC: We collect from animal-liberation groups, Aryan Nation and militia groups, but that is just for our research purposes. We don't make it available to outsiders. Government lawyers advise us against giving that kind of information out to them or to the outside world. It's a civil liberty issue.

CQ: Even if that material is open source material, available to anyone who finds their Web site?

HC: Even if it is open source.

But the advent of YouTube in 2005 changed the situation dramatically, Conway wrote, playing an increasing role in distributing terrorist content. Not only did YouTube become an immediate repository for large amounts of jihadist video content, but the social-networking aspects of the site allowed a dialogue between posters and viewers of videos.[53]

Terrorists-linked groups also have used mass e-mailings to reach broad audiences, according to Denning. "The Jihadist Cyber-Attack Brigade, for example, announced in May 2008 they had successfully sent 26,000 e-mails to 'citizens of the Gulf and Arab countries explaining the words of our leader Usama Bin Ladin.'"[54]

Terrorists and Cybercrime

Terrorists increasingly have turned to the Internet to raise funds, often through cybercrime. "We should be extremely concerned about the scope of the credit-card fraud problem involving terrorists," according to Dennis Lormel, a retired special agent in the FBI. Although there is "limited or no empirical data to gauge the extent

Political Change Is Main Attack Motivation

Four out of six types of cyber attacks or threats are politically motivated. Attackers typically use "malware," or malicious software that spreads viruses, or denial-of-service attacks to disrupt Web sites of individuals, companies, governments and other targets.

Cyber Threat	Motivation	Target	Method
Cyberterror	Political or social change	Innocent victims	Computer-based violence or destruction
Hacktivism*	Political or social change	Decision-makers or innocent victims	Web page defacements or denial of service
Black Hat Hacking**	Ego, personal enmity	Individuals, companies, governments	Malware, viruses, worms or hacking
Cybercrime	Economic gain	Individuals, companies	Malware for fraud or identity theft; denial of service for blackmail
Cyber Espionage	Economic or political gain	Individuals, companies, governments	Range of techniques
Information War	Political or military gain	Infrastructures, information-technology systems and data (private or public)	Range of techniques

Hacking to promote an activist's political ideology.

** *Hacking just for the challenge, bragging rights or due to a personal vendetta.*

Source: Franklin D. Kramer, Stuart H. Starr and Larry Wentz, eds., "Cyber Threats : Defining Terms," Cyberpower and National Security (2009)

of the problem . . . there are compelling signs that an epidemic permeates," he wrote.[55]

In his jailhouse autobiography, Imam Samudra — convicted of masterminding the 2002 nightclub bombings in Bali, Indonesia, that killed 202 people — includes a rudimentary outline of how to commit online credit-card fraud, or "carding."

"If you succeed at hacking and get into carding, be ready to make more money within three to six hours than the income of a policeman in six months," Samudra writes. "But don't do it just for the sake of money." Their main duty, he tells readers, is to raise arms against infidels, "especially now the United States and its allies."[56] Although Samudra's laptop revealed an attempt at carding, it's not clear he ever succeeded.

But others have. Younis Tsouli, a young Moroccan immigrant in London who made contact with al Qaeda online, and two associates used computer viruses and stolen credit-card accounts to set up a network of communication forums and Web sites that hosted "everything from tutorials on computer hacking and bomb making to videos of beheadings and suicide bombing attacks in Iraq," said Lormel.[57]

The three hackers ran up $3.5 million in charges to register more than 180 Web site domains at 95 different Web hosting companies and purchased hundreds of prepaid cellphones and more than 250 airline tickets. They also laundered money through online gaming sites.[58]

Even though both Samudra and Tsouli are in jail, "they left their successful tradecraft on Web pages and in chat rooms for aspiring terrorists to learn and grow from," noted Lormel.[59]

CURRENT SITUATION

Alternative Voices

Western governments and terrorism experts are concerned that the United States and other nations are not providing a counter message to online militant Islamists.

"The militant Islamist message on the Internet cannot be censored, but it can be challenged," says Johnny Ryan, a senior researcher at the Institute of International and European Affairs in Dublin, Ireland. But governments and societies, he says, for the most part, have ceded the dialogue in cyberspace to extremists, who are highly skilled at crafting their message.

That message "is mostly emotional," according to Frank Cilluffo, director of the Homeland Security Policy Institute at The George Washington University in Washington, D.C. It "uses images, visuals and music to tell a powerful story with clear-cut heroes and villains."

Societies interested in countering that message should not shy away from emotion either, he argues. "Who are the victims of al Qaeda?" Cilluffo asks, "and why don't we know their stories?" Western and Arab-Muslim media rarely reveal victims' names unless they are famous or foreign, he points out. Personal stories about victims "from the World Trade Center to the weddings, funerals, schools, mosques and hotels where suicide bombers have brought untold grief to thousands of families, tribes and communities throughout the Muslim world" could be told in online social networks, he suggested, "creating a Facebook of the bereaved that crosses borders and cultures."[60]

Raising doubts is "another powerful rhetorical weapon," says Ryan, who suggests exploiting the chat rooms and discussion forums frequented by prospective militants and sympathizers. Moderate Islamic voices should question the legitimacy of al Qaeda's offensive jihad, disseminate the arguments of Muslim scholars who renounce violence and challenge militant Islamists' version of historical relations between the West and Islam, according to Ryan.[61]

The U.S. Department of State has begun its own modest online effort. In November 2006 it created a Digital Outreach Team with two Arabic-speaking employees. The team now has 10 members who actively engage in conversations on Arabic-, Persian- and Urdu-language Internet sites, including blogs, news sites and discussion forums. Team members identify themselves as State Department employees, but instead of posting dry, policy pronouncements they create "engaging, informal personas for [their] online discussions." The team's mission

The Top 10 Jihadi Web Forums

The most influential jihadi online forums serve as virtual community centers for al Qaeda and other Islamic extremists, according to Internet Haganah — an online network dedicated to combating global jihad. Jihadi Web addresses, which are often blocked, change frequently.

1 al-Faloja
Highly respected among terrorists; focuses on the Iraq War and the Salafi-jihadi struggle.

2 al-Medad
Was associated with Abu Jihad al-Masri, the al-Qaeda propaganda chief killed in a U.S. missile strike in Pakistan on Oct. 30, 2008; disseminates Salafi-jihadi ideology.

3 al-Shouaraa
Originally named el-Shouraa, it was blocked, but later reemerged with a new name; has North African influences; no longer active.

4 Ana al-Muslm
Very active; was used by al Qaeda to communicate with Abu Musab al-Zarqawi (Osama bin Laden's deputy in Iraq) until he was killed by U.S. forces in 2006.

5 al-Ma'ark
Has been slowly and steadily building an online following in recent years.

6 al-Shamukh
Successor to al-Mohajrun, a militant Islamic organization that was banned in the U.K. in 2005; provides radio broadcasts.

7 as-Ansar
Features English and German invitation-only spin-off sites; a favorite among Western jihadists.

8 al-Mujahideen
Attracts a strong contingent of Hamas supporters, with an overall global jihad perspective; especially focused on electronic jihad.

9 al-Hanein
Has a significant amount of jihadi content tinged by Iraqi, Egyptian and Moroccan nationalism.

10 at-Tahaddi
Sunni jihadist; recruits from Somali, Taliban and other terrorist groups.

Source: "Top Ten List of Jihadi Forums," Internet Haganah, a project of The Society for Internet Research, Aug. 3, 2009, http://internethaganah .com/harchives/006545. html; Jamestown Foundation

Hamaad Munshi — a British national convicted in 2008 of possessing materials likely to be used for terrorism — was 16 when he was arrested after participating in an online British extremist group. The trial revealed that Munshi had downloaded details on how to make napalm and grenades and wished to become a martyr by fighting abroad.

is "to explain U.S. foreign policy and to counter misinformation," according to the State Department.[62]

No one knows the full impact of the team's efforts, but the project has come in for criticism. "They should be larger," says Matt Armstrong, an analyst and government advisor who writes a blog on public diplomacy at mountainrunner.us, "and they should be coordinated to a much greater degree with the production side of the State Department." The team's Internet conversations should directly shape a post on the State Department Web site or on its radio program, he says.

But Duncan MacInnes, principal deputy coordinator at the State Department's Bureau of International Information Programs, says the scale of the Digital Outreach Team is about right, although it could use one or two

more Persian speakers and possibly expand into more languages. "Having too many people blogging in a fairly small blogosphere would raise our profile, and we felt [it] would create a reaction against us. You don't want to overdo it." Also, he says, the team does not work in isolation. It writes a biweekly report about the issues, concerns and misunderstandings members encounter online, which goes to hundreds of people inside the State Department.

Others question whether the government should be the one to hold this dialogue. "The state is not in a position to be the primary actor here because it lacks credibility in online forums," says Ryan.

"The best approach is to provide young people with the information and the intellectual tools to challenge this material themselves on various Web forums," says Bergin, of the Australian Strategic Policy Institute. "It's got to be provided by stakeholders in the Muslim community themselves, from community workers, religious figures and parents."

The Sakinah Campaign

Many terrorism analysts cite Saudi Arabia's Sakinah Campaign as a model program. Internet use in the kingdom has grown rapidly since access first became available there 10 years ago. Since 2000, the kingdom's total number of Internet users has risen from roughly 200,000 to more than 7 million today, out of an overall population of nearly 29 million.[63]

Meanwhile, extremist Web sites in the kingdom have multiplied from 15 sites in 1998 to several thousand today, even though the Saudi government controls Internet access and blocks sites featuring gambling, pornography and drug and alcohol use, according to Christopher Boucek, a researcher at the Carnegie Endowment for International Peace. Extremist sites "often appear faster than they can be identified and blocked," said Boucek.[64]

Responding to that trend, the Sakinah Campaign since 2004 has used volunteer Islamic scholars "to interact online with individuals looking for religious knowledge, with the aim of steering them away from extremist sources." These scholars have "highly developed understandings of extremist ideologies, including the religious interpretations used to justify violence and terrorism," according to Boucek.[65] The campaign is officially an independent, nongovernmental project, even though several government ministries encourage and support it.

Is cyberterrorism a significant global threat?

YES   Mohd Noor Amin
Chairman, International Multilateral Partnership Against Cyber Threats Selangor, Malaysia

NO   Tim Stevens
Associate, Centre for Science and Security Studies, King's College London

Written for *CQ Global Researcher*, November 2009

Alarm bells on cyberterrorism have been sounding for more than a decade, and yet, hacktivism aside, the world still has not witnessed a devastating cyber attack on critical infrastructure. Nothing has occurred that caused massive damage, injuries and fatalities resulting in widespread chaos, fear and panic. Does that mean the warnings were exaggerated?

On the contrary, the convergence of impassioned politics, hacktivism trends and extremists' growing technological sophistication suggests that the threat of cyberterrorism remains significant — if not more urgent — today. Although hacktivists and terrorists have not yet successfully collaborated to bring a country to its knees, there is already significant overlap between them. Computer-savvy extremists have been sharpening their skills by defacing and hacking into Web sites and training others to do so online. Given the public ambitions of groups like al Qaeda to launch cyber attacks, it would be folly to ignore the threat of a major cyber assault if highly skilled hackers and terrorists did conspire to brew a perfect storm.

Experts are particularly concerned that terrorists could learn how to deliver a simultaneous one-two blow: executing a mass, physical attack while incapacitating the emergency services or electricity grids to neutralize rescue efforts. The scenario may not be so far-fetched, judging from past cyber attacks or attempts, although a certain level of technical skill and access would be needed to paralyze part of a nation's critical infrastructure. However, as shown by an oft-cited 2000 incident in Australia, a single, disgruntled former employee hacked into a wastewater management facility's computer system and released hundreds of thousands of gallons of raw sewage onto Sunshine Coast resort grounds and a canal.

Vital industrial facilities are not impenetrable to cyber attacks and, if left inadequately secured, terrorists and hackers could wreak havoc. Similarly, the 2008 cyber attacks that caused multicity power outages around the world underscore the vulnerabilities of public utilities, particularly as these systems become connected to open networks to boost economies of scale.

If this past decade of terrorist attacks has demonstrated the high literacy level, technological capability and zeal of terrorists, the next generation of terrorists growing up in an increasingly digitized and connected world may hold even greater potential for cyberterrorism. After all, if it is possible to effect visibly spectacular, catastrophic destruction from afar and still remain anonymous, why not carry it out?

Written for *CQ Global Researcher*, November 2009

Cyberterrorism is the threat and reality of unlawful attacks against computer networks and data by an individual or a non-governmental group to further a political agenda. Such attacks can cause casualties and deaths through spectacular incidents, such as plane crashes or industrial explosions, or secondary consequences, such as crippled economies or disrupted emergency services.

We have seen many attempts to disrupt the online assets of governments, industry and individuals, but these have mercifully not yet caused the mass casualties predicted by the term "cyberterrorism." The assumption that terrorists might use cyberspace in such attacks is not in question, but the potential threat that cyberterrorism poses is accorded disproportionate weight in some circles.

Cyberterrorism resulting in civilian deaths is certainly one possible outcome of the convergence of technology and political aggression. That it has not happened yet is a function of two factors. First, the ongoing vigilance and operational sophistication of national security agencies have ensured that critical infrastructure systems have remained largely unbreached and secure. And second, like all self-styled revolutionaries, terrorists talk a good talk.

Although a terrorist group might possess both the intent and the skill-sets — either in-house, or "rented" — there is little evidence yet that any group has harnessed both to serious effect. Most attacks characterized as "cyberterrorism" so far have amounted to mere annoyances, such as Web site defacements, service disruptions and low-level cyber "skirmishing" — nonviolent responses to political situations, rather than actions aimed at reaping notoriety in flesh and blood.

It would be foolish, however, to dismiss the threat of cyberterrorism. It would also be disingenuous to overstate it. Western governments are making strides towards comprehensive cyber security strategies that encompass a wide range of possible scenarios, while trying to overcome agency jurisdictional issues, private-sector wariness and the fact that civilian computer systems are now seen as "strategic national assets."

As it becomes harder to understand the complexities of network traffic, identify attack vectors, attribute responsibility and react accordingly, we must pursue integrated national and international strategies that criminalize the sorts of offensive attacks that might constitute cyberterrorism. But designating the attacks as terrorism is a taxonomic firewall we should avoid.

According to Abdullah Ansary, a lawyer and former lecturer at King Abdul-Aziz University in Saudi Arabia, al Qaeda has issued several statements over the Internet cautioning their followers not to engage in dialogues with members of the Sakinah Campaign, a sign that the campaign is having an impact on al Qaeda's membership.[66] The campaign itself periodically releases the number of people it says it has turned away from extremism. In January 2008, it announced it had "convinced some 877 individuals (722 male and 155 female) to reject their radical ideology across more than 1,500 extremists Web sites."[67]

But in 2007, after the government arrested members of seven terrorist cells operating in the kingdom, several columnists complained that the Sakinah Campaign and other government supported programs trying to reform extremists were ineffective and not getting to the root of the problem. According to translations from the Middle East Media Research Institute, columnist Abdallah bin Bajad Al-'Utaibi wrote in the Saudi daily *Al-Riyadh*: "There are schoolteachers, imams in the mosques, preachers and jurisprudents who do nothing but spread hatred and *takfir** in our society. They should be prosecuted for their actions, which lay down the foundations for terrorism."[68]

Ansary said the government must make wider reforms if it wants to prevent young people from turning to extremism. The government must "speed up the process of political reform in the country, widening popular participation in the political process, improving communication channels of both the government and the public, creating effective communication among branches of government, continuing the efforts in overhauling the Saudi educational system and boosting the role of women in the society."[69]

In late 2006, the Sakinah Campaign expanded its role and created its own Web site designed to "serve as a central location for people to turn to online with questions about Islam."[70]

Government-funded Sites

Similar Web sites have been set up in other countries to offer alternative messages to terrorist propaganda.

The Islamic Religious Council of Singapore — the country's supreme Islamic authority, whose members are appointed by the country's president — has several interactive Web sites to counter extremist strands of Islam. The sites feature articles, blogs and documentary videos targeted at young people and host an online forum where religious scholars answer questions about Islam. One site specifically challenges the ideology of Jemaah Islamiyah, the jihadist group responsible for the deadly 2002 nightclub bombing in Bali and the July 2009 bombings of the Marriott and Ritz Carlton hotels in Jakarta. The organization wants to establish a pan-Islamic theocratic state across much of Southeast Asia.[71]

But the effectiveness of such sites is difficult to gauge. "To a certain extent it is helping to drown out extremist voices online," says Osman, of Nanyang Technological University in Singapore, "but for those who are actively seeking extremist ideology, these kinds of Web sites don't appeal to them."

A similar project in the United Kingdom also meets with skepticism. On its Web site, the Radical Middle Way calls itself "a revolutionary grassroots initiative aimed at articulating a relevant mainstream understanding of Islam that is dynamic, proactive and relevant to young British Muslims."[72] It rejects all forms of terrorism, and its site has blogs, discussions, videos, news and a schedule of its events in the U.K. Its two dozen supporters and partners are mostly Muslim organizations as well as the British Home Office, which oversees immigration, passports, drug policy and counterterrorism, among other things.

"We are arguing that this is not money well spent," says Neumann of King's College. "The kind of money the government is putting into the Web site is enormous, and the site doesn't attract that much traffic."

The government money has also caused at least some young people to question the group's credibility. One blogger called the group "the radical wrong way" and wrote that "because the funding source is so well known, large segments of alienated British Muslims will not have anything to do with this group. . . . If anything, such tactics will lead to even further alienation of young British Muslims — who will rightly point out that this kind of U.S./U.K.-funded version of Islam is just another strategy in the ongoing war on Islam."[73]

Neumann and Bergin recommend instead that governments give out many small grants to different Muslim organizations with ideas for Web sites and see if any can grow to significance without dependence on government funds.

---

* *Takfir* is the act of identifying someone as an unbeliever.

In the end, individual governments' direct role in providing an online alternative narrative to terrorist ideology may, out of necessity, be quite small because of the credibility issue, say analysts. Instead, they say, governments could fund Internet literacy programs that discuss hate propaganda, adjust school curriculums to include greater discussion of Islam and the West and encourage moderate Muslim voices to take to the Web. Cilluffo, of the Homeland Security Policy Institute, said the United Nations could lead the way, sponsoring a network of Web sites, publications and television programming.

"The United Nations can and should play a significant role," Cilluffo said, "bringing together victims to help meet their material needs and raising awareness by providing platforms through which to share their stories."[74]

Above, an Internet café in Sydney. Many Australians oppose government plans to build what critics call the Great Aussie Firewall — a mandatory Internet filter that would block at least 1,300 Web sites prohibited by the government.

AFP/Getty Images/Torsten Blackwood

OUTLOOK
Pooling Resources

Web sites that promote terrorism are here to stay, although governments and Internet companies will occasionally shut one down if it violates the law or a terms-of-service agreement. Such decisions can only be reached after prolonged monitoring and "must weigh the intelligence value against the security risk posed by the Web site," says Jordanian terrorism expert Bakier.

But monitoring the thousands of Web sites, discussion forums, chat rooms, blogs and other open sources of the Web requires trained personnel with expertise in the languages, cultures, belief systems, political grievances and organizational structures of the terrorist groups online. Because such personnel are scarce, most experts agree that nations should pool their resources. "It is hardly possible for one individual member state to cover all suspicious terrorism-related activities on the Internet," according to a European Union (EU) report.[75]

Good intentions aren't enough. "There are lots of conferences, lots of declarations, lots of papers, but in reality, you have different counterterrorism agencies not sharing information, competing, afraid of each other, sometimes in the same state and also across borders," says Haifa University's Weimann.

Europol, the EU police agency, began a program in 2007 called Check the Web, which encourages member nations to share in monitoring and evaluating open sources on the Web that promote or support terrorism. The online portal allows member nations to post contact information for monitoring experts; links to Web sites they are monitoring; announcements by the terrorist organizations they are tracking; evaluations of the sites being monitored and additional information like the possibility of legal action against a Web site.

Weimann, who calls the program a "very good idea and very important," says he cannot directly evaluate its progress, since access is restricted to a handful of counterterrorism officials in each member nation. But he does speak to counterterrorism experts at workshops and conferences, where he hears that "international cooperation — especially in Europe — is more theoretical than practical."

When asked if barriers exist to such cooperation, Dublin City University's Conway says, "Emphatically, yes! These range from protection-of-institutional-turf issues — on both a national and EU-wide basis — to potential legal constraints." For instance, she says, some member states' police are unsure whether or not they need a court order to monitor and participate in a Web forum without identifying themselves. Others disagree about the definition of a terrorist and what kinds of sites should be watched.

These barriers may not be the program's only problem. "It might be a disadvantage that so far just EU countries participate," according to Katharina von Knop, a professor of international politics at the University of the Armed Forces, in Munich, Germany, thus limiting the expertise available.[76]

NOTES

1. Abdul Hameed Bakier, "An Online Terrorist Training Manual — Part One: Creating a Terrorist Cell," *Terrorism Focus*, vol. 5, no. 13, The Jamestown Foundation, April 1, 2008. The ek-Is.org Web site has also gone under various other names, including ekhlass.org.

2. *Ibid.*

3. Bakier, *op. cit.*, "Part Two: Assassinations and Robberies," vol. 5, no. 14, April 9, 2008.

4. Bakier, *op. cit.*, "Part Three: Striking U.S. Embassies," vol. 5, no. 15, April 16, 2008.

5. Gabriel Weimann, *Terror on the Internet*, United States Institute of Peace Press (2006), p. 51.

6. *Ibid.*, p. 30.

7. University of Arizona, "Artificial Intelligence Lab Dark Web Project," www.icadl.org/research/terror/.

8. "The 9/11 Commission Report," www.9-11commission.gov/report/index.htm.

9. Anne Stenersen, "The Internet: A virtual training camp?" Norwegian Defense Research Establishment, Oct. 26, 2007, p. 3, www.mil.no/multimedia/archive/00101/Anne_Stenersen_Manu_101280a.pdf.

10. Dorothy Denning, "Terror's Web: How the Internet Is Transforming Terrorism," Handbook on Internet Crime, 2009, p. 19, http://faculty.nps.edu/dedennin/publications/Denning-TerrorsWeb.pdf.

11. *Ibid.*, p. 4.

12. "Violent Islamic Extremism, the Internet, and the Homegrown Terrorist Threat," U.S. Senate Committee on Homeland Security and Governmental Affairs, May 8, 2008, pp. 2, 13, http://hsgac.senate.gov/public/_files/IslamistReport.pdf.

13. "Safeguarding Online: Explaining the Risk Posed by Violent Extremism," Office of Security and Counter Terrorism, Home Office, Aug. 10, 2009, p. 2, http://security.homeoffice.gov.uk/news-publications/publication-search/general/Officers-esafety-leaflet-v5.pdf?view=Binary.

14. *Ibid.*

15. Peter Neumann and Tim Stevens, "Countering Online Radicalisation: A Strategy for Action," The International Centre for the Study of Radicalisation and Political Violence, Kings College London, 2009, p. 14, www.icsr.info/news/attachments/1236768445ICSROnlineRadicalisationReport.pdf.

16. Clodagh Hartley, "Govt Can't Stop 'Web of Terror,'" *The Sun* (England), March 20, 2009, p. 2.

17. "Interview given by Mme. Michèle Alliot-Marie, French Minister of the Interior, to Le Figaro," French Embassy, Feb 1, 2008, www.ambafrance-uk.org/Michele-Alliot-Marie-on-combating.html.

18. Greg Goth, "Terror on the Internet: A Complex Issue, and Getting Harder," IEEE Computer Society, March 2008, www2.computer.org/portal/web/csdl/doi/10.1109/MDSO.2008.11.

19. Howard Altman, "Al Qaeda's Web Revival," *The Daily Beast*, Oct. 2, 2009, www.thedailybeast.com/blogs-and-stories/2009-10-02/is-this-al-qaedas-website.

20. Gregory McNeal, "Cyber Embargo: Countering the Internet Jihad," *Case Western Reserve Journal of International Law*, vol. 39, no. 3, 2007-08, p. 792.

21. *Brandenburg v. Ohio*, www.oyez.org/cases/1960-1969/1968/1968_492/.

22. "Safeguarding Online: Explaining the Risk Posed by Violent Extremism," *op. cit.*, p. 3.

23. Elizabeth Renieris, "Combating Incitement to Terrorism on the Internet: Comparative Approaches in the United States and the United Kingdom and the Need for an International Solution," *Vanderbilt Journal of Entertainment and Technology Law*, vol. 11:3:673, 2009, pp. 687-688.

24. Fergus Watts, "Caught out by net plan," *Herald Sun* (Australia), Dec. 29, 2008, p. 20, www.heraldsun.com.au/opinion/caught-out-by-net-plan/story-6frfifo-1111118423939.

25. Weimann, *op. cit.*, p. 180.

26. "Jordanian accused in Dallas bomb plot goes to court," CNN, Sept. 25, 2009, www.cnn.com/2009/CRIME/09/25/texas.terror.arrest/index.html.

27. http://smallbusiness.yahoo.com/tos/tos.php.

28. Neumann and Stevens, *op. cit.*, p. 32.

29. Maura Conway, "Terrorism & Internet Governance: Core Issues," U.N. Institute for Disarmament Research, 2007, p.11. www.unidir.org/pdf/articles/pdf-art2644.pdf.

30. Isambard Wilkinson, "Pakistan sets death penalty for 'cyber terrorism,'" *Telegraph.co.uk*, Nov 7, 2008, www.telegraph.co.uk/news/worldnews/asia/pakistan/3392216/Pakistan-sets-death-penalty-for-cyber-terrorism.html.

31. "Cyber attacks and cyber terrorism are the new threats," *India eNews*, March 26, 2009, www.indiaenews.com/print/?id=187451.

32. Linda McGlasson, "ATM Fraud Linked in RBS WorldPay Card Breach," Bank info Security, Feb. 5, 2009, www.bankinfosecurity.com/articles.php?art_id=1197.

33. Dorothy Denning, "A View of Cyberterrorism Five Years Later," 2007, pp. 2–3, http://faculty.nps.edu/dedennin/publications/Denning-TerrorsWeb.pdf.

34. Steven Bucci, "The Confluence of Cyber-Crime and Terrorism," Heritage Foundation, June 15, 2009, p. 6, www.heritage.org/Research/NationalSecurity/upload/hl_1123.pdf.

35. *Ibid.*, p. 5.

36. *Ibid.*, p. 6.

37. Dorothy Denning, *op. cit.*, p. 15.

38. *Ibid.*

39. Denning, "Terror's Web: How the Internet is Transforming Terrorism," *op. cit.*, p. 2.

40. *Ibid.*

41. Weimann, *op. cit.*, p. 15.

42. Evan Kohlmann, " 'Homegrown' Terrorists: Theory and Cases in the War on Terror's Newest Front," *The Annals of the American Academy of Political and Social Science*, July 2008; 618; 95. p. 95.

43. Denning, "Terror's Web: How the Internet is Transforming Terrorism," *op. cit.*, p. 3.

44. Kohlmann, *op. cit.*, p. 101.

45. *Ibid.*

46. David Talbot, "Terror's Server," *Technology Review.com*, Jan. 27, 2005, www.militantislammonitor.org/article/id/404.

47. Anthony Bergin, *et al.*, "Countering Internet Radicalisation in Southeast Asia," The Australian Strategic Policy Institute Special Report, March 2009, p. 5.

48. *Ibid.*, p. 6.

49. Weimann, *op. cit.*, pp. 75-76.

50. Weimann, *op. cit.*, p. 75.

51. Rita Katz and Josh Devon, "WWW.Jihad.com," *National Review Online*, July 14, 2003, http://nationalreview.com/comment/comment-katz-devon071403.asp.

52. Maura Conway and Lisa McInerney, "Jihadi Video & Auto-Radicalisation: Evidence from an Exploratory YouTube Study," 2008, p. 1, http://doras.dcu.ie/2253/2/youtube_2008.pdf.

53. *Ibid.*, p. 2.

54. Denning, "Terror's Web: How the Internet is Transforming Terrorism," *op. cit.*, p. 5.

55. Dennis Lormel, "Terrorists and Credit Card Fraud . . . A Quiet Epidemic," Counterterrorism Blog, Feb. 28, 2008, http://counterterrorismblog.org/2008/02/terrorists_and_credit_card_fra.php.

56. Alan Sipress, "An Indonesian's Prison Memoir Takes Holy War Into Cyberspace," *The Washington Post*, Dec. 14, 2004, p. A19, www.washingtonpost.com/wp-dyn/articles/A62095-2004Dec13.html.

57. Lormel, *op. cit.*

58. Dennis Lormel, "Credit Cards and Terrorists," Counterterrorism Blog, Jan. 16, 2008, http://counterterrorismblog.org/2008/01/credit_cards_and_terrorists.php.

59. Dennis Lormel, "Terrorists and Credit Card Fraud . . . ," *op. cit.*

60. Frank Cilluffo and Daniel Kimmage, "How to Beat al Qaeda at Its Own Game," *Foreign Policy*, April 2009, www.foreignpolicy.com/story/cms.php?story_id=4820.

61. Johnny Ryan, "EU must take its anti-terrorism fight to the Internet," *Europe's World*, Summer 2007, www.europesworld.org/EWSettings/Article/tabid/191/ArticleType/ArticleView/ArticleID/21068/Default.aspx.

62. Digital Outreach Team, U.S. Department of State, www.state.gov/documents/organization/116709.pdf.

63. "Middle East Internet Usage and Population Statistics," *Internet World Stats*, www.internetworldstats.com/stats5.htm.

64. Christopher Boucek, "The Sakinah Campaign and Internet Counter-Radicalization in Saudi Arabia," *CTC Sentinel*, August 2008, p. 2, www.carnegieendowment.org/files/CTCSentinel_Vol1Iss9.pdf.

65. *Ibid.*, p. 1.

66. Abdullah Ansary, "Combating Extremism: A brief overview of Saudi Arabia's approach," *Middle East Policy*, Summer 2008, vol. 15, no. 2, p. 111.

67. *Ibid.*

68. Y. Admon and M. Feki, "Saudi Press Reactions to the Arrest of Seven Terrorist Cells in Saudi Arabia," Inquiry and Analysis, no. 354, MEMRI, May 18, 2007.

69. Ansary, *op. cit.*, p. 111.

70. Boucek, *op. cit.*, p. 3.

71. Bergin, *op. cit.*, p. 19.

72. www.radicalmiddleway.co.uk.

73. "A radical wrong way," Progressive Muslims: Friends of Imperialism and Neocolonialism, Oct. 31, 2006, http://pmunadebate.blogspot.com/2006/10/radical-wrong-way.html.

74. Cilluffo and Kimmage, *op. cit.*

75. "Council Conclusions on Cooperation to Combat Terrorist Use of the Internet ("Check the Web")," Council of the European Union, May 16, 2007, p. 3, http://register.consilium.europa.eu/pdf/en/07/st08/st08457-re03.en07.pdf.

76. Katharina von Knop, "Institutionalization of a Web-Focused, Multinational Counter-Terrorism Campaign," *Responses to Cyber Terrorism* (2008), p. 14.

BIBLIOGRAPHY
Books

Jewkes, Yvonne, and Majid Yar, eds., *The Handbook on Internet Crime, Willan Publishing*, 2009.
British criminology professors have compiled essays by leading scholars on issues and debates surrounding Internet-related crime, deviance, policing, law and regulation in the 21st century.

Kramer, Franklin D., Stuart H. Starr and Larry K. Wentz, eds., *Cyberpower and National Security, Potomac Books*, 2009.
Experts write about cyber power and its strategic implications for national security, including an assessment of the likelihood of cyberterrorism.

Sageman, Marc, *Leaderless Jihad: Terror Networks in the Twenty-First Century, University of Pennsylvania Press*, 2008.
A senior fellow at the Center on Terrorism, Counter-Terrorism, and Homeland Security in Philadelphia examines the impact of the Internet on global terrorism, including its role in radicalization, and strategies to combat terrorism in the Internet age.

Weimann, Gabriel, *Terror on the Internet, United States Institute of Peace Press*, 2006.
A professor of communication at Haifa University in Israel explores how terrorist organizations exploit the Internet to raise funds, recruit members, plan attacks and spread their message.

Articles

Boucek, Christopher, "The Sakinah Campaign and Internet Counter-Radicalization in Saudi Arabia," *CTC Sentinel*, August 2008.
Saudi Arabia enlists religious scholars to engage in dialogue on the Internet with individuals seeking out religious knowledge in order to steer them away from extremist beliefs.

Cilluffo, Frank, and Daniel Kimmage, "How to Beat al Qaeda at Its Own Game," *Foreign Policy*, April 2009, www.foreignpolicy.com.
Two American terrorism experts recommend using Web sites, chat rooms, social networking sites, broadcasting

and print to tell the stories of Muslim victims of militant Islamist terror attacks.

Goth, Greg, "Terror on the Internet: A Complex Issue, and Getting Harder," *IEEE Distributed Systems Online*, vol. 9, no. 3, 2008.
Counterterrorism agencies cringe when posturing by politicians leads to the dismantling of terrorist Web sites they've been monitoring.

Labi, Nadya, "Jihad 2.0," *The Atlantic Monthly*, July/August, 2006.
With the loss of training camps in Afghanistan, terrorists turned to the Internet to find and train recruits.

Talbot, David, "Terror's Server — How radical Islamists use Internet fraud to finance terrorism and exploit the Internet for Jihad propaganda and recruitment," *Technology Review.com*, Jan. 27, 2008.
Terrorists use the Internet for fundraising, propaganda and recruitment, but government and the Internet industry responses are limited by law and technology.

Reports and Studies

Bergin, Anthony, *et al.*, "Countering Internet Radicalisation in Southeast Asia," Australian Strategic Policy Institute, March 2009.
The director of research at the institute traces the evolution of extremist and terrorist-linked content from static Web sites to the more dynamic and interactive parts of the Internet.

Boyne, Shawn Marie, "The Criminalization of Speech in an Age of Terror," Indiana University School of Law-Indianapolis, working paper, June 12, 2009.
A law professor compares prosecution of incitement to terror in Germany, the U.K. and the United States.

Conway, Maura, "Terrorism & Internet Governance: Core Issues," *Disarmament Forum*, 2007.
A terrorism expert at Dublin City University in Ireland explores the difficulties of Internet governance in light of terrorists' growing use of the medium.

Denning, Dorothy, "Terror's Web: How the Internet is Transforming Terrorism," *Naval Postgraduate School*, 2009.
A professor of conflict and cyberspace discusses the implications of shutting sites down versus continuing to monitor sites or encouraging moderate voices to engage in dialogue online with terrorist sympathizers.

Neumann, Peter R., and Tim Stevens, "Countering Online Radicalisation: A Strategy for Action," *The International Centre for the Study of Radicalisation and Political Violence*, 2009.
Shutting down terrorist sites on the Internet is expensive and counterproductive, according to the authors.

Renieris, Elizabeth, "Combating Incitement to Terrorism on the Internet," *Vanderbilt Journal of Entertainment and Technology Law*, vol. 11:3:673, 2009.
The author compares U.S. and U.K. laws used to prosecute incitement to terrorism on the Internet.

For More Information

Australian Strategic Policy Institute, 40 Macquarie St., Barton ACT 2600, Australia; (61) 2 6270 5100; www.aspi .org.au. Nonpartisan policy institute set up by the Australian government to study the country's defense and strategic policy choices.

EuroISPA, 39, Rue Montoyer, B-1000 Brussels, Belgium; (32) 2 503 2265; www.euroispa.org. World's largest association of Internet service providers.

Homeland Security Policy Institute, George Washington University, 2300 I St., N.W., Suite 721, Washington, DC 20037; (202) 994-2437; www.gwumc.edu/hspi. A think tank that analyzes homeland security issues.

Institute for International and European Affairs, 8 North Great Georges St., Dublin 1, Ireland; (353) 1 8746756; www.iiea.com. A think tank that analyzes how global and European Union policies affect Ireland.

International Centre for Political Violence and Terrorism Research, Nanyang Technological University, South Spine S4, Level B4, Nanyang Ave., Singapore 639798; (65) 6790 6982; www.pvtr.org. Studies threats and develops countermeasures for politically motivated violence and terrorism.

International Centre for the Study of Radicalisation and Political Violence, King's College London, 138-142 Strand, London, WC2R 1HH, United Kingdom; (44) 207 848 2098; http://icsr.info/index.php. A think tank set up by King's College London, the University of Pennsylvania, the Interdisciplinary Center Herzliya (Israel) and the Jordan Institute of Diplomacy.

Internet Haganah, http://internet-haganah.com/haganah/ index.html. Tracks, translates and analyzes extremist Islamic sites on the Web.

The Jamestown Foundation, 1111 16th St., N.W., Suite #320, Washington, DC 20036; (202) 483-8888; www .jamestown.org. Informs policy makers about trends in societies where access to information is restricted.

Middle East Media Research Institute, P.O. Box 27837, Washington, DC 20038-7837; (202) 955-9070; www.memri .org. Provides translations of Arabic, Persian, Turkish and Urdu-Pashtu media and analyses political, ideological, intellectual, social, cultural and religious trends in the Middle East.

NEFA Foundation, (212) 986-4949; www1.nefafoundation .org. Exposes those responsible for planning, funding and executing terrorist activities, with a particular emphasis on Islamic militant organizations.

Norwegian Defense Research Establishment, FFI, P.O. Box 25, NO-2027 Kjeller, Norway; (47) 63 80 70 00; www .mil.no/felles/ffi/english. The primary institution responsible for defense-related research in Norway.

Organization for Security and Co-operation in Europe, Action Against Terrorism Unit, Wallnerstrasse 6, 1010 Vienna, Austria; (43) 1 514 36 6702; www.osce.org/atu. Coordinates anti-terrorism initiatives among European nations.

Voices From Abroad:

NADEZDA NIKISHINA

Program Coordinator International Academy of Television and Radio, Russia

Terrorist groups use the Web
"Immediate action [is needed] to create the necessary legal environment on [an] international level. All terrorist organizations and extremist groups have Internet sites."

Cyprus News Agency October 2008

K. M. CHANDRASEKHAR

Union Federal Cabinet Secretary, India

Cyberterror threatens infrastructure
"Cyber attacks and cyberterrorism are the new looming threats on the horizon. There could be attacks on critical infrastructure such as telecommunications, power distribution, transportation, financial services, essential public utility services and others."

The Asian Age (India) March 2009

SWANAND SHINDE

Software Engineer, India

Cyberterrorists change as technology advances
"The recent nationwide attacks and blasts have revealed [a] nexus between terrorists, cyber experts and [the] underworld. The latest tool they have is hoax warning e-mails."

The Times of India, May 2009

"THIS IS MY LATEST EDICT CONDEMNING GODLESS WESTERN TECHNOLOGY... TWITTER IT TO THE NETWORKS AND POST IT ON OUR WEBSITE..."

Cagle Cartoons/Bill Shorr

ASIF ALI ZARDARI

President, Pakistan

Death for cyberterrorists
"Whoever commits the offense of cyberterrorism and causes the death of any person shall be punishable with death or imprisonment for life, and with a fine."

Press Trust of India November 2008

PROFESSOR IBIDAPO-OBE

University of Lagos, Nigeria

Technology is a boon and burden
"The rapid growth and use of computers, access to the Internet and other telecommunications technologies are promoting advances in virtually every aspect of society. . . . Unfortunately, many of the attributes of this

technology — low cost, ease of use and anonymous nature, among others — make it an attractive medium for fraudulent scams, child sexual exploitation, cyber-suicide and, increasingly, a new concern known as 'cybersecurity and cybercrime.' "

Vanguard (Nigeria) December 2008

GORDON BROWN

Prime Minister
United Kingdom

Cyberspace and national security are linked
"Just as in the nineteenth century we had to secure the seas for our national safety and prosperity, and in the twentieth century we had to secure the air, in the twenty-first century we also have to secure our position in cyber-space in order to give people and businesses the confidence they need to operate safely there. That is why today I am announcing — alongside our updated National Security Strategy — the UK's first strategy for cybersecurity."

M2 Presswire (U.K.), June 2009

SAM ROGGEVEEN

Former Senior Analyst, Office of National Assessments, Australia

Cyberterrorism can't be prevented
"Aren't we better off making our systems more survivable and redundant rather than trying to protect them? . . .

This goes beyond cyberterrorism and on to the terrorism threat as a whole.

Bulletin Wire (Australian Associated Press), April 2008

YOO HO-JIN

National Intelligence Service, South Korea

South Korea vulnerable
"Our country [is] vulnerable. Some . . . government branches failed to function when we recently simulated a cyber attack on them. This is a grave threat to our national security."

Yonhap News Agency (South Korea), June 2009

SULEYMAN ANIL

Head, NATO Computer Incident Response Capability Technical Center, Belgium

Cyberterror needs global response
"Cyberdefense is now mentioned at the highest level. . . . We have seen more of these attacks, and we don't think this problem will disappear soon. Unless globally supported measures are taken, it can become a global problem."

The Guardian (United Kingdom), March 2008

5

Drone Warfare

Thomas J. Billitteri

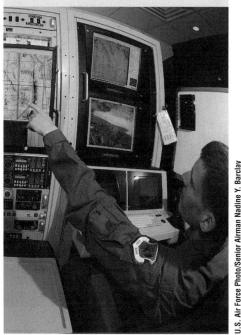

Pilots fly drones over Pakistan, Afghanistan and Iraq from computer consoles at Creech Air Force Base near Las Vegas and other locations. The Obama administration has carried out at least 101 drone strikes on suspected militants in Pakistan. Critics say the attacks cause high civilian casualties and are ineffective in eliminating top Al Qaeda leaders. Drone supporters say strikes are precise, cause limited collateral damage and save the lives of U.S. soldiers.

From *CQ Researcher*,
August 6, 2010.

Mustafa Abu al-Yazid ranked high on the roster of global terrorists. He was jailed in connection with the 1981 assassination of Egyptian President Anwar Sadat, thought to have managed finances for the Sept. 11 attacks on the United States and, as the No. 3 official in Al Qaeda, was widely viewed as a prime conduit to Osama bin Laden.[1]

Yazid's life apparently came to an end in May when a missile from a CIA drone aircraft hit him in the lawless tribal region of western Pakistan. Al Qaeda claimed Yazid's wife, three of his daughters, a granddaughter and other children and adults also died.

The attack on Yazid, also known as Sheikh Sa'id al-Masri, was part of a massive and controversial expansion in the use of "unmanned aerial vehicles," often called UAVs or drones, for battlefield reconnaissance and targeted killing of suspected militants.*

The boom in drones has stirred a variety of concerns among critics, but the greatest has been over strikes carried out covertly by the CIA under a classified, but widely reported, program of strikes against suspected militants inside Pakistan. Critics say the intelligence agency's drone attacks violate the laws of war because they are executed by civilian agents and occur inside another nation's sovereign territory. Others, however, defend the strikes as lawful acts of war and national self-defense in the fight against the Taliban and Al Qaeda.[2]

So far, the Obama administration has carried out at least 101 drone strikes in Pakistan, more than twice the 45 executed by the Bush administration from 2004 through 2008, according to the New America Foundation, a Washington think tank.[3] Allegations of high civilian casualty rates have heightened the drone controversy.

U.S. Air Force Photo/Senior Airman Nadine Y. Barclay

Drone Attacks Increasing in Pakistan

At least 50 drone attacks have targeted Pakistan thus far in 2010, nearly the same amount as in all of 2009. Since 2004, from 1,040 to as many as 1,579 people have been killed in the attacks; an estimated one-third of the casualties were civilians.*

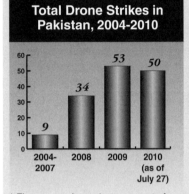

Total Drone Strikes in Pakistan, 2004-2010

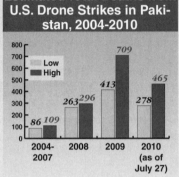

Estimated Total Deaths from U.S. Drone Strikes in Pakistan, 2004-2010

* Figures are based on accounts from reliable media organizations.

Source: "The Year of the Drone: An Analysis of U.S. Drone Strikes in Pakistan, 2004-2010," New America Foundation, 2010

About a third of those killed by CIA strikes since 2004 were non-militants, foundation researchers concluded.

Meanwhile, some question the attacks' effectiveness at stemming Al Qaeda and the Taliban insurgency. The Reuters news agency found that the CIA had killed roughly a dozen times more low-level fighters than mid- to high-level leaders since the summer of 2008, when drone strikes in Pakistan intensified.[4]

Critics also argue that drone strikes are fueling anti-American sentiment and spurring more terrorism. They point to Faisal Shahzad, the Pakistan immigrant living in Connecticut who tried to set off a car bomb in New York's Times Square in May. Shahzad, who pleaded guilty, suggested U.S. drone strikes in Pakistan and elsewhere helped motivate him.[5]

But drone supporters argue that strikes are precise, limited in collateral damage compared to conventional bombing or artillery attacks and save the lives of U.S. soldiers.

On Aug. 3, the American Civil Liberties Union and the Center for Constitutional Rights filed a lawsuit with potentially broad implications in the debate over targeted killing. The suit contests a Treasury Department rule requiring lawyers to get a special license before they can provide legal services benefiting a U.S.-born radical Muslim cleric thought to be hiding in Yemen whom the Obama administration has reportedly placed on a kill list.

The New York Times said the suit could test "some of the most deeply contested disputes to arise in the conflict against Al Qaeda — including whether the entire world is a battlefield for legal purposes, or whether terrorism suspects who are found away from combat zones must, in the absence of an imminent threat, instead be treated as criminals and given trials."[6]

The growing use of unmanned warplanes is part of a much broader embrace of drone technology for both military and civilian uses — everything from environmental monitoring and U.S. border patrol to drug interdiction and post-disaster searches. But it is the expanding robotic technology for war that is stirring the greatest debate.

In recent years the U.S. military has spent billions of dollars to expand its fleet of unmanned planes, which has gone from 167 aircraft in 2002 to more than 7,000 now. Last year, the Air Force trained more pilots to fly unmanned planes than traditional fighter pilots.[7]

Drone technology itself is astonishing in its capacity to reconnoiter and kill. In the case of the Predator and its even more powerful brother, the Reaper, controllers sit at computer consoles at U.S. bases thousands of miles from harm's way and control the aircraft via satellite communication. With the ability to remain aloft for long hours undetected on the ground — Predators can fly at altitudes of about 50,000 feet — the planes can do everything from snap high-resolution reconnaissance photos of insurgents' vehicles to shoot Hellfire missiles at them.

A secret archive of classified military documents controversially released in July by the group WikiLeaks revealed the lethal power of the Predator. As reported by *The New York Times*, in early winter 2008 a Predator spotted a group of insurgents suspected of planting roadside bombs near an American military outpost in Afghanistan. "Within minutes after identifying the militants, the Predator unleashed a Hellfire missile, all but evaporating one of the figures digging in the dark," *The Times* said. "When ground troops reached the crater caused by the missile, costing $60,000, all that was left was a shovel and a crowbar." [8]

The Times noted that the U.S. Air Force flies some 20 Predator and Reaper aircraft a day in Afghanistan, almost twice as many as it did a year ago, and that allies such as Britain and Germany have their own fleets. The leaked incident reports, the newspaper said, show that missions include snapping reconnaissance photos, gathering electronic transmissions, sending images of ongoing battles to field commanders and attacking militants with bombs and missiles, plus supporting U.S. Special Operations missions.

"Killer drones are the future of warfare," Afsheen John Radsan, a former CIA lawyer who teaches at the William Mitchell College of Law in St. Paul, Minn., told a House panel in April. [9]

But overshadowing that future is a fierce debate over how, where and by whom drones are being used. Of particular concern is the CIA's drone program, which reportedly has targeted suspected militants in western Pakistan and other remote trouble spots where the United States is not engaged in open hostilities, including Yemen, where a 2002 drone strike killed a group of Al Qaeda suspects that included a U.S. citizen. [10]

The CIA attacks have raised important legal questions about the role of targeted killing in the fight against the Taliban and Al Qaeda. Administration officials contend that such killings are legal under established principles of self-defense, international laws of armed conflict and the Authorization for Use of Military Force — the so-called "law of 9/11" passed by Congress following the 2001 terrorist attacks.

In March, Harold Koh, the State Department's legal adviser, defended the administration's use of unmanned aircraft for targeted attacks, asserting that the United States "may use force consistent with its inherent right to self-defense under international law." [11] And CIA Director Leon E. Panetta called drone strikes "the only game in town in terms of confronting and trying to disrupt the Al Qaeda leadership." [12]

But critics say CIA attacks inside Pakistan violate international laws of armed conflict because the United States is not at war with Pakistan, is not using its drones as part of Pakistan's own military operations and its drone strikes are carried out by civilians in secret far from active battlefields. "You can never, at the end of the day, find a legal basis for the CIA to be doing this," argues Mary Ellen O'Connell, a law professor at the University of Notre Dame, who says militants like Yazid should be pursued through law enforcement means, not covert attacks.

In a report this spring, Philip Alston, the United Nations special rapporteur on extrajudicial executions, sharply criticized targeted killings of terrorism suspects and the use of drones to carry them out, citing "the displacement of clear legal standards with a vaguely defined licen[s]e to kill, and the creation of a major accountability vacuum." [13] He also warned against "a 'Playstation' mentality to killing" with drone technology. [14] A CIA spokeswoman told *U.S. News & World Report* that "without discussing or confirming any specific action, this agency's operations are . . . designed from the very start to be lawful and are subject to close oversight." [15]

In a groundbreaking exposition of the CIA's drone program, *New Yorker* reporter Jane Mayer wrote last fall that "embrace of the Predator program has occurred with remarkably little public discussion, given that it represents a radically new and geographically unbounded use of state-sanctioned lethal force. And, because of the CIA program's secrecy, there is no visible system of accountability in place, despite the fact that the agency has killed many civilians inside a politically fragile, nuclear-armed country with which the U.S. is not at war." [16]

On Capitol Hill, where hearings on drone policy were held this spring, U.S. Rep. John F. Tierney D-Mass., chairman of the House Subcommittee on National Security and Foreign Affairs, noted that "the use of unmanned weapons to target individuals — and, for that matter, the targeting of individuals in general — raises many complex legal questions. We must examine who can be a legitimate target, where that person can be legally targeted and when the risk of collateral damage is too high." [17]

At least 40 other nations, including China, Russia and Iran, have "begun to build, buy and deploy" unmanned planes, according to Brookings Institution senior fellow P. W. Singer. [18] Last year, U.S. fighter jets shot down an unarmed Iranian spy drone over Iraq.[19] And drones are in the arsenals of non-state actors, including Hezbollah, the Lebanese paramilitary group. National-security experts worry that if drones fall into the hands of terrorists, the United States itself could be at risk of attack. "Simple logic tells us that every day drones become a greater threat," says Gary Solis, a former law professor at the U.S. Military Academy at West Point who now teaches at the Georgetown University Law Center.

"What you have moving forward is a debate not just about what can these systems do, but who can use them," says Singer, author of *Wired for War: The Robotics Revolution and Conflict in the 21st Century*. "That question of who can use them covers the gamut from the military to the federal government to local police forces to civilian actors."

As the use of drones grows, here are some of the questions that policy makers, legal analysts and human-rights advocates are weighing:

Do drone strikes comply with international law?

As legal scholars and human-rights advocates debate the use of drones, they are especially focused on strikes thought to be carried out by the CIA inside Pakistan. Several key questions are at issue:

- Is targeting suspected militants a matter of military necessity or do other reasonable alternatives, such as capture and arrest, exist?
- Is the intensity of the attacks — along with any civilian casualties and collateral damage — proportional to the threat posed by the militants being targeted?
- Are drone operators working for the CIA — and not the U.S. military — in compliance with international law, including, under certain circumstances, the laws of war governing "lawful combatants"?
- Are suspected militants hiding in the Pakistani border region directly engaged in hostilities with the United States, making them legal targets for attack?
- Does it matter if the Pakistani government sanctions American drone strikes within its borders?

Answering such questions is made difficult because two separate legal principles may be used to address them. International Humanitarian Law — the so-called law of armed conflict — has been shaped by international

agreement over many decades. It gives "lawful combatants" — generally uniformed soldiers who are part of a country's armed forces — the right to strike other combatants or civilians who are taking direct part in hostilities. The other is the principle of self-defense, under which nations may claim the right to use lethal force not only in an active combat zone but also outside it to protect vital national interests.

In his speech in March, the State Department's Koh rested his defense of drone attacks on both. He did not expressly name the CIA's covert drone program in Pakistan, and he cited "obvious limits to what I can say publicly" on the subject of targeted killing of suspected militants. But he asserted that drone strikes "comply with all applicable law, including the laws of war."

Koh went on to say that "the United States has the authority under international law, and the responsibility to its citizens, to use force, including lethal force, to defend itself." The "organized terrorist enemy . . . does not have conventional forces," he said, but "plans and executes its attacks . . . while hiding among civilian populations. That behavior simultaneously makes the application of international law more difficult and more critical for the protection of innocent civilians."

Many legal scholars agree with Koh's view that U.S. drone attacks, even by the CIA inside Pakistan, are legitimate and legal under international law and/or the principle of self defense.

Kenneth Anderson, a law professor at American University and a visiting fellow at the conservative Hoover Institution at Stanford University, contends that the strikes are legal under a doctrine of self-defense that he says goes back many decades in American policy. He argues that terrorists in western Pakistan and other locations, such as Yemen and Somalia, pose a direct threat to U.S. security even though they operate in sovereign countries outside areas where the U.S. military is formally engaged in open hostilities.

Anderson says he is reaffirming a self-defense doctrine laid out in 1989 by then-State Department legal adviser Abraham Sofaer, who said the United States supports "the right of a State to strike terrorists within the territory of another State where the terrorists are using that territory as a location from which to launch terrorist attacks and where the State involved has failed to respond effectively to a demand that the attacks be stopped."[20]

Radsan, the Minnesota law professor, who served as CIA assistant general counsel from 2002 to 2004, says he thinks both the international law of armed conflict and the principle of self-defense could justify U.S. drone attacks in western Pakistan, though he leans toward international law. "I'm concerned that the self-defense theory is too broad," he says.

But his larger concern is that U.S. law has fallen behind in the development of drone technology, particularly when that technology is deployed by non-military agents like the CIA. "As a country we should come up with a hybrid legal model" that blends principles of armed conflict and due process protections, he says. "Let's put some checks in place that may be more cumbersome than the checks we would have on conventional military operations."

William C. Banks, director of the Institute for National Security and Counterterrorism at Syracuse University, views the use of drones for targeted killing as legal as long as it is in the context of an armed conflict. And, he says, "We are clearly in an armed conflict against Al Qaeda and the Taliban." A "more subtle" and "debatable" question, he adds, is whether the battlefield extends into Pakistan. But Banks argues that it does because terrorists have launched attacks into Afghanistan, as well as against the Pakistani government, from hideouts in the Pakistani border region.

"The basic task under [International Humanitarian Law] is whether there's a persistent use of force in a given battle space," he says. "The facts on the ground meet that standard."

Still, in congressional testimony last spring, Banks noted that "contemporary laws have not kept up with changes in the dynamics of military conflicts. Nowhere is the weakness of the legal regime more glaring than in its treatment of targeted killing." Banks noted that U.S. law, international laws and international laws governing armed conflict overlap, a phenomenon "fraught with dispute and contentiousness. . . .

"There has been little deliberative attention to modernizing the law to reflect the modern battlefield," he told a House panel. "Congress would do all of us an important favor by devoting attention to articulating policy and legal criteria for the use of force against non-state terrorists."[21]

Many analysts believe Pakistan has quietly condoned at least some drone strikes while not doing so publicly for fear of heightening anti-Western tensions in the country. While some argue that U.S. drone strikes within Pakistan's border would be illegal if the Pakistani government hasn't expressly approved them, Banks said they are acts of "valid self-defense" by the United States under International Humanitarian Law.

However, other legal experts argue that drone strikes, carried out by the civilian CIA and away from where the U.S. military is engaged in active combat, are illegal.

O'Connell of the University of Notre Dame is prominent among them. She argues that members of the CIA, as civilians, are not "lawful combatants" under international law, meaning their drone killings are "unlawful."

The U.S. military — but not the CIA — could be lawful combatants inside Pakistan, but only if Pakistan asked for help in suppressing a challenge to its civilian government, O'Connell contends. She sharply disagrees with the view that any basis exists in the law of self-defense for using drones on Pakistani territory. "The U.S. may only invoke self-defense for the use of force on Pakistani territory if Pakistan is responsible for an armed attack on the U.S.," she says. "It is armed attack that triggers the right of self-defense."

U.N. special rapporteur Alston, in a news release, expressed concern about the secrecy shrouding the CIA drone program. "[T]he international community does not know when and where the CIA is authorized to kill, the criteria for individuals who may be killed, how it ensures killings are legal and what follow-up there is when civilians are illegally killed." He added that "in a situation in which there is no disclosure of who has been killed, for what reason and whether innocent civilians have died, the legal principle of international accountability is, by definition, comprehensively violated."[22]

And in a letter this spring to President Obama challenging the legality of targeted killing of suspected terrorists, the American Civil Liberties Union argued that "the entire world is not a war zone, and wartime tactics that may be permitted on the battlefields in Afghanistan and Iraq cannot be deployed anywhere in the world where a terrorist suspect happens to be located."[23]

Are drones an effective counter-terrorism tool?

David Kilcullen, a former counter-insurgency adviser to Gen. David H. Petraeus, made headlines last year when

light for the allies of Allah, to illuminate their path

A missile strike by a CIA-operated drone aircraft apparently killed Mustafa Abu al-Yazid, Al Qaeda's third-ranking leader, in May in the lawless tribal region of western Pakistan. Al Qaeda claimed Yazid's wife, three of his daughters, a granddaughter and other children and adults also were killed. Yazid is believed to have managed finances for the Sept. 11 attacks on the United States and served as a prime conduit to terrorist leader Osama bin Laden.

he told a congressional panel that drone strikes in Pakistan were backfiring. "We need to call off the drones," he said, explaining that his objection against targeting militants wasn't moral or legal, but practical.

"I realize that they do damage to the Al Qaeda leadership," he said. "Since 2006, we've killed 14 senior Al Qaeda leaders using drone strikes [and] in the same period we've killed 700 Pakistani civilians in the same area. The drone strikes are highly unpopular. They are deeply aggravating to the population. And they've given rise to a feeling of anger that coalesces the population around the extremists and leads to spikes of extremism."[24]

How many civilians have died from drone strikes in Pakistan and elsewhere is something of a guessing game. With the CIA program under a shroud of secrecy and the task of distinguishing friend from foe often difficult, especially along the Afghanistan-Pakistan border region, civilian casualties can't be determined with certainty — a factor that influences where various analysts come down on the effectiveness of drones as an anti-terror tool.

In mid-July, the New America Foundation researchers said the drone program in Pakistan had, by their count, reportedly killed at least 1,040 people since 2004, of whom reliable press accounts described about two-thirds as militants or suspected militants, indicating that about one-third were not militants.[25]

The researchers, Peter Bergen and Katherine Tiedemann, said drone accuracy had improved "even as the pace of the program has increased over the past two years," with 43 percent of fatalities reported to be militants or suspected militants in 2008, compared with 62 percent in 2009 and about 90 percent through mid-2010. That suggested that non-militant deaths had dropped to about 10 percent this year, they said.[26]

Kilcullen's testimony and pronouncement of 700 Pakistani civilian deaths is oft cited in the debate over drones, but C. Christine Fair, an assistant professor in Georgetown University's Security Studies Program, wrote this spring that the conclusion that "drone strikes produce more terrorists than they eliminate . . . would be a damning argument — if the data weren't simply bogus." She argued that the only public data on civilian casualties from drone attacks in Pakistan come from the Pakistani Taliban and that "high-level Pakistani officials have conceded to me that very few civilians have been killed by drones, and their innocence is often debatable."[27]

Yet critics of drone strikes argue that no matter how successful they may be at killing individual militants, they sow the seeds for new rounds of extremism and militancy.

Of particular concern is the use of drones as part of a counterinsurgency strategy, an approach used in Afghanistan that has put a premium on protecting civilians as a way to promote the rule of law and choke off insurgent influence. That strategy was a hallmark of Gen. Stanley A. McChrystal, fired in June after he and some of his staff criticized the Obama administration's war strategy in a magazine interview. To what degree Petraeus, McChrystal's replacement, will continue the counterinsurgency approach remains unclear.

O'Connell says that it appears drone strikes undermine efforts to root out militant extremists in western Pakistan and to build trust for the United States in Afghanistan.

"If the drones create such passion for revenge and anger because they are robot killing machines in which there's an unfair advantage toward the warrior operating them and if they are disproportionately killing civilians, are they in fact creating more resistance?" she asks. "Are they helping to fuel the insurgency?"

Radsan, the Minnesota law professor and former CIA lawyer, says the strategy of using drones to eliminate terrorists must be viewed through both a short and long lens. "In the short term, we're killing bad people," he says. "We don't have other means of getting to [those] people. But I accept in the long term if we're creating more recruits, the counterterrorism strategy will create problems for our counterinsurgency strategy. The military is aware of that."

Radsan says he views the effectiveness of drone strikes according to a "sliding scale," depending on whether the target is a high-value figure such as bin Laden or his deputy, Ayman al Zawahiri, or a lower-level militant. "There's a point," he says, "at which [drone] use becomes counterproductive for counterinsurgency purposes."

Daniel L. Byman, director of the Center for Peace and Security Studies at Georgetown University, also draws distinctions in analyzing drone use.

"I distinguish between deterrence — stopping [people] from joining these groups — and disruption, where it just makes [the groups] less effective," he says. "I'm not sure it has any deterrent effect — it may. But I do believe the disruptive effect is considerable."

Still, as Byman wrote last year, targeted killings "are a poor second to arrests. Dead men tell no tales and thus are no help in anticipating the next attack or informing us about broader terrorist activities" But when arrest is impossible, the result is the kind of "terrorist haven" that exists along the Afghanistan-Pakistan border, and "killing terrorist operatives is one way to dismantle these havens."

Even so, Byman wrote, "we must not pretend the killings are anything but a flawed short-term expedient that at best reduces the Al Qaeda threat — but by no means eliminates it. . . . The real answer to halting Al Qaeda's activity in Pakistan will be the long-term support of Pakistan's counterinsurgency efforts." Meanwhile, "targeted killings are one of America's few options left."[28]

Is drone technology ethical for use in war?

Last year, Britain's Lord Bingham, a retired senior judge, suggested drones could, like cluster bombs and land mines, come to be viewed as "so cruel as to be beyond the pale of human tolerance."

"It may be — I'm not expressing a view — that unmanned drones that fall on a house full of civilians [are] a weapon the international community should decide should not be used," he said.[29]

Of course, not all unmanned planes flying in war zones are used to kill. They may be used to scope out potential targets for manned aircraft, for example, or to survey battlefield terrain. But Bingham's comment raises a fundamental issue in the debate about unmanned military aircraft: whether the technology itself is inappropriate for use in war.

Many military experts argue that drones are simply a new kind of weapon, not unlike machine guns and tanks once were. Koh, the State Department legal adviser, pointed out that "there is no prohibition under the laws of war on the use of technologically advanced weapons systems in armed conflict . . . so long as they are employed in conformity with applicable laws of war."[30]

But some critics are concerned about the moral implications of using weapons that put civilians — but not the weapons' operators — at risk. "According to the just-war principles, it is better to risk the lives of one's own combatants than the lives of enemy noncombatants," *The Christian Century* magazine opined. "But this moral calculus is completely tossed aside in the case of drone warfare, since drone operators don't risk their lives at all."[31]

Some experts contend that as drones and other robotics expand as tools of war, so too does the illusion in the public's mind that war can be fought without a steep price.

In *Wired for War*, his book on how the robotic revolution is shaping the future of armed conflict, the Brookings Institution's Singer quotes a former defense official who supports unmanned systems because "they save lives" but is concerned about how they shape perceptions of war both at home and abroad. The robotic revolution "will further disconnect the military from society," the former official told Singer. "People are more likely to support the use of force as long as they view it as costless."

What's more, as Singer explained, "a new kind of voyeurism allowed by the new technologies will make the public more susceptible to false selling of how easy a potential war will be." As the former defense official said, "There will be more marketing of wars. More 'shock and awe' talk to defray discussion of the costs." In addition, the former official worried that robotic technology may cause leaders to think that 'warfare is easy.' "[32]

In the book, Singer also writes about how footage of drone strikes and clips of combat scenes are available on

Drones Being Drafted for Non-Military Duties

But U.S. flight-safety officials are moving cautiously.

In Antarctica, pilots and scientists on research missions risk death if something goes wrong with their planes. Crashes in the globe's frozen reaches are "often beyond rescue capabilities," said Elizabeth Weatherhead, an environmental scientist at the University of Colorado at Boulder.[1]

But now drone aircraft are taking some of the danger out of polar exploration.

"A multinational, robotic air corps" is quietly invading the polar regions, *Scientific American* noted. "Some catapult from ships; some launch from running pickup trucks; and some take off the old-fashioned way, from icy airstrips. The aircraft range from remote-controlled propeller planes — of the type found at Toys "R" Us — to sophisticated high-altitude jets. All are specially outfitted, not with weapons but with scientific instruments."[2]

The polar drones are part of a growing wave of unmanned aircraft for non-military duties. Advocates say pilotless planes are good for a wide range of jobs, from monitoring forest fires, hurricanes and oil spills to patrolling borders and assessing earthquake damage.

Yet in the United States, skies already are crowded with conventional aircraft, and the Federal Aviation Administration is moving cautiously on allowing drones to share that space.

"There is a tremendous pressure and need to fly unmanned aircraft in [civilian] airspace," Henry Krakowski, who heads the nation's air traffic control system, recently told European aviation officials. "We are having constant conversations and discussions, particularly with the Department of Defense and the Department of Homeland Security, to figure out how we can do this safely with all these different sizes of vehicles."[3]

Krakowski acknowledged that some want the Federal Aviation Administration (FAA) to proceed quickly with the approval process. "I think industry and some of the operators are frustrated that we're not moving fast enough," he said in a media interview, "but safety is first. This isn't Afghanistan. This isn't Iraq. This is a part of the world that has a lot of light airplanes flying around, a lot of business jets."

The FAA reportedly is evaluating more than 150 requests from groups seeking to fly unmanned planes, and in June the agency said it was working with Insitu, a Boeing Co. subsidiary that manufactures drones, on a two-year study of the issue.[4] However, pilotless cargo and passenger flights are not the study's aims, it said.[5]

Routine access to the national airspace system by unmanned craft "poses technological, regulatory, workload and coordination challenges," the Government Accountability Office (GAO) stated. "No technology has been identified as a suitable substitute for a person on board the aircraft in seeing and avoiding other aircraft."

The GAO also noted that communication and control links to unmanned craft "are vulnerable to unintentional or intentional radio interference that can lead to loss of control of an aircraft and an accident."[6]

In 2007 the National Transportation Safety Board cited operator error and poor oversight by Customs and Border Protection officials in a Predator-B crash near Nogales, Ariz.[7]

Still, demand for more drone flights over U.S. territory is growing, especially along U.S. borders. U.S. Customs and Border Protection (CBP), part of the Department of Homeland Security, flies three Predator-B aircraft on patrol missions along the Southwest border from Arizona to eastern Texas and two on the U.S.-Canada border. A Predator patrol of the Texas border from El Paso to Brownsville is also scheduled to begin.

In addition, the CBP has a maritime "Guardian" version of the plane, equipped with special sea-search radar, which flies from Florida and is used for drug interdiction and search missions, among other things. It also has helped monitor the BP oil spill in the Gulf of Mexico, a spokesman said. Another Guardian is scheduled for delivery before the end of this year, and funding for a third is included in the fiscal 2011 budget request, an agency official told a House panel in July.

Together, he said, CBP planes have enabled the agency "to support the response to large-scale natural events such

You Tube, turning "war into a sort of entertainment, or 'war porn' as soldiers call it."[33]

"We're seeing fundamental changes in the age-old meaning of going to war," Singer says in an interview.

"It's changing for the nation . . . but also for the individual. That phrase — 'to go to war' — for the last 5,000 years meant going to a place of such danger that you might never come home again, might never see your as hurricanes, floods and the oil spill in the Gulf of Mexico," plus positioned it "to confront ever-changing threats to the homeland in the future."[8]

Some fret that as drones shrink in size and grow in sophistication, Americans' privacy could be in jeopardy.

"The U.S. government has a history of commandeering military technology for use against Americans," wrote John W. Whitehead, a constitutional lawyer and founder of the Rutherford Institute, a conservative civil-liberties organization. "We saw this happen with tear gas, tasers and sound cannons. . . . Now the drones . . . are coming home to roost."[9]

Whitehead pointed to a North Carolina county that reportedly has used a drone to monitor gatherings of motorcycle riders, testing of a drone for police work in Los Angeles, "insect-like drones . . . seen hovering over political rallies in New York and Washington" and creation by University of Maryland engineering students of "the world's smallest controllable surveillance drones, capable of hovering to record conversations or movements of citizens."

(The university said the "monocopter" device, inspired by the spiraling flight of maple tree seeds, can carry out surveillance maneuvers for defense, fire monitoring and search and rescue.[10])

"Unfortunately, to a drone, everyone is a suspect because drone technology makes no distinction between the law-abiding individual and the suspect," Whitehead argued. The "crucial question," he concluded, "is whether Americans will be able to limit the government's use of such surveillance tools or whether we will be caught in an electronic nightmare from which there is no escape."

Others aren't worried about the possibility of government drones encroaching on privacy.

"I'm no more concerned about that than the government being intrusive of my phone calls or coming into my home with some kind of surveillance," says retired Air Force Gen. Charles Wald, director and senior adviser to the aerospace and defense industry for Deloitte Services and former deputy commander of the U.S. European Command. "I think our government's responsible."

— *Thomas J. Billitteri*

Then-President George W. Bush, right, and Homeland Security Secretary Michael Chertoff, left, inspect an unmanned drone used to monitor illegal immigration along the Arizona-Mexico border.

[2] *Ibid.*

[3] Quoted in Joan Lowy, "FAA under pressure to open U.S. skies to drones," The Associated Press, June 14, 2010, http://apnews.myway.com/article/20100614/D9GB009G0.html.

[4] Tom Fontaine, "FAA evaluating requests to put drones in U.S. skies," *Pittsburgh Tribune-Review*, June 14, 2010, www.pittsburghlive.com/x/pittsburghtrib/s_685948.html#.

[5] *Ibid.*

[6] "Unmanned Aircraft systems: Federal Actions Needed to Ensure Safety and Expand Their Potential Uses Within the National Airspace System," U.S. Government Accountability Office, May 2008, p. 3, www.gao.gov/new.items/d08511.pdf.

[7] Del Quentin Wilber, "NTSB Cites Lax Safety Controls, Pilot Error in Ariz. Drone Crash," *The Washington Post*, Oct. 17, 2007, www.washingtonpost.com/wp-dyn/content/article/2007/10/16/AR2007101602040.html.

[8] Testimony of Major Gen. Michael C. Kostelnik (Ret.), assistant commissioner, Office of Air and Marine, U.S. Customs and Border Protection, before House Committee on Homeland Security, Subcommittee on Border, Maritime and Global Counterterrorism, July 15, 2010, http://homeland.house.gov/SiteDocuments/2010071 5103917-58435.pdf.

[9] John W. Whitehead, "Drones Over America: Tyranny at Home," Rutherford Institute, June 28, 2010, www.rutherford.org/articles_db/commentary.asp?record_id=661.

[10] "Spiraling Flight of Maple Tree Seeds Inspires New Surveillance Technology," press release, University of Maryland, A. James Clark School of Engineering, Oct. 19, 2009, www.eng.umd.edu/media/pressreleases/pr101909_mapleseed.html.

[1] Davide Castelvecchi, "Invasion of the Drones: Unmanned Aircraft Take Off in Polar Exploration," *Scientific American*, March 10, 2010, www.scientificamerican.com/article.cfm?id=invasion-of-the-drones.

family. . . . But for the individual now — not all, but for an increasing set — going to war is the act of waking up, getting in your car and driving to sit behind a computer screen and engaging in what is war, then driving home. I'm not saying this is an awful thing. It's different, and it presents new challenges" for everything from leadership to stress management to "crucial questions of personnel and promotion policies."

Some critics say the rise of unmanned systems has far-reaching political and policy implications. "Drones are a technological step that further isolates the American people from military action, undermining political checks on contemporary warfare," argues Mary L. Dudziak, a professor of law, history and political science at the University of Southern California's Gould School of Law. "And the isolation of the people, historians of war have argued, helps enable ongoing, endless war."[34]

But as with any emerging war technology, drones require a nuanced evaluation, many ethicists say.

Edward Barrett, director of research at the U.S. Naval Academy's Stockdale Center for Ethical Leadership, told a House panel that "unmanned systems are consistent with a society's duty to avoid unnecessary risks to its combatants" and that research suggests such systems can "enhance awareness and restraint" among soldiers engaged in "virtual warfare." But he also said unmanned systems "could encourage unjust wars" and "facilitate the circumvention of legitimate authority and pursuit of unjust causes."[35]

BACKGROUND

Early Prototypes

A s futuristic as unmanned warplanes may be, they are not exactly new. Their roots go back nearly a century. Near the end of World War I (1914-1918) inventor Charles Kettering tested a pilotless biplane called the Kettering Bug that, by the standards of the day, was on the leading edge of military technology.

Six feet across, five feet long and powered by a two-cycle Ford engine, it was designed to take off from a track and fly toward enemy lines. At a set time, the wings would detach and the plane, which could carry a 250-pound warhead, would hit the ground and explode. The U.S. Army built some 50 Kettering Bugs, but World War I ended before the Bug was used in combat.[36]

In the years leading up to World War II (1941-1945), Reginald Denny, a British pilot and Hollywood actor, developed a radio-controlled drone for hobbyists. In 1940 he marketed his OQ-2 Radioplane, or "Dennymite," to the Army for use in target practice. Once World War II began, the plane became the first mass-produced unmanned aircraft in history.[37]

The Aphrodite Project, which used well-worn B-17 and B-24 bombers, was another World War II-era drone project. The planes were loaded with explosives and two-man crews flew them part-way to their targets, bailing out over British territory. A following aircraft guided the Aphrodite planes toward the enemy by radio signal. Eleven such bombers were launched, but they had little success. One mission led to the death of Joseph Kennedy Jr., elder brother of the future president, when an Aphrodite bomber he was flying exploded over England.[38]

World War II also saw the use of the first operational cruise missiles, introduced by the Nazi regime against Britain and other European targets. The V-1 "buzz bomb" carried a one-ton, high-explosive warhead and could travel 150 miles, but was extremely inaccurate. The far more potent V-2, deployed in 1944, was powered by a liquid propellant rocket engine and launched from mobile platforms. Its range was 200 miles.[39]

The German military also developed a radio-guided armor-piercing bomb called the "Fritz X," for use against Allied ships. The bombs sank an Italian battleship and damaged another in 1943, "but Allied air defenses soon made further use very difficult," said the Smithsonian's National Air and Space Museum.[40]

Drone development proceeded in fits and starts after World War II. During the Vietnam War, which ended in 1975, an unmanned reconnaissance plane called the Fire Fly flew more than 3,400 missions, but 16 percent of the planes crashed, according to *Wired for War.*[41] In the late 1970s, the Army planned development of a small propeller-driven reconnaissance drone called the Aquila, but military planners kept adding expensive technological requirements, Singer wrote. Finally, after spending more than $1 billion for a few prototypes, the military canceled the project.[42]

Still, the 1980s saw a resurgence in interest in unmanned aircraft. In the 1982 war in Lebanon, the Israeli Air Force used a drone called the Pioneer, powered by a 26-horse-power snowmobile engine. The U.S. Navy bought several, and the Reagan administration ramped up drone research.[43]

During the 1991 Persian Gulf War, Pioneer planes scoped out targets for shelling of Iraqi forces by ships. "In one case, a group of Iraqi soldiers saw a Pioneer flying overhead and . . . waved white bed sheets and undershirts at the drone," Singer wrote. "It was the first time in history that human soldiers surrendered to an unmanned system."[44]

CHRONOLOGY

1900s-1940s *World wars lead investors and military planners to develop early drone technology.*

1918 U.S. Army builds pilotless biplanes, but World War I ends before they are used in combat.

1940 British pilot and Hollywood actor Reginald Denny markets "Radioplane" to the Army for use in target practice; breakout of World War II makes it the world's first mass-produced unmanned plane.

1943 German radio-guided bomb called the "Fritz X" sinks Italian battleship.

1944 Joseph Kennedy Jr., older brother of the future president, dies when his bomb-laden plane, intended to be guided by radio toward enemy territory once its crew bailed out, explodes over England. . . . Nazi regime sends V-1 "buzz bombs" and more powerful V-2 rockets at London and other Allied targets.

1950s-1980s *Drone development proceeds in fits and starts.*

1962 First industrial robot, the Unimate, used by General Motors.

1972 Laser-guided bombs help destroy Thanh Hoa Bridge in Vietnam after years of attempts by the U.S. military.

1975 Vietnam War ends; unmanned "Fire Fly" reconnaissance plane flew 3,400 missions during the conflict, but 16 percent of the planes crashed. . . . *Viking* space probes employ robotics.

1979 Army begins developing the Aquila, a small propeller-driven reconnaissance drone; cost and technical issues force abandonment of the project.

1982 Israelis' use of Pioneer drone in Lebanon war leads U.S. Navy to purchase several of the unmanned planes; Reagan administration bolsters drone research.

1990s-2000s *Unmanned military aircraft become more lethal as Defense Department spends $3 billion on drone technology.*

1991 U.S. military uses Pioneer drones in Persian Gulf War to scope out targets for naval shelling of Iraqi forces.

1995 Early version of Predator drone used for reconnaissance during NATO air campaign against Bosnian Serbs; Global Positioning System, providing navigation data for military and civilian use, including drones, reaches full capability.

2001-Present *Sept. 11 terrorist attacks spur rapid escalation in drone use in wars against Taliban, Al Qaeda.*

2001 Hellfire laser-guided missile successfully test-fired from Predator drone. . . . Al Qaeda launches simultaneous attacks against targets in the United States on Sept. 11. . . . U.S. and coalition forces invade Afghanistan on Oct. 7.

2002 Predator strike in Yemen kills Qaed Salim Sinan al-Harethi, an Al Qaeda leader suspected in the 2000 bombing of the *USS Cole*, plus five other suspected militants.

2003 U.S.-led invasion of Iraq begins; use of unmanned military aircraft soars.

2004 Predator strike in Pakistan reportedly kills four, including Taliban leader Nek Muhammad.

2005 U.S. Customs and Border Protection agency begins using Predator aircraft to patrol U.S.-Mexico border.

2006 Ayman al Zawahiri, Al Qaeda's No. 2 leader, and Abu Khabab al Masri, an Al Qaeda expert in weapons of mass destruction, escape drone attack that reportedly kills at least 18; al Masri dies in another drone attack in 2008.

2008 Military's reliance on unmanned aircraft reportedly exceeds more than 500,000 hours of flight, largely in Iraq.

2009 Predators begin patrolling U.S.-Canada border. . . . Pakistan Taliban chief Baitullah Mehsud killed in drone attack.

2010 Drone strikes in Pakistan since 2004 reportedly approach 150 as war in Afghanistan nears its ninth anniversary.

Drone Pilots Challenge Air Force Culture

"I wouldn't go back to flying fighter jets."

There are fighter pilots and then there are drone pilots. Between the two is a cultural gap the Air Force is trying to bridge.

The clash between the old and the new became especially apparent in 2006 after an air strike that killed Abu Musab al-Zarqawi — the Iraqi leader of an Al Qaeda affiliate. After land-based crews of the unmanned Predator drone spent hundreds of hours searching for al-Zarqawi, an F-16 released a bomb that killed him.

The F-16 pilot received the Distinguished Flying Cross; the Predator pilots received thank you notes from a general based in the region. Military officials concluded that even though the drone crews engaged in missions of a combative nature, they weren't physically in combat and weren't in harm's way. [1] Appreciation for drone pilots, however, is gradually changing, even within a hidebound Air Force culture that exalts fighter and bomber pilots.

Pilots of drones being flown in Afghanistan and Pakistan typically operate from bases in the United States, 7,500 miles away from the action. Operating a drone may be an enhanced version of the latest Xbox flight simulator, but pilots say it's no game. "You know that there's no reset button," says Col. Christopher R. Chambliss, a former F-16 fighter pilot and now commander of a drone squadron at Creech Air Force Base, near Las Vegas, the first base in Air Force history that exclusively flies unmanned aircraft.

"When you let a missile go, and it's flying over the head of friendly forces and it's flying over the enemy to kill somebody or break something, you know that that's real life, and there's no take-back there." [2]

Lt. Col. Chris Gough, who flew F-16 combat missions over Kosovo and now operates a Predator drone at Creech, adds, "I've never been more engaged in a conflict in my life. Physiologically, the stimulus and response are exactly the same." [3]

As an indication of the Air Force's commitment to drone warfare, it bought more unmanned aircraft than traditional fighter jets for the first time in 2010. [4]

The increasing use of drones in part reflects frustration felt by Defense Secretary Robert M. Gates, who has complained that the Air Force seemed more concerned with buying expensive fighter planes for future use than contributing to the wars currently under way.

"I've been wrestling for months to get more intelligence, surveillance, and reconnaissance assets into the theater," he told officers at Maxwell Air Force Base in Alabama in April 2008. "Because people were stuck in old ways of doing business, it's been like pulling teeth." [5]

For now, though, traditional pilots are still top dog.

"The culture is still one dominated by aviators," observes James Hasik, an industry consultant and author of *Arms and Innovation: Entrepreneurship and Alliances in the Twenty-First Century Defense Industry.*

Pleased with the Pioneer, the Defense Department spent more than $3 billion in the 1990s on unmanned aircraft. [45]

Predator Era

The Predator era began in the mid-1990s, driven by a constellation of developing forces. Among them: the development of Global Positioning System (GPS) technology that uses satellites for pinpoint navigational accuracy; the growth and ubiquity of computer power and its increasing adoption by the military; pressure on the Pentagon to spend more efficiently on new battlefield technology; and political pressure to adopt unmanned systems, in part to reduce combat casualties and attract tech-savvy recruits into the armed forces.

But the drone revolution's flight path was turbulent. For one thing, early problems with the technology cast doubt on its reliability. An early version of the Predator was used for reconnaissance in 1995 during a NATO air campaign in the Balkan war against Bosnian Serbs. But "it was unable to fly almost 60 percent of its missions because its wings iced up so easily," the Center for Public Integrity, a journalistic watchdog group in Washington, wrote in 2006, citing a Defense Department report. The center's article focused on travel spending for congressional staff members by the Predator's builder, San Diego-based General Atomics. [46]

In February 2001 a Hellfire laser-guided missile was successfully test-fired from a Predator drone, and by the end of the year the Sept. 11 terrorist attacks on the United

"But there have been past paradigm-shifting technologies that have stuck with the military in peacetime for the big war people want to prepare for. This is one of them."

While the Air Force prefers to use commissioned aviators with cockpit experience to fly the Predator and other drones, it has had to call on National Guard and Reserve crews to satisfy the growing demand for drones.

And from an economic standpoint, drones make sense. "The writing's on the wall," Hasik says. "Regular fighter jets are simply becoming too expensive to buy in large quantities, and the Air Force must lean more toward less-costly alternatives."

Former fighter pilots who have now been assigned to drones are becoming receptive to the change. "I wouldn't [go back to flying fighter jets]," says Chambliss. [6]

But the new generation of drone pilots, however, is unlikely to reach parity with traditional fighter pilots until drone operators rise to the top ranks, which are still largely controlled by fighter jockeys.

"If you want to change the culture, you must change the people within it. It's going to be a while until the culture changes," says Hasik. "The number of generals with drones as their specialty is still in the single digits."

For the time being, the huge demand for drones has left many pilots on the ground at Creech, away from the action that would help them ascend to the top ranks.

Still, their place in the Air Force culture seems increasingly secure.

"As long as there's a war in Afghanistan, there's going to be a place for these guys," Hasik says.

— Darrell Dela Rosa

Defense Secretary Robert Gates has pressed the Air Force to use drones to gather more intelligence.

[1] See Greg Jaffe, "Drone Pilots Rise on Winds of Change in Air Force," *The Washington Post*, Feb. 28, 2010, p. A1.

[2] See "America's New Air Force," "60 Minutes," CBS, Aug. 16, 2009, www.cbsnews.com/video/watch/?id=5245555n&tag=related;photovideo.

[3] *Ibid.*

[4] *Ibid.*

[5] Mark Thompson, "Why the Air Force Bugs Gates," *Time*, April 21, 2008, www.time.com/time/nation/article/0,8599,1733747,00.html.

[6] "60 Minutes," *op. cit.*

States had thrown the development and use of unmanned aircraft — particularly armed ones — into high gear.[47]

In the first year of war, armed Predators destroyed roughly 115 targets in Afghanistan.[48] Soon, their use outside of the Afghan battlefield opened a debate that continues today over targeted killings.

In November 2002, a Hellfire missile fired from a Predator based in Djibouti struck a vehicle speeding through a desert in Yemen, targeting Qaed Salim Sinan al-Harethi, a leader of Al Qaeda in Yemen and a suspect in the October 2000 bombing of the Navy destroyer *USS Cole*. Also in the car were five other men, including a suspected Al Qaeda operative who held U.S. citizenship.[49]

A month after Harethi's demise it was disclosed that the Bush administration had prepared a secret list of terrorist targets the CIA was authorized to pursue, *The New York Times* reported at the time. "The creation of the secret list is part of the expanded CIA effort to hunt and kill or capture Qaeda operatives far from traditional battlefields, in countries like Yemen," the newspaper noted. It added that the Bush administration's decision "to authorize, under certain circumstances, the killing of terrorist leaders threatens to thrust it into a murky area of national security and international law."[50]

The Times noted that the Bush administration had criticized Israel's targeting of Palestinian leaders. But the newspaper quoted an unnamed former senior official as saying such criticism had died down as the Bush White House sought to bring Al Qaeda to heel. Yet, *The Times* continued, some national security lawyers said putting

The Drone Fleet

The three main unmanned aerial vehicles (UAVs), or drones, used by the U.S. Air Force and the Central Intelligence Agency are the Predator (top), a medium-altitude craft that can shoot two laser-guided Hellfire missiles and take high-resolution reconnaissance photos; the Reaper (middle), a larger version of the Predator that carries four Hellfire missiles; and the Global Hawk, a high-altitude, long-endurance craft that gathers and transmits reconnaissance and surveillance data.

together lists of people subject to lethal force could "blur the lines drawn by government's ban on assassination," a prohibition imposed by President Gerald Ford. "In the view of some lawyers, it applies not only to foreign leaders, but to civilians."

Quoted right after that point, ironically, was Koh, the State Department adviser who recently laid out the Obama administration's legal rationale for CIA drone strikes in Pakistan. In 2002, as a professor of international law at Yale University who had served in the State Department during the Clinton administration, Koh was expressing skepticism about the Bush administration's actions.

Declared Koh back then: "The inevitable complication of a politically declared but legally undeclared war is the blurring of the distinction between enemy combatants and other non-state actors. The question is, what factual showing will demonstrate that they had warlike intentions against us, and who sees that evidence before any action is taken?"[51]

In whatever way legal analysts and administration officials have viewed drone strikes, one thing has been clear: The use of unmanned military aircraft has grown apace in the past half-dozen or so years, with a mix of strategic successes and failures and technological advantages and vulnerabilities.

Tactical Missteps

Unmanned aircraft have been used to take out a number of so-called high-value terrorist targets, among them Baitullah Mehsud, Pakistan's Taliban chief, suspected in the assassination of former Pakistani prime minister Benazir Bhutto. He was killed by a CIA drone strike in summer 2009. "Pakistan considered the Al Qaeda-linked Mehsud its No. 1 internal threat," MSNBC noted, pointing out that his demise was "a severe blow to extremists threatening the stability of [nuclear-armed Pakistan] and a possible boost to U.S.-Pakistan cooperation in fighting insurgents who wreak havoc along the Afghan border."[52]

David Rohde, a *New York Times* reporter held captive by the Taliban for seven months before escaping in June 2009, said in a PBS interview that Mehsud's killing "did have a significant impact. . . .

"I saw firsthand in North and South Waziristan [in the Pakistani tribal region] that the drone strikes do have a major impact. They generally are accurate. The strikes

USAF Photo/Tech. Sgt. Sabrina Johnson

Getty Images/Ethan Miller

Getty Images/USAF

that went on killed foreign militants or Afghan or Pakistani Taliban around us. There were some civilians killed, but generally the Taliban would greatly exaggerate the number of civilians killed. They inhibited their operations. Taliban leaders were very nervous about being tracked by drones. So they are effective in the short term. . . . They do eliminate some top leaders." Still, Rhode continued, "as we've seen by Baitullah Mehsud, new leaders emerge, and I think the only long-term solution is to have Pakistani forces in North Waziristan regain control of that area. I don't think the answer is, you know, endless drone strikes."[53]

Sometimes, drones have led to charges of serious tactical missteps. In 2002 Daraz Khan and two Afghan men were collecting scrap metal when a Hellfire missile fired from a Predator drone killed all three. As reported by *The New York Times*, "American government officials said one of the people in the group was tall and was being treated with deference by those around him. That gave rise to speculation that the attack might have been directed at Osama bin Laden, who is 6-feet-4." The 5-foot-11 Khan, and not bin Laden, was the tall man.

A week later a Pentagon official said the drone had detected "a meeting on a hillside" and that "the initial indications afterwards would seem to say that these are not peasant people up there farming." But Khan's niece said, "Why did you do this? Why did you Americans kill Daraz? We have nothing, nothing. . . . We did nothing to deserve this."[54]

This spring a military report said a U.S. Predator crew, "ignored or downplayed" information that Afghan civilians were in a convoy hit by helicopter fire in February. At least 23 people died in the blast. The drone was monitoring the convoy at the time.[55]

Besides posing strategic obstacles, military action involving drones also poses formidable technical challenges. While drone experts say the technology is getting more sophisticated each year, the reliability of unmanned aircraft remains an issue.

"Some [drone aircraft] crash or collide, forcing American troops to undertake risky retrieval missions before the Taliban can claim the drone's weaponry," *The New York Times* noted in summarizing the classified documents released by WikiLeaks.[56]

The *Los Angeles Times* reported in July that 38 Predator and Reaper drones had crashed during combat missions in Afghanistan and Iraq, and another nine crashed during training at U.S. bases. Each crash cost between $3.7 million and $5 million, the newspaper said. It added that altogether 79 drone accidents costing at least $1 million each had occurred, according to the Air Force.

"Pentagon accident reports reveal that the pilotless aircraft suffer from frequent system failures, computer glitches and human error," the newspaper stated. "Design and system problems were never fully addressed in the haste to push the fragile plane into combat over Afghanistan shortly after the Sept. 11 attacks. . . . Air Force investigators continue to cite pilot mistakes, coordination snafus, software failures, outdated technology and inadequate flight manuals."

The newspaper said accident rates for drones are falling, but total mishaps are rising because the aircraft are being put to more and more use. At least 38 drones are in the air over Afghanistan and Iraq at any one time, and flight hours over the two countries more than tripled between 2006 and 2009, according to the newspaper. Last year, drones flew 185,000 hours over Afghanistan and Iraq, it said.

Accident rates per 100,000 hours fell to 7.5 for the Predator and 16.4 for the Reaper in 2009, the newspaper said, citing Air Force data. Air Force officers said the Predator rate is comparable to that of the F-16 fighter jet in the same stage, the newspaper said.

"These airplanes are flying 20,000 hours a month, OK?" retired Rear Adm. Thomas J. Cassidy Jr., president of the aircraft systems group at General Atomics Aeronautical Systems in San Diego, maker of the Predator and Reaper, told the newspaper. "That's a lot of flying. Some get shot down. Some run into bad weather. Some, people do stupid things with them. Sometimes they just run them out of gas."[57]

Last year it was reported that Shiite militants in Iraq, allegedly with Iranian backing, had intercepted live video feeds from Predator drones by using readily available software such as SkyGrabber costing as little as $25.95. Military officials said they were working to improve encryption of the feeds and said they saw no evidence that militants had been able to interfere with drone flights.[58]

Lt. Gen. David Deptula, Air Force deputy chief of staff for intelligence, surveillance and reconnaissance, told a reporter with an industry trade publication that the intercepted videos led to no "significant impacts" on operations or tactics, and he challenged the notion that insurgents had "compromised" intelligence data. "What do you mean the 'compromise of the data?' " Deptula asked the reporter. "Nothing is compromised. I want to get information out to the joint forces on the ground, you follow me? If someone does pick [the video feed] up and they don't know the context of how the information is being used, what's the compromise?"[59]

Still, *The Wall Street Journal* wrote that "the drone intercepts mark the emergence of a shadow cyber war within the U.S.-led conflicts overseas. They also point to a potentially serious vulnerability in Washington's growing network of unmanned drones."[60]

CURRENT SITUATION

Spending Increases

As the technology advances, federal spending on robotic planes and other hardware is expected to skyrocket.

"I see the investment in unmanned anything — vehicles, ground, airborne, undersea — only increasing, and along with that will be an increase in the funding line for data fusion, analysis and information, and then you have to have satellite bandwidth as well," says retired Air Force Gen. Charles F. "Chuck" Wald, director and senior adviser to the aerospace and defense industry for Deloitte Services and former deputy commander of the U.S. European Command.

"Right now we're still in the first generation of unmanned technology," notes Lindsay Voss, a research analyst with the Association for Unmanned Vehicle Systems International, a nonprofit group in Arlington, Va.

The Pentagon's 2011 budget, released early this year, included plans for a doubling of production of unmanned aircraft. In fact, the Air Force, for the first time, proposed buying more unmanned planes than conventional piloted combat craft. The Air Force planned to double production of the Reaper, and the Army planned to buy 26 extended-range Predators, according to the *Los Angeles Times*. Overall, the newspaper reported, Pentagon spending on Reapers and Predators will grow to $1.4 billion in 2011, up from $877.5 million in 2010.[61]

"We will continue to see significant growth for some years into the future even as the wars in Iraq and Afghanistan eventually wind down," Defense Secretary Robert Gates said of unmanned aircraft. Drones not only are useful in dealing with international conflict but also for fighting drug trafficking and providing help in natural disasters, he said. "The more we have used them, the more we have identified their potential in a broader and broader set of circumstances."[62]

In a report this year, the Teal Group Corp., an aerospace and defense-market analysis firm in Fairfax, Va., estimated that worldwide spending on unmanned aerial vehicles will more than double over the next decade, from current annual expenditures of $4.9 billion to $11.5 billion, totaling more than $80 billion in the next 10 years. It suggested that the United States will account for 76 percent of research, development, test and evaluation spending on unmanned aerial technology over the next decade and about 58 percent of procurement.

Steve Zaloga, a senior analyst at Teal and coauthor of the study, said Teal expects sales of unmanned aerial systems to "follow recent patterns of high-tech arms procurement worldwide, with Europe representing the second-largest market, . . . followed very closely by Asia-Pacific. Africa and Latin America are expected to be very modest markets."[63]

How efficiently the military is adopting drone technology, however, is a matter of concern in government circles. A 2009 report by a government watchdog group found that the Army and Air Force had not done enough to collaborate on their acquisition of unmanned aircraft and could do more to achieve "commonality" and savings in their drone programs. Most of 10 unmanned aircraft acquisition programs the Government Accountability Office (GAO) reviewed "had experienced cost increases, schedule delays, performance shortfalls or some combination of these problems," a GAO official said.[64]

The GAO also noted that the Defense Department, in its fiscal 2011 budget request, indicated that it expected to need more than $24 billion for unmanned aircraft systems through 2015.[65]

Next Generation

In the longer term, military planners envision a massive expansion in the role of drones in combat operations. An

Are drone strikes in Pakistan legal?

YES Kenneth Anderson
Professor of Law, Washington College of Law, American University

Written for *CQ Researcher*, August 2010

The Obama administration has embraced the counterterrorism strategy of targeted killing using drone aircraft for many reasons. One is that it is successful and, as senior Obama officials have repeatedly said, one of the very few, if not the only, option for direct attack against Al Qaeda leadership.

A second reason why the Obama administration has embraced targeted killing is that it is targeted. The technology represents a step forward in discrimination in targeting that should be understood as a major humanitarian advance. Any collateral civilian death is tragic, but the alternative in Pakistan and Afghanistan is not non-violence but instead a rolling artillery barrage by the Pakistani army, with the results already seen in its campaign in the Swat Valley.

For 25 years, humanitarian advocates have been urging the United States to come up with less damaging and more discriminating ways of waging war. Targeted killing from drones is an enormous humanitarian step forward in that effort. Criticism that it still allows civilian collateral deaths is merely to engage in the fantasy game of "so what have you done for me lately?" Worse still is the claim that it allows the United States. to use violence without exposing its own people to risk. Not subjecting U.S. servicemen and women to unnecessary risk, while ratcheting down risk to civilians, is a bad thing? Why?

The Obama administration's senior lawyers, including Harold Koh, a leading human rights scholar and current legal adviser to the State Department, have made a close review of the law regarding targeted killing, both in the abstract and in its application in actual targeting by both the U.S. military and the CIA. They have concluded that it is lawful, in the abstract and as carried out. Targeted killing using Predator drone aircraft, Koh has said, is justified as attacks against combatants in an armed conflict by the military or associated U.S. forces, or as acts of force in legitimate self-defense by the CIA, or both. Warning is not required, nor is there an obligation to seek to arrest or detain prior to attacking with deadly force, and American citizens who take up the fight against the United States abroad are subject to the same conditions.

These legal propositions are correct, and represent the views of the United States going back many decades. Likewise, the legal proposition that if a state is unable or unwilling to control its territory where terrorists take safe haven, those havens are not immune from attack.

NO Mary Ellen O'Connell
Professor of Law, University of Notre Dame

Written for *CQ Researcher*, August 2010

In armed conflict, lawful combatants may target and kill other combatants. In the absence of hostilities, authorities are restricted in using lethal force to when it is absolutely necessary, such as to save a life immediately.

Despite these clear, fundamental principles, the United States has used unmanned aerial vehicles or drones to kill suspected terrorists far from any hostilities and not when absolutely necessary. On Nov. 3, 2002, the CIA, based in Djibouti, fired a missile from a drone into a passenger vehicle on a road in remote Yemen killing all six passengers, including a U.S. citizen. The U.N. Special Rapporteur on extrajudicial, summary, or arbitrary executions reported the killings were extrajudicial executions.

Nevertheless, the United States has persisted in using drones outside of hostilities. Indeed, the practice has increased in the Obama administration. U.S. officials argue the United States has the right to use military force far from hostilities based on the international law of self-defense. Yet, the right to use military force for self-defense means using force on the territory of a state responsible for an armed attack. The United States began its use of force in Afghanistan in 2001 because it held Afghanistan responsible for the 9/11 attacks. The United States continues to use force in Afghanistan today, however, based on an invitation to assist in defeating an insurgency — not the right of self-defense. The U.S. does not hold any of the states where it is using drones responsible for an attack on the United States.

Pakistan has possibly requested some drone strikes to assist in its military campaign against insurgents there. But these strikes are still unlawful because the CIA is conducting them. The CIA has no right to kill in combat. Nor would simply exchanging the military for the CIA entirely solve the problem. Even more important, military force must only be used as part of Pakistan's own hostilities.

Attacks in Yemen and Somalia have also been separate from those countries' hostilities; authorities in those states have no right to consent to killing by drones outside of hostilities.

The American public should know that those who defend the U.S. use of drones for targeted killing as consistent with international law are a distinct minority. The vast majority, certainly of independent scholars in the world who specialize in the international law on the use of force, reject targeted killing far from the battlefield.

Getty Images/Ethan Miller

The F-16 jet fighter remains the combat workhorse of the Air Force. More than 4,400 F-16s have been built since 1976, but the Air Force has stopped buying the highly maneuverable craft as it prepares for the next-generation fighter. Meanwhile, the Air Force is stepping up its use of drone aircraft.

82-page Air Force study released last year outlined potential drone development through 2047. Titled the "Unmanned Aircraft System Flight Plan," it "explains how ever-larger and more sophisticated flying robots could eventually replace every type of manned aircraft in its inventory — everything from speedy, air-to-air fighters to lumbering bombers and tankers," according to *Wired.com*.

That's not to say every manned craft will indeed be replaced with a drone, *Wired* cautioned. "Emphasis [is] on 'might' and 'could,' " it said, noting that "some of the missions tapped for possible, future drones are currently considered sacrosanct for human pilots. Namely: dog fighting and nuclear bombing."

"We do not envision replacing all Air Force aircraft with" unmanned aircraft systems, Col. Eric Mathewson told *Wired*. "We do plan on considering [unmanned aircraft systems] as alternatives to traditionally manned aircraft across a broad spectrum of Air Force missions . . . but certainly not all."[66]

Deptula, the Air Force deputy chief of staff, said early this year that a "degree of infatuation" with unmanned technology existed in the military and that some missions, such as those involving the transportation of nuclear weapons, would probably require pilots in the cockpit.

"Sure, we could do it," he said of using unmanned planes for nuclear missions. "Why would you? Technology might allow us to do something, but we have to apply common sense as to whether or not it fits into the overall defense equation."[67]

Wald, a decorated military pilot with more 3,600 flight hours, including 430 combat hours, says dog fighting with unmanned planes poses special challenges. "It's so three-dimensional and rapid," he says. "For a dog fight to occur you'd have to have 360-degree sensing without any latency. That will take a lot of computing [power]."

Still, he says, "I don't necessarily rule out anything. That will take a long time, but there'll be a trend to try to get that." A key reason, he says, is that the capabilities of unmanned systems will exceed those of human pilots and manned aircraft — the capacity to withstand extreme gravitational forces, for instance, and the potential to stay in the air much longer than conventional planes.

As the revolution in drone technology proceeds, manufacturers are working to figure out how to enhance the capability of unmanned aircraft. As Deptula noted, "We are at a stage today dealing with remotely piloted aircraft, unmanned aerial systems, where we were in 1918, 1920, with manned aircraft."[68]

Voss, of the Association for Unmanned Vehicle Systems International, says "the big focus right now is on how to increase endurance. What kind of propulsion or power system is going to be incorporated that allows [unmanned aircraft] to go up into the air" and stay there "in some cases for maybe days or even months or years?"

Another major focus is on incorporating additional "subsystems" — or payloads — onto remotely piloted aircraft, Voss says. While the major focus has been on the aircraft themselves "because that's what everybody sees," she says, "where there's really big advancements being made is in the area of payloads: cameras, thermal imagers, communications-relay payloads, chemical and biological sensors," and so on. "At the end of the day, the aircraft is just a means to an end."

While much of the focus has been on military applications in overseas war zones, domestic use of unmanned planes also has garnered considerable attention. Among the biggest issues on the domestic front is how the Federal Aviation Administration (FAA) can safely incorporate unmanned aircraft into the same airspace that conventional planes use.

In Congress, lawmakers have introduced several bills that would direct the FAA to come up with an overall plan for integrating unmanned planes into the aviation system.[69]

A key domestic use of unmanned craft is border patrol. Unmanned craft already are used to patrol the U.S.-Canada border and part of the U.S.-Mexico boundary, and in June the FAA, under pressure from congressional lawmakers and others from Texas, approved an unmanned craft to monitor 1,200 miles of border from El Paso to Brownsville, as well as the Texas Gulf Coast, according to news reports and statements from U.S. Sen. John Cornyn, R-Texas, and U.S. Rep. Henry Cuellar, D-Texas.[70]

Cornyn had held up Senate confirmation of Michael Huerta, Obama's choice for deputy FAA administrator, until the aviation administration approved the Predator flights along the Texas border.

OUTLOOK

Many Questions

On both the global war front and the domestic front, the revolution in unmanned aviation that began in the 1990s will only get broader and more sophisticated in the years ahead, experts say. And as it does, questions of the proper use of drone aircraft — the legal and ethical dimensions of Predator-fired weapons, the safety of unmanned craft in civilian air space, the ethics of pilotless surveillance and the notion of robotic planes carrying human passengers — will become more and more pressing.

One issue that is sure to get more attention is how effective unmanned planes — especially armed ones — are at defeating terrorism. "In the end, they're a tactic," said Bruce Riedel, a former CIA officer and current Brooking Institution senior fellow who led an Obama administration strategy review on Afghanistan and Pakistan last year. "They can be a very effective tactic, but they're not really a strategy. It's a little bit like going after a beehive one bee at a time. You may be successful, but it's gonna take a long time to go at it that way."[71]

A 2008 RAND Corp. study analyzed terrorist groups that existed worldwide between 1968 and 2006 and concluded that "military force was rarely the primary reason" such groups ended. Rather, most ended "because of operations carried out by local police or intelligence agencies or because they negotiated a settlement with their governments," the study said. It added, "these findings suggest that the U.S. approach to countering [Al Qaeda] has focused far too much on the use of military force. Instead, policing and intelligence should be the backbone of U.S. efforts."[72]

Another question is whether the United States, with all of its pioneering technology in unmanned aviation, will itself fall prey to rogue actors who get their hands on the same technology.

"What about other countries doing this back at us?" asks Radsan, the law professor and former CIA lawyer. "Think of the Chinese or Iran. It is frightening. Now go further: Imagine if the Taliban or Al Qaeda get" the ability to launch drone attacks. "If we have too many drones, it could be bad for everybody."

Radsan says policy makers should be working on putting together an international agreement to spell out the legal dimensions of drone usage by all nations in warfare, similar to pacts that limit space warfare and nuclear arms. But he is less than hopeful. He points out how hard it has been to forge a universal ban on landmines.

Some experts are more sanguine about the potential risks of unmanned aviation. "There's always going to be risk at some level," says Voss of the Association for Unmanned Vehicle Systems International. "If we have an adversary looking for a way to harm the U.S., they can find creative ways of doing that. Could they potentially use an unmanned system? They could, but they could use a manned system just as easily."

NOTES

1. "Senior Afghan al-Qaeda leader 'killed in Pakistan,'" BBC News, June 1, 2010, http://news.bbc.co.uk/2/hi/world/middle_east/10200712.stm. See also Eric Schmitt, "American Strike Is Said to Kill a Top Qaeda Leader," *The New York Times*, May 31, 2010, www.nytimes.com/2010/06/01/world/asia/01qaeda.html; and Zeeshan Haider, "U.S. believes it killed al Qaeda No. 3," Reuters, June 1, 2010, www.reuters.com/article/idUSTRE65007720100601.

2. For background, see the following *CQ Researcher* reports: Peter Katel, "America at War," July 23, 2010, pp. 605-628; Thomas J. Billitteri, "Afghanistan Dilemma," Aug. 7, 2009, pp. 669-692; Peter Katel, "Rise in Counterinsurgency," Sept. 5, 2008, pp. 697-720; Peter Katel, "Cost of the Iraq War," April 25, 2008, pp. 361-384; and Robert Kiener, "Crisis in Pakistan," *CQ Global Researcher*, December 2008, pp. 321-348.

3. Peter Bergen and Katherine Tiedemann, "The Year of the Drone," New America Foundation, 2010, http://counterterrorism.newamerica.net/drones. Bergen is the CNN national security analyst and is a senior fellow at the New America Foundation.

4. Adam Entous, "Special Report: How the White House Learned to Love the Drone," Reuters, http://static.reuters.com/resources/media/editorial/20100518/Drones.pdf.

5. Andrea Elliott, "Militant's Path From Pakistan to Times Square," *The New York Times*, June 22, 2010, www.nytimes.com/2010/06/23/world/23terror.html.

6. Charlie Savage, "Rule Limiting Legal Services in Terror Cases Is Challenged," *The New York Times*, Aug. 3, 2010, www.nytimes.com/2010/08/04/world/asia/04terror.html?hp.

7. Drone inventory figures and pilot-training facts are from statement of Rep. John F. Tierney, D-Mass., chairman, House Subcommittee on National Security and Foreign Affairs, Committee on Oversight and Government Reform, hearing on "Rise of the Drones: Unmanned Systems and the Future of War," March 23, 2010, http://oversight.house.gov/images/stories/subcommittees/NS_Subcommittee/3.23.10_Drones/3-23-10_JFT_Opening_Statement_FINAL_for_Delivery.pdf.

8. C. J. Chivers, *et al.*, "View Is Bleaker Than Official Portrayal of War in Afghanistan," *The New York Times*, July 25, 2010, www.nytimes.com/2010/07/26/world/asia/26warlogs.html?_r=1&scp=4&sq=wikileaks&st=cse.

9. Statement of Afsheen John Radsan before the House Subcommittee on National Security and Foreign Affairs, "Loftier Standards for the CIA's Remote-Control Killing," April 28, 2010, www.oversight.house.gov/images/stories/subcommittees/NS_Subcommittee/4.28.10_Drones_II/Radsan_Statement_for_the_Record.pdf.

10. "U.S. defends Yemen strike," BBC News, Nov. 10, 2002, http://news.bbc.co.uk/2/hi/americas/2439305.stm.

11. Harold Hongju Koh, "The Obama Administration and International Law," U.S. Department of State, March 25, 2010, www.state.gov/s/l/releases/remarks/139119.htm.

12. Mary Louise Kelly, "Officials: Bin Laden Running Out of Space to Hide," National Public Radio, June 5, 2009, www.npr.org/templates/story/story.php?storyId=104938490.

13. Philip Alston, "Report of the Special Rapporteur on extrajudicial, summary or arbitrary executions," United Nations General Assembly, Human Rights Council, May 28, 2010, p. 3. See also Charlie Savage, "U.N. Report Highly Critical of U.S. Drone Attacks," *The New York Times*, June 2, 2010, www.nytimes.com/2010/06/03/world/03drones.html.

14. *Ibid.*, p. 25.

15. Quoted in Alex Kingsbury, "CIA Drone Strikes Draw United Nations Fire," *U.S. News & World Report*, June 10, 2010, http://politics.usnews.com/news/articles/2010/06/10/cia-drone-strikes-draw-united-nations-fire.html.

16. Jane Mayer, "The Predator War," *The New Yorker*, Oct. 26, 2009, p. 38.

17. Statement of Rep. John F. Tierney, D-Mass., Chairman, Subcommittee on National Security and Foreign Affairs, U.S. House of Representatives, April 28, 2010, http://oversight.house.gov/images/stories/subcommittees/NS_Subcommittee/4.28.10_Drones_II/Opening_Statement.pdf.

18. P. W. Singer, "Defending Against Drones," *Newsweek*, Feb. 25, 2010, www.newsweek.com/2010/02/25/defending-against-drones.html.

19. "U.S.: We shot down Iranian drone over Iraq," CNN, March 16, 2009, www.cnn.com/2009/WORLD/meast/03/16/iran.iraq/index.html.

20. Sofaer is quoted in Kenneth Anderson, "Predators over Pakistan," *The Weekly Standard*, March 8, 2010, p. 31.

21. Testimony of William C. Banks, Committee on Oversight and Government Reform, Subcommittee on National Security and Foreign Affairs, U.S. House of Representatives, April 28, 2010, http://insct.syr.edu/events&lectures/Rise%20of%20the%20drones%20testimony%20042810%20william%20banks.pdf.

22. "U.N. expert criticizes 'illegal' targeted killing policies and calls on the U.S. to halt CIA drone killings," news release, United Nations Office at Geneva, June 2, 2010, www.unog.ch/unog/website/news_media .nsf/(httpNewsByYear_en)/73F4C83992E3BFB0C 1257736004F8D41?OpenDocument.

23. Letter from Anthony D. Romero, ACLU executive director, to President Barack Obama, April 28, 2010, www.aclu.org/files/assets/2010-4-28-ACLULetterto PresidentObama.pdf.

24. Doyle McManus, "U.S. drone attacks in Pakistan 'backfiring,' Congress told," *Los Angeles Times*, May 3, 2009, http://articles.latimes.com/2009/may/03/ opinion/oe-mcmanus3.

25. Bergen and Tiedemann, *op. cit.*

26. Peter Bergen and Katherine Tiedemann, "Drone war hitting its targets," CNN, June 9, 2010, www.cnn .com/2010/OPINION/06/09/bergen.drone.war/ index.html.

27. C. Christine Fair, "Drone Wars," *Foreign Policy*, May 28, 2010, www.foreignpolicy.com/articles/2010/05/ 28/drone_wars.

28. Daniel L. Byman, "Do Targeted Killings Work?" *ForeignPolicy.com*, July 14, 2009, www.brookings .edu/opinions/2009/0714_targeted_killings_byman .aspx. Byman is a senior fellow in the Brookings Institution's Saban Center for Middle East Policy.

29. Murray Wardrop, "Unmanned drones could be banned, says senior judge," *Telegraph*, July 6, 2009, www.telegraph.co.uk/news/newstopics/politics/ defence/5755446/Unmanned-drones-could-be- banned-says-senior-judge.html.

30. Koh, *op. cit.*

31. "Remote-control warfare," *The Christian Century*, May 18, 2010, http://christiancentury.org/article .lasso?id=8443.

32. P. W. Singer, *Wired for War* (2009), pp. 315-316.

33. *Ibid.*, p. 320.

34. Mary L. Dudziak, "On drones and the war power," Legal History Blog, Sept. 27, 2009, http://legalhistory blog.blogspot.com/2009/09/on-drones-and-war- power.html.

35. Statement of Edward Barrett before House Committee on Oversight and Government Reform, Subcommittee on National Security and Foreign Affairs, March 23, 2010, http://oversight.house.gov/images/stories/ subcommittees/NS_Subcommittee/3.23.10_Drones/ Barrett.pdf.

36. John DeGaspari, "Look, Ma, No Pilot!" *Mechanical Engineering*, November 2003, www.memagazine .org/backissues/membersonly/nov03/features/lookma/ lookma.html.

37. Singer, *op. cit.*, p. 49.

38. DeGaspari, *op. cit.*

39. "V-1 Missile" and "V-2 Missile," National Air and Space Museum, www.nasm.si.edu/collections/artifact .cfm?id=A19600341000 and www.nasm.si.edu/ collections/artifact.cfm?id=A19600342000.

40. "Bomb, Guided, Fritz X (X-1)," National Air and Space Museum, www.nasm.si.edu/collections/ artifact.cfm?id=A19840794000.

41. Singer, *op. cit.*, pp. 54-55.

42. *Ibid.*, p. 55.

43. Andrew Callam, "Drone Wars: Armed Unmanned Aerial Vehicles," *International Affairs Review*, winter 2010, www.iar-gwu.org/node/144. The review is a graduate-student-run publication of George Washington University's Elliott School of International Affairs.

44. Singer, *op. cit.*, p. 57.

45. Callam, *op. cit.*

46. Steve Henn and Robert Brodsky, "Top Gun of Travel," Center for Public Integrity, June 5, 2006, http://projects.publicintegrity.org/powertrips/ report.aspx?aid=170. The report focused on spending for congressional staff members by the Predator's builder, San Diego-based General Atomics.

47. Callam, *op. cit.*

48. Singer, *op. cit.*, p. 35.

49. Seymour M. Hersh, "Manhunt," *The New Yorker*, Dec. 23, 2002, www.newyorker.com/archive/2002/ 12/23/021223fa_fact. See also David Johnston and David E. Sanger, "Yemen Killing Based on Rules Set Out by Bush," *The New York Times*, Nov. 6, 2002, www .nytimes.com/2002/11/06/international/middleeast/

06YEME.html; and James Risen and David Johnston, "Bush Has Widened Authority of CIA to Kill Terrorists," *The New York Times*, Dec. 15, 2002, www.nytimes.com/2002/12/15/international/15INTE.html.

50. *Ibid.*

51. Quoted in *ibid.*

52. "Death of Taliban chief a blow to extremists," MSNBC, Aug. 7, 2009, www.msnbc.msn.com/id/32320879/.

53. "Fresh Air," PBS, May 6, 2010, www.npr.org/templates/transcript/transcript.php?storyId=126536285.

54. John F. Burns, "U.S. Leapt Before Looking, Angry Villagers Say," *The New York Times*, Feb. 17, 2002, www.nytimes.com/2002/02/17/world/a-nation-challenged-the-manhunt-us-leapt-before-looking-angry-villagers-say.html?scp=1&sq=daraz%20kahn&st=cse.

55. The Associated Press, "Drone crew blamed in Afghan civilian deaths," *USA Today*, May 29, 2010, www.usatoday.com/news/world/afghanistan/2010-05-29-afghanistan-civilian-deaths_N.htm.

56. Chivers, *et al.*, *op. cit.*

57. David Zucchino, "War zone drone crashes add up," *Los Angeles Times*, July 6, 2010, http://articles.latimes.com/2010/jul/06/world/la-fg-drone-crashes-20100706.

58. Siobhan Gorman, Yochi J. Dreazen and August Cole, "Insurgents Hack U.S. Drones," *The Wall Street Journal*, Dec. 17, 2009, http://online.wsj.com/article/SB126102247889095011.html.

59. Stephen Trimble, "Hacked Predator video no concern: USAF intel chief," FlightGlobal.com, Dec. 12, 2009, www.flightglobal.com/articles/2009/12/18/336394/hacked-predator-video-no-concern-usaf-intel-chief.html.

60. Gorman, Dreazen and Cole, *op. cit.*

61. Julian E. Barnes, "Pentagon budget calls for more unmanned aircraft," *Los Angeles Times*, Feb. 2, 2010, http://articles.latimes.com/2010/feb/02/nation/la-na-budget-pentagon2-2010feb02.

62. *Ibid.*

63. "Teal Group Predicts Worldwide UAV market Will Total Over $80 Billion In Its Just Released 2010 UAV Market Profile And Forecast," press release, Teal Group, Feb. 1, 2010, www.tealgroup.com/index.php?option=com_content&view=article&id=62:uav-study-release&catid=3&Itemid=16.

64. Michael J. Sullivan, statement before House Subcommittee on National Security and Foreign Affairs, "DOD Could Achieve Greater Commonality and Efficiencies among its Unmanned Aircraft Systems," March 23, 2010, www.gao.gov/new.items/d10508t.pdf. The July 2009 GAO report is at www.fas.org/irp/gao/gao-09-520.pdf.

65. Sullivan, *ibid.*

66. David Axe, "Air Force Plans for All-Drone Future," Danger Room blog, *Wired.com*, July 17, 2009, www.wired.com/dangerroom/2009/07/air-force-plans-for-all-drone-future.

67. Megan Scully, "General warns of unmanned aircraft 'infatuation,'" *Congress Daily*, Feb. 18, 2010, www.govexec.com/dailyfed/0210/021810cdpm2.htm.

68. *Ibid.*

69. "FAA Pressed to Allow Drone Flights in U.S.," CBS News/AP, June 14, 2010, www.cbsnews.com/stories/2010/06/14/national/main6579920.shtml.

70. See Dave Michaels, "FAA approves Predator drone to monitor Texas border," Airline Biz blog, *Dallas Morning News*, June 23, 2010, http://aviationblog.dallasnews.com/archives/2010/06/faa-approves-predator-drone-to.html; and press release, Sen. John Cornyn, "Cornyn Announces FAA Approval of Predator Flights Along Entire Texas-Mexico Border," June 23, 2010, http://cornyn.senate.gov/public/index.cfm?p=NewsReleases&ContentRecord_id=894a8499-f19a-4292-8a2a-052eaa0d76f0.

71. Quoted in Kelly, *op. cit.*

72. Seth G. Jones and Martin C. Libick, "How Terrorist Groups End," *Research Brief*, Rand Corporation, 2008, www.rand.org/pubs/research_briefs/RB9351/index1.html.

BIBLIOGRAPHY

Books

Singer, P. W., *Wired for War: The Robotics Revolution and Conflict in the 21st Century*, Penguin, 2009.
A senior fellow at the Brookings Institution explores the tactical, political, economic and legal implications of a massive shift toward unmanned military systems.

Articles

Entous, Adam, "Special Report: How the White House Learned to Love the Drone," *Reuters*, May 18, 2010, www.reuters.com/article/idUSTRE64H5SL 20100518.
A Reuters analysis of government data shows the CIA has killed roughly 12 times more low-level fighters than mid-to-high-level Al Qaeda and Taliban leaders since drone strikes grew more intense in mid-2008.

Fair, C. Christine, "Drone Wars," *Foreign Policy*, May 28, 2010, www.foreignpolicy.com/articles/2010/05/28/drone_wars.
A Georgetown University professor of security studies argues that data suggesting high civilian casualty rates from drone attacks in Pakistan are at best unreliable and contends that while "drone strikes may not be perfect . . . they're likely the most humane option available" in the country's remote tribal region.

Gorman, Siobhan, Yochi J. Dreazen and August Cole, "Insurgents Hack U.S. Drones," *The Wall Street Journal*, Dec. 17, 2009, http://online.wsj.com/article/SB126102247889095011.html.
Using $26 software, Iranian-backed militants in Iraq intercepted video feeds from U.S. Predator drones, marking "the emergence of a shadow cyberwar within the U.S.-led conflicts overseas" and pointing "to a potentially serious vulnerability in Washington's growing network of unmanned drones."

Harris, Shane, "Are Drone Strikes Murder?" *National Journal*, Jan. 9, 2010.
"[A] broad range of important international actors are raising fundamental questions about the legality of drone strikes," says this analysis.

Mayer, Jane, "The Predator War," *The New Yorker*, Oct. 26, 2009, p. 36.
An investigative reporter offers a ground-breaking look at the CIA's drone program in Pakistan, writing that "there is no longer any doubt that targeted killing has become official U.S. policy."

Robertson, Nic, "How robot drones revolutionized the face of warfare," *CNN*, July 26, 2009, www.cnn.com/2009/WORLD/americas/07/23/wus.warfare.remote.uav/index.html.
Defense Secretary Robert Gates has said the next generation of fighter planes will be the last manned fighter aircraft, and a top Air Force official says "the next phase will enable a single drone to provide as many as 60 simultaneous live video feeds directly to combat troops."

Savage, Charlie, "U.N. Report Highly Critical of U.S. Drone Attacks," *The New York Times*, June 2, 2010, www.nytimes.com/2010/06/03/world/03drones.html?scp=1&sq=u.n.%20report%20highly%20critical%20of%20u.s.%20drone%20attacks&st=cse.
Philip Alston, the UN's special representative on extrajudicial executions, called for greater restraint by the American government on the use of drones to attack suspected militants.

Scully, Megan, "General warns of unmanned aircraft 'infatuation,'" *Congress Daily*, Feb. 18, 2010, www.govexec.com/dailyfed/0210/021810cdpm2.htm.
Lt. Gen. David Deptula, who oversees the Air Force's fleet of drones, cautioned the U.S. military to use "common sense" in planning for the future of unmanned aircraft.

Reports and Studies

"DOD Could Achieve Greater Commonality and Efficiencies among Its Unmanned Aircraft Systems," *U.S. Government Accountability Office*, March 23, 2010, www.gao.gov/new.items/d10508t.pdf.
The Defense Department is investing heavily in unmanned aircraft systems but needs to do a better job of increasing collaboration and commonality among the military services' drone-acquisition programs.

"Unmanned Aircraft systems: Federal Actions Needed to Ensure Safety and Expand their Potential Uses within the National Airspace System," *U.S. Government Accountability Office*, **Maya 2008, www.gao .gov/new.items/d08511.pdf.**

Unmanned aircraft "pose technological, regulatory, workload and coordination challenges that affect their ability to operate safely and routinely" in civilian airspace in the United States, says the federal watchdog agency.

Alston, Philip, "Report of the Special Rapporteur on extrajudicial, summary or arbitrary executions," *United Nations Human Rights Council*, **May 28, 2010, www2.ohchr.org/english/bodies/hrcouncil/docs/ 14session/A.HRC.14.24.Add6.pdf.**

A UN special representative examines the implications of drones and other lethal-force technology in so-called targeted killings.

For More Information

Association for Unmanned Vehicle Systems International, 2700 S. Quincy St., Suite 400, Arlington, VA 22206; (703) 845-9671; www.auvsi.org. Membership organization that promotes unmanned systems and related technology.

Brookings Institution, 1775 Massachusetts Ave., N.W., Washington, DC 20036; (202) 797-6000; www.brookings. edu. Centrist think tank that provides research, data and other resources on security and political conditions in Afghanistan and Pakistan and global counterterrorism.

Center for Peace and Securities Studies, Georgetown University, Edmund A. Walsh School of Foreign Service, 3600 N St., N.W., Washington, DC 20007; (202) 687-5679; http://cpass.georgetown.edu/. Conducts research and classes on security issues.

Institute for National Security and Counterterrorism, Syracuse University, 402 McNaughton Hall, Syracuse, NY 13244-1030; (315) 443-2284; http://insct.syr.edu. Studies national and international security and terrorism.

New America Foundation, 1899 L St., N.W., Suite 400, Washington, DC 20036; (202) 986-2700; http://counterterrorism.newamerica.net/drones. Counterterrorism Strategy Initiative includes extensive study on drones.

Rutherford Institute, P.O. Box 7482, Charlottesville, VA 22906-7482; (434) 978-3888; www.rutherford.org. Conservative civil liberties organization.

Stockdale Center for Ethical Leadership, U.S. Naval Academy, 121 Blake Road, Annapolis, MD 21402; (410) 293-6085; www.usna.edu/ethics. Promotes the ethical development of military leaders.

6

Prosecuting Terrorists

Kenneth Jost

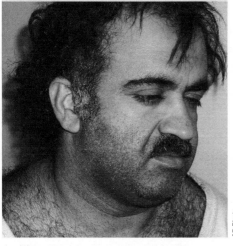

AP Photo

Republican lawmakers say al Qaeda terrorist Khalid Sheikh Mohammed, seen shortly after his capture in Pakistan in 2003, should be treated as an enemy combatant and tried in the military commissions established during the Bush administration. But administration officials and Democratic lawmakers say criminal prosecutions have produced hundreds of convictions since 9/11 compared to only three in the military system.

From *CQ Researcher*,
March 12, 2010. (Updated May 16, 2011)

H e has been described as Osama bin Laden's chief executive officer, the man who conceived the plan to crash hijacked airliners into buildings symbolic of America's political, military and financial power.

Some 18 months after the 9/11 attacks, Pakistani intelligence agents, working with the U.S. Central Intelligence Agency, captured Kuwait-born Khalid Sheikh Mohammed at an al Qaeda safe house in Rawalpindi. Rousted out of bed in the middle of the night, he looked like a street person — not the scion of a well-to-do Pakistani family once known for his expensive tastes and elegant dress.[1]

For the next three years, KSM — as U.S. officials and news media dubbed him — was held at a secret CIA site, reportedly in Poland, where interrogators waterboarded him 183 times in the first month of his captivity. In September 2006 he was transferred to the U.S. prison camp at the Guantánamo Bay naval base in Cuba, to be held awaiting trial.

The trial — on 2,973 counts of murder and other charges — began before a military judge on June 5, 2008, but was thrown into disarray six months later, when Mohammed announced that he and his four co-defendants wanted to plead guilty. A month later, the judge, Army Col. Stephen Henley, agreed to put the trial on hold in response to President Obama's decision, on his first full day in office, to suspend the military trials of all suspected "enemy combatants" being held at Guantánamo.

Now, a year after Obama's interim move, the proceedings against KSM remain in limbo thanks to the full-throttle controversy that erupted after Attorney General Eric Holder announced plans to try

Military Commissions Convicted Three

Three of the terrorism suspects who were detained at Guantánamo Bay — Ali Hamza Ahmad Suliman al Bahlul, Salim Ahmed Hamdan and David Hicks — have been convicted after trials before military commissions. Hicks, known as the "Australian Taliban," and Hamdan, identified as the driver for al Qaeda leader Osama bin Laden, have served their sentences already and been released to their home countries. Al Bahlul awaits a decision on his appeal to his life sentence before a U.S. military judge panel. Hamdan's appeal of his conviction is pending before the same panel; Hicks waived his right of appeal after pleading guilty.

Terrorists Convicted in
Military Commissions at Guantánamo Bay

AFP/Getty Images

al Bahlul
Nationality: Yemeni
Conviction date: Nov. 3, 2008
Charges: 35 counts of solicitation to commit murder, conspiracy and providing material support for terrorism.
Current status: Sentenced to life in prison; appeal pending before panel of military judges; argued Jan. 26.

AFP/Getty Images

Hamdan
Nationality: Yemeni
Conviction date: Aug. 6, 2008
Charges: Providing material support for terrorism.
Current status: Returned to Yemen and released; appeal pending before panel of military judges; argued Jan. 26.

Getty Images

Hicks
Nationality: Australian
Conviction date: March 30, 2007
Charges: Providing material support for terrorism.
Current status: Returned to Australia and released

Source: News reports

the five alleged 9/11 conspirators in a federal court in New York City. In announcing his decision on Nov. 13, Holder said the defendants would "answer for their alleged crimes in a courthouse just blocks away from where the twin towers [of the World Trade Center] once stood."[2]

New York City Mayor Michael Bloomberg and Police Commissioner Raymond Kelly welcomed Holder's decision, but many New Yorkers expressed concerns about the costs and risks of a sensational trial in Lower Manhattan. Some families of 9/11 victims also voiced criticism, saying enemies of the United States deserved military tribunals, not civilian courts.

Holder faced a buzz saw of criticism when he appeared before the Senate Judiciary Committee a week later to defend his decision — which he said he made without consulting the White House. Sen. Jeff Sessions of Alabama, the committee's ranking Republican, called the decision "dangerous," "misguided" and "unnecessary."[3]

Criticism of the decision intensified — and became even more overtly politicized — after the Christmas Day arrest of Umar Farouk Abdulmutallab for the attempted bombing of a Northwest Airlines flight bound from Amsterdam to Detroit. Republican lawmakers and former GOP officials, including former Vice President Dick Cheney and former Attorney General Michael Mukasey, strongly criticized the decision to treat Abdulmutallab as a criminal suspect instead of as an enemy combatant. A major focus of the criticism was the decision to advise Abdulmutallab of his Miranda rights not long after his arrest.

GOP lawmakers raised the stakes on the issue by introducing legislation in Congress to prohibit the use of any funds to try KSM in civilian courts. With administration officials and Democratic lawmakers making little headway in quieting the criticism, the White House let it be known in early February that Obama was personally reviewing the planned location for the trial as part of the broader issue of where and how to try the remaining prisoners at Guantánamo.[4]

The trials have been delayed by controversies that began immediately after President George W. Bush decided to use the base to house alleged enemy combatants captured in the Afghanistan war or rounded up from other locations. Instead of using civilian courts or regular military courts — courts-martial — Bush used his power as commander in chief to create military commissions to try the detainees, with fewer procedural rights than courts-martial.[5]

Critics, including a wide array of civil liberties and human rights organizations, denounced the military commissions as a second-class system of justice. They also lent their support to legal challenges filed by some of the prisoners that eventually resulted in Supreme Court decisions guaranteeing judicial review of their cases and forcing some changes in the rules for the commissions.

Because of the legal uncertainties, the military commissions did not produce their first conviction until March 2007 when David Hicks, the so-called Australian Taliban, pleaded guilty to providing material support for terrorism. Two other Guantánamo prisoners were convicted on material-support counts the next year: Salim Ahmed Hamdan, former driver to bin Laden, and Ali Hamza Ahmad Suliman al Bahlul, an al Qaeda filmmaker and propagandist.

Even as the Guantánamo cases moved at a glacial pace, the Bush administration was using federal courts to prosecute hundreds of individuals arrested in the United States on terrorism-related charges. Among the first was Richard Reid, the so-called shoe bomber, who was charged with attempting to blow up a commercial aircraft en route to the United States on Dec. 22, 2001. Reid, an admitted al Qaeda supporter, is now serving a life sentence.

At various points, Bush himself touted the administration's record of convicting hundreds of individuals in terrorism-related cases in criminal courts. In a budget document in 2008, the Justice Department put the number of convictions or guilty pleas at 319 out of 512 individuals prosecuted.[6]

Guidelines Adopted for Detainee Prosecutions

The Justice and Defense departments adopted broadly written guidelines in July 2009 to be used in deciding whether a Guantánamo detainee was to be tried in a civilian court or before a military tribunal. The protocol begins with "a presumption that, where feasible, referred cases will be prosecuted in" federal criminal courts. The two-page agreement lists three categories of factors to be considered in deciding whether "other compelling factors make it more appropriate to prosecute a case in a reformed military commission":

Strength of interest, including where the offense occurred, where the defendant was apprehended and which agency or agencies investigated the case.

Efficiency, including protection of intelligence sources, foreign policy concerns and "legal or evidentiary problems that might attend prosecution in the other jurisdiction."

Other prosecution considerations, including the charges that can be brought and the sentences that can be imposed in one or the other forum.

Source: "Determination of Guantánamo Cases Referred for Prosecution," July 20, 2009, www.justice.gov/opa/documents/taba-prel-rpt-dptf-072009.pdf

More recently, a report written for Human Rights First counted 195 convictions or guilty pleas in al Qaeda- or Taliban-related terrorism cases through July 2, 2009, along with 19 acquittals or dismissals. The report, written by two lawyers who had previously served as federal prosecutors in New York, concluded that the criminal justice system "is well-equipped to handle a broad variety of cases arising from terrorism" associated with al Qaeda or similar groups.[7]

Despite that record, GOP lawmakers, ex-Bush administration officials and conservative experts and advocates are arguing strongly for the use of military commissions to try Abdulmutallab and, apparently, most of the prisoners held at Guantánamo. "Wartime alien enemy combatants should be tried by military commissions in the safety of Guantánamo Bay," says Andrew McCarthy, a contributing editor with *National Review Online* and former federal prosecutor.[8]

While in the U.S. attorney's office in Manhattan, McCarthy was lead prosecutor in the 1995 trial of Omar Abdel Rahman, the so-called Blind Sheik, along with nine others for plotting to blow up various civilian targets in the New York City area. Rahman was convicted of seditious conspiracy and is now serving a life sentence.[9]

Human rights advocates, however, say military commissions have failed to produce results while tarnishing the United States' image both at home and abroad. "The only choice should be trial in civilian courts," says Laura Olson, senior counsel for the rule of law program at the Washington-based Constitution Project. "They're both tougher and more reliable than military commissions."

The Obama administration says civilian trials are the presumptive forum for terrorism cases but is continuing the use of what it calls "reformed" military commissions for some cases. A protocol adopted jointly by the Justice and Defense departments in July 2009 says forum selection will depend on a number of factors, including the agency or agencies involved in the investigation and the charges and sentences available in one or the other forum. Holder designated several Guantánamo prisoners for trial by military commissions on the same day he announced the decision to try KSM in New York City.

Meanwhile, administration officials also are saying that 50 or more Guantánamo prisoners may be held indefinitely without trial because they cannot be prosecuted successfully but are too dangerous to release.[10] Conservatives say the prolonged detentions are justifiable as long as the United States is effectively at war with al Qaeda. Civil liberties advocates strongly disagree.

President Obama cheered human rights groups with his initial moves on counterterrorism policies, especially his pledge to close the Guantánamo prison camp within a year. Now that the deadline has been missed and other policies recalibrated, Obama is drawing some complaints from liberal advocacy groups along with sharp criticism from Republicans and conservative groups for the planned use of federal courts to try enemy combatants.

Here are some of the major issues the administration faces:

Should suspected terrorists be tried in civilian courts?

When the FBI got wind of a group of Yemeni Americans who had trained at an al Qaeda camp in 2001 and returned to their homes in the Buffalo, N.Y., suburb of Lackawanna, Bush administration's officials were divided on what to do.

Vice President Dick Cheney and Defense Secretary Donald Rumsfeld wanted to use troops to arrest the men and treat them as enemy combatants to be tried before a military commission. President Bush, however, sided with Attorney General John Ashcroft and FBI Director Robert Mueller, who favored using federal agents to arrest the men and trying them in a federal court.

In the end, the men were arrested without incident on Sept. 14, 2002, and over the next year pleaded guilty and received prison sentences ranging from seven to 10 years for supporting a foreign terrorist organization. They also cooperated with authorities in providing information about al Qaeda, and three of them testified in the 2008 military commission trial of the al Qaeda filmmaker Bahlul.[11]

Supporters of criminal prosecutions — including but not limited to human rights and civil liberties groups — say prosecutions such as the Lackawanna Six case prove civilian courts can mete out effective, tough justice in terrorism-related cases without shortchanging constitutional rights.

"The criminal justice system is reasonably well-equipped to handle most international terrorism cases," New York attorneys Richard B. Zabel and James J. Benjamin Jr. wrote in the Human Rights First report in May 2008. A year later, the two former federal prosecutors reiterated that civilian court prosecutions had generally led to "just, reliable results" without causing security breaches or other harms to national security.[12]

National security-minded critics and some non-ideological experts counter that the rights accorded defendants in the criminal justice system do pose potential obstacles to successful prosecutions in some terrorism cases. "Civilian trials should be a secondary option," says David Rivkin, a former Justice Department official in the Bush administration now affiliated with the hawkish Foundation for the Defense of Democracies. Among other problems, Rivkin says classified information is harder to protect in a civilian court than in a military commission despite a federal law, the Classified Information Procedure Act (CIPA), which limits disclosure in federal trials.

"The federal courts have some real limitations," agrees Benjamin Wittes, a research fellow at the Brookings Institution and author of several influential reports about war-on-terror policies. He cites as examples the beyond-a-reasonable-doubt standard used in criminal prosecutions and the stricter standard on use of evidence obtained under coercive interrogation. Still, Wittes adds, the problems are "not as big as conservatives claim."

Critics assailed the decision to try the 9/11 conspiracy case in New York City in particular as a security risk. Rivkin complains of "the logistical nightmare" that would be created by a trial in a major metropolitan area such as New York.

When Holder visited New York to discuss plans for the trial in December, however, a Justice Department spokesman declared, "We have a robust plan developed by both federal and local officials to ensure that these trials can be safely held in New York, and everyone is committed to doing that."[13]

Above any practical considerations, however, critics such as Rivkin say simply that criminal prosecutions signal a wrong approach in the nation's fight against al Qaeda. "This is a long and difficult war," he says. "It is essential for any administration to inculcate the notion that this is a real war. And it is utterly jarring in that context to take enemy combatants, particularly high-value ones, and treat them as common criminals."

Benjamin counters that the criminal justice system in fact amounts to one of the United States' most effective weapons in the war on terror. "We are at war," he says. "One of the unique features of this particular war is that many of the people on the other side are violating our criminal law. If we can develop the evidence and successfully put them away, why in the world would we foreclose ourselves from doing that?"

Should suspected terrorists be tried in military tribunals?

Attorney General Holder's decision to try seven Guantánamo detainees in military commissions represents only a modest step toward resolving the cases of the remaining prisoners there. But the trials, if completed, would more than double the number of cases resolved by military tribunals since President Bush authorized them less than two months after the 9/11 attacks.

Supporters say history, law and national security justify the use of military tribunals to try enemy combatants. They blame opponents for the legal controversies that have limited their use so far.

"The record has been underwhelming," concedes ex-Justice Department attorney Rivkin. "Why should we be surprised? There has been a concentrated effort from day one to litigate against them."

Human rights and civil liberties groups counter that the military tribunals were flawed from the outset and, despite some recent reforms, still have significant problems and will face additional legal challenges.

"They remain vulnerable to constitutional challenge," says Olson of the Constitution Project. "We're going to have to go through this litigation for years and years."

In contrast to the three men convicted so far by military commissions, the prisoners that Holder designated in his Nov. 13 announcement for trial by military commissions include figures alleged to have played significant roles in al Qaeda operations. They include Abd al Rahim al Nashiri, a Yemeni accused of plotting the October 2000 attack on the *USS Cole*, and Noor Uthman Mohammed, a Sudanese alleged to have assisted in running an al Qaeda training center in Afghanistan.

The accusations against some of the others, however, depict them as hardly more than al Qaeda foot soldiers. The group includes Omar Khadr, the youngest Guantánamo detainee, who was captured at age 15 after a firefight in Afghanistan. Now 23, the Canadian citizen faces a charge of providing support for terrorism by throwing a grenade that killed a U.S. soldier. The charge goes against the United Nations' position that children should not be prosecuted for war crimes.[14]

In announcing his decisions on the legal forum to be used, Holder gave no explanation of the reasons for designating some of the prisoners for trial by military commissions. But he did say that recent changes approved by Congress for the commissions "will ensure that commission trials are fair, effective and lawful." Those changes include limits on use of hearsay and coerced testimony and greater access for defendants to witnesses and evidence.

Despite the changes, human rights advocates continue to oppose use of the military commissions. "We don't quarrel with military justice," says Ben Winzer, a staff attorney with the American Civil Liberties Union's (ACLU) national security project. "The problem is that even the modified military commissions are being used to paper over weaknesses in the government's evidence."

"Most of the growing pains have been alleviated," counters Rivkin. "The solution now is to stand them up,

AFP/Getty Images/Don Emmert

Omar Abdel Rahman, the so-called Blind Sheik, was convicted in a civilian criminal trial in 1995 along with nine others for plotting to blow up various civilian targets in the New York City area. Rahman is now serving a life sentence. Andrew McCarthy, the then-lead prosecutor for the U.S. attorney's office, is now a contributing editor with *National Review Online*, a conservative publication. He now says, "Wartime alien enemy combatants should be tried by military commissions in the safety of Guantánamo Bay."

make them work, give them the right resources and get out of the way."

For his part, Brookings Institution expert Wittes says the military commissions "have significantly underperformed to date" and continue to face a host of practical and legal difficulties. "We worry that the military commissions will present issues of their own, particularly with respect to challenges to the lawfulness and integrity of the system itself," he says. "And the rules have been used so little that there are a lot of issues about how the system works."

Among the most important pending issues is the question whether material support of terrorism — a mainstay of criminal prosecutions — is an offense that

can be tried in a military tribunal. The review panel established to hear appeals from the military commissions currently has that issue under advisement after arguments in two cases in January.

"No one questions that these are crimes, but there are special rules that come into play when we start talking about what crimes military commissions can prosecute," says Stephen Vladeck, a law professor at American University in Washington. "I think there are far fewer cases in which the government realistically has a choice between civilian and military courts than we might think, if for no other reason than the jurisdiction of military commissions is actually tightly circumscribed by the Constitution."

Should some Guantánamo detainees be held indefinitely without trial?

In his first major speech on how to deal with the Guantánamo prisoners, President Obama called in May 2009 for "prolonged detention" for any detainees "who cannot be prosecuted yet who pose a clear danger to the American people." Obama said he would work with Congress to "construct a legitimate legal framework" for such cases, but added: "I am not going to release individuals who endanger the American people."[15]

In the nine months since, neither Congress nor the president has put any appreciable work into possible legislation on the issue. Now, administration officials are estimating 50 or more detainees will have to be held without trial, but they have not listed names or described procedures being used to designate individuals for that category.

The ACLU and other human rights groups immediately denounced Obama's remarks on the issue and continue to oppose detention without trial. The administration's conservative critics approve of holding some prisoners without trial but fault the administration for its efforts to transfer others to their home countries or other host nations because they might return to hostilities against the United States.

"The term is detention for the duration of hostilities," says Rivkin. "Those rules have been in place since time immemorial. They are not meant to punish anybody; they are designed to prevent someone from going back to the battlefield."

Rivkin says the policy of transferring prisoners to other countries — begun by the Bush administration and continued by Obama — amounts to "a revolving door" for terrorists. "We know for sure that they go back

Khalid Sheikh Mohammed and the 9/11 Attacks

Khalid Sheikh Mohammed, self-described mastermind of the Sept. 11 terrorist attacks, faces trial in federal court on 2,973 counts of murder and other charges along with his four co-defendants. Kuwait-born KSM first claimed to have organized the 9/11 attacks during interrogations in which he was waterboarded 183 times. In March 2007, at a hearing at the Guantánamo Bay prison, he said he was responsible for the attacks "from A to Z" — as well as for 30 other terrorist plots. The five co-defendants now face nine charges including conspiracy, terrorism, providing material support for terrorism and murder. Controversy erupted over Attorney General Eric Holder's plan to hold the trial in New York City, and the location of the trial is now being reconsidered. KSM's four co-defendants are:

• **Ramzi Bin al-Shibh (Yemen)** — Alleged "coordinator" of the attacks after he was denied a visa to enter the United States.
• **Walid bin Attash (Saudi Arabia)** — Charged with selecting and training several of the hijackers of the attacks.
• **Ali Abdul Aziz Ali (Pakistan)** — Allegedly helped hijackers obtain plane tickets, traveler's checks and hotel reservations. Also taught them the culture and customs of the West.
• **Mustafa Ahmed al-Hawsawi (Saudi Arabia)** — Allegedly an organizer and financier of the attacks.

to combat," Rivkin says. "This is the first war in human history where we cannot hold in custody a captured enemy. That's a hell of a way to run a war."

ACLU lawyer Winzer calls Obama's detention-without-trial proposal "an extraordinarily controversial statement in a country governed by the rule of law." Anyone "truly dangerous" should be and likely can be prosecuted, Winzer says. "Our material-support laws are so broad that if we don't have legitimate evidence to convict [detainees] under those laws, it's hard to accept that they are too dangerous to release."

Allegations that some of the released Guantánamo prisoners have returned to hostilities against the United States stem from studies released by the Pentagon during the Bush administration and sharply challenged by some human rights advocates. The final of three studies, released in January 2009 only one week before Bush was to leave office, claimed that 61 out of 517 detainees released had "returned to the battlefield."

But an examination of the evidence by Mark Denbeaux, a law professor at Seton Hall University in South Orange, N.J., and counsel to two Guantánamo detainees, depicts the Pentagon's count as largely unsubstantiated. In any event, Denbeaux says the Pentagon's count is exaggerated because it includes former prisoners who have done nothing more after their release than engage in propaganda against the United States.[16]

Supporters of detention without trial cite as authority the first of the Supreme Court's post-9/11 decisions,

Hamdi v. Rumsfeld.[17] In that 2004 ruling, a majority of the justices agreed that the legislation Congress passed in 2001 to authorize the Afghanistan war included authority for the detention of enemy combatants. In the main opinion, Justice Sandra Day O'Connor said a detainee was entitled to some opportunity to contest allegations against him, but did not specify what kind of procedure.

The court rulings appear to support the government's power "to hold people indefinitely without charge if they are associated with al Qaeda or the Taliban in the same way that a solider is associated with an army," says Benjamin, coauthor of the Human Rights First report. Law professor Vladeck agrees, but says the number of people in that category is likely to be "small."

Brookings Institution expert Wittes defends the practice "philosophically" but acknowledges practical problems, including public reaction both in the United States and abroad. "The first risk is that it's perceived as the least legitimate option, domestically or internationally," he says. "It's not the way you like to do business."

The evidence needed to justify detention has been the major issue in the dozens of habeas corpus petitions filed by Guantánamo prisoners. Federal district judges in Washington who have been hearing the cases have mostly decided against the government, according to a compilation coauthored by Wittes.[18]

Wittes has long urged Congress to enact legislation to define the scope of indefinite detention. In an unusual interview, three of the judges handling the cases agreed. "It should be Congress that decides a policy such as this," Judge Reggie Walton told the online news site *ProPublica*.[19]

But David Cole, a law professor at Georgetown University in Washington and prominent critic of the detention policies, disagrees. The issues, Cole says, "require careful case-by-case application of standards. It's a job for judges, not Congress."[20]

BACKGROUND

Power and Precedent

The United States faced the issue of how to deal with captured members or supporters of al Qaeda or the Taliban with no exact historical parallel as guidance. The use of military tribunals for saboteurs, spies or enemy sympathizers dated from the American Revolution but had been controversial in several instances, including during the Civil War and World War II. After World War II, military commissions became — in the words of Brookings expert Wittes — "a dead institution." The rise of international terrorism in the 1980s and '90s was met with military reprisals in some instances and a pair of notable U.S. prosecutions of Islamist extremists in the 1990s.[21]

As commander of the revolutionary army, Gen. George Washington convened military tribunals to try suspected spies — most notably, Major John André, Benedict Arnold's coconspirator, who was convicted, sentenced to death and hanged. During the War of 1812 and the First Seminole War (1817-1818). Gen. Andrew Jackson was criticized for expansive use of his powers as military commander — most notably, for having two British subjects put to death for inciting the Creek Indians against the United States. During the occupation of Mexico in the Mexican-American War, Gen. Winfield Scott established — without clear statutory authority — "military councils" to try Mexicans for a variety of offenses, including guerrilla warfare against U.S. troops.

The use of military tribunals by President Abraham Lincoln's administration during the Civil War provoked sharp criticism at the time and remains controversial today. Lincoln acted unilaterally to suspend the writ of habeas corpus in May 1861, defied Chief Justice Roger Taney's rebuke of the action and only belatedly got Congress to ratify his decision. More than 2,000 cases were tried by military commissions during the war and Reconstruction. Tribunals ignored some judicial orders to release prisoners.

Lincoln, however, overturned some decisions that he found too harsh. As the war continued, the Supreme Court turned aside one challenge to the military commissions, but in 1866 — with the war ended — held that military tribunals should not be used if civilian courts are operating.[22]

During World War II, President Franklin D. Roosevelt prevailed in three Supreme Court challenges to expansive use of his powers as commander in chief in domestic settings. Best known are the court's decisions in 1943 and 1944 upholding the wartime curfew on the West Coast and the internment of Japanese-Americans. Earlier, the court in 1942 had given summary approval to the convictions and death sentences of German saboteurs captured in June and tried the next month before hastily convened military commissions. Roosevelt's order convening the seven-member tribunals specified that the death penalty could be imposed by a two-thirds majority instead of the normal unanimous vote. The Supreme Court heard habeas corpus petitions filed by seven of the eight men but rejected their claims in a summary order in the case, *Ex parte Quirin*, on July 31. Six of the men had been executed before the justices issued their formal opinion on Oct. 29.[23]

International law governing wartime captives and domestic law governing military justice were both significantly reformed after World War II in ways that cast doubt on the previous ad hoc nature of military commissions. The Geneva Conventions — signed in 1949 and ratified by the Senate in 1954 — strengthened previous protections for wartime captives by, among other things, prohibiting summary punishment even for combatants in non-traditional conflicts such as civil wars. The Uniform Code of Military Justice, approved by Congress in 1950, brought civilian-like procedures into a system previously built on command and discipline. The United States went beyond the requirements of the Geneva Conventions in the Vietnam War by giving full prisoner-of-war status to enemy captives, whether they belonged to the regular North Vietnamese army or the guerrilla Vietcong.

International terrorism grew from a sporadic problem for the United States in the 1970s to a major concern in the 1980s and '90s. The results of foreign prosecutions in two of the major incidents in the '80s left many Americans disappointed. An Italian jury imposed a 30-year sentence in 1987 on Magid al-Molqi after the Palestinian confessed to the murder of U.S. citizen Leon Klinghoffer during the 1985 hijacking of the cruise ship *Achille Lauro*; the prosecution had sought a life term. The bombing of

Pan Am Flight 103 over Scotland in 1988 — and the deaths of 189 Americans among the 270 victims — resulted in the long-delayed trial of Abdel Basset Ali al-Megrahi, former head of the Libyan secret service. Megrahi was indicted in 1991 in the United States and Scotland, extradited only after protracted diplomatic negotiations and convicted and sentenced to life imprisonment in 2001. He was released on humanitarian grounds in 2009, suffering from purportedly terminal pancreatic cancer.

Two prosecutions in the United States stemming from the 1993 bombing of the World Trade Center produced seemingly stronger verdicts. Omar Abdel Rahman, the so-called Blind Sheik, was convicted in federal court in New York City along with nine others in 1995 for conspiracy to carry out a campaign of bombings and assassinations within the United States. Abdel Rahman is now serving a 240-year prison sentence. Two years later, Ramzi Ahmed Yousef was convicted on charges of masterminding the 1993 bombing and given a life sentence. Even after the second verdict, however, questions remained about whether the plot had been sponsored by a foreign state or international organization.[24]

Challenge and Response

The Bush administration responded to the 9/11 attacks by declaring an all-out war on terrorism that combined separate strategies of detaining captured "enemy combatants" at Guantánamo outside normal legal processes and prosecuting hundreds of individuals in federal courts on terrorism-related charges. The improvised system of military tribunals at Guantánamo drew political and legal challenges that stalled their work, resulting in only three convictions late in Bush's time in office. Meanwhile, criminal cases proceeded in federal courts with relatively few setbacks and little hindrance from criticism by some civil libertarians of overly aggressive prosecutions.[25]

Even as the Guantánamo military tribunals were being formed, the administration was initiating criminal prosecutions in other al Qaeda or Taliban-related cases. In the most important, the government indicted Zacarias Moussaoui, sometimes called the 20th hijacker, on Dec. 11, 2001, on conspiracy counts related to the 9/11 attacks. The prosecution dragged on for more than four years, extended by Moussaoui's courtroom dramatics and a fight over access to classified information that ended with a ruling largely favorable to the government. The trial ended on May 3, 2006, after a jury that had deliberated for

seven days imposed a life sentence instead of the death penalty — apparently rejecting the government's view of Moussaoui as a central figure in the 9/11 attacks.

Two other early prosecutions ended more quickly. British citizen Richard Reid, the so-called shoe bomber, was charged in a federal criminal complaint on Dec. 24, 2001, two days after his failed explosive attack on American Airlines Flight 63. In January, Attorney General John Ashcroft announced that U.S. citizen John Walker Lindh, the so-called American Taliban captured in Afghanistan, would be tried in a civilian court in the United States. Both men entered guilty pleas in 2002; Lindh was given a 20-year sentence while Reid was sentenced in January 2003 to life in prison.

The government started two other early cases in the criminal justice system and moved them into the military system only to return later to civilian courts. Ali Saleh Kahlah al-Marri, a Qatari student attending college in Illinois, was detained as a material witness in December 2001 and indicted two months later on credit-card charges. Bush's decision in 2003 to designate him as an enemy combatant led to a protracted appeal that the Obama administration resolved in 2009 by indicting al-Marri on a single count of conspiracy to provide material support for terrorism. In a similar vein, U.S. citizen José Padilla was arrested at the Chicago airport on May 8, 2002, on suspicion of plotting a radioactive attack; designated an enemy combatant a month later and then indicted after drawn-out legal challenges that reached the Supreme Court. Padilla was convicted of terrorism conspiracy charges and given a 17-year prison sentence; al-Marri drew 15 years after pleading guilty.

Meanwhile, the military tribunals had been stymied by a succession of legal challenges before the Supreme Court and responses by the administration and Congress to the justices' rulings. In the pivotal decision in Hamdan's case, the court ruled in June 2006 that the military commissions as then constituted were illegal because the president had not shown a need to depart from established rules of military justice.[26] Reconstituted under the Military Commissions Act of 2006, the tribunals finally produced their first conviction in March 2007 when the Australian Hicks pleaded guilty to a single material-support count. Under a plea agreement and with credit for time served, he was allowed to return to Australia to serve the remaining nine months of a seven-year sentence.

Two more convictions followed in 2008, both after trials. Hamdan was convicted in August of conspiracy

CHRONOLOGY

1970s-2000 *International terrorism era begins, with attacks on civilian aircraft, facilities; prosecutions in foreign, U.S. courts get mixed results.*

1988 Bombing of Pan Am Flight 103 over Scotland kills 270, including 189 Americans; Scottish court later convicts and sentences to life former head of Libyan secret service; ill with cancer, he was released from Scottish jail in 2009.

1995 Civilian court convicts Omar Abdel Rahman and nine others for conspiring to blow up World Trade Center, other sites, in 1993.

1997 Ramzi Ahmed Yousef draws life sentence after 1997 conviction in civilian court for masterminding 1993 trade center bombing.

2000-Present *Al Qaeda launches 9/11 attacks; Bush, Obama administrations prosecute terrorism cases mainly in civilian courts.*

September-October 2001 Nearly 3,000 killed in al Qaeda's Sept. 11 attacks. . . . Congress on Sept. 14 gives president authority to use force against those responsible for attacks.

November-December 2001 President George W. Bush on Nov. 13 authorizes military commissions to try enemy combatants captured in Afghanistan, elsewhere. . . . U.S. Naval Base at Guantánamo Bay is chosen as site to hold detainees. . . . Zacarias Moussaoui indicted in federal court in Virginia on Dec. 11 for conspiracy in 9/11 attacks. . . . "Shoe bomber" Richard Reid arrested Dec. 21 for failed attack on American Airlines Flight 63.

2002 First of about 800 prisoners arrive in Guantánamo; first of scores of habeas corpus cases filed by detainees by mid-spring. . . . José Padilla arrested at Chicago airport May 8 in alleged radioactive bomb plot; case transferred to military courts. . . . John Walker Lindh, "American Taliban," sentenced Oct. 4 by a civilian court to 20 years in prison.

2003 Federal judge in Boston sentences Reid to life in prison on Jan. 31.

2004 Supreme Court rules June 28 that U.S. citizens can be held as enemy combatants but must be afforded hearing

before "neutral decisionmaker" (*Hamdi v. Rumsfeld*); on same day, court rules Guantánamo detainees may use habeas corpus to challenge captivity (*Rasul v. Bush*).

2006 Moussaoui is given life sentence May 3. . . . Supreme Court rules June 29 that military commissions improperly depart from requirements of U.S. military law and Geneva Conventions (*Hamdan v. Rumsfeld*). . . . Congress passes Military Commissions Act of 2006 in September to remedy defects.

2007 First conviction in military commission: Australian David Hicks sentenced on March 30 to nine months after guilty plea to material support for terrorism. . . . Padilla convicted in federal court Aug. 16 on material support counts; later sentenced to 17 years.

2008 Supreme Court reaffirms June 12 habeas corpus rights for Guantánamo detainees (*Boumediene v. Bush*). . . . Two more convictions of terrorists in military commissions: Hamdan convicted on material support counts Aug. 6, sentenced to a seven-and-a-half-year term; al Qaeda propagandist Ali Hamza al Bahlul convicted Nov. 3, given life sentence.

January-June 2009 President Obama pledges to close Guantánamo within a year, suspends military commissions pending review (Jan. 21). . . . Obama in major speech says some detainees to be held indefinitely without trial (May 21).

July-December 2009 Defense and Justice departments agree on protocol to choose civilian or military court (July 20). . . . Military Commission Act of 2009 improves defendants' protections (October). Attorney General Eric Holder announces plan to try Khalid Sheikh Mohammed (KSM), four others in federal court in Manhattan for 9/11 conspiracy (Nov. 13); other alleged terrorists designated for military commissions; plan for N.Y. trial widely criticized. . . . Umar Farouk Abdulmutallab arrested Dec. 25 in failed bombing of Northwest Flight 253; decision to prosecute in civilian court criticized, defended.

2010 Administration mulls change of plans for KSM trial. . . . U.S. appeals court backs broad definition of enemy combatant in first substantive appellate-level decision in Guantánamo habeas corpus cases (Jan. 5). . . . Military review panel weighs arguments on use of "material support of terrorism" charge in military commissions (Jan. 26).

2010

June 21 — Faisal Shahzad pleads guilty to 10 terrorism-related counts for May 1 attempted car bomb attack in Times Square; is given life sentence on Oct. 5.

Nov. 17 — Investigating officer recommends court martial and possible death penalty for Maj. Nidal Malik Hasan for Nov. 5, 2009, shooting rampage at Fort Hood, Texas.

2011

Jan. 7 — President Obama signs defense authorization bill with restrictions on civilian trials, transfers for Guantánamo prisoners.

March 7 — Obama orders military trials to resume at Guantánamo with new review procedures for prisoners unable to be tried.

April 4 — Attorney General Eric Holder refers 9/11 conspiracy charges against Khalid Sheikh Mohammed, four others to military commissions; criticizes congressional restrictions on civilian trials.

April 20 — Abd al-Rahim al-Nashiri is charged in military commission with murder, terrorism, other counts in Oct. 12, 2000, bombing of *U.S.S. Cole.*

May 1 — Osama bin Laden is killed by U.S. Navy Seals in walled compound in Abbottabad, Pakistan.

May 5 — Anwar Awlaki, a U.S.-born militant Islamic cleric, escapes without injury after missile attack by U.S. drones in Yemen.

and material support but acquitted of more serious charges and given an unexpectedly light sentence of 61 months. With credit for time served, he was transferred to his native Yemen in late November to serve the last month of his term. Earlier, a military tribunal on Nov. 3 had convicted Bahlul of a total of 35 terrorism-related counts after the former al Qaeda propaganda chief essentially boycotted the proceedings. The panel returned the verdict in the morning and then deliberated for an hour before sentencing the Yemeni native to life imprisonment.

As the Bush administration neared an end, the Justice Department issued a fact-sheet on the seventh anniversary of the 9/11 attacks touting its "considerable success in America's federal courtrooms of identifying, prosecuting and incarcerating terrorists and would-be terrorists." The report listed the Padilla and Moussaoui cases among eight "notable" prosecutions in recent years. It also briefly noted the department's cooperation with the Defense Department in developing procedures for the military commissions, defending against challenges to the system and jointly bringing charges against KSM and other high-value detainees.[27]

In an important post-election setback, however, a federal judge in Washington ruled on Nov. 20, 2008, in favor of five of the six Algerians whose habeas corpus petitions had led to the Supreme Court decision guaranteeing judicial review for Guantánamo detainees. Judge Richard Leon said the government had failed to present sufficient evidence to show that the six men, arrested in Bosnia in January 2002, had planned to travel to Afghanistan to fight against the United States. He found sufficient evidence, however, that one of the prisoners had acted as a facilitator for al Qaeda. Three of the five were returned to Bosnia in December; two others were transferred to France in May and November 2009.[28]

Change and Continuity

In his first days in office, President Obama began fulfilling his campaign pledge to change the Bush administration's legal policies in the war on terror. Obama's high-profile decisions to set a deadline for closing Guantánamo, shut down the secret CIA prisons and prohibit enhanced interrogation techniques drew support from Democrats and liberals and sharp criticism from Republicans and conservatives. By year's end, the roles were reversed, with support from the right and criticism from the left of Obama's decision to continue use of military tribunals and claim the power to detain suspected terrorists indefinitely without trial. Meanwhile, the government was continuing to win significant terrorism-related convictions in

The Case Against the 'Christmas Day' Bomber

Critics say prosecutors mishandled Abdulmutallab's arrest.

Caught in the act of trying to bomb a Northwest Airlines aircraft, Umar Farouk Abdulmutallab would appear to offer prosecutors a slam dunk under any of several terrorism-related charges. Indeed, there were dozens of witnesses to his capture.

But the case against the baby-faced Nigerian-born, Yemeni-trained al Qaeda supporter became enmeshed in post-9/11 American politics almost immediately after his Christmas Day flight landed in Detroit.[1]

President Obama invited the subsequent criticism by initially labeling Abdulmutallab as "an isolated extremist" on Dec. 26 before learning of his training in al Qaeda camps in Yemen and history of extreme Islamist views. Homeland Security Secretary Janet Napolitano compounded the administration's political problems by saying on Dec. 27 that Abdulmutallab's capture showed that "the system worked" — a statement she quickly worked hard to explain away, given that a U.S. airliner had nearly been bombed.

The administration also faced criticism for intelligence analysts' failure to block Abdulmutallab from ever boarding a U.S.-bound aircraft after having received a warning from the suspect's father, a prominent Nigerian banker, of his son's radicalization. Obama moved to stanch the criticism by commissioning and quickly releasing a review of the intelligence agencies' "failure to connect the dots" and by ordering other steps, including a tightening of airline security procedures.

The politicization of the case intensified, however, with a broadside from former Vice President Dick Cheney sharply attacking the administration's decision to treat Abdulmutallab as a criminal suspect instead of an enemy combatant to be tried in a military tribunal. Obama "is trying to pretend we are not at war," Cheney told *Politico*, the Washington-based, all-politics newspaper.

"He seems to think if he has a low-key response to an attempt to blow up an airliner and kill hundreds of people, we won't be at war. He seems to think if he gives terrorists the rights of Americans, lets them lawyer up and reads them their Miranda rights, we won't be at war."[2]

White House press secretary Robert Gibbs responded promptly by accusing Cheney of playing "the typical Washington game of pointing fingers and making political hay." But the response did nothing to stop Republican politicians and conservative commentators from keeping up a drumbeat of criticism for several weeks into the new year, focused in particular on the decision to advise Abdulmutallab of his right to remain silent and to confer with a lawyer.

The criticism appears to have been based in part on an erroneous understanding of when FBI agents advised the 21-year-old Abdulmutallab of his Miranda rights. For weeks, critics said he had been "Mirandized" within 55 minutes of his arrest. Only in mid-February did the administration release a detailed, materially different timeline.[3]

The administration's account showed that Abdulmutallab was questioned for 55 minutes and provided some

federal courts but suffering setbacks in many habeas corpus cases brought by Guantánamo prisoners.

Even with the Guantánamo and interrogation policies under attack, the Justice Department was achieving some significant successes in prosecutions that carried over from the Bush administration. The new administration sidestepped a Supreme Court test of the power to detain U.S. residents by transferring al-Marri to civilian courts in late February and securing his guilty plea in April. Also in April, Wesam al-Delaema, an Iraqi-born Dutch citizen, was given a 25-year prison sentence for planting roadside bombs aimed at U.S. troops in his native country.

Al-Delaema had fought extradition from the Netherlands and was to be returned there to serve what was expected to be a reduced sentence. The case marked the first successful prosecution for terrorist offenses against U.S. forces in Iraq.

In May, the government won convictions — after two prior mistrials — in its case against the so-called Liberty City Six (originally, Seven), who were charged with plotting to blow up the Sears Tower in Chicago and selected federal buildings. The jury in Miami convicted five of the men but acquitted a sixth. On the same day, a federal jury in New York City convicted Oussama Kassir, a information about his rights before being taken away for surgery. When he returned after the four-hour procedure — a total of nine hours after his arrest — Abdulmutallab declined to answer further questions.

Without regard to the precise timing, critics said Abdulmutallab should have been treated outside the criminal justice system to maximize his value as a source of intelligence. Former Attorney General Michael B. Mukasey said the administration had "no compulsion" to treat Abdulmutallab as a criminal defendant "and every reason to treat him as an intelligence asset to be exploited promptly." The administration claimed that Abdulmutallab did begin providing actionable intelligence after family members were brought to the United States from Nigeria, but Mukasey said the five-week time lag meant that "possibly useful information" was lost.[4]

Administration supporters noted, however, that the Bush administration handled all suspected terrorists arrested in the United States as criminal defendants with the concomitant necessity to advise them of their Miranda rights. The administration's defense was substantiated by John Ashcroft, Mukasey's predecessor as attorney general. "When you have a person in the criminal justice system, you Mirandize them," Ashcroft told a reporter for *Huffington Post* when questioned at the conservative Tea Party Conference in Washington in mid-February.[5]

U.S. Marshals Service via Getty Images

Umar Farouk Abdulmutallab, a 23-year-old Nigerian, is charged with attempting to blow up a Northwest Airlines flight as it was landing in Detroit last Christmas Day.

Administration critics appeared to say little about the precise charges brought against Abdulmutallab. He was initially charged in a criminal complaint Dec. 26 with two counts: attempting to blow up and placing an explosive device aboard a U.S. aircraft. Two weeks later, a federal grand jury in Detroit returned a more detailed indictment charging him with attempted use of a weapon of mass destruction and attempted murder of 269 people. If convicted, he faces a life sentence plus 90 years in prison. No trial date is set.

— *Kenneth Jost*

[1] Some background drawn from a well-documented Wikipedia entry: http://en.wikipedia.org/wiki/Umar_Farouk_Abdulmutallab.

[2] Mike Allen, "Dick Cheney: Barack Obama 'trying to pretend,'" *Politico*, Dec. 30, 2009, www.politico.com/news/stories/1209/31054.html, cited in Philip Elliott, "White House Hits Back at Cheney Criticism," The Associated Press, Dec. 30, 2009.

[3] Walter Pincus, "Bomb suspect was read Miranda rights nine hours after arrest," *The Washington Post*, Feb. 15, 2010, p. A6.

[4] Michael B. Mukasey, "Where the U.S. went wrong on Abdulmutallab," *The Washington Post*, Feb. 12, 2010, p. A27.

[5] Ryan Grim, "Ashcroft: 'When You Have a Person in the Criminal Justice System, You Mirandize Them,'" *Huffington Post*, Feb. 19, 2010, www.huffingtonpost.com/2010/02/19/ashcroft-when-you-have-a_n_469384.html.

Lebanese-born Swede, of attempting to establish a terrorist training camp in Oregon. Material-support charges were the major counts in both cases. Kassir was sentenced to life in September; of the six defendants in the Miami case, sentences handed down on Nov. 20 ranged from 84 to 162 months.

By summer, the Justice Department conceded that it would be late with an interim report on closing Guantánamo. In acknowledging the delay in a background briefing on July 20 — the eve of the due date for the report — administration officials claimed some progress in resettling some of the detainees but confirmed expectations to hold some of the prisoners indefinitely. The administration did release the two-page protocol from the Defense and Justice departments on prosecuting Guantánamo cases, with its stated "presumption" in favor of civilian prosecutions "where feasible." The memo outlined a variety of factors to consider in choosing between civilian courts or "reformed" military commissions. With Guantánamo dominating the coverage, the memo drew little attention.[29]

Meanwhile, federal judges in Washington, D.C., were giving mixed verdicts as more of the long-delayed habeas corpus cases by Guantánamo detainees reached

Material-Support Law Called Anti-Terror "Weapon of Choice"

Critics say the broadly written law criminalizes lawful speech.

Oussama Kassir never took up arms against U.S. forces in Afghanistan and never carried out a terrorist attack against Americans in the United States or abroad. But he is serving a life prison sentence today after a federal court jury in New York City found him guilty of attempting to establish a jihadist training camp in Oregon and distributing terrorist training materials over the Internet.

To put Kassir behind bars, federal prosecutors used a broadly written law that makes it a crime to provide "material support" — broadly defined — to any group designated by the government as a "terrorist organization." The law, first passed in 1994 and amended several times since, accounts for roughly half of the al Qaeda-related terrorism convictions since 2001, according to a study by two ex-prosecutors written for the Washington-based group Human Rights First.[1]

The material-support law is "the anti-terror weapon of choice for prosecutors," says Stephen Vladeck, a law professor at American University in Washington, D.C. "It's a lot easier to prove that a defendant provided material support to a designated terrorist organization than to prove that they actually committed a terrorist act."

Kassir, a Lebanese-born Swedish citizen, was convicted on May 12, 2009, after a three-week trial. The evidence showed he came to the United States in 1999 and bought a parcel of land in Oregon with plans to take advantage of lax U.S. gun laws to train Muslim recruits in assembling and disassembling AK-47 rifles. He also established six different Web sites and posted materials about how to make bombs and poisons.

The defense denied that Kassir conspired to train recruits and claimed the Web sites contained only readily available information. The jury deliberated less than a day before returning guilty verdicts on a total of 11 counts. U.S. District Judge John Keenan sentenced him to life imprisonment on Sept. 15.[2]

On the same day as the Kassir verdict, a federal court jury in Miami returned guilty verdicts against five of the so-called "Liberty City Six," who had been charged with plotting to blow up the Sears Tower in Chicago and selected federal buildings. In the Human Rights First report, New York lawyers Richard Zabel and James J. Benjamin Jr. note that the trial shows the importance of the material-support charge because prosecutors won convictions against only two defendants on an explosives charge and against only one defendant for seditious conspiracy.

Zabel and Benjamin, who both served in the U.S. attorney's office in New York City, say the material-support law has similarly been used to convict defendants for such actions as providing broadcasting services to a terrorist organization's television station or traveling to Pakistan for training in a jihadist camp. The law was also invoked against Lynne Stewart, a well-known defense lawyer, for transmitting messages to her terrorism-case client, Omar Abdel Rahman, the "Blind Sheik."

The law defines material support to include not only financial contributions but also any "property" or "service," including "personnel" and "training, expert advice or assistance." Medicine and religious materials are exempted.

---

decision stage.[30] In the first of the rulings after Obama took office, Judge Leon ruled on Jan. 28 that evidence of serving as a cook for al Qaeda was sufficient to hold a prisoner for "material support" of terrorism. In 14 cases over the next year, however, the government lost more — eight — than it won (six). In five of the cases granting habeas corpus, judges found the government's evidence either insufficient or unreliable. In one, the judge specifically found the government's evidence had been obtained by torture or under the taint of prior torture. In the two other cases, one of the detainees was found to have been expelled from al Qaeda, while the other was no longer a threat because he was cooperating with U.S. authorities.

Some civil liberties and humanitarian groups contend the law sweeps too broadly. Material support is defined "so expansively and vaguely as to criminalize pure speech furthering lawful, nonviolent ends," the bipartisan Constitution Project says in a recent report. The report recommends amending the law to exempt "pure speech" unless intended to further illegal conduct. It also calls for giving groups the opportunity to contest designation as a terrorist organization.[3]

Appellate courts have generally upheld broad readings of the statute. In a decision in December 2007, however, the San Francisco-based U.S. Court of Appeals for the Ninth Circuit ruled that some of the law's terms — "training," "service," and "expert advice or assistance" — were impermissibly vague or overbroad.

The ruling came in a suit filed originally in 1998 by the Humanitarian Law Project on behalf of individuals or U.S.-based groups that sought to provide assistance to two designated terrorist organizations: the Kurdistan Workers' Party in Turkey or the Liberation Tigers of Tamil Eelam in Sri Lanka. The plaintiffs claimed they wanted to counsel both groups on use of international law and nonviolent conflict resolution.

The Supreme Court agreed to hear the government's appeal of the case as well as the plaintiffs' cross-appeal of the part of the ruling that upheld a broad construction of the term "personnel." The case was argued on Feb. 23; a decision is due by the end of June.[4]

Meanwhile, a military appeals panel is weighing challenges to the use of material-support counts in military commission proceedings. The United States Court of Military Commission Review heard arguments on Jan. 26 in appeals by two of the three men convicted so far in

Oussama Kassir is serving a life sentence after a federal court jury in New York City found him guilty last year of attempting to establish a jihadist training camp in Oregon and distributing terrorist training materials over the Internet.

AFP/Getty Images/Vadim Kramer

military commissions: Salim Ahmed Hamdan, former driver for al Qaeda leader Osama bin Laden, and al Qaeda filmmaker and propagandist Ali Hamza Ahmad Suliman al Bahlul.

Hamdan, who was freed in late 2008 after about seven-and-a-half years in captivity, and al Bahlul, who was sentenced to life imprisonment, both contend that material support for terrorism is outside the military tribunals' jurisdiction because it is not a traditional war crime. The cases were argued before separate three-judge panels, which gave no indication when rulings would be expected.[5]

— Kenneth Jost

[1] Richard B. Zabel and James J. Benjamin Jr., "In Pursuit of Justice: Prosecuting Terrorism Cases in the Federal Courts," Human Rights First, May 2008, p. 32, www.humanrightsfirst.info/pdf/080521-USLS-pursuit-justice.pdf. See also by same authors "In Pursuit of Justice: Prosecuting Terrorism Cases in the Federal Courts: 2009 Update and Recent Developments," July 2009, www.humanrightsfirst.org/pdf/090723-LS-in-pursuit-justice-09-update.pdf.Background drawn from both reports.

[2] The press release by the U.S. Attorney for the Southern District of New York can be found at www.humanrightsfirst.org/pdf/090723-LS-in-pursuit-justice-09-update.pdf. See also "Man convicted in NY of trying to start terror camp," The Associated Press, May 12, 2009.

[3] "Reforming the Material Support Laws: Constitutional Concerns Presented by Prohibitions on Material Support to 'Terrorist Organizations,'" Constitution Project, Nov. 17, 2009, www.constitutionproject.org/manage/file/355.pdf.

[4] The case is *Holder v. Humanitarian Law Project*, 08-1498. For materials on the case, including links to news coverage, see SCOTUSWiki, www.scotuswiki.com/index.php?title=Holder_v._Humanitarian_Law_Project.

[5] Material in Bahlul's case can be found at www.defense.gov/news/CMCRHAMZA.html/; materials in Hamdan's case at www.defense.gov/news/commissionsHamdan.html.

In order to prevent leaks, Holder made his decision to try KSM in a federal court with little advance notice to New York City officials. He explained later to the Senate Judiciary Committee that a federal court trial would give the government "the greatest opportunity to present the strongest case in the best forum." The explanation left Republicans, conservatives and many New Yorkers unconvinced of the benefits, dismayed at the potential costs and appalled at the idea of according full legal rights to a self-proclaimed enemy of the United States. Civil liberties and human rights groups applauded the decision while giving little attention to Holder's simultaneous move to try the alleged *USS Cole* plotter and others in military commissions that the groups had called for abolishing.

The political attacks over the administration's handling of Abdulmutallab's case added to the pressure against trying KSM in New York City. Behind the scenes, Justice Department officials were looking for alternate, more remote sites for a possible civilian trial. And by February Holder was being deliberately ambiguous about whether the case would be tried in a civilian court at all.

"At the end of the day, wherever this case is tried, in whatever forum, what we have to ensure is that it's done as transparently as possible and with adherence to all the rules," Holder said on Feb. 11.[31] "If we do that, I'm not sure the location or even the forum is as important as what the world sees in that proceeding."

CURRENT SITUATION

Watching Appeals

Lawyers for the government and for Guantánamo detainees are watching the federal appeals court in Washington and a specially created military appeals panel for the next major developments on the rules for prosecuting terrorism cases.

The government scored a major victory in early January when the U.S. Circuit Court of Appeals for the District of Columbia decisively backed the government's power to detain a low-level member of a pro-Taliban brigade captured during the Afghanistan war and held at Guantánamo for more than eight years.

Later in the month, the U.S. Court of Military Commission Review heard arguments on Jan. 26 from two of the men convicted so far in the military tribunals challenging the government's power to prosecute material support for terrorism in military instead of civilian courts. Separate three-judge panels convened to hear the appeals by al Qaeda propagandist Bahlul and former bin Laden driver Hamdan gave no indication when they would rule on the cases.

With several other habeas corpus cases pending before the D.C. Circuit, the appeals court is likely to determine both the direction and the pace of the next stage of the litigation from Guantánamo prisoners, according to Brookings Institution scholar Wittes.

If other judges follow the lead of the conservative-dominated panel in the Jan. 5 decision, many of the outstanding issues regarding the government's power to hold enemy combatants could be resolved quickly, Wittes says. But different rulings by panels in other cases could add to what he calls the "cacophony" surrounding the habeas corpus cases and force the Supreme Court to intervene to resolve the conflicts.

The appeals court's decision rejected a habeas corpus petition by Ghaleb Nassar Al-Bihani, a Yemeni native who served as a cook for a Taliban brigade. He argued that he should be released because the war against the Taliban has ended and, in any event, that he was essentially a civilian contractor instead of a combatant.

In a 25-page opinion, Judge Janice Rogers Brown rejected both arguments. Brown, a strongly conservative judge appointed by President George W. Bush, said Bihani's admitted actions of accompanying the brigade to the battlefield, carrying a weapon and retreating and surrendering with the brigade showed that he was "both part of and substantially supported enemy forces."

As for the status of the war, Brown said, it was up to Congress or the president to decide whether the conflict had ended, not the courts. In a significant passage, Brown also said that U.S. instead of international law determined the president's authority to hold enemy combatants. "The international laws of war as a whole have not been implemented domestically by Congress and are therefore not a source of authority for U.S. courts," Brown wrote.

Judge Brett Kavanaugh, another Bush-appointed conservative, joined Brown's opinion. Judge Stephen Williams, who was appointed by President Ronald Reagan, agreed on the result but distanced himself from Brown's comments on the impact of international law. He noted that Brown's "dictum" — the legal term for a passage unnecessary to the decision in the case —"goes well beyond what the government has argued in the case."[32]

Wittes says the ruling is "a huge development if it stands." The appellate panel, he says, was "signaling" to the federal district court judges in Washington handling habeas corpus cases to "lighten up" on the government. District court judges have ruled against the government in somewhat over half of the cases decided so far.

The appeals court for the military commissions was created by the 2006 law overhauling the rules for the tribunals, but it had no cases to review until after Hamdan's and Bahlul's convictions in 2008.

Cole Bombing Case, Six Others Set for Tribunals

Abd al Rahim al Nashiri, the alleged mastermind of the October 2000 suicide attack on the *USS Cole*, is one of seven Guantánamo detainees designated by Attorney General Eric Holder for trial by military commissions. Seventeen U.S. sailors were killed in the attack on the warship as it lay docked in Aden, Yemen.

The Saudi-born al-Nashiri, now 45, allegedly served as al Qaeda's chief of operations in the Arabian peninsula before his capture in the United Arab Emirates in November 2002. He was held in a secret CIA prison (reportedly in Thailand) until being brought to Guantánamo in 2006.

The CIA has confirmed that al-Nashiri was waterboarded. He claims that he falsely confessed to the *Cole* attack and six other terrorist incidents as a result. It is also reported that he was the target of a mock execution by CIA interrogators.

The six other prisoners designated for trial by military commissions are:

- **Ahmed al Darbi (Saudi Arabia)** — Accused of plotting to bomb oil tankers in the Strait of Hormuz.
- **Mohammed Kamin (Afghanistan)** — Charged with planting mines in Afghanistan.
- **Omar Khadr (Canada)** — Accused of killing a U.S. soldier with a grenade in Afghanistan in 2002; Khadr was 15 at the time.
- **Noor Uthman Mohammed (Sudan)** — Charged with assisting in running al Qaeda training center.
- **Obaidullah (Afghanistan)** — Charged with possessing anti-tank mines.
- **Ibrahim al Qosi (Sudan)** — Accused of acting as Osama bin Laden's bodyguard, paymaster and supply chief.

In their appeals, both men claim that their convictions for material support for terrorism were improper because the offense is not a traditional war crime prosecutable in a military court. Bahlul also argues that the First Amendment bars prosecuting him for producing a video documentary for al Qaeda that recounts the bombing of the *USS Cole* and calls for others to join a jihad against the United States.

The government counters by citing cases from the Civil War and World War II to argue that providing support to unlawful enemy combatants has been prosecutable in military courts even if the term "material support for terrorism" was not used. As to Bahlul's free-speech argument, the government contends that the First Amendment does not apply to enemy "propaganda."[33]

Bahlul is also challenging the life sentence imposed in November 2008; Hamdan was freed later that month after being credited with the seven years he had already been held at Guantánamo.

Wittes says the government has "a big uphill climb" on the material-support issue. He notes that in the Supreme Court's 2006 decision in Hamdan's case, four of the justices questioned whether military tribunals could try a conspiracy charge, another of the generally phrased offenses the

government has used in terrorism cases. Material support for terrorism would be harder to justify, he says.

Wittes adds that it is important to resolve the issue quickly if the military commissions are to be used in other cases. "What you don't want to happen is to have a whole lot of people sentenced in military commissions and then find out that the charges are invalid," he says.

Making a Deal?

The Obama administration may be on the verge of deciding to try Khalid Sheikh Mohammed and four other alleged 9/11 conspirators in a military tribunal in an effort to gain Republican support for closing Guantánamo prison camp.

Administration officials are reportedly near to recommending that Obama reverse Attorney General Holder's Nov. 13 decision to hold the 9/11 conspiracy trial in federal court in hopes of securing support for closing Guantánamo from an influential Republican senator, South Carolina's Lindsey Graham.[34]

Graham, a former military lawyer, has strongly advocated use of military tribunals for detainees held at Guantánamo but has not joined other Republicans in attacking Obama's pledge to close the facility. GOP

Should terrorism suspects ordinarily be tried in civilian courts?

YES
Laura Olson
Senior Counsel, Rule of Law Program
Constitution Project

Written for *CQ Researcher*, March 2010

Civilian courts are the proper forum for trying terrorism cases. Trial in our traditional federal courts is a proven and reliable way to provide justice, while ensuring our national security. This is in stark contrast to the new military commissions that were re-created for the third time in the Military Commissions Act (MCA) of 2009. Like their predecessors, these new commissions remain vulnerable to constitutional challenge.

We should not place some of the most important terrorism trials, and arguably the most important criminal trials, in our nation's history in the untested and uncertain military commissions system.

Since 2001, trials in federal criminal courts have resulted in nearly 200 convictions of terrorism suspects, compared to only three low-level convictions in the military commissions. Two of those three are now free in their home countries. This record demonstrates that prosecutions in our traditional federal courts are tough on terrorists.

To date, the rules to accompany the MCA of 2009 remain to be approved. Therefore, military commission judges are without guidance on how to proceed with these cases. Meanwhile, our traditional federal courts move ahead, applying long-established rules on procedure and evidence. For example, the Classified Information Procedures Act (CIPA) elaborates the procedures by which federal courts admit evidence while protecting national security information from improper disclosure. The MCA of 2009 incorporates CIPA procedures on dealing with classified information into the military commissions system, but military judges have little or no experience with these procedures. Federal judges have worked with CIPA for the last 30 years.

Our Constitution provides a safe and effective way to prosecute terrorism suspects. In fact, Ahmed Kfalfan Ghailani, a former Guantánamo detainee, is now being held in New York City for his trial in federal court there. The judge has issued a protective order on all classified information, and there have been no reports of any increased safety risks or expenses associated with this trial.

I agree with the nearly 140 former diplomats, military officials, federal judges and prosecutors and members of Congress, as well as bar leaders, national-security and foreign-policy experts, and family members of the 9/11 attacks that signed Beyond Guantánamo: A Bipartisan Declaration. This unique and bipartisan group is in favor of trying terrorism suspects in our traditional federal courts. Federal trials are the only way to ensure swift and constitutional trials of terrorism suspects.

NO
Sen. John McCain, R-Ariz.

From statement in support of the Enemy Belligerent Interrogation, Detention and Prosecution Act, March 4, 2010

This legislation seeks to ensure that the mistakes made during the apprehension of the Christmas Day bomber, such as reading him a Miranda warning, will never happen again and put Americans' security at risk.

Specifically, this bill would require unprivileged enemy belligerents suspected of engaging in hostilities against the U.S. to be held in military custody and interrogated for their intelligence value by a "high-value detainee" interagency team established by the president. This interagency team of experts in national security, terrorism, intelligence, interrogation and law enforcement will have the protection of U.S. civilians and civilian facilities as their paramount responsibility. . . .

A key provision of this bill is that it would prohibit a suspected enemy belligerent from being provided with a Miranda warning and being told he has a right to a lawyer and a right to refuse to cooperate. I believe that an overwhelming majority of Americans agree that when we capture a terrorist who is suspected of carrying out or planning an attack intended to kill hundreds if not thousands of innocent civilians, our focus must be on gaining all the information possible to prevent that attack or any that may follow from occurring. . . . Additionally, the legislation would authorize detention of enemy belligerents without criminal charges for the duration of the hostilities consistent with standards under the law of war which have been recognized by the Supreme Court.

Importantly, if a decision is made to hold a criminal trial after the necessary intelligence information is obtained, the bill mandates trial by military commission, where we are best able to protect U.S. national security interests, including sensitive classified sources and methods, as well as the place and the people involved in the trial itself.

The vast majority of Americans understand that what happened with the Christmas Day bomber was a near catastrophe that was only prevented by sheer luck and the courage of a few of the passengers and crew. A wide majority of Americans also realize that allowing a terrorist to be interrogated for only 50 minutes before he is given a Miranda warning and told he can obtain a lawyer and stop cooperating is not sufficient. . . .

We must ensure that the broad range of expertise that is available within our government is brought to bear on such high-value detainees. This bill mandates such coordination and places the proper focus on getting intelligence to stop an attack, rather than allowing law enforcement and preparing a case for a civilian criminal trial to drive our response.

lawmakers have been pushing legislative proposals to block use of funds for closing Guantánamo or for holding the 9/11 conspiracy trial in federal court.

The administration's possible reversal on the KSM trial is drawing a heated response from civil liberties and human rights groups. The decision would "strike a blow to American values and the rule of law and undermine America's credibility," according to the ACLU.

Elisa Massimino, president and CEO of Human Rights First, says failure to support Holder's decision would set "a dangerous precedent for future national security policy."

In the wake of the strong criticism of holding the KSM trial in New York City, Justice Department lawyers and others had been reported to be holding onto the plan for a federal court trial, but in a different location. Among the sites reported to have been under consideration were somewhere else in southern New York, Northern Virginia and western Pennsylvania.[35]

Any of those sites would satisfy the constitutional requirement that trial of a federal criminal case be held in "the district wherein the crime shall have been committed." Besides the World Trade Center in New York City, the 9/11 hijackers also crashed a plane into the Pentagon in Northern Virginia and into a rural location in western Pennsylvania.

Graham, first elected to the Senate in 2002, argued during the Bush administration for a greater role for Congress in defining detention policies. Since Obama's election, he is widely reported to have formed a working relationship on several issues with White House chief of staff Rahm Emanuel, a former colleague in the House of Representatives. Emanuel was described in a flattering profile in *The Washington Post* and elsewhere as having disagreed with Obama's pledge to close Guantánamo and with Holder's decision to try KSM in federal court.[36]

Beyond the KSM trial and Guantánamo issue, Graham is continuing to call for congressional legislation to govern the handling of detention issues. "I want Congress and the administration to come up with a detainee policy that will be accepted by courts and so that the international community will understand that no one is in jail by an arbitrary exercise of executive power," Graham told *The New York Times*.[37]

As outlined, the legislation would authorize holding terrorism suspects inside the United States without charging them with a crime or advising them of Miranda rights;

FEMA News Photo/WireImage/Andrea Booher

Controversy erupted after Attorney General Eric Holder announced plans to try the five alleged 9/11 conspirators in a federal court "just blocks away from where the twin towers [of the World Trade Center] once stood." New York City Mayor Michael Bloomberg and Police Commissioner Raymond Kelly welcomed Holder's decision, but many New Yorkers expressed concern about the costs and risks of a sensational trial in Lower Manhattan.

establish standards for choosing between military or civilian court for prosecution; and authorize indefinite detention under standards subject to judicial review. Civil liberties and human rights groups remain opposed to indefinite-detention proposals.

Administration officials were quoted in news accounts as saying Obama hopes to have the KSM trial issue resolved before he begins a trip to Asia on March 18. But officials quoted in *The Washington Post* cautioned against expecting a "grand bargain" with Graham on the full range of detention issues in the near future.

OUTLOOK

Bringing Justice to Bear

When he defended the administration's decision to try Khalid Sheikh Mohammed in a civilian court, deputy national intelligence director John Brennan made clear that he expected the trial would be fair and just, but the result certain and severe.

"I'm confident that he's going to have the full weight of American justice," Brennan said on NBC's "Meet the Press" on Feb. 7. Asked by host David Gregory whether Mohammed would be executed, Brennan initially skirted the question but eventually concluded, "I'm convinced and confident that Mr. Khalid Sheikh Mohammed is going to meet his day in justice and before his maker."[38]

Despite the assurance from Brennan, Attorney General Holder and other administration officials, Americans apparently lack the same confidence in the federal court system. An ABC/*Washington Post* poll conducted in late February showed Americans favoring military over civilian trials for terrorism suspects by a margin of 55 percent to 39 percent. In a similar poll in the fall, Americans showed a statistically insignificant preference for military trials: 48 percent to 47 percent.[39]

A survey by Democratic pollsters similarly finds a majority of respondents opposed to Obama's policy on interrogation and prosecution of terrorism suspects (51 percent to 44 percent). But the survey, conducted in late February for the Democratic groups Democracy Corps and Third Way, also found majority approval of Obama's handling of "national security" (57 percent to 40 percent) and "fighting terrorism" (54 percent to 41 percent).

In a memo, leaders of the two organizations advise Obama to move the issue away from "civilian" versus "military" trials. Instead, they say the administration should "place the debate over terrorism suspects into the broader context of tough actions and significant results."[40]

Even before the memo's release, civil liberties and human rights groups were following the strategy in public lobbying of Obama as the administration was weighing where to hold the KSM trial. In a March 5 conference call for reporters arranged by Human Rights First, three retired military officers all depicted the military commissions as an unproven forum for prosecuting terrorists. "This is not ready for prime time," said Human Rights First President Massimino.

The ACLU followed with a full-page ad in the Sunday edition of *The New York Times* that compared the 300 terrorism cases "successfully handled" in the criminal justice system to "only three" in military commissions. "Our criminal justice system will resolve these cases more quickly and more credibly than the military commissions," the March 7 ad stated.

Meanwhile, former prosecutor McCarthy conceded in a speech sponsored by a college-affiliated center in Washington, "I don't think the military commission system performed well. By and large, the civilian system has performed well."

Speaking March 5 at the Kirby Center for Constitutional Studies and Citizenship at Hillsdale College in Michigan, McCarthy nevertheless reiterated that discovery procedures available to defendants argued against use of criminal prosecutions. "When you're at war, you can't be telling the enemy your most sensitive national intelligence," the *National Review* columnist said. Massimino noted, however, that a new military commissions law passed in 2009 dictates that defendants are to have access to evidence "comparable" to that provided in civilian courts.

The White House now says a decision on the KSM trial is "weeks" away. On Capitol Hill, Sen. Graham is continuing to push for a deal that would swap Republican support for closing Guantánamo for the administration's agreement to try KSM and other high-level terrorism suspects in military commissions. But Graham has yet to gain any public support for the plan from GOP colleagues.

McCarthy mocks Graham's proposed deal. He says the White House has already "stood down" on the military commissions issues and is only deferring a decision in hopes of getting GOP support for closing Guantánamo. "It makes no sense to horse-trade when Obama was being pushed toward military commissions by reality," McCarthy writes.[41]

Fellow conservative Rivkin also expects military commissions to become the norm for terrorism suspects. "My hope is that we'll come to our senses," he says. The current policies "are not consonant with the traditional law-of-war architecture, and they're not consistent with prevailing in this war."

Liberal groups continue to strongly oppose use of military commissions, but acknowledge congressional politics may determine decision-making. "There's no question that Congress has been trying to hold hostage the president's national security agenda," Massimino says.

For his part, former Assistant U.S. Attorney Benjamin doubts that military commissions will prove as useful as conservatives expect. "It would be great if the military commissions develop into a forum that works," he says. "But I have my doubts about how quickly or how smoothly that will happen."

UPDATE

The Obama administration has reluctantly bowed to Congress and given up for now any federal court prosecutions of suspected terrorists held at the U.S. Naval Base at Guantánamo Bay, Cuba. Instead, the Guantánamo detainees will be tried before military tribunals at the base.

Congress effectively blocked civilian trials for Guantánamo detainees with a provision attached to the defense authorization bill that bars bringing any Guantánamo detainee into the United States. [42]

President Obama and Attorney General Eric Holder both criticized the provision, but Holder agreed to nullify the federal court indictment of Khalid Sheikh Mohammed, the self-proclaimed architect of al-Qaida's Sept. 11, 2001, attacks on the United States. Instead, Holder on April 4 referred the conspiracy case against Mohammed and four co-defendants to the Defense Department for prosecution.

Two weeks later, military prosecutors on April 20 filed formal charges in what is likely to be the first major terrorism case to be tried in a military commission since procedural changes that Congress approved at the Obama administration's behest in 2009. Abd al-Rahim al-Nashiri was charged with murder, terrorism and other war crimes in connection with the October 2000 bombing of the *U.S.S. Cole*, which killed 17 U.S. sailors and injured 41 others.

Meanwhile, the government continued winning federal court convictions in domestic terrorism, including a guilty plea and life sentence in the case against a Pakistani immigrant for a failed car bomb attack in New York City's Times Square on May 1, 2010. Military prosecutors were also preparing a capital murder case against U.S. Army Maj. Nidal Hasan, a Muslim later linked to anti-American views, for a November 2009 shooting rampage at Fort Hood, Texas, in which 13 people were killed and 32 others wounded.

The government averted what would have been a difficult prosecutorial decision with the May 1 killing of Al-Qaida leader Osama bin Laden by U.S. Navy Seals after CIA agents tracked him to a walled compound in Abbottabad, Pakistan. The question of what kind of proceeding, if any, to institute against bin Laden, if captured alive, had been discussed but not resolved during much of the decade-long hunt. Holder, among others, had publicly predicted that bin Laden would not be captured alive. [43]

The administration was also targeting other Al-Qaida leaders abroad. Anwar Awlaki, a U.S.-born leader of Al-Qaida on the Arabian Peninsula, was the target of a missile attack from U.S. drones flying over Yemen on May 6. He escaped uninjured, but two other militants were killed. [44]

9/11 Conspiracy Trial

The 9/11 conspiracy case against Mohammed — dubbed "KSM" in news coverage — emerged as the critical test of the Obama administration's determined preference to bring terrorism cases in federal court instead of in the military commission system established under President George W. Bush.

Holder's decision in November 2009 to try KSM and four co-defendants in federal court in Manhattan touched off a political firestorm, especially among New York officials. The criticism, combined with general sentiment against affording full legal rights to suspected terrorists, led bipartisan majorities in Congress to block bringing Guantánamo detainees into the United States for trial or imprisonment.

In announcing the change of course on April 4, Holder said he stood by his original decision to bring the case in federal court but conceded that the law left him no alternative to referring the case to military prosecutors. "We simply cannot allow a trial to be delayed any longer for the victims of the 9/11 attacks or for their family members, who have waited for nearly a decade for justice," Holder said. [45]

In tandem with the announcement, the government moved in federal court in New York City to unseal the indictment previously approved by a federal grand jury against KSM and the four co-defendants and then to

A memorial recognizes the victims of a Nov. 5, 2009, shooting rampage at Fort Hood, Texas. Military prosecutors have been preparing a capital murder case against Maj. Nidal M. Hasan, a U.S. Army psychiatrist accused in the shootings.

have it dismissed. The 81-page indictment listed 10 counts — including murder, terrorism and aircraft piracy — and closed with a listing by name of the 2,976 persons killed in the attack.

Mohammed was charged in the indictment with having initially proposed to bin Laden the use of hijacked airplanes to destroy buildings. Mohammed allegedly trained the hijackers, directed their preparations and oversaw funding and logistical support for the mission.

The others named in the indictment were Walid bin Attash, charged with collecting information on airport and airplane security measures; Ramzi bin al-Shibh and Ali Abdul Azis Ali, both charged with sending money to the hijackers from abroad; and Mustafa al Hawsawi, charged with helping the hijackers travel to the United States and facilitating their efforts upon arrival. [46]

Holder said Justice Department prosecutors had worked with Defense Department lawyers in preparing the case and would continue to assist in preparations for the military commission. By mid-May, no charges had been brought in the military system.

U.S.S. Cole Bombing Trial

Nashiri was accused in the April 20 charges of directing the planning and preparation for the bombing of the *Cole* as it lay in the Port of Aden, Yemen, on Oct. 12, 2000. He was also charged with similar roles in an attempted attack on a second U.S. warship, the *U.S.S.*

The Sullivans, on Jan. 3, 2000, and an attack on a French civilian oil tanker on Oct. 6, 2002. The attack on the tanker killed a crew member and spilled about 90,000 gallons of oil into the Gulf of Aden. [47]

Along with the 9/11 case, the Nashiri charges refocused attention on the military commission system after a period of near dormancy under the Obama administration. The administration suspended prosecutions in the military system as it sought and won enactment of procedural reforms in the Military Commissions Act of 2009.

In 2010, military prosecutors secured guilty pleas and substantial sentences in two cases before military commissions. Ibrahim Ahmed Mahmoud al-Qosi, bin Laden's former bodyguard, pleaded guilty on July 7 to one count of providing material support for terrorism and was sentenced to 14 years in prison. Omar Khadr pleaded guilty on Oct. 26 to five counts, including murder and material support for terrorism, in connection with the killing of a U.S. serviceman during a firefight in July 2002; Khadr, 15 at the time of his capture, was sentenced to an additional eight years' imprisonment.

The sworn charges against Nashiri were submitted to a retired military lawyer, Bruce MacDonald, who assumed the position of "convening authority" for the military commissions in late March 2010. MacDonald is to decide what charges, if any, to refer for trial and to appoint commission members.

Both the Nashiri and KSM trials will present issues arising from the detention and coercive interrogation of both men in secret CIA prisons before their transfers to Guantánamo. Mohammed was subjected to waterboarding; Nashiri was waterboarded and also subjected to a mock execution in which CIA operatives held a power drill and gun to his head.

Domestic Terrorism Cases

With the military commission system only beginning to gear up at Guantánamo, Justice Department prosecutors have been winning significant terrorism-related convictions in civilian courts in the United States, including cases against U.S. citizens. [48]

In the most recent major cases, Farooque Ahmed, a naturalized U.S. citizen born in Pakistan, was sentenced to 23 years in prison after pleading guilty in federal court in Alexandria, Va., to two terrorism-related counts for conspiracy to bomb Washington, D.C.-area subway stations. Ahmed plotted the bombings with men he thought were Al-Qaida operatives but were actually government agents. In court, Ahmed admitted that he wanted "to kill as many Americans as possible." [49]

Earlier, Faisal Shahzad, also a Pakistani-born naturalized U.S. citizen, was given a life sentence on Oct. 5, 2010, for attempting to detonate a car bomb in New York City's Times Square on May 1. Shahzad, describing himself as a "Muslim soldier," had pleaded guilty in federal court in New York on June 21 to 10 counts. Shahzad had built the bomb on his own; it failed to detonate.

The government won a less impressive victory on Nov. 17, 2010, when a federal court jury in New York City convicted Ahmed Khalfan Ghailani of only one of more than 280 counts stemming from the 1998 bombings of U.S. embassies in Kenya and Tanzania. Ghailani, so far the only Guantánamo detainee to be tried in a civilian court, was sentenced on Jan. 25 to life imprisonment. [50]

Still awaiting trial is Umar Farouk Abdulmutallab, the so-called "Underwear Bomber," who was arrested on Dec. 25, 2009, for attempting to detonate plastic explosives hidden in his underwear while on a flight from Amsterdam to Detroit. A federal grand jury in Detroit indicted Abdulmutallab on Jan. 6, 2010, on six counts, including attempted murder and attempted use of a weapon of mass destruction. In September 2010, he fired his court-appointed counsel and was given permission to represent himself. [51]

Meanwhile, Hasan is awaiting a decision by the commander of Fort Hood on whether his capital trial will be held at the base or elsewhere. Hasan's military lawyer says the Army psychiatrist cannot receive a fair trial at the base. Hasan presented no defense at a so-called Article 32 hearing — akin to a grand jury proceeding, but open to the public — held in October and November 2010. The hearing ended with a recommendation by the presiding officer that Hasan be tried on 13 counts of murder and 32 counts of attempted murder. [52]

NOTES

1. Some background information drawn from Farhan Bokhari, *et al.*, "The CEO of al-Qaeda," *Financial Times*, Feb. 15, 2003. See also the Wikipedia entry on Khalid Sheikh Mohammed and sources cited there, http://en.wikipedia.org/wiki/Khalid_Sheikh_Mohammed.

2. Quoted in Devlin Barnett, "NYC trial of 9/11 suspects faces legal risks," The Associated Press, Nov. 14, 2009. For Holder's prepared remarks, see U.S. Department of Justice, "Attorney General Announces Forum Decisions for Guantánamo Detainees," Nov. 13, 2009, www.justice.gov/ag/speeches/2009/ag-speech-091113.html.

3. Quoted in Carrie Johnson, "Holder Answers to 9/11 Relatives About Trials in U.S.," *The Washington Post*, Nov. 19, 2009, p. A3. See also Charlie Savage, "Holder Defends Decision to Use U.S. Court for 9/11 Trial," *The New York Times*, Nov. 19, 2009, p. A18.

4. See Anne E. Kornblut and Carrie Johnson, "Obama to help pick location of terror trial," *The Washington Post*, Feb. 12, 2010, p. A1.

5. For background, see these *CQ Researcher* reports: Kenneth Jost, "Closing Guantánamo," Feb. 27, 2009, pp. 177-200; Peter Katel and Kenneth Jost, "Treatment of Detainees," Aug. 25, 2006, pp. 673-696; and Kenneth Jost, "Civil Liberties Debates," Oct. 24, 2003, pp. 893-916.

6. "FY 2009 Budget and Performance Summary: Part One: Summary of Request and Performance," U.S. Department of Justice, www.justice.gov/jmd/2009summary/html/004_budget_highlights.htm. See also Mark Hosenball, "Terror Prosecution Statistics Criticized by GOP Were Originally Touted by Bush Administration," *Declassified* blog, Feb. 9, 2010, http://blog.newsweek.com/blogs/declassified/archive/2010/02/09/terror-prosecution-statistics-criticized-by-gop-were-originally-touted-by-bush-administration.aspx.

7. Richard B. Zabel and James J. Benjamin Jr., "In Pursuit of Justice: Prosecuting Terrorism Cases in the Federal Courts: 2009 Update and Recent Developments," Human Rights First, July 2009, www.humanrightsfirst.org/pdf/090723-LS-in-pursuit-justice-09-update.pdf. See also by the same authors, "In Pursuit of Justice: Prosecuting Terrorism Cases in the Federal Courts," Human Rights First, May 2008, www.humanrightsfirst.info/pdf/080521-USLS-pursuit-justice.pdf.

8. Andy McCarthy, "No Civilian Trial — In NYC or Anywhere Else," *Conservative Blog Watch*, Jan. 30, 2010, www.conservativeblogwatch.com/2010/01/30/no-civilian-trial-in-nyc-or-anywhere-by-andy-mccarthy.

9. See Benjamin Weiser, "A Top Terrorism Prosecutor Turns Critic of Civilian Trials," *The New York Times*, Feb. 20, 2010, p. A1.

10. See Del Quentin Wilber, " '08 habeas ruling may snag Obama plans," *The Washington Post*, Feb. 13, 2010, p. A2.

11. The defendants and their respective sentences were Mukhtar Al-Bakri and Yahya Goba (10 years each), Sahim Alwan (9-1/2 years), Shafal Mosed and Yaseinn Taher (eight years each) and Faysal Galab (seven years). For a full account, see Matthew Purdy and Lowell Bergman, "Where the Trail Led: Between Evidence and Suspicion, Unclear Danger: The Lackawanna Terror Case," *The New York Times*, Oct. 12, 2003, sec. 1, p. 1. See also Lou Michel, "Lackawanna officials say troops in city was bad idea," *Buffalo News*, July 26, 2009, p. A1.

12. *In Pursuit of Justice, op. cit.*, p. 2; *In Pursuit of Justice: 2009 Update, op. cit.*, p. 2.

13. Quoted in Bruce Golding, "Holder tours federal courthouse ahead of 9/11 terror trial," *The New York Post*, Dec. 9, 2009.

14. See Peter Finn, "The boy from the battlefield," *The Washington Post*, Feb. 10, 2010, p. A1.

15. "Remarks by the President on National Security," National Archives, May 21, 2009, www.whitehouse.gov/the_press_office/Remarks-by-the-President-On-National-Security-5-21-09/. For coverage, see Sheryl Gay Stolberg, "Obama Would Move Some Terror Detainees to U.S.," *The New York Times*, May 22, 2009, p. A1.

16. Department of Defense comments on the study are at www.defense.gov/Transcripts/Transcript.aspx?TranscriptID=4340. See also Joseph Williams and Bryan Bender, "Obama Changes US Course on Treatment of Detainees," *The Boston Globe*, Jan. 23, 2009, p. A1. See Mark Denbeaux, Joshua Denbeaux and R. David Gratz, "Released Guantánamo Detainees and the Department of Defense: Propaganda by the Numbers?," Jan. 15, 2009, http://law.shu.edu/publications/GuantánamoReports/propaganda_numbers_11509.pdf.

17. The case is 542 U.S. 507 (2004). For an account, see Kenneth Jost, *Supreme Court Yearbook 2003-2004*, CQ Press.

18. Benjamin Wittes, Robert Chesney and Rabea Benhalim, "The Emerging Law of Detention: The Guantánamo Habeas Cases as Lawmaking," Brookings Institution, Jan. 22, 2010, www.brookings.edu/papers/2010/0122_Guantánamo_wittes_chesney.aspx. See Benjamin Wittes and Robert Chesney, "Piecemeal detainee policy," *The Washington Post*, Jan. 27, 2010, p. A17.

19. Chisun Lee, "Judges Urge Congress to Act on Indefinite Detention," *ProPublica*, Jan. 22, 2010, www.propublica.org/feature/judges-urge-congress-to-act-on-indefinite-terrorism-detentions-122. Walton, an appointee of President George W. Bush, was joined in the interview by Chief Judge Royce Lamberth, an appointee of President Ronald Reagan, and Judge Ricardo Urbina, an appointee of President Bill Clinton.

20. David Cole, "Detainees: still a matter for judges," *The Washington Post*, Feb. 9, 2010, p. A16.

21. Background drawn in part from Jennifer K. Elsea, "Terrorism and the Law of War: Trying Terrorists as War Criminals before Military Commissions," Congressional Research Service, Dec. 11, 2001, www.fas.org/irp/crs/RL31191.pdf. See also Louis Fisher, *Military Tribunals and Presidential Power: American Revolution to the War on Terrorism* (2005). Wittes's quote is from his book *Law and the Long War: The Future of Justice in the Age of Terror* (2008), p. 42.

22. The decision is *Ex parte Milligan*, 71 U.S. 2 (1866). *The New York Times'* contemporaneous account is reprinted in Kenneth Jost, *The New York Times on the Supreme Court 1857-2006* (2009), CQ Press, pp. 58-59.

23. The citation is 317 U.S. 1 (1942). The opinion was issued on Oct. 29, almost three months after the July 31 decision. The rulings on the curfew and internments are *Hirabayashi v. United States*, 320

U.S. 81 (1943), and *Korematsu v. United States*, 323 U.S. 214 (1944).

24. Joseph P. Fried, "Sheik Sentenced to Life in Prison in Bombing Plot," *The New York Times*, Jan. 18, 1996, p. A1, and Christopher S. Wren, "Jury Convicts 3 in a Conspiracy to Bomb Airliners," *The New York Times*, Sept. 6, 1996, p. A1. See also Benjamin Weiser, "Judge Upholds Conviction in '93 Bombing," *The New York Times*, April 5, 2003, p. A1.

25. Accounts drawn from *Pursuit of Justice* (2008), *op. cit.*, supplemented by Wikipedia entries or contemporaneous news coverage.

26. The decision is *Hamdan v. Rumsfeld*, 548 U.S. 557 (2006). For an account, see Kenneth Jost, *Supreme Court Yearbook 2005-2006*, CQ Press.

27. U.S. Department of Justice, "Fact Sheet: Justice Department Counter-Terrorism Efforts Since 9/11," Sept. 11, 2008, www.justice.gov/opa/pr/2008/September/08-nsd-807.html.

28. The Supreme Court decision is *Boumediene v. Bush*, 553 U.S. — — (2008). For an account, see Kenneth Jost, *Supreme Court Yearbook 2007-2008*, CQ Press. For Leon's decision granting habeas corpus to five of the six prisoners, see "Emerging Law of Detention," *op. cit.*, p. 99; William Glaberson, "Judge Declares Five Detainees Held Illegally," *The New York Times*, Nov. 21, 2008, p. A1.

29. See Peter Finn, "Report on U.S. Detention Policy Will Be Delayed," *The Washington Post*, July 21, 2009, p. A2.

30. For summaries of individual cases, see "Emerging Law of Detention," *op. cit.*, appendix II, pp. 88-105.

31. Quoted in Kornblut and Johnson, *op. cit.*

32. The decision is *Al Bihani v. Obama*, D.C. Cir., Jan. 5, 2010, http://pacer.cadc.uscourts.gov/docs/common/opinions/201001/09-5051-1223587.pdf. For coverage, see Del Quentin Wilber, "Court upholds ruling to detain Yemeni suspect," *The Washington Post*, Jan. 6, 2010, p. A3.

33. Material in Bahlul's case can be found at www.defense.gov/news/CMCRHAMZA.html/; materials in Hamdan's case had not been posted by the deadline for this report.

34. See Anne E. Kornblut and Peter Finn, "Obama aides near reversal on 9/11 trial," *The Washington Post*, March 5, 2010, p. A1; Charlie Savage, "Senator Proposes Deal on Handling of Detainees," *The New York Times*, March 4, 2010, p. A12.

35. Richard A. Serrano, "Experts make case for N.Y. terror trial," *Los Angeles Times*, March 3, 2010, p. A12.

36. Jason Horwitz, "Obama's 'enforcer' may also be his voice of reason," *The Washington Post*, March 2, 2010, p. A1.

37. Savage, *op. cit.* (March 4).

38. Transcript: www.msnbc.msn.com/id/35270673/ns/meet_the_press//.

39. http://blogs.abcnews.com/thenumbers/2010/03/911-and-military-tribunals.html

40. "The Politics of National Security: A Wake-Up Call," Democracy Corps/Third Way, March 8, 2010, www.democracycorps.com/strategy/2010/03/the-politics-of-national-security-a-wake-up-call/?section=Analysis. The memo was signed by Stanley B. Greenberg, James Carville and Jeremy Rosner of Democracy Corps, and Jon Cowan, Matt Bennett and Andy Johnson of Third Way.

41. Andrew McCarthy, "Hold the Champagne on Military Commissions — It's a Head Fake," *The Corner*, March 5, 2010, http://corner.nationalreview.com.

42. For previous coverage, see Kenneth Jost, "Closing Guantánamo: Update," *CQ Researcher*, March 15, 2011.

43. See "Testy words over fate of bin Laden," The Associated Press, March 17, 2010. Holder made the remark to the House Appropriations Justice Subcommittee. Appearing before the Senate Judiciary Committee four weeks later, Holder somewhat softened the prediction. "We hope to capture him and interrogate him," Holder said. But, he added, "It is highly unlikely he will be taken alive." See Michael Muskal, "Civilian Sept. 11 trial still possible," *Los Angeles Times*, April 15, 2011, p. A8.

44. For coverage, see David S. Cloud, "Cleric was target of U.S. strike," *Los Angeles Times*, May 7, 2011, p. A1.

45. U.S. Department of Justice, "Statement of the Attorney General on the Prosecution of the 9/11 Conspirators," April 4, 2011, www.justice.gov/iso/opa/ag/speeches/2011/ag-speech-110404.html. For coverage, see Charlie Savage, "In a Reversal, Military Trials for 9/11 Cases," *The New York Times*, April 5, 2011, p. A1.

46. The indictment and motion to dismiss the indictment were posted to a national security law listserv maintained by Robert Chesney, a law professor at the University of Texas-Austin: https://webspace.utexas.edu/rmc2289/KSM%20S14%20Indictment%20%282%29.pdf; https://webspace.utexas.edu/rmc2289/Nolle%20and%20Unsealing%20Order%20-%204-4-11.pdf.

47. Department of Defense, "DOD Announces Charges Sworn Against Detainee Nashiri," April 20, 2011, www.defense.gov/releases/release.aspx?releaseid=14424; sworn charge sheet: www.defense.gov/news/20110420_Sworn_Charge_Sheet.pdf. For coverage, see Peter Finn, "Guantánamo detainee faces capital charges in Cole attack," *The Washington Post*, April 21, 2011, p. A3; Richard Serrano, "U.S. revives Guantánamo tribunal," *Los Angeles Times*, April 21, 2011, p. 8.

48. For background, see Peter Katel, "Homegrown Jihadists," *CQ Researcher*, Sept. 3, 2010, pp. 701-724.

49. See Dana Hedgepath, "Va. man gets 23 years in bombing plot," *The Washington Post*, April 12, 2011, p. B1.

50. Geraldine Baum and Richard Serrano, "Life term in embassy bombings," *Los Angeles Times*, Jan. 26, 2011, p. A10; Benjamin Weiser, "U.S. Jury Acquits Former Detainee of Most Charges," *The New York Times*, Nov. 18, 2011, p. A1.

51. See Charlie Savage, "Nigerian Man Is Indicted in Attempted Plane Attack," *The New York Times*, Jan. 7, 2010, p. A14. Other information from Wikipedia entry.

52. See David Zucchino, "Death penalty recommended in Ft. Hood attack," *Los Angeles Times*, Nov. 18, 2010, p. A21; "Ft. Hood suspect's lawyers decline to put on a defense," *ibid.*, Nov. 16, 2010, p. A7.

BIBLIOGRAPHY

Books

Fisher, Louis, *Military Tribunals and Presidential Power: American Revolution to the War on Terrorism*, University of Kansas Press, 2005.
The veteran separation-of-powers specialist at the Library of Congress examines the development of the president's wartime authority in legal matters. Includes chapter notes, 10-page bibliography and list of cases.

Wittes, Benjamin, *Law and the Long War: The Future of Justice in the Age of Terror*, Penguin Press, 2008.
A leading researcher on national security at the Brookings Institution provides a critical examination of detention and interrogation policies along with his arguments for Congress to pass legislation to authorize administrative detention of suspected enemy combatants and to create a national security court to try terrorism cases. Includes detailed notes. Wittes is also editor of *Legislating the War on Terror: An Agenda for Reform* (Brookings, 2009).

Yoo, John, *War by Other Means: An Insider's Account of the War on Terror*, Kaplan, 2005.
Yoo, a law professor at the University of California-Berkeley who served as deputy assistant attorney general for the Office of Legal Counsel during the George W. Bush administration, provides a combative account of his role in detention and interrogation policies and a strong argument for presidential wartime powers vis-à-vis Congress and the courts. Includes detailed notes. Yoo's other books include *Crisis and Command: The History of Executive Power from Washington to George W. Bush* (Kaplan, 2009); and *The Powers of War and Peace: Foreign Affairs and the Constitution after 9/11* (University of Chicago (2005).

Articles

Mayer, Jane, "The Trial," *The New Yorker*, Feb. 5, 2010, www.newyorker.com/reporting/2010/02/15/100215fa_fact_mayer.
The magazine's prolific staff writer details the legal reasoning behind, and political implications of, Attorney General Eric Holder's decision to prosecute Khalid Sheikh Mohammed and four other alleged 9/11 conspirators in a civilian court instead of a military tribunal.

Reports and Studies

Elsea, Jennifer K., "Comparison of Rights in Military Commission Trials and Trials in Federal Criminal Courts," *Congressional Research Service*, Nov. 19, 2009, http://assets.opencrs.com/rpts/R40932_20091119.pdf.
The 23-page report provides a side-by-side comparison of the rights accorded to defendants respectively in federal criminal courts under general federal law or in military commissions under the Military Commissions Act of 2009. Elsea, a legislative attorney with CRS, also wrote two previous reports on military commissions: "The Military Commissions Act of 2006 (MCA): Background and Proposed Amendments" (Sept. 8, 2009), http://assets.opencrs.com/rpts/R40752_2009 0908.pdf; and "Terrorism and the Law of War: Trying Terrorists as War Criminals before Military Commissions" (Dec. 11, 2001), www.fas.org/irp/crs/RL31191.pdf.

Laguardia, Francesca, Terrorist Trial Report Card: September 11, 2001-September 11, 2009, *Center on Law and Security, New York University School of Law*, January 2010, www.lawandsecurity.org/publications/TTRCFinalJan14.pdf.
The series of reports studies data from federal terrorism prosecutions in the post-9/11 years and analyzes trends in the government's legal strategies.

Wittes, Benjamin, Robert Chesney and Rabea Benhalim, "The Emerging Law of Detention: The Guantánamo Habeas Cases as Lawmaking," *Brookings Institution*, Jan. 22, 2010, www.brookings.edu/papers/2010/0122_guantanamo_wittes_chesney.aspx.
The comprehensive report examines and identifies unsettled issues in decisions by federal courts in Washington, D.C., in several dozen habeas corpus cases filed by Guantánamo detainees. Wittes is a senior scholar and Benhalim a legal fellow at Brookings; Chesney is a law professor at the University of Texas-Austin.

Zabel, Richard B., and James J. Benjamin Jr., "In Pursuit of Justice: Prosecuting Terrorism Cases in the Federal Courts: 2009 Update and Recent Developments," *Human Rights First*, July 2009, www.humanrightsfirst.org/pdf/090723-LS-in-pursuit-justice-09-update.pdf.
The 70-page report by two New York City lawyers who formerly served as federal prosecutors finds federal courts to have a "track record of serving as an effective and fair tool for incapacitating terrorists." The report updates the authors' original, 171-page report, "In Pursuit of Justice: Prosecuting Terrorism Cases in the Federal Courts" (May 2008), www.humanrightsfirst.info/pdf/080521-USLS-pursuit-justice.pdf.

On the Web

Two newspapers — *The New York Times* and *The Miami Herald* — maintain Web sites with comprehensive information on Guantánamo detainees: http://projects.nytimes.com/guantanamo and www.miamiherald.com/guantanamo/. The Pentagon maintains a Web site on military commissions: www.defense.gov/news/courtofmilitarycommissionreview.html.

For More Information

American Civil Liberties Union, 125 Broad St., 18th Floor, New York, NY 10004; (212) 549-2500; www.aclu.org. Advocates for individual rights and federal civilian trials for suspected terrorists.

Brookings Institution, 1775 Massachusetts Ave., N.W., Washington, DC 20036; (202) 797-6000; www.brookings .edu. Public policy think tank focusing on foreign policy and governance.

Constitution Project, 1200 18th St., N.W., Suite 1000, Washington, DC 20036; (202) 580-6920; www.constitutionproject.org. Promotes bipartisan consensus on significant constitutional and legal issues.

Foundation for Defense of Democracies, P.O. Box 33249, Washington, DC 20033; (202) 207-0190; www.defend

democracy.org. Nonpartisan policy institute dedicated to promoting pluralism, defending democratic values and opposing ideologies that threaten democracy.

Human Rights First, 333 Seventh Ave., 13th Floor, New York, NY 10001; (212) 845 5200; www.humanrightsfirst .org. Advocates for the U.S. government's full participation in international human rights laws.

National Institute of Military Justice, Washington College of Law, American University, 4801 Massachusetts Ave., N.W., Washington, DC 20016; (202) 274-4322; www.wcl.american .edu/nimj. Promotes the fair administration of justice in the military system.

7

Future of Globalization

Reed Karaim

Vietnamese workers in Vietnam's Mekong Delta region process shrimp bound for American dinner plates. International trade has tumbled dramatically since the current recession began, declining by margins not seen since the Great Depression. Some economists suggest international trade is entering an era of "deglobalization" — a sustained retreat from global trade and economic integration fed by increasingly nationalistic policies and rising protectionism.

From *CQ Researcher*,
September, 2009.

I n a two-bedroom Mumbai apartment in 1982, young entrepreneurs Ashank Desai and two partners launched Mastek, one of India's first software companies. Today, its nearly 4,000 employees handle information-technology operations for firms around the world, many in the United States and the United Kingdom.

If Mastek is a symbol of the outsourcing phenomenon sweeping the global workplace, Caterpillar embodies the traditional, heavy manufacturing that first made America an economic powerhouse. Catepillar's big, yellow "Cats" — backhoes, bulldozers and loaders — are still ubiquitous in the United States, but these days two-thirds of Caterpillar's business comes from foreign sales.

Mastek and Caterpillar, in fact, are both examples of modern, highly globalized firms. And both companies are dealing with a world economy that looks far different than it did two years ago.

In the wake of the global recession, international trade has fallen off a cliff, tumbling by margins not seen since the Great Depression. The falloff, combined with other factors, has led some economists and historians to suggest international trade is entering an era of "deglobalization" — a sustained retreat from global trade and economic integration fed by increasingly nationalistic policies and rising protectionism. The result, they say, will increase not only economic stress but also political tensions around the world. International sales and profits have tumbled at both Mastek and Caterpillar in the last year. But as officials at the two firms contemplate the future, they see two scenarios. From India, where the economy has continued growing despite the downturn, Desai is optimistic the "Great Recession," will end within a year.

Trillion-dollar 'Club' Has Three Members

Germany, China and the United States export more than $1 trillion worth of goods and services, according to the most recent data available from the Central Intelligence Agency. Eight countries export more than $400 billion in goods.

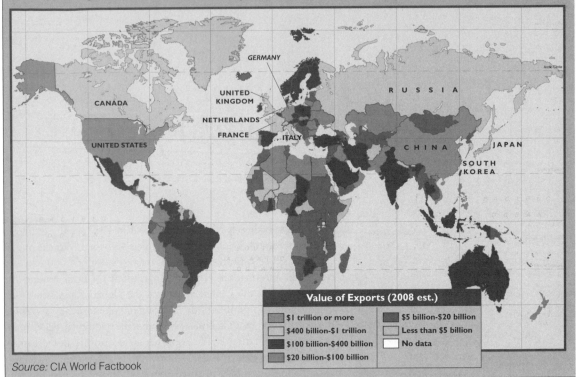

Value of Exports (2008 est.)

- $1 trillion or more
- $400 billion-$1 trillion
- $100 billion-$400 billion
- $20 billion-$100 billion
- $5 billion-$20 billion
- Less than $5 billion
- No data

Source: CIA World Factbook

"If that happens," he says, "I don't think things will change much. We'll get back to where we were."

But from his office in Washington, Bill Lane, Caterpillar's director of governmental affairs, sees more cause for concern. "There's increasing evidence that the world could be turning inward," Lane says, "and where you will see that first is in countries embracing protectionist measures. Some of that's already happening."

Analysts who believe deglobalization lies ahead say it is being driven by more than just the recession. "Two phenomena are overlapping," says Harold James, a British professor of history and international affairs at Princeton University. "One is a crisis in the financial system that drove global integration over the past four decades; the other is worry about the character of globalization itself and a backlash against it. I think the

financial crisis is the tipping point that moved things in the direction of deglobalization, but there were already substantial pressures pushing in that direction."

In a recent article James became one of the first scholars to suggest the trade collapse heralds something more lasting.[1] Other economic analysts support his view, as do many longtime critics of globalization, but for different reasons.

James' theory — also laid out in his soon-to-be-published book *The Creation and Destruction of Value: The Globalization Cycle* — has its skeptics. "If you see globalization as primarily a matter of trade flows, then, yes, it has slowed down," says Moisés Naím, editor of *Foreign Policy* magazine. "But it's really a web of interactions between institutions and individuals in a whole variety of arenas. I see it as a political and technological revolution that's essentially irreversible."

Deglobalization undoubtedly would represent a sea change in the course of history. Since World War II, global trade has grown steadily, spurred by a Western political consensus that trade promotes both peace and prosperity. In the last two decades, this process has accelerated dramatically, with China, India and other emerging economies becoming aggressive players in global markets.

But the World Trade Organization (WTO), which monitors world trade, is now predicting global trade will contract by 10 percent in 2009. [2] Other forecasts are even bleaker. The Organisation for Economic Co-operation and Development (OECD), a group of 30 nations working to promote democracy and open markets, predicts a 16 percent falloff in world trade this year.[3]

Global trade is declining faster than at the beginning of the Great Depression, according to Kevin O'Rourke, a professor of economics at Trinity College in Dublin, Ireland, and Barry Eichengreen, a professor of economics and political science at the University of California, Berkeley.

They examined a host of factors, such as industrial output and stock market levels, and concluded that the downturn is, in fact, another depression.[4] Of all the indicators, "the one that really stands out is the world trade index. It is clearly falling more rapidly than world trade in the Great Depression," says O'Rourke. "It's really the most alarming aspect of the day."

The Depression was the last great era of deglobalization, with disastrous worldwide economic and political consequences. But while O'Rourke sees many similarities between the Great Depression and today's collapse, he is careful to point out that the current governmental responses have been very different.

In the 1930s, countries around the world retreated behind tariffs and other trade barriers, led by the protectionist Smoot-Hawley Tariff Act of 1930 in the United States. "There have been some protectionist actions here and there, but there's nothing dramatic like what happened in the '30s," says O'Rourke, who considers it an "open question" whether a period of deglobalization is coming.

Economists are perhaps most alarmed by the fact that world trade has fallen more precipitously than the overall global economy has contracted, suggesting

The World's Top 20 Exporters		
Rank	Country	Exports
		In $billions (2008 est.)
1	Germany	$1,500.0
2	People's Republic of China	$1,400.0
3	United States	$1,300.0
4	Japan	$776.8
5	France	$761.0
6	Italy	$566.1
7	Netherlands	$537.5
8	Russia	$476.0
9	United Kingdom	$468.7
10	Canada	$461.8
11	South Korea	$419.0
12	Belgium	$372.9
—	Hong Kong*	$362.1
13	Saudi Arabia	$311.1
14	Mexico	$294.0
15	Spain	$292.8
16	Republic of China (Taiwan)	$255.7
17	Singapore	$235.8
18	United Arab Emirates	$207.7
19	Brazil	$200.0
20	Malaysia	$195.7

*Listed separately from mainland China

Source: CIA World Factbook

strongly that something more fundamental is occurring.

However, an analysis by Joseph Francois, an economics professor at Johannes Kepler University in Linz, Austria, indicates the decline is not as out of line as it appears. Rather, Francois says, trade has fallen off most sharply in those sectors that have been hardest hit by the recession, such as automobiles, machinery and tools.[5]

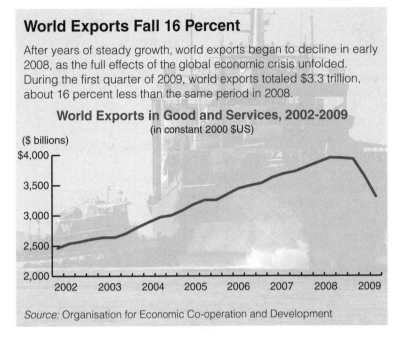

World Exports Fall 16 Percent

After years of steady growth, world exports began to decline in early 2008, as the full effects of the global economic crisis unfolded. During the first quarter of 2009, world exports totaled $3.3 trillion, about 16 percent less than the same period in 2008.

World Exports in Good and Services, 2002-2009
(in constant 2000 $US)

Source: Organisation for Economic Co-operation and Development

Leaders of the industrialized nations, known as the G-20, met in Washington in November and vowed not to repeat the protectionist mistakes made during the Great Depression. [6] By February, however, a World Bank study found that between October 2008 and February 2009 at least 17 of the G-20 nations had implemented 47 protectionist measures at the expense of other countries, and more were proposed. [7]

Still, protectionist impulses have been largely contained so far, most economists note. "Even if you look at the 'surge' in trade remedies, they don't really cover a lot of trade," says Francois. "These actions are like steam valves, allowing governments to blow off some of the protectionist pressure they're feeling, while still maintaining the basic system."

But to globalization's longtime critics, the world economic order is collapsing from the weight of its own excesses and inequities. "The whole idea that we've got a free market is a misnomer, because it's actually bound by rules that protect corporate power and not the rights of people," says David Korten, author of the new book *Agenda for a New Economy: From Phantom Wealth to Real Wealth.*

Until now the anti-globalization movement — a loose coalition of disparate groups, ranging from anarchists to union members seeking labor protections in international trade agreements — has been unable to derail the political consensus favoring expanded trade. Now, however, those who see deglobalization on the horizon worry that anti-globalization sentiment and other political pressures could usher in a new world order characterized by greater international tension and conflict.

"I'm absolutely convinced that eras of deglobalization are much more destructive and difficult for people living in them than periods of globalization," says Princeton's James. He doesn't see the world economy getting back to normal anytime soon.

As analysts study the global economy, here are some of the questions they are trying to answer:

Does rising protectionism threaten global economic recovery?

Some analysts worry that recently adopted protectionist measures may signal that more protectionism is on the way.

James says last November's G-20 meeting reminded him of the World Economic Conference organized by the League of Nations in 1927, in which the major industrial nations pledged to reduce tariffs — a proclamation that proved empty after the global economy crashed. He sees a similar hollowness to the G-20 declaration.

The G-20 "vowed to stand by free trade, and within a day or so Russia imposed a whole series of tariffs on automobiles, and India imposed a whole set of protectionist regulations," he says. "It was a kind of political verbiage that was disconnected from what immediately happened."

But Douglas Irwin, a Dartmouth College professor specializing in trade history, believes international structures now in place will prevent a tariff war like the one that broke out in the 1930s. "We have the World Trade Organization," he says, "and in previous times, most notably the Depression, there wasn't such an organization, and it wasn't clear you'd be retaliated against if you took protectionist action. Today, it's very clear that if you violate a rule, you are going to be penalized."

Jaime Daremblum, a Costa Rican author of several works on economics and former ambassador to the United States, notes that much of world trade nowadays is governed through regional pacts, such as the North American Free Trade Agreement (NAFTA).[8] Although trade issues can still flare up, he says, larger trading blocs created through regional agreements like the European Union or NAFTA have "taken a lot of trade off the table," when it comes to retaliatory battles.

But other analysts see a threat from so-called soft, or indirect, protectionism. "It's protectionism with a smile," says Caterpillar's Lane. "In today's world, no one will give a speech openly promoting protectionism and isolationism, but they will support policies that have the same effect." Soft protectionism includes industrial policies that favor domestic companies or shield them from larger economic forces, such as the original "Buy American" provisions in the U.S. stimulus package, which mandated that U.S. materials be used for any public-works projects funded by the act.[9]

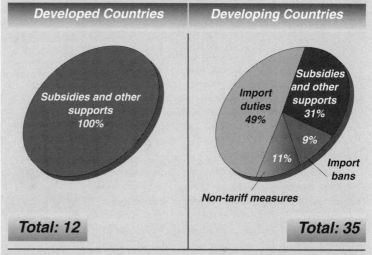

Crisis Triggers Protectionist Measures

Developed and developing nations implemented 47 protectionist measures during the height of the global economic crisis last winter. Developed countries adopted subsidies totaling $48 billion worldwide. Developing countries adopted a variety of measures, including import duties and subsidies. Russia raised tariffs on used autos, and Argentina used non-tariff measures, such as imposing licensing requirements on textiles, TVs, toys and shoes.

Types of Trade Protections Implemented
(October 2008-February 2009)

Developed Countries | **Developing Countries**

Subsidies and other supports 100%

Import duties 49%

Subsidies and other supports 31%

9%

11%

Import bans

Non-tariff measures

Total: 12

Total: 35

Source: "Trade Protection: Incipient but Worrisome Trends," The World Bank, March 2, 2009

Nearly all of the stimulus packages passed by Western industrial nations in response to the recession included some protectionist measures, notes Austin Hughes, chief economist for KBC Bank Ireland. He considers indirect protectionism one of the threats to economic recovery. "It's almost inevitable, really," Hughes says, "that as governments get more involved in bailing out sectors of their economy, they become more susceptible to this sort of thing."

The German stimulus plan, for example, is "designed to primarily benefit the German auto industry," according to *Der Spiegel*, the leading German newspaper.[10] And French President Nicolas Sarkozy caused a furor when he announced his country's stimulus benefits would include nationalist requirements at odds with European Union principles of economic integration.

"We want to stop moving factories abroad, and perhaps we will bring them back," Sarkozy said, specifically citing French auto companies that have moved production to the Czech Republic, a fellow EU member.[11]

But Irwin believes most world leaders recognize that trade inequities did not cause the Great Recession. "It's not a problem of too many imports," he says. "Cracking down on trade is not going to solve the problem."

If the global economy begins to turn around within the next year or so, Irwin predicts that protectionist impulses will quickly fade. But Lane is not so sure, noting that political leaders are becoming reluctant to actively champion free trade. "Normally, during an economic downturn, the reaction from policy makers is to promote exports by opening foreign markets, and one of the easiest ways to do that is to negotiate trade barriers

Does a 'Level Playing Field' Exist in Global Trade?

Critics say rules often favor competitors.

A merican critics of free-trade policies often say they only want to establish "a level playing field" so U.S. and foreign businesses all compete under the same rules.

When American companies compete with Chinese manufacturers, for instance, the Chinese companies have an advantage because of exploitative government labor policies, argues Sen. Byron Dorgan, D-N.D. In his book *Take this Job and Ship It: How Corporate Greed and Brain Dead Politics are Selling Out America*, Dorgan writes that government policies in China allow "for children to work, or for workers to be put in unsafe workplaces, or for companies to pollute the air and water, or jail [for] those who try to start a union. Manufacturing is less expensive in China precisely because workers are exploited.[1]

But what constitutes a "level" playing field in trade, and are U.S. companies really being forced to compete at a disadvantage? The answers aren't as simple as they may seem.

Free-trade policies today are based on the classical economic theory of "comparative advantage," developed by 19th-century English political economist David Ricardo. The theory states that each nation has natural advantages and disadvantages when it comes to producing different crops and goods. Prosperity, Ricardo argued, is achieved if each nation concentrates on its strengths by producing crops and products it can create the most efficiently (cheaply) and selling them in the international marketplace.

For example, Ricardo noted, England's lush, cool landscape was perfect for raising sheep, while Portugal enjoyed other natural advantages for growing grapes. While wine could be made in England and sheep raised in Portugal, the economic efficiency and thus the wealth of both nations

would increase if each nation played to its strength and traded its key product for the other's country's specialty.

Trade today is vastly more complicated than exchanging wine and wool, encompassing services and complex manufactured goods made from raw materials that can come from dozens of countries. But Ricardo's theory remains at the heart of free-trade ideology, particularly the idea that

Cotton farmers in Burkina Faso gather cotton bolls for market. Farmers in the West African nation and other developing countries say they can't compete with cotton farmers in industrialized countries, particularly those in the United States, who receive hefty government subsidies.

free trade allows a country to concentrate on areas in which the field is tilted decidedly in its favor. The concept of a level playing field is largely irrelevant under Ricardo's theory, say some economists.

away," he says. "That's not going on right now. The bilateral free-trade agreements before Congress aren't moving forward, and the WTO talks are stalled."[12]

In India, Mastek's Desai believes globalization will prevail, since he's seen the difference it has made in his country's burgeoning IT industry. "Maybe there was a time when globalization's benefits just went one way, to the wealthier nations," he says. "But now the benefits are

spread across so many countries. There's so much more diversity, I don't think protectionism will really take hold unless the recession lasts three or four years."

Some economists see a shorter window of opportunity. If global economic conditions continue to deteriorate for another year, says Irish economist O'Rourke, "not only would protectionism be likely, it would be almost inevitable. I don't think you could expect

"The idea of competitive or uncompetitive applied to a country is problematic," says Arvind Panagariya, a former economist at the World Bank, the Asian Development Bank and the World Trade Organization.[2] "In an industry, you can be competitive or uncompetitive, but as a nation you can't be." Nations can always find areas where a trading partner seems to have an unfair advantage, he says. For instance, while U.S. free-trade critics cite a lack of safety and labor standards in competing nations, "If you are India or China, you could say, 'There's no level playing field because America has so much money to invest in new technology, and we've got such limited capital, it's not fair.' "

Likewise, cotton farmers in a developing country who don't receive government subsidies say it's unfair for them to have to compete with cotton farmers in industrialized countries, particularly the United States, who get hefty government subsidies.

But critics of globalization believe the theory of comparative advantage isn't working. As proof, critics like Dorgan cite the $673 billion U.S. trade deficit, the result of U.S. imports exceeding exports.[3] "Yes, they can create an economic advantage," Dorgan writes. "But it is not a *natural* competitive advantage."[4]

However, Jaime Daremblum, former Costa Rican ambassador to the United States, says trade agreements can help reduce such disparities. "Free-trade agreements like CAFTA [Central American Free Trade Agreement] are not just about trade," Daremblum says. "They're also plans for governance, in terms of improving the judiciary, improving the enforcement of labor laws and labor standards, improving transparency and accountability. The field is being leveled as we speak."

But many free-trade critics see such trade rules as unfair intrusions into national policies. If CAFTA, NAFTA (North American Free Trade Agreement) and other trade pacts are leveling the playing field, they are doing so by encouraging a "race to the bottom," forcing wages and standards in the wealthier nations down to those in the poorest

Farmers halt traffic in Zagreb, Croatia, on June 10, 2009, to protest plummeting milk and wheat prices. Such well-organized resistance from farm groups in developed countries prevents officials from lowering agricultural subsidies that harm Third World farmers.

nations, according to Lori Wallach, head of Global Trade Watch for Public Citizen, a U.S. advocacy group.

Wallach claims advocates of free trade cite the wrong statistic to prove it's working. "They look at the volume of trade flows between countries, but that is not the measure of the success of a trade agreement," she says. Instead, the question should be: "Did it raise incomes?" U.S. median wages have now declined to 1972 levels, and income inequality has drastically increased since NAFTA and the World Trade Organization accords were adopted, she says.

To Wallach and other critics of current trade policy, the increase in income inequality helps prove the playing field remains far from level.

[1] Byron Dorgan, *Take this Job and Ship It: How Corporate Greed and Brain Dead Politics are Selling Out America* (2006), pp. 42-43.

[2] Panagariya is now an economics professor at Columbia University.

[3] Christopher Rugaber, "U.S. Trade Deficit Fell Sharply in 2008," The Associated Press, March 18, 2009.

[4] Dorgan, *op. cit.*

political leaders not to succumb to the pressure that would ensue."

Are some protectionist measures appropriate in today's economy?

Arvind Panagariya, an Indian economist at Columbia University who has worked for both the World Bank and the World Trade Organization, notes that WTO rules

allow "countries, in certain situations, to safeguard domestic companies from foreign competition" during times of economic distress.

The so-called safeguard provisions allow restrictions on certain imports if they threaten serious injury to a domestic industry. But the restrictions must be temporary, providing the domestic industry time to adjust to new conditions. Countries also may restrict imports if they believe a foreign company is "dumping" goods into their market at subsidized or unfairly low prices.[13]

In 2002 when the U.S. steel industry sought protection from foreign imports, President George W. Bush used the safeguard provisions to impose temporary tariffs on imports.[14] Some critics said the action betrayed the administration's free-trade principles.[15] But Kevin Dempsey, senior vice president for public policy and general counsel for the American Iron and Steel Institute, says Bush made the right choice. "The U.S. industry worked hard during that period to become more competitive," he says, "It gave us time to restructure."

In the current recession, the U.S. automobile tire industry has applied for similar relief from Chinese imports. Manufacturers of several different steel products also have brought dumping charges against Chinese competitors, which the Commerce Department is reviewing.[16]

Dempsey believes such actions are necessary and legitimate, particularly in today's economic climate. "Unfortunately, when companies invoke their rights under WTO law to insure that other countries' actions don't harm them, a lot of people refer to this as protectionism," he says. "But bringing an anti-dumping case or a safeguard case can be an important way to make sure we have fair competition."

Panagariya is skeptical, noting "a big surge in anti-dumping actions" since the economic crisis began. "There are signs people may be abusing the privilege." Even if these actions meet the WTO definition of a legal action, he believes they are usually counterproductive. "In the end, two can play the same game," he says. "You're simply inviting retaliation, and it's ultimately detrimental to everyone."

The Obama administration moved aggressively early in its term to back the U.S. auto industry, believing its survival was essential to the nation's economic health. The industry's troubles were, in part, the result of the financial crisis, which dried up credit, and not of the industry's making, Dempsey notes. "We support the efforts to help the U.S. auto industry to restructure," he says. "It's critical to give them breathing room to adjust, and under these circumstances, it's warranted."

But Panagariya believes subsidized loans and other aid provided to domestic auto industries by the United States, Germany, France, Australia and Brazil were protectionist,

discriminating against foreign manufacturers selling cars in those countries. The actions "will almost certainly be challenged and found to break WTO rules," he predicted.[17]

Other analysts, however, think even stronger measures are needed to protect domestic industries. The Trade Reform, Accountability, Development and Employment (TRADE) Act, supported by organized labor and other U.S. interest groups, would require the president to renegotiate NAFTA and other trade agreements with more stringent environmental, labor and safety standards for nations exporting goods into the United States. The legislation, which has more than 100 House cosponsors, also sets out what could not be included in trade agreements, such as requirements that economic sectors be privatized or deregulated.

Lori Wallach, director of Global Trade Watch for Public Citizen, a U.S. consumer advocacy organization that has lobbied for legislation to dramatically revamp U.S. trade law, rejects the notion that such measures will hurt global commerce.

"The question isn't whether there's going to be trade," she says. "The question is 'Under what rules?' The TRADE Act is about taking a different approach, fixing the rules to get agreements that are consistent with the goals and values of the American people."

But Boris Kozolchyk — director of the National Law Center for Inter-American Free Trade at the University of Arizona in Tucson — believes the effort is protectionist and will fail.

"In today's global economy, there's always going to be a replacement buyer or seller to take your place," he says. "It would be a loss economically for whoever tries it."

Will globalization survive the world economic crisis?

The recession, by numerous measures, is the worst economic crisis since the Great Depression. But economists disagree over what impact the recession will have and whether globalization will be one of its casualties. Those who believe deglobalization could worsen see political and economic conditions combining to create a fundamental breakdown in the existing order.

"It is now clear that the global economic crisis will be deep and prolonged and that it will have far-reaching geopolitical consequences," former U.S. Deputy Treasury Secretary Roger Altman wrote recently.

"The long movement toward market liberalization has stopped, and a new period of state intervention, re-regulation and creeping protectionism has begun. Indeed, globalization itself is reversing. The long-standing wisdom that everyone wins in a single world market has been undermined."[18]

Altman and others see deglobalization as the start of a new geopolitical era that will be accompanied by escalating conflicts over key natural resources and the ascendancy of China to a position of greater worldwide influence. In effect, they say, the world's economic problems and geopolitical tensions will create a feedback loop of growing distrust and disagreement, pushing the world into the deglobalized era. In this scenario, countries with a smaller economic base, particularly developing nations, will be especially hard hit.

In Honduras, however, former trade minister Norman García sees nothing so severe in his crystal ball. Despite the severity of the recession, he says, "We haven't really felt that much effect in our trade with the United States. We're still maintaining the same levels." Honduras' primary exports are clothing and agricultural goods, and its primary markets are the United States and Europe, he says.

Indeed, García says that while trade is down overall, "No trading partner has enacted any protectionist measures that have had any effect on us," thanks mostly to the Central American Free Trade Agreement (CAFTA). The pact includes the United States, Honduras and five other countries.[19] The Honduran government was determined to sign CAFTA for that very reason, García says.

"What we were doing is guaranteeing that that market was here to stay for good," he says. Because of such agreements, including the WTO, he says, "I don't think this so-called deglobalization will get any momentum."

But David Smick, an economic policy strategist and author of the 2008 book *The World Is Curved: Hidden Dangers to the Global Economy*, has less faith. "The whole economic model under which the world has operated in the last two decades is crash landing," he says. "The global emerging-market export model is in real trouble."

In that model, he explains, less developed nations such as China promoted rapid growth by setting up their economy "as an export platform, heavily dependent on the U.S. consumer." The model depended on several factors, including a favorable rate of currency exchange

Farmers — Both Rich and Poor — Demand Protection

European milk producers seeking protection from falling milk prices clash with police outside European Commission headquarters in Brussels, Belgium, on July 22, 2009 (top). As economic stress increases, farmers in poor countries are also flexing their political muscle. In New Delhi, thousands of protesting Indian farmers on Dec. 16, 2008, demand help in competing in global markets (bottom). Among other things, they were seeking higher subsidies, lower diesel prices and interest-free agricultural loans.

with the dollar to keep exports relatively inexpensive. [20] But most critically, it depended on Americans' voracious consuming habits and their willingness to pile up debt as they kept buying. The debt habit was fed by easy credit, underwritten by ever-appreciating home equity.

But the housing bubble has burst, and Americans appear to have changed their buying habits, at least for the moment. "There are surveys showing Americans are pulling back, and they're finding pleasure in pulling back," Smick says. "A large part of the world is in denial about this. They think the U.S. consumer is coming back. Well, the U.S. consumer is never coming back in the same way because U.S. regulators are never going to allow that kind of over-leveraging again."

The contraction of that export market, he believes, will significantly strain export-dependent countries such as China, Germany and Korea, along with many smaller developing nations. "I really think we are entering a period of deglobalization," Smick says. "The question is just how fast and to what extent."

But Alan Winters, an economist at the University of Sussex in the United Kingdom, is more optimistic about the future, citing the G-20's April pledge of additional aid to help developing nations weather the crisis. [21] "There's certainly room to do more, but we have avoided a meltdown," he says.

Moreover, he says, the world's two rising economic powers, China and India, have tremendous incentives to avoid a retreat from globalization. "When people ask me, 'Is this the end of capitalism as we know it?' I say, 'No, capitalism is safe in the hands of the Chinese. They know they've done incredibly well out of the global markets, and the Indians know that, too."

But after considerable time in China, Smick believes China's ability to adjust to the changing trade picture is complicated by an authoritarian political structure, an aging population and a bureaucratic culture that can still discourage individual innovation.

The United States remains the engine of the global economy, he says, and American political leaders are losing their determination to resist Americans' rising protectionist sentiment. But without U.S. leadership, he warns, the global consensus in favor of free trade could splinter.

"Today there are just so many parallels to where we were in the '30s, when every country paid attention to their own bilateral priorities," Smick says. "I'm afraid that's the world we're moving in again."

BACKGROUND

Ancient Traders

Globalization is either a modern phenomenon or nearly as old as civilization itself — depending on one's viewpoint.

Many economists see globalization as the unprecedented level of worldwide economic and financial integration, fueled by technological advances, witnessed in the last 30 years. Others view globalization as the age-old exchanging of goods and ideas by people from different parts of the world. As financial historian William J. Bernstein puts it: Globalization "is a process that has been slowly evolving for a very, very long time." [22]

In his 2008 book *A Splendid Exchange, How Trade Shaped the World*, Bernstein traces the role of trade in world affairs since the dawn of recorded history, depicting a surprising range and diversity of trading in the ancient world.

Bronze-age Mesopotamians actively traded grain, metals and goods across southern Arabia. The Roman Empire traded across Europe, much of Africa and as far away as India and China. In 30 B.C., "Rome was flooded with pepper, exotic animals and precious jewels from the Orient," Bernstein writes. "Chinese silk was the most famous and coveted of these commodities." [23]

In more recent times, the disruptive impacts of international trade were felt long before modern treaties like the North American Free Trade Agreement sought to promote open trade between nations. More than 200 years ago, for example, a flood of cheaper tanned hides from the Americas undercut Europe's leather industry. "If *The New York Times* columnist Thomas Friedman had been writing in 1800, he would have had little trouble explaining the flattening of world commerce to European tanners," Bernstein observes. [24] (Friedman, *The New York Times* columnist and author of *The World Is Flat, A Brief History of the Twenty-first Century*, embraces globalization as a nearly unstoppable revolution brought forth by a convergence of new technologies and an emerging world order.)

"Globalization is such a diverse, broad-based, and potent force that not even today's massive economic crash will dramatically slow it down," writes *Foreign Policy* editor Naím. "Love it or hate it, globalization is here to stay." [25]

But historians such as Bernstein and Princeton's James believe the longer view reveals many eras of globalization, usually followed by periods in which trade and other contacts declined significantly. In the period around 30 B.C., for example, trade expanded within the Roman Empire, followed by a period in which it slowed to a trickle, Bernstein notes, as Rome fell into decline following

CHRONOLOGY

1920s *Trade flourishes until Great Depression hits.*

October 1929 U.S. stock market crashes.

1930s *Protectionism worsens the Depression.*

1930 Smoot-Hawley Tariff Act in U.S. raises more than 900 import duties; other nations later follow suit.

1929-1934 World trade drops 66 percent.

1940s *Nations seek to build postwar international economic relationships.*

1944 Allied nations meet in Bretton Woods, N.H., to create international monetary and financial structure.

1947 General Agreement on Tariffs and Trade (GATT) encourages free trade by reducing tariffs.

1950s-1960s *Growing economic and political cooperation expands ties among Western nations.*

1951 Six countries form European Coal and Steel Community, the precursor of the Common Market.

1957 European Economic Community, or Common Market, expands economic cooperation and cross-border trade.

1962 Trade Expansion Act empowers President John F. Kennedy to negotiate major tariff reductions. . . . European Union gives members joint control over food production and prices.

1967 Kennedy round of trade talks, honoring the slain president, conclude.

1970s-1980s *Open markets and political changes in West appear to reverse economic stagnation, while dramatic reforms unleash China's economy. Soviet Union and former satellite nations embrace free markets, open trade.*

1973 Arab oil embargo causes gas shortages and worsens economic malaise known as "stagflation."

1978 China initiates free-market reforms.

1985 Soviet leader Mikhail Gorbachev initiates reforms that lead to the USSR's collapse in 1991.

1989 U.S. and 11 Pacific nations form Asia Pacific Economic Cooperation forum to discuss free trade.

1990s *Global trade grows, but backlash develops.*

1992 A European Union treaty moves toward a common currency. Union eventually grows to 27 nations.

1994 North American Free Trade Agreement eliminates most trade barriers between U.S., Canada and Mexico.

1995 The 123-member World Trade Organization (WTO) replaces GATT.

1999 Anti-globalization protesters shut down WTO Seattle meeting.

2000s *Recession undercuts global trade.*

2001 Trade talks begin in Doha, Qatar, to lower remaining trade barriers.

2007 U.S. housing prices begin to collapse, rattling U.S. financial institutions.

2008 Worst recession in nearly 80 years hits world economy. Banking institutions worldwide face insolvency. . . . Doha round talks collapse.

2009 Global trade plummets in the first two quarters and is expected to drop 10 percent or more for the year. . . . China and Western nations initiate massive stimulus spending to revive their econo-mies. By mid-summer signs of recovery are mixed with economic difficulties, prompting some experts to predict deglobalization will fracture the global status quo.

Rejecting Globalization Produces Winners and Losers

Developing nations could suffer economically and politically.

For two decades, Ireland flourished as "the poster child for globalization," in the words of Irish economist Austin Hughes. Today, the country's battered economy reflects the sharp reversal of fortune that can come with a collapse in world trade.

Ireland's embrace of policies that opened the island to global markets and international investment had turned its economy into the "Celtic Tiger." But the global economic downturn sent Ireland's property values plummeting, its banks required a government bailout and unemployment has soared to close to 12 percent.

"There was a sense that we had discovered the crock of gold at the end of the rainbow," Hughes says. "Now there's this fatalism that says it was just a crock."

Some desperate economies that once embraced globalization are now beginning to turn inward, in a trend called deglobalization, in which they adopt restrictive tariffs and other protective policies. If the trend continues, experts say, there will be winners and losers on both the global and national stages. The losers will far outnumber the winners, according to many mainstream economists, but in anything as vast and complicated as the global economy, some industries and even nations will find themselves with a relative advantage in the new status quo.

Ireland is hardly the only nation that will face a significant economic adjustment if the recession triggers an era of deglobalization. Several smaller Western nations, including Iceland and Latvia, are in similar straits, and many of the world's successful economies are highly export dependent, notes David Smick, an international economic strategist. Exports provide more than 40 percent of the gross domestic product (GDP) in China, Germany and Korea, among other nations, he says.

Boris Kozolchyk, director of the National Law Center for Inter-American Free Trade in Tucson, Ariz., believes developing countries would be big losers in an era of deglobalization. Many Latin American countries, for example, have staked their economic and political development on free trade.

Kozolchyk says the banking crisis that sparked the recession illustrates intertwined global relationships. "There was a chain of finance: you had Wells Fargo Bank

the death of Emperor Marcus Aurelius. [26] And other periods of robust globalization — including the era of trade expansion that occurred during the Renaissance and the emergence of French and English colonial empires in the 18th century — also eventually slowed or ended dramatically, James observes.

"All of these previous globalization episodes came to an end, almost always with wars . . . accompanied by highly disruptive and contagious financial crises," he writes.[27]

Depression and Protection

Whether globalization is an old story or uniquely modern, the contemporary chapter clearly begins about 80 years ago, with a worldwide economic disaster.

Contrary to popular belief, the Great Depression of the 1930s wasn't started by protectionist tariffs and other trade barriers rising around the globe. The economic debacle was well under way when President Herbert Hoover signed the 1930 Smoot-Hawley act, which increased nearly 900 different import tariffs on foreign goods.

Authors Rep. Willis Hawley, R-Ore., and Sen. Reed Smoot, R-Utah, reaped political infamy for their efforts, but the measure reflected lawmakers' widespread protectionist sentiments. Thomas Hall, a professor of economics at Miami University in Ohio and co-author of *The Great Depression: An International Disaster of Perverse Economic Policies*, believes it was more the Depression that caused Smoot-Hawley, rather than the reverse. "Smoot-Hawley providing financing to Banco Atlántida in Honduras, which was financing local businesses," he says. "Now it's all come to a halt."

Kozolchyk also fears developing nations could lose politically, as their economic struggles lead them to turn away from democracy in search of other solutions. "This has already started happening," he says, citing the influence of Venezuelan President Hugo Chávez. "You definitely have a return to demagoguery and authoritarian government, all in the name of false economic development."

Large and economically diverse nations will be hurt less. Only 11 percent of the U.S. GDP is tied to exports, according to Smick. "We will be hurt," he says, "but we will be less vulnerable than most of the rest of the world."

Within the U.S. economy, however, certain industries would be disproportionately affected by deglobalization. Exports in medical equipment, industrial engines and aircraft engines all grew significantly last year. [1] Other industries, however, were already heavily export driven. For example, nearly 40 percent of the computer and electronics-industry jobs in the United States are dependent upon exports, according to government statistics. Heavy manufacturing, the chemical industry and the U.S. leather goods trade also count on exports for a substantial share of their business. [2]

Even distinctly American industries are global enterprises these days and could suffer if the world deglobalizes. Hollywood made nearly twice as much money on its movies overseas as it did in the United States. [3] If deglobalization triggers a rise in economic and cultural nationalism, the entertainment industry could be a big loser.

The winners? It depends on your perspective on globalization. David C. Korten — a longtime critic of "corporate globalization" and author of *Agenda for a New Economy: From Phantom Wealth to Real Wealth* — sees a retreat from international markets sparking a more sustainable lifestyle in the United States and abroad. The trend would embrace smaller-scale, local agriculture and green technologies, including alternative-energy production and more efficient building practices. In the view of anti-globalists like Korten, the final winners would include Americans, who would enjoy better-quality lives.

Others take a more cynical view of how winners would be determined. "It really depends on which industries have the political clout to get the best protectionism," says Douglas Irwin, a specialist in trade policy at Dartmouth College.

---

[1] "U.S. Export Fact Sheet," International Trade Administration, U.S. Department of Commerce, Feb. 11, 2009, http://trade.gov/press/press_releases/2009/export-factsheet_021109.pdf.

[2] "Total Jobs Supported by Manufactured Exports, 2006," Office of Industry and Trade Information, U.S. Department of Commerce, www.trade.gov/td/industry/otea/jobs/Reports/2006/jobs_by_industry.html.

[3] "Entertainment Industry Market Statistics 2007," Motion Picture Association of America, p. 3, www.mpaa.org/USEntertainmentIndustryMarketStats.pdf.

---

had been kicking around in Congress for some years," he says. "What the Depression did was align the political forces to get it passed."

The measure became law despite desperate opposition from financial and economic circles, remarkably including 1,028 economists who signed an open letter calling on Hoover not to sign the bill. Thomas Lamont, a partner at J. P. Morgan and an economic adviser to the president, recalled: "I almost went down on my knees" to beg Hoover to veto the bill. [28]

Hoover, however, had long harbored protectionist sentiments and signed the bill into law. As opponents had predicted, the act led to a trade war, with nations around the world raising their own import barriers in retaliation.

Economists differ on how much responsibility Smoot-Hawley bears for the calamitous collapse in world trade in the 1930s. U.S. imports from Europe declined from a 1929 high of $1.3 billion to just $390 million in 1932 — a precipitous 69 percent drop. U.S. exports to Europe declined 65 percent — from $2.3 billion to $784 million — over the same period. Overall, world trade fell a breathtaking 66 percent from 1929 to 1934. [29]

But many historians have noted that the real impact of Smoot-Hawley was to turn nations inward at a time of international political and economic crisis. In its 1941 obituary for Hawley, *Time* went so far as to call Smoot-Hawley "one of the most enormous acts of isolationism in U.S. history." The magazine even suggested that the act set the world on course for the worst war in history. "Economic nationalism, forced into full flower by the Smoot-Hawley Tariff, became the physical basis for the ideology of fascism," *Time* intoned. "The lines were written, the stage was set for World War II."[30]

Whether that verdict was too harsh — and most historians would argue the conditions that gave birth to fascism ranged beyond isolationist trade policies — it reflects postwar convictions. The democracies of the West, led by the United States, emerged from World War II convinced that protectionist tariffs had not only exacerbated the worst economic collapse in modern history but also helped lead to a catastrophic war.

For the rest of the 20th century, trade policy would be seen through the lens of the negative impact of protectionism. With only occasional demurrals, the Free World agreed that trade must be kept open to maintain peace and prosperity. In the aftermath of the war, the West would go about setting up the international structures to make that happen.

From GATT to WTO

The years immediately after World War II produced watershed events in international integration. The United Nations held its first General Assembly in 1946.[31] The North Atlantic Treaty Organization (NATO) set up its collective defense agreement in 1949. And the forerunner of the European Economic Community was formed in 1951.

But before the war had even ended, representatives of the 44 Allied nations met in tiny Bretton Woods, N.H., in July 1944, to hammer out the postwar economic order, establishing the International Monetary Fund (IMF) and the International Bank for Reconstruction and Development (the World Bank).

The delegates also established a new global monetary system. Because the United States had become far and away the world's most powerful economy and also held most of the world's gold reserves, Bretton Woods tied the world's currencies to the dollar, which the delegates agreed should be convertible into gold at $35 per ounce. The goal was to prevent the wild currency fluctuations that had contributed to instability in the 1930s. The IMF was charged with maintaining the system of exchange rates.[32]

Guiding all these efforts was the belief that a stable global economic system, allowing a free exchange of goods and services, was essential to world order. "Unhampered trade dovetailed with peace. High tariffs, trade barriers and unfair economic competition with war," U.S. Secretary of State Cordell Hull later wrote in his autobiography.[33]

Three years after Bretton Woods, 23 nations met in Geneva, Switzerland, to finalize work on a General Agreement on Tariffs and Trade (GATT). It established basic trade rules and included 45,000 tariff concessions, eliminating or reducing duties on $10 billion worth of products being traded at the time — about one-fifth of the worldwide total.[34]

GATT membership would grow dramatically through the years, as would its scope, which was expanded in a series of negotiations known as "trade rounds," named after the cities in which they were convened. For nearly half a century, GATT would provide the basic framework for world trade.

Dartmouth trade historian Irwin notes that GATT didn't always succeed in boosting trade. For instance, its inability to eliminate agricultural subsidies, still widely protected around the globe, is considered one of the treaty's largest failings. And its provisions are often ignored by some countries during economic stress, such as in the late 1970s and early '80s, when sluggish growth again led to a rise in protectionism.[35]

But overall the picture has been positive. "There's been a demonstrable lowering of trade barriers over the last 60 or so years, and GATT was largely responsible," says Irwin. World trade has expanded dramatically in the 60 years since GATT was first signed, growing 8 percent a year through the 1950s and '60s.[36]

"It added stability to the system," he notes, making people "more willing to make investments in other countries, which has helped the developing world, in particular."

But GATT was only meant to be a stop-gap measure. The architects of the postwar world order envisioned an International Trade Organization (ITO), operating as a U.N. agency, which would serve as a third pillar of the world economy alongside the IMF and the World Bank. The draft charter for the ITO included rules on employment, business practices, international investment and services.[37] Eventually, ITO negotiations foundered on the sheer magnitude of the concept. However, nearly half a century later, the international community would return to the idea, creating the World Trade Organization in 1995 as the successor to GATT.

The WTO represented the culmination of the original postwar vision of a new level of international commerce. But at the end of the millennium the world was a much different place than in the years immediately after World War II. And since its inception, the WTO has attracted ardent critics and supporters.

But on one thing they all agree: the WTO in the 21st century faces a series of challenges that reflect the stresses of the global economic and political order.

Governing Trade Today

In recent years, countries have focused more on crafting regional and bilateral trade agreements, while international trade talks have languished. In fact, regional free-trade agreements have proliferated so rapidly they've become an alphabet soup of acronyms: NAFTA, CAFTA, SAFTA (the South Asia Free Trade Agreement) and more.

Bilateral free-trade agreements have also proliferated. The United States, for example, now has trade agreements — both bilateral and multilateral — with 17 countries, and three more are pending in Congress.[38] Many other countries have similar agreements with neighboring countries or important trading partners.

As the number of trade agreements has multiplied, the size of global markets has grown dramatically. Before the collapse of the Soviet Union in 1991 and the opening up of the Chinese and Indian economies, a large share of the world's population was essentially shut off from international trade. As a result of political changes in those countries, however, more than 1.5 billion people joined the competitive global work force.[39] Many smaller, developing nations also turned to low-cost global exports in an attempt to raise living standards.

Simultaneously, the World Trade Organization has expanded its reach into areas such as the trade in services and intellectual-property rights. The expanded authority, however, required new rules that reach much farther into the internal practices and regulation of national economies.

"Until the mid-1990s, trade rules were about trade. They set tariffs, that sort of thing," says Wallach at Global Trade Watch. "Now you have a whole bunch of policies that have nothing to do with how goods move between countries. They have to do with domestic policies."

WTO rules on intellectual property, for instance, have been particularly controversial because they can involve patents for lifesaving drugs and can restrict or increase the cost of medicine in many parts of the world. Proponents view the WTO's intellectual-property-rights provisions as essential to boosting trade, encouraging innovation and promoting the adoption of best practices around the globe. Opponents see them as a form of exploitation by multinational corporations.

Trade agreements and other WTO policies have caused job losses in certain economic sectors in participating countries, such as the U.S. textile industry, and have contributed to downward pressure on wages, particularly in developed nations.

Not surprisingly, a backlash developed against the WTO and the whole idea of globalization. The scope of the anti-globalization movement and the depth of its frustration became apparent during the 1999 WTO meeting in Seattle, where a massive, largely peaceful protest was marked by violent outbursts that so rattled officials they ended the conference early.[40]

Globalization's critics cite the economic crisis that hit in 2007 and '08 as proof of its failure, while supporters urged that eight-year-long trade negotiations, known as the Doha round, be concluded to help lift the world out of the recession.

Although these debates reflect modern tensions, Bernstein points out that anti-globalization protests have occurred for centuries. "Today's debates over globalization repeat, nearly word for word in some cases, those of earlier eras," he writes. "Wherever trade arrives, resentment, protectionism and their constant companions — smuggling, disrespect for authority and occasionally war — will follow."

Yet Bernstein also notes, "The instinct to truck and barter is part of human nature; any effort to stifle it is doomed to fail in the long run."[41]

CURRENT SITUATION
Clouded Forecast

Several analysts say evidence suggests the recession in the United States, China and other nations could be coming to an end. In early August, the U.S. government said the nation's economic output shrank only 1 percent in the second quarter of the year, a dramatic improvement over the 6.4 percent contraction in the previous quarter.[42]

In one of the most protectionist responses to the global economic crisis, Ecuador's government in February imposed restrictions on most imported items. Now many imports — like this hair conditioner and deodorant being sold in a store in Quito — are more expensive.

Moreover, the U.S. stock market recorded its best July in 20 years, and home prices appeared to be creeping upward.[43] A number of major banks also have recorded profits, leading some to predict the financial system has stabilized. Since the United States is the largest driver of the global economy, these signs indicate a recovery may be in the cards for the last half of 2009 or early 2010.

Two of the world's emerging economic powerhouses, India and China, also offer reason for optimism. In June, the World Bank raised its 2009 growth forecast for China from 6.5 percent to 7.2 percent.[44] In July, Chinese manufacturing expanded at its fastest rate in a year, according to a survey.[45] Also in July, the IMF revised its projection for India's economic growth for 2009 upward to 5.4 percent while forecasting an overall global contraction of 1.4 percent.[46]

"My take is that the U.S. will come out of this in another six months to a year, and the large majority of nations will start pulling out once the U.S. economy does," says Panagariya, the former World Bank and WTO economist.

But for every patch of blue sky visible on the economic horizon there remains a cloud. U.S. consumer spending, which comprises 70 percent of economic activity, has continued to fall. And with U.S. unemployment not expected to peak until later this year or early in 2010, a consumer-driven recovery will be delayed. The Obama administration's $787 billion stimulus package now accounts for 20 percent of U.S. output, but federal officials acknowledge that the current level of deficit spending is unsustainable in future years.[47]

Meanwhile, credit markets remain tight, both globally and in the United States, limiting money for new investments, particularly in riskier economies. Conditions continue to look bleak in many leading Western industrial nations. The IMF predicts continued contraction of 4 percent or more this year in Germany, Japan, the United Kingdom, Russia and Italy — among other nations — with negative or only negligible growth seen in 2010.[48]

"There's all this talk right now about 'green shoots' [signs of economic recovery] and the end of the recession, and I understand why people feel this way: They hope they can get back to normal very quickly," says James, the Princeton University economic historian, "but I just don't think they're going to be able to do that."

Indeed, the overall world economy looks remarkably grim by any historical measure. As of June, the declines in world industrial output and other key indicators were slightly worse than during the Great Depression at the same point in its history, according to one analysis.[49] In a late June assessment, the World Bank noted that "unemployment continues to rise throughout the world, housing prices in many countries are still falling . . . bank balance sheets are fragile."[50]

Several factors could derail the beginnings of a recovery, analysts say, especially rising energy costs. In early August, Fatih Birol, chief economist for the International Energy Agency, warned that rising oil prices — which had reached $73 a barrel — threaten economic recovery. Sustained oil prices above $70 a barrel could strangle a recovery, he says.[51]

Even if the recession is ending, the recovery is widely expected to be feeble, barely relieving public suffering or discontent. "While the global economy is likely to begin expanding again in the second half of 2009, the recovery is expected to be subdued as global demand remains depressed, unemployment remains high and recession-like conditions continue until 2011," Hans Timmer, director of the World Bank's Development Prospects Group, said recently.[52]

In this environment, the determination of the world's political leaders to maintain global trade could be critical. But the latest signals can be read both ways.

Will a period of deglobalization disrupt world trade?

YES Harold James
Professor of History and International Af
Author, The Creation and Destruction of
Value: The Globalization Cycle

Written for *CQ Researcher*, September 2009

NO Moisés Naím
Editor in Chief, Foreign Policy Author, Illicit: How
Smugglers, Traffickers and Copycats Are
Hijacking the Global Economy

Excerpted with permission from *Foreign*
Policy #171 (March/April 2009) www.foreignpolicy.com

Globalization is a very old phenomenon. It has also produced tremendous benefits in terms of poverty reduction in many countries. But historically, globalization is also vulnerable to terrible and costly backlashes, as in the late 18th century, when it was interrupted by wars and revolutions, or in the early 20th century, when the very integrated world of the late 19th century was pulled apart by the First World War and by the Great Depression. We might think of the globalization phenomenon as cyclical.

Because so much recent globalization was driven by financial flows, the financial meltdown is a very serious setback. The most immediate impact of the financial collapse of September 2008 was on world trade, with a 30 percent decline in the last quarter of 2008, and only very fragile signs of recovery in 2009. The World Trade Organization estimates that global trade will be 10 percent lower in 2009 than in 2008.

The measures that governments take against the crisis are likely to produce a longer-term deglobalization trend. State rescues of entire banking systems will tend to produce a different financial system, in which large parts of finance are renationalized. Italian and French taxpayers will not want to see their money used to bail out remote East European debtors. Banks rescued by governments are under substantial pressure to cut back foreign lending and increase domestic loans.

Fiscal stimulus packages have a similar effect, in that they are intended to benefit domestic producers and involve the assumption of additional debt, which constitutes a long-term liability of domestic taxpayers. In consequence, many of the large stimulus packages are accompanied by more or less explicit provisions ("Buy America" or "Buy China") that attempt to ensure domestic, not foreign, producers are stimulated.

The reactions against globalization are as much driven by a new psychology as by economic reality or a precise weighing of the costs and benefits of globalization. Crises give rise to conspiracy theories, often directed against foreigners or foreign countries. Many Americans argue that the mess is the fault of Chinese surpluses. Many people in other countries already argue that they are being hit by a U.S. crisis made in America. We will see trade protectionism and massive and powerful xenophobic sentiment. Perhaps many former so-called "globalization critics" will see just how good the integration was when it starts to fall apart.

Rumors of globalization's demise — such as Princeton economic historian Harold James' recent obituary for "The Late, Great Globalization" — have been greatly exaggerated. . . .

All kinds of groups are still connecting, and the economic crisis will not slow their international activities. . . . It might even bolster them. Global charities, for instance, will face soaring demand for their services. . . . At a time when cash is king and jobs are scarce, globalized criminals will be one of the few . . . sources of credit, investment and employment in some places. . . .

It's true that private flows of credit and investment across borders have temporarily plummeted. . . . But as private economic activity falls, the international movement of public funds is booming. Last fall, the U.S. Federal Reserve and the central banks of Brazil, Mexico, Singapore and South Korea launched $30 billion worth of currency arrangements for each country designed to stabilize their financial markets. Similar reciprocal deals now tie together central banks throughout Asia, Europe and the Middle East.

Yes, some governments might be tempted to respond to the crisis by adopting trade-impairing policies, imposing rules that inhibit global financial integration or taking measures to curb immigration. The costs of doing so, however, are enormous and hard to sustain in the long run. What's more, the ability of any government to shield its economy and society from outside influences and dangers has steadily evaporated in the past two decades. . . .

Globalization is such a diverse, broad-based and potent force that not even today's massive economic crash will dramatically slow it down or permanently reverse it. . . .

But claims about the return of strong governments and nationalism are equally overstated. Yes, China might team up with Russia to counterbalance the United States in relation to Iran, but meanwhile the Chinese and U.S. economies will be joined at the hip (China holds more than a trillion dollars of U.S. debt, and the United States is the main destination for its exports). . . .

The bottom line: Nationalism never disappeared. Globalization did not lessen national identities; it just rendered them more complex. . . . Globalization and geopolitics coexist, and neither is going anywhere.

Chinese factory workers in Huaibei manufacture clothes for export to the United States. China's rapid growth has been based on an export-driven economy that heavily depended on Americans' voracious consuming habits. U.S. demand for Chinese products declined during the recession, however, prompting China to protect its textile and other labor-intensive industries with tax rebates.

Trade Policy Pressure

In July, U.S. Trade Representative Ron Kirk addressed workers at a steel plant outside Pittsburgh, Pa. The steel industry continues to be hit hard by foreign imports and has been pushing the administration to act against what it considers unfair competition from China. Kirk's language was as combative as any heard from a White House trade official in some time.

The United States will get tough on foreign governments that ignore trade rules, he said, and would no longer wait for a complaint to be filed but would proactively identify and investigate potential violations of labor rules in countries with free-trade agreements with the United States.

"We will take new steps to protect the rights of American farmers and small-business owners. We will hold our trading partners to their word on labor standards," Kirk said. "And we will use work we're already doing to fight even harder for the men and women who fuel our economy and support their families."[53]

Kirk's speech could be read as a tilt toward the wing of the Democratic Party that has pushed for more aggressive action to level the playing field in trade. Even before Kirk spoke, some free-trade supporters worried the Obama administration was less committed to the idea of free trade than its predecessors.

"I do not believe the current administration is at all protectionist," says Lane, the governmental affairs director for Caterpillar. "But by the same token, there's been a reluctance to engage their core constituencies on these measures. What's missing so far is advocacy. So far, they haven't made it a priority."

Yet some observers saw the speech as an attempt to reassure labor unions and other Democratic Party interest groups before a push by the administration for ratification of bilateral trade agreements with Panama, Colombia and South Korea.[54] The deals, signed by the Bush administration, are pending in Congress but have been put on hold by a wary Democratic leadership.

The G-20 will meet again later this month in Pittsburgh, where President Obama is expected to discuss his administration's trade agenda.

Doha Stalls

More than eight years after negotiators began working on the latest international trade agreement, known as the Doha round, the adjective most commonly attached to the negotiations is "stalled."

In mid-summer, WTO Director-General Pascal Lamy laid out what he described as a road map for negotiations to be completed in 2010. But his plan was met with only muted responses from the world's leading industrial nations.

Yet finishing Doha is critical in helping the world economy recover and preventing deglobalization, says Winters, the economist at Sussex University in the U.K., who studies the problems of developing nations. "If the Doha round fails, it's not clear that we can maintain the status quo," he says. "Doha helps us head off a big increase in protectionism that could occur if we don't get it."

The Doha impasse centers on disagreements between developed and developing nations, which believe they were promised certain concessions in return for opening up their economies in the last round. Perhaps the most highly publicized dispute is over EU and U.S. agricultural price supports. Many developed nations use price supports, import quotas and other programs to protect producers of some farm commodities from cheaper foreign imports.

For example, government programs in the United States subsidize politically powerful cotton producers, helping to depress the world price for cotton and hurting producers in Africa and India. The African nations, in particular, have been pushing for reduced cotton price supports in the developed nations. A 2007 study by Oxfam, a London-based nongovernmental organization dedicated to fighting global poverty, estimated that if the United States — the world's largest cotton-exporting nation — eliminated its cotton subsidies, the price for West African cotton would increase by 5 to 12 percent, dramatically improving the lives of the region's cotton farmers.[55]

Winters believes the disagreement over agricultural policy in developed countries has come to carry more weight than it should. Rather than pressing the developed nations to make politically difficult reforms, Winters thinks developing nations should concentrate on getting rid of quotas, tariffs and other more traditional agricultural trade barriers. "Most African nations are net food importers," he says. "For a good part of the developing world, it's really far more important that the West open up its markets than it is that they lower their agricultural subsidies."

While most analysts are pessimistic that Doha will move forward anytime soon, others remain hopeful. Jagdish Bhagwati, a professor at Columbia University who has been an adviser for both GATT and the WTO, notes that no trade round has ever failed.

"They often break down, are often thought to be in intensive care where the pessimists predict that they will expire," he wrote with Panagariya, "and they come back like the proverbial cat and are concluded. Doha will be no exception."[56]

But others see a watershed moment. Smick, the author and global economic policy strategist, sees the economic crisis combining with existing tensions to splinter the international political consensus in favor of continuing trade liberalization, even though globalization has lifted millions of people around the world out of poverty.

"You're seeing the collapse of world trade authority with Doha, unless there's a miracle," Smick says, "and it doesn't look like that's going to happen."

OUTLOOK

Era of Deglobalization?

Experts who fear the world is headed into a period of deglobalization paint a gloomy picture of increased international tensions, conflict and nationalist fervor. Great Power politics — specifically the United States and China — will predominate, and governments will aggressively intervene in their national economies as state power grows.

Princeton professor James says a drop in international commerce combined with growing demand for limited resources such as oil is a recipe for increased international hostility. "Issues like the fuel supply or the supply of food — countries have and may again go to war about exactly this," says James.

Developing countries will be hit particularly hard, according to former Clinton deputy Treasury secretary Altman. "Already unstable nations, such as Pakistan, could disintegrate. And poverty will rise sharply in a number of African nations," he wrote in a recent issue of *Foreign Affairs*.[57]

Like James, Altman sees one nation in particular emerging in a more powerful position. "The one clear winner is China, whose unique political-economic model has come through unscathed," he wrote.

A recent report of the U.S. National Intelligence Council considers it a "relative certainty" that the global tensions predicted by James and Altman lie ahead. The report, "Global Trends 2025: A Transformed World," concludes that world population — expected to increase by 1.2 billion people by 2025 — will put increasing pressure on energy, food and water resources. But the council is less certain that the world will retreat from global markets, calling it one of the "key uncertainties" of the next 16 years.[58]

Deglobalization would be a welcome development for globalization's longtime critics. Walden Bello, a sociology professor at the University of the Philippines and a leading critic of globalization, called the current crisis proof that globalization has "ended in massive failure." The crisis is an opportunity for developing nations to build regional relationships that go beyond trade to shared economic and social goals, promoting greater equity and justice, he says, citing recent efforts by Venezuelan President Hugo Chávez to build regional economic relationships.[59]

Other globalization critics see the crisis as the end of an unsustainable system of corporate economic domination and excessive consumption. Korten, the author and longtime critic of "corporate globalization," thinks the world will eventually embrace a radically different approach. "Food sources would be primarily local," he says. People would rely more on renewable energy, including solar and wind. "It would mean much more energy-efficient buildings and a far greater attention to . . . sustainable development."

In Korten's vision, global prosperity would depend not on what a country sells abroad but what it produces close to home. "The economy would be much more based on what our real needs are," he says.

But other experts predict a less calamitous or revolutionary future. Panagariya, the Columbia University economist, says under the most pessimistic scenario the U.S. economy would follow the route of the Japanese in the 1990s, with a lost decade of little or no economic growth. But he considers that unlikely.

"The U.S. is a lot more proactive policywise," Panagariya says. "It's willing to take a lot more risks, and the U.S. markets are a lot more flexible."

He also doesn't expect any significant changes in habits, among nations or individuals. "If housing prices go up," he says, "I think we'll go on a spending spree again."

Ireland did as well as any nation under globalization, but its crash has been as severe as any in Europe. Looking ahead, Irish economist Hughes hopes the future is found in the middle ground.

"I don't think the question is whether globalization is the right thing or not, but whether you can have a trajectory that's more sustainable and deals with the downsides of globalization," he says. "I'm suggesting that wise counsel prevails and people realize they have to learn to move it forward at a walking pace, rather than just rocket forward."

NOTES

1. Harold James, "The Late Great Deglobalization," *Current History*, January 2009.

2. Jonathan Lynn and Kazunori Takada, "World trade to shrink 10 pct, Asia leads recovery: WTO," Reuters, July 22, 2009, www.reuters.com/article/businessNews/idUSSP48113720090722.

3. Angel Gurría and Jørgen Elmeskov, "Economic Outlook No. 85," Organisation for Economic Co-operation and Development, June 24, 2009, www.oecd.org/dataoecd/36/57/43117724.pdf.

4. Barry Eichengreen and Kevin O'Rourke, "A Tale of Two Depressions," at VoxEU.org, Centre for Economic Policy Research, June 4, 2009, www.voxeu.org/index.php?q=node/3421.

5. Joseph Francois, "The Big Drop: Trade and the Great Recession," *The Random Economist*, May 2, 2009, www.intereconomics.com/blogs/jff/2009/05/big-drop-trade-and-the-great-recession.html.

6. "Statement from G-20 Summit," Nov. 15, 2008. The complete text can be found at www.cfr.org/publication/17778/.

7. Elisa Gamberoni and Richard Newfarmer, "Trade Protection: Incipient but Worrisome Trends," *Tradenotes*, No. 37, The World Bank, March 2, 2009, www.voxeu.org/index.php?q=node/3183.

8. For background, see Mary H. Cooper, "Rethinking NAFTA," *CQ Researcher*, June 7, 1996, pp. 481-504.

9. Those provisions were subsequently modified, at the insistence of the Obama administration, to include a stipulation that they must comply with WTO rules.

10. Wolfgang Münchau, "Europe and the Protectionism Trap," Spiegel Online International, Feb. 13, 2009, www.spiegel.de/international/europe/0,1518,607457,00.html.

11. *Ibid.*

12. The latest round of WTO-sponsored trade talks, known as the Doha round, have been stalled over disagreements between developing and developed countries.

13. "Anti-dumping, subsidies, safeguards: contingencies, etc," "Understanding the WTO: the Agreements," www.wto.org/english/theWTO_e/whatis_e/tif_e/agrm8_e.htm.

14. "President Announces Temporary Safeguards for Steel Industry," White House press release, March 5, 2002, http://georgewbush-whitehouse.archives.gov/news/releases/2002/03/20020305-6.html.

15. Daniel J. Ikenson, "Sordid Steel Shenanigans," Fox News Online, Sept. 18, 2002, www.cato.org/pub_display.php?pub_id=3608.

16. Daniel Lovering, "Steel Product Makers Claim China Dumping Goods," *Manufacturing.net*, June 9, 2009.

17. Jagdish Bhagwati and Arvind Panagariya, "Legal Trade Barriers Must Be Kept in Check," *The Financial Times*, June 11, 2009, www.ft.com/cms/s/0/bcdf98c8-56b2-11de-9a1c-00144feabdc0.html.

18. Roger Altman, "Globalization in Retreat, Further Geopolitical Consequences of the Financial Crisis," *Foreign Affairs*, July/August 2009, p. 2.

19. The agreement is formally known as the CAFTA-DR, and the other signatories are Costa Rica, El Salvador, Guatemala, Nicaragua and the Dominican Republic.

20. For background, see Peter Behr, "The Troubled Dollar," *CQ Global Researcher*, October 2008, pp. 271-294.

21. For background, see Peter Behr, "Fixing Capitalism," *CQ Global Researcher*, July 2009, pp. 177-204.

22. William Bernstein, *A Splendid Exchange, How Trade Shaped the World* (2008), p. 14.

23. *Ibid.*, p. 8.

24. *Ibid.*, pp. 13-14.

25. Moisés Naím, "Think Again: Globalization," *Foreign Policy*, March/April 2009, www.foreignpolicy.com/story/cms.php?story_id=4678.

26. Bernstein, *op. cit.*, p. 8.

27. James, *op. cit.*, p. 21.

28. "The Battle of Smoot-Hawley," *The Economist*, Dec. 18, 2009, www.economist.com/displayStory.cfm?story_id=12798595.

29. Statistical information on U.S. and international trade volumes from the U.S. Department of State Historical Timeline, http://future.state.gov/when/timeline/1921_timeline/smoot_tariff.html.

30. "The Congress: Death of a Woodcutter," *Time*, Aug. 4, 1941.

31. "Milestones in United Nations History, a Selective Chronology," www.un.org/Overview/milesto4.htm.

32. "The Bretton Woods Conference," from the U.S. Department of State Timeline of U.S. Diplomatic History, www.state.gov/r/pa/ho/time/wwii/98681.htm. For background, see Behr, "The Troubled Dollar," *op. cit.*

33. Cordell Hull, "The Memoirs of Cordell Hull: Vol. 1" (1948), p. 81.

34. "The GATT Years: From Havana to Marrakesh," Understanding the WTO, World Trade Organization, www.wto.org/english/thewto_e/whatis_e/tif_e/fact4_e.htm.

35. Douglas Irwin, "GATT Turns 60," *The Wall Street Journal*, April 9, 2007, http://online.wsj.com/article/SB117607482355263550.html.

36. "The GATT Years: From Havana to Marrakesh," *op. cit.*

37. *Ibid.*

38. For a list see Office of the United States Trade Representative, www.ustr.gov/trade-agreements/free-trade-agreements.

39. Tom Friedman, *The World Is Flat: A Brief History of the Twenty-first Century* (2007), p. 212.

40. For background, see Brian Hansen, "Globalization Backlash," *CQ Researcher*, Sept. 28, 2001, pp. 761-784.

41. Bernstein, *op. cit.*, p. 367.

42. Catherine Rampell and Jack Healy, "In Hopeful Sign, Output Declines at Slower Pace," *The New York Times*, Aug. 1, 2009, p. A1, www.nytimes.com/2009/08/01/business/economy/01econ.html.

43. Nick Timraos and Kelly Evans, "Home Prices Rise Across U.S.," *The Wall Street Journal*, July 29, 2009, p. A1.

44. *China Quarterly Update*, The World Bank, June 2009, http://go.worldbank.org/9FV11IHMF0.

45. Joe McDonald, "Survey: China manufacturing improved in July," The Associated Press, Aug. 3, 2009.

46. "World Economic Outlook Update," International Monetary Fund, July 8, 2009, www.imf.org/external/pubs/ft/weo/2009/update/02/pdf/0709.pdf.

47. Rampell and Healy, *op. cit.* U.S. Treasury Secretary Timothy Geithner, speaking on ABC's "This Week," Aug. 2, 2009.

48. "World Economic Outlook Update," *op. cit.*

49. Eichengreen and O'Rourke, *op. cit.*

50. "Global Development Finance 2009: Outlook Summary," The World Bank, June 22, 2009, http://go.worldbank.org/HCR2ABQPX0.

51. Kate Mackenzie, "Global economy at risk from oil price rise," *The Financial Times*, Aug. 3, 2009, www.ft.com/

cms/s/0/1281aad6-8049-11de-bf04-00144feabdc0
.html.

52. "The Financial Crisis: Charting a Global Recovery," The World Bank, June 22, 2009, http://go.world-bank.org/KUG53HWZY0.

53. A complete text of Kirk's speech can be found at www.ustr.gov/about-us/press-office/speeches/tran-scripts/ 2009/july/ambassador-kirk-announces-new-initiatives-trade.

54. Ian Swanson, "Kirk Sooths on Trade," *The Hill*, July 16, 2009, http://thehill.com/the-executive/kirk-soothes-on-trade-2009-07-16.html.

55. Julian M. Alston, Daniel A. Sumner and Henrich Brunke, "Impacts of Reductions in US Cotton Subsidies on West African Cotton Producers," Oxfam America, 2007.

56. Jagdish Bhagwati and Arvind Panagariya, "Doha: The Last Mile," *The New York Sun*, Aug. 21, 2008, www .nysun.com/opinion/doha-the-last-mile/84314/.

57. Altman, *op. cit.*

58. "Global Trends 2025: A Transformed World," National Intelligence Council, www.dni.gov/nic/ PDF_2025/2025_Global_Trends_Final_Report.pdf.

59. Walden Bello, "Challenges of Regional Integration," presented July 21, 2009, to the Universidad de Deportes, Asunción, Paraguay, reprinted by Focus on the Global South, http://focusweb.org/index.php.

BIBLIOGRAPHY

Books

Bernstein, William, *A Splendid Exchange, How Trade Shaped the World*, Grove Press, 2008.
An American financial theorist comprehensively examines how trade has influenced world events throughout history.

Dorgan, Byron, *Take This Job and Ship It: How Corporate Greed and Brain-dead Politics are Selling Out America*, Thomas Dunn Books, St. Martin's Press, 2006.
The populist Democratic senator from North Dakota takes on what he considers the misguided political choices and false perceptions about world trade that have cost Americans jobs and income.

Ferguson, David, and Thomas Hall, *The Depression: An International Disaster of Perverse Economic Policies*, University of Michigan Press, 1998.
Two economists examine policy decisions that helped to create the Great Depression and then make it worse.

Friedman, Thomas, *The World Is Flat: A Brief History of the Twenty-first Century*, Picador, 2007.
The New York Times columnist's international best-seller presents a largely optimistic take on the globalization phenomenon.

James, Harold, *The Creation and Destruction of Value, The Globalization Cycle*, Harvard University Press, forthcoming, September 2009.
The British professor of history and international affairs at Princeton University who started the current debate about deglobalization puts the current crisis into historical context.

Korten, David, *Agenda for a New Economy: From Phantom Wealth to Real Wealth*, Berrett-Koehler, 2009.
An intellectual leader of the opposition to what he terms "corporate globalization" offers a radically different view of economic prosperity, focused not on corporate profits but on quality of life.

Smick, David, *The World Is Curved, Hidden Dangers to the Global Economy*, Portfolio, 2008.
In what amounts to a response to Friedman's book, a global economic policy strategist and free-trade proponent presents reasons to worry about globalization's future.

Articles

"The Battle of Smoot-Hawley," *The Economist*, Dec. 18, 2009.
The article examines how Congress passed and President Herbert Hoover signed one of the world's most disastrous anti-trade measures.

Altman, Roger, "Globalization in Retreat: Further Geopolitical Consequences of the Financial Crisis," *Foreign Affairs*, July/August 2009.
A former deputy U.S. Treasury secretary under President Bill Clinton sees a "new period of state intervention, re-regulation and creeping protectionism" under way.

Irwin, Douglas, "GATT Turns 60," *The Wall Street Journal*, April 9, 2009.
A Dartmouth College professor who specializes in trade history traces the beginnings of modern globalization from the GATT negotiations after World War II.

James, Harold, "The Late, Great Globalization," *Current History*, January 2009.
A Princeton history professor suggests a period of deglobalization is beginning in which trade will decline and tensions between nations will rise as they compete for critical resources.

Naím, Moisés, "Think Again: Globalization," *Foreign Policy*, March/April, 2009.
The magazine's editor, a former minister of trade and industry in Venezuela, argues that globalization is more than an economic phenomenon but an unstoppable cultural and technological transformation.

Reports and Studies

Eichengreen, Barry, and Kevin O'Rourke, "A Tale of Two Depressions," VoxEU.org, June 4, 2009.
Irish and American economists examine a series of key economic indicators that reveal how closely the current economic downturn tracks the first years of the Great Depression.

Gameroni, Elisa, and Richard Newfarmer, "Trade Protection: Incipient but Worrisome Trends," *Tradenotes, No. 37,* The World Bank, March 2, 2009.
The authors examine protectionist measures taken since the economic downturn started.

Gurría, Angel, and Jørgen Elmeskov, "Economic Outlook No. 85," *Organisation for Economic* Co-operation and Development, June 24, 2009.
The OECD's secretary general (Gurría) and the head of its Economics Department examine major trends in the world economy.

Mattoo, Aaditva, and Arvind Subramian, "Multilateralism Beyond Doha," "Working Paper No. 153," Center for Global Development, October 2008.
The authors contend the international trading system has failed to adapt to changing world economic conditions and suggest what should be done.

For More Information

Focus on the Global South, http://focusweb.org. An anti-globalization research and activist group with offices in Thailand, the Philippines and India, which aims to transform the global economy "from one centered around the needs of transnational corporations to one that focuses on the needs of people, communities and nations."

Organisation for Economic Co-operation and Development, 2, rue André Pascal F 75775 Paris Cedex 16, France; 33 1 45 24 82 00; www.oecd.org. Organization made up of 30 industrialized countries that provides economic research and advises governments on handling the economic, social and governance challenges associated with a globalized economy.

Peterson Institute for International Economics, 1750 Massachusetts Ave., N.W., Washington, DC 20036-1903; (202) 328-9000; www.iie.com. A private, nonpartisan research institution devoted to the study of international economic policy; advocates expanded global trade.

Public Citizen's Global Trade Watch, 1600 20th St., N.W., Washington, DC 20009; (202) 588-1000; www.citizen.org/trade. Nongovernmental organization that promotes democracy "by challenging corporate globalization, arguing that the current globalization model is neither a random inevitability nor 'free trade.' "

World Trade Organization, Centre William Rappard, Rue de Lausanne 154, CH-1211 Geneva 21, Switzerland; (41-22) 739 51 11; www.wto.org. A 153-member international organization established to set global trade rules and manage disputes.

Voices From Abroad:

PETER MANDELSON
Business Secretary United Kingdom

The problem with protectionism.
"Economic nationalism did not cause the long economic slump of the 1930s, but it deepened it, and acted as a barrier to the return to growth. It also exemplified the most important problem with protectionism, which is that it is highly contagious."

Jakarta Post (Indonesia), June 2009

HU JINTAO
President China

BRIC countries should take the lead.
"We [BRIC countries] should . . . take the lead in recovering from the global financial crisis. This is not only for our own need, but also contributes to world economic recovery."

Asia Pulse (Australia), June 2009

ELFREN S. CRUZ
Professor of Strategic Management
De La Salle University Philippines

Deglobalization leads to immediate solutions.
"Absolutely nobody can claim that he or she can predict what will happen to the world in the next couple of years. But, I believe that there is a strong possibility that as the recession and financial crisis continues to worsen, governments will turn to deglobalization as a means of satisfying their peoples' demand for more immediate solutions."

BusinessWorld (Philippines), February 2009

The Khaleej Times/UAE/Paresh Nath

ROLAND RUDD
Chairman Business for New Europe
United Kingdom

Free-trade advocates need the European Union.
"In seeking ways of maintaining free trade and eschewing protectionism, politicians should embrace the EU to achieve these goals. In the current climate of national protectionism, we need a stronger EC to maintain the integrity of the single market."

Daily Telegraph (England), February 2009

MANMOHAN SINGH
Prime Minister India

Reversing impact not easy.
"Some action by the developed countries — particularly the withdrawal of capital resources from developing countries by the banks of the developed countries — is equally

worrisome. We have entirely agreed that protectionism of all sorts including financial protectionism has to be avoided."

PTI news agency (India), April 2009

GERARD LYONS

**Chief Economist Standard Chartered Bank
United Kingdom**

Protectionism must end.
"Protection measures only give you short-term wins. They might help you today, they won't help you tomorrow. Protectionism isn't evil but it needs to be stopped."

Thai Press Reports, March 2009

STUART HARBINSON

Former Adviser World Trade Organization

The WTO is to blame.
"The global economic crisis showed cracks in the system. Weaknesses in the system, such as the length of time taken to produce a (WTO) settlement and a lack of compensation, should be seriously reviewed."

South China Morning Post, June 2009

PASCAL LAMY

Director-General World Trade Organization

We must open our borders.
"In a financial crisis, and at times of economic distress — in particular at a time of soaring world food prices — what impoverished consumers desperately need is to see their purchasing power enhanced and not reduced. What is needed in times of crises is to enable consumers to purchase more for less. The temptation to shut our borders does exactly the opposite. There is no doubt therefore that the current hurricane that has hit financial markets must not dissuade the international community from pursuing greater economic integration and openness."

Speech before WTO Public Forum, September 2008

8

Future of the Euro

Sarah Glazer

An election worker counts ballots after Ireland's general election on Feb. 25, in which the ruling party suffered a crushing defeat amid public anger over the country's economic crisis. Ireland's new prime minister, Enda Kenny, resisted pressure at an EU summit the following month to raise Ireland's low corporate tax rate — which attracts corporations like Google to Dublin — as the price for lowering the interest rate charged by the EU to Ireland for its bailout.

From *CQ Researcher*,
May 17, 2011.

When two German lawmakers suggested last year that Greece sell off some of its islands and artworks in exchange for a bailout from the European Union, the suggestion caused much hilarity in the European press.

"We give you cash, you give us Corfu . . . and the Acropolis too," cackled a headline in the German newspaper *Bild*. The British *Guardian* couldn't resist calling the proposal "My Big Fat Greek Auction," noting a Greek island could be picked up for as little as $2 million.

Dimitris Droutsas, Greece's deputy foreign minister, was not amused. "Suggestions like this are not appropriate at this time," he told German television.[1]

The dust-up epitomized the conflicts between the weak and the economically strong economies in the eurozone — the 17 European Union (EU) members that have adopted the euro as their currency. The tensions have escalated over the past year as Greece, Ireland and Portugal have received handouts from their EU brethren to help deal with domestic debt and budget crises. Now Greece apparently will need even more money to finance its debt, aggravating tensions and raising questions about whether richer countries will support yet more loans.

"The political understandings that underpin the European Union are beginning to unravel," declared *Financial Times* columnist Gideon Rachman on April 17, the day Finland's nationalist True Finns party — which had campaigned strongly against a bailout for Portugal — made spectacular gains in the general election. The victory intensified doubts at the time over whether Europe could agree on a solution to the debt crisis, since bailouts require

Eurozone Power Most of EU Economy

Seventeen of the 27 European Union (EU) members,represing a poulation of about 330 million,
have adopted the euro currency.Seven other countries are expected to join the eurozone
over the next seven years.Euro countries account for 75 percent of the EU's gross domestic product,
making the world's second-most-important currency after the U.S.dollar. Sweden, Denmark and the
United Kingdom have declined to join the eurozone. Portugal, ireland and Greece are experiencing
debt problem and have asked for bailouts.Some worry Spain could be next

The European Union and the Eurozone

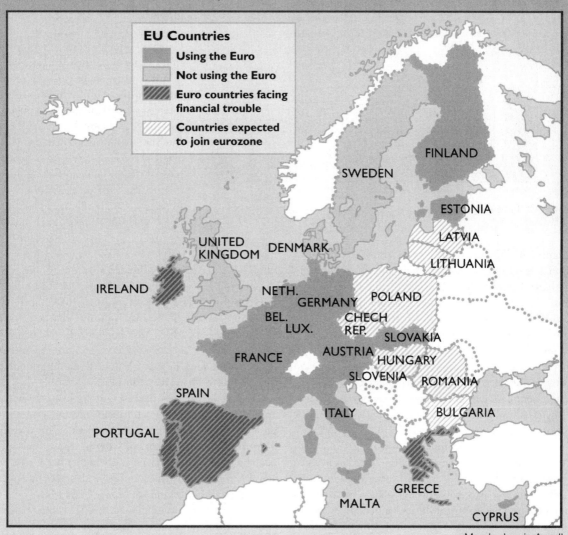

EU Countries

- Using the Euro
- Not using the Euro
- Euro countries facing financial trouble
- Countries expected to join eurozone

Source: European Commission

Map by Lewis Agrell

Failing Economies Loaded With Debt

Portugal, Ireland, Greece and Spain failed last year to meet the European Union (EU) goal of limiting countries' public debt to 60 percent of national output, or gross domestic product (GDP). Greece's debt-to-GDP ratio was the EU's highest, at 144 percent of GDP. Nordic countries such as Finland and Sweden had far lower ratios. But Germany, critical of countries with high debts, had a higher ratio than Spain. By comparison, the U.S. debt was 58.9 percent of GDP — just below the EU target.

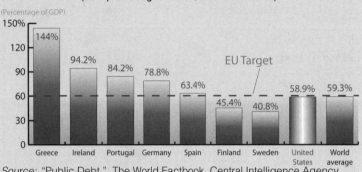

Public Debt for Select Countries
(as a percentage of GDP, 2010 Estimates)

Source: "Public Debt," The World Factbook, Central Intelligence Agency, May 2011

eurozone, a German voter is just as likely to be asked to bail out the Greek government — or, ultimately, to shore up a Greek bank.

The current crisis grew out of the inability of highly indebted governments like Greece, Ireland and Portugal to raise enough money in the bond markets to pay their debts and government obligations after the global recession sent tax revenues plunging. It began a year ago, when Greece — facing default after revelations that the nation's finances were in much worse shape than the previous administration had claimed — received a €110 billion ($145 billion) bailout loan from the EU and the International Monetary Fund (IMF). Then in November, Ireland — whose hyper-inflated housing bubble burst during the world credit crisis — received a €67.5 billion ($88.42 billion) EU/IMF rescue. Finally, Portugal's Socialist government last month came to the EU hat in hand, realizing it would not be able to pay its bondholders this June. On May 3, the EU and IMF agreed to loan Portugal €78 billion ($115 billion). The May 14 arrest of IMF Managing Director Dominique Strauss-Kahn on charges of the attempted rape of a New York hotel maid could complicate upcoming EU/IMF talks over revamping Greece's bailout loan, since he was a crucial figure in arranging the bailouts for the three countries.[3]

Despite the bailouts, interest rates for loans to Greece and Portugal have continued to soar, effectively preventing them from resuming normal borrowing. "Apparently bond traders are skeptical of whether those [bailout] guarantees will be sufficient and whether the Germans and other Europeans will stand behind larger and larger guarantees, if they become necessary," says Moss.

In exchange for the bailouts, the EU is demanding painful austerity measures that some economists say could trigger up to 10 more years of recession and huge cuts in treasured pension, unemployment, education and health-care programs. Nevertheless, although EU

unanimous approval by all 17 members of the eurozone.[2] Those fears were calmed, somewhat, when Finland's Parliament voted May 12 to support the Portugal bailout. But the vote came amid growing opposition in Germany to a possible second bailout for Greece and concerns that all three countries could make return visits to the euro till.

"My fear is the euro could sow seeds of division between members," says Simon Tilford, chief economist at the Centre for European Reform, a London think tank. "My question for the euro is whether it was ever realistic for such a heterogeneous group of nations," he says.

The growing resentments between rich and poor countries feed into a lingering question that has plagued the eurozone experiment since it was created in 1999: Can a common market like the eurozone function without a common government? In the United States, points out Harvard Business School professor of business administration David Moss, "There is a lot of anxiety and anger that Americans feel in bailing out Wall Street banks, but at least they're American banks." In the officials in Brussels insist such budget-cutting conditions will prevent defaults, investors recently have come to believe that a Greek default is "inevitable," according to the *Financial Times*.[4]

Indeed, some experts foresee the collapse of banks in wealthier nations like Germany, which loaned billions to the four faltering countries — Portugal, Ireland, Greece and Spain (known by their acronym, the PIGS) — during the credit boom years. Because of those banks' high exposure to troubled governments' bonds, EU leaders want to stave off default at all costs, experts say. The EU's solution is "a Ponzi scheme [that] could in theory go on forever," the former governor of Argentina's central bank, Mario Biejer, recently charged, suggesting that accepting a default might be "preferable to increasing the burden on future taxpayers."[5]

The eurozone was conceived as a way to turn the European Union into a formidable world economic power.[6] But the current crisis has highlighted what some economists say is the system's inherent weakness: the failure to form a United States of Europe with overarching power to balance the vast differences in wealth between the poor South and the rich North. The euro imposed a single currency on diverse countries without creating a centralized government with the power to collect taxes and decide how to spend them.

Ardent proponents of the euro knew from the beginning that eventually they would have to create "a federal fiscal system," says British economic historian Niall Ferguson, author of *The Cash Nexus* and a professor of history at Harvard. "But they didn't say it publicly, because no ordinary voter wants to be in the United States of Europe."

"Politicians knew that they risked running afoul of voters if they surrendered too much sovereignty," writes Mary Elise Sarotte, a professor of International Relations at the University of Southern California.[7] Instead, member countries have continued to guard jealously their power to tax and spend.

The recent deals among EU countries in the wake of the crisis show that member states continue to be reluctant to surrender sovereignty "in key areas such as pensions, labor and wage policy, or taxation," said the European Policy Centre, a Brussels think tank.[8]

EU diplomats say the current crisis presents an opportunity to fix those weaknesses. But some experts say the price demanded by the EU — austerity budgets and repayment of huge loans to the EU — will be so high that debt-laden countries like Portugal, Greece and Ireland will eventually abandon the euro currency.

"It's a question of time before the Irish or the Greeks or the Portuguese say, 'We can't do any more of this [debt- and budget-cutting] adjustment,' " says Desmond Lachman, resident scholar at the American Enterprise Institute (AEI), a conservative think tank in Washington. Or the Germans will simply "get tired of financing this."

The conflict already has had serious political repercussions for leaders in the eurozone. In February, the Irish government fell. A month later Portugal's Socialist Prime Minister José Sócrates was forced to resign. Also in March, German Chancellor Angela Merkel's Christian Democratic Party lost a crucial provincial election in a former party bastion — a loss partly blamed on German voters' resistance to paying higher taxes to rescue crisis-ridden Greece and Ireland.[9]

"The German voter has had enough of writing checks for people in the rest of Europe that he or she regards as lazy," says Ferguson.

Brussels diplomats refer to the tension between what countries must give up to make a common currency work and what is politically feasible as "Juncker's curse," after Luxembourg Prime Minister Jean-Claude Juncker's quip, "We all know what to do, but we don't know how to get re-elected once we have done it."[10]

However, that logjam may have broken, say EU diplomats, citing the recent bailouts and efforts to more closely monitor weaker states' balance sheets to prevent future disasters. "We are strengthening and broadening the surveillance framework of the euro in ways that would not have been thought possible before this crisis," maintains Silvia Kofler, minister counselor and head of press and public diplomacy at the EU delegation to the United States.

Yet, those very budget-cutting, debt-reducing measures could force the weaker countries to desert the euro, some fear. At some point, the troubled countries "are going to say, 'We're going through these tremendous recessions in order to pay interest to foreign bankers.' That's a very difficult political sell to maintain," observes Lachman.

And, unlike the U.S. dollar regime, the EU has no common military or coercive power that could be used

'Desperate Generation' Hits the Streets in Portugal

Youths complain of low pay, few jobs.

Twenty-three-year-old João Moreira considered himself lucky to get a job as a school teacher after obtaining his master's degree in education in Porto, Portugal's second-largest city.

But he was appalled when he discovered that he would earn less than the minimum wage. At €330 a month ($440) he is forced to live at home with his mother in his second year of teaching high-school students.

On March 12, Moreira and other recent university graduates used Facebook to organize street demonstrations to protest the dismal economic conditions facing his generation. The protests attracted between 300,000-400,000 demonstrators in Portugal's 10 major cities, surprising even the organizers themselves.

The organizers, all in their 20s, called themselves *geração à rasca* — loosely translated as the "desperate generation" or "generation in a jam." They say they were inspired by the Portuguese band Deolinda's popular song "What a Fool I Am," whose lyrics, "I'm from the unpaid generation," spoke to their precarious work situation.

"There are no jobs for young people in Portugal, and when you have a job, you have a job like mine — a low-paid job," says Moreira. "We can't see a future for ourselves; we have no prospects." Two of his fellow organizers were headed to wealthier countries — Germany and Denmark — to work.

Besides unemployment, demonstrators complained about the lack of job security. The number of so-called "green receipts" jobs — temporary consultant jobs without benefits — has swelled, and the protesters say many are trapped in these jobs for years. Youths also complain of another form of exploitation in their eyes: unpaid or low-paid internships.

"We have 35-year-olds who graduated 10 or 15 years ago who are still in internships because there's no other way of getting into the job market," says Paula Gil, 26, a petite, serious-eyed organizer of the Lisbon protests, who has a master's degree in international relations and is working in a year-long paid internship with a nongovernmental, international development organization.

"It is slavery," when you're working for free, says Gil. In a paid internship like hers, she says, payroll taxes take 50 percent of her pay even though "you don't get access to unemployment insurance or sick leave, you can be fired at any time and you don't get social security benefits."

Such dead-end jobs delay young people's decisions, experts note. "They can't marry because banks won't give them a mortgage," further contributing to Portugal's low fertility rate, observes Ana Catarina Santos, a political journalist for TSF, a radio news station in Lisbon. [1]

But not all university graduates foresee such a grim future. Several graduate students in economics at Nova University School of Business and Economics in Lisbon — Portugal's most selective business school — are optimistic about finding jobs, but expect they probably will have to go abroad to find their "dream job." None had attended the recent demonstrations.

Employers are simply trying to get around Portugal's rigid labor and benefit rules that make it expensive to hire and difficult to fire employees, these students say, echoing the view of the European Union, which is expected to

to force member states to stay in the eurozone, notes Harvard's Moss. "In this country, an attempted secession was put down by force during the Civil War. One has to wonder whether there is a limit to how far integration can go in Europe without a common government and without the threat of coercive power."

"The euro is like a sick patient on the couch, and the doctors don't agree on the diagnosis or prescription," Charles Grant, director of the Centre for European Reform, told a London School of Economics audience on March 15. And the crisis, he noted, comes as Europe's military and diplomatic power are dwindling, along with its economic competitiveness.

The fallout from the crisis has been multifaceted. The seven other EU members expected to adopt the euro sometime in the next seven years may now be less willing demand that Portugal move towards a more flexible labor market. Those labor laws need to change, says Nova student Rafael Barbosa, 21. "When you march against symptoms, nothing will get done," he says.

"It is very difficult for a boss to fire a worker in Portugal because they're protected by law by unions and lawyers," explains Santos, coauthor of the 2010 book, *Dangerous Ideas to Save Portugal.* Under existing law, if an employer fires a worker the boss must pay close to twice the employee's salary for every year worked, Santos notes. If the employer tries to challenge the requirement in court, it could take up to 10 years to get through the appeal process.

Indeed, there's "a cultural expectation" among the Portuguese that they'll have a job for life, especially in the bloated government sector, Santos says. It's partly a legacy of the 1974 revolution against the 42-year dictatorship of António de Oliviera Salazar and of the socialist rhetoric in liberated Portugal's constitution, which strongly guarantees workers' rights. About 13 percent of Portugal's workforce is employed in government jobs, from which it is almost impossible to be fired, according to Santos.

But Portugal's recently requested bailout from the European Union will likely require reform of the country's rigid labor rules — similar to recent labor reforms in Spain — and reductions in worker benefits.

Portugal also has suffered from a decade of poor economic growth, largely the result of its failure to improve the productivity of industries like textiles, which have become increasingly uncompetitive in the face of cheap Chinese exports.

Protest leaders have steered clear of offering political solutions to these economic realities. Their primary purpose, they say, was to start a discussion at the grass roots. They presented parliament with hundreds of survey sheets filled out by protesters, who were asked to suggest solutions. It's unclear what kind of reception their proposals, which Santos expects to be "a bit utopian," will receive from the new government after the June 5 elections. The new

Protesters in downtown Lisbon are just some of the 300,000-400,000 demonstrators who took to the streets of 10 major cities in Portugal on March 12, 2011, to protest the lack of job opportunities for young people. The turnout surprised even the organizers, who used Facebook to advertise the protests.

government will have to devise a strict austerity package to meet EU bailout conditions.

Still, the March demonstrations, notable for their lack of violence, touched a chord among other generations, too. "You could see a 40-year-old mother worried that her sons were unemployed, and you could see pensioners who earn only €300 a month," reports Santos. "It was diverse — each group protesting a different thing, a bit messy but very genuine. It showed Portuguese society has a lot of problems."

— Sarah Glazer

---

[1] The fertility rate refers to the average number of children born per woman in the population during her life. From 2005-2010, Portugal's fertility rate averaged 1.38 children per woman. A fertility rate below 1.8 is considered insufficient to replace the current population. For fertility rates, See "Pensions at a Glance, 2011," Organisation for Economic Co-operation and Development, 2011, p. 163.

to abandon their own currencies.[11] And EU enthusiasm for admitting new, less prosperous countries appears to have cooled somewhat. Meanwhile, right-wing nationalist parties — many of them skeptical of the euro and opposed to helping struggling neighbors — are making big strides across Europe.

Is the eurozone headed for yet more internal conflict or greater unity? Here are some of the questions being posed in governments, academia and the international community:

Will the Eurozone survive in its current form?

Even before Portugal was bracing for a new round of budget cuts in exchange for an EU bailout, some experts were predicting the eurozone's poorest country would defect if the EU's budget discipline became too draconian.

Budget Deficits Hobble Troubled Euro Countries

Portugal, Ireland and Greece are experiencing both debt crises and budget deficits. Greece and Portugal have the biggest deficits — more than 10 percent of their national output, or gross domestic product (GDP). The European Union recommends that member countries' budget shortfalls not exceed 3 percent of GDP. The U.S. budget deficit is 3.4 percent of GDP. Finland, Germany and the Netherlands have budget surpluses.

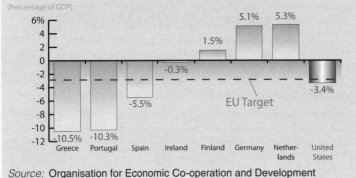

Budget Deficits (or Surpluses) for Select Countries
(as a percentage of GDP, 2010)

Source: Organisation for Economic Co-operation and Development

Current EU budget rules require member countries to reduce their public debt to no more than 60 percent of national output — or gross domestic product (GDP) — and to keep their budget deficits from exceeding 3 percent of GDP.[12]

Portugal, Ireland, Greece and Spain have a long way to go to meet those goals. And reaching them could take up to 10 years of stunted economic growth while they pay back their debts, slash their budgets and raise taxes, some economists say.

Such strict budget and debt ceilings, however, will block the PIGS from using economic tools governments historically have utilized to lift their nations out of recession: deficit spending to stimulate the economy.

"These countries are now forced in a vicious way to use austerity when you shouldn't have it; austerity makes things worse and undermines the political basis of the support you need for the eurozone," says Paul De Grauwe, a professor of economics at the University of Leuven, in Belgium.

Indeed, AEI's Lachman predicts that Greece, Ireland, Portugal and probably Spain will drop out of the eurozone because they won't be able to survive the inevitable years of recession that will follow such austerity programs.

The eurozone "can't survive in its present form," he says. "For me, it's a question of just the timing when that occurs."

Others, such as EU diplomat Kofler, consider the idea of defection "really difficult to take seriously." If a nation left the euro, she says, its "existing debt level would remain in euros, regardless of what new currency it introduced after leaving the euro area." Since the new currency likely would devalue against the euro — by 50 percent according to some estimates — the cost of paying back interest and principal on the existing debt would "skyrocket," she predicts.[13] The result would be steep inflation, collapsed banking sectors and the flight of capital, EU officials warn.[14]

Irish economist David McWilliams, however, advocates that Ireland leave the euro and pay back its debtors in a new devalued Irish currency, essentially forcing debtors to accept a loss. Adopting a new, weaker currency, McWilliams predicts, would make Ireland "cheaper overnight for people to do business in."[15]

Yet, even an early euroskeptic like economist Ferguson considers exiting too expensive and unlikely, partly because of a widely expressed fear of crisis contagion.

Others cite practical problems like printing new currency and redesigning vending machines. De Grauwe, another early euroskeptic, says these arguments remind him of the stories of Soviet couples who wanted to divorce but couldn't because of the impossibility of finding a second apartment. "You were condemned to stay together, and you hated each other. If that's the future of the eurozone, I'm not optimistic," he says. "In the end, the [weaker countries] will say, 'To hell with it: Even if the practical problems are high, we just don't want it anymore.'"

On the other hand, De Grauwe and other euroskeptics have suggested, stronger economies like Germany are suffering from "integration fatigue" and might leave the eurozone to avoid paying bailout costs. Euro defenders counter that richer countries won't let a collapse happen if only for their own self-interest: Bailouts for Greece help German banks, which own large amounts of the PIGS' debt in the form of government bonds and loans. If any one of the troubled countries defaults and leaves the euro, German banks would suffer huge losses.[16]

By sharing the euro with poorer economies, Germany also benefits from using a weaker currency, making its exports cheaper than if German exports were priced in a more expensive deutschmark. "It's a great advantage; that's why they'll never leave it," says Carlo Bastasin, an economist and senior fellow at the Brookings Institution, a moderate think tank in Washington.

Observers on both sides say the eurozone is at a critical political juncture. The current crisis is "analogous to the New Deal period in the United States," says Simon Hix, a professor of European and Comparative Politics at the London School of Economics. "There were huge battles over whether the U.S. government would take on . . . fiscal responsibilities [for other states,] because until then the U.S. federal budget was tiny."

And despite the current raging debate, Hix maintains, there's a surprising amount of consensus among political rivals about accepting the EU's new levels of austerity. Even in Portugal, the opposition Social Democratic Party — which is favored to win the June election and which helped sink the government's last austerity package — has accepted the need for bailout austerity.

"If that broad level of consensus carries on in Europe among voters like this, we have a good chance of getting through this," Hix says, "because you have publics that are willing to accept the tough political decisions needed to make these things work."

Skeptics, however, think the strains of trying to yoke such different economies to the euro are fomenting, not calming, new political tensions. "You're getting two Europes: the North that is doing OK and the South that is going down the drain," says Lachman. "That's not the way to have a political union."

Are some countries worse off under the euro?

When it comes to Ireland's current economic crisis, the government's biggest mistake was joining the euro in the first place, according to Sean Barrett, an economist at Trinity College, Dublin.

"Since joining the euro we've conducted an experiment by blowing up the laboratory," he says, pointing out that Ireland went from full employment and a balanced budget before adopting the euro to 14.5 percent unemployment and insolvency today.

As Nobel Prize-winning American economist Milton Friedman warned in 2001, countries need different monetary policies depending on whether their economies are fast-growing and inflationary — which need higher interest rates to cool them down — or slow-growing, needing low rates to help heat up the economy by encouraging borrowing, investment and consumption.[17]

Today Friedman's predictions seem prescient. Known during boom times as the "Celtic Tiger," Ireland was growing exponentially on a virtual tsunami of cheap money during the 1990s-2000s, which triggered a disastrous property bubble. The government should have raised interest rates to slow down the borrowing frenzy, euro critics say, but it no longer had that power since the European Central Bank (ECB) sets interest rates for the euro countries.

"Ireland needed to cool down in the years after it joined the euro, but Germany needed to warm up," notes Barrett. Now the situation is reversed, with the European Central Bank responding more to Germany's fast-growth situation than to Ireland's dismal recession.

ECB President Jean-Claude Trichet encountered a storm of criticism — mainly from Ireland and Spain — when the bank on April 7 raised Europe's interest rates by a quarter of a percentage point to 1.25 percent. The increase was expected to hit the two countries especially hard because of the large number of homeowners with variable-rate mortgages.[18]

"There's a double whammy [in Ireland] for homeowners in that the main banks here can increase their rates but also the European Central Bank can increase its rates," which are reflected in variable-rate mortgages, says Aoife Walsh, spokesperson for Respond! Housing Association, which advises Irish homeowners.

By contrast, Germany welcomed the interest rate hike as a way to cool inflation. Trichet said his action was aimed at the eurozone as a whole, where inflation has exceeded the bank's 2 percent target.

Adopting the euro also meant governments could no longer devalue their own currencies — a primary tool nations use to recover from a recession because it makes their exports cheaper and therefore more competitive. When Ireland devalued its currency, the punt, during its 1990s recession, Barrett notes, it stimulated "pretty strong growth."

In addition, say economists, the EU's Germanic obsession with living within one's budget has shifted attention away from encouraging economic growth, which would require deficit spending.

Portugal, for example, has suffered from a decade of slow growth. After years as Europe's sweatshop, selling cheap shoes and textiles, Portugal recently has found itself underpriced by China. And Portugal's failure to reconfigure its industries as high-end, high-fashion brands, as Italy has done, has forced many small companies to shut down and others to suffer. But that kind of investment seems unlikely when demand is low and the cost of borrowing is high.

During the boom years, with exceptionally low interest rates, those in the weaker eurozone countries were practically "paid to borrow," says Tilford, of London's Centre for European Reform. The resulting borrowing-fueled consumption disguised both the lack of underlying growth and the need for structural reforms, such as making hiring and firing more flexible.

"Spain, Italy and Portugal saw the euro as a way of avoiding reforms and being free of currency crises, but it doesn't shield them from the credit crisis," he says.

By contrast, some non-euro EU economies — notably Sweden, Poland and Britain — grew faster in 2010 than eurozone countries.[19] The U.K. also has embarked on an austerity budget, but it can devalue its currency to make its exports more competitive, which the euro countries aren't free to do.

Other economists say the euro is being blamed unfairly for an economic crash that had more to do with the international credit crisis and the failure of domestic regulators. In the case of Ireland, "joining the euro meant we had greater access" to funding from abroad, acknowledges Philip Lane, a professor of economics at Trinity College, Dublin. German banks lent to Irish banks at low rates, who in turn lent cheaply and recklessly to property developers and homeowners. But, "That doesn't mean we had to take it up. It's the role of the regulator to be the grown-up," he says, by requiring a sensible fit between the income of the borrower and the value of the property, something Ireland's regulators failed to do.

"The world was awash in credit," he says, and borrowing standards were being loosened internationally. Iceland, for example, experienced a phenomenal credit crash even though it wasn't on the euro, he points out.

Once Ireland got into trouble, he notes, it benefited from eurozone membership by being able to borrow from the European Central Bank when borrowing in the bond markets became too expensive.

John Fitz Gerald, an economist at the Economic and Social Research Institute, a think tank in Dublin, says his group warned as early as 1996 that once on the euro the Irish government would have to take other steps to cool borrowing, like taxing homeowners' mortgage-interest payments.

"It's not rocket science," he says, but the government paid no attention. "Don't blame the euro for bad government. Bad government gives you bad results."

Will the EU approach solve the debt crisis?

"Trouble paying your debt? Here borrow some more: How about €80 billion?" asked the *Financial Times* the day after Portugal asked the EU for a $119 billion loan. The eurozone's policymakers should ask themselves whether overindebted Portugal, Ireland and Greece can really do everything expected of them in drastic austerity plans and still pay back their EU loans on time, the *FT* warned.[20]

Some economists say the EU bailout formula "shows no sign of working," according to *The New York Times*, and some say it's making the problem worse.[21]

Under the weight of steep budget cuts over the past two years, the EU's first bailout recipient, Greece, has suffered a 6-percent contraction in real GDP, while Ireland's economy has shrunk by 11 percent. "This is now seriously undermining those countries' tax bases as well as their political willingness to stay the course of [budget-cutting] adjustment," concluded AEI's Lachman.[22] In fact, he predicts, under the EU's prescription, Greece's economy "will collapse."

Already, "Greece has basically ground to a halt," *FT* writer Vincent Boland said on May 9, after the euro plunged on rumors Greece was in so much trouble it would leave the eurozone.[23]

The EU insistence on governments living within their budgets has deprived these countries of deficit spending, says the University of Leuven's De Grauwe.

Deficit spending is used by governments to "make sure those who are unemployed have some purchasing power to buy goods and services to permit the economy to start growing again," he says. "You don't do that only out of altruism, but also out of a rational calculus that it stabilizes the economy."

Eurozone ministers acknowledged on May 8 that Greece's bailout was insufficient and that the government would need more EU cash to pay its debts into next year. EU ministers planned to meet in May to find a solution, since it was clear Greece could not borrow in the bond markets at the prohibitively high interest rates it was being charged. Amid heightened speculation that Greece would default, eurozone leaders said they were also considering easing Greece's repayment terms.[24]

That renewed crisis — a year after Greece received its bailout, plus Ireland's recent request for easier payback terms — signal that the bailout approach is failing, critics say. "Greece and Ireland are already bailed out and look like they won't be able to finance themselves next year," because of skyrocketing borrowing costs, says Raoul Ruparel, an analyst at Open Europe, a London think tank focused on the European Union.

Increasingly, some prominent economists are urging that these countries need a restructuring — a polite term for default.

"There needs to be a frank acknowledgement that these debts are unsustainable," says University of California, Berkeley, economist Barry Eichengreen. So far, he says, the EU's emphasis on budget cuts is "reducing the cost of everything but the debt; that's another reason why the current strategy will not work."

With an orderly debt restructuring, much like a personal bankruptcy, the EU could tell the countries' creditors, or bondholders, that if they don't want to suffer a total loss from a likely default, "take 60 cents on the dollar plus a guarantee that this debt is secure" — backed by the full faith and credit of the eurozone member countries.

Once the debt load is reduced in this manner, Eichengreen says, countries like Greece and Ireland can grow again.

A default — or restructuring — would actually be cheaper for Portugal than the current EU-style bailouts, argues a recent paper by Open Europe's Ruparel. The country's overall debt burden would decline, eventually

New York City detectives hold IMF Managing Director Dominique Strauss-Kahn after he was arrested on May 15 and charged with the attempted rape of a hotel chambermaid. Strauss-Kahn, who is being held without bond, was a crucial figure in advocating the bailouts for Greece as well as Ireland and Portugal, and his arrest could complicate upcoming EU/IMF talks over easing the terms of Greece's bailout loan.

AFP/Getty Images/Jewel Samad

driving down the nation's borrowing costs. It would also shift some of the burden of the loss that default inevitably brings to investors, who would not get back all their money, and away from taxpayers who now are bearing the burden of repaying their government's loans in full.[25]

Ruparel says much of the opposition to restructuring comes from the banking sector, "particularly in Germany, where banks are heavily exposed to these [troubled] countries. The government knows if a restructure were to happen, the banks would suffer serious losses."

In their 2011 book, *This Time Is Different*, American economists Carmen M. Reinhart and Kenneth S. Rogoff find that sovereign defaults have been a common government feature for more than eight centuries. Reinhart says a default could end the market speculation that escalates governments' borrowing costs — and their pain — once and for all. "You may be postponing going to the dentist, and it is not going to be a pretty experience, " says Reinhart, "but once you do, it's over and you move on."

Some economists are horrified by the idea of letting any country default, because they fear failures would spread like a contagious virus. For example, if Portugal defaulted many experts fear Spain, whose banks have high exposure to Portuguese government bonds, would be the next to fall.

Italian economist Bastasin says, "It would be politically disruptive and have terrible consequences on those countries."

EU diplomats have strongly resisted any suggestion of default or restructuring for Greece or Portugal. The EU does not contemplate the possibility of restructuring until 2013, when the EU proposes to establish a permanent bailout fund — the European Stability Mechanism (ESM).

Critics say that's too little too late. And most observers agree the fund wouldn't be big enough to bail out a large economy like Spain. Some experts say they won't worry about the eurozone's future until Spain, a much bigger economy than any of the other PIGS, appears to be in serious trouble. As in Ireland, Spain's housing bubble — concentrated in coastal resort/retirement areas — pulled down home prices. Spanish savings banks are heavily exposed to domestic property losses, so a sharp decline in housing prices could trigger difficulties that could spread to the eurozone. However, Spain has begun to reform its extremely rigid labor market and enacted deficit-controlling cost-cutting measures. So far Spain's borrowing costs have remained below 5 percent, far less than the other PIGS' double digit rates.[26]

Officials in Brussels say the new proposed bailout fund, created from contributions and guarantees from all eurozone countries — represents the kind of "fiscal union" the eurozone has long been criticized for lacking. But De Grauwe, author of the classic textbook *Economics of Monetary Union*, now in its eighth edition, disagrees.

"It's a far cry from the kind of budgetary union the United States would have with automatic transfers" from one state to another, he says. "The ESM is a mechanism to manage crisis not to prevent crisis."

Ironically, when the fund was first proposed last year, it triggered a crisis of its own after investors learned it contemplated restructuring after 2013. Private holders of government bonds feared a default would cost them money. The borrowing costs for struggling eurozone members surged on that news.

As De Grauwe puts it, each time a new country runs into trouble, "we fight, then the markets are uncertain what's going to happen. As a result, they dump bonds of countries in trouble, and we get involved each time in a major financial crisis."

Some economists would favor the introduction of a so-called eurobond, which would be backed by all the countries of the eurozone. That would avoid the kind of market attacks on individual countries' bonds that have occurred in the past year. De Grauwe sees a eurobond as a partial step toward the political union the eurozone has always lacked, yet "more realistic than full budgetary union like in the U.S."

BACKGROUND

Bending Union Rules

History offers few examples of successful efforts among nations to share a single currency on the scale of today's eurozone. It does offer, however, "several examples of monetary unions between sovereign states disintegrating," writes historian Ferguson in his 2001 history of money, *The Cash Nexus.*[27] The unions usually fell apart when one member suffering from deficits bent the rules and began printing its own money, essentially devaluing the currency.

The closest precedent to the eurozone, the so-called Latin Monetary Union (1865-1927), made the coinages of six European governments freely exchangeable within a single area that encompassed France, Belgium, Switzerland, Italy, the Papal States and Greece. Like the eurozone, the Latin Union began with a political motivation — the dream of a "European Union."

Eventually the extravagance of the Italian and Papal governments became too costly for the other member states. The Papal government financed its debts by debasing its coinage, while Italy issued its own paper currency. Under these strains, the union had effectively stopped functioning by World War I and was pronounced dead, belatedly, in the 1920s.[28]

In more recent times, several unions have been short-lived. Around the time of the fall of the Berlin Wall, three separate monetary unions — one among the former members of the Soviet Union, and one each among the countries that make up the former Yugoslavia and Czechoslovakia — broke apart after weaker members raised revenue by printing money. Looking back at that history, Ferguson predicted in 2001 that "the strains caused by unaffordable social security and pension systems," which would grow with Europe's aging population, could similarly break up the eurozone.[29]

Governments have long used the tactic of debasing their currencies — which spurred many of the past breakups — to reduce their debts. Ancient Roman emperors had reduced the silver content of the denarius coin by nearly 99 percent between the reign of Marcus Aurelius and the time of Diocletian. Struggling to pay his debts, King Henry VIII in the 1540s reduced the gold and silver content of England's new coins, giving them a face value twice that of the metal they contained.[30]

Today, printing more paper money to devalue one's currency is a technologically advanced way of debasing coinage. But eurozone governments lost the option of devaluing their currency when they adopted the euro — a loss that has exacerbated their current troubles.

Bloodshed Averted

After World War II, European leaders were determined to prevent future bloodshed by creating greater cooperation among their nations. In 1951 six countries — France, Germany, Italy, Netherlands, Belgium and Luxembourg — agreed to run their coal and steel industries under a common plan so no country could create weapons against another. For the first time, the six nations agreed to give up some of their sovereignty in a common effort.

Following the success of the coal and steel treaty, the six nations in 1957 signed the Treaty of Rome, creating the European Economic Community (EEC) or Common Market, pledging cooperation in the free movement of goods, services and people across borders.[31]

Throughout the 1960s and into the '70s, the EEC continued to break down trade barriers and add new members. In 1968 the six Common Market countries removed customs duties on goods imported across their borders. Trade grew rapidly both among the six and with the rest of the world.[32]

By 1988, the Single Market Act contained a commitment to monetary unification but included no deadline for introducing it. The deciding event came in 1989 with the fall of the Berlin Wall and the prospect of a reunified Germany for the first time in 40 years.[33]

Germany's reunification required the consent of the four post-World War II occupying powers: France, Britain, the United States and the Soviet Union. When Germany sought French approval for reunification, the creation of a European monetary union — something long sought

Weeds grow unchecked in the streets and yards of new houses offered at discount prices in Ballindine, County Mayo, Ireland — remnants of the country's hyper-inflated housing bubble that caused average home prices to nearly triple. When the bubble burst, home prices and tax revenues plummeted and Ireland's debt and interest rates skyrocketed, forcing it to seek an EU/IMF rescue.

Getty Images/Tim Graham

by France as a way to increase its own political influence — became France's quid pro quo.

"Now that Germany's land area, population and economic capacity were set to expand at a stroke, it became even more urgent to lock it into Europe" to prevent German imperial ambitions — which had flourished during two world wars — from re-emerging, writes University of California economist Eichengreen.[34]

Why was France so committed to a monetary union? Ferguson notes that one ardent single-currency proponent, French Socialist Jacques Delors, thought the euro would protect Europe's extensive welfare state because all members would be tied to the same highly taxed, "centralized, redistributive and, in some ways, socialist system."[35]

Paradoxically, the eurozone's political leaders have taken more of a free-market approach, judging by recent EU requirements that debt-laden economies slash their social-welfare benefits and reduce expensive payroll taxes paid by businesses for those benefits. "When the countries joined, they effectively signed up to much more liberal [free-market] economic policies — free trade and flexible labor markets — but they don't seem to realize that" or acknowledge it to their voters, says Tilford of London's Centre for European Reform.

Of course, there were also some mutual benefits, even for Germany. "What you got was lower borrowing costs for the indebted nations and a weaker currency for

CHRONOLOGY

1945s-1959s *In aftermath of World War II, European leaders decide to forge greater economic cooperation to prevent more bloodshed.*

1951 Six countries (France, Germany, Italy, the Netherlands, Belgium and Luxembourg) agree to run coal and steel industries under a common pact to prevent one country from forging weapons to use against another.

1957 The six coal and steel compact nations adopt Treaty of Rome, creating the European Economic Community (EEC) — the "Common Market" — to allow free movement of goods and people across borders.

1960-1979 *Economic growth and trade grow rapidly; EEC expands.*

1968 The six EEC members remove customs duties among themselves.

1973 Denmark, Ireland and U.K. join the EEC.

1980s *Berlin Wall falls; Germany agrees to monetary union; EEC membership expands.*

1980 Greece joins EEC, bringing membership to 10.

1986 Portugal and Spain become EEC's 11th and 12th members.

1988 Single Market Act commits to a European monetary union but no deadline for achieving it.

1989 Berlin Wall falls. France approves German reunification in exchange for German agreement to establish a common European currency.

1990s *European Monetary Union and euro established.*

1992 Treaty — signed at Maastricht, Netherlands — re-names EEC the European Community under the newly created European Union (in 2009 the EC is absorbed into the EU), commits it to monetary union by 1999 and sets rules for participating countries.

1997 Stability Pact establishes stricter maximum debt and budget deficit targets for EU members, but they're never enforced.

Jan. 1, 1999 Euro introduced in 11 countries for commercial/financial transactions, but U.K. retains the British pound as its currency.

2000s *World financial crisis dries up credit; housing bubbles burst in Ireland, Spain; EU bails out Greece, Ireland.*

2001 Greece becomes 12th country to join euro but its financial qualifications are later found deceptive.

2002 Euro notes and coins introduced into general circulation.

September 2008 Major financial crisis strikes Europe, as mortgage, credit and housing bubbles burst; Lehman Bros. fails; Irish government guarantees banks' deposits and bonds.

2009 Greece's new government reveals budget deficit is twice what the previous government had reported.

2010 EU and IMF bail out Greece with €110 billion ($160 billion) loan. EU approves new lending to euro countries to prevent the financial crisis from spreading. . . . EU agrees to bail out Ireland (Nov. 28).

2011 José Sócrates' Socialist government in Portugal collapses after his austerity package fails to pass (March 23). . . . EU summit agrees to establish permanent bailout fund to safeguard euro and help struggling countries (March 24-25). . . . Portugal asks EU for bailout (April 6). . . . Greek borrowing costs soar on news it failed to meet its EU deficit-reduction target. Borrowing costs for Portugal and Ireland reach euro-era highs on fears all three countries might default (April 27). . . . EU discusses more aid for Greece (May 7-9). . . . Finnish Parliament supports Portugal bailout, despite opposition from nationalist True Finns party (May 12). . . . IMF head Dominique Strauss-Kahn is arrested for attempted rape in New York, complicating bailout negotiations (May 14). . . . Portugal general election scheduled (June 5). . . . Portugal must redeem €7 billion ($10 billion) in maturing bonds; bailout loan seen as crucial (June 15).

Germany," says Ferguson. That meant German exports were cheaper, making them more competitive.

Until the last 50 years, most Western European countries were not economically viable on their own, and some, like Britain and France, used colonial empires to fuel their domestic economies, points out London School of Economics professor Hix. The Common Market, and later the EU, accomplished the same thing without bloodshed.

Indeed, without the creation of this internal market, the German, French, British and Italian economies "would not be large enough to sustain the standards of living which their citizens take for granted," Hix writes.[36]

Birth of the Euro

On Feb. 7, 1992, the Treaty on European Union was signed by the members of the Common Market, under the renamed European Union, at Maastricht, Netherlands. The treaty established rules for a single currency and set 1999 as the deadline for introducing the euro. Britain was exempted from the currency, while Denmark was to decide by referendum.

Both Britain and Denmark obtained legal exemptions from joining the euro. Denmark, a small but proud country, voted in 2002 not to join the euro.[37] Under Conservative Prime Minister John Major, Britain had participated in an earlier version of monetary union, the European Monetary System. But after a speculators' attack on the pound, Britain took its currency out of the joint system in 1992. "Tony Blair could credit his victory in the 1997 general election to the damage done to the Conservative government of John Major by the 1992 crisis," Eichengreen writes.

The so-called Maastricht Criteria set conditions for participating in the monetary union, including caps on budget deficits (no more than 3 percent of GDP), public debt (no more than 60 percent of GDP) and limits on inflation and long-term interest rates. But members had trouble following these conditions.

As the University of Southern California's Sarotte has observed, "Policymakers wanted the new currency to succeed and started using the number of members and applicants as an oversimplified metric of success, thereby allowing weaker economies to join without due scrutiny. Such laxness allowed the entry not only of members with debt-to-GDP ratios well in excess of 60 percent

(Belgium, Italy) but also of applicants such as Greece, which not only flouted the rules but also falsified its records."[38]

Once accepted into the union, weaker member states could borrow at roughly the same interest rate as Germany, due to the European Central Bank's practice of treating the sovereign debt of all eurozone members equally. This meant that spending increased without regard to what the countries could actually afford.

The budgeting criteria were strengthened, at least in theory, at the request of the Germans in a 1997 Stability Pact, which established fines on those who violated the criteria. But fines have never been imposed, so the Maastricht Criteria have been observed mostly in the breach — even by the Germans.

After German reunification, the high cost of economic reconstruction in East Germany drove up Germany's borrowing costs, forcing Germany to ask, humiliatingly, for lenient implementation of the Stability Pact it had instigated. The EU agreed. Afterward, it was much harder for subsequent German governments to act in a holier-than-thou fashion toward any other member with economic woes. The fact that the French also found themselves in a fiscal hole for much of the 1990s only compounded the problem.

Thus, the Maastricht Criteria were only minimally enforced. But some experts say the caps were unrealistic from the outset. "The aging population of Europe plus the welfare state translated into deficits that were going to be way larger than 3 percent of GDP," says Ferguson, who predicted in 2000 that problems would surface within a decade.

On Jan. 1, 1999, the euro was introduced in 11 countries for commercial and financial transactions. Notes and coins entered general circulation in 2002.

Bubbles and Bailouts

When Greece became the 12th country to adopt the euro in 2001, no one guessed that it held the seeds of a disaster that would severely test the future of the monetary union.

Three years later it was discovered that Greece's financial reports, which had seemed to meet the eurozone's conditions for entry, were inaccurate. And in 2009 Greece's new Socialist government revealed that the national budget deficit would be 12.7 percent of GDP — twice the

Ireland Struggles With Public and Private Debt

"Reckless lending" and cronyism are blamed.

According to a joke told around Dublin these days, second prize for winning the Irish sweepstakes is five apartments. First prize? Zero apartments.

It's a painful truth that during Ireland's roaring "Celtic Tiger" years, the entire country was caught up in a property-buying frenzy and easy credit — until it all ended in the economic crash of 2008-09.

Since property values plummeted, one of every two homeowners is in "negative equity," with the amount they owe on their mortgage greater than the value of their house. Many families can't pay their debts because they have lost a job, had their salary cut or seen their house value drop by 50 percent from the peak.

"We've seen cases of middle-income families that have their own mortgage to pay plus three more mortgages" on houses they bought to rent out, says Paul Joyce, senior policy researcher at Free Legal Advice Centers (FLAC) in Dublin, a network of volunteer lawyers that advises people on how to get out of debt. During the boom years, investment advisors regularly touted property purchases as a nest egg for retirement, he says. But potential tenants and homebuyers have evaporated, including the immigrant construction workers who returned to Eastern Europe when the housing industry collapsed.

The stories of property magnates and government regulators drinking together at lavish racetrack fundraisers for Fianna Fáil, the previous government's party, are rife — a relationship many blame for a housing bubble the government either didn't see coming or didn't want to burst. [1] "It was cronyism at its worst," says Joan Collins, a member of Parliament who represents Dublin's South Central neighborhood, one of Ireland's poorest. She blames "all this madness" on tax breaks the Fianna Fáil government gave developers to build new housing, hotels and private hospitals.

Less well-known is the extent to which the government turned to private developers to build public housing. The wreckage of that failed effort can be seen at St. Michael's public housing complex in Dublin, where a developer demolished eight of 10 apartment blocks, then walked away bankrupt when the economy crashed, leaving a vast wasteland and former tenants scattered into temporary rentals. "Now a community has been devastated," Collins says.

At one of Dublin's largest public housing complexes, Dolphin House, where residents had long complained of backed-up sewage seeping into their 1940s-era apartments, the City Council also turned to a developer for the solution. The developer planned to replace the existing 436 apartments and build an additional 600 private apartments to be sold to well-heeled professionals, since the location is desirable — just five minutes by light rail from downtown. [2]

The residents were still in the planning stage when the housing bubble burst. The developers vanished. "We missed the boat," admits Veronica Lally, 41, a resident of Dolphin House. "The Dublin City Council is bankrupt. There's no money to maintain these properties," she says, holding little hope for repair of the archaic plumbing system.

Like many Irish taxpayers, Lally, a community employment adviser, expresses rage that she'll be paying thousands of euros in taxes "for a developer that was greedy" and the ensuing bank crisis. She holds government, developers and trade unions equally responsible. [3]

"They got into bed the three of them and ripped the heart out of this country; and young people are shipping off to America and Australia — all our good talent going, because there's nothing here for them," she continues. Now the bankers must be bailed out and the money the government borrowed from the European Union to prop up the banks "paid back to Europe."

Like Dublin's council, the national government made the mistake of failing to build up its budget surpluses during the good times for a rainy day, some economists say.

"The government should have targeted the housing market by taxing mortgage interest payments. Instead they

previous government's estimate, and more than four times larger than the EU's target.

The announcement caused Greece's bond rating to plummet, and the risk of a default surfaced for the first time. This occurred as an international credit and financial crisis was building in 2007 and became official in September 2008, when Lehman Brothers, a big U.S. investment bank, collapsed, and credit dried up around the world.

Starting as early as 2005, imbalances were already building between stolid, economically successful Germany subsidized mortgage interest payments," says John Fitz Gerald, an economist at the Economic and Social Research Institute, a Dublin think tank. If the government had followed his advice, "they would have given households higher interest rates de facto," he says, which would have made households more cautious about taking on too big a mortgage. Then, "when the economy slowed down, the government would have had a surplus they could have used."

"Reckless lending" by banks is a common phrase heard in Ireland these days. Many blame the failed Anglo-Irish Bank for its maverick lending strategy of dropping traditional credit requirements, such as putting a down payment on a home mortgage — a practice that put pressure on other Irish banks to do the same.

Besides middle-class homeowners, Ireland has a new and growing working class saddled with exorbitant amounts of personal debt, often piled up on multiple credit cards. "A lot of people in working-class areas had access to subprime lenders and to credit they wouldn't have had before," Joyce says. "A lot of individuals won't be able to pay the money back; it was lent quite recklessly with very little regard to lending standards."

Ireland's debt problem is compounded by the fact that the country lacks modern bankruptcy laws that would allow an individual to wipe out his personal debts, Joyce says. And "non-recourse" lending, common in the United States, is totally unknown in Ireland. It allows a homeowner to mail his keys back to the bank and walk away without paying the rest of the mortgage. Even if an Irish bank forecloses on a house and sells it — typically for a fraction of its original value — the homeowner is still responsible for the remainder of the mortgage.

"That's really why people are concerned," says Aoife Walsh, spokesperson for Respond! Housing Association, which advises troubled homeowners. "They know that not only could they lose the roof over their heads, but they'll have this massive debt hanging over them for the rest of their lives."

Although the new Fine Gael/Labour coalition government elected Feb. 25 has pledged to "fast-track" personal bankruptcy reform, no legislation is pending yet. The

Community organizer Wally Bowden stands in front of an abandoned building at Dolphin House, a public housing complex in Dublin, Ireland. A developer had planned to renovate the complex, add profit-making apartments and turn the building into a private clinic. When the property market crashed, the developer abandoned the project.

International Monetary Fund's bailout loan for Ireland, however, called for such legislation to be introduced by March 2012.

— Sarah Glazer

[1] Christopher Caldwell, "Not Too Big to Fáil," *The Weekly Standard*, Feb. 21, 2011, www.weeklystandard.com/articles/not-too-big-f-il_547 416.html.

[2] "Dolphin Decides: The Final Report," Dolphin House Community Development Association, 2009, p. 8, www.pcc.ie/dolphindecides/dolphin.html.

[3] The bill to the government for bailing out Irish banks reached €70 billion in March, equal to €17,000 for each citizen. See Larry Elliott and Jill Treanor, "Ireland forced into new €21 billion bailout by debt crisis," *Guardian*, March 31, 2011, www.guardian.co.uk/world/2011/mar/31/ireland-new-bailout-euro-crisis?INTCMP=SRCH.

and weaker economies in southern eurozone countries on such crucial measures as competitiveness, trade surpluses and deficits.

With a Greek default looming and fears that such a crisis might prove contagious, European heads of state on April 11, 2010, agreed to establish a crisis mechanism to safeguard the zone's financial stability by lending funds to member states in serious financial distress. On May 2, it was announced that Greece would receive an EU/IMF bailout loan of €110 billion.[39]

AFP/Getty Images/Louisa GGouliamaki

AFP/Getty Images/Christina Quicler

Strikes and Protests

A man hauls around fake euro notes (top) during a demonstration in Seville called by Spanish unions on June 8, 2010, to protest government austerity cuts. Garbage went uncollected and hospital services were limited throughout the country as thousands of public workers protested the cuts, designed to reduce Spain's deficit. BBVA is Spain's second-largest bank. In Athens, Greece, a cardboard coffin symbolizes the death of the euro during a protest march on March 30, 2010 (bottom). Government austerity measures in Greece have sparked several general strikes and street protests.

On May 9, 2010, officials established the European Financial Stability Facility (EFSF) — a three-year, €440 billion ($592 billion) fund to lend to troubled euro countries (other than Greece). That would be supplemented with a €250 billion ($337 billion) IMF commitment. After recent growing concerns that the fund's lending

capacity might be insufficient, EU leaders this March committed themselves to finding a compromise by the summer to boost its lending ability.[40]

Last July 23 the EU announced the results of its "stress tests" on 91 European banks to determine whether the banks were resilient enough to weather future economic shocks. All but seven passed the tests, which the EU represented as a sign of the banks' solidity.[41] But the spectacular crash just a few months later of several Irish banks raised skepticism about the value of future tests.

Between 2003 and 2007 Ireland experienced a property-driven boom. By 2007, average house prices were nearly triple 2000 levels. The Irish economy became increasingly dependent on the construction sector — representing almost a quarter of its economy. By 2007, government revenues were heavily dependent on windfall taxes from the housing market.

When the housing bubble burst, tax revenues plummeted, ending a decade of budget surpluses.[42] But none of this could have happened without German banks lending to Irish banks cheaply and massively.

"People have not commented enough on how unusual it is for banks to get their growth driven by lending from other banks," says William Black, associate professor of economics and law at the University of Missouri, Kansas City, and a former senior financial regulator during the U.S. savings and loan crisis of the 1980s.

As a result, Irish banks grew to be much larger, relative to Ireland's small economy, than U.S. banks.[43]

By the end of September 2008, troubled Irish banks were unable to access financial markets, which were frozen by the international credit crunch. The government agreed to a blanket guarantee on all the banks' deposits as well as to most private bondholders of the six major banks — a move that has been severely criticized for essentially putting the entire burden for bank losses on Irish taxpayers.[44]

Black, an outspoken critic of the move, says bondholders who made risky investments are "supposed to be wiped out. To do anything else is to give people a complete bonanza."

Throughout 2010, the impact of the Greek sovereign debt crisis, coupled with the market's realization that Ireland's generous bank guarantees would severely strain its finances, sent interest rates on Irish government bonds soaring. By autumn it was clear the country was running out of money and was effectively shut out of the financial markets. The government had no choice but to seek help from the new EU bailout fund.

On November 28, the EU and the IMF agreed to bail out Ireland, the second eurozone member to come hat in hand. Under the agreement, it would receive a loan of €67.5 billion ($88.42 billion).[45]

CURRENT SITUATION

Cutting Deals

Eurozone leaders are taking steps to shore up the eurozone's struggling members and will meet in June to put the finishing details on a permanent fund to help future governments that run into difficulty.

But troubles continue to plague countries that have received bailouts and embarked on austerity programs. In April and May, the bond markets were punishing both Ireland and Greece with double-digit interest rates, even as steadfast Germany was paying only around 3.4 percent on its government debt.[46]

Nearly a year after Greece received its bailout deal, its borrowing costs on April 14 had soared to more than 13 percent on 10-year government bonds — the highest since it joined the euro in 2001. The surge followed suggestions by German Finance Minister Wolfgang Schäuble that Greece might have to restructure (default on) its debt. Thus, it appeared increasingly likely that the Greek government would be shut out of the financial markets in 2012, when it needs to raise €25-30 billion ($35 billion-$43 billion).[47]

With a national debt mounting to more than 150 percent of GDP, Greece appeared condemned to years of zero growth and recession, fueled by deep spending cuts and tax increases.[48] Its jobless rate rose to 15.1 percent in January, the highest level since 2004, when the country's national statistics agency began collecting unemployment figures.[49] Given the dismal statistics, European officials admitted on May 7 that Greece probably would need a new cash bailout of tens of billions of euros, possibly with easier repayment terms.[50]

However, EU officials continued to resist any talk of a Greek restructuring plan, even though market speculation that a default was inevitable intensified on May 9, as interest rates on Greek bonds continued to rise.[51]

And in the week following the flurry of EU meetings on the Greek crisis, German leader Merkel, facing opposition to any further bailouts from her junior coalition party, the Free Democrats, denied that Germany was ready to give Greece more aid. She said she was awaiting an EU report on the situation due in June.[52]

EU leaders had already agreed on March 11 to reduce Greece's bailout interest rate by 1 percentage point and extend the payback period to 7.5 years. In exchange, the EU demanded that Greece privatize government assets to yield €50 billion ($69 billion) by 2015 — which led to the German politicians' suggestion, mocked in the press, that Greece sell some of its islands and art treasures.[53]

Some economists said the €50 billion target, amounting to about 20 percent of Greek GDP, would be difficult to reach. As Greece was headed for a revamped bailout in May, European leaders complained that the government's delay in selling off its public holdings was one reason it failed to meet its deficit-reduction target. Intense opposition from public unions over cost-cutting measures also has hampered Greece from meeting EU budget targets.[54]

In March Ireland had refused a similar deal — reducing its bailout loan interest rate — when told it would have to eliminate its corporate tax haven in return. In the wake of the Greek crisis in May, Irish Prime Minister Enda Kenny was intensifying pressure on EU leaders to reduce Ireland's interest bill, saying there was a question as to whether Ireland could repay its bailout loan at the current rate. But in exchange he was once again expected to face pressure from French leaders to "harmonize" Ireland's corporate tax system with the rest of the EU.[55]

France fears that lower-tax regimes like Ireland's could undercut France's own ample social welfare state, says Hix, of the London School of Economics. "In France, a lot of the costs of their generous social welfare state are imposed on business in corporate taxes and in unemployment insurance paid by business," he notes.

Despite the deals cut in early March, EU leaders failed to calm the markets. As the details of the deal trickled out in early March, Moody's downgraded both Greece's and Spain's credit ratings, citing increased risk of default (Greece), and higher estimates of the Spanish banking system's capital needs.

On March 23 Portugal's prime minister resigned after Parliament failed to approve his party's fourth austerity

Would Ireland have been better off without the euro?

YES
Sean Barrett
Senior Lecturer, Economics Department, Trinity College, Dublin, Ireland

Written for *CQ Global Researcher*, May 2011

Ireland joined the euro as a political gesture to a currency that accounted for less than a third of its trade. University of Chicago economist Milton Friedman warned in the *Irish Times* on Sept. 5, 2001, that "the euro was adopted really for political purposes, not economic purposes, as a step towards the myth of the United States of Europe. In fact I believe that its effect will be exactly the opposite. The need for different policies like tightening monetary policy in Ireland or a more flexible monetary policy in Italy will produce political tensions that will make it more difficult to achieve political unity."

Today these tensions have increased German reluctance to fund further rescues after Greece and Ireland. Germany needs higher interest rates in order to curb inflation. Ireland needs lower interest rates to tackle a 14.5 percent unemployment rate. The peripheral countries need a weaker euro to grow, but the euro is strengthening. When Ireland joined as a full-employment, solvent country it did not need either reduced interest rates or the large capital inflow arising from membership.

Friedman was pessimistic about any way out for Ireland. "Ireland is stuck with the euro. How would you break out, and start all over again to establish a new monetary system, the punt?* You are not going to give it up. You have locked yourselves together and thrown away the key."

Having joined the euro without economic analysis, Ireland then celebrated a hard-currency union with soft-currency policies. The Organisation for Economic Co-operation and Development's (OECD) 2008 "Report on Public Management in Ireland" found that between 1995 and 2005 the public-expenditure policies in Ireland and Germany were polar opposites. Real annual public expenditure in Ireland increased by 5 percent a year and contracted by 0.5 percent a year in Germany. Ireland lacked fiscal discipline.

Meanwhile, less than 2 percent of the massive capital inflow resulting from euro membership was invested in industry and agriculture. Ireland had the highest home-price increases in the OECD countries, with Dublin second-hand house prices rising from €104,000 ($121,000) in 1997 to €512,000 ($645,000) in 2006.

Ireland joined the euro without analysis, pursued economic policies the opposite of those of Germany — the bulwark of the euro — and has no exit strategy. It is a lethal policy combination.

---

* The Irish pound also is known as the punt.

NO
Philip R. Lane
Professor of International Macroeconomics, Trinity College Dublin, Ireland

Written for *CQ Global Researcher*, May 2011

At a superficial level, membership in Europe's Economic and Monetary Union (EMU)* may seem to have directly contributed to the boom-bust cycle in Ireland. However, had Ireland not joined the euro, the current banking crisis could have been amplified by a currency crisis. Moreover, an independent currency would not have offered a guarantee against the onset of the mid-2000s credit boom.

The credit boom affected many non-euro economies in Europe, including Iceland and countries in Central and Eastern Europe. In addition, many nations have experienced twin banking and currency crises, in which collapsing currencies raised the local burden of foreign-currency debts, inducing a more severe crash. Moreover, even under an independent monetary policy, it is not clear that the central bank would have been able to neuter the housing boom solely through its interest rate policy, since a large interest rate hike might have caused a big recession without cooling down the housing market.

Membership in the monetary union also has provided considerable stability during this crisis period. Most directly, the European Central Bank has provided substantial cheap funding to Irish banks during the crisis. In contrast, non-euro countries such as Latvia and Iceland suffered far harsher crises, since these economies had no similar source of external funding. In addition, highly indebted Irish households have benefited from low ECB interest rates during the crisis.

However, it is important to emphasize that Ireland took excessive macroeconomic risks during the first decade of the single currency, particularly by failing to regulate the banking sector to guard against systemic risk factors. This was especially problematic under the EMU, because Irish banks' newly expanded access to area-wide financial markets amplified the scope of their risk-taking. In addition, Ireland's fiscal policy was insufficiently counter-cyclical. These twin policy weaknesses both failed to curb the boom and exacerbated the scale of the crisis. Ireland learned a harsh lesson from the crisis: It should never again tolerate weak banking regulation or imprudent fiscal policies. Indeed, Ireland is now undergoing extensive institutional reforms in order to ensure that such a crisis does not recur in the future.

---

* The EU-established monetary system that introduced the euro.

package. The failure was blamed on lack of cooperation from opposition Social Democrats, who are favored to win the June 5th general election.

Then in the run-up to the EU's March 24-25 summit on Portugal's bailout, Portugal's credit rating was downgraded by both the Moody's and Fitch ratings agencies. Standard & Poor's went further, downgrading Portugal's bonds to one notch above junk status on March 29. The actions sent Portugal's borrowing costs soaring, forcing the country's caretaker government to seek a bailout loan in April.[56]

In late March eurozone leaders also agreed to create a permanent rescue fund, the European Stability Mechanism (ESM), which in 2013 would replace the temporary fund known as the EFSF. It would have an effective lending capacity of €500 billion ($688 billion). But leaders postponed decisions on the funds' details, saying the effective lending capacity of the temporary fund and of the permanent facility would be finalized by the end of June.[57]

Eurozone leaders also agreed on the so-called Euro Plus Pact — touted earlier in the year by French and German leaders as the Competitiveness Pact — which commits eurozone countries to closer economic cooperation. In provisions that go to the heart of nations' traditional sovereignty, the pact calls on participating states to limit public-sector wage increases, lower taxes on labor, develop a common corporate tax base, revise pension systems with an eye to future costs and establish some form of debt brake in their national fiscal rules.

Both the French and Germans claimed victory, even though the pact did not include any enforcement mechanisms — such as fines or sanctions — included in the original German proposal.

"They've totally watered down the idea that they should all coordinate what they do in their domestic policy," says Hix. "They'll monitor what each other [does] but in a very soft-power way. There's no way they're going to enforce sanctions on what people do with their labor market policies and their tax policy."

By June, new bank stress tests are expected to be carried out by the EU's newly created European Banking Authority, but some observers doubt they will be tough enough to restore confidence in Europe's banking system. The EU's 2010 stress tests were widely criticized when only seven of 91 banks failed the tests. All of Ireland's banks passed the tests, for instance, yet by year's end they required huge bailouts.[58]

Government Killer?

Whether or not the euro is a "government-killing mechanism" as historian Ferguson terms it, several recent government defeats have been attributed to the sovereign debt crises in the euro countries.

In Spain, where unemployment is running at 20 percent, the austerity program arguably made the Socialist Prime Minister José Luis Rodríguez Zapatero so unpopular he has said he won't run for a third term.

Right-wing populist parties — which combine their anti-bailout messages with anti-immigrant sentiments — have made gains, especially in countries with stronger economies. The most recent sign of rising nationalism occurred May 12, when Denmark re-erected border controls with other EU countries, a measure pushed by the right-wing, anti-immigrant Danish People's Party. The action came just as EU interior ministers agreed to reinstate passport controls among 22 EU countries that since 1995 have enjoyed unfettered travel. The measure was designed to restrict the recent flood of North African immigrants fleeing political upheavals and followed an earlier spat between Italy and France over whether the rising tide of Tunisian immigrants arriving on Italy's shores should be able to migrate easily to the other EU countries.[59]

On March 23, the Socialist government of Portuguese Prime Minister Sócrates collapsed after it could not muster support for a fourth austerity package in Parliament. The opposition Social Democrats, now favored to win the June 5 election, particularly opposed cuts that fell hard on pensioners.[60]

Concern about Portugal's ability to pay €7 billion ($10 billion) on bonds maturing on June 15 led to the government's request in April for an EU rescue package, because the newly elected government was not expected to be in place in time for the June deadline.[61] EU officials hoped to approve a final Portuguese rescue package amounting to €78 billion ($115 billion) at a May 16 meeting of eurozone finance ministers.[62] But Finland's finance minister warned that the package must be "harder and more comprehensive than the one the parliament voted against," which included a tax of up to 10 percent on pensions over €1,500 a month and a freeze on smaller pensions.[63]

The latest potential setback for a resolution of the debt crisis came in mid-April, when the True Finns party, which campaigned against a bailout for Portugal, made spectacular gains in the general election. With their jingoistic motto, "The Finnish cow should be milked in Finland," the party rose to a 19 percent share of the vote from only 4 percent in 2007, making it a close third behind the two leading parties. Finland, unlike other countries, requires parliamentary approval to take part in bailouts, which require unanimous support of all 17 eurozone members.[64]

However, on May 12, Finland's Parliament voted to support Portugal's bailout, after the conservative NCP party agreed with the Social Democrats to include conditions requiring Portugal to sell off assets to repay EU countries and to begin talks with private investors.[65] Nevertheless, the True Finns' gains had already triggered a renewed outbreak of the sovereign debt crisis in the eurozone, as the costs of borrowing for debt-laden countries like Greece rose to record levels again.

On May 9, Standard & Poor's downgraded Greece's bond status further into junk status territory — from BB- to B — saying Greece may need to renege on at least half of its €327 billion ($470 billion) debt mountain, implying big losses for investors.[66]

OUTLOOK

Nationalist Obstructionism?

The recent rise of nationalist parties in Europe raises questions about how willing prosperous Europeans will be to bail out their poorer brethren, but also, more broadly, how much unity Europe really wants. Anti-EU rhetoric coupled with anti-immigrant right-wing messages make it appear that this is "Europe's own Tea Party moment."[67]

If nationalism holds sway in any country, a single government could block the rescue packages. Most EU supporters were confident that an effort to put the bailout funds on a firm legal ground, via a pending amendment to remove the EU treaty's prohibition on bailouts, will be approved. But one country could block the change.[68]

In addition, unanimous approval is needed to loan money to any troubled country after 2013, when the permanent bailout fund is set to open. This provision was aimed at reassuring richer eurozone countries like Austria,

Finland, Germany and the Netherlands that they can't be forced to provide loans.[69]

Nationalists in debt-laden countries may argue that the bailout austerity measures are too harsh. Will voters stand for such harsh cuts? Ana Caterina Santos, a journalist for the Portuguese radio news station TSF, thinks they will.

"What scares us most is Greece — we don't want to be seen as Greek people," with all the connotations of the profligate southern stereotype, she says. "We have this idea: We Portuguese are more European than the Greeks. [W]e want to prove we can change."

That could be harder than people think. Most Portuguese see free health and education as two sacred untouchables, according to Santos. Unfortunately, that's where the big savings can be found, experts say, along with pensions, which are already very low by European standards.

Europe's lack of unity was further underscored in mid-April when Hungarian Prime Minister Viktor Orbán, whose country currently holds the EU presidency, said the EU's willingness to welcome new members was weaker than at any time in past 15 years.[70]

But the euro's troubles have also given some EU members pause about whether they're ready to adopt the currency, legally a requirement of EU membership (except for Britain and Denmark, which have legal exemptions.)

"The Poles and the Czechs continue to say, 'We'll join.' But they're not going to rush into it," predicts economist Tilford.

"The walking-wounded banks are the second part of the crisis," predicts Ferguson. "Before the end of this year, we'll have to sit down and admit which banks in Europe are bust."

As the continent struggles with the economic crisis, Europe's inferiority complex about its shrinking importance, squeezed between the great economic powers of China and the United States, has intensified. "[W]ill Europe be unable to cope with the dynamism of other regions of the world and be paralyzed at home by national populism and selfishness, leading it to resign itself to being nothing more than a regional power?" Michel Barnier, EU commissioner for the internal market, asked on May 9.

He urged the European Union to move toward greater cooperation, including adopting a common defense policy. "Will Europe be a continent under the influence of the United States, China and even of Russia?" he asked.[71]

To the contrary, according to American economist Eichengreen, the euro — alongside the dollar and the Chinese renminbi — will be one of the three currencies that will dominate world trade in the future. Already, the euro is widely used outside of the eurozone. Some 37 percent of all international bonds are in euros, according to Eichengreen, partly to appeal to European investors.

But what about Europe's failure to come up with an overarching federal government like that in the United States? Won't that hold the eurozone back?

"There are different flavors of capitalism and different flavors of monetary union," says Eichengreen. In his view, European countries "don't need to turn into a United States of Europe to make a monetary union work."

The eyes of the world are on Europe to see what kind of recipe for unity it will devise and whether it will work.

NOTES

1. Julia Finch, "Greece Told to Sell off Islands and Artwork," *Guardian*, March 4, 2010, www.guardian .co.uk/world/2010/mar/04/greece-greek-islands-auction.

2. Gideon Rachman's Blog, "The European Union in Deep Trouble," *ft.com*, April 17, 2011, http://blogs .ft.com/rachmanblog/2011/04/the-european-union-in-deep-trouble/.

3. "Wires: Portugal Agrees to Bailout Loan," *ft.com*, May 3, 2011, http://ftalphaville.ft.com/blog/2011/05/ 03/558136/wires-portugal-agrees-to-bailout-loan/. Robin Harding, *et al.*, "IMF head's arrest hits debt talks," *Financial Times*, May 15, 2011, www.ft.com/ cms/s/0/415d008c-7e97-11e0-9e98-00144feabdc0 .html#ixzz1MX9YTphe.

4. "Jump in Greek Yields Spurs Restructure Talk," *Financial Times*, May 3, 2011, www.ft.com/cms/ s/0/6cd219e4-75a7-11e0-80d5-00144feabdc0.html# axzz1LUBTvdlc.

5. Mario Biejer, "Europe is running a giant Ponzi scheme," *Financial Times*, May 5, 2011, www.ft.com/ cms/s/0/ee728cb6-773e-11e0-aed6-00144feabdc0 .html#axzz1LUBTvdlc.

6. Estonia became the 17th country to adopt the euro on Jan. 1, 2011. Under EU law, all other members of the 27-nation EU — except for Britain and Denmark — are required to adopt the euro after meeting the budgetary and economic criteria set by the European Union.

7. Mary Elise Sarotte, "Eurozone Crisis as Historical Legacy," *Foreign Affairs*, Sept. 29, 2010, www .foreignaffairs.com/print/66715?page-2.

8. "A Quantum Leap in Economic Governance; But Questions Remain," European Policy Centre, March 28, 2011, pp. 8-9, www.epc.eu/documents/uploads/ pub_1247_post-summit_analysis_-_28_march_2011 .pdf.

9. The state is Baden-Württemberg. A similar defeat occurred in Rhineland-Palatine. See "Germany: The Lights Go Out," *Financial Times*, March 28, 2011, www.ft.com/cms/s/0/828b8746-596b-11e0-bc 39-00144feab49a.html#axzz1JCQeKBqX. Also see, "Angela's Trauma," *The Economist*, March 28, 2010, www.economist.com/blogs/newsbook/2011/03/ germanys_regional_elections?page=1.

10. "The Quest for Prosperity," *The Economist*, March 15, 2007, www.economist.com/node/8808044.

11. For background, see "Europe Will Work," *Nomura Global Economics*, March 2011, p. 19, www.nomura .com/europe/resources/pdf/Europe%20will%20 work%20FINAL_March2011.pdf.

12. GDP is the total value of an economy's output of goods and services. It is considered a key indicator of economic growth.

13. It's estimated that the new currencies of Spain, Portugal and Ireland would fall as much as 50 percent and Greece's as much as 80 percent. See Simon Tilford, "How to Save the Euro," Centre for European Reform, September 2010, p. 14, www.cer.org.uk/ pdf/essay_euro_tilford_14sept10.pdf.

14. *Ibid.*

15. David McWilliams, "Ditching the Euro Could Boost Our Failing Economy," May 6, 2009, www .davidmcwilliams.ie/2009/05/06/ditching-the-euro-could-boost-our-failing-economy.

16. "Europe's Banks: Follow the Money," *The Economist*, April 16, 2011, p. 80, www.economist.com/node/ 18560535?story_id=18560535&CFID=16840511 6&CFTOKEN=43737452.

17. See Conor O'Clery, "U.S. Economist Expounds on Great Euro Mistake," *The Irish Times*, Sept. 5, 2001, p. 17, www.irishtimes.com/newspaper/archive/2001/0905/Pg017.html#Ar01700.

18. "Trichet Defends ECB Rate Increase," *Financial Times*, April 7, 2011, www.ft.com/cms/s/0/e4c95f16-6143-11e0-ab25-00144feab49a.html#axzz1Ipf7zFRy.

19. www.economist.com/blog/dailychart/2010/12/Europes_economies.

20. Lex, "Portugalling: Debts are Not Sustainable," *Financial Times*, April 7, 2011, www.ft.com/cms/s/3/26efc574-6126-11e0-8899-00144feab49a.html#axzz1Ipf7zFRy.

21. Steven Erlanger, "In Portugal Crisis, Worries on Europe's 'Debt Trap,'" *The New York Times*, April 8, 2011, www.nytimes.com/2011/04/09/world/europe/09portugal.html?_r=1&scp=1&sq=%22In%20Portugal%20Crisis,%20worries%20on%20europe%27s%20debt%20trap%22&st=cse.

22. Desmond Lachman, "Waiving the Rules for Portugal," *Financial Times*, April 7, 2011, www.ft.com/cms/s/0/e44bab88-6103-11e0-8899-00144feab49a.html#ixzz1JIf33xid.

23. The rumors were denied by both Greek and EU officials. See "Video: Greece Needs Revised Bailout," *ft.com*, May 9, 2011, http://video.ft.com/v/936381701001/Greece-needs-revised-bail-out.

24. Peter Spiegel, *et al.*, "European Officials to Revamp Greek Aid," *Financial Times*, May 8, 2011, www.ft.com/cms/s/0/b445945c-7978-11e0-86bd-00144feabdc0.html#axzz1LrivhFKc.

25. Raoul Ruparel, "Stopping the Rot? The Cost of a Portuguese Bail-Out and Why it is Better to Move Straight to Restructuring," Open Europe, March 2011, www.openeurope.org.uk/research/portugalrestructure.pdf.

26. FT Alphaville, "A Proclamation from Spain's Ministry of Public Works," *Financial Times*, May 11, 2011, p. 35. Also see Martin Wolf, "The Eurozone's Journey to Defaults," *Financial Times*, May 11, 2011, p. 15.

27. Niall Ferguson, *The Cash Nexus: Money and Power in the Modern World 1700-2000* (2001), p. 340.

28. *Ibid.*, pp. 334-335.

29. *Ibid.*, p. 336. For background, see Alan Greenblatt, "The Graying Planet," *CQ Global Researcher*, March 15, 2011, pp. 133-156; and Sarah Glazer, "Social Welfare in Europe," *CQ Global Researcher*, Aug. 1, 2010, pp. 185-210.

30. Ferguson, *op. cit.*, p. 150.

31. For background, see B. W. Patch, "European Economic Union," *Editorial Research Reports*, March 27, 1957, available at *CQ Researcher Plus Archive*.

32. For background, see I. B. Kobrak, "Common Market: Start of a New Decade," *Editorial Research Reports*, Feb. 8, 1967, available at *CQ Researcher Plus Archive*.

33. For background, see Mary H. Cooper, "A Primer on German Reunification," *Editorial Research Reports*, Dec. 22, 1989, available at *CQ Researcher Plus Archive*.

34. Barry Eichengreen, *Exorbitant Privilege* (2011), pp. 88-89.

35. Delors later became president during the 1980s of the European Commission, a policy-setting branch of the then-Common Market and later the EU, whose membership consists of one commissioner per member state. The presidency of the commission has been compared to the post of prime minister in a parliamentary government.

36. Simon Hix, *What's Wrong with the European Union & How to Fix It* (2010), pp. 10-11, 15.

37. See www.worldpress.org/Europe/232.cfm.

38. Mary Elise Sarotte, "Eurozone Crisis as Historical Legacy," *Foreign Affairs*, Sept. 29, 2010, www.foreignaffairs.com/print/66715?page=2.

39. The €110 billion package, formally agreed to May 10, 2010, consists of €80 billion from euro area countries and €30 billion from the IMF.

40. "A Quantum Leap in Economic Governance, but Questions Remain," European Policy Centre, March 28, 2013, p. 4, www.epc.eu/documents/uploads/pub_1247_post-summit_analysis_-_28_march_2011.pdf.

41. Patrick Jenkins, "Seven Banks Fail EU Stress Tests, *Financial Times*, July 23, 2010, www.ft.com/cms/s/0/c14b9464-9678-11df-9caa-00144feab49a,s01=2.html#axzz1LsWojoIn.

42. Constantin Gurdgiev, *et al.*, "The Irish Economy: Three Strikes and You're Out?" Social Science Research Network, March 6, 2011, http://ssrn.com/abstract=1776190.

43. "How Ireland's Bank Bailout Shook the World," National Public Radio, Nov. 23, 2010, www.npr.org/blogs/money/2010/11/23/131538931/how-the-irish-bank-bailout-shook-the-world.

44. Gurdgiev, *op. cit.*

45. The total rescue package came to €85 billion, including €17.5 billion from the Irish government. Of the €67.5 billion in external assistance: €22.5 billion came from the European Financial Stability Mechanism (EFSM) contributed by EU members; €22.5 billion from the International Monetary Fund (IMF); and €22.5 billion from the European Financial Stability Fund (EFSF) and bilateral loans contributed by eurozone members.

46. See Landon Thomas Jr., "In U.K. Budget Cuts, Test Case for America," *International Herald Tribune*, April 15, 2011, p. 1.

47. Jennifer Hughes, "Greek debt hit by restructuring fears," *Financial Times*, April 14, 2011, www.ft.com/cms/s/0/086d7be6-667b-11e0-ac4d-00144feab49a.html#axzz1JVwZGUMq.

48. "Reuters Breaking Views: Not Yet Time for a Greek Restructuring," *International Herald Tribune*, April 15, 2011, p. 18. See Erlanger, *op. cit.*, for 150 percent figure.

49. "Greece Hit by Fear of Debt Overhaul," *International Herald Tribune*, April 15, 2011, p. 15.

50. Steven Erlanger, "Greek Leader Irked by Speculation on Debt," *The New York Times*, May 7, 2011, www.nytimes.com/2011/05/08/business/global/08greece.html?scp=1&sq=erlanger%20greece&st=cse.

51. *Ibid.* Also See Richard Milne, "S&P Cuts Greece Rating Two Notches," *Financial Times*, May 9, 2011, www.ft.com/cms/s/0/3997499c-7a47-11e0-bc74-00144feabdc0.html#axzz1LrivhFKc.

52. Judy Dempsey, "Germany Rejects Talk of Easing Bailout Terms," *The New York Times*, May 10, 2011, www.nytimes.com/2011/05/11/business/global/11euro.html.

53. Ralph Atkins and Kerin Hope, "Greek Goal of Return to Market in Doubt," *Financial Times*, April 13, 2011, www.ft.com/cms/s/0/c08e2970-65f2-11e0-9d40-00144feab49a.html#axzz1LsWojoIn.

54. Kerin Hope, "Greece in Line of Fire over Inability to Hit Targets," *Financial Times*, May 9, 2011, www.ft.com/cms/s/0/889c47f4-7a60-11e0-af64-00144feabdc0,s01=1.html#axzz1LrivhFKc.

55. Philip Inman, "EU Under pressure to Slash Ruinous Irish and Greek Bailout Bills," *Guardian*, May 9, 2011, www.guardian.co.uk/business/2011/may/09/eu-pressure-slash-irish-greek-bailout-bills?INTCMP=SRCH.

56. European Policy Centre, *op. cit.*, p. 2.

57. *Ibid.*

58. *Ibid.*, pp. 11-12.

59. The May 12 proposal, described as a "last resort" for emergencies, still needs approval from EU prime ministers and the European Parliament. See Ian Traynor, "Europe Moves to End Passport-Free Travel in Migrant Row," *Guardian*, May 12, 2011, www.guardian.co.uk/world/2011/may/12/europe-to-end-passport-free-travel.

60. Raphael Minder, "Austerity Debate Fells Portugal's Premier," *The New York Times*, March 23, 2011, www.nytimes.com/2011/03/24/world/europe/24portugal.html?_r=1&scp=3&sq=Socrates%20resigns&st=cse.

61. Peter Wise, "Portugal's Borrowing Costs Rise," *Financial Times*, April 15, 2011, www.ft.com/cms/s/0/6a38d2a0-675f-11e0-9bb8-00144feab49a.html#axzz1JVwZGUMq.

62. For Portugal's €78 billion package, the EU has pledged a total of €52 billion; the IMF contribution will be €26 billion over three years. See, IMF Survey Magazine, "IMF Outlines Joint Support Plan with EU for Portugal," May 6, 2011, www.imf.org/external/pubs/ft/survey/so/2011/INT050611A.htm.

63. Peter Wise, "Portuguese Prepare for Tighter Belts," *Financial Time*, April 8, 2011, www.ft.com/cms/s/0/4067461c-6211-11e0-8ee4-00144feab49a.html#axzz1JVwZGUMq.

64. See "Frustrated Finland," *Financial Times*, April 18, 2011.

65. "Finnish Parties Agree to Support Bail-out for Portugal," BBC News, May 12, 2011, www.bbc.co .uk/news/world-europe-13372218.

66. Inman, *op. cit.*

67. Peter Spiegel, "Anger Begins to Infect Europe's Prosperous Core," *Financial Times*, April 11, 2011, www.ft.com/cms/s/0/c9ec3d9e-6463-11e0-a69a-00144feab49a.html#axzz1JUlJGMDc.

68. The amendment is needed to counter challenges that have already arisen in German courts. See European Policy Centre, *op. cit.*

69. European Policy Centre, *op. cit.*, p. 5.

70. Stephen Castle, "Hungary Urges Balkan E.U. Entry," *The New York Times*, April 14, 2011, hwww .nytimes.com/2011/04/15/world/europe/15iht-hungary15.html?_r=1&scp=1&sq=Stephen%20 Castle%20Hungary&st=cse.

71. Stephen Castle, "EU Official Urges More Unity," *The New York Times*, May 9, 2011, www.nytimes .com/2011/05/10/world/europe/10iht-union10 .html?_r=1&emc=tnt&tntemail0=y.

BIBLIOGRAPHY

Bibliography

Eichengreen, Barry, *Exorbitant Privilege: The Rise and Fall of the Dollar*, Oxford University Press, 2011.
A professor of economics and political science at the University of California, Berkeley, predicts that the euro will become one of three leading international currencies along with the dollar and the Chinese renminbi.

Ferguson, Niall, *The Cash Nexus: Money and Power in the Modern World, 1700-2000*, Penguin, 2001.
A Harvard professor of international history, who predicted 10 years ago that the eurozone would run into problems, finds that prior attempts to form monetary unions have failed.

McWilliams, David, *Follow the Money: The Tale of the Merchant of Ennis*, Gill & Macmillan, 2010.
In this amusing account of Ireland's economic crash, an Irish columnist says the previous government's finance minister was clueless about how to respond and predicts

Ireland will become "a large debt-servicing machine for a generation."

Reinhart, Carmen M., and Kenneth S. Rogoff, *This Time Is Different: Eight Centuries of Financial Folly*, Princeton University Press, 2009.
An economist at the Peterson Institute for International Economics (Reinhart) and a Harvard University professor of economics find that government defaults have been surprisingly frequent over time in their study of 66 countries.

Articles

Erlanger, Steven, "In Portugal's Crisis, Worries on Europe's 'Debt Trap,' " *The New York Times*, April 8, 2011, www.nytimes.com/2011/04/09/world/europe/ 09portugal.html?_r=1&scp=2&sq=steven%20 erlanger%20euro&st=cse.
Economists fear Portugal will follow Greece and Ireland into a "debt trap."

Heise, Michael, "Why the Euro Will Survive," *The Wall Street Journal*, Jan. 6, 2011, http://online.wsj .com/article/SB1000142405274870472310457606 1440431381526.html.
The chief economist at Germany's giant Allianz insurance company says breaking up the eurozone would hurt its members, and budget retrenchment for debt-ridden countries will help them in the long run.

Lachman, Desmond, "Waiving the Rules for Portugal," *Financial Times*, April 7, 2011.
A resident fellow at the American Enterprise Institute says austerity budgets imposed on bailout countries like Greece and Ireland are making it harder for those economies to recover.

Lewis, Michael, "When Irish Eyes are Crying," *Vanity Fair*, March 2011, www.vanityfair.com/business/ features/2011/03/michael-lewis-ireland-201103.
In his usual amusing style, journalist Lewis describes how Ireland got into its current economic mess.

McNamara, Kathleen R., "Can the Eurozone be Saved?" *Foreign Affairs*, April 7, 2011, www.foreign affairs.com/articles/67710/kathleen-r-mcnamara/ can-the-eurozone-be-saved.
The director of Georgetown University's Mortara Center for International Studies says the eurozone has failed to

create the kind of unified federal government necessary for a monetary union to work, but that a common euro-bond will solve the problem.

Münchau, Walter, "The Eurozone's Quack Solutions Will Be No Cure," *Financial Times*, April 24, 2011.
A respected economics columnist says the eurozone's solutions to the debt crisis will not calm the bond market's fears.

Reports and Studies

"Europe Will Work," *Nomura*, March 2011, www .nomura.com/europe/resources/pdf/Europe%20 will%20work%20FINAL_March2011.pdf.
Asia's largest global investment bank concludes that the eurozone probably will not break up but needs to strengthen its governance.

"A Quantum Leap in Economic Governance — But Questions Remain," *European Policy Centre*, March 28, 2011, www.epc.eu/pub_details.php?cat_id=5& pub_id=1247.
This summary of the European Union's March summit agreements on how to tackle the euro debt crisis includes criticisms of the proposed solutions.

Ruparel, Raoul, "Stopping the Rot? The Cost of a Portuguese Bail-Out and Why It Is Better to Move Straight to Restructuring," Open Europe, March 2011, www.openeurope.org.uk.
It would be cheaper for Portugal to default than to accept a bailout loan from the European Union, concludes an analyst at the London think tank Open Europe.

Tilford, Simon, "How to Save the Euro," *Centre for European Reform*, September 2010, www.cer.org.uk/ about_new/about_cerpersonnel_tilford_09.html.
The gap between the rhetoric of integration and the reality of national interests is proving lethal to the eurozone, argues the chief economist for a London think tank.

For More Information

Centre for Economic Policy Research, 77 Bastwick St., London EC1V 3PZ, United Kingdom; +44 (0)20 7183 8801; www.cepr.org. Network of more than 700 European researchers who study issues such as the euro. Has set up VoxEU.org website for commentary by leading economists.

Economics Without Boundaries With David McWilliams; www.davidmcwilliams.ie/2010/09/08/economics-without-boundaries-with-david-mcwilliams. Blog of Irish economics columnist who has been highly critical of the government's handling of Irish debt and economic crisis.

European Council, Rue de la Loi 175, B-1048 Brussels, Belgium; (32-2) 281 61 11; www.european-council.europa. eu/home-page.aspx?lang=en. Composed of the heads of member states of the European Union; defines the general political directions and priorities of the EU; posted the March 25 summit agreement on the euro at www.consilium.europa. eu/uedocs/cms_data/docs/pressdata/en/ec/120296.pdf.

European Union, http://europa.eu/index_en.htm. Web portal that links to all EU agencies.

European Union Delegation to the United States of America, 2175 K St., N.W., Washington, DC 20037; (202) 862-9500; www.eurunion.org/eu. Provides information about the EU to Americans.

European Policy Centre, Résidence Palace, 155 rue de la Loi, B-1040, Brussels, Belgium; +32 (0) 2 231 0340; www .epc.eu. Independent Brussels think tank devoted to European integration.

Open Europe, 7 Tufton St., London SW1P 3QN, U.K.; (44) 207 197 2333; www.openeurope.org.uk. Independent think tank with offices in London and Brussels.

Respond! Housing Association, Airmount, Dominick Pl., Waterford, Ireland; (353) 0818 357901; www.respond .ie. Ireland's largest nonprofit public housing association; has built nearly 5,200 homes nationwide for traditional families, single-parent families, the elderly, homeless and disabled.

Voices From Abroad:

DOMINIQUE STRAUSS-KAHN

Managing Director International Monetary Fund

Praise Greece

"The Greek government should be commended for committing to an historic course of action that will give this proud nation a chance of rising above its current troubles and securing a better future for the Greek people."

The Boston Globe, May 2010

Bulgaria/Christo Komarnitski

ANGELA MERKEL

Chancellor Germany

Germany is ready

"We now have a mechanism of collective solidarity for the euro. And we all are ready, including Germany, to say that we now need a permanent crisis mechanism to protect the euro."

The Washington Post November 2010

SIMON TILFORD

Chief Economist, Centre for European Reform United Kingdom

Euro's Survival

"I don't think it's sustainable in the absence of a much greater degree of political and economic integration. It's very hard for any economy to flourish in the teeth of fiscal austerity of this magnitude — let alone those that can't devalue."

The New York Times November 2010

OLLI REHN

Commissioner for Economic and Monetary Affairs, European Commission

Containing the fire

"The recovery is taking hold, and it is progressing, but at the same time it is essential that we contain the financial bush fires so that they will not turn into a Europe-wide forest fire."

Thai Press Reports December 2010

SIMON WARD

Chief Economist Henderson Global Investors United Kingdom

Weak won't leave

"I don't believe that the weak countries will leave the euro. If it's anyone it'll be Germany, which is worried about financing the bailouts, so it may be attractive for it to return to the deutschemark."

Express on Sunday (U.K.) November 2010

MARKUS KERBER

Professor of Finance Berlin Technical University Germany

Germany is not alone

"German guilt has been turned into too much money over too many years. But this is over. All of a sudden Germans are grasping the figures. The Dutch and the

Austrians are fundamentally in the same situation. They don't want to see the monetary union turn into a transfer union."

The Christian Science Monitor May 2010

COLM MCCARTHY

Lecturer in Economics University College Dublin, Ireland

Blame the real estate bubble
"The credit-fuelled property bubble is the direct and indirect source of Ireland's debt crisis. If the bubble had been prevented by the bankers or their regulators, Ireland would now be suffering a mild recession rather than an existential threat to economic sovereignty."

Sunday Independent (Ireland) November 2010

FRANÇOIS FILLON

Prime Minister, France

Greece is unique
"Portugal's situation is nothing like that of Greece. . . . There is no reason to speculate against Spain and Portugal.

. . . These countries' debt is perfectly within the average for the eurozone."

Daily Telegraph (England) May 2010

NICOLAS VERON

Economist Bruegel Belgium

Remaining intact
"The market perception now is the eurozone is not going to break up. We can safely say that if a country left the euro, it would be economically disruptive."

The Associated Press December 2010

9

Climate Change

Reed Karaim

Erosion is washing away beachfront land in the Maldives. The island nation in the Indian Ocean faces possible submersion as early as 2100, according to some climate change predictions. President Mohamed Nasheed said the voluntary emission cuts goal reached in Copenhagen last December was a good step, but at that rate "my country would not survive."

From *CQ Researcher*,
February, 2010. (Updated May 16, 2011)

It was the global gathering many hoped would save the world. For two weeks in December, delegates from 194 nations came together in Copenhagen, Denmark, to hammer out an international agreement to limit global warming. Failure to do so, most scientists have concluded, threatens hundreds of millions of people and uncounted species of plants and animals.

Diplomatic preparations had been under way for years but intensified in the months leading up to the conference. Shortly before the sessions began, Yvo de Boer, executive secretary of the United Nations Framework Convention on Climate Change — the governing body for negotiations — promised they would "launch action, action and more action," and proclaimed, "I am more confident than ever before that [Copenhagen] will be the turning point in the fight to prevent climate disaster."[1]

But delegates found themselves bitterly divided. Developing nations demanded more financial aid for coping with climate change. Emerging economic powers like China balked at being asked to do more to limit their emissions of the greenhouse gases (GHGs) — created by burning carbon-based fuels — blamed for warming up the planet. The United States submitted proposed emissions cuts that many countries felt fell far short of its responsibility as the world's dominant economy. As negotiations stalled, frustration boiled over inside the hall and on the streets outside, where tens of thousands of activists had gathered to call world leaders to action. A historic opportunity — a chance to reach a global commitment to battle climate change — seemed to be slipping away.

Then, on Dec. 18 — the final night of the conference — leaders from China, India, Brazil, South Africa and the United States emerged

Reuters/Reinhard Krause

Major Flooding, Drought Predicted at Century's End

Significant increases in runoff — from rain or melting snow and ice — are projected with a high degree of confidence for vast areas of the Earth, mainly in northern regions. Up to 20 percent of the world's population lives in areas where river flood potential is likely to increase by the 2080s. Rainfall and runoff are expected to be very low in Europe, the Middle East, northern and southern Africa and the western United States.

Projected Changes in Annual Runoff (Water Availability), 2090-2099
(by percentage, relative to 1980-1999)

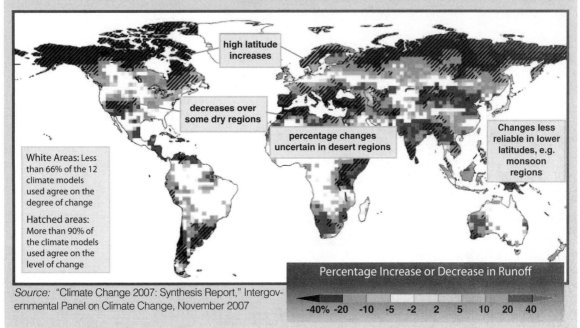

high latitude increases

decreases over some dry regions

percentage changes uncertain in desert regions

Changes less reliable in lower latitudes, e.g. monsoon regions

White Areas: Less than 66% of the 12 climate models used agree on the degree of change

Hatched areas: More than 90% of the climate models used agree on the level of change

Percentage Increase or Decrease in Runoff

-40% -20 -10 -5 -2 2 5 10 20 40

Source: "Climate Change 2007: Synthesis Report," Intergovernmental Panel on Climate Change, November 2007

from a private negotiating session with a three-page, non-binding accord that rescued the meeting from being judged an abject failure.

But the accord left as much confusion as clarity in its wake. It was a deal, yes, but one that fell far short of the hopes of those attending the conference, and one largely lacking in specifics. The accord vowed to limit global warming to 2 degrees Celsius (3.6 Fahrenheit) above pre-Industrial Revolution levels, provide $30 billion in short-term aid to help developing countries cope with the effects of climate change — with more promised longer-term — and included significant reporting and transparency standards for participants, including emerging economic powers such as China and India.

The accord did not, however:

- Include earlier language calling for halving global greenhouse gas emissions by 2050;
- Set a peak year by which greenhouse gases should begin to decline;
- Include country-specific targets for emission reductions (signatories began filling in the numbers by the end of January);
- Include a timetable for reaching a legally binding international treaty, or
- Specify where future financial help for the developing world to cope with climate change will come from.[2]

Called back into session in the early morning hours, delegates from much of the developing world reacted

Carbon Emissions Rising; Most Come from China

Global emissions of carbon dioxide (CO_2) — the most common greenhouse gas (GHG) blamed for raising the planet's temperature — have grown steadily for more than 150 years. Since 1950, however, the increases have accelerated and are projected to rise 44 percent between 2010 and 2030 (top graph). While China emits more CO_2 than any other country, Australians produce the most carbon emissions per person (bottom left). Most manmade GHG comes from energy production and transportation (pie chart).

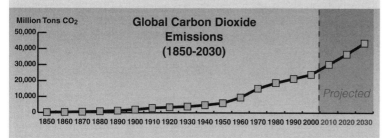

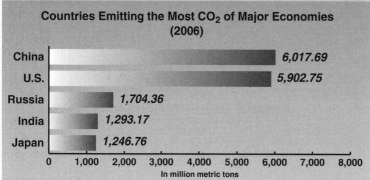

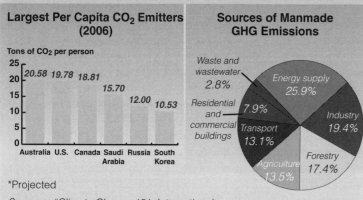

*Projected

Sources: "Climate Change 101: International Action," Pew Center on Global Climate Change, undated; "Climate Change 2007: Synthesis Report," Intergovernmental Panel on Climate Change, November 2007; Union of Concerned Scientists

with dismay to a deal they felt left their countries vulnerable to catastrophic global warming.

"[This] is asking Africa to sign a suicide pact — an incineration pact — in order to maintain the economic dependence [on a high-carbon economy] of a few countries," said Lumumba Di-Aping, the Sudanese chair of the G77 group of 130 poor countries.[3]

British Prime Minister Gordon Brown, however, hailed the deal as a "vital first step" toward "a green and low-carbon future for the world."[4] A total of 55 countries, including the major developed nations, eventually signed onto the deal.

But at the Copenhagen conference, delegates agreed only to "take note" of the accord, without formally adopting it.

Since then, debate has raged over whether the accord represents a step backward or a realistic new beginning. "You had the U.S., China and India closing ranks and saying it's too hard right now to have a binding agreement," says Malini Mehra, an Indian political scientist with 20 years of involvement in the climate change debate. "It's really worse than where we started off."

Others are more upbeat. Michael Eckhart, president of the American Council on Renewable Energy, points out that the convention had revealed how unworkable the larger effort — with 194 participants — had become. "The accord actually sets things in motion in a direction that is realistic," he says. "To have these major nations signed up is fantastic."

Copenhagen clearly demonstrated how extremely difficult and complex global climate negotiations can be. Getting most of the world's nations to agree on anything is no easy task, but climate change straddles the biggest geopolitical fault lines of our age: the vast economic disparity between the developed and developing worlds, questions of national sovereignty versus global responsibility and differences in political process between democratic and nondemocratic societies.

Climate change also involves a classic example of displaced hardship — some of the worst effects of global warming are likely to be felt thousands of miles from those nations that are most responsible for the higher temperatures and rising seas, making it easier for responsible parties to delay action. Finally, tackling the problem is likely to take hundreds of billions of dollars.

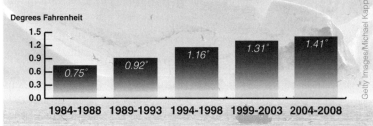

Warming Trends Continue to Accelerate

During the last 25 years the Earth's average temperature steadily increased — and at increasingly higher increments — compared to the average temperature from 1880-1910. From 2004-2008, the increase was about 1.4 degrees F., or nearly double the increase from 1984 to 1988.

Average Temperature Increases in Five-year Periods, Relative to the Average Temperature in 1880-1910

Degrees Fahrenheit

1984-1988	1989-1993	1994-1998	1999-2003	2004-2008
0.75°	0.92°	1.16°	1.31°	1.41°

Source: "Realities vs. Misconceptions About the Science of Climate Change," Pew Center on Global Climate Change, August 2009

None of this is comforting to those already suffering from climate change, such as Moses Mopel Kisosion, a Maasai herdsman who journeyed from Kenya to tell anyone who would listen how increasingly severe droughts are destroying his country's traditional way of life. But it does explain why reactions to the Copenhagen Accord — which even President Barack Obama acknowledged is simply a "beginning" — have varied so widely.[5]

For some U.S. environmental groups, the significance of the accord was in the commitment Obama secured from emerging economies to provide greater transparency and accountability, addressing one of the U.S. Senate's objections to earlier climate change proposals. The Senate never ratified the previous international climate agreement, known as the Kyoto Protocol.

Carl Pope, executive director of the Sierra Club, called the accord "historic — if incomplete," but said, "Now that the rest of the world — including countries like China and India — has made it clear that it is willing to take action, the Senate must pass domestic legislation as soon as possible."[6]

But to nongovernmental organizations focused on global poverty and economic justice, the accord represented an abdication of responsibility by the United States and other developed countries. Tim Jones, chief climate officer for the United Kingdom-based anti-poverty group World Development Movement, called the accord "a shameful and monumental failure that has condemned millions of people around the world to untold suffering."[7]

Easily lost in the heated rhetoric, however, is another part of the Copenhagen story: The conference illustrated how a consensus now unites most of the globe about the threat climate change poses. And although skeptics continue to speak out the scientific community has overwhelmingly concluded that average global temperatures are rising and that manmade emissions — particularly carbon dioxide from burning coal, oil and other fossil fuels — are largely to blame. According to a comprehensive assessment released in June 2009 by the U.S. Global Change Research Program, "Observations show that warming of the climate is unequivocal."[8] The conclusion echoes earlier findings by the U.N.'s Intergovernmental Panel on Climate Change (IPCC).[9]

The costs of climate change, both economic and in human lives, already appear significant. Disasters tied to climate change kill around 300,000 people a year and cause roughly $125 billion in economic losses, according to the Global Humanitarian Forum, a Geneva-based think tank led by former U.N. Secretary General Kofi Annan.[10] Evidence widely cited during the conference

Protesters outside the U.N. Climate Change Conference in Copenhagen on Dec. 10, 2009, call for rich countries to take responsibility for their disproportionate share in global warming. Greenhouse gas emissions by industrial countries are causing climate changes in poor countries thousands of miles away. The nonbinding Copenhagen Accord calls for $10 billion a year for the next three years to help them deal with climate change.

strengthens the conclusion the world is heating up. The World Meteorological Organization (WMO) reported that the last decade appeared to be the warmest on record, continuing a trend. The years 2000 through 2009 were "warmer than the 1990s, which were warmer than the 1980s, and so on," said Michel Jarraud, the secretary general of the WMO, as Copenhagen got under way.[11] Other reports noted that sea levels appeared likely to rise higher than previously estimated by 2100, with one estimating seas could rise more than six feet by then. The Antarctic ice shelves and the Greenland ice sheet are also melting faster than the U.N. scientific body previously found.[12]

Copenhagen also provided evidence of a growing international political consensus about climate change. About 120 heads of state attended the final days of the conference, hoping to sign their names to an agreement, an indication of the seriousness with which the global community now views the issue.

"It was remarkable the degree to which Copenhagen galvanized the public," says David Waskow, Oxfam America's climate change policy adviser, who attended the conference. "That's true with the literally millions who came out to show their support for strong action on climate change around the world. It's true with the

number of heads of state who showed up, and even in terms of the number of developing countries making substantial offers to tackle their emissions."

As observers try to determine where the world is headed on climate change and how the Copenhagen Accord helps or hinders that effort, here are some of the questions they are considering:

Is the Copenhagen Accord a meaningful step forward in the fight against global warming?

No one claims that a three-page accord that leaves out hard emission-reduction targets or a firm timetable is the final answer to global climate change. But does it bring the world closer to adequately addressing the problem?

Accord supporters range from the dutiful to the enthusiastic. But the unifying thread is a feeling that the accord is better than no deal at all, which is where the conference seemed to be headed until the 11th-hour negotiations.

"If the standard is — were we going to get a blueprint to save the world? The fact is, we were never going to meet it. None of the documents circulating were a feasible basis for agreement among the major players," says Michael A. Levi, director of the Program on Energy Security and Climate Change for the U.S. Council on Foreign Relations. "What we ended up with is something that can be useful if we use it the right way. It has pieces that empower all sorts of other efforts, like increased transparency, some measure of monitoring and reporting. It sets a political benchmark for financing. It can be a meaningful step forward."

Levi also notes that countries signing the accord agreed to fill in their targets for emissions cuts (as the major signatories and other nations did at the end of January), addressing one of the main criticisms of the deal.

But the Indian political scientist Mehra says even if countries abide by their commitments to cut emissions, the accord will not meet its target of holding global warming to 2 degrees Celsius (3.6-degrees Fahrenheit), which U.N. scientists consider the maximum increase that could avoid the worst effects of climate change, including a catastrophic rise in sea levels and severe damage to world food production.

She cites an IPCC conclusion that says in order to meet the 2-degree goal industrialized countries must reduce their emissions to 25-40 percent of 1990 levels by 2020 and by 50 percent by 2050. "What we actually got in the various announcements from the developed nations are far below that, coming in at around 18 percent," Mehra says.

Indeed, research by Climate Interactive — a joint effort by academic, nonprofit and business entities to assess climate policy options — found that the countries' commitments would allow temperatures to rise about 3.9 degrees Celsius (7 degrees Fahrenheit) by 2100 — nearly twice the stated goal.[13] "If you're looking at an average of 3 to 4 degrees, you're going to have much higher rises in significant parts of the world. That's why so many of the African negotiators were so alarmed by this," says Mehra. "It's worse than where we started because it effectively sets in stone the lowest possible expectations."

But other analysts point out that President Obama and other leaders who backed the accord have acknowledged more must be done.[14] They add that focusing on the initial emissions goals ignores the areas where the deal breaks important ground. "A much bigger part of the story, I think, is the actual money the developed world is putting on the table, funds for mitigation and adaptation," says Mike Hulme, a professor at the University of East Anglia in Great Britain who has been studying the intersection between climate and culture. "This is as much part of the game as nominal reduction targets."

The accord calls for $10 billion a year to help poorer, more vulnerable countries cope with climate change over the next three years, rising to $100 billion a year by 2020. The money will come from "a wide variety of sources, public and private, bilateral and multilateral, including alternative sources of finance," according to the agreement.[15]

Equally important, say analysts, is the fact that the agreement sets new standards of participation and accountability for developing economies in the global warming fight. "The developing countries, particularly China, made a step forward and agreed not only to undertake some actions to reduce emissions, but to monitor and report those. I think that's significant," says Stephen Eule, a U.S. Chamber of Commerce climate expert and former George W. Bush administration climate official.

However, to many of the accord's critics, the accord mostly represents a failure of political leadership. "It was hugely disappointing. Watching world leaders lower expectations for three months coming into this, and then actually having them undershoot those expectations was unbelievable," says Jason Blackstock, a research scholar at the International Institute for Applied Systems Analysis in Austria, who studies the intersection of science and international affairs. He places some of the blame at the feet of President Obama: "This is clearly not one of his top issues, and that's disappointing."

But Thomas Homer-Dixon, who holds an international governance chair at the Balsillie School of International Affairs in Waterloo, Canada, and studies climate policy, believes critics are underestimating the importance of leaders from around the globe sitting down face-to-face to tackle the problem. "Symbolically, that photograph of the leaders of those countries sitting around the table with their sleeves rolled up was enormous," he says. "All of a sudden we're having a direct conversation among the actors that matter, both in the developed and developing world."

He also credits the conference for tackling difficult questions such as how much money developed countries need to transfer to the developing world to fight climate change and how much countries have to open themselves up to international inspection. "There's been sort of an agreement not to talk about the hard stuff," he says, "and now, at Copenhagen, it was finally front and center."

But to those who believe that the time for talk is running out, the dialogue meant nothing without concrete results. "This [deal], as they themselves say, will not avert catastrophic climate change," said Kumi Naidoo, Greenpeace International's executive director. "That's the only thing on which we agree with them. Everything else is a fudge; everything else is a fraud, and it must be called as such."[16]

Is the U.N.'s climate change negotiating framework outdated?

Although delegations from most of the world's nations came to Copenhagen, the final deal was hammered out by the leaders of only five countries. Those nations — the United States, China, India, Brazil and South Africa — provide a snapshot of the changing nature of geopolitical power.

Although they had been involved in larger group discussions of about 30 nations, the traditional European powers and Japan were not involved in the final deal. The five key players represented the world's largest economy (the United States), the largest emitter of greenhouse gases and second-biggest economy (China) and significant emerging economies in South America (Brazil), Africa (South Africa) and India, with the world's second-largest population.

The five-nation gathering could be seen as an effort to fashion a thin cross-section of the global community. But the U.N.-sponsored Copenhagen conference was supposed to embody the entire world community. To some observers, the fact that the accord was fashioned outside the official sessions appeared to be an attempt to undermine the U.N. effort.

Anne Petermann, co-director of the Global Justice Ecology Project, an international grassroots organization, notes the Bush administration also worked outside the U.N., setting up a smaller meeting of major economies to discuss climate change. "It wasn't particularly surprising the U.S. negotiated an accord that was completely outside the process," she says. "This wasn't the first time that the U.S. had come in with a strategy of undermining the U.N. Framework Convention."

To other analysts, however, the ability of the small group of leaders to come together where the larger conference had failed shows that the U.N. effort no longer fits the crisis. "The Framework Convention is actually now an obstacle to doing sensible things on climate change," says East Anglia's Hulme. "Climate change is such a multifaceted problem that we need to find sub-groups, multiple frameworks and initiatives to address it."

To others, the U.N. effort remains both the best chance for the world to reach a binding climate change agreement and essential to proceeding. "Because you've really got to have a global solution to this problem, it's essential that all the interested parties, including the most vulnerable countries, be around the table," says Oxfam's Waskow. "There's no question the U.N. Framework Convention, which has been working on this for many years, is the right place for that."

But Homer-Dixon, of the Balsillie School of International Affairs, believes the U.N. Framework process "has too many parties." He expects that on the negotiating side "we're going to migrate to something like the G-20 [economic forum], which includes all the major emitters. It would make sense to have the G-20 responsible."

However, Kassie Siegel, the climate law expert for the Center for Biological Diversity, a U.S. environmental group, thinks critics underestimate the U.N. effort. "Both the U.N. Framework Convention and the Intergovernmental Panel on Climate Change have been building capacity since 1992," she says. "There's not any other institution that came close to their experience on this issue. The U.N. Framework process is the best and fastest way forward."

Supporters also note that the United States and other signatories to the Copenhagen Accord have called for efforts to continue toward reaching a binding agreement at the next U.N. climate gathering in Mexico City at the end of this year. "I don't think the U.N. negotiations are irrelevant because the U.S. is still engaged in the Framework Convention," says Nicola Bullard, a climate change analyst and activist with Focus on the Global South, a nongovernmental group in Bangkok, Thailand.

But Eckhart believes the results in Copenhagen mean that key countries will now focus most of their efforts outside the U.N. framework. "I doubt Mexico City is still relevant," he says. "What can they get done in Mexico City that they couldn't get done in Copenhagen?"

The relationship between the Copenhagen Accord and the U.N. Framework Convention is somewhat ambiguous. Jacob Werksman, a lawyer specializing in international environmental and economics law at the World Resources Institute, concludes the conference's decision to only "take note" of the accord means that some provisions, including the call for setting up a Copenhagen Green Climate Fund to manage billions of dollars in aid through the U.N. mechanism, cannot occur without a conference decision to accept the accord.

U.N. Secretary General Ban Ki-moon has called on all U.N. countries to back the accord.[17] But some analysts believe the U.N. Framework Convention can't legally adopt it until the Mexico City conference, which would push the Climate Fund and possibly other accord provisions down the road another year — a delay climate change activists say the world can't afford.

Would a carbon tax reduce emissions more effectively?

Obscured by the immediate furor over Copenhagen is a longer-term debate over whether the developed world is taking the right tack in its approach to reducing emissions.

The most popular approach so far has been the so-called cap-and-trade programs.[18] Progressively lower caps on overall emissions allow power companies and other entities to trade their emission quotas, creating a market-based approach to cutting greenhouse gases. Several European nations have embraced "cap-and-trade," and the climate change legislation that passed the U.S. House last June takes such an approach. But the system has been criticized for its complexity and susceptibility to manipulation and abuse.

Some analysts believe a carbon tax — a levy on carbon-emitting fuels, coupled with a system to rebate most of the tax back to consumers, is a more straightforward and effective way to control emissions. Robert Shapiro, former undersecretary of commerce during the Clinton administration and chair of the U.S. Climate Task Force, advocates such a program and works to educate the public on the need for action on climate change.

Shapiro's plan would use 90 percent of the carbon tax revenue to cut payroll taxes paid by workers and businesses, with the remaining 10 percent going to fund research and development of clean energy technology. The tax would provide a price incentive for discouraging the use of carbon emitting fuels and encouraging the use of green energy, while the tax cut would keep the approach from unduly burdening lower-income Americans. "A carbon tax would both directly reduce greenhouse gas emissions and provide powerful incentives for technological progress in this area," Shapiro wrote. "It offers the best way forward in both the national and global debate over climate change."[19]

However, carbon tax opponents argue it would be no more effective than cap-and-trade and would lead to a huge expansion of government. Analysts at the Heritage Foundation, a conservative U.S. think tank, wrote that a carbon tax "would cause significant economic damage and would do very little to reduce global temperatures." Even coupling it with a payroll tax cut, they continue, "would do little to offset the high energy prices that fall particularly hard on low-income households." The real agenda of a carbon tax, they charge, is "about raising massive amounts of revenue to fund a huge expansion in government."[20]

Several Scandinavian countries have adopted carbon taxes, with mixed results. Norway has seen its per capita

Residents grin and bear flooding in Jakarta, Indonesia, in December 2007. Similar scenes would be played out in coastal cities and communities around the world if climate change causes glaciers and polar ice caps to melt, which many researchers predict. Analysts say the worst effects of climate change are expected to be felt in Asia.

CO_2 emissions rise significantly. But Denmark's 2005 emissions were 15 percent below what they were in 1990, and the economy still remained strong.[21]

But to Bullard, at Focus on the Global South, a carbon tax is the approach most likely to spur changes in personal behavior. "Reducing consumption is really important, reducing our own dependence on fossil fuels," she says. "I think it's very important to have a redistributive element so that working people and elderly people don't end up with a huge heating bill. But it's really a simpler and more effective route than a complicated solution like cap-and-trade."

However, Bill McKibben — an American environmentalist and the founder of 350.org, an international campaign dedicated to scaling back GHG emissions — says a carbon tax faces an almost insurmountable political hurdle in the United States. "Even I can't convince myself that America is going to sit very long with something called a carbon tax," he says.

McKibben thinks "cap and rebate" legislation recently introduced by Sens. Maria Cantwell, D-Wash., and Susan Collins, R-Maine, would be more palatable to voters. It would cap total emissions — a limit that would be tightened over time — with the government auctioning off available carbon credits. The money raised would be rebated to consumers to offset any higher energy bills.[22]

Climate Change Could Force Millions to Relocate

"Climate Refugees" from Africa to the Arctic could be affected.

Maasi herdsman Moses Mopel Kisosion had never been outside Kenya before. He'd never ridden on a plane. But he flew across parts of two continents to deliver a message to anyone who would listen at the Copenhagen climate conference in December.

Climate change, he believes, is destroying the ability of his people, the Kajiado Maasi, to make a living. "I am a pastoralist, looking after cattles, walking from one place to another looking for grass and pastures," Kisosion said. "And now, for four years, we have a lack of rain, so our animals have died because there's no water and no grass. . . . We are wondering how our life will be because we depend on them."[1]

The Maasi are hardly alone in worrying if they will be able to continue living where they are. From small South Pacific island nations to the Arctic, hundreds of millions of people might have to relocate to survive as a result of climate change. If global warming predictions prove accurate, some researchers believe the world could soon find itself dealing with a tidal wave of "climate refugees."

A study by the U.N. Office for the Coordination of Humanitarian Affairs and the Internal Displacement Monitoring Centre found that "climate-related disasters — that is, those resulting from hazards that are already being or are likely to be modified by the effects of climate change — were responsible for displacing approximately 20 million people in 2008."[2]

Norman Myers, a British environmentalist, sees the situation worsening as the effects of climate change grow. In a 2005 study, he concluded that up to 200 million people could become climate refugees.[3] But he recently revised his estimate significantly. "We looked at the best prognosis for the spread of desertification and sea level rise, including the associated tsunamis and hurricanes, and we meshed those figures with the number of people impoverished or inhabiting coastal zones," says Myers. "We believe we could see half a billion climate refugees in the second half of the century."

The human displacement is likely to take place over several decades, experts say, and determining who is a climate refugee and who is simply a political or economic refugee could be difficult. International organizations have just begun the discussion about their status and what kind of assistance they might require.

The European Commission is funding a two-year research project, "Environmental Change and Forced Migration Scenarios," based on case studies in 24 vulnerable countries.[4] An African Union Summit in Kampala, Uganda, also met last October to consider how it would address the growing number of displaced Africans.[5]

Wahu Kaara, a Kenyan political activist, says the need for action is pressing. Kenya has recorded four major droughts in the last decade, significantly higher than the average over the previous century. "Very many people are dislocated and have to move to where they can salvage their lives," she says. "We have seen people die as they walk from one place to another. It's not a hardship; it's a catastrophe. They not only have lost their animals, they have lost their lives, and the framework of their lives for those who survive."

While Africa already may be suffering population movement due to climate change, the worst consequences are

Congressional efforts, however, have focused on cap-and-trade. But as wariness grows in the U.S. Senate toward the ramifications of cap-and-trade, Shapiro believes a carbon tax could prove a more appealing option. "A real public discussion and debate about a carbon tax tied to offsetting cuts in payroll or other taxes," he said, "could be the best news for the climate in a very long time."[23]

BACKGROUND

Road to Copenhagen

The road to Copenhagen was a long one. In one sense, it began with the Industrial Revolution in the 18th and 19th century, which brought with it the increased burning of coal and the beginning of large-scale carbon dioxide emissions in Europe and America. It also started with likely to be felt in Asia, analysts say. Rising sea levels threaten low-lying coastal areas, which constitute only 2 percent of the land surface of the Earth but shelter 10 percent of its population. About 75 percent of the people living in those areas are in Asia.[6]

The Maldives, a nation of low-lying islands in the Indian Ocean that could be submerged if predictions prove accurate, has taken the lead in trying to organize smaller island nations in the global warming debate. President Mohamed Nasheed initially supported the Copenhagen Accord and its 2-degree Celsius target for limiting global warming as a beginning. But before the deal was struck, he declared, "At 2 degrees, my country would not survive."[7]

Rising sea levels threaten every continent, including the Americas. Until recently, Kivalina Island, an eight-mile long barrier island in northern Alaska, had survived the punishing storms that blew in from the ocean because of ice that formed and piled up on the island.[8]

Inupiat hunters from the island's small village began noticing changes in the ice years ago, says the island's tribal administrator, Colleen Swan, but the change has accelerated in recent years. "In early September and October, the ice used to start forming, but now it doesn't form anymore until January and it's not building up," she says. "When that happened, we lost our barrier from fall sea storms, and our island just started falling apart. We started losing a lot of land beginning in 2004."

The U.S. Army Corps of Engineers is building a seawall to protect what's left of Kivalina, but Swan says it is expected to buy only 10 or 15 years. "People in the United States are still debating whether climate change is happening. The U.N. is focusing on the long-term problem of emissions," Swan says, "but we're in the 11th hour here. The bottom line is we need someplace to go."

— *Reed Karaim*

A house tumbles into the Chukchi Sea in Shishmaref, Alaska. Like other victims of climate change, residents may have to abandon the tiny community due to unprecedented erosion caused by intense storms.

AP Photo/Diana Haecker

[1] Moses Mopel Kisosion spoke in a video blog from Kilmaforum09, the "people's forum" on climate change held in Copenhagen during the official conference. It is available online at http://en.cop15.dk/blogs/view+blog?blogid=2929.

[2] "Monitoring disaster displacement in the context of climate change," the U.N. Office for the Coordination of Humanitarian Affairs and The Internal Displacement Monitoring Centre, September 2009, p. 12.

[3] Norman Myers, "Environmental Refugees, an Emergent Security Issue," presented at the 13th Economic Forum, Prague, May 2005.

[4] "GLOBAL: Nowhere to run from nature," IRIN, Nov. 9, 2009, www.irinnews.org/report.aspx?ReportId=78387.

[5] "AFRICA: Climate change could worsen displacement — UN," IRIN, Nov. 9, 2009, www.irinnews.org/report.aspx?ReportId=86716.

[6] Anthony Oliver-Smith, "Sea Level Rise and the Vulnerability of Coastal Peoples," U.N. University Institute for Environment and Human Security, 2009, p. 5, www.ehs.unu.edu/file.php?id=652.

[7] "Address by His Excellency Mohamed Nasheed, President of the Republic of Maldives, at the Climate Vulnerable Forum," Nov. 9, 2009, www.actforclimatejustice.org/2009/11/address-by-his-excellency-mohamed-nasheed-president-of-the-republic-of-maldives-at-the-climate-vulnerable-forum/.

[8] See John Schwartz, "Courts As Battlefields in Climate Fights," *The New York Times*, Jan. 26, 2010.

scientific speculation in the 1930s that manmade emissions could be changing the planet's climate.

Those first studies were widely discounted, a reflection of the difficulty humanity has had coming to grips with the idea it could be changing the global climate. But by the mid-1980s, thanks in large part to the work of David Keeling at the Mauna Loa Observatory in Hawaii, the world had a nearly three-decade record of rising carbon dioxide levels in the atmosphere.[24] Scientists were also reporting an overall warming trend in the atmosphere over the last 100 years, which they considered evidence of a "greenhouse effect" tied to CO_2 and other manmade emissions.

Humankind began a slow, often painful struggle to understand and deal with a global challenge. From the beginning, there were doubters, some well-intentioned, some with a vested interest in making sure that the world

CHRONOLOGY

1900-1950s *Early research indicates the Earth is warming.*

1938 British engineer Guy Stewart Callendar concludes that higher global temperatures and rising carbon dioxide levels are probably related.

1938 Soviet researchers confirm that the planet is warming.

1957 U.S. oceanographer Roger Revelle and Austrian physicist Hans Suess find that the oceans cannot absorb carbon dioxide as easily as thought, indicating that manmade emissions could create a "greenhouse effect," trapping heat in the atmosphere.

1958 U.S. scientist David Keeling begins monitoring atmospheric carbon dioxide levels, creating a groundbreaking record of their increase.

1960s *Climate science raises the possibility of global disaster.*

1966 U.S. geologist Cesare Emiliani says ice ages were created by tiny shifts in Earth's orbit, backing earlier theories that climate reacts to small changes.

1967 Leading nations launch 15-year program to study the world's weather.

1968 Studies show Antarctica's huge ice sheets could melt, raising sea levels.

1970s-1980s *Research into climate change intensifies, and calls for action mount.*

1975 A National Aeronautics and Space Administration (NASA) researcher warns that fluorocarbons in aerosol sprays could help create a greenhouse effect.

1979 The National Academy of Sciences finds that burning fossil fuels could raise global temperatures 6 degrees Fahrenheit in 50 years.

1981 U.S. scientists report a warming trend since 1880, evidence of a greenhouse effect.

1985 Scientists from 29 nations urge governments to plan for warmer globe.

1988 NASA scientist James Hansen says global warming has begun; he's 99 percent sure it's manmade.

1988 Thirty-five nations form a global panel to evaluate climate change and develop a response.

1990s *As the world responds to global warming, industry groups fight back.*

1990 The carbon industry-supported Global Climate Coalition forms to argue that climate change science is too uncertain to take action.

1995 The year is the hottest since the mid-19th century, when records began being kept.

1997 More than 150 nations agree on the Kyoto Protocol, a landmark accord to reduce greenhouse gases. The U.S. signs but never ratifies it.

2000s *The political battle over climate change action escalates worldwide.*

2000 Organization of Petroleum Exporting Countries (OPEC) demands compensation if global warming remedies reduce oil consumption.

2006 National Academy of Sciences reports the Earth's temperature is the highest in 12,000 years, since the last Ice Age.

2007 A U.N. report concludes that global warming is "unequivocal" and human actions are primarily responsible.

2009 The 194 nations attending the Copenhagen Climate Change Conference cannot agree on a broad treaty to battle global warming. After two weeks of contentious discussion, five nations create a nonbinding climate change accord, which 55 nations eventually sign, but which falls far short of delegates' hopes.

2010 The U.N effort to get a global, legally binding climate change treaty is scheduled to continue in November-December in Mexico City.

2009

December — The U.N. climate change conference in Copenhagen fails to reach a comprehensive legally binding accord to limit global warming.

2010

February — Yvo de Boer, the Dutch diplomat who led the U.N. Framework Convention on Climate Change effort for four years, resigns less than two months after Copenhagen, furthering the sense of a process in disarray.

November — A Republican majority, largely skeptical about climate change, sweeps into the U.S. House of Representatives, reducing the chance of comprehensive legislation to deal with greenhouse gas emissions any-time soon.

December — U.N. conference in Cancún, Mexico, agrees to take modest steps in the battle against climate change; supporters hail the agreement as a sign the U.N. process is still alive.

December — Environmental Protection Agency (EPA) says it will act to curb greenhouse gas emissions at power plants and oil refineries, possibly as early as 2011.

2011

January — National Climate Data Center announces that 2010 tied with 2005 as the hottest and wettest year on record, based on average annual precipitation.

February — Another investigation — the sixth — concurs that no scientific misconduct was revealed by researchers in connection with "climategate," the controversy that erupted in 2009 when more than 1,000 climatologists' emails were made public. Skeptics had claimed the emails cast doubt on the legitimacy of climate change findings.

April — U.S. House of Representatives blocks the EPA from regulating greenhouse gases, but a similar measure fails in the Senate.

December — Representatives from the 194 nations participating in the U.N. process are scheduled to meet in Durban, South Africa, to continue efforts to forge a meaningful international agreement to reduce manmade greenhouse gases and limit global warming.

continued to burn fossil fuels. Even as the scientific consensus on climate change has grown stronger, and many nations have committed themselves to tackling global warming, the issue continues to provoke and perplex.

Climate and Culture

In her book *Field Notes from a Catastrophe, Man, Nature and Climate Change*, American writer Elizabeth Kolbert visits, among other spots, Greenland's ice fields, a native village in Alaska and the countryside in northern England, surveying how global warming is changing the Earth. In the opening section, she admits her choices about where to go to find the impact of climate change were multitudinous.

"Such is the impact of global warming that I could have gone to hundreds if not thousands of other places," Kolbert writes, "From Siberia to the Austrian Alps to the Great Barrier Reef to the South African *fynbos* (shrub lands)."[25]

Despite mounting evidence, however, climate change remains more a concept than a reality for huge parts of the globe, where the visible impacts are still slight or nonexistent. Research scholar Blackstock, whose work focuses on the intersection between science and

international affairs, points out that for many people this makes the issue as much a matter of belief as of fact.

"It really strikes to fundamental questions on how we see the human-nature interface," he says. "It has cultural undertones, religious undertones, political undertones." Blackstock thinks many climate scientists have missed this multifaceted dimension to the public dialogue. "Pretending this is just a scientific debate won't work," he says. "That's important, but we can't have that alone."

The heart of the matter, he suggests, is how willing we are to take responsibility for changes in the climate and how we balance that with other values. This helps to explain the varying reactions in the United States, which has been reluctant to embrace limits on carbon emissions, and Europe, which has been more willing to impose measures. "You're seeing the cultural difference between Europe and America," Blackstock says, "the American values of individualism and personal success versus the communal and collective good, which Europe has more of a sense of being important."

Other analysts see attitudes about climate deeply woven into human culture. The University of East Anglia's Hulme, author of *Why We Disagree About Climate Change*, notes that

Climate Scientists Thinking Outside the Box

"Geoengineering" proposes futuristic solutions that sound like science fiction.

Imagine: A massive squadron of aircraft spewing sulfur particles into the sky. An armada of oceangoing ships spraying sea mist into the air. A swarm of robotic mirrors a million miles out in space reflecting some of the sun's harmful rays away from the Earth. Thousands of giant, air-filtering towers girdling the globe.

The prospect of devastating global warming has led some scientists and policy analysts to consider the kind of planet-altering responses to climate change that were once the province of science fiction. The underlying concept, known as "geoengineering," holds that manmade changes in the climate can be offset by futuristic technological modifications.

That idea raises its own concerns, both about the possibility of unintended consequences and of technological dependence. But from an engineering perspective, analysts say the sulfur particle and sea vapor options — which would reflect sunlight away from the Earth, potentially cooling the planet — appear feasible and not even that expensive.

"Basically, any really rich guy on the planet could buy an ice age," says David Keith, a geoengineering expert at the University of Calgary, estimating that sulfur injection could cost as little as $1 billion or so a year. "Certainly, it's well within the capability of most nations."

"Technologically, it would be relatively easy to produce small particles in the atmosphere at the required rates," says Ken Caldiera, a climate scientist at the Carnegie Institution for Science's Department of Global Ecology in Stanford, Calif. "Every climate-model simulation performed so far indicates geoengineering would be able to diminish most climate change for most people most of the time."

To spread sulfur, planes, balloons or even missiles could be used.[1] For sea vapor, which would be effective at a lower altitude, special ships could vaporize seawater and shoot it skyward through a rotor system.[2]

A global program of launching reflective aerosols higher into the atmosphere would cost around $5 billion annually — still small change compared to the economic costs of significant global warming, says Caldiera. Other geoengineering options are considerably more expensive. The cost of launching the massive (60,000 miles by 4,500 miles) cloud of mirrors into space to block sunlight would cost about $5 trillion.[3] Building air-scrubbing towers would also be expensive and would require improved technology.[4]

climate and weather have been critical to humanity for most of its history. The seasons, rains and hot or cold temperatures have been so essential to life — to the ability to obtain food and build stable communities — that they have been attributed to deities and formed the basis for religious ceremonies. Even in the modern age, Hulme says, "People have an instinctive sense that weather and climate are natural phenomena, that they work at such scales and complexity that humans could not possibly influence them."

He points out that weather was once the realm of prophets, "and part of our population is still resistant to the idea that science is able to predict what the weather will be. This deep cultural history makes climate change a categorically different phenomenon than other scientifically observed data."

Climate is also often confused with weather. England, for example, has a temperate, damp climate, but can have

dry, hot years. The human inclination is to believe what's before our eyes, so every cold winter becomes a reason to discount global warming.

Sander van der Leeuw, director of the School of Human Evolution and Social Change at Arizona State University in Tempe, Ariz., notes that facing climate change also means contemplating the costs of consumerism. "Those of us in the developed world have the most invested in this particular lifestyle," he says. "If that lifestyle has to change, we'll be facing the most wrenching dislocations."

Van der Leeuw, who worked for the European Union on climate change issues in the 1990s, is actually optimistic about the progress the world has made on climate change in the face of these challenges. "It's a very long process," he says, "but I'm encouraged by my students. It's wonderful to see how engaged they are, how open to thinking differently on

But cost is not what worries those studying geoengineering. "Everyone who's thinking about this has two concerns," says Thomas Homer-Dixon, a political scientist at Canada's Balsillie School of International Affairs in Waterloo, Ontario. "One is unintended consequences — because we don't understand climate systems perfectly — something bad could happen like damage to the ozone layer. The second is the moral-hazard problem: If we start to do this, are a lot of people going to think it means we can continue the carbon party?"

Keith thinks the consequences could be managed. "One of the advantages of using aerosols in the atmosphere is that you can modulate them," he says. "If you find it's not working, you can stop and turn the effect off." But he shares a concern with Caldiera and Homer-Dixon that geoengineering could be used as an excuse to avoid reducing carbon-dioxide emissions.

Geoengineering also raises geopolitical concerns, in part because it could be undertaken unilaterally. Unlike lowering greenhouse gas emissions, it doesn't require a global agreement, yet its effects would be felt around the planet — and not evenly.

That could aggravate international tensions: Any sustained bad weather in one nation could easily raise suspicion that it was the victim of climate modifications launched by another country. "If China, say, were to experience a deep drought after the deployment of a climate-intervention system," says Caldiera, "and people were starving as a result, this could cause them to lash out politically or even militarily at the country or countries that were engaged in the deployment."

Such scenarios, along with the fear of undercutting global negotiations to reduce emissions, make serious international consideration of geoengineering unlikely in the near term, says Homer-Dixon. But if the direst predictions about global warming prove accurate that could change. "You could see a political clamor worldwide to do something," he says.

Some scientists believe stepped-up geoengineering studies need to start soon. "We need a serious research program, and it needs to be international and transparent," says Keith. "It needs to start small. I don't think it needs to be a crash program, but I think there's an enormous value in doing the work. We've had enough hot air speculation. We need to do the work. If we find out it works pretty well, then we'll have a tool to help manage environmental risk."

— Reed Karaim

[1] Robert Kunzig, "A Sunshade for Planet Earth," *Scientific American*, November 2008.

[2] *Ibid.*

[3] *Ibid.*

[4] Seth Borenstein, "Wild ideas to combat global warming being seriously entertained," *The Seattle Times*, March 16, 2007, http://seattletimes.nwsource.com/html/nationworld/2003620631_warmtech16.html.

these issues. I know we have very little time, but history is full of moments where we've reacted in the nick of time."

However, there are still those who doubt the basic science of climate change.

The Doubters

To enter the world of the climate change skeptics is to enter a mirror reflection of the scientific consensus on the issue. Everything is backwards: The Earth isn't warming; it may be cooling. If it is warming, it's part of the planet's natural, long-term climate cycles. Manmade carbon dioxide isn't the heart of the problem; it's a relatively insignificant greenhouse gas. But even if carbon dioxide is increasing, it's beneficial for the planet.

And that scientific consensus? It doesn't exist. "What I see are a relatively small number, perhaps a few hundred at most, of extremely well-funded, well-connected evangelistic scientists doing most of the lobbying on this issue," says Bob Carter, a geologist who is one of Australia's more outspoken climate change skeptics.

Many scientists who take funds from grant agencies to investigate global warming, he says, "don't speak out with their true views because if they did so, they would lose their funding and be intimidated."

It's impossible to know if people are keeping views to themselves, of course. But professional science has a method of inquiry — the scientific method — and a system of peer review intended to lead to knowledge that, as much as possible, is untainted by prejudice, false comparison or cherry-picked data. The process isn't always perfect, but it provides our best look at the physical world around us.

In December 2004, Naomi Oreske, a science historian at the University of California, San Diego, published an analysis in *Science* in which she reviewed 928 peer-reviewed climate studies published between 1993 and 2003. She did not find one that disagreed with the general consensus on climate change.[26]

The U.S. National Academy of Sciences, the Royal Society of London, the Royal Society of Canada, the American Meteorological Society, the American Association for the Advancement of Science and 2,500 scientists participating in the IPCC also have concluded the evidence that humans are changing the climate is compelling. "Politicians, economists, journalists and others may have the impression of confusion, disagreement or discord among climate scientists, but that impression is incorrect," Oreske wrote, after reviewing the literature.[27]

The debate over climate change science heated up last fall, when, shortly before the Copenhagen conference, hackers broke into the University of East Anglia's computer network and made public hundreds of e-mails from scientists at the school's climate research center — some prominent in IPCC research circles. Climate change skeptics were quick to point to the "Climategate" e-mails as evidence researchers had been squelching contrary opinions and massaging data to bolster their claims.

Reviews by *Time*, *The New York Times* and the Pew Center on Climate Change, however, found the e-mails did not provide evidence to alter the scientific consensus on climate change. "Although a small percentage of the e-mails are impolite and some express animosity toward opponents, when placed into proper context they do not appear to reveal fraud or other scientific misconduct," the Pew Center concluded.[28]

Some skeptics are scientists, but none are climate researchers. Perhaps the most respected scientific skeptic is Freeman Dyson, a legendary 86-year-old physicist and mathematician. Dyson does not dispute that atmospheric carbon-dioxide levels are rapidly rising and humans are to blame. He disagrees with those who project severe consequences. He believes rising CO_2 levels could have some benefits, and if not, humanity could bioengineer trees that consume larger amounts of carbon dioxide or find some other technological solution. He is sanguine about the ability of the Earth to adapt to change and is suspicious of the validity of computer models.

"The climate-studies people who work with models always tend to overestimate their models," Dyson has said. "They come to believe models are real and forget they are only models."[29]

Unlike Dyson, many climate change skeptics are connected to groups backed by the oil, gas and coal industries, which have worked since at least 1990 to discredit global warming theories. A 2007 study by the Union of Concerned Scientists found that between 1998 and 2005 ExxonMobil had funneled about $16 million to 43 groups that sought to manufacture uncertainty about global warming with the public.[30]

The tactics appear to be patterned after those used by the tobacco industry to discredit evidence of the hazards of smoking. According to the study, ExxonMobil and others have used ostensibly independent front groups for "information laundering," as they sought to sow doubts about the conclusions of mainstream climate science.

Several prominent climate change skeptics — including physicist S. Fred Singer and astrophysicists Willie Soon and Sallie Baliunas — have had their work published by these organizations, some of which seem to have no other purpose than to proliferate the information. "By publishing and re-publishing the non-peer-reviewed works of a small group of scientific spokespeople, ExxonMobil-funded organizations have propped up and amplified work that has been discredited by reputable climate scientists," the study concludes.[31]

Is the world cooling? Is global warming a natural phenomenon? Is more CO_2 really good for the planet? Science and media watchdog groups have published detailed rebuttals to the claims of climate change skeptics.[32] To cite one example, assertions that the Earth is actually cooling often use 1998 as the base line — a year during the El Niño weather system, which typically produces warmer weather. The Associated Press gave temperature numbers to four statisticians without telling them what the numbers represented. The scientists found no true declines over the last 10 years. They also found a "distinct, decades-long" warming trend.[33]

James Hoggan, a Canadian public relations executive who founded DeSmogblog to take on the skeptics, feels climate scientists have done a poor job of responding to the skeptics, too often getting bogged down in the minutiae of detail. "We need to start asking these so-called skeptics a number of basic questions," says Hoggan, the author of

Climate Cover-Up: The Crusade to Deny Global Warming. "The first one is, 'Are you actually a climate scientist?' The second one is, 'Have you published peer-reviewed papers on whatever claims you're making?' And a third one is, 'Are you taking money directly or indirectly from industry?'"

Untangling the Threads

Since nations first began to seriously wrestle with climate change, most of the effort has gone into fashioning a legally binding international treaty to cut greenhouse gas emissions while helping poorer nations cope with the effects of global warming.

The approach has a powerful logic. Climate change is a worldwide problem and requires concerted action around the planet. Assisting those most likely to be affected — populations in Africa and Asia who are among the poorest on the globe — is also a burden that is most equitably shared.

But the all-in-one-basket approach also comes with big problems. The first is the complexity of the negotiations themselves, which involve everything from intellectual-property rights to hundreds of billions of dollars in international finance to forest management. Global nations have been meeting on these issues for nearly two decades without a breakthrough deal.

Some observers believe the best chance for moving forward is untangling the threads of the problem. "We don't have to try to set the world to rights in one multilateral agreement," says East Anglia's Hulme. "It's not something we've ever achieved in human history, and I doubt we can. It seems more likely it's acting as an unrealistic, utopian distraction."

Analysts cite the 1987 Montreal Protocol, which phased out the use of chlorofluorocarbons that were damaging the ozone layer, as an example of a successful smaller-scale deal.

So far, the effort to control global warming has focused on limiting carbon-dioxide emissions from power plants and factories. But CO_2 accounts for only half of manmade greenhouse gas emissions.[34] The rest comes from a variety of sources, where they are often easier or cheaper to cut.

Black carbon, mainly produced by diesel engines and stoves that burn wood or cow dung, produces from one-eighth to a quarter of global warming.[35] Promoting cleaner engines and helping rural villagers move to cleaner-burning

Hunger and Thirst

A young Turkana girl in drought-plagued northern Kenya digs for water in a dry river bed in November 2009 (top). Momina Mahammed's 8-month-old son Ali suffers from severe malnutrition in an Ethiopian refugee camp in December 2008 (bottom). Food and water shortages caused by climate changes are already affecting many countries in Africa. A sudanese delegate to the Copenhagen Climate Change Conference called the nonbinding accord reached at the convention "an incineration pact" for poor countries.

stoves would cut global warming gases, yet hardly requires the wrenching shift of moving from coal-fired electricity. Hydrofluorocarbons (HFCs) are more than a thousand times more potent as greenhouse gases than CO_2, but are used in comparably minuscule amounts and should be easier to limit.

"Why are we putting all the greenhouse gases into one agreement? CO_2 is very different from black soot, or

More Countries Agree to Emissions Cuts

The nonbinding climate agreement reached in Copenhagen, Denmark, on Dec. 18 was originally joined by 28 countries, which were to send the United Nations by the end of January their individual goals for reducing carbon emissions by 2020. But other nations also were invited to sign on by submitting their own plans to cut emissions. On Feb. 1, the U.N. reported that a total of 55 nations had submitted targets for cutting greenhouse gases. Analysts say while these countries produce 78 percent of manmade carbon emissions, more cuts are needed. The U.N. will try to use the accord as a starting point for a binding treaty at the next international climate conference in Mexico City, Nov. 29-Dec. 10.

Key provisions in the Copenhagen Accord:

- Cut global greenhouse gas emissions so global temperatures won't rise more than 2 degrees Celsius above the pre-Industrial Revolution level.
- Cooperate in achieving a peak in emissions as soon as possible.
- Provide adequate, predictable and sustainable funds and technology to developing countries to help them adapt to climate change.
- Prioritize reducing deforestation and forest degradation, which eliminate carbon-consuming trees.
- Provide $30 billion in new and additional resources from 2010 to 2012 to help developing countries mitigate climate change and protect forests; and provide $100 billion a year by 2020.
- Assess implementation of the accord by 2015.

Sources: "Copenhagen Accord," U.N. Framework Convention on Climate Change, Dec. 18, 2009; "UNFCCC Receives list of government climate pledges," press release, United Nations Framework Convention on Climate Change, Feb. 1, 2010, http://unfccc.int/files/press/news_room/press_releases_and_advisories/application/pdf/pr_accord_100201.pdf

methane or HFCs," Hulme says. "Tropical forests, why do they have to be tied to the climate agenda? They sequester carbon, yes, but they're also valuable resources in other regards."

Those who support negotiating a sweeping climate change accord believe that untangling these threads could weaken the whole cloth, robbing initiative from critical parts of the deal, such as assistance to developing countries. But Hulme believes the poorer parts of the world could benefit.

"We can tend to the adaptation needs of the developing world without having them hitched to the much greater complexity of moving the economy in the developed world away from fossil fuels," he says.

Other analysts, however, are unconvinced that climate change would be easier to deal with if its constituent

issues were broken out. "There are entrenched interests on each thread," says Blackstock, at Austria's International Institute in Applied Systems Analysis. "That's the real problem at the end of the day."

CURRENT SITUATION

Next Steps

The whole world may be warming, but as has been said, all politics is local — even climate change politics. "It's still the legislatures of the nation states that will really determine the pace at which climate policies are driven through," notes the University of East Anglia's Hulme. "In the end, that's where these deals have to make sense."

Nations around the globe are determining their next steps in the wake of Copenhagen. Most greenhouse gases, however, come from a relative handful of countries. The United States and China, together, account for slightly more than 40 percent of the world's manmade CO_2 emissions.[36] If India and the European Union are added, the total tops 60 percent.[37] The post-Copenhagen climate change status is different for each of these major players.

China — China presents perhaps the most complex case of any of the countries central to climate change. It was classified as a developing country in the Kyoto Protocol, so it was not required to reduce carbon emissions.[38] But as the country's economy continued to skyrocket, China became the world's largest carbon dioxide emitter in 2006, passing the United States.[39]

But with roughly 700 million poorer rural citizens, promoting economic growth remains the Chinese government's essential priority. Nevertheless, shortly before Copenhagen, China announced it would vow to cut CO_2 emissions by 40 to 45 percent *per unit of gross domestic product* below 2005 levels by 2020. The complicated formula meant that emissions would still rise,

Is the Copenhagen Accord a meaningful step forward in halting climate change?

YES Ban Ki-moon
Secretary-General, United Nations

NO Nnimmo Bassey
Chair, Friends of the Earth International

From opening remarks at press conference, U.N. Climate Change Conference, Copenhagen, Dec. 19, 2009

Written for *CQ Global Researcher,* February 2010

The Copenhagen Accord may not be everything that everyone hoped for. But this decision of the Conference of Parties is a new beginning, an essential beginning.

At the summit I convened in September, I laid out four benchmarks for success for this conference. We have achieved results on each.

- All countries have agreed to work toward a common, long-term goal to limit global temperature rise to below 2 degrees Celsius.
- Many governments have made important commitments to reduce or limit emissions.
- Countries have achieved significant progress on preserving forests.
- Countries have agreed to provide comprehensive support to the most vulnerable to cope with climate change.

The deal is backed by money and the means to deliver it. Up to $30 billion has been pledged for adaptation and mitigation. Countries have backed the goal of mobilizing $100 billion a year by 2020 for developing countries. We have convergence on transparency and an equitable global governance structure that addresses the needs of developing countries. The countries that stayed on the periphery of the Kyoto process are now at the heart of global climate action.

We have the foundation for the first truly global agreement that will limit and reduce greenhouse gas emission, support adaptation for the most vulnerable and launch a new era of green growth.

Going forward, we have three tasks. First, we need to turn this agreement into a legally binding treaty. I will work with world leaders over the coming months to make this happen. Second, we must launch the Copenhagen Green Climate Fund. The U.N. system will work to ensure that it can immediately start to deliver immediate results to people in need and jump-start clean energy growth in developing countries. Third, we need to pursue the road of higher ambition. We must turn our back on the path of least resistance.

Current mitigation commitments fail to meet the scientific bottom line.

We still face serious consequences. So, while I am satisfied that we have a deal here in Copenhagen, I am aware that it is just the beginning. It will take more than this to definitively tackle climate change.

But it is a step in the right direction.

The Copenhagen Accord is not a step forward in the battle to halt climate change. Few people expected the Copenhagen climate talks to yield a strong outcome. But the talks ended with a major failure that was worse than predicted: a "Copenhagen Accord" in which individual countries make no new serious commitments whatsoever.

The accord sets a too-weak goal of limiting warming to 2 degrees Celsius, but provides no means of achieving this goal. Likewise, it suggests an insufficient sum for addressing international solutions but contains no path to produce the funding. Individual countries are required to do nothing.

The accord fails the poor and the vulnerable communities most impacted by climate change. This non-agreement (it was merely "noted," not adopted, by the conference) is weak, non-binding and allows false solutions such as carbon offsetting. It will prove completely ineffective. Providing some coins for developing countries to mitigate climate change and adapt to it does not help if the sources of the problem remain unchecked.

The peoples' demands for climate justice should be the starting point when addressing the climate crisis. Instead, in Copenhagen, voices of the people were shut out and peaceful protests met brutal suppression. Inside the Bella Center, where the conference took place, many of the poor countries were shut out of back-room negotiations. The accord is the result of this anti-democratic process.

The basic demands of the climate justice movement remain unmet. The U.N. climate process must resume, and it must accomplish these goals:

- Industrialized countries must commit to at least 40 percent cuts in emissions by 2020 by using clean energy, sustainable transport and farming and cutting energy demand.
- Emission cuts must be real. They cannot be "achieved" by carbon offsetting, such as buying carbon credits from developing countries or by buying up forests in developing countries so they won't be cut down.
- Rich countries must make concrete commitments to provide money for developing countries to grow in a clean way and to cope with the floods, droughts and famines caused by climate change. Funding must be adequate, not the minuscule amounts proposed in the accord.

Wealthy nations are most responsible for climate change. They have an obligation to lead the way in solving the problem. They have not done so with the Copenhagen Accord.

but at a slower rate. China subsequently committed to this reduction when confirming its Copenhagen pledge at the end of January.

U.N. climate policy chief de Boer hailed the move as a critical step. But the United States — especially skeptical members of the U.S. Congress — had hoped to see more movement from China and wanted verification standards.

Some participants say China's recalcitrance is why Copenhagen fell short. The British seemed particularly incensed. Ed Miliband, Great Britain's climate secretary, blamed the Chinese leadership for the failure to get agreement on a 50-percent reduction in global emissions by 2050 or on 80-percent reductions by developed countries. "Both were vetoed by China," he wrote, "despite the support of a coalition of developed and the vast majority of developing countries."[40]

But the Global Justice Ecology Project's Petermann places the blame elsewhere. "Why should China get involved in reducing emissions if the U.S. is unwilling to really reduce its emissions?" she asks.

Jiang Lin, director of the China Sustainable Energy Program, a nongovernmental agency with offices in Beijing and San Francisco, thinks China's leaders take the threat of climate change seriously. "There's probably a greater consensus on this issue in China than the United States," says Jiang. "The Chinese leadership are trained engineers. They understand the data."

Jiang points out that China already is seeing the effects predicted by climate change models, including the weakening of the monsoon in the nation's agricultural northwest and the melting of the Himalayan glaciers. "The Yellow River is drying up," he adds. "This is very symbolic for the Chinese. They consider this the mother river, and now almost half the year it is dry."

The Copenhagen Accord is not legally binding, but Jiang believes the Chinese will honors its provisions. "When they announce they're committed to something, that's almost as significant as U.S. law," he says, "because if they don't meet that commitment, losing facing is huge for them."

While attention has focused on international negotiations, China is targeting improved energy efficiency and renewable power. In 2005, China's National People's Congress set a goal of generating 20 gigawatts of power through wind energy by 2020. The goal seemed highly ambitious, but China expected to meet it by the end of 2009 and is now aiming for 150 gigawatts by 2020. The target for solar energy has been increased more than 10-fold over the same period.[41]

Coal still generates 80 percent of China's power, and the country continues to build coal-fired plants, but Chinese leaders clearly have their eyes on the green jobs that President Obama has promoted as key to America's future.[42] "Among the top 10 solar companies in the world, China already has three," says Jiang, "and China is now the largest wind market in the world. They see this as an industry in which China has a chance to be one of the leaders."

The United States — To much of the world, the refusal of the United States so far to embrace carbon emission limits is unconscionable. U.S. emissions are about twice Europe's levels per capita, and more than four times China's.

"The United States is the country that needs to lead on this issue," says Oxfam's Waskow. "It created a lot of problems that the U.S. wasn't able to come to Copenhagen with congressional legislation in hand."

In the Copenhagen Accord, President Obama committed the United States to reduce its carbon dioxide emissions to 17 percent below 2005 levels by 2020. That equates to about 4 percent below 1990 levels, far less stringent than the European and Japanese pledges of 20 percent and 25 percent below 1990 levels, respectively. However, Congress has not passed global warming legislation. Last year, the House of Representatives passed a bill that would establish a cap-and-trade system, which would limit greenhouse gases but let emitters trade emission allowances among themselves. The legislation faces stiff opposition in the Senate, however.

In 1997, after the Kyoto Protocol was adopted, the Senate voted 95-0 against signing any international accord unless it mandated GHG emission reductions by developing countries as well. Securing such commitments in Copenhagen — especially from China, along with improved verification — was considered critical to improving the chances a climate change bill would make it through the Senate.

Some analysts also blamed the lack of U.S. legislation for what was considered a relatively weak American proposal at Copenhagen. "Obama wasn't going to offer more than the U.S. Senate was willing to offer," says the

International Institute for Applied System's Blackstock. "He could have done more and said, 'I cannot legally commit to this, but I'll go home and fight for it.' He didn't."

But Obama's negotiating effort in Copenhagen impressed some observers. "He could have stood back and worried about looking presidential," says the American Council on Renewable Energy's Eckhart. "He didn't. He rolled up his sleeves and got in there and tried to do good for the world."

Early reviews of the Copenhagen Accord were favorable among at least two key Republican senators, Lisa Murkowski of Alaska and Richard Lugar of Indiana. "Whenever you have developing countries, and certainly China and India stepping forward and indicating that they have a willingness to be a participant … I think that that is progress," said Murkowski.[43]

Still, analysts remain skeptical whether it will make a real difference on Capitol Hill. "I don't see Congress doing anything, even in line with the position in the Copenhagen Accord unless Obama makes it his 2010 priority," says 350.org's McKibben. "There's no question it's going to be hard because it's going to require real change."

The administration is planning to regulate some greenhouse gases through the Environmental Protection Agency (EPA). The Center for Biological Diversity has petitioned the EPA to make further use of regulation to reduce greenhouse emissions. "The president has the tools he needs. He has the Clean Air Act," says the center's Siegel. "All he has to do is use it."

However, some Senate Republicans are already calling for a resolution to undo the EPA's limited actions, and polls show a rising number of Americans skeptical about global warming, particularly Republicans.[44] Given the highly polarized nature of American politics, any significant move on climate change is likely to prove a bruising battle. President Obama has made promoting green energy jobs a priority, but with health care and joblessness still leading the administration's agenda, further action on climate change seems unlikely in the next year. Chances for major legislative action shrunk even further with the election of Republican Scott Brown, a climate change skeptic, to the Senate from Massachusetts. Brown's win ended the democrats' 60-vote, filibuster-proof majority.[45]

India — Although India's economy has grown almost as rapidly as China's in recent years, it remains a much poorer country. Moreover, its low coastline and dependence on seasonal monsoons for water also make it sensitive to the dangers of global warming. Jairam Ramesh, India's environment minister, said, "The most vulnerable country in the world to climate change is India."[46]

India's leaders announced recently they will pursue cleaner coal technology, higher emissions standards for automobiles and more energy-efficient building codes. Prior to Copenhagen, India also announced it would cut CO_2 emissions per unit of GDP from 2005 levels, but rejected legally binding targets.

After the negotiations on the accord, Ramesh told the *Hindustan Times* that India had "upheld the interest of developing nations."[47] But some analysts said India had largely followed China's lead, a position that could cost India some prestige with other developing nations, whose cause it had championed in the past.

"The worst thing India did was to align itself uncritically to China's yoke," says Indian political scientist Mehra, "because China acted purely in its own self interest."

The European Union — European leaders are calling for other countries to join them in backing the Copenhagen Accord, but they've hardly tried to hide their disappointment it wasn't more substantial. The European Union had staked out one of the stronger positions on emissions reductions beforehand, promising to cut emissions by 20 percent from 1990 levels to 2020, or 30 percent if other countries took similarly bold action. They also wanted rich nations to make 80 to 95 percent cuts in GHG emissions by 2050.[48]

Some national leaders also had expended political capital on global warming before the conference. French President Nicolas Sarkozy had announced a proposal to create a French "carbon tax" on businesses and households for use of oil, gas and coal. The proposal was blocked by the French Constitutional Council, but Sarkozy's party plans to reintroduce it this year.[49]

In the United Kingdom, Prime Minister Brown's government passed legislation committing to an 80 percent cut in U.K. greenhouse gas emissions by 2050.[50] Brown also pressed publicly for $100 billion a year in aid to the developing world to cope with climate change.

The European efforts were designed to lead by example. But analysts say the approach yielded little fruit in Copenhagen. "The European perspective that they could lead by example was the wrong strategy. This was a negotiation. Countries do not check their national

Causes of Climate Change

Rapidly industrializing China has surpassed the United States as the world's largest emitter of carbon dioxide—one of the greenhouse gases (GHG) responsible for rising world temperatures. Although most GHGs are invisible, air pollution like this in Wuhan, China, on Dec.3, 2009 (above) often includes trapped greenhouse gases. The destruction of tropical rainforests decreases the number of trees available to absorb carbon dioxide. Palm oil trees once grew on this 250-acre plot being cleared for farming in Aceh, Indonesia (below).

interests at the door when they enter the U.N.," says the Chamber of Commerce's Eule, who worked on climate change in the Bush administration.

Although Europe's leaders finally backed the accord and formally pledged 20 percent emission reductions, they had only limited influence on the deal's final shape. "Europe finds itself now outside the driver's seat for how this is going to go forward," says Hulme at the University of East Anglia. "I think in Brussels [home of the E.U. headquarters], there must be a lot of conversations going on about where Europe goes from here." He believes

Europe's stricter emissions regulations could now face a backlash.

Framework Conference chief de Boer, who is a citizen of the Netherlands, captured the resignation that seemed to envelope many European diplomats during his post-Copenhagen comments to the press. Before the climate conference kicked off, de Boer had predicted that Copenhagen would "launch action, action and more action" on climate change.

But in his December 19 press conference, when asked what he hoped could be accomplished in the year ahead, he responded, "Basically, the list I put under the Christmas tree two years ago, I can put under the Christmas tree again this year."

OUTLOOK

Too Late?

The world's long-term climate forecast can be summed up in a word: warmer. Even if the nations of the world were to miraculously agree tomorrow to reduce global greenhouse gas emissions, global warming could continue for some time because of the "lag" in how the climate system responds to GHG emission reductions.

In the last decade, researchers have poured a tremendous amount of effort into trying to foresee where climate change could take us. But the projections come with an element of uncertainty. Still, taken together, the most startling forecasts amount to an apocalyptic compendium of disaster. Climate change could:

- Lead to droughts, floods, heat waves and violent storms that displace tens of millions of people, particularly in Asia and sub-Saharan Africa;
- Create a high risk of violent conflict in 46 countries, now home to 2.7 billion people, as the effects of climate change exacerbate existing economic, social and political problems;[51]
- Cause the extinction of about a quarter of all land-based plant and animal species — more than a million — by 2050;[52]
- Effectively submerge some island nations by 2100,[53] and create widespread dislocation and damage to coastal areas, threatening more than $28 trillion worth of assets by 2050; and[54]

- Cause acidification of the oceans that renders them largely inhospitable to coral reefs by 2050, destroying a fragile underwater ecosystem important to the world's fisheries.[55]

If temperatures climb by an average of 3.5 to 4 degrees Celsius (6.3 to 7.2 Fahrenheit) by the end of the century, as some projections predict, it would mean "total devastation for man in parts of the world," says the Global Justice Ecology Project's Petermann. "You're talking about massive glaciers melting, the polar ice caps disappearing. It would make life on this planet completely unrecognizable."

But some analysts, while endorsing the potential dangers of climate change, still back away from the view that it's a catastrophe that trumps all others. "The prospective tipping points for the worst consequences are just that, prospective tipping points, and they're resting on the credibility of scientific models," says East Anglia University's Hulme. "We should take them seriously. But they're not the Nazis marching across Belgium. We need to weigh our response within the whole range of needs facing the human race."

The critical question likely to determine the shape of the planet's future for the rest of this century and beyond is when humans will stop pouring greenhouse gases into the atmosphere. If done soon enough, most scientists say, climate change will be serious but manageable on an international level, although billions of dollars will be needed to mitigate the effects in the most vulnerable parts of the globe.

But if emissions continue to rise, climate change could be far more catastrophic. "It is critically important that we bring about a commitment to reduce emissions effectively by 2020," said IPCC Chairman Rajendra Pachauri, shortly before Copenhagen.[56]

To accomplish Copenhagen's goal of holding warming to 2 degrees Celsius, Pachauri said emissions must peak by 2015. The agreement, however, sets no peaking year, and the emission-reduction pledges by individual nations fall short of that goal, according to recent analysis by Climate Interactive, a collaborative research effort sponsored by the Sustainability Institute in Hartland, Vt.[57]

World leaders acknowledge they need to do more, and some observers remain hopeful the upcoming climate conference in Mexico City could provide a breakthrough

that will avert the worst, especially if pressure to act continues to grow at the grassroots level. "Right now there is a massive gulf between where the public is and where the political process is," says India's Mehra. "But I think [in 2010] you will see government positions mature. And I think you will see more politicians who have the conviction to act."

Canadian political scientist Homer-Dixon considers bold action unlikely, however, unless the world's major emitting nations, including the United States and China, start suffering clearly visible, serious climate-change consequences.

"In the absence of those really big shocks, I'm afraid we're probably achieving about as much as possible," he says. "Because of the lag in the system, if you wait until the evidence is clear, it's too late."

UPDATE

The long-term forecast for planet Earth remains the same: warmer climate, with increased severe weather events likely. But the outlook for government action on the problem of global climate change is cloudier and has cooled on a couple of fronts.

On the international level, the U.N.-led effort to forge a comprehensive accord to battle climate change has focused on incremental steps, after falling short of its most ambitious goals at a discordant Copenhagen conference in 2009. Leaders of the U.N. Framework Convention on Climate Change — the governing body for international treaty negotiations — sought to temper expectations during the most recent climate change conference, held last year in Cancún, Mexico.

In the United States, the chances of comprehensive climate change legislation being enacted have been put in a deep freeze by a new, Republican-led House of Representatives that includes key members openly dismissive of the idea of climate change being affected by human activity.

Meanwhile, 2010 tied with 2005 as the warmest year on record, according to the National Climactic Data Center, marking the 34th year in a row that the global temperature was above average.[58]

The scientific consensus that climate change is occurring and that human activity is most likely responsible

Yvo de Boer, a Dutch diplomat who led the U.N. Framework Convention on Climate Change, speaks at a press briefing during a conference in Copenhagen on Dec. 19, 2009. De Boer resigned less than two months later, furthering a sense that U.N. efforts to deal with climate issues were in disarray.

remains firm. "A few years ago, we were seeing a lot of new research, papers coming out that indicated, wow, everything is happening faster than we thought. That trend has solidified," says Jay Gulledge, senior scientist and director for science and impacts at the Pew Center on Global Climate Change.

Extreme Weather More Likely

Although no earth-shattering new findings have come to light, climate researchers continue to advance their understanding of what's happening in the atmosphere and the likely consequences for life on Earth.

"There's some recent work that's provided computer-modeling support for the conjecture that climate change is making extreme weather events more likely," Gulledge says.

A study in the *Journal of Great Lakes Research*, for example, looked at the likelihood of more extreme heat waves such as the unprecedented event that killed nearly 800 people in Chicago in July 1995. Such extreme weather could become more commonplace, researchers have concluded, depending on the rise in greenhouse gas emissions, the carbon dioxide and other gases that heat up the Earth's atmosphere. "Before the end of the century, 1995-like heat waves could occur every other year on average under lower emissions and as frequently as three times per year under higher" emissions,

researchers concluded. Thousands could die as a result, they said. [59]

Other research indicates that global warming is helping to spread malaria into Africa's highland areas, where it has been almost unknown. Experts believe the death toll from the disease, which already kills about 1 million people a year, could rise dramatically because upland inhabitants have developed less resistance to the disease.[60]

New research also shows that climate change is affecting a wide variety of plants and animals. In fact, changes in the planet's temperatures may be ushering in a wave of mass extinctions like those that have occurred only rarely in the planet's history, according to a new study. Scientists caution that a complex interplay of factors is at work. But other research has bolstered the conclusion that global warming is challenging lots of different species, and many scientists believe it is playing a significant role in extinction rates.[61]

All in all, much of the recent research supports the idea that the risks to Earth from climate change aren't "far away in the future," says Gulledge, "but are already here in some cases."

International Negotiations

The last two U.N. climate change conferences provide a study in contrasts and an example of hard lessons learned.

In 2009 the Copenhagen conference kicked off with high hopes that world leaders would sign a landmark agreement setting firm targets for reducing manmade greenhouse gases and a timetable for reaching a legally binding treaty to cut those emissions.

Instead, the negotiations nearly collapsed in acrimony, exposing fault lines between the developed and developing worlds and between China and leading Western nations. As thousands of activists from around the world filled the streets of Copenhagen to urge the delegates to act, negotiators inside the meeting hall haggled in increasing frustration.

In the end, the so-called Copenhagen Accord was negotiated at the 11th hour by a small group of world leaders, including President Barack Obama and Chinese Premier Wen Jiabao. It kept the international dialogue alive and included a pledge to provide billions in aid to help developing countries cope with climate change, along with new reporting and transparency standards for participating countries.

AFP/Getty Images/Olivier Morina

But it failed to include a timetable for reaching a legally binding treaty and in most other ways fell short of expectations. Many nations reacted with dismay. Africa was being asked "to sign a suicide pact," declared Sudanese delegate Lumumba Di-Aping, referring to the dire consequences of higher temperatures on his desert nation and other African countries. A bitterly divided conference agreed only to "take note" of the accord, not adopt it.

A year later, the U.N. conference in Cancún was notable for the relative modesty of its goals and the low-key manner in which leading nations approached the session, inviting none of the large expectations that attended Copenhagen. Instead, negotiators focused on smaller steps, including strengthening nations' non-binding pledges to reduce greenhouse gas emissions, creating a mechanism to spread clean-energy technology and formally establishing the new Green Climate Fund to help poor countries deal with climate change. It also clarified reporting and verification requirements important to U.S. negotiators.[62]

Participants declared they were back on track. "This is not the end, but it is a new beginning," said Christiana Figueres, executive secretary of the U.N. Framework Convention on Climate Change. "Governments have given a clear signal that they are headed towards a low-emissions future together."[63]

But skeptics noted that negotiators from the 194 participating countries reached agreement only by once again avoiding the hard questions. "They kicked the can down the road," says Patrick J. Michaels, a senior fellow in environmental studies at the Cato Institute, a libertarian think tank in Washington. "What we're seeing, pretty much globally, is a retreat from expansive global-warming policies and global agreements."

Michaels attributes this to a shift in world public opinion against the idea that climate change requires immediate action. "The more realistic people on this planet are saying we have to see what climate change is going to take place," he says.

But Elliot Diringer, vice president for international strategies at the Pew center, believes Cancún helped re-establish the relevance of the U.N. negotiations. "Essentially what happened in Cancún," he says, "was importing the Copenhagen Accord into the U.N. process and taking some initial steps to implement its essential elements."

Diringer acknowledges that negotiators in Cancún sidestepped difficult issues, specifically binding commitments to limit emissions. "And I'm glad they did because for a long time the process seemed stuck in a binding or nothing mode," he says. "Ultimately, we'd like to see this resolve in the direction of binding commitments, but that's going to take time, and concrete, incremental steps can help us get there."

Outside the U.N. process, some nations are making progress on an individual basis or within smaller groups. For example, the Arctic Council, an organization of eight nations with northern territories that ring the Arctic Circle, recently agreed to reduce emissions of black carbon — essentially soot — a significant contributor to Arctic global warming.[64]

The U.N. effort will reconvene in Durban, South Africa, later this year to continue working toward a more substantial agreement. Pressure will be ratcheted up in 2012, when the initial commitment period of the Kyoto Protocol expires. Under the protocol, 37 industrialized nations (but not the United States) promised to cut greenhouse gases, but some have indicated they will not renew their Kyoto commitments.[65]

"The question for Durban is whether this new sense of realism carries over," Diringer says, "or do we fall back into this binding-or-nothing syndrome?"

U.S. Impasse

The prospect, already slight, that Congress would pass comprehensive climate change legislation this session died in January when the Republicans swept back into control of the U.S. House of Representatives.

Skepticism about global warming runs high among congressional Republicans, and they have pressed the administration on a couple of fronts. The budget deal hammered out between Republicans and Democrats in April eliminated funding for the National Oceanic and Atmospheric Administration's Climate Service and the position of assistant to the president for energy and climate change. It significantly reduced U.S. commitments to international climate change efforts. [66]

House Republicans also have voted to block Environmental Protection Agency (EPA) plans to regulate and limit greenhouse gases as pollutants under the Clean Air Act. But President Obama threatened to veto the bill, and the Senate failed to pass similar legislation.[67]

Given the mood in Washington, the likelihood of the bipartisan effort that would be necessary to move a bill limiting manmade greenhouse gases forward seems remote. "We don't expect to see any major legislation in this Congress," says Diringer.

But further Republican efforts to curb the EPA's regulatory effort also seem unlikely to succeed. "That's not going to happen unless there's a president and a Senate of a different persuasion," says Michaels.

In other words, the current impasse is almost certain to continue, at least until the 2012 elections.

NOTES

1. Yvo de Boer, the United Nation's Framework Convention on Climate Change video message before the opening of the Cop15 conference, Dec. 1, 2009, www.youtube.com/climateconference#p/u/11/xUTXsdkinq0.

2. The complete text of the accord is at http://unfccc.int/resource/docs/2009/cop15/eng/l07.pdf.

3. John Vidal and Jonathan Watts, "Copenhagen closes with weak deal that poor threaten to reject," *The Guardian*, Dec. 19, 2009, www.guardian.co.uk/environment/2009/dec/19/copenhagen-closes-weak-deal.

4. *Ibid.*

5. "Remarks by the President," The White House Office of the Press Secretary, Dec. 18, 2009, www.whitehouse.gov/the-press-office/remarks-president-during-press-availability-copenhagen.

6. http://action.sierraclub.org/site/MessageViewer?em_id=150181.0.

7. See Jones' complete comments at http://wdm.gn.apc.org/copenhagen-'deal'-'shameful-and-monumental-failure'.

8. Jerry Melillo, Karl Thomas and Thomas Peterson, editors-in-chief, "Global Climate Change Impacts in the United States," U.S. Global Change Research Program, executive summary, June 16, 2009, www.education-research-services.org/files/USGCRP_Impacts_US_executive-summary.pdf.

9. Intergovernmental Panel on Climate Change staff, "Climate Change 2007: Synthesis Report," The U.N. Intergovernmental Panel on Climate Change, Nov. 17 2007, www.ipcc.ch/pdf/assessment-report/ar4/syr/ar4_syr_spm.pdf.

10. "Climate Change responsible for 300,000 deaths a year," Global Humanitarian Forum, http://ghfgeneva.org/NewsViewer/tabid/383/vw/1/ItemID/6/Default.aspx.

11. Andrew C. Revkin and James Kanter, "No Slowdown of Global Warming, Agency Says," *The New York Times*, Dec. 8, 2009, www.nytimes.com/2009/12/09/science/earth/09climate.html.

12. "Key Scientific Developments Since the IPCC Fourth Assessment Report," in Key Scientific Developments Since the IPCC Fourth Assessment Report, Pew Center on Global Climate Change, June 2009.

13. "Final Copenhagen Accord Press Release," The Sustainability Institute, Dec. 19, 2009, http://climateinteractive.org/scoreboard/copenhagen-cop15-analysis-and-press-releases.

14. "Remarks by the President," *op. cit.*

15. "Copenhagen Accord," draft proposal, United Nations Framework Convention on Climate Change, Dec. 18, 2009, p. 3. http://unfccc.int/resource/docs/2009/cop15/eng/l07.pdf.

16. Kumi Naidoo, speaking at Copenhagen in a video blog posted by Greenpeace Australia, www.facebook.com/video/video.php?v=210068211237.

17. Ban Ki-moon, remarks to the General U.N. Assembly, Dec. 21, 2009, www.un.org/News/Press/docs/2009/sgsm12684.doc.htm.

18. Jennifer Weeks, "Carbon Trading, Will it Reduce Global Warming," *CQ Global Researcher*, November 2008.

19. Robert Shapiro, "Addressing the Risks of Climate Change: The Environmental Effectiveness and Economic Efficiency of Emissions Caps and Tradable Permits, Compared to Carbon Taxes," February 2007, p. 26, http://67.23.32.13/system/files/carbon-tax-cap.pdf.

20. Nicolas Loris and Ben Lieberman, "Capping Carbon Emissions Is Bad, No Matter How You Slice the Revenue," Heritage Foundation, May 14, 2009, www.heritage.org/Research/EnergyandEnvironment/wm2443.cfm.

21. Monica Prasad, "On Carbon, Tax and Don't Spend," *The New York Times*, March 25, 2008, www.nytimes.com/2008/03/25/opinion/25prasad.html.

22. "Cantwell, Collins Introduce 'Cap and Rebate' Bill," Clean Skies, Energy and Environment Network, Dec. 11, 2009, www.cleanskies.com/articles/cantwell-collins-introduce-cap-and-rebate-bill.

23. Robert J. Shapiro, "Carbon Tax More Likely," *National Journal* expert blog, Energy and the Environment, Jan. 4, 2010, http://energy.national-journal.com/2010/01/whats-next-in-the-senate.php-1403156.

24. A concise history of Keeling and his work is at "The Keeling Curve Turns 50," Scripps Institution of Oceanography, http://sio.ucsd.edu/special/Keeling_50th_Anniversary/.

25. Elizabeth Kolbert, *Field Notes from a Catastrophe: Man, Nature, and Climate Change* (2006), p. 2.

26. Naomi Oreskes, "Beyond the Ivory Tower: The Scientific Consensus on Climate Change," *Science*, Dec. 3, 2004, www.sciencemag.org/cgi/content/full/306/5702/1686.

27. *Ibid.*

28. "Analysis of the Emails from the University of East Anglia's Climatic Research Unit," Pew Center on Global Climate Change, December 2009, www.pewclimate.org/science/university-east-anglia-cru-hacked-emails-analysis.

29. Quoted by Nicholas Dawidoff, "The Civil Heretic," *The New York Times Magazine*, March 23, 2009, p. 2, www.nytimes.com/2009/03/29/magazine/29Dyson-t.html?pagewanted=1&_r=1.

30. "Smoke, Mirrors & Hot Air: How ExxonMobil Uses Big Tobacco's Tactics to Manufacture Uncertainty on Climate Science," Union of Concerned Scientists, January 2007, p. 1, www.ucsusa.org/assets/documents/global_warming/exxon_report.pdf.

31. *Ibid.*

32. Many are summarized in a policy brief by the non-profit Pew Center on Global Climate Change, "Realities vs. Misconceptions about the Science of Climate Change," August 2009, www.pewclimate.org/science-impacts/realities-vs-misconceptions.

33. Seth Borenstein, "AP IMPACT: Statisticians Reject Global Cooling," The Associated Press, Oct. 26, 2009, http://abcnews.go.com/Technology/wireStory?id=8917909.

34. Unpacking the problem," *The Economist*, Dec. 5-11, 2009, p. 21, www.economist.com/specialreports/displaystory.cfm?story_id=14994848.

35. *Ibid.*

36. It is important to note that if CO_2 emissions are calculated on a per capita basis, China still ranks far below most developed nations. The highest emitter on a per capita basis is Australia, according to the U.S. Energy Information Agency, with the United States second. See www.ucsusa.org/global_warming/science_and_impacts/science/each-countrys-share-of-co2.html.

37. A chart of the top 20 CO_2 emitting countries is at www.ucsusa.org/global_warming/science_and_impacts/science/graph-showing-each-countrys.html.

38. "China ratifies global warming treaty," CNN.com, Sept. 4, 2002, http://archives.cnn.com/2002/WORLD/africa/09/03/kyoto.china.glb/index.html.

39. "China overtakes U.S. in greenhouse gas emissions," *The New York Times*, June 20, 2007, www.nytimes.com/2007/06/20/business/worldbusiness/20iht-emit.1.6227564.html.

40. Ed Miliband, "The Road from Copenhagen," *The Guardian*, Dec. 20, 2009, www.guardian.co.uk/commentisfree/2009/dec/20/copenhagen-climate-change-accord.

41. "A Long Game," *The Economist*, Dec. 5-11, 2009, p. 18.

42. *Ibid.* Keith Bradsher, "China Leading Global Race to Make Clean Energy," *The New York Times*, Jan. 31, 2010, p. A1.

43. Darren Samuelsohn, "Obama Negotiates 'Copenhagen Accord' With Senate Climate Fight in Mind," *The New York Times*, Dec. 21, 2009, www.nytimes.com/cwire/2009/12/21/21climatewire-obama-negotiates-copenhagen-accord-with-senat-6121.html.

44. Juliet Elperin, "Fewer Americans Believe in Global Warming, Poll Shows," *The Washington Post*, Nov.

25, 2009, www.washingtonpost.com/wp-dyn/con
tent/article/2009/11/24/AR2009112402989.html.

45. Suzanne Goldenberg, "Fate of US climate change
bill in doubt after Scott Brown's Senate win," *The
Guardian*, Jan. 20, 2010, www.guardian.co.uk/envi
ronment/2010/jan/20/scott-brown-climate-change-
bill.

46. "India promises to slow carbon emissions rise," BBC
News, Dec. 3, 2009, http://news.bbc.co.uk/2/
hi/8393538.stm.

47. Rie Jerichow, "World Leaders Welcome the
Copenhagen Accord," Denmark.dk, Dec. 21, 2009,
www.denmark.dk/en/menu/Climate-Energy/
COP15-Copenhagen-2009/Selected-COP15-news/
World-leaders-welcome-the-Copenhagen-Accord
.htm.

48. "Where countries stand on Copenhagen," BBC
News, undated, http://news.bbc.co.uk/2/hi/science/
nature/8345343.stm.

49. James Kantor, "Council in France Blocks Carbon
Tax as Weak on Polluters," *The New York Times*,
Dec. 31, 2009, www.nytimes.com/2009/12/31/
business/energy-environment/31carbon.html.

50. Andrew Neather, "Climate Change could still be
Gordon Brown's great legacy," *The London Evening
Standard*, Dec. 15, 2009, www.thisislondon.co.uk/
standard/article-23783937-climate-change-could-
still-be-gordon-browns-great-legacy.do.

51. Dan Smith and Janini Vivekananda, "A Climate of
Conflict, the links between climate change, peace
and war," *International Alert*, November 2007, www
.international-alert.org/pdf/A_Climate_Of_
Conflict.pdf.

52. Alex Kirby, "Climate Risk to a Million Species,"
BBC Online, Jan. 7, 2004, http://news.bbc.co.uk/2/
hi/science/nature/3375447.stm.

53. Adam Hadhazy, "The Maldives, threatened by
drowning due to climate change, set to go carbon-
neutral," *Scientific American*, March 16, 2009, www
.scientifi camerican.com/blog/post.cfm?id=maldives-
drown ing-carbon-neutral-by-2009-03-16.

54. Peter Wilkinson, "Sea level rise could cost port cities
$28 trillion," CNN, Nov. 23, 2009, www.cnn

.com/2009/TECH/science/11/23/climate.report
.wwf.allianz/index.html.

55. "Key Scientific Developments Since the IPCC
Fourth Assessment Report," *op. cit.*

56. Richard Ingham, "Carbon emissions must peak by
2015: U.N. climate scientist," Agence France-Presse,
Oct. 15, 2009, www.google.com/hostednews/afp/arti
cle/ALeqM5izYrubhpeFvOKCRrZmWSYWCkPoRg.

57. "Final Copenhagen Accord Press Release," *op. cit.*

58. Doyle Rice, "2010 tied for Earth's warmest year on
record," *USA Today*, Jan. 13, 2011, www.usatoday
.com/tech/science/environment/2011-01-12-2010-
warmest-year-climate-change_N.htm.

59. Katherine Hayhoe, *et al.*, "Climate change, heat
waves, and mortality projections for Chicago,"
Journal of Great Lakes Research 36 (2010), pp. 65-73,
www.as.miami.edu/geography/research/climatol-
ogy/JGR_manuscript.pdf.

60. Paul Epstein and Dan Ferber, "Malaria on the Rise
as East African Climate Heats Up," *Scientific
American*, April 1, 2011, www.scientificamerican.
com/article.cfm?id=east-africa-malaria-rises-under-
climate-change.

61. Carl Zimmer, "Multitude of Species Face Climate
Threat," *The New York Times*, April 4, 2011, www
.nytimes.com/2011/04/05/science/earth/05climate
.html.

62. Elliot Diringer, *et al.*, "Summary: Cancún Climate
Change Conference," The Pew Center on Global
Climate Change, December 2010, www.pewcli
mate.org/international/cancun-climate-confer
ence-cop16-summary.

63. "UN Climate Change Conference in Cancún delivers balanced package of decisions, restores faith in
multilateral process," press release, United Nations
Framework Convention on Climate Change, Dec.
11, 2010, http://unfccc.int/files/press/news_room/
press_releases_and_advisories/application/pdf/pr_
20101211cop16_closing.pdf.

64. See Joby Warrick, "In Greenland, many like it
warmer," *The Washington Post*, May 13, 2011, p. A6.

65. Suzanne Goldenberg, "Cancún climate change conference: Russia will not renew Kyoto protocol,"

Guardian.co.uk, Dec. 10, 2010, www.guardian.co
.uk/environment/2010/dec/10/cancun-climate-
change-conference-kyoto.

66. "Climate Action in Congress," Pew Center on
Global Climate Change, www.pewclimate.org/
federal/congress.

67. John Broder, "House Votes to Bar E.P.A. From
Regulating Industrial Emissions," *The New York
Times*, April 7, 2011, www.nytimes.com/2011/
04/08/us/politics/08emit.html.

BIBLIOGRAPHY

Books

Hoggan, James, *Climate Cover-Up: The Crusade to
Deny Global Warming*, Greystone Books, 2009.
A Canadian public relations executive who founded the
anti-climate-skeptic Web site DeSmogblog takes on
what he considers the oil and gas industry's organized
campaign to spread disinformation and confuse the public about the science of climate change.

Hulme, Mike, *Why We Disagree About Climate
Change: Understanding Controversy, Inaction and
Opportunity*, Cambridge University Press, 2009.
A professor of climate change at East Anglia University
in Great Britain looks at the cultural, political and scientific forces that come into play when we consider climate
and what that interaction means for dealing with climate
change today.

Kolbert, Elizabeth, *Field Notes from a Catastrophe:
Man, Nature and Climate Change*, Bloomsbury, 2006.
A *New Yorker* writer summarizes the scientific evidence on
behalf of climate change and looks at the consequences for
some of the world's most vulnerable locations.

Michaels, Patrick J., and Robert C. Balling, *Climate
of Extremes: Global Warming Science They Don't
Want You to Know*, The Cato Institute, 2009.
Writing for a libertarian U.S. think tank, the authors
argue that while global warming is real, its effects have
been overstated and do not represent a crisis.

Articles

"Stopping Climate Change, A 14-Page Special
Report," *The Economist*, Dec. 5, 2009.

The authors provide a comprehensive review of the state
of global climate change efforts, including environmental, economic and political conditions.

Broder, John and Andrew Revkin, "A Grudging
Accord in Climate Talks," *The New York Times*, Dec.
19, 2009.
The Times assesses the Copenhagen Accord and reports
on the final hours of the climate change convention.

Kunzig, Robert, "A Sunshade for Planet Earth,"
Scientific American, November 2008.
An award-winning scientific journalist examines the
various geoengineering options that might reduce global
warming, their costs and possible consequences.

Schwartz, John, "Courts as Battlefields in Climate
Fights," *The New York Times*, Jan. 26, 2009.
A reporter looks at environmental groups' and other
plaintiffs' efforts to hold corporations that produce
greenhouse gases legally liable for the effects of climate
change on vulnerable areas, including Kivalina Island off
the coast of Alaska.

Walsh, Bryan, "Lessons from the Copenhagen
Climate Talks," *Time*, Dec. 21, 2009.
Time's environmental columnist provides predictions
about the future of the climate change battle, based on
the final Copenhagen Accord.

Walsh, Bryan, "The Stolen Emails: Has 'Climategate'
been Overblown," *Time Magazine online*, Dec. 7, 2007.
The stolen East Anglia University e-mails, the author
concludes, "while unseemly, do little to change the overwhelming scientific consensus on the reality of manmade climate change."

Reports and Studies

"Climate Change 101: Understanding and
Responding to Global Climate Change," Pew Center
on Global Climate Change, January 2009.
This series of reports aims to provide an introduction to
climate change science and politics for the layman.

"World Development Report 2010: World Development
and Climate Change," *World Bank*, November 2009,
http://econ.worldbank.org/WBSITE/EXTERNAL/
EXTDEC/EXTRESEARCH/EXTWDRS/EXTWDR20
10/0,,contentMDK:21969137~menuPK:5287816~page

PK:64167689~piPK:64167673~theSitePK:5287 741,00.html.
This exhaustive, 300-page study examines the consequences of climate change for the developing world and the need for developed nations to provide financial assistance to avert disaster.

Bernstein, Lenny, *et al.*, "Climate Change 2007: Synthesis Report," The Intergovernmental Panel of Climate Change, 2007, www.ipcc.ch/pdf/assessment-report/ar4/syr/ar4_syr_spm.pdf.
The international body tasked with assessing the risk of climate change caused by human activity gathered scientific research from around the world in this widely quoted report to conclude, "warming of the climate system is unequivocal."

Thomas, Karl, Jerry Melillo and Thomas Peterson, eds., "Global Climate Change Impacts in the United States," United States Global Change Research Program, June 2009, www.globalchange.gov/publications/reports/scientific-assessments/us-impacts.
U.S. government researchers across a wide range of federal agencies study how climate change is already affecting the United States.

For More Information

Cato Institute, 1000 Massachusetts Avenue, N.W., Washington, DC 20001; (202) 842-0200; www.cato.org/globalwarming. A conservative U.S. think tank that maintains an extensive database of articles and papers challenging the scientific and political consensus on climate change.

Climate Justice Now; www.climate-justice-now.org. A network of organizations and movements from around the world committed to involving people in the fight against climate change and for social and economic justice at the grassroots level.

Climate Research Unit, University of East Anglia, Norwich, NR4 7TJ, United Kingdom; +44-1603-592722; www.cru.uea.ac.uk. Recently in the news when its e-mail accounts were hacked; dedicated to the study of natural and manmade climate change.

Greenpeace International, Ottho Heldringstraat 5, 1066 AZ Amsterdam, The Netherlands; +31 (0) 20 7182000; www.greenpeace.org/international. Has made climate change one of its global priorities; has offices around the world.

Intergovernmental Panel on Climate Change, c/o World Meteorological Organization, 7bis Avenue de la Paix, C.P. 2300 CH- 1211, Geneva 2, Switzerland; +41-22-730-8208; www.ipcc.ch. U.N. body made up of 2,500 global scientists; publishes periodic reports on various facets of climate change, including a synthesis report summarizing latest findings around the globe.

Pew Center on Global Climate Change, 2101 Wilson Blvd., Suite 550, Arlington, VA, 22201; (703) 516-4146; www.pewclimate.org. Nonprofit, nonpartisan organization established in 1998 to promote research, provide education and encourage innovative solutions to climate change.

United Nations Framework Convention on Climate Change, Haus Carstanjen, Martin-Luther-King-Strasse 853175 Bonn, Germany; +49-228-815-1000; http://unfccc.int/2860.php. An international treaty that governs climate change negotiations.

Voices From Abroad:

JOHN ASHE

Chair, Kyoto Protocol Talks

A reason for hope
"Given where we started and the expectations for this conference, anything less than a legally binding and agreed outcome falls far short of the mark. On the other hand . . . perhaps the bar was set too high and the fact that there's now a deal . . . perhaps gives us something to hang our hat on."

BBC, December 2009

Peter Broelman, Australia

JOHN SAUVEN

Executive Director Greenpeace UK

Copenhagen = Crime Scene
"Copenhagen is a crime scene tonight, with the guilty men and women fleeing to the airport. It seems there are too few politicians in this world capable of looking beyond the horizon of their own narrow self-interest, let alone caring much for the millions of people facing the threat of climate change."

The Guardian (England), December 2009

MOHAMED NASHEED

President, Maldives

A critical number
"Anything above 1.5 degrees [Celsius], the Maldives and many small islands and low-lying islands would vanish. It is for this reason that we tried very hard during the course of the last two days to have 1.5 degrees in the document. I am so sorry that this was blatantly obstructed by big-emitting countries."

BBC, December 2009

JOSÉ MANUEL BARROSO

President European Commission

All countries have a role
"Developed countries must explicitly recognise that we will all have to play a significant part in helping to finance mitigation action by developing countries. . . . The counterpart is that developing countries, at least the economically advanced amongst them, have to be much clearer on what they are ready to do to mitigate carbon emissions as part of an international agreement."

Business Day (South Africa), September 2009

NELSON MUFFUH

Senior Climate Change Advocacy Advisor Christian Aid England

Climate change kills 300,000 a year
"Already 300,000 people die each year because of the impact of climate change, most in the developing world. The lack of ambition shown by rich countries in Copenhagen means that number will grow."

The Observer (England), December 2009

NICOLAS SARKOZY

President, France

A vital contract

"The text we have is not perfect. . . . If we had no deal, that would mean that two countries as important as India and China would be freed from any type of contract . . . [and] the United States, which is not in Kyoto, would be free of any type of contract. That's why a contract is absolutely vital."

BBC, December 2009

STANISLAS KAMANZI

Environment and Lands Minister, Rwanda

Progress regardless of Copenhagen

"Our policy is that every industrialized investment in the country should come up with an environment friendly technology. So, with or without Copenhagen, we are safe with policies in place."

New Times (Rwanda), December 2009

KYERETWIE OPOKU

Member, Forest Watch Ghana

Relationships are key

"I accept the technological challenges and all that, but the real challenges are restructuring relationships. If we don't resolve these, forget about going to Copenhagen and getting a deal."

Public Agenda (Ghana), October 2009

VICTOR FODEKE

Chief Climate Officer, Nigeria

Kyoto: the only hope

"The Kyoto Protocol is the only hope of the developing countries; it is the only legally binding instrument requiring developed countries to cut their emission, killing it is dashing the hope of developing countries."

Daily Trust (Nigeria), December 2009

10

Sub-Saharan Democracy

Jason McLure

AFP/Getty Images/Jekesai Njikizana

Zimbabwe's authoritarian President Robert Mugabe (center), refused to accept defeat during his country's disputed 2008 presidential election, setting a bad precedent, according to democracy advocates, for other African leaders seeking to retain power. After international condemnation, Mugabe agreed to appoint his opponent, Morgan Tsvangirai as prime minister. Like many of Africa's other post-independence dictators — so-called "Big Men" — Mugabe has ruled Zimbabwe for 28 years as a one-party authoritarian.

From *CQ Researcher*,
February 15, 2011.

Elections are supposed to choose one winner. But the presidential run-off in Ivory Coast last Nov. 28 left a bizarre predicament: Two candidates claimed victory. Each held an inauguration and appointed separate cabinets, leaving the lush West African country in limbo.

The farce continued after the country's electoral commission declared opposition leader and former Prime Minister Alassane Ouattara the winner on Dec. 2. Incumbent President Laurent Gbagbo, who had postponed elections for five years, promptly challenged the results in a constitutional court, which declared him the winner, with 51 percent of the vote. Street protests and a violent crackdown by security forces ensued. Most foreign leaders congratulated Ouattara, a U.S.-educated economist and technocrat, but the Ivorian army remained with Gbagbo.

Meanwhile, Gbagbo remained in the presidential palace in the nation's commercial and administrative capital, Abidjan, surrounded by security forces, while Ouattara holed up in the nearby Golf Hotel, surrounded by barbed wire and guarded by U.N. peacekeepers.

But the standoff was not new for the world's largest cocoa producer, known officially as Côte d'Ivoire. During the 2000 presidential election, Gbagbo and Gen. Robert Guei both claimed victory and held competing swearing-in ceremonies — though street protests eventually persuaded Guei to step aside.

"It's a shame that as Africa tries hard to tear itself away from despotism, leaders are reluctant to uphold democracy," Kenya's second-largest newspaper, *The Standard*, editorialized. "It is another statistic on the continent's soaring catalogue of shame."[1]

Few Sub-Saharan Nations Are 'Free'

Only nine of the 48 countries in Sub-Saharan Africa are rated as "free" by the human rights organization Freedom House. The free countries — three in West Africa, three in southern Africa and three island nations — represent 12 percent of the vast region's population. More than 750 million people — more than three-quarters of sub-Saharan inhabitants — live in countries deemed "not free" or "partly free."

Levels of Freedom in Sub-Saharan Africa, 2010

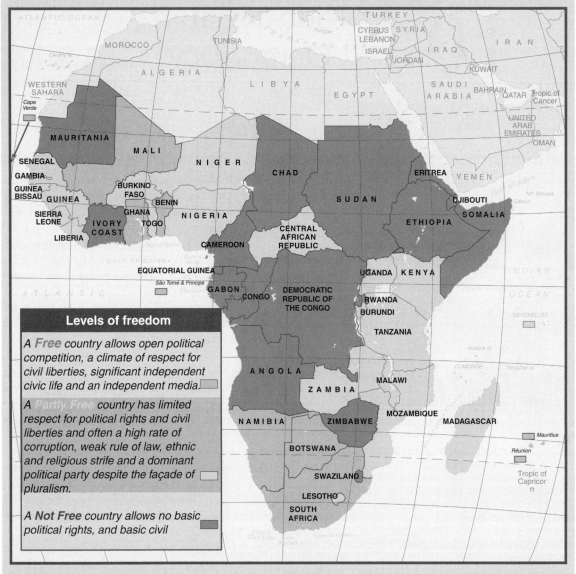

Levels of freedom

A *Free* country allows open political competition, a climate of respect for civil liberties, significant independent civic life and an independent media.

A *Partly Free* country has limited respect for political rights and civil liberties and often a high rate of corruption, weak rule of law, ethnic and religious strife and a dominant political party despite the façade of pluralism.

A *Not Free* country allows no basic political rights, and basic civil

Source: "Freedom in the World 2011," Freedom House, Jan. 13, 2011

Ivory Coast gained independence from France in 1960. The nation of 22 million people was for decades among Africa's wealthiest and most stable countries, often called the "Ivorian miracle." Its history exemplifies the political difficulties experienced in much of sub-Saharan Africa. Félix Houphouët-Boigny, the country's first president, ruled as a moderate, anti-communist dictator for 33 years, well into his eighties.

But as is often the case in the region, the eventual transition of leadership was chaotic. Houphouët-Boigny did not groom a successor nor prepare for a transition to democracy, and after his death in 1993, the introduction of elections and multiparty politics contributed to instability. The country fractured along ethnic and religious lines, largely between the predominantly Christian south and Muslim north. Gbagbo, a Christian from the Bete ethnic group, comes from the south. Supporters of Ouattara, a Muslim and a Dioula, live mostly in the north, held by rebels who initiated a civil war less than two years after Gbagbo became president.[2]

Autocratic "Big Men" like Houphouët-Boigny ruled much of Africa during the decades after independence in the 1960s and '70s. When the Berlin Wall fell in 1989, signaling the beginning of the Soviet Union's disintegration, not a single African president had permitted his people to vote him out of power.[3]

"The old saying was that at independence Africa pursued the one-person, one-vote, one-time approach to free elections," says Tibor Nagy, a former U.S. ambassador to Ethiopia and Guinea. "That lasted until the collapse of the Soviet Union [in 1991], when African states could no

Press Freedom Is Rare in Sub-Saharan Africa

Only two mainland sub-Saharan countries — Mali and Ghana — enjoy press freedom, a major prerequisite for democracy, according to the international human rights organization Freedom House. Three other countries in the 48-nation region have a free press: the island nations of Cape Verde, São Tomé/Príncipe and Mauritius. Eritrea, Equatorial Guinea and Zimbabwe have the least media freedom in the region.

Sub-Saharan Countries With the Freest, Least Free Media, 2010
(The lower the rating the freer the press)

Country	Freedom House rating	Press Freedom status
TOP 10 (Most Press Freedom)		
Mali	25	Free
Ghana	26	Free
Mauritius	27	Free
Cape Verde	28	Free
São Tomé and Príncipe	28	Free
South Africa	32	Partly Free
Benin	33	Party Free
Namibia	34	Partly Free
Botswana	39	Partly Free
Burkina Faso	41	Partly Free
BOTTOM 10 (Least Press Freedom)		
Swaziland	76	Not Free
Chad	77	Not Free
Ethiopia	78	Not Free
Democratic Republic of the Congo	81	Not Free
The Gambia	81	Not Free
Rwanda	83	Not Free
Somalia	84	Not Free
Zimbabwe	84	Not Free
Equatorial Guinea	90	Not Free
Eritrea	94	Not Free

Source: "Freedom of the Press 2010," Freedom House, May 2010

longer play off the East vs. the West, and the dictators realized things had to change or their days were numbered."

As the Cold War ended and the superpowers no longer felt compelled to support dictators who supported them, democracy began to surge in Africa.

AFP/Getty Images/Yasuyoshi Chiba

AFP/Getty Images/Roberto Schmidt

Before and After

Kenya's disputed 2007 presidential election triggered ethnic violence that left at least 1,000 people dead and 600,000 homeless, sparking international outrage over alleged ethnic cleansing (top). Stability returned after an awkward power-sharing arrangement left incumbent Mwai Kibaki as president and opposition leader Raile Odinga as prime minister. The 2008 peace agreement that ended the violence also called for a new constitution, along with other wide-ranging electoral, judicial and land reform measures to improve governance in East Africa's largest economy. A supporter of the new constitution (bottom) participates in a rally in Nairobi on Aug. 1, 2010. Three days later the voters overwhelmingly approved the constitution in a peaceful referendum.

Between 1990 and 1994, more than half of Africa's sub-Saharan nations underwent regime change, sparking an expansion of civil liberties through the decade, according to Freedom House, a Washington-based advocacy group

that tracks human rights and democratic reforms around the world.[4]

"One clear measure of the spread of democratic politics is the acceptance of the ballot box as the only means of acquiring political legitimacy," says Emmanuel Gyimah-Boadi, director of the Ghana Center for Democratic Development, which oversees the Afrobarometer opinion poll monitoring African attitudes toward democracy. "It's also clear from the Afrobarometer data that popular rejection of alternative forms of rule has also been resoundingly strong. Military rule, one-person rule, one-party rule — all these other forms of government have been quite thoroughly repudiated."

The march to freedom stalled, however, in recent years and has begun to reverse. "The trajectory has been basically positive until about 2005, and in the last three or four years there has been a decline," says Arch Puddington, research director at Freedom House.

To be sure, political systems have been successfully transformed in some African countries, notably Mali, South Africa, Ghana and Benin. All four have had at least two consecutive democratically elected governments.

But there have been more backsliders than success stories. For instance, Kenya's disputed 2007 election triggered ethnic violence that left 1,000 people dead. Zimbabwe's 2008 presidential election ended in a months-long standoff after President Robert Mugabe lost a first-round of voting and then terrorized the opposition into withdrawing before a run-off. More recently, Ethiopia's ruling party and its allies won more than 99 percent of parliamentary seats in rigged national elections in 2010, only five years after holding the freest polls in the country's history.[5]

According to Freedom House, only nine of sub-Saharan Africa's 48 countries were "free" in 2010, down from 11 in 2005. Sixteen African countries had declining scores in civil rights and political liberties, such as freedom of expression and quality of elections, while only four nations showed improvement, according to Freedom House's 2010 report. The decline occurred even as the continent experienced 5.8 percent annual economic growth between 2004 and 2009, considerably higher than the 3.7 percent average global growth rate.[6]

"It's been a case of two steps forward in the early 1990s and one step back in the past decade," says Kathryn Sturman, a researcher at the South African Institute of International Affairs in Braamfontein. "You have people holding elections, so the issue in 2010 is not whether there will be an election, it's whether it will be free and fair."

Africa's intense ethnic loyalties present a major obstacle to democratic development. Many Africans identify first with their tribe, not with their nationality. When Europeans colonized Africa at the end of the 19th century, they arbitrarily lumped rival ethnic groups together into single political entities and divided some groups between multiple countries. Colonial administrations then operated as autocratic fiefdoms focused on the maximum production of raw materials.

"Not only do you throw together people who are historical enemies, but you create all infrastructure and lines of communications to focus on extracting the countries' natural resources," says Nagy. "You send colonial officials who are the dregs of the service and can't make it anywhere else, and you empower them with dictatorial powers and security laws that the Africans inherit after independence."

Today foreign powers continue to play a significant role in African governance. The United States, China and former colonial powers France and the United Kingdom have major economic and political interests on the continent, and the U.N. operates six peacekeeping missions in sub-Saharan Africa (one each in Western Sahara, Ivory Coast, Liberia and Democratic Republic of Congo and two in Sudan).

And some experts say booming world prices and increased demand for African

Demand for Democracy Outstrips Supply

An average of 70 percent of the residents in 20 select sub-Saharan African countries prefer democracy over other forms of government (top), but only 59 percent say they live in a full or almost full democracy (bottom). The highest support for democracy was in southern African countries such as Botswana and Zambia.

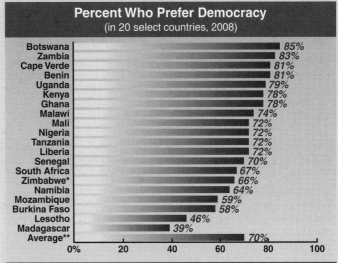

Percent Who Prefer Democracy
(in 20 select countries, 2008)

Country	Percent
Botswana	85%
Zambia	83%
Cape Verde	81%
Benin	81%
Uganda	79%
Kenya	78%
Ghana	78%
Malawi	74%
Mali	72%
Nigeria	72%
Tanzania	72%
Liberia	72%
Senegal	70%
South Africa	67%
Zimbabwe*	66%
Namibia	64%
Mozambique	59%
Burkina Faso	58%
Lesotho	46%
Madagascar	39%
Average**	70%

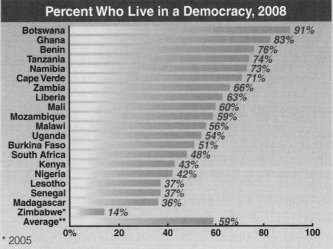

Percent Who Live in a Democracy, 2008

Country	Percent
Botswana	91%
Ghana	83%
Benin	76%
Tanzania	74%
Namibia	73%
Cape Verde	71%
Zambia	66%
Liberia	63%
Mali	60%
Mozambique	59%
Malawi	56%
Uganda	54%
Burkina Faso	51%
South Africa	48%
Kenya	43%
Nigeria	42%
Lesotho	37%
Senegal	37%
Madagascar	36%
Zimbabwe*	14%
Average**	59%

* 2005

** Does not include Zimbabwe

Source: "Neither Consolidating Nor Fully Democratic: The Evolution of African Political Regimes, 1999-2008," Afrobarometer, May 2009

Democratic Models Are All in West Africa

Ghana, Mali and Benin have peacefully turned over party power.

It was the closest presidential election in African history, and the campaign preceding it was marked by harsh rhetoric. But Ghana's 2008 election bore little resemblance to Kenya's 2007 election, with its deadly aftermath of ethnic violence. [1]

The race between Nana Akufo-Addo of the ruling New Patriotic Party and John Atta Mills of the opposition National Democratic Congress was nail-bitingly close after Akufo-Addo narrowly won a first round of voting. But in the run-off election three weeks later, Mills squeaked by him, winning by 50.2 percent to 49.8 percent.

But despite the razor-thin margin of victory, Akufo-Addo conceded. So too did outgoing President John Kufuor, who was from the same party as Akufo-Addo. There were no outbreaks of ethnic violence, no barrage of lawsuits demanding recounts and no interference by security forces. The media was free to report, and the electoral commission operated independently and transparently.

"Very often when we look at Africa we lose hope," Jean Ping, chairman of the African Union Commission, told a press conference following badly flawed 2010 elections in Sudan. "We don't need to lose hope."

Indeed, nine sub-Saharan African countries are consolidating democratic gains, according to the Washington-based democracy advocacy group Freedom House. [2] South Africa, Namibia, Botswana, Mauritius, Cape Verde and São Tomé/Príncipe are often rightfully praised for their political freedoms and smooth transitions from one leader to the next. However, politics in all three of the southern African countries are dominated by a single party, while Mauritius, Cape Verde and São Tomé/Príncipe are tiny island states.

That makes the achievements of West Africa's Ghana, Mali and Benin all the more impressive. All three have successfully transferred presidential power from one party to another via the ballot box. In Ghana, it's happened twice, in Benin three times.

They also provide counter-examples to the widely held view that nations must first attain a level of economic security before democracy can take root. Mali is among the world's poorest nations, while Ghana only attained the status of "middle-income" country (as defined by the World Bank) in 2010 — a full decade after its first democratic transition.

Even as many other countries on the continent have seen democratic freedoms retreat, multiparty systems in

commodities have hurt African democracy, even though they have boosted economic growth. Western buyers are less inclined to push the region's authoritarian leaders to democratize when facing stiff competition from other buyers like China, which remains neutral on democratic reforms.

As sub-Saharan Africa has begun to regress politically, here are some of the questions being debated:

Can Africa move beyond ethnic politics?

Africa has unparalleled human diversity — an estimated 2,000 languages are spoken on the continent, with more than 200 spoken in Democratic Republic of Congo (DRC) alone. But ethnic differences have long been a source of political friction.

Ethnic tension in Rwanda between Hutus and Tutsis led to the 1994 genocide that killed some 800,000 Tutsi and moderate Hutus. [7] In Sudan, an estimated 2 million people died in a 20-year-long civil war between the predominately Arab and Muslim north and the black and mainly Christian and animist south. Another 300,000 reportedly have died over the past decade due to war between the Sudanese government and rebels from several ethnic minority groups in the western region of Darfur. [8] Somalia has been in a state of constant civil war since 1991, driven largely by clan rivalries. [9]

Even in countries such as Kenya and Ivory Coast, which experienced decades of stability after independence, ethnic tensions have led to political crises in recent years. "Ethnicity is holding its own as a potent political force in Africa," says David Shinn, a former U.S. ambassador to Burkina Faso and Ethiopia. "Few African countries have managed to overcome this scourge."

In fact, many Africans — even in the continent's most stable and democratic countries — consider their ethnic identity as equally or more important than their

Mali, Benin and Ghana seem to be strengthening with each passing election. The success of those nations' democracies provides a powerful example to strongmen elsewhere on the continent, who cling to power by arguing that only authoritarianism can bring Africa stability and that Africans are not ready for democracy.

Having military men who are willing to exit politics gracefully seems to help. Benin's Lt. Gen. Mathieu Kérékou was Africa's first post-independence leader to allow himself to be voted from office. In Ghana, former president Jerry Rawlings came to power via a coup d'etat, ruled as a military leader for 11 years before twice winning disputed elections in the 1990s. But he stepped down in 2000, after then opposition leader Kufuor beat Mills, Rawlings' vice president.

Mali also had military leaders who were willing to step aside for civilians. After leading a coup that ousted former dictator Moussa Traore in 1991, Gen. Amadou Toumani Touré held multiparty polls the following year and handed power over to former opposition leader Alpha Konaré. A grateful population elected Touré to succeed Konaré in 2002.

"It's something of an achievement for Africa that you can count a handful of countries that have gone through power alternations," says Emmanuel Gyimah-Boadi, director of the Ghana Center for Democratic Development, who oversees the Afrobarometer opinion poll monitoring

Election officers count votes at a polling station in Accra, Ghana, on Dec. 7, 2008. The West African country has twice transferred presidential power peacefully from one party to another via the ballot box, providing a counter-example to recent African elections marred by intimidation and violence.

African attitudes toward democracy. "It's no longer unthinkable."

— *Jason McLure*

[1] Jeffrey Gettelman, "Disputed Vote Plunges Kenya Into Bloodshed," *The New York Times*, Dec. 31, 2007, www.nytimes.com/2007/12/31/world/africa/31kenya.html?_r=1.

[2] "Freedom in the World 2011 Survey Release," Freedom House, Jan. 13, 2011, www.freedomhouse.org/template.cfm?page=594.

national identity: Slightly more than half of Africans polled by Afrobarometer in 2005 and 2006 said they had a stronger or equally strong attachment to their ethnic group as their national identity.[10] Strong ethnic attachments can hamper the development of democracy if elections become mere ethnic headcounts, with winners dividing the spoils.

Further hampering the development of democracy, experts say, are the arbitrary boundaries of African states — imposed when colonial powers divvied up the continent in the late 1800s. The selection of boundaries that were not based on existing ethnic or cultural geography prevented the emergence of strong national identities in African countries. Moreover, where ethnic groups were left straddling national boundaries, civil wars often have spilled over into neighboring states, as occurred in 2006, when Chad was drawn into the conflict in neighboring Sudan's Darfur region.[11]

"Africa as it exists today is a pure fiction," says Barak Hoffman, executive director of the Center for Democracy and Civil Society at Georgetown University. "The lines are ones that Europeans drew. Prior to the 20th century, states lived and died on their own internal organization. Post-World War II African states don't die, because we've used an enormous amount of foreign aid and U.N. troops to prop up the governments."

Africans have rarely determined their own national borders. In fact, it has only happened twice since the colonial era. In 1993, Eritreans voted overwhelmingly for independence from Ethiopia (which itself had never been colonized by Europeans, although it was occupied by Italy from 1936-1941). And in January of this year, South Sudan voted to secede from the north, an election mandated by an internationally brokered peace agreement following Sudan's 20-year civil war.

In many cases, colonial administrators used rivalries between African ethnic groups, playing one group against another in order to consolidate colonial rule. Belgium used traditional Tutsi rulers to control its Rwandan colony, exacerbating tensions with the country's Hutu majority.

In other cases, European colonizers lumped hostile groups together into a single nation, setting the stage for eventual civil war. In Nigeria, for example, seven years after independence the country's third-largest ethnic group, the Igbo, tried to secede and form their own country of Biafra. At least 500,000 people died of starvation and related causes after the Nigerian government blockaded the breakaway region. The rebels surrendered in 1970 after two and a half years of war.

But some sub-Saharan countries have overcome their ethnic conflicts. In South Africa, where colonial rule lasted the longest, national liberation parties such as the African National Congress were able to effectively unite previously competing black ethnic groups against European colonial governments and white rule.

Yet the strength and cohesiveness that helped such parties overcome ethnic divisions sometimes has harmed post-independence democracy, says Sturman, of the South African Institute of International Affairs. In Zimbabwe, for instance, liberation leader Mugabe became president after wresting power from the white-ruled Rhodesian government. After independence, however, he created a one-party state under the Zimbabwe African National Union-Patriotic Front (ZANU-PF).

"Following independence, people vote for the national liberation movement year after year until it's entrenched," Sturman says. "The problem is very visible in Zimbabwe, where for 20 years people voted for [Mugabe's] ZANU-PF, and then by 2000 it was too late for real democracy because ZANU was too strong, and they could gerrymander constituencies."

Strategies to mitigate the effects of ethnicity in politics vary from country to country. Two states with poor democratic records, Ethiopia and Nigeria, have nonetheless won praise from some for their efforts to defuse ethnic tensions. Under a system known as ethnic federalism, Ethiopia has been divided into regions based on ethnicity. Control of land, local policing, elementary education and marriage devolves to local authorities. However, the system has been criticized for not protecting the rights of minority groups in the regions and for overemphasizing ethnicity in decisions, such as who should receive university scholarships and government jobs.

"This is highly controversial, but given the abject failure of centralized African states, it's well-worth pursuing," says former U.S. ambassador to Ethiopia Nagy.

Similarly in Nigeria, he says, the ruling People's Democratic Party's unwritten requirement to rotate the presidency between the Muslim north and Christian/animist south every two terms has helped the once-coup-plagued country maintain civilian rule for 11 years. Until the policy was adopted, no civilian government had left power peacefully in Nigeria's first four decades of independence from Britain.

But Nigeria's system will be tested this year: Southerner Goodluck Jonathan, the incumbent, has upset the rotational principle by seeking reelection to a term informally reserved for a northern candidate.

Does natural resource wealth hamper African democracy?

Despite sub-Saharan Africa's reputation as an economic basket-case, the region averaged 5.8 percent growth per year from 2004 to 2009, significantly higher than the rate in U.S. and major European economies.[12] Oil-exporting countries grew the fastest — averaging 7.9 percent per year — thanks to rising crude prices and new production in Angola, Chad and Equatorial Guinea.

But, as in other regions, the discovery of oil has not coincided with an expansion of democratic rights. Seven of the eight-largest oil producers in Africa — Chad, Sudan, Equatorial Guinea, Angola, Cameroon, Gabon and DRC — are classified as "not free" by Freedom House. The exception — Nigeria — draws a "partly free" designation.

"There is a myth out there, I call it the 'Beverly Hillbillies' myth, that the discovery of oil is going to lead to democracy and prosperity," says Stephen Kretzmann, executive director of OilChange International, a Washington-based group that monitors the oil industry. "Unfortunately you can't just drill your way to democracy and prosperity."

Indeed, Kretzmann's research parallels other studies showing oil-exporting countries less likely to be democratic and more prone to conflict.[13] In many countries oil benefits only a politically connected few in the capitals and ports that support the oil industry. The establishment of a large middle class is often viewed as a key element in democracy building. Yet oil production creates few jobs for local people. It requires expensive equipment such as offshore drilling platforms but only a small work force, often mainly foreign workers and engineers with specialized training.[14] Instead of investing oil wealth in improving education, health and infrastructure, most leaders use it to strengthen security forces so they can overpower political opponents.

Oil also has fueled ethnic conflict in Africa, notably in Nigeria's oil-rich Niger Delta and the Angolan enclave of Cabinda. In both regions people living closest to the oil production have been angered by the persistence of local poverty and pollution, despite their proximity to billions of dollars in petroleum wealth.

Further, the demand for oil from China's rapidly expanding economy has heightened competition with oil-importing Western nations, such as the United States, Britain and France. Indeed, resource-hungry China has become a major trading partner in Africa in recent years, buying timber, so-called rare earth minerals and oil, including the majority of Sudan's petroleum exports. And because communist China doesn't complicate its business dealings with political demands, Africa's other major trading partners — the United States and European Union — have quieted their demands for democratic reforms in exporting countries like Angola.[15]

"There has been a lessening of international pressure for democracy," says the South African Institute of International Affairs' Sturman. "The U.S. and EU countries that previously would have imposed more conditions before investing in a country are now investing anywhere" they can.

The decline of democracy is especially evident in oil-rich Equatorial Guinea, where opponents of dictator Teodoro Obiang Nguema face "abduction, detention, torture and execution," according to Amnesty International. Obiang and his cronies deposited tens of millions of dollars of the country's oil wealth into overseas bank accounts, according to a 2004 probe by the U.S. Senate Government Affairs Permanent Subcommittee on Investigations, while nearly two-thirds of the population live in extreme poverty, and infant and

Rebels in Nigeria's oil-rich Niger Delta have declared a full-scale "oil war" until the government addresses poverty and pollution in the region. The discovery of oil in Africa has brought neither democracy nor peace and prosperity. Seven of the eight-largest African oil producers are classified as "not free" by the human rights advocacy group Freedom House. Nigeria is considered "partly free" but has fought the rebels in the delta region for years.

child mortality equals that of the war-ravaged Democratic Republic of Congo.[16] Meanwhile, according to *Foreign Policy* magazine, Obiang's son spent more on real estate and cars between 2004 and 2006 than the government spent on education.[17]

Nonetheless, doing business with American oil producers such as Exxon Mobil and Hess has kept U.S. relations with Obiang's government warm. The Obama administration's ambassador to Equatorial Guinea recently called the country an "ally," even as he urged Obiang to develop a "more robust civil society."[18]

Last June, in what some are calling an attempt at image doctoring, Obiang promised to carry out political reforms in the coming decade, spend more on the poor and allow the International Red Cross to investigate alleged human rights violations.[19]

Equatorial Guinea's African neighbors have been no more critical than the United States. On January 30 they elected Obiang to a one-year term as president of the African Union.

But some analysts hope Africa's most democratic countries, at least, can beat the so-called resource-curse. South Africa (gold), Zambia (copper) and Botswana (diamonds) have all scored high on democracy indicators, despite their rich natural resources.

"Botswana would seem to be a good model," says John Harbeson, a former U.S. Agency for International Development (USAID) official who oversaw democracy programs in Africa. "While Botswana is maintaining its democratic credentials, its corruption ranking remains strong."

A key test of the resource curse will be Ghana, a democratic country with a much larger and more diverse population than Botswana. Ghana began pumping offshore oil from its Jubilee field in December. Flanking Ivory Coast on the east, Ghana has functioned as a democracy for nearly two decades and peacefully transferred power between rival parties in 2000 and 2008. Though corruption is a problem, the country is considered less corrupt than more developed countries like Italy, Thailand and Brazil, according to Transparency International.[20] "Ghana is an important test case if it can be the first in Africa to maintain relatively democratic government and avoid the oil curse," says former ambassador Shinn.

In addition to its experience with democracy, Ghana is also fortunate, ironically, that its oil find, which will generate about 120,000 barrels of crude per day and about $1 billion in revenue, is relatively modest compared with Nigeria or Angola, which each receive more than 15 times as much oil money.[21] Many hope Ghana's smaller find won't overwhelm the country's political class and small-farmer-led cocoa sector, while allowing strong oversight over how the new revenue is spent.

Is democracy the best form of government for spurring economic growth in Africa?

Africa is the poorest continent in the world, with about half its population living in poverty, according to the World Bank. Moreover, poverty levels have remained stable since 1981, despite recent economic growth.[22]

China's Rising Influence Could Slow Democracy

China's share of Sub-Saharan Africa's trade quadrupled between 2000 and 2009, even though the European Union remained Africa's largest trading partner. Some experts say the growth of China's economic influence in the region relieves pressure on authoritarian African governments to democratize, because — unlike the U.S. and other Western trading partners — China does not link progress toward democratization to its business dealings with other countries.

China's Share of Trade in Sub-Saharan Africa, 2000-2009

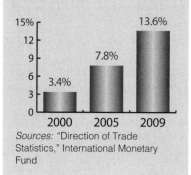

Sources: "Direction of Trade Statistics," International Monetary Fund

The persistence of hunger, disease and low living standards in Africa underscores the question of how tightly democracy and poverty are linked. Since the 1950s the debate has been shaped by "modernization theory," which argues that rising wealth leads to an educated middle class that demands political freedom and control over its governance, eventually ousting repressive governments.

But the rapid economic development of nondemocratic societies, such as China — and to a lesser degree Russia — in the past two decades has challenged that idea. The Chinese Communist Party lifted more than 600 million people out of poverty between 1981 and 2005, even as the party retained its authoritarian grip over the political system.[23] That success hasn't gone unnoticed in Africa.

"They're providing a model by their own success as an authoritarian, state-driven capitalist system that does provide an alternative," says Freedom House's Puddington.

Indeed, recent research has shown that the link between economic growth and political freedom is actually quite weak — and may be getting weaker.[24] Some of the African countries that have made the greatest strides in reducing poverty in recent years — such as Rwanda, Ethiopia and Uganda — have been the most notable backsliders on democratic freedoms.[25]

Ethiopia, which appears to be modeling its political and economic system on China, says it has averaged more than 10 percent growth per year for the past five years — in what is one of the world's poorest countries. Even allowing for some exaggeration, such growth is remarkable. By contrast, economic growth in Senegal, Benin and Ghana — three of the continent's freest states — has averaged about half that over the same period.

Ethiopia's Prime Minister Meles Zenawi criticizes what he calls the failure of "neo-liberal" reforms advocated by the World Bank and other Western-dominated institutions, which promote free markets and, to a lesser degree, free politics.[26] Meles has instead shifted the continent's second-most populous country toward that of a "developmental state," which mixes foreign investment with the championing of government- and ruling-party-owned companies in key sectors. He's similarly shifted Ethiopia away from the path of liberal democracy towards "revolutionary democracy," virtually eliminating the organized opposition.[27]

Angola, one of China's biggest oil suppliers, has also moved toward greater authoritarianism as its trade ties with China have grown.[28]

"A number of African leaders who would like to maintain pseudo-democracies are looking at the Chinese model," says former Ambassador Nagy. "They know that economic advancement is a much higher goal for their people than genuine democracy, so the China factor can at least delay Africa's political transformation."

China's influence in Africa has grown along with its trade presence. Trade with Africa (including North Africa) topped $115 billion in 2010, up from $18.5 billion in 2003.[29] "It is apparent to me that the Chinese are indifferent to democratization," former USAID official Harbeson says. "At best they may be helping African leaders to thumb their noses at the whole architecture of Western human rights and democracy norms."

The Chinese economy's resilience during the global economic crisis that began in 2008 and the backlash against the U.S. invasion of Iraq in 2003 have also changed perceptions. "The financial and economic crisis has increased the attractiveness of the Chinese model of authoritarian capitalism," the Economist Intelligence Unit's 2010 report on global democracy said.[30] "Democracy promotion by the Western world was already discredited by the experience in the Middle East in recent years. The economic crisis has undermined further the credibility of efforts by developed nations to promote their values abroad."

Yet, democracy advocates warn, what's succeeded in China, with its ethnic homogeneity and centuries of history as a nation-state, may not prove as durable in multiethnic Africa.

For the Chinese Communist Party, economic growth is key to its survival. "The party knows that it needs to create jobs," says Hoffman, of Georgetown University. "If governments in Africa faced that same exigency, they'd find the same way to create those jobs. Governments in Africa don't face that same pressure, in part because Western aid gives them alternative" sources of government funds.

In addition, China's model shows that while some authoritarian governments can drive economic growth and rapidly reduce poverty, its model doesn't allow governments that don't produce growth to be replaced. Zimbabwe's gross domestic product dropped by half between 2000 and 2009, as President Mugabe's government stole elections, seized farmland from whites and printed money so rapidly that inflation reached 231 million percent in 2008.[31]

"Authoritarianism begets more authoritarianism," says Shinn. "At some point, there is a breaking point unless there is movement, even slow movement, toward increasing participation of the people in government."

BACKGROUND

Ancient Africa

The rise of complex political entities in Africa came at different times in different regions. The first great kingdom south of the Sahara emerged at Axum, in what is now northern Ethiopia, as early as the 2nd century A.D. By the 4th century the Axumites had converted to Christianity and would eventually expand their empire across the Red Sea to include parts of the Arabian Peninsula.[32]

In West Africa the first empire to emerge was the kingdom of Ghana, established around 800 A.D in what is now western Mali and southeastern Mauritania.[33] Ghana's kings drew their wealth from the region's vast gold deposits and control of the trans-Saharan salt trade. The empire was destroyed in 1240 A.D. by a Mandingo chieftain named Sundiata Keita, who then established the Kingdom of Mali, the region's first great Muslim state, reflecting the spread of Islam to the lands just south of the Sahara Desert.[34]

CHRONOLOGY

1400s-1700s *Europeans begin trading with Africa, eventually shifting focus from trading in gold and ivory to slaves, taking an estimated 11.5 million people from Africa, undermining local governance.*

1800s *Europeans begin colonizing Africa.*

1807 Slavery is banned in British Empire.

Nov. 1884-January 1885 European powers meet in Berlin to establish rules for colonizing Africa; "scramble for Africa" begins.

1950s-1960s *Era of independence begins. U.S. and Soviet pressure forces Europeans to give up their African colonies.*

1957 Britain grants independence to Ghana. Most British colonies become independent by 1965.

1958 Guinea becomes independent. Most French African colonies gain independence by 1960.

1960 Belgian Congo gains independence but plunges into civil war.

1970s-1980s *One-party governments or dictatorships take control in most of Africa, usually supported by the Cold War superpowers.*

1975 Portugal's last African colonies — Angola and Mozambique — become independent.

1980 Zimbabwe is established with black-majority rule after guerrilla war.

1990s *End of the Cold War eliminates U.S.-Soviet rivalries. African democracy grows.*

1990 Namibia becomes independent after civil war against South Africa's apartheid government. Benin's long-time president Mathieu Kérékou becomes first incumbent president in Africa to be peacefully voted out of power.

1991 Rebels depose Ethiopia's military dictator Mengistu Haile Mariam. . . . Zambian President Kenneth Kaunda is defeated in multiparty elections.

1994 South Africa holds first multiracial parliamentary elections; Nelson Mandela becomes president. Malawi's "Life President" H. Kamuzu Banda loses office in multiparty elections.

1999 Military rule in Nigeria ends after multiparty elections.

2000s *Democratic gains slow, begin to reverse.*

2002 Kenya's Daniel arap Moi retires after 24 years as president; his chosen successor Uhuru Kenyatta loses multiparty elections to Mwai Kibaki. Mali has second democratic transition since 1991.

2005 Following disputed elections, Ethiopian security forces shoot unarmed protesters, helping to extend 14-year rule of Prime Minister Meles Zenawi. Allies of Uganda's Yoweri Museveni, already in power for 19 years, eliminate presidential term limits. Togo's Gnassingbé Eyadéma, leader for 38 years, dies and is succeeded by his son.

2007 Nigerian presidential elections are marred by large-scale fraud, installing political unknown Umaru Yar'Adua — anointed by his predecessor Olusegun Obasanjo. Disputed Kenya elections trigger ethnic violence that kills 1,000 and displaces up to 600,000.

2008 Massive crackdown on supporters of opposition leader Morgan Tsvangirai, winner of a first-round poll, leads him to withdraw from presidential run-off. He and President Robert Mugabe eventually establish a power-sharing government.

2010 Deeply flawed elections enable incumbents to win more than 90 percent of the vote in Rwanda, Burundi and Ethiopia. Opposition parties boycott Sudan's first election in 24 years. Ivory Coast President Laurent Gbagbo refuses to cede power after losing election.

2011 Presidential elections are scheduled to take place in 15 African countries.

Africa's Gulag State Shuns Democracy

Tiny Eritrea hasn't held an election in 17 years.

A former ambassador died when he didn't receive medicine for his chronic asthma. The former vice president died after not receiving medicine for a swelling on his neck. A journalist hung himself in a doorway with his tee-shirt. One of the highest-ranking women in the liberation movement and a former transportation minister both died of heat exhaustion.

Such was the fate of just a few of the 35 prisoners at Eritrea's secret Era-Ero prison camp, operated by one the world's most repressive regimes, according to Eyob Bahda, a former prison guard. Little more than a collection of metal shipping containers and cement-block structures on a broiling desert plain near the Red Sea, the camp houses the country's most sensitive political prisoners.

"They are left for death," Bahda said in a meeting with reporters in Ethiopia in May 2010. "The government knows everything."

The camp was built to house senior government officials and journalists arrested over the past decade for demanding reforms from President Isaias Afewerki, who for 17 years has ruled the tiny, tulip-shaped, former Italian colony with an iron fist. [1] Of the 35 prisoners who have been taken into custody by the military intelligence group that runs the camp, only 20 are still alive, according to Bahda.

Eritrea's ministry of information did not respond to e-mails requesting comment on Bahda's report. But his story is consistent with reports by human rights organizations, even as it provides a greater degree of detail.

The weakest prisoners at Era-Ero are kept in the shipping containers, he says. All are kept in their three-square-yard cells 23-hours a day. Though prisoners are not tortured, they also do not receive medical treatment, and temperatures often reach 115 degrees Fahrenheit. Food rations are meager.

While nearly every African government now holds regular elections — regardless of how flawed — Eritrea's insular regime has not held a single national poll since the country gained independence from Ethiopia after a 1993 referendum. The vote followed a 30-year war of independence — Africa's longest civil war — in the country located on the northwestern tip of Africa's Horn.

However, the absence of polls is just one in a variety of alleged human rights abuses by Afewerki's government, which has turned the country into a "giant prison," according to Ben Rawlence, an Africa researcher for New York-based Human Rights Watch. [2]

According to the human rights advocacy group, independent media offices were shuttered in 2001, when the first group of political detainees were arrested. Foreign journalists are regularly kicked out of the country or denied access, and a veil of secrecy blankets the regime. Freedom of religion is restricted — with the president appointing Christian and Muslim religious leaders — and citizens need permits to travel inside the country or go overseas. Those fleeing the country face a shoot-to-kill policy by the security forces, according to Human Rights Watch. Nearly all men age 18 and over are conscripted into the army or the government's national service. [3]

Bahda escaped from his guard unit under the pretext of attending a wedding. He then snuck across the border into Ethiopia, well-aware that his family would be fined for his desertion. Even the prison guards, he says, aren't free in Eritrea.

"We were also prisoners there," he says. "I was afraid I'd die with those people."

— *Jason McLure*

---

[1] For background, see Jason McLure, "The Troubled Horn of Africa, *CQ Global Researcher*, June 2009, pp. 149-176.

[2] Ben Rawlence, "Slender Land, Giant Prison," Human Rights Watch, www.hrw.org/en/news/2009/05/06/eritrea-slender-land-giant-prison.

[3] "Service for Life," Human Rights Watch, April 16, 2009, www.hrw.org/en/reports/2009/04/16/service-life-0.

Meanwhile, in Central Africa's Great Lakes region, near present-day Rwanda and Uganda, the Bantu people established their first kingdoms around 1300. In southern Africa, the first major empire was that of Great Zimbabwe, which reached its height in the mid-15th century along the Zambezi River.[35]

These precolonial-era African kingdoms and other entities practiced various forms of governance. Many

Africans lived in stateless societies, clusters of villages or towns where people did not recognize a supreme leader beyond that of the village chief. And in some of the African kingdoms, such as the Solima Yalunka in Sierra Leone, a monarch ruled but consulted on important decisions with a council of elders. In the area near modern Guinea, Liberia and Sierra Leone, secret societies known as *poro* made important decisions such as war declarations.[36]

States usually did not have standing armies that allowed monarchs to impose their will. At the local level, a village headman, aided by heads of families and community leaders, handled governance.

In most precolonial African societies, women had little voice in governance, although there were exceptions. Among the Yoruba of modern Nigeria the *iyalode*, or female representative, had jurisdiction over women's issues and a place on the ruling council. In some cases women also fought in armies — with the Dahomey Amazons of modern Benin being the best known example.

The first Europeans to make contact with Africa were the Portuguese, who began exploring coastal African communities in the 15th century. In 1469, Portugal granted a Lisbon merchant, Fernã Gomes, a five-year monopoly on trade south of the island of Arguin, off Mauritania. In return Gomes promised to pay the crown 500 crusados and explore 100 leagues (about 300 miles) of coastline per year — a seemingly stiff price, given that almost nothing was known of the area. But the potential for profits from an unexplored region fueled discoveries: Within 20 years the explorer Bartholomew Diaz had rounded the Cape of Good Hope, and by 1498 Vasco de Gama had reached India by sailing around southern Africa.[37]

The Slave Trade

Contact with Europeans would have a profound impact on the political life of Africans. The English, French and Dutch soon followed the Portuguese in pursuit of African gold and ivory. But by the 17th century the Europeans had shifted to trade in a more lucrative cargo: human beings.[38]

Up to 11.5 million Africans were exported from Africa between 1600 and 1870 to work as slaves in plantations in the Americas.[39] The impact of the slave trade on Africa's Atlantic coast varied. The area near modern Senegal and Gambia provided many of the slaves in the early years of the trade.[40] In the 1700s, civil war among the Yoruba in

what is now Nigeria provided a large number of slaves for export via ports in today's Benin, as did British slave forts in Ghana. Portugal's abolition of the slave trade north of the equator in 1815 fueled commerce in human beings from areas further south in modern-day Angola, Gabon and Democratic Republic of Congo.

The slave trade fomented warfare and ethnic tension within Africa and upended political stability in many affected areas, as increasingly wealthy traders prospered at the expense of less powerful groups. The trade even felled the mighty kingdoms of the Ngoyo and Kakongo in what today are Angola and the DRC. But for others — such as the Ashanti kingdom in what is now Ghana, the Dahomey kingdom of modern Benin and the Oyo kingdom of modern Nigeria — the slave trade with Europeans helped local monarchs consolidate control and expand their influence.[41]

Southern and eastern Africa were largely unaffected by the trans-Atlantic slave trade. In South Africa, however, contact with Europeans brought Dutch (in 1657) and later British (beginning in 1820) settlers who would clash both with each other and with Bantu-speaking groups who had migrated south from central Africa.[42] In East Africa, Ethiopia would remain largely insulated from European contact until the mid-19th century, while the Swahili-speaking coast of what is now Kenya and Tanzania had greater links with the Arabian Peninsula until the age of European imperial control in the late 1800s.

'Scramble for Africa'

From the 1500s onward, Africans and Europeans were increasingly bound in a series of unequal relationships. However, beyond a few coastal areas and swathes of white-settled South Africa, Europeans did not exert direct political control over sub-Saharan Africa until the late 1800s.

By that time European rivalries and hunger for natural resources had led to a "scramble for Africa," with its abundant gold, ivory, timber and empty tracts of fertile land for farming. In November 1884 the main European powers in Africa: Great Britain, France, Germany, Portugal and Belgium's King Leopold II[43] attempted to formalize their conflicting commercial, missionary and diplomatic interests at a conference in Berlin.[44] Underpinning the colonial mission were pseudo-scientific ideas of European racial superiority, a desire to "civilize" African societies that were technologically primitive and the hope that

Europe might gain economically from exploiting Africa's raw materials while selling manufactured goods to its inhabitants.

By 1912, Europeans ruled virtually all of sub-Saharan Africa except independent Ethiopia.[45] An estimated 10,000 independent African political/ ethnic groups had been consolidated into 40 European colonies, often with disregard to the location of common ethnic and language groups. France alone claimed 3.75 million square miles of African territory, primarily in the West.[46]

The Europeans faced armed resistance in virtually every colony and maintained power only through the use of superior arms and strategic alliances with traditional rulers. The British favored a system of indirect rule, whereby British district administrators used local African leaders to collect taxes and keep order in their domains. Incredibly, the system allowed Britain to rule its 43 million African colonial subjects in the 1930s with only 1,200 British officials.[47]

Financial self-sufficiency was the primary goal of European colonial administrations; public services such as health and education largely were left to small groups of missionaries. European-owned companies controlled most commerce and emphasized the production of cash crops such as coffee, cocoa and rubber or raw materials such as timber and minerals — an economic system whose legacy is still visible today in much of Africa.

Bumpy Road to Independence

World War I altered the colonial map by stripping Germany of its colonial possessions in what are now Namibia, Cameroon, Togo, Tanzania, Rwanda and Burundi. Italian dictator Benito Mussolini briefly occupied Ethiopia in the late 1930s.

But World War II — a catalyst for African independence — was to have a profound, long-term impact on Africa. Nearly 400,000 Africans joined the British army, and African units helped defeat the Italians in Ethiopia and restore the rule of Emperor Haile Selassie. They also noted that independence movements in other poor countries, like India and Burma, had won pledges of self-governance from the Crown.[48]

The war also crippled the British and French economies and spurred the rise of the United States and Soviet Union — emerging superpowers that opposed colonialism. Under the 1941 Atlantic Charter between President Franklin D. Roosevelt and British Prime Minister Winston Churchill, Britain and the United States would "respect the right of all peoples to choose the form of government under which they will live."[49] Anti-colonialism, meanwhile, was a tenet of Soviet communism and inspired the establishment of pro-communist African nationalist movements.

Belated reform efforts by colonial administrations — ending slave labor, investing in infrastructure and social services and offering a larger governance role to Africans — proved to be too little too late. Independence in sub-Saharan Africa came first in Ghana, formerly Britain's Gold Coast colony. There Kwame Nkrumah, a charismatic U.S.-educated lawyer, emerged from a British prison in 1951 to become prime minister of the country's colonial government and lead it to independence in 1957.

Ghana's relative wealth, its sizable number of educated leaders and its ethnic homogeneity helped smooth its transition as Africa's first independent state. Ghana's experience became a model for others as Nkrumah used his new position to help spur a wave of independence for European colonies elsewhere in Africa.

By 1960 France had granted independence to most of its colonies in West and Central Africa, and by the mid-1960s Belgium had exited from its territories. British rule had ended in East and West Africa. In 1963, the Organization of African Unity was established in Ethiopia by 32 now-independent African states (including those of North Africa) with a mandate to support the freedom of Africa's remaining colonies and to foster continental unity.

In many cases the transition of political authority was remarkably peaceful. Nonetheless, the newly independent states faced enormous challenges, including the need for infrastructure, health care and education for their largely illiterate populations. They also faced the question of how they might integrate politically. In French-speaking West Africa, Ivorian Houphouët-Boigny — leader of the region's wealthiest territory at the time — defeated an attempt to form a union among France's eight West African states.[50] While the move guaranteed that Ivory Coast wouldn't have to share its lucrative cocoa and coffee revenues with its poorer neighbors, it ensured that the region would be divided into several small, weak states vulnerable to foreign domination.

Ethnic tensions, competition for influence between the United States and the Soviet Union and the lingering influence of European colonial governments created a toxic and more violent environment elsewhere in Africa. While Ghana and Ivory Coast managed their transitions to nation-states relatively smoothly, the DRC, Angola and South Africa had rough going.

The sprawling DRC, one of Africa's wealthiest nations in natural resources, gained its independence in June 1960. But it was among the continent's least-governable, with dozens of ethnic groups living in an area more than three times the size of France, a tiny group of educated citizens and virtually no roads or phones. Riots against the colonial authorities and a mutiny by security services followed, and the copper-rich Katanga region, backed by European business interests, tried to secede from the new state.[51]

Prime Minister Patrice Lumumba, who led the country's sole national democracy movement, was arrested in December of 1960 and murdered in early 1961, reportedly with the complicity of U.S. and Belgian officials. In 1965, Col. Joseph-Désiré Mobutu took power in a coup, renamed the country Zaire and ruled as a pro-U.S. dictator (under the name Mobutu Sese Seko) until the 1990s.

According to former congressional staffer and Africa policy specialist Stephen R. Weissman, "The murder of Patrice Lumumba . . . crystallized an eventual 35-year U.S. commitment to the perpetuation of that regime [which] would tear civil society apart, destroy the state and help pave the way for a regional war that would kill millions of people." Noting the role played by the U.S., Belgian and Congolese governments in the assassination, Weissman said Lumumba "continues to be honored around the world because he incarnated — if only for a moment — the nationalist and democratic struggle of the entire African continent against a recalcitrant West."[52]

In Angola, Portuguese rule slowly disintegrated during the 1960s and '70s as Europe's weakest colonial power battled three rival nationalist groups. During that period the conflict morphed from a war of liberation against colonial forces into a civil war between competing Angolan groups. Although Portugal officially granted Angola independence in 1975, the conflict between Angolan factions hardly paused.

The United States, white-ruled South Africa and Zaire's Mobutu supported two Angolan factions — Uniao Nacional para a Independencia Total de Angola (UNITA)

and Frente Nacionale de Licertacao de Angola (FNLA) — while the Soviet Union and Fidel Castro's Cuba provided cash and troops to the Movimento Popular de Libertacao de Angola (MPLA).[53] By the time the conflict ended in 2002 — 27 years after independence — up to 1.5 million people had died and 4 million had been displaced.[54]

South Africa's history was vastly different from that of much of the continent, because of large-scale white settlement in the 1800s. By 1911, there were more than a million whites — about a fifth of the population — and the country had become a self-governing part of the British Commonwealth in 1910. But only whites were allowed to vote.[55]

In 1948, a vicious policy of racial categorization and segregation known as apartheid was instituted. It required blacks to carry passes when traveling and live in racially zoned areas. Blacks, mixed-race people and those of Indian or Asian background were barred from jobs, schools and public facilities reserved for whites. Backed by an extensive police state, apartheid would endure for nearly five decades, until black resistance and the collapse of U.S. support for the government at the end of the Cold War led to the end of apartheid and the selection of Nelson Mandela as president in the country's first multiracial elections in 1994.

'Big Men'

Cold War rivalry between the United States and the Soviet Union seriously hampered the development of democracy across the African continent. Angola's civil war was not the only African conflict fomented by Cold War tensions. South Africa and Zaire (today's DRC) were not the only authoritarian regimes propped up by the superpowers.

Foreign aid and arms from the U.S. and Soviet blocs ensured that authoritarian rulers had the means to violently repress their opponents — and, hence, little need to win popular support. In the process, Western democracies found themselves providing military and financial support to some of the continent's most dictatorial — albeit staunchly anti-communist — governments.[56]

As a result, the first-generation of post-independence African leaders often came to power talking of democracy and then promptly turned away from it after assuming control. Successive leaders in many countries came to power either through military coups or civil war, sometimes with superpower funding.

From the early 1960s until the collapse of the Soviet Union, Africa was ruled by the so-called Big Men who dealt ruthlessly with political opponents, feisty media and disloyal military officers. They stacked electoral commissions, cowed the judiciary and universities, enriched their families and top deputies, squandered money on arms and secret police and used state-owned television stations as outlets for one-sided demagoguery. The United States and its European allies nominally pushed for democratic reforms, fearing a leadership change would weaken anti-Soviet governments or even usher in communist governments.

Among the client regimes supported by the United States and its Cold War allies, France and the United Kingdom, were Zaire's Mobutu (1965-1997), Ethiopia's Haile Selassie (1930-1974), Gabon's Omar Bongo (1967-2009), Ivory Coast's Houphouët-Boigny (1960-1993), Central African Republic's Jean-Bedel Bokassa (1966-1979), Cameroon's Ahmadou Ahidjo (1960-1982) and Malawi's Hastings Kamuzu Banda (1966-1994).

Soviet-backed dictators included Mozambique's Samora Machel, Ethiopia's Mengistu Haile Mariam (1974-1991) and Guinea's Ahmed Sékou-Touré (1958-1984).

Still others — such as Tanzania's Julius Nyerere (1961-1985), Zambia's Kenneth Kaunda (1964-1991) and Ghana's Kwame Nkrumah (1957-1966) — tried to chart a middle-path and joined the Non-Aligned Movement, though they created single-party states to remain in power. [57]

'Second Liberation'

The collapse of the Soviet Union in the late 1980s and early '90s led to sweeping political changes across Africa. The United States and Russia both scaled back military and diplomatic support for presidents with dubious human rights records, and international pressure grew for real democratic reforms and multiparty elections around the world. Televised images of former dictators fleeing from office across Eastern Europe put Africa's autocrats on notice.

The change set the stage for what some hoped would be Africa's "second liberation." Benin, a small former French colony in West Africa, was the first to break the

Mobutu Sese Soku — who took power in the Belgian Congo in a coup d'etat in 1965 — is sworn in for his third seven-year term on Dec. 5, 1984. The dictator renamed the country Zaire (renamed Democratic Republic of Congo after he was deposed) and ruled for 32 years — one of many strongmen who led Africa during the post-independence era. The United States and its allies supported Mobutu and others during the Cold War because of their anti-communist stance.

AFP/Getty Images

mold. Lt. Gen. Mathieu Kérékou had ruled autocratically since taking power in a 1972 coup. Yet in March of 1991, after being beaten in an election 2 to 1 by former World Bank economist Nicephore Soglo, Kérékou stepped down. It was the first peaceful removal of an incumbent president in Africa since independence from colonial rule.[58]

By the fall of 1994, a dozen African nations had established multiparty democracies. In Zambia, Kaunda, the country's president since independence, stepped down after being defeated in October 1991 by union leader Frederick Chiluba. In April 1994, South Africa held its first multiracial elections following the end of apartheid, and the following month in Malawi, self-styled "Life President" Banda was defeated by businessman Bakili Muzuli.

Africa's Newest Nation Faces a Tough Road Ahead

Peaceful vote leads to South Sudan's secession from the Arab north.

South Sudan's road to independence was one of the longest and bloodiest in the history of Africa's liberation movements. About 2 million people died — one in five of the inhabitants — during the 22-year war between the Arab, Muslim-dominated north and the black, Christian and animist south, which ended when a peace accord was signed in 2005.

The horrific death toll made south Sudan's January independence referendum all the more emotional for the 3.9 million people who supported independence. "We lost a lot of people," Lt. Col. William Ngang Ayuen, a soldier, told The Associated Press, as he struggled to maintain his composure outside a polling place. "Today is good for them." [1]

Final results of the referendum, announced on Feb. 7, showed that 98.8 percent of the voters chose to separate from the north, clearing the way for Africa's newest nation to become independent on July 9. [2]

But, while jubilation over independence was testimony to the restorative power of the ballot box, the new nation faces massive challenges. Decades of warfare have left the landlocked region one of the poorest and least-developed corners of the world.

A 15-year-old girl in southern Sudan has a higher chance of dying in childbirth than of completing school, according to the United Nations. [3] Only 8 percent of women are literate, and one in seven children die before age 5. The Texas-size new country has less than 50 miles of paved roads and an estimated 5 billion barrels of petroleum reserves. But the pipelines that transport the crude to ports on the Red Sea run through territory controlled by its old enemies in Khartoum. [4]

The prospects for democracy are as bleak as the country's development indicators. The government of southern Sudan depends on oil revenue for 98 percent of its budget. [5] Corruption in the south is rampant, and the government is dominated by former rebels from the Sudanese People's Liberation Army. Tension remains rife in a region with dozens of ethnic groups, some of whom were armed by Khartoum to attack their neighbors during the country's civil war. [6]

"To have an oil economy in a newly independent state without institutions is not a recipe for stability," says one European diplomat, who declined to be identified. Pessimists predict

Kyodo via AP Images/Tomoaki Nakano

Residents in Juba, South Sudan, celebrate the news that 98.8 percent of voters peacefully chose in a January referendum to secede from the north. The oil-rich south — scene of a brutal 20-year civil war with the north — will become Africa's newest country in July.

South Sudan could descend into chaos and become a failed state like nearby Somalia.

For the moment, the people of southern Sudan appear optimistic about the future. "We have suffered for 55 years at the hands of our Arab brothers," Augustine Ngor, a 70-year-old man in Bahr el Ghazal state, told *The Guardian* newspaper. "And now at last we will have our freedom." [7]

— Jason McLure

[1] Jason Straziuso and Maggie Fick, "For Jubilant Voters in S. Sudan, New Country Nears," The Associated Press, Jan. 10, 2011, www .msnbc.msn.com/id/40990533/ns/world_news-africa/.

[2] "'A New Country Is Being Born,'" *The Washington Post*, Feb. 8, 2011.

[3] "Scary Statistics — Southern Sudan," United Nations, September 2010, www.unsudanig.org/library/index.php?fid=documents.

[4] Alan Boswell, "South Sudan Buys Russian Helicopters Ahead of a Planned Vote on Secession," Bloomberg News, Sept. 3, 2010, www .bloomberg.com/news/2010-09-03/southern-sudan-buys-russian-helicopters-ahead-of-planned-secession-vote.html.

[5] Maram Mazen and Jared Ferrie, "South Sudan Votes in Referendum to Declare Oil-Rich Region's Independence," Bloomberg News, Jan. 9, 2011, www.bloomberg.com/news/2011-01-08/sudan-s-referendum-begins-as-oil-rich-southern-region-eyes-independence.html.

[6] "Sudan: Mounting Ethnic Tensions in the South," IRIN, June 24, 2009, www.irinnews.org/PrintReport.aspx?ReportID=84971.

[7] Xan Rice, "Sudan Vote: Celebrations Across South as Millions Flock to Polling Stations," *The Guardian*, Jan. 9, 2011, www.guardian.co.uk/world/2011/jan/09/sudan-vote-celebrations-south.

Does Western aid improve African democracy and good governance?

YES — Gregory Adams
Director of Aid Effectiveness Oxfam America Hussein Khalid Executive Director Muslims for Human Rights Kenya

Written for *CQ Global Researcher*, February 2011

Aid to Africa does not create democracy and good governance. Africans create democracy and good governance by holding their leaders accountable, respecting the rule of law, defending basic rights and meeting citizens' needs. But Africans often have used Western aid to better govern their countries.

- In Mozambique the Administrative Tribunal has received aid from Sweden, Germany, Norway, Finland and others to better scrutinize government actions and reduce corruption. By 2008, it was conducting 350 audits, covering about 35 percent of the budget. The tribunal's latest annual report found increasing accountability across the political spectrum.
- In Liberia, the U.S. Treasury Department's Office of Technical Assistance helped create an electronic link between the Ministry of Finance and the Central Bank in 2005. The change eliminated reliance on easily-forged paper receipts, and provided for electronic cross-checks between accounts. This reduced the potential for fraud and offered taxpayers a one-stop tax preparation and payment option.
- In Kenya, Muslims for Human Rights (MUHURI) received Western aid to conduct social audits of funds intended to promote grassroots development. By involving local communities in evaluating their elected representatives, MUHURI is empowering Kenyans to hold their leaders accountable. During the 2007 elections, a majority of those audited lost their seats as a direct result of findings that exposed corruption among leaders.
- In Malawi, donors have supported community scorecards, enabling citizens to provide feedback on government services. In one stakeholder meeting, the scorecard revealed that teachers were sending students nearly two miles away from the school to fetch water for the teachers' houses before classes. Since the scorecards were implemented, the community has appealed for a water borehole near the school and the practice of having students fetch water for teachers has mostly stopped.

In each example, success was contingent upon Africans themselves — both inside and outside government — seizing the initiative for change. If donors invest the time and energy to find capable and willing partners from both government and civil society, these partnerships can yield significant lasting change to help Africans take charge of their own futures.

NO — Babatunde Olugboji
Long-time African human rights activist; Recently joined Human Rights Watch

Written for *CQ Global Researcher*, February 2011

Sub-Saharan Africa receives the highest share of foreign aid globally — about one-third of net foreign aid in 2000-2007 — and receives the most aid per capita. But I am not convinced that aid furthers the growth of African democracy.

African aid has multiple, contradictory effects. It affects state formation and disintegration, state-society relations and regional geopolitics. Aid also helps in emergencies, prevents (and fuels) conflict and provides services, infrastructure and capital.

But, according to some critics, aid can also be a tool of foreign policy or represent economic and cultural domination. Countries like Uganda and Ethiopia, which receive a substantial portion of their budgets from foreign aid, are hailed by Western donors as economic models. But both are virtually one-party states.

Africa's problems cannot be solved from Washington, London or Paris. Internally-generated solutions are far more sustainable. Moreover, foreign aid often favors the giver rather than the receiver. About 75 percent of the $27.7 billion spent by the United States on foreign assistance in the 1980s "was spent in the United States to purchase food and equipment sent abroad or the salaries of aid workers," according to a Clinton Administration report.

In addition, the number of major official donors' implementing agencies has expanded exponentially over the last three decades, to more than 100. Each recipient country deals with an average of 26 different official donors. More than 35,000 separate official aid transactions occurred in 2004, said one study, which quotes astonishing figures showing how African ministries are overloaded by aid proliferation. For example, Tanzania had more than 2,000 ongoing donor projects in the early 1990s, while Mozambique's ministry of health was managing more than 400 projects at one point.

The resources Africa desperately needs for self-sustaining growth can be found in Africa itself. While African leaders are — rightly — being blamed for corruption, little attention has been paid to Western nations and institutions that indirectly aid corruption in Africa. Many Western nations happily accommodate corrupt African companies and officials when they are allies, especially in the so-called war on terror. Western banks gladly open their vaults to illicit deposits from African dictators, safe in the knowledge that age-old banking secrecy laws will block prying eyes. Bank executives know that in all probability such monies will never be repatriated.

The real question should be: Does the West really care if Africa is democratizing?

Progress, however, was uneven. In Niger and Mali, newly elected governments still struggled with ethnic conflict. In Cameroon, Gabon and Ghana, incumbents clung to power amid charges of election irregularities. In the DRC, ethnic divisions stifled under the Mobutu regime led to clashes and eventually a horrific civil war that continues two decades later.

Nevertheless, by 2005 the number of African countries categorized as "free" had grown to 11, up from 2 in 1988.

CURRENT SITUATION

Democracy Retreats

The declining trend toward democracy that began earlier in the decade appears to be continuing, calling into question the durability of the progress made in the 1990s and the legitimacy of the 15 African elections that will be held this year.

"The year 2010 featured a continued pattern of volatility and decline for sub-Saharan Africa," said Freedom House in its "Freedom in the World 2011" report. "The region as a whole registered declines in both political rights and civil liberties indicators."

While more than half of African countries introduced presidential term limits between 1990 and 1994, 12 governments reversed themselves and abolished term limits in the 10 years ending in 2009, according to the South African Institute of International Affairs.[59] The backsliders include Cameroon's President Paul Biya, who had the distinction of instituting term limits on his rule in 1996 and then abolishing them in 2008 as his scheduled retirement loomed.

"The stars that people were looking to a decade ago — Ethiopia, Kenya, Uganda — they're not going in the right direction," says Georgetown University's Hoffman. "These were going to be the generation of reformers. But power corrupts."

Experts say a variety of factors in the early 2000s tripped up Africa on its way to democracy, starting with the U.S. government's long and bloody military effort to install democracy in Iraq. Many began to question the moral authority of the West's efforts to promote democracy. "Our misadventure in Iraq, democracy at the barrel of a gun, did much to de-legitimize democracy promotion in the U.S. and the welcoming of democracy support by recipient countries," says former USAID official Harbeson.

Meanwhile, after the Soviet Union collapsed, African leaders watched in alarm as so-called "color revolutions" erupted in one former communist regime after another. Between 2003 and 2005, popular uprisings ousted authoritarian leaders in Ukraine ("Orange Revolution"), Georgia ("Rose Resolution") and Kyrgyzstan ("Tulip Revolution"). The Africans could not help but note that after the uprisings, long-simmering ethnic tensions — held in check by years of one-party rule — frequently burst to the surface.

"There is not going to be a 'Rose Revolution' or a 'Green Revolution' or any colour revolution in Ethiopia after the election," Ethiopian Prime Minister Meles Zenawi said in May 2005 as the opposition took to the streets to protest his reelection, which extended his 14-year rule.[60] The election had widely been seen as the freest ever in Africa's second-most-populous country. Security forces responded to the protests by killing nearly 200 people and arresting much of the opposition leadership.

Western donors did not withdraw aid to the regime, and within days Uganda's leading opposition leader Kizza Besigye was arrested on treason charges, less than four months before the first multiparty elections since President Yoweri Museveni took power in 1986. Museveni won an easy victory in February 2006 after his allies amended the constitution to allow him to stand for a third term. The charges against Besigye were later dropped.

In 2007 two key countries held flawed elections, despite having held internationally lauded polls earlier in the decade. In Nigeria, Africa's most-populous country, efforts by the incumbent Olusegun Obasanjo to change the constitution so he could remain in office for a third-term were defeated. His handpicked successor, Umaru Yar'Adua, an obscure state governor, won the election with 70 percent of the vote, despite concerns over his health. A European Union (EU) electoral observation mission concluded the results were not credible, due to a "lack of essential transparency, widespread procedural irregularities, substantial evidence of fraud, widespread voter disenfranchisement, lack of equal conditions for political parties and candidates and numerous incidents of violence" that killed at least 200 people. The report said political parties should "end the practice of hiring thugs to perpetrate electoral violence."[61]

Even more disturbing was the widespread violence that broke out in December 2007 after a disputed election in Kenya, long one of Africa's most stable and prosperous nations. President Mwai Kibaki, elected five years earlier in a widely lauded poll, appeared to have been beaten by opposition leader Raile Odinga, who was backed by the long-marginalized Luo ethnic group in the country's west and Muslims along its Indian Ocean coast.

Yet, according to EU election observers, the country's electoral commission swung tens of thousands of votes to Kibaki by altering results, giving him a 2-percentage-point victory.[62] He was hastily sworn-in for a second term in a secret ceremony televised by the state broadcaster.[63] A wave of ethnic violence ensued, leaving more than 1,000 people dead across the country and displacing up to 600,000. A modicum of stability returned two months after the election when Kibaki and Odinga agreed to an awkward power-sharing arrangement, under which Kibaki remained president and Odinga was named prime minister. Though it ended the bloodshed, the deal set an unfortunate precedent for Africa: An incumbent president need not stand down just because he lost an election.

African democracy also began to falter when the broad coalitions that helped force the Big Men from power had little to unify them once an autocrat stepped down. In Kenya Odinga and Kibaki — who had been allies against the 24-year rule of former President Daniel arap Moi — later became political enemies. "You have coalitions who throw out autocrats, but then they have to decide how to rule themselves," says Hoffman. The new leaders then rule less through repression and more by "throwing around a lot of patronage and corruption."

Kenya's power-sharing agreement helped set the stage for a similar problematic electoral outcome in Zimbabwe in 2008. Mugabe, who had led the liberation movement to topple the white-minority run Rhodesian government in 1980, was expected to face his toughest electoral challenge, given the country's economic collapse during the previous decade. In a first round of voting, opposition leader Morgan Tsvangirai topped Mugabe by a significant 48 percent to 43 percent margin.

But Tsvangirai halted his bid to end Mugabe's 28-year rule after Mugabe's security forces and supporters unleashed a wave of violence, beating thousands of opposition supporters and leaving at least 86 dead. Tsvangirai withdrew

"No to a dictatorship. Long life to democracy," says a placard during post-election protests outside the U.N. offices in Bouake, Ivory Coast, on Dec. 2, 2010. During the 33-year rule of longtime President Felix Houphouët-Boigny, the Ivory Coast was a bastion of peace and relative prosperity, the so-called "Ivoirian miracle." After Houphouët-Boigny's death in 1993, the country eventually descended into a civil war that has divided the nation along ethnic and religious lines. U.N. peacekeepers are monitoring the uneasy peace.

from the run-off, taking refuge briefly in the Dutch embassy in Harare.[64] Mugabe claimed victory, despite international condemnation.

Under pressure from African and Western governments and with food supplies in the country running low, Mugabe signed a Kenya-style power-sharing deal with Tsvangirai, under which Mugabe remained president but Tsvangirai was given the less powerful post of prime minister.[65]

Botswana President Ian Khama was one of the few African leaders to directly criticize Mugabe's actions. "If a ruling party thinks it's likely to lose, and then uses its position as a ruling party to manipulate the outcome of the election . . . , [it is] not the way to go," he told the *Financial Times* in 2009.[66] "This power-sharing thing is a bad precedent for the continent."

Doing Elections

Since 2008, the number of authoritarian regimes in sub-Saharan Africa has grown from 22 to 25, according to

> **Africa's post-colonial rulers include an "assortment of military fufu-heads, Swiss Bank-socialists, crocodile liberators [and] vampire elite."**
>
> **— George Ayittey, Ghanaian economist**

the Economist Intelligence Unit's 2010 Democracy Index. And just five out of 44 countries measured by the London-based consulting group had free and fair elections: Botswana, South Africa, Ghana and the island nations of Mauritius and Cape Verde.

"Many elections are rigged, and defeated incumbents often still refuse to accept defeat," the report said.[67]

"The democratization process on the continent is not faring very well," says Jean Ping, the Gabonese chairman of the African Union Commission, which helped to craft the power-sharing agreements in Kenya and Zimbabwe and pushes African governments to adhere to pan-African treaties on democracy and human rights. "The measures that we take here are taken in a bid to make sure that we move forward. The crises, they are repeating themselves."

The problems in Kenya, Nigeria, Ivory Coast and Ethiopia are particularly distressing because those countries are among the continent's most influential. "A disturbing development is the failure of the largest and most strategically significant African countries to develop stronger and more mature democratic institutions," says Puddington, the Freedom House researcher. "They do have elections, but they are inevitably flawed, with high levels of political violence."

Ivory Coast's wasn't the only election in 2010 to highlight current difficulties. In Rwanda, Burundi and Ethiopia, incumbent leaders Paul Kagame, Pierre Nkurunziza and Zenawi used a mix of coercion and threat to systematically exclude opposition parties from taking part in the vote while stacking the courts and electoral commissions to ensure they would ratify the results. All three leaders won more than 90 percent of the vote.[68]

"The really powerful governments learned how to do elections," Richard Dowden, director of the London-based Royal African Society, said after Ethiopia's most recent poll.[69]

Meanwhile in Togo President Faure Gnassingbé, who took power in 2005 when his father, Gnassingbé Eyadéma, died after ruling the country for 38 years, handily won reelection in an election in which the fairness was disputed by the opposition.[70] A similar "hereditary presidency" exists in Gabon, where Ali Ben Bongo won a disputed presidential election in 2009 after the death of his father, Omar Bongo, who had ruled for 42 years. Likewise in Senegal, President Abdoulaye Wade, 84, once viewed as a staunch democrat, now appears to be grooming his son Karim to succeed him.[71]

"African socialism and single-party democracy didn't really change underlying colonial patterns of authoritarian executive rule so much as adapt them to new purposes and fly them under new ideological covers," says Harbeson. "We now know beyond a shadow of a doubt that multiparty elections per se don't undo these colonial structures either."

Polls elsewhere in 2010 had more positive outcomes. In Guinea — where a politically inspired massacre and mass rapes occurred in 2009 — the country teetered on the brink of open ethnic warfare after the announcement of its election results in November.[72] Yet tensions eased after Cellou Dalein Diallo, the loser of the run-off, conceded.

War-torn Sudan's first election in 24 years in April 2010 was largely peaceful, albeit tainted by a boycott by major opposition parties. Although President Omar al-Bashir — under indictment by the International Criminal Court for war crimes in Darfur — was returned to power, the election set the stage for southern Sudan's peaceful independence vote in January.[73]

In Tanzania, President Jakaya Kikwete — whose Chama Cha Mapinduzi (CCM) party has ruled the country in varying forms since 1964 — was reelected with 61 percent of the vote. Yet opposition parties ran unexpectedly strong in urban areas and among educated voters — heralding more competitive elections in the future.[74]

As 2011 begins, all eyes will be focused on the 15 presidential elections scheduled to take place in sub-Saharan Africa this year. Polls are expected to be held in Benin, Cameroon, Cape Verde, Central African Republic, Chad, DRC, Djibouti, Gambia, Liberia, Madagascar, Niger, Nigeria, Uganda, Zambia and Zimbabwe.

OUTLOOK

Cheetahs vs. Hippos

How governance in Africa evolves in the coming decades will depend on the outcome of the conflict between what Ghanaian economist George Ayittey calls the continent's "cheetahs" and "hippos."

Cheetahs, as Ayittey defines them, are a new generation of meritocratic African elites. "They brook no nonsense about corruption, inefficiency, ineptitude, incompetence or buffoonery," he writes. "The Cheetahs do not look for excuses for government failure by wailing over the legacies of the slave trade, Western colonialism, imperialism, the World Bank, or an unjust international economic system."[75]

Hippos, Ayittey continues, represent the post-colonial African ruling class that enriched themselves through corruption, manipulation of state-power and donor funds. They are, as he colorfully described them in a 2007 speech, "an assortment of military fufu-heads, Swiss Bank-socialists, crocodile liberators [and] vampire elite."[76]

"Hippos are near-sighted — and sit tight in their air-conditioned government offices, comfortable in their belief that the state can solve all of Africa's problems," he wrote earlier this year.[77] "All the state needs is more power and more foreign aid. And they would ferociously defend their territory, since that is what provides them with their wealth. . . . They care less if the whole country collapses around them, but are content as long as their pond is secure."

Analysts disagree as to what extent hippos will continue to shape the future of African governance. "There was a certain sense that we're going to see democracy grow and grow," says Gyimah-Boadi, of Afrobarometer. "But I think, in the end, autocratic rulers have found ways to forestall progress, especially by . . . keeping political power largely concentrated at the center."

Gyimah-Boadi foresees a continuation of "super-tense elections, all kinds of attempts to abridge constitutions so as to enable rulers and governments to exercise power, and very dramatic . . . attempts to evade constitutional limits on tenure."

Bruce Gilley, an African politics researcher at Portland State University, argues that Mugabe's ability to cling to power despite diplomatic isolation and sanctions has set a bad precedent for leaders like Kagame, Museveni, Gbagbo and Zenawi.

"It is easy to dismiss him as a relic of the past, but Mugabe is actually an augur of the future," writes Gilley.[78] "At independence Mugabe was a great conciliator who spoke of good governance and an end to conflict. Over time, this cheetah became a hippo. Others are now following."

The growing influence in Africa of rising global economic powers is bringing greater demand for African oil, minerals and coffee, but less international pressure for democratic reforms. "China's involvement — and perhaps that of countries like Brazil, India and the Arab world as well — may be problematic for democracy," says, former USAID democracy expert Harbeson.

But others foresee a brighter future, as the continents' governments are eventually turned over to a less-insular, better prepared group of leaders. "Africa has had several generations of truly abysmal political leadership," says Puddington of Freedom House. "As you move further from the post-colonial generation and get young people who are educated and see how other countries work, I think you'll see more leaders who are committed to democracy."

"Enlightened African leaders will spur democratic reforms," says Shinn, the longtime U.S. African diplomat. "Without enlightened leadership that really believes in democratic principles, I doubt there will be much improvement. Too many leaders are interested in remaining in power at any cost."

The challenge for Africa's democrats now is not to oust independence-leaders-turned-Big-Men but to provide a check on presidential powers by strengthening democratic institutions such as parliaments, the judiciary, electoral commissions and citizens' groups, some experts say.

Others see the recent retreat in political freedoms as just a temporary recession in a trend towards greater democratic governance, citing countries like Ghana and Mali, whose free press and domestic human rights groups will provide a model for their neighbors.

"Most of Africa will be greatly improved. Overall trends will be more positive than the last decade," says Nagy, the former U.S. diplomat in Africa. "The scales have finally tipped. The Ghana models will become much more the norm than the Ivory Coast or Kenya models."

NOTES

1. "Ivory Coast: Africa's Latest Case of Bungled Elections," *The Standard* (Nairobi, Kenya), Dec. 4, 2010, www.standardmedia.co.ke/editorial/InsidePage.php?id=2000023976&cid=16&story=Ivory%20Coast:%20Africa.

2. George E. Curry, "Exclusive Interview: Embattled Ivory Coast President Explains His Victory," *New Journal and Guide*, 2011, www.njournalg.com/index.php?option=com_content&view=article&id=4503:exclusive-interview-embattled-ivory-coast-president-explains-his-victory&catid=41:national-news&Itemid=29.

3. Martin Meredith, *The Fate of Africa* (2005), pp. 378-379.

4. Michael Bratton and Nicolas van de Walle, *Democratic Experiments in Africa* (1997), p. 4.

5. Jason McLure, "Ethiopia: Supreme Court To Hear Election Challenge," *The New York Times*, June 16, 2010, p. A6.

6. "Freedom in the World 2011 Survey Release," Freedom House, Jan. 13, 2011, www.freedomhouse.org/template.cfm?page=594.

7. For background, see Sarah Glazer, "Stopping Genocide," *CQ Researcher*, Aug. 27, 2004, pp. 685-708.

8. For background, see Karen Foerstel, "Crisis in Darfur," *CQ Global Researcher*, Sept. 1, 2009, pp. 243-270.

9. For background, see Jason McLure, "The Troubled Horn of Africa," *CQ Global Researcher*, June 1, 2009, pp. 149-176.

10. Amanda Lea Robinson, "National Versus Ethnic Identity in Africa," *Afrobarometer Working Papers*, September 2009, www.isn.ethz.ch/isn/Digital-Library/Publications/Detail/?ots591=0C54E3B3-1E9C-BE1E-2C24-A6A8C7060233&lng=en&id=106155.

11. Alan Boswell, "Chad, Sudan Signal End to Proxy Wars," VOANews.com, Voice of America, www.voanews.com/english/news/africa/east/Chad-Sudan-Signal-End-to-Proxy-Wars-84017867.html.

12. "Regional Economic Outlook: Sub-Saharan Africa," International Monetary Fund, October 2010, www.imf.org/external/pubs/ft/reo/2010/AFR/eng/sreo1010.htm. Note: IMF regional data does not include Sudan.

13. Stephen Kretzmann, "Drilling into Debt," OilChange International, July 2005, available at: http://priceofoil.org/educate/resources/drilling-into-debt/.

14. John Ghazvinian, *Untapped: The Scramble for Africa's Oil* (2007).

15. For background, see Karen Foerstel, "China in Africa," *CQ Global Researcher*, Jan. 1, 2008, pp. 1-26.

16. Terence O'Hara and Kathleen Day, "Ex-Riggs Manager Won't Testify About Accounts," *The Washington Post*, July 16, 2004, p. A1, www.washingtonpost.com/wp-dyn/articles/A53345-2004Jul15.html. Also see "Money Laundering and Foreign Corruption: Enforcement and Effectiveness of the Patriot Act, Case study involving Riggs Bank," Permanent Subcommittee on Investigations, Senate Government Affairs Committee, July 14, 2004, http://levin.senate.gov/newsroom/supporting/2004/071504psireport.pdf.

17. Tutu Alicante and Lisa Misol, "Resource Cursed," *Foreign Policy*, Aug. 26, 2009.

18. Alberto M. Fernandez, "Remarks by Ambassador Alberto M. Fernandez at the 4th of July Reception," U.S. State Department, http://malabo.usembassy.gov/ambassador/statements.html.

19. Celia W. Dugger, "African Leader Hires Adviser and Seeks an Image Change," *The New York Times*, June 28, 2010.

20. "Transparency International's 2010 Corruption Perceptions Index," www.transparency.org/policy_research/surveys_indices/cpi/2010/results.

21. Jason McLure, "Ghana's New Oil Wealth May Trigger Borrowing Spree," Bloomberg.com, Dec. 15, 2010, www.bloomberg.com/news/2010-12-15/ghana-oil-wealth-may-trigger-borrowing-spree-not-fund-future-generations.html.

22. Shaohua Chen and Martin Ravallion, "The Developing World Is Poorer Than We Thought, But No Less Successful in the Fight Against Poverty," World Bank, August 2008, http://siteresources.worldbank.org/JAPANINJAPANESEEXT/Resources/515497-1201490097949/080827_The_Developing_World_is_Poorer_than_we_Thought.pdf.

23. *Ibid.*

24. Bruce Bueno de Mesquita and George Downs, "Development and Democracy," *Foreign Policy*, September/October 2005.

25. "Efficiency Versus Freedom," *The Economist*, Aug. 5, 2010, www.economist.com/node/16743333.

26. Akwe Amosu, "China in Africa: It's (Still) the Governance, Stupid," *Foreign Policy in Focus*, March 9, 2007, www.fpif.org/reports/china_in_africa_its_still_the_governance_stupid.

27. Helen Epstein, "Cruel Ethiopia," *New York Review of Books*, May 13, 2010.

28. "Angola: Authoritarian Alliances," *Africa Confidential*, March 2, 2007.

29. "China-Africa Trade Hits Record High," *People's Daily Online*, Dec. 24, 2010, http://english.people-daily.com.cn/90001/90776/90883/7241341.html.

30. "The Democracy Index 2010: Democracy in Retreat," *The Economist Intelligence Unit*, 2011.

31. Sebastien Berger, "Zimbabwe Inflation Hits 231 Million Percent," *The Telegraph*, Oct. 9, 2008.

32. Colin McEvedy, *The Penguin Atlas of African History* (1995), p. 40.

33. John Addison, *Ancient Africa* (1970), p. 37.

34. Basil Davidson, *The African Past* (1964), p. 73.

35. Addison, *op. cit.*, pp. 99-103, 115-116.

36. Unless otherwise noted, this section is drawn from C. Magbaily Fyle, *Introduction to the History of African Civilization: Precolonial Africa*, University Press of America (1999), pp. 86-97.

37. McEvedy, *op. cit.*, pp. 70-73.

38. Davidson, *op. cit.*, pp. 176-177.

39. For further detail see: Philip Curtin, *The Atlantic Slave Trade: A Census* (1969).

40. Roland Oliver and Michael Crowder (eds.), *The Cambridge Encyclopedia of Africa* (1981), pp. 146-148.

41. *Ibid.*, p. 149.

42. Gideon Were, *A History of South Africa* (1974), pp. 22, 53.

43. The Congo Free State, which lasted from 1885 to 1909, was a private colonial project of King Leopold II, though the Belgian government provided financing. For further reading on Leopold's brutal rule, see Adam Hochschild, *King Leopold's Ghost* (1998).

44. Thomas Pakenham, *The Scramble for Africa: White Man's Conquest of the Dark Continent from 1876 to 1912* (1991), pp. 239-255.

45. Parts of South Africa were under independent white rule. Liberia, established as a homeland for freed American slaves in the 1840s, was nominally independent at this time though in practice it functioned as a U.S. protectorate.

46. Meredith, *op. cit.*, p. 2.

47. *Ibid.*, pp. 5-6.

48. *Ibid.*, p. 8.

49. The Atlantic Charter, Aug. 14, 1941, U.S. National Archives, www.archives.gov/education/lessons/fdr-churchill/images/atlantic-charter.gif.

50. Meredith, *op. cit.*, p. 64.

51. Oliver and Crowder, *op. cit.*, p. 260.

52. Stephen R. Weissman, "New Evidence Shows U.S. Role in Congo's Decision to Send Patrice Lumumba to His Death," *allAfrica.com*, Aug. 1, 2010, http://allafrica.com/stories/201008010004.html.

53. Meredith, *op. cit.*, pp. 312-318.

54. "Angola," *The World Factbook*, CIA, www.cia.gov/library/publications/the-world-factbook/geos/ao.html.

55. Leonard Thompson, *A History of South Africa* (2001), p. 298.

56. See Michael Clough, *Free at Last? U.S. Policy Toward Africa and the End of the Cold War* (1992).

57. Meredith, *op. cit.*

58. For background on post-Cold War democratization in Africa, see Kenneth Jost, "Democracy in Africa," *CQ Researcher*, March 24, 1995, pp. 241-272.

59. Kathryn Sturman, "Term Limits — Who Needs Them?" South African Institute of International Affairs, Aug. 25, 2009, www.saiia.org.za/diplomatic-pouch/term-limits-who-needs-them.html.

60. "Protests Banned in Ethiopia," Agence France-Presse, May 15, 2005, www.news24.com/Africa/News/Protests-banned-in-Ethiopia-20050515.

61. John Attard-Montalto and Vittorio Agnoletto, "Presidential and National Assembly Elections in Nigeria," (and accompanying press release) European Parliament, May 8, 2007, www.europarl.europa.eu/intcoop/election_observation/missions/2004-2009/20070421_nigeria_en.pdf.

62. "Kenya: Final Report on the General Elections 27 December, 2007," European Union Election Observation Mission, April 3, 2008, www.eueomkenya.org/Main/English/PDF/Final_Report_Kenya_2007.pdf.

63. "Kenya's Elections: Twilight Robbery, Daylight Murder," *The Economist*, Jan. 3, 2008, www.economist.com/node/10438473.

64. Alan Cowell and Barry Bearak, "A Grim Image of Politics in Zimbabwe," *The New York Times*, June 27, 2008, www.nytimes.com/2008/06/27/world/africa/27zimbabwe.html.

65. Karin Brulliard, "Power-Sharing Deal is Signed in Zimbabwe," *The Washington Post*, Sept. 16, 2008, www.washingtonpost.com/wp-dyn/content/article/2008/09/15/AR2008091500504.html.

66. Tom Burgis, "Harare Power-Sharing Comes Under Fire," *Financial Times*, March 8, 2009, www.ft.com/cms/s/0/c4eb75d8-0c01-11de-b87d-0000779fd2ac.html#axzz1D0JpjuYO.

67. Economist Intelligence Unit, *op. cit.*,

68. "U.S. Expresses Concern About Rwanda Election," Reuters, Aug. 14, 2010, www.reuters.com/article/2010/08/14/us-rwanda-election-usa-idUSTRE67D0DX20100814?type=politicsNews&feedType=RSS&sp=true; also see Jina Moore, "Burundi Election Lacks Critical Ingredient: Presidential Candidates," *The Christian Science Monitor*, June 23, 2010, www.csmonitor.com/World/Africa/2010/0623/Burundi-election-lacks-critical-ingredient-presidential-candidates; "Premier's Party Sweeps Ethiopian Vote," *The New York Times*, May 26, 2010, www.nytimes.com/2010/05/26/world/africa/26ethopia.html.

69. Jason McLure, "Why Democracy Isn't Working," *Newsweek*, June 18, 2010, www.newsweek.com/2010/06/18/why-democracy-isn-t-working.html.

70. John Zodzi, "Togo Leader Gnassingbe Re-elected in Disputed Poll," Reuters, March 6, 2010, www.reuters.com/article/2010/03/06/us-togo-idUSTRE62520G20100306?pageNumber=2.

71. "President's Son Says He'll Join Senegal's Government," Agence France-Presse, May 1, 2009, www.france24.com/en/20090501-presidents-son-says-he-will-join-new-government-.

72. Ougna Camara and Jason McLure, "Guinea President Konate Declares State of Emergency," Bloomberg News, Nov. 17, 2010, www.bloomberg.com/news/2010-11-17/guinea-s-president-konate-declares-emergency-amid-post-election-violence.html. For background, see Jina Moore, "Confronting Rape as a War Crime," *CQ Global Researcher*, May 1, 2010, pp. 105-130.

73. Opheera McDoom, "Sudan Poll Does Not Meet World Standards: Observers," Reuters, April 17, 2010, www.reuters.com/article/2010/04/17/us-sudan-elections-idUSTRE63F1FC20100417?feedType=RSS&feedName=topNews.

74. "Tanzania's Kikwete Wins Second Presidential Term," VOA News, Nov. 5, 2010, www.voanews.com/english/news/africa/Tanzanias-Kikwete-Extends-Lead-in-Presidential-Election-106760463.html.

75. George Ayittey, "Why Africa Needs 'Cheetahs,' Not 'Hippos,' " CNN.com, Sept. 6, 2010, http://edition.cnn.com/2010/OPINION/08/25/ayittey.cheetahs.hippos/index.html.

76. "George Ayittey on Cheetahs vs. Hippos," Speech to TEDGlobal 2007 Conference in Arusha, Tanzania. Video available at www.ted.com/talks/george_ayittey_on_cheetahs_vs_hippos.html.

77. *Ibid.*, Ayittey, CNN.com.

78. Bruce Gilley, "The End of the African Renaissance," *Washington Quarterly*, October 2010, www.twq.com/10october/docs/10oct_Gilley.pdf.

BIBLIOGRAPHY

Books

Ayittey, George, *Africa Unchained: The Blueprint for Africa's Future*, Palgrave MacMillan, 2006.
Ghanaian economist George Ayittey is unsparing in his criticism of the failures of modern African governance, 50 years after the end of colonialism. Freeing African

economies from their governments' shackles would raise living standards for the continent's poorest, he argues.

Collier, Paul, *Wars, Guns, and Votes, HarperPerennial*, 2009.
Oxford Professor Paul Collier argues that sham democracies in the world's poorest countries, many of them in Africa, are prone to higher levels of political violence. Rigged elections lead to disillusionment, resentment and eventually bad governance.

Maathai, Wangari, *The Challenge for Africa*, Pantheon, 2009.
Nobel prize-winning environmentalist and human rights campaigner sees hope for the continent in reforming local governance and promoting grassroots development. She criticizes colonialism and Western hypocrisy towards Africa but also finds fault with modern African cultures tolerate corruption and environmental degradation.

Meredith, Martin, *The Fate of Africa, PublicAffairs*, 2005.
This sweeping history takes the reader on a continent-wide journey, beginning at independence and ending with civil wars in Darfur, Liberia and Sierra Leone. Key leaders, including Ghana's Kwame Nkrumah, Zimbabwe's Robert Mugabe and Ivory Coast's Felix Houphouët-Boigny are given unflinching treatment.

Pakenham, Thomas, *The Scramble for Africa: White Man's Conquest of the Dark Continent from 1876 to 1912, RandomHouse*, 1991.
This classic history of African colonialism — from King Leopold's grab for the Congo to British domination of South Africa — details how the continent was divided arbitrarily by the European powers, with long-lasting effects on African governance.

Wrong, Michela, *It's Our Turn to Eat: The Story of a Kenyan Whistleblower, HarperCollins*, 2009.
This biography of Kenyan journalist and iconoclastic anti-corruption activist John Githongo illuminates the failed dream of democracy in Kenya — once considered East Africa's most stable government — and highlights the corruption and ethnic division that plague Kenyan politics.

Articles

Epstein, Helen, "Cruel Ethiopia," *The New York Review of Books*, May 13, 2010.

The writer documents in detail how the World Bank and other Western aid agencies were complicit in Ethiopia's development into an authoritarian one-party state after the country's abortive multiparty elections in 2005.

McLure, Jason, "Why Democracy Isn't Working," *Newsweek*, June 18, 2010.
The United States and its allies are accepting democracy's retreat in Africa. Confirmed autocrats remain close U.S. allies in part because of the need for natural resources, help in fighting terrorists like al-Qaeda and an entrenched aid bureaucracy.

Sanders, Edmund, "Democracy is Losing Ground Across Africa," *Los Angeles Times*, July 13, 2008.
China's growing influence, along with African leaders' reluctance to criticize each other, helps explain why many democratic gains on the continent have been reversed.

Reports and Studies

"Freedom in the World 2011: The Authoritarian Challenge to Democracy," *Freedom House*, 2011, www.freedomhouse.org/template.cfm?page=594.
The democracy promoting advocacy group's annual report shows that only nine of 48 sub-Saharan countries were considered "free" in 2010. Last year was the fifth consecutive year liberties declined globally, the longest regression in the report's nearly four-decade history.

Bratton, Michael, and Robert Mattes, "Neither Consolidating Nor Fully Democratic: The Evolution of African Political Regimes, 1999-2008," *Afrobarometer*, May 2009, www.afrobarometer.org/index.php?option=com_docman&Itemid=37.
A polling project founded by a network of African research organizations provides a wealth of survey data on how citizens in 19 (mostly free or partly free) countries view their own governance.

Rawlence, Ben, and Chris Albin-Lackey, "Nigeria's 2007 General Elections: Democracy in Retreat," *African Affairs 106* (424), 2007, pp. 497-506.
Two Human Rights Watch officials painstakingly detail the myriad ways the ruling party in Africa's most populous state cheated in its last election.

For More Information

African Union, P.O. Box 3243, Addis Ababa, Ethiopia; +251 11 551 77 00; www.africa-union.org. Pan-African body that promotes political and economic cooperation between the 53 member nations; mediates election disputes.

Freedom House, 1301 Connecticut Ave., N.W., Sixth Floor, Washington, DC 20036; (202) 296-5101; www.freedom-house.org. Founded in 1941, tracks liberties across the globe based on a checklist of political and civil rights; publishes an annual survey, "Freedom in the World."

Human Rights Watch, 350 Fifth Ave., 34th Floor, New York, NY 10118-3299; (212) 290-4700; www.hrw.org. Uses its own on-the-ground research to provide periodic reports on human rights developments in Africa and around the world.

Institute for Security Studies, P.O. Box 1787, Brooklyn Square, Tshwane (Pretoria) 0075, South Africa; +27 012 346 9500; www.iss.co.za. One of Africa's leading foreign policy think tanks; provides a range of views on democracy and other African issues.

Mo Ibrahim Foundation, 3rd Floor North, 35 Portman Square, London W1H 6LR, United Kingdom; +44 20 7535 5088; www.moibrahimfoundation.org. Sudanese-born telecom tycoon Ibrahim has donated part of his fortune to improving African governance. Foundation offers the world's richest prize — $5 million over 10 years and $200,000 for life thereafter — to democratically-elected African heads of state who serve their countries well and then leave office. The organization also publishes an index ranking African countries on their governance.

National Endowment for Democracy, 1025 F St., N.W., Suite 800, Washington DC 20004; (202) 378-9700; www.ned.org. A private, nonprofit foundation funded mainly by the U.S. Congress; finances democracy projects in more than 90 countries and publishes the *Journal of Democracy.*

South African Institute of International Affairs, P.O. Box 31596, Braamfontein 2017, South Africa; +27 11 339 2154; www.saiia.org. An Africa-focused think tank that studies African governance, parliamentary performance and natural resource management.

Voices From Abroad:

GUILLAUME SORO

Prime Minister Ivory Coast

At a crossroads

"This is what's at stake: Either we assist in the installation of democracy in Ivory Coast or we stand by indifferent and allow democracy to be assassinated."

Virginian-Pilot, January 2011

Florida Today/Parker

DONKRIS MEVUTA

Executive Director Friends of the Land (environmental NGO), Ghana

Blessing or curse?

"Politicians have left people expecting very high returns. The very limited space the people have for participation [in managing the impact of the oil industry] is a recipe for disappointment and conflict. Oil is a blessing, but the way we manage the environmental and social impacts will show whether it is a curse."

The Christian Science Monitor December 2010

HAJO ANDRIANAINARIVELO

Minister of Land Management, Madagascar

No advice wanted

"One has the right to strike if one feels his liberty is not respected, so we had the right to take the future in our hands. As for SADC [the Southern African Development Community], we don't need democracy lessons from the likes of Zimbabwe or Swaziland."

The Christian Science Monitor November 2010

CHINUA ACHEBE

Novelist, Nigeria

Patience needed

"This is not a time to bemoan all the challenges ahead. It is a time to work at developing, nurturing and sustaining democracy. But we also must realize that we need patience and cannot expect instant miracles. Building a nation is not something a people do in one regime, in a few years, even. . . . Sustaining democracy in Nigeria will require more than just free elections. It will also mean ending a system in which corruption is not just tolerated, but widely encouraged and hugely profitable."

The New York Times January 2011

KAMALI

Resident, Nairobi, Kenya

Coups still necessary

"Coups are there because of lack of democracy. To avoid coups, [the African Union] should emphasize building true democratic institutions. Currently, coups are still needed in Africa."

New York Amsterdam News February 2010

PACOME BIZIMUNGU

Physiotherapy student
Kigali Health Institution Rwanda

Steps toward democracy

"We make our decision according to the strength of the candidates — there is no issue of ethnicity. We are in a process. We have not reached real democracy yet, but I think this is the first step to democracy."

The Christian Science Monitor August 2010

DAVID DADGE

Director, International Press Institute, Austria

Democracy leads to development

"From the statistics, it is now clear that there's a correlation between poor leadership of a country and press freedom. It is high time these leaders cultivated some sense of democracy as this will ultimately lead to the development of their nations."

The Nation (Kenya), March 2010

ELIJAH OMAGOR

Partner Ezel Associates (think tank) Uganda

Oil curse makes leaders unresponsive

"Oil revenues therefore turn out to be a curse when leaders enjoy free reign over national resources. This lack of accountability is a recipe for the oil curse because personalisation of national resources always results in politicians becoming unresponsive and unaccountable to their electorate. This is especially so because political relationships in our part of the world tend to be vertical such that those in power allocate resources downwards in exchange for political support. This means that even basic functions of government are fulfilled in exchange for political support and those who are politically well-connected reap big."

The Monitor (Uganda) March 2010

11

Europe's Immigration Turmoil

Sarah Glazer

African migrants at a detention camp in Malta await immigration processing, which can take up to 18 months. Hundreds of African "boat people" arrive each year on the Mediterranean island — the European Union's smallest member state — after risking their lives at sea trying to migrate to the EU, primarily from North Africa.

AFP/Getty Images/Robyn Beck

From *CQ Researcher*,
December 2010.

Shooting at mosques and killing *muezzins* aren't usually part of election campaigns in Austria. * But such measures were featured in "Bye Bye Mosque," an online video game launched by the anti-immigrant Freedom Party (FPÖ) during September elections in the industrial state of Styria.

Local party leader Gerhard Kurzmann — who says a multicultural society "can only be a criminal society" — defended the game, which closed with the message "Styria is full of minarets and mosques. So that this doesn't happen (in reality): Vote . . . the FPÖ!"[1]

The game was taken down shortly after protests from the opposing Green Party, which pointed out that there are no minarets in Styria. But Kurzmann's party apparently benefited from the heated debate about the game: For the first time since 2005 the Freedom Party gained a seat in the nine-member provincial government. Even in cosmopolitan Vienna, where the party pushed for referendums banning minarets, it won more than a quarter of the vote in October's provincial elections, spurring speculation the party could dramatically affect national elections in three years.[2]

Fringe factions like the Freedom Party have been gaining support across Western Europe, most surprisingly in two countries traditionally known for their tolerance — Sweden and the Netherlands. And while Swedish and Austrian mainstream parties so far have resisted including such minority parties in their governments, Dutch politician Geert Wilders — charged this year with inciting racial hatred for his rabidly anti-Muslim statements — has become the main power broker in his country's coalition government.[3]

France, Germany and Britain Saw Largest Influx

More than 3.5 million immigrants became permanent citizens of European Union countries between 2004 and 2008, nearly 60 percent of them settling in France, Germany and the United Kingdom. The migrants were from both EU and non-EU countries. Countries with fewer job opportunities, such as Poland and Romania, saw only modest increases.

Number of New Citizens in EU Countries, 2004-2008

Source: Eurostat, August 2010

Rhetoric and anti-immigrant code words once reserved for right-wing, xenophobic parties have seeped into the speeches of mainstream politicians. German Chancellor Angela Merkel's uncharacteristically blunt remark in October that the nation's "multicultural" experiment — to "live happily side-by-side" with foreign workers — has "utterly failed" was widely interpreted as a criticism of the nation's 4 million Muslims, most of Turkish origin. Referring to America's own recent brouhaha over a proposed mosque near Ground Zero, *Boston Globe* religion columnist James Carroll commented, "On both sides of the Atlantic, a rising tide of xenophobic hostility toward immigrants is threatening to swamp the foundation of liberal democracy."[4]

While it's tempting to draw parallels to the recent upsurge in American anti-Muslim hostility, important differences exist between U.S. Muslims — mainly educated and professional — and Europe's Muslims, workers who migrated primarily from rural villages in countries like Turkey, Algeria and Bangladesh. European Muslims are "more like the black communities of the United States — in terms of handicaps and social problems," such as high unemployment, school dropout and welfare dependency rates, notes Shada Islam, senior program executive at the European Policy Centre think tank in Brussels. And Europe's Muslims don't enjoy as much mainstream political support as American Muslims do.

"I haven't heard a single European politician stand up and say what Mayor [Michael] Bloomberg of New York and others say in the United States" in defending Muslims who want to build a mosque near Ground Zero, observes Islam.

European immigration experts are particularly disturbed by the growing power of anti-immigrant parties.

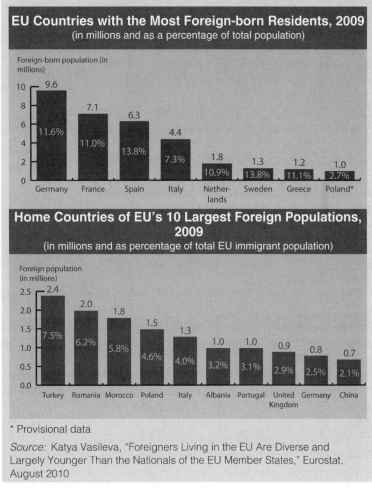

Germany Has the Most Foreign-Born Residents

Nearly 10 million foreign-born residents live in Germany — more than in any other European Union (EU) country. More than 2 million Turks live in the EU, making Turkey the largest source of EU immigrants.

EU Countries with the Most Foreign-born Residents, 2009
(in millions and as a percentage of total population)

Foreign-born population (in millions)

Germany	France	Spain	Italy	Netherlands	Sweden	Greece	Poland*
9.6	7.1	6.3	4.4	1.8	1.3	1.2	1.0
11.6%	11.0%	13.8%	7.3%	10.9%	13.8%	11.1%	2.7%

Home Countries of EU's 10 Largest Foreign Populations, 2009
(in millions and as percentage of total EU immigrant population)

Foreign population (in millions)

Turkey	Romania	Morocco	Poland	Italy	Albania	Portugal	United Kingdom	Germany	China
2.4	2.0	1.8	1.5	1.3	1.0	1.0	0.9	0.8	0.7
7.5%	6.2%	5.8%	4.6%	4.0%	3.2%	3.1%	2.9%	2.5%	2.1%

* Provisional data

Source: Katya Vasileva, "Foreigners Living in the EU Are Diverse and Largely Younger Than the Nationals of the EU Member States," Eurostat, August 2010

For instance, Wilders' party won promises from the new Dutch government to cut immigration from non-Western (presumably Muslim) countries in half and to make it harder for workers from those countries to bring over their spouses. "For the first time we have a government that is singling out a specific group of citizens; . . . it's pure discrimination," says Jan Willem Duyvendak, a sociology professor at the University of Amsterdam.

Even more disturbing, say experts, is the trend of mainstream politicians adopting similar anti-immigrant positions. The National Front, France's most right-wing party,

Afghan migrants receive food handouts from a nongovernmental organization in Calais, France, in November, 2009, after riot police bulldozed a makeshift camp used as a base to sneak across the English Channel into Britain. Resentment toward immigrants has grown in recent years throughout Europe as the weak economy intensifies unemployment.

has declined in popularity since it peaked in 2002, when its leader Jean-Marie Le Pen came in second in presidential elections. But if it no longer garners as much support, that's in part because French President Nicolas Sarkozy "gives people a respectable way" of echoing the party's anti-immigrant sentiments, says Philippe Legrain, the British author of the 2007 book, *Immigrants: Your Country Needs Them.*

"There's a great temptation among mainstream politicians to adopt the rhetoric and the xenophobic diatribes of populist parties," says Islam, who is "very alarmed" by this trend. "People in these uncertain times want to know there is one guilty party," and Muslims have become a convenient scapegoat, she says.

In the past year, anti-immigrant hostility has emerged in various rhetorical and legislative forms in several European countries:

- In the Netherlands, the coalition government that took power in October agreed to Wilders' demands to pursue headscarf bans and measures making it harder for immigrants' spouses to join them. The

agreement followed the strong third-place showing of Wilders' Freedom Party in national elections.[5]

- In France, Sarkozy expelled Romanian and Bulgarian Roma, also known as Gypsies, a move that violated European Union agreements on antidiscrimination and the free movement of EU citizens between countries, according to human rights groups. The parliament banned the public wearing of the Muslim burqa, a full-body covering that exposes only the eyes through a mesh screen.
- In a referendum in Switzerland, nearly 58 percent of voters supported a ban on new minarets on mosques in 2009, and a majority say they want to ban the burqa.[6]
- In Sweden, the anti-immigrant Swedish Democrat Party doubled its support in September from the last election — to nearly 6 percent — allowing members to sit in parliament for the first time. The party's campaign called for banning full-face veils, new mosques and most new immigration from Muslim countries.[7] Also in Sweden, authorities warned in October that in 15 separate shootings this year one or more snipers had targeted "dark-skinned" residents of Malmo, killing one and wounding eight.[8]
- In Britain, Conservative Prime Minister David Cameron was elected after promising to cut immigration from hundreds of thousands to "tens of thousands," and his government temporarily capped non-EU immigration — to become permanent next year.
- In Italy, Roman officials bulldozed 200 Roma squatter camps, which some say was aimed at getting them to leave Italy.[9]

Meanwhile, recent polls show that sizable percentages of Europeans feel immigrants drain welfare benefits, damage the quality of life and make it harder to get jobs. In a *Financial Times* poll in September about 63 percent of Britons thought immigration had harmed the National Health Service and the education system. In Spain, where 20 percent of the workers are jobless, 67 percent of respondents thought immigration made it harder to find a job, and nearly a third said immigration lowers wages.[10]

Paradoxically, Western Europe's anti-immigrant fervor is peaking just as the recession has been slowing immigration and even reversing immigrant flows in some countries. Ireland and Germany, for instance — where booming economies attracted foreign workers for years — are now seeing more out-migration than in-migration, as the economies of those countries slow down or, in the case of Ireland, flounder.[11]

Experts point out that the number of immigrants entering Western Europe from majority Muslim countries is dwarfed by the number coming from non-Muslim countries, especially from the EU. (European Union governments are required by law to accept other EU citizens, as well as all political refugees deemed eligible for political asylum.)[12] For example, Germany now has more people emigrating back to Turkey than Turks entering Germany, and the other countries sending the most migrants to Germany last year — Poland, Romania, Bulgaria and the United States — weren't Muslim at all.[13] Austria, home of the anti-Muslim Freedom Party, has more immigrants arriving from Germany than from Turkey.[14]

Some experts blame growing anti-immigrant hostility on the insecurity voters feel about jobs, pensions and benefits in budget-cutting Europe.[15]

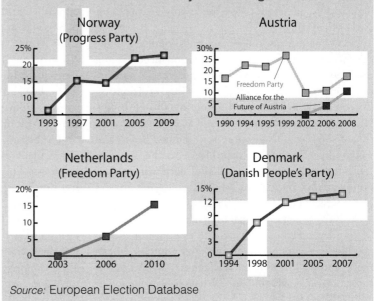

Anti-Immigration Parties Score Election Gains

Right-wing, anti-immigrant political parties have made significant gains in recent parliamentary elections in several traditionally liberal European nations. The Freedom Party in the Netherlands, for example, garnered 16 percent of the vote in the latest election, up from zero percent seven years earlier. Two parties in Austria — the Freedom Party and the Alliance for the Future of Austria — combined to earn more than one-quarter of the votes in 2008.

Percent of Votes Won by Anti-Immigrant Parties

Source: European Election Database

Others say Europeans worry about losing their national identities in increasingly diverse societies that don't subscribe to America's melting-pot cultural heritage.

Sarkozy's mass expulsion of the Roma was widely viewed as a ploy to satisfy right-wing voters, as was his support for banning burqas and stripping French citizenship from naturalized citizens who commit violent crimes. "Sarkozy, with very low approval ratings, is trying to shore up or gain support among the far right and supporters of the National Front," says John R. Bowen, a Washington University, St. Louis, anthropologist and author of the 2007 book *Why the French Don't Like Headscarves.* "The burqa ban looks like it's about Islam, but all of these [initiatives] are really about immigrants and about a deal for the far right."

Still, much of Europe's recent anti-immigrant hostility has focused on Muslims, and that often seems to include

Muslims born on the continent or who are citizens. In the Netherlands, Wilders once proposed taxing headscarves for "polluting" the landscape. Similar sentiments in Germany helped to boost former central banker Thilo Sarrazin's new book, *Germany Does Away with Itself,* to the top of bestseller lists. The book claims Muslim immigrants are "dumbing down" society and coming to Germany only for its generous welfare benefits.[16]

"The Turks are taking over Germany . . . with a higher birth rate," Sarrazin has said. "I don't want the country of my grandchildren and great-grandchildren to be largely Muslim, or that Turkish and Arabic will be spoken in large areas, that women will wear headscarves and the daily rhythm is set by the call of the *muezzin.*"[17]

Sarrazin's book dared to break a politically correct silence about Germany's real problems with its Turkish population: high rates of unemployment and welfare dependency combined with low education levels, even among second- and third-generation immigrants.[18] In a survey released in October, 30 percent of respondents believed Germany was "overrun by foreigners" seeking welfare benefits,[19] and 58.4 percent thought German Muslims' religious practices should be "significantly curbed."[20] Newspapers are filled with politicians' statements about Muslim immigrants' inability to integrate — ironically, just when Turkish migration has declined dramatically, and more people are leaving Germany for Turkey than entering.[21]

Some mainstream politicians and economists argue that Western Europe's aging population needs young migrants to expand the work force, pay social security taxes and keep the economy growing, considering Europe's low birth rates and coming retiree bulge. "Europe's feeble demographic outlook" means that continued support of its generous state-funded health and welfare benefits is "incompatible" with the desire to "ring-fence their national cultures with controls on immigration," editorialized Tony Barber, former Brussels bureau chief of the *Financial Times*.[22]

Yet perceptions of immigration are often more about fear and protecting one's culture than about demographics or economics. Statistics "don't address the feeling of unease that voters have [about] 'What kind of society are we developing into? What's happening to our culture?'" says Heather Grabbe, executive director of the Open Society Institute, a think tank in Brussels concerned with immigrants' rights. Much anti-immigrant sentiment perceives Islam as an alien, threatening ideology, even though many Muslims were born in Europe.

"This is not about recent migration," says Grabbe. "This is about several generations of migration and people who are in many cases very well-integrated into communities." And the right's political rhetoric about national identity "hasn't been opposed effectively by any other kind of discussion, particularly on the left."

As Western Europeans struggle with their fears about immigration and its impact on their economies, jobs and culture, here are some of the questions being asked:

Does Europe need its immigrants?

Former central banker Sarrazin's bestseller claiming immigrants "drag down" Germany triggered an eruption in the blogosphere from Germans who say they've had

enough immigration. Yet large swathes of eastern Germany are becoming depopulated due to the country's extremely low birth rate and greater out-migration than in-migration over the last two years.

Demographer Reiner Klingholz, director of the Berlin Institute for Population Development, suggests Germany follow the American example of the Wild West: encourage settlement and "massive" in-migration.[23] Even if Germany could increase its annual net immigration rate back up to the levels of a few years ago (about 100,000-200,000), Klingholz calculates, the population would decline by 12 million by 2050 — a "bloodletting" similar to emptying Germany's 12 largest cities. Young, booming nations like India, China and Brazil will have a clear economic advantage, he says, and when they also begin to age and need to recruit young workers from abroad, there will be no workers left to immigrate into "good old Europe."

The recent fiscal crisis has shined a laser on two trends that will force all European governments deeper into debt: Europe's burgeoning aging population and fertility rates that are too low to replace the current populations.[24] Thus, governments across Europe face the specter of having to support a huge generation of retiring baby boomers with too few young workers to pay the social security taxes needed to support them. Many countries have already turned to immigrants to solve some of their labor shortages, such as Turkish taxi drivers in Berlin and African chambermaids in Italy.

Because immigrants tend to be younger than native-born populations, they can offer an important solution to the looming pension and demographic crises, some experts argue. According to the most recent figures from Eurostat, the EU's statistical office, the median age for foreigners living in the European Union is 34.3, about six years younger than that of the national population.[25] The percentage of older persons in Europe's population is expected to rise even more in nearly all of the EU, primarily because people are living longer and birth rates are declining. But migration will help sustain population growth — where it exists — between now and 2030, according to Eurostat.[26]

In a new report, experts at the Organisation for Economic Co-operation and Development (OECD) in Paris say migration is the key to long-term economic growth. For their own economic self-interest, the report urges, European countries should be opening — not closing — citizenship to foreigners. And, the authors argue, governments should be helping immigrants who have lost jobs by giving them the same unemployment benefits they give to natives — another inflammatory issue among voters this year.[27]

"There is no escaping the fact that more labour migration will be needed in the future in many OECD countries, as the recovery progresses and the current labor market slack is absorbed," said John P. Martin, OECD's director of employment, in an editorial.[28] "In a world where labour is becoming scarcer, immigrants are a valuable resource, and employers need to see this."

Yet skeptics suggest that as more women enter the labor force and as native-born Europeans begin working beyond their traditional retirement age, which is generally in the late 50s, more immigrant workers may not be needed at all. In Austria, life expectancy is now about 20 years past the average retirement age of 58 for women and 59 for men, so many older people probably will remain in the work force years longer than in the past, says Wolfgang Lutz, demographer at the International Institute of Applied Systems Analysis in Laxenburg, Austria, outside Vienna. And as for women entering the work force, countries like Germany and Austria — with their traditions of stay-at-home mothers — have a long way to go to catch up with Scandinavian countries, where women play an equal part with men in the work force, he points out.

"Reforms to labor markets to reduce barriers to working — like childcare policies for women — are going to be more important, quantitatively, than immigration," says Madeleine Sumption, policy analyst at the Migration Policy Institute in Washington, D.C. "If immigration were to solve the problem alone, the scale of numbers you'd have to have coming in would be politically impossible."

It's also possible that technology will improve future productivity, enabling Europe to produce the same amount of goods and services with fewer workers. Under that scenario, says Lutz, "The low birth rate may be the best thing that could happen to Europe. Otherwise there would be lots of unemployment."

Moreover, countries like Germany are getting the wrong kind of migrants — low-skilled, uneducated workers that don't contribute much to the economy or taxes, says Ruud Koopmans, director of migration and integration research at the Social Science Research Center in Berlin. "We need immigrants, it's quite clear; but we do not need the immigrants we are getting so far," he says. "Europe has not succeeded in being attractive

enough for highly skilled immigrants from India or other Asian countries. Usually, we're getting immigrants for whom there are no shortages in the labor market."

Skeptics of the immigration solution also question whether underpaid, low-skilled immigrants can really bail out governments from their pension shortfall, since the taxes they pay will be relatively small due to their low incomes. With immigrants' unemployment rates running at twice those of European natives in the recent crisis, they could eat up more in welfare benefits than they pay in taxes, suggest some experts and anti-immigrant voices in Britain.[29]

A recent British study examined the impact of Eastern European immigration into the U.K., where in 2004 a flood of young Poles and other Eastern Europeans began entering Britain after their countries joined the EU. Although Polish immigrants often generated resentment among working class voters, the study found that immigrants from the new EU countries had actually contributed more in taxes than they consumed in welfare benefits. According to the study, these immigrants were 60 percent less likely than natives to collect state benefits, tax credits or subsidized housing.

"They made a positive contribution to public finance," according to study author Christian Dustmann, professor of economics at University College London. Eastern European immigrants paid 37 percent more in taxes than they received in public goods and services in 2008-2009.[30]

Despite these positive findings, Dustmann doesn't think immigration can solve the problem of aging societies needing younger immigrant labor. "It's only a quick fix," not a long-term solution, he says, because immigrants will eventually age and will also require social security. "I don't think immigrants can solve our demographic problems."

Still, foreign workers could defuse another demographic time bomb, argues author Legrain: the need for workers to care for the elderly. The demand for such workers will skyrocket in the health and elder-care industries, he predicts, as the share of Europe's population over age 80 almost triples by 2050.[31]

"Many of these jobs are low-skilled, low-paid jobs that Europeans don't want to do," he argues. "Who's going to work in the care homes?"

But Sir Andrew Green, chairman of Migration Watch, a British group that wants to cut migration, says access to cheap migrants is precisely why these kinds of jobs are so "appallingly badly paid." He considers it

Homeless Migrants in Britain Feel the Pain

With winter coming, jobless immigrants are sleeping on the street.

When 22-year-old Polish immigrant Michal Anisko showed up in October at a homeless day shelter in Slough, England, he was a far cry from the stereotypically successful "Polish plumber" often blamed in British tabloids for depriving native workers of jobs.

His weather-beaten face showed the strain of having slept on park benches for four months, ever since returning to this charmless, industrial suburban town outside London — known for its factories, plentiful jobs and big Polish community. After finding only spotty employment in his native Poland for a year, England had drawn him back with memories of an earlier year of steady work in restaurant kitchens, car-washes and construction. But that was before the recession hit Slough; when he returned this summer, the temp agency that had found him those jobs had shut down.

Even the Polish food shop window, which he remembered crammed with help-wanted placards, was comparatively bare. "These days there are only a few jobs posted, and when I ring up, they say someone already took the job," he said through an interpreter. Desperate, Anisko took an illegal job as a construction day laborer, but when he asked for his pay, his employers beat him up.

Slough is only one barometer of Britain's economic downturn since 2004, when Poland and seven other former Soviet bloc countries joined the European Union and thousands of Poles — just granted the right to work anywhere in the EU — were attracted to England's booming economy. [1] Three or four years ago only one or two Eastern European migrants per day came through the door of Slough's Save Our Homeless shelter seeking a hot meal or a shower.

"We're now looking at 30 or 40 a day using our service, because they're sleeping on the street," Mandy McGuire, who runs the shelter, said in October. Typically, the men, most of them older and more street-hardened than Anisko, have lived in Slough for four or five years and once earned enough at low-skilled jobs to send money home and rent a room. "But now the work's gone, their accommodations are gone; they're turning to alcohol," McGuire says. "The more they're turning to alcohol, the less employable they're becoming."

London has seen a similar trend. At the latest count, 954 people — about a quarter of those found sleeping on the street — were from Eastern Europe, according to London's Combined Homeless and Information Network. That is more than triple the number counted in 2006-2007. Across the country, 84 percent of homeless day centers have reported an increase in the number of Eastern European migrants using their services, according to Homeless Link, which represents 480 homeless organizations in the U.K. [2]

Because Anisko's past employers paid in cash, which was off-the-books, he's not eligible for unemployment or housing benefits available to registered immigrants who have worked legally for a year — another contradiction to the widespread British view of immigrants as "welfare scroungers." Anisko's ineligibility for welfare is typical of homeless migrants from Eastern Europe, either because their jobs are illegal or migrants can't afford the $145 fee to register as a worker, experts say.

The European Commission has said Britain's policy of denying housing, homeless assistance and other social benefits to immigrants from Eastern Europe who have not been registered workers for at least 12 months is discriminatory and violates EU rules on free movement and equal treatment. The United Kingdom has two months to bring its legislation in line with EU law, the commission said on Oct. 28. Otherwise, the commission may decide to refer the U.K. to the EU's Court of Justice. [3]

Also in October, the Polish charity Barka UK offered Anisko a free plane ticket back to Poland and help finding work there. But he refused, saying it would be even more difficult to find a job back home. Six of his fellow migrants from Slough had accepted Barka's offer and flew home the previous week, according to McGuire.

"immoral" to import what he calls "an underclass" to care for the elderly.

"In the short term it does make elder care affordable," he says, "but in the long term it's a bad policy" that will contribute to Britain's projected population growth and the nation's already crowded highway and mass transit systems. "And we are a small island," he notes, citing statistics showing that Britain is about twice as densely populated as France and about 12 times as crowded as the United States.

While most of Britain's approximately 1 million Polish immigrants have fared well in England, about 20 percent — generally older men who don't speak English — have failed to find a steady source of income, according to Ewa Sadowska, chief executive of Barka UK. [4]

"This is a communist generation that spent most of their lives under a regime where everything was taken care of by the state," she says. Some were lured to London by sham employers who advertised British jobs in Polish newspapers, then took their money and passports when they arrived in England, according to Sadowska.

After the Soviet Union began disintegrating in 1989, Barka UK was founded in Poland by her parents, two psychologists, to help homeless, troubled individuals. Barka was first invited to London in 2007 by one of the local councils in a neighborhood where homeless Polish immigrants were sleeping on the streets. Since then, Barka has been working in a dozen London boroughs and in nearby Slough and Reading at the invitation of local governments, which fund their outreach work.

Besides a free plane ticket, Barka offers help in Poland with alcohol and drug addiction. Unregistered migrants in Britain don't qualify for rehab or detox programs under England's National Health Service. Often, homeless migrants are ashamed to go back home and be seen by their families as economic failures, says Sadowska.

"We help them to understand it's pointless to stay in London and die on the street," says Sadowska. So far, 1,248 mainly Polish migrants have returned to Eastern Europe with Barka's help.

Slough residents have complained of drunken noisemakers and rat infestations at makeshift homeless camps. Slough's local newspaper ran a front-page picture on Sept. 24 of a homeless camp beneath a discarded billboard under the headline "How Can We Be Proud of This?" [5]

Asked if Slough is funding Barka just to export a local nuisance, McGuire said: "We're certainly not saying, 'Go back to Poland and stay there.' We're saying, 'Go back, get yourself sorted out. If you've got an alcohol problem, address that; maybe get trained with a skill that's needed over here so it's comparatively easy to find work.' "

The temperature had just dropped to freezing the previous October night. As winter approaches, McGuire says,

Discouraged by Britain's sagging job market, Polish immigrants in London board a bus to return to Poland on May 20, 2009. Thousands of Polish workers flocked to Britain after Poland's entrance into the European Union in 2004 eliminated barriers to Poles working in other EU countries.

"My personal concern is that those that don't want to go back will be freezing to death out there."

— Sarah Glazer

[1] The eight Eastern European countries that joined the EU in 2004, thereby granting their citizens working rights in the U.K. are: Czech Republic, Estonia, Hungary, Latvia, Lithuania, Poland, Slovakia and Slovenia. In 2007, Bulgaria and Romania were accepted into the EU, but with only limited working rights in the U.K. The homeless figures in this sidebar include migrants from all new EU countries in Eastern Europe . See www.belfasttelegraph.co.uk/business/help-advice/employment-issues/eu-nationals-and-their-rights-to-work-14314169.html#ixzz13Xz341HR.

[2] "Snap 2010," Homeless Link, www.homeless.org.uk/snap-2010.

[3] "Commission Requests UK to End Discrimination on Other Nationals' Right to Reside as Workers," news release, European Commission, Oct. 28, 2010;

http://ec.europa.eu/social/main.jsp?langId=en&catId=457&newsId=917&furtherNews=yes.

[4] The Civic Institute for Monitoring and Recommendations estimates that about 20 percent of approximately 1 million Polish migrants who live in the U.K. don't speak English, lack a stable income, have health problems (including addictions) and lack access to organized information sources.

[5] "How Can We Be Proud of This?" *Slough Observer*, Sept. 24, 2010, p. 1, www.sloughobserver.co.uk/news/roundup/articles/2010/09/25/48537-how-can-we-be-proud-of-this-/.

Ironically, both sides in the debate admit, when governments try to limit low-skilled immigration, they send culturally hostile signals to the very same high-skilled workers they hope to attract to their country. "If you're an Indian IT specialist, why go to Germany?" Legrain asks. "Even in a high paid job, you'll be made to feel unwelcome, you'll feel excluded from the rest of society" and will pay higher income tax than in the United States, "where you'll have no problem fitting in."

Germany's Turks Reverse Course

Reflecting Germany's poor job market, 10,000 more people have been emigrating from Germany to Turkey each year since 2008 than have been arriving. German anti-immigrant sentiment is growing, despite the fact that only 30,000 Turks immigrated into Germany last year — about half as many as in 2002.

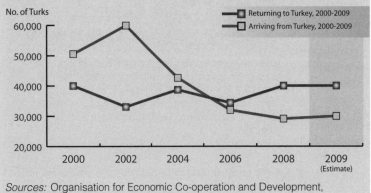

Sources: Organisation for Economic Co-operation and Development, Destatis

"That's the striking thing: Europe is so terrified of immigrants, and increasingly immigrants don't want to come to Europe," he observes.

Should European governments do more to integrate immigrants?

Chancellor Merkel's remark that multiculturalism has "utterly failed" in Germany reflects a growing sentiment that foreigners and their children should assimilate more into German society. Referring to the nation's majority population as "we," Merkel went on to tell the youth branch of her party, "We feel tied to Christian values. Those who don't accept them don't have a place here." That comment seemed to put the blame squarely on Turks, not Germans, for their failure to assimilate.[32]

Yet, for many years Turkish *Gastarbeiters* (guestworkers) were not even allowed to seek German citizenship, and children born in Germany to Turkish immigrant parents did not automatically become German citizens. A 2000 law that made it easier for Turks to become German citizens spurred an initial surge of applications, but applications have declined steadily in recent years, primarily because Germany does not permit dual citizenship.[33]

Many Turks do not want to give up their Turkish citizenship, even if that means being required to do military service in Turkey.

"We have two nationalisms clashing," says Berlin sociologist Koopmans: "Germans saying, 'You have to make a choice,'" and Turks, who "are also very nationalistic."

Turks without German citizenship cannot vote in Germany or play a part in the political process. "They're still not politically integrated, and that affects the degree of identification of Turks in Germany with their home country," Koopmans acknowledges. First- and second-generation Turkish immigrants share some of the blame for that, he says.

The tendency for Turkish pride to come before German identification was recently illustrated by a widely viewed video clip of young German-speaking Turks booing German-Turkish soccer star Mesut Özil, as he played for the German team in the World Cup.

"Mesut Özil is no Turk!" shouted young Turks decked out in the colors of the Turkish flag, angry at Özil for choosing to play for Germany rather than Turkey. To many Germans, the film clip was yet another sign that Turks don't want to integrate.[34]

But that's not the whole story, says German economist Sabine Beppler-Spahl, an editor at the libertarian German magazine *Novo Argumente*. At her children's predominantly Turkish public school in Berlin, Turkish children arrived waving German flags and rooted for the team during the World Cup, she reports. Germans are just as much to blame for creating two parallel societies, she suggests.

"A lot of middle-class German people moving to the suburbs have virtually no contact with Turks," she says. "Their kids don't go to school with them and don't have Turkish friends in their immediate circle. Middle-class Germans agree with [former German central banker] Sarrazin because they go into the city and see women with headscarves" and are frightened by the sight of young Turks hanging out on the streets, whom they assume are unemployed, on welfare and have criminal tendencies.

In an effort to require greater "integration" of immigrants into their societies, some European governments have begun to require courses on their national culture and language and citizenship tests as a precondition for emigrating to their country. The Netherlands, once known for its tolerance, led the way in this trend in March 2006, requiring applicants for family reunification to take an "integration" test at a Dutch embassy abroad as a precondition for being granted even a temporary residence permit. Since then similar policies have been adopted by Finland, Denmark, Austria, Germany and France.[35]

In the Dutch citizenship tests, would-be immigrants must understand that it is acceptable for unmarried and gay couples to live together, that women enjoy equal rights and that domestic violence (including honor killings and female genital mutilation) will be punished. In the Netherlands, Austria and Germany, religiously conservative Muslims are "a particular target group of these tests," according to a study.[36]

In the Netherlands, "what began as an immigration-integration policy has turned into the opposite: a no-immigration policy," concluded migration expert Christian Joppke, a professor of political science at the American University of Paris. The integration tests and other requirements are aimed at keeping out low-skilled family immigrants, particularly Muslims of Turkish and Moroccan origin, he said.[37]

To Dutch sociologist Duyvendak, such tests are clearly discriminatory. "The wrong answers on these multiple-choice tests . . . have implicit prejudices about Muslims," he says. "People taking the test feel they're depicted as backward and intolerant." Several years ago, the Netherlands garnered international attention for a video it showed would-be immigrants abroad of topless women sunbathing and gay couples kissing. "You can only understand this when you see how monocultural the Dutch are," Duyvendak says, a homogenous culture with clearly progressive values.

But other experts say language requirements and citizenship tests help immigrants achieve economic independence. A recent study by Koopmans found that countries like Germany, Austria and France, which make

AFP/Getty Images/Denis Charlet

A Roma girl plays with her doll on Sept. 8, 2010, in an illegal camp in Lille, France. After France began expelling illegal Roma immigrants in July, the European Parliament on Sept. 9 demanded that France suspend the expulsions. Italian police also recently demolished illegal Roma settlements on the outskirts of Rome in an effort to force the Roma back to Romania and Bulgaria.

welfare benefits or visas dependent on a certain amount of assimilation (such as language tests and obligatory integration courses) tend to produce better results for immigrants than countries like Sweden, with traditionally easy access to citizenship and generous welfare benefits. Countries like Germany, which have stricter immigration prerequisites, have more immigrants who are employed, less crime among immigrants and less residential segregation, Koopmans finds.[38]

While some politicians may see these requirements as a way to keep Muslims out, Koopmans defends them: "It's an attempt by European countries to do something the classical immigration countries like Canada and Australia have done all along, namely selective immigration," or recruiting the highly skilled workers they need, not low-skilled immigrants who will become welfare dependent.

New Integration Policies Seen as Discriminatory

Critics say the tough rules target non-EU immigrants.

British university graduate Emily Churchill began to cry when she heard the announcement that starting this fall, foreign spouses must pass an English test overseas before being allowed to join their British spouses.

Last summer she married an aspiring Palestinian filmmaker named Basel whom she had met while studying abroad in Syria the previous winter and with whom she speaks Arabic. The British government has refused their first two attempts to obtain a visa for him. The English test "epitomized how I felt we'd been treated by the system and the government approach to make spousal immigration as difficult as possible," she says.

In announcing the new requirement, Home Secretary Theresa May said it "will help promote integration, remove cultural barriers and protect public services." [1] But because the rule applies only to non-EU immigrants, Churchill feels it is more about discrimination than integration. "If Basel were British or Italian, we would not be apart," she wrote on a *Guardian* newspaper blog. [2] Under European Union agreements, immigrants from EU member countries are allowed free movement within the EU.

Some experts charge that marriage rules like this — along with strict age limits and required integration courses for would-be immigrant spouses — are discriminatory because they are aimed only at non-EU immigrants. Such restrictions also get vocal support from anti-immigrant politicians with growing electoral power in several European countries. For example, the Netherlands government has agreed in principle to the anti-immigrant Freedom Party's demand to follow Denmark's example by raising the age for immigrant spouses from 21 to 24. The Dutch marriage partner would also have to earn 120 percent of the minimum wage.

"If you're 23 and want to bring your bride from Turkey or Morocco and you don't earn enough, you cannot marry the partner you want," says Jan Willem Duyvendak, a sociology professor at the University of Amsterdam. "Whereas, if you're 24 and want to bring someone from Bulgaria, Rumania or a European country, then it is possible. That shows how discriminatory it is."

But Ruud Koopmans, director of migration research at the Social Science Research Center in Berlin, says the measures are "a good thing because many of these migrants came from rural regions not knowing how to read and write. Almost certainly they will end up dependent on social welfare with integration problems." France, too, has introduced language tests as a prerequisite for entry for prospective marriage migrants. Under pressure from the anti-immigrant Danish People's Party, the Danish government is dropping its age minimum of 24 — but only for those immigrant spouses who speak Danish and have high levels of education and work experience. [3] The policies are aimed at reducing the number of immigrants with low skill levels "for whom there is no demand in the labor market," Koopmans says.

In Germany, newly arrived immigrants from non-EU countries must, at the discretion of immigration authorities, participate in a government-funded integration course that includes 600 hours of German language instruction and a 30-hour orientation on German culture, history and law. Thousands of people are on waiting lists for the courses, but budget cuts suggest the waiting lists will only get longer, according to *Der Spiegel*, Germany's leading news magazine. [4]

Anti-discrimination laws limit the extent to which such restrictions can target only immigrants, Koopmans says, so some countries pass sweeping laws, such as the Dutch decision to abolish welfare benefits for anyone under 27. Though it sounds draconian, the law appears to have improved immigrants' employment rates and reduced dependence on welfare. However, Duyvendak points out, the job market was already booming when the law was passed.

— Sarah Glazer

[1] "UK Marriage Visa Applicants will have to pass English tests," June 10, 2010, www.workpermit.com/news/2010-06-10/uk/uk-marriage-visa-applicants-english-language-test.htm.

[2] Emily Churchill, "Being with your spouse is a right, not a privilege," *Guardian*, June 14, 2010, www.guardian.co.uk/commentisfree/2010/jun/14/foreign-spouse-language-tests-immigration-system.

[3] "PM: 24-year-rule expands to points system," *Copenhagen Post Online*, Nov. 8, 2010, www.cphpost.dk/news/politics/90-politics/50410-pm-24-year-rule-expands-to-.

[4] "Migrants on the Waiting List," *Spiegelonline*, Oct. 25, 2010, www.spiegel.de/international/germany/0,1518,725118,00.html and "German Integration Summit Delivers Little," *Spiegelonline*, Nov. 4, 2010, www.spiegel.de/international/germany/0,1518,727238,00.html.

Most of today's European immigration involves relatives of current residents, and governments are trying to make it more difficult for those family members to emigrate. Often the would-be immigrant is a bride-to-be from the home country. Even Muslims born in the Netherlands or Germany tend to import wives from their parents' native land. About 80 percent of second-generation Turks and Moroccans in the Netherlands marry someone from their country of origin, Koopmans notes. Typically, they are highly religious, have low levels of education and can't speak the language of their new country — all factors associated with high welfare dependency and the delay of assimilation for generations.

"The children of these immigrants will be raised in the Berber dialect and start with the same disadvantage as children of the first generation," he says. So language and other assimilation requirements are "good for educational and labor market integration."

Unlike the United States, where the immigrant bears the cost of not learning English — in the form of poorer job prospects — welfare-generous Europe pays the bill, through higher welfare costs if an immigrant doesn't assimilate, Koopmans argues. "That gives receiving societies more of a right to make demands on immigrants than in the United States, where it's your choice," whether to learn English or adjust to American ways, he says.

But Beppler-Spahl says Germany's citizenship tests are a superficial response designed to assuage Germans' fears about immigrants not integrating that doesn't solve the country's real problems. "Our problem is we're not using the potential we have," she says. "If we have young Turkish children, we should ask ourselves, 'Why are they failing in German schools, and what can we do about that?' "

Sarrrazin's controversial assertion that Germany is being "dumbed down" by a lower-intelligence population of Turks intensifies the perception that the problem lies with the immigrants rather than with Germany's educational system, she contends. "I don't believe Sarrazin's theory that, 'There's a limited intelligence pool, and we're getting the low end of a nation's limited intelligence pool,' " says Beppler-Spahl. "That's wrong. . . . Why say that people from poor families will stay poor and will never make it? That's where the racism starts flowing in."

Should immigrants be required to follow local customs?

Liberals, feminists and anti-immigrant conservatives can become strange bedfellows when it comes to one issue in Europe: banning the burqa. Dutch right-wing populist Wilders sounds like some feminists when he argues that the burqa is "a medieval symbol, a symbol against women."[39]

France, which banned headscarves for students attending public schools in 2004, recently banned public wearing of the burqa. Italy, Belgium, the Netherlands, Austria, Denmark and Switzerland have considered similar legislation.

Some see the move as a thinly veiled anti-Muslim policy, others as a strike for women's freedom and integrating Muslims into mainstream society. Washington University anthropologist Bowen described France's national unity around the headscarf ban as stemming from the French philosophy that citizens must all subscribe to the same values. That desire for "shared values" played strongly in the French support of the burqa ban, he says.

"In France everyone is expected to potentially interact with everyone else; wearing a burqa is cutting oneself off from that sort of interaction. That's the justification the justice minister gave when it was being debated," Bowen explains. "All the other arguments — it oppresses women, it's against human dignity — really don't work because no women are complaining. How can you say it harms them if no one's complaining?"

But some Muslim women, like Algerian-American law professor Karima Bennoune, do see the veil as inherently oppressive. She remembers driving into Algiers during the Algerian civil war of the 1990s, when armed fundamentalist groups were killing women who went out unveiled. "I knew that my bare head, like those of the thousands of Algerian women who refused to submit, was marked with a target," she writes.[40]

In a 2007 law review article, Bennoune, who teaches at Rutgers School of Law in Newark, N.J., strongly supported the French headscarf ban. Before the ban, she wrote, gangs of young men in immigrant neighborhoods of Paris had taken to raping young girls who wore

CHRONOLOGY

19th Century *European nations colonize much of the Muslim world, providing source of immigrant labor.*

1830 French control of Algeria, Morocco and Tunisia leads to exodus of Muslim immigrants to France.

1950s-1960s *After deaths of millions of working-age men in World War II, Europe recruits immigrants to rebuild economy. Number of Turkish "guestworkers" in Germany surges. European resentment against immigrants grows.*

1954-55 Germany begins recruiting temporary foreign workers from Italy and Spain, later from Turkey.

1961 Germany signs a recruitment agreement with Turkey to import guest workers for two-year periods.

1970s-1980s *Jobs for immigrants dwindle in recession; Europe limits workers' immigration but lets in families, causing more Muslim immigration. Palestinian intifadas, riots in Britain, Saudi money for fundamentalist Wahhabi teachings stoke religious extremism.*

1974 France, Netherlands institute "immigration stop" policies. Immigration from Muslim countries triples in France, increases tenfold in the Netherlands in next three decades.

1977 France offers to pay immigrants to leave — with little success.

1990s-2000s *Terrorist attacks focus governments to monitor extremism among Muslim residents. Thousands of migrants from Eastern Europe move West; Europe begins requiring immigrants to integrate. Anti-immigrant parties make electoral gains, even as global economic crisis slows immigration to Europe.*

1995-1996 Radical Algerian group seeking Islamist state explodes bombs in Paris subways and trains.

1998 Al Qaeda calls on Muslims to kill Americans and their allies.

2000 Germany makes it easier for Turkish guestworkers and their children to become citizens.

Sep. 11, 2001 Al Qaeda attacks World Trade Center and Pentagon, killing nearly 3,000 people.

2002 Far-right Dutch leader Pim Fortuyn, who criticized Muslims for not assimilating, is murdered.

2004 Thousands of Eastern Europeans move to Western Europe to work. France bans headscarves in schools. . . . Madrid subway bombings kill 191; radical Islamist kills Dutch filmmaker Theo Van Gogh.

2005 London's "7/7" transit bombings kill 52; disaffected African immigrants riot in Paris suburbs.

2006 Netherlands requires applicants for family reunification to pass integration test abroad.

2007 EU admits Bulgaria and Romania but with limited working rights. . . . Radical immigrants try to blow up Glasgow, Scotland, airport. . . . Germany, Denmark foil extremist terrorist plots.

2008 As worldwide recession begins, migration starts to slow.

2009 Swiss ban new minarets on mosques. . . . Immigration to Spain, Ireland falls drastically; unemployment among foreign-born youth exceeds 40 percent in Spain, 37 percent in Sweden.

2010 Anti-immigrant parties make electoral gains in Sweden, Netherlands, Austria. . . . Conservatives take power in Britain with pledge to reduce immigration. . . . French President Sarkozy expels Roma from France. . . . French parliament bans the burqa in public. . . . German bestseller spurs debate on Muslim integration. . . . Migration Policy Institute says European immigration has come to a "virtual halt." . . . British government places temporary ceiling on skilled immigrants from outside EU, prompting industry protests. . . . New Dutch government pledges to halve non-Western immigration. . . . European Commission withdraws threat of legal action against France for expulsion of Roma. . . . France pledges to bring its immigration law in line with EU rules. . . . German Chancellor Merkel says multiculturalism has failed.

miniskirts or went to the movies. Many French Muslim women's groups supported the ban on the grounds that girls were frequently forced by their family or an older brother to wear the headscarf. The French Algerian feminist Fadela Amara called the veil a "visible symbol of subjugation."[41]

More recently, leading German feminists Alice Schwarzer and Necla Kelek came out in support of proposed burqa bans in Germany. Kelek said the garment has nothing to do with religion and comes out of an ideology where "women in public don't have the right to be human."[42]

Human rights groups, however, have generally opposed both headscarf and burqa bans. "Treating pious women like criminals won't help integrate them," said Judith Sunderland, senior researcher with the Europe and Central Asia division of Human Rights Watch in April.[43]

These same human rights groups, Bennoune counters, "would not come out in favor of Christian prayer in American schools . . . or the right to wear a swastika [once a religious symbol, now a political one] in a European classroom, because they understand the potential impact on other students and are able to appreciate the political meaning in context."[44]

Patrick Weil, a University of Paris immigration historian, said the French headscarf ban was largely a reaction to gangs of young Muslim men threatening Muslim girls who did not wear a scarf in school. "The law was endorsed by the majority of Muslims; it preserved the freedom of Muslim girls," maintains Weil, author of the 2008 book *How to Be French, Nationality in the Making Since 1789*, who served on the commission that advised the government to institute the ban. And the law has been enforced over the last six years with very little protest, he has pointed out.[45]

Devout Muslim girls who still want to wear the headscarf can attend the religious schools that operate in France under contract to the government, he points out (though most such schools are Christian): "We have a dual system that works well."

To Weil and other supporters, the headscarf ban was about upholding a basic French principle: separation between government and religion within state schools. But as for adult women walking in the streets, he sees the burqa ban as an assault on women's basic freedom to wear what they want. "I think it's unconstitutional. I don't like the burqa, and very few people in France are in favor of it, but I say these women have the right to go in the street dressed as they wish," he says. "That's a fundamental human right."

Paradoxically, of the fewer than 2,000 women who don burqas in France today, a quarter of them are converts to Islam, and two-thirds have French nationality, according to government estimates.[46]

"These are a small number of young women — several hundred — trying out their relationship to their religion and to the rest of society," Bowen says. "To stigmatize them seems wrong-headed from the point of view of social psychology." Some research indicates that young Muslim women may use headscarves as a way to negotiate with their families for more freedom, to attend university, for example. Banning the veil will, if anything, prompt a more fundamentalist reaction among such women, some critics predict.

After the French Senate passed the burqa ban in September, some Muslim women said they would remain cloistered in their homes rather than go out unveiled, boding badly for increased integration.[47]

In a 2006 court case, *Begum v. Headteacher*, the British House of Lords upheld a British high school's authority to prohibit a young girl from wearing a *jilbab* (a dark cloak) to school and found that the prohibition did not violate human rights.[48] Yet in a country like Britain, with its long tradition of freedom of expression, most people disapprove of the government banning the wearing of burqas in public, judging from polls and recent interviews.[49]

Muslim groups in Britain protested in 2006 when Labour member of Parliament and ex-foreign secretary Jack Straw said he asked Muslim constituents to remove their veils from their faces when they came to his office. Some Muslim community spokesmen claimed Straw was being discriminatory. Straw argued that face-to-face communication was better when you could "see what the other person means, and not just hear what they say."[50]

BACKGROUND

Colonial Roots

Modern Muslim migration in Europe began in the late 19th century as a result of Europe's colonial and trading activities. Those historic patterns largely explain the different ethnic groups that migrated to each country and, to some degree, their acceptance by those societies.

Gypsies Face Poor Education, Discrimination

In traditional clans, girls drop out of school early.

Twenty-four-year-old Sara Kotowicz seems like any other fashionably dressed Londoner finishing her university education. But she is a rare exception in her clan of Polish Roma, or Gypsies. Girls in her large extended family are expected to marry by 15 or 16, have children right away and stop attending school — despite living in 21st-century London.

Kotowicz, whose family migrated to England when she was 11, married at 17, the upper age-limit for acceptable marriage in her family. But her decision to pursue a degree in interior design during her first year of marriage subjected her to severe criticism.

"Within the community you're expected to do the duties of a wife. There's no time for school," says Kotowicz, whose one concession to Gypsy attire is her long black skirt. Each morning as she left for class, she faced a scolding from her mother-in-law — "You should think of washing clothes, looking after your husband" — harassment that drove her and her husband, uncharacteristically, to move out of his family's home.

Throughout Europe, experts say, the lack of education is probably the single greatest impediment to the advancement of the Roma, along with discrimination.[1] British professionals who work with Romanian and Polish Roma immigrants say it's sometimes difficult to convince Roma parents to allow their children to attend school, because in their home countries — Poland, Romania, Hungary and Slovakia — Roma children often were consigned to segregated schools or backwater classes for the mentally handicapped.

For traditional Roma families where girls are commonly expected to marry as early as 14, girls who become mothers enjoy high status, says Michael Stewart, an anthropologist at University College London, who studies the Eastern European Roma. "There's enormous value in traditional Romany communities in becoming mothers — literally reproducing the community" — one that faced extermination under the Nazis and persecution under communist regimes.

"Twenty years ago I never found a 16- or 17-year-old girl who was unmarried," says Heather Ureche, a consultant with the charity Equality, which helps Eastern European Roma migrants in Britain.[2] "Now I do. It's changing slowly, but we still have quite a way to go."

"A lot of people in Eastern Europe say the Roma are not educated, the parents don't want their children in school, don't value education. That's not true — in general," says Stewart. "The problem is they're very badly treated — humiliated and put into separate classes for the hard-to-educate."

In Romania, few Roma children continue school after age 9 or 10, according to Ureche. Moreover, she says, "Roma parents are often worried about sending young girls into coed school settings just after puberty for fear they'll get in trouble with non-Roma boys."

Children in Roma culture generally are given great independence at an early age and are expected to have the maturity needed to be a parent by 14, experts report. "If you're an academically ambitious 13-year-old girl in a traditional Romany family, it is really tough," Stewart observes. "You have a battle on your hands to persuade your parents to let you go on and study." Some younger Roma from traditional families are bucking the trend, such as Viktoria Mohacsi, who represented Hungary as a member of the European Parliament from 2004 to 2009.[3]

Getting a high school education is becoming more acceptable for Roma girls in London, says Kotowicz, who is a youth advocacy worker for the Roma Support Group, a London charity. But she still has trouble persuading teenage girls from her community to continue their education.

By the late 1800s, France, Britain and the Netherlands had gained control over most of the world's Muslims. France conquered Algiers in 1830, eventually leading to French control of Algeria, Morocco and Tunisia. The British colonized India (which included modern-day Pakistan and Bangladesh). The Dutch dominated trade in Southeast Asia, where today's Indonesia — the world's most populous Muslim nation — became a Dutch colony after the Dutch East India Company relinquished control. By the end of the 19th century, France was importing low-paid workers from Algeria and other African territories, while other European countries recruited workers from their colonies and territories.

However, Europe — where residents had long been immigrating to the United States in search of a better life — did not become a major immigrant destination

A recent visit to a house in North London illustrated some of the striking differences in how Romanian Roma families raise their children. As school was letting out, an array of spirited children, ages 4-16, some related to the family and some not, paraded through the tiny kitchen. All seemed perfectly comfortable eating something from the refrigerator, whether they lived there or not.

Unlike British and American culture, where childhood is viewed as a separate phase of life that can last until age 18, for the Roma "young children have enormous autonomy," Stewart explains. "Children are never told off, never told, 'You mustn't do that.' Children learn not to do things through making mistakes rather than through constant correction; the assumption is that by the age of 10 or 13 Romany people are autonomous moral agents — what we would call adults."

These cultural values sometimes create serious problems for Roma families in Britain, says Sywia Ingmire, coordinator of the Roma Support Group. "Children are the responsibility of every adult visiting the home; children are passed from hand to hand," she says. But sometimes "bewildered social workers" think a child is being trafficked. For instance, in 2008 several large extended Roma families were living together in the town of Slough. In a series of dawn raids on 17 houses, 24 Roma adults were arrested, supposedly for taking Roma children from their families and forcing them into a life of crime. But nine days later, none of the 24 adults arrested at the scene had been charged with child trafficking offenses, and all but one child had been returned to the Roma community in Slough.[4]

"These stories about rings of trafficking people are often built more on exaggeration and fantasy than a good empirical basis," says Stewart, who finds that children who beg and steal are a small minority of Europe's Roma population.

Yet the view of Roma children as beggars and thieves is widespread in Europe. In a recent street survey in three cities, more than 60 percent of those questioned associated

School uniforms identify two Roma sisters — Violeta Stelica, 8, (right), and Nicoleta Mihai, 6, (left) — as public school students in North London on Oct. 11, 2010. But in traditional Roma families across Europe, girls often drop out in order to get married, sometimes as early as age 14.

Gypsies with negative activities like thievery. [5]In Europe, Ureche says, prejudice against Gypsies "is the last bastion of racism."

— *Sarah Glazer*

[1]Angela Doland, "Lack of Schooling Seen as Root of Gypsy Woes," The Associated Press, Oct. 9, 2010, www.google.com/hostednews/ap/article/ALeqM5hA_jAjgctB4r_ZYfw645v7vLBlWAD9IOJLD01?docId=D9IOJLD01.

[2]See Equality's website, at http://equality.uk.com/Welcome.html.

[3]"Interview: Viktoria Mohacsi," *Foreign Policy*, Oct. 20, 2010, www.foreignpolicy.com/articles/2010/10/20/interview_viktoria_mohacsi.

[4]Helen Pidd and Vikram Dodd, "From Brilliant Coup to Cock-up. How the Story of Fagin's Urchins Fell Apart," *Guardian*, Feb. 2, 2008, www.guardian.co.uk/uk/2008/feb/02/immigration.ukcrime.

[5]Heather Ureche, "Racism in a Velvet Glove," *Oxfam Poverty Post*, Sept. 10, 2009, www.oxfamblogs.org/ukpovertypost/2009/09/racism-in-a-velvet-glove%E2%80%A6/.

until the 1950s, when it needed workers to help rebuild cities and economies ravaged by World War II. After the wartime deaths of thousands of working-age men, England sought workers from throughout the British Empire, in part because they would speak English: Indians and Pakistanis came from the 1950s on, Bangladeshis from the 1970s. For much the same reason, in the postwar economic boom, France, Germany and the Netherlands

also recruited immigrants from their former colonies, and in some cases, the mother countries gave preferential treatment to former colonists wanting to enter the country to work.

Some former colonials integrated more quickly into their new home countries than others. Muslims from francophone Africa, for instance, have been more interested in becoming part of France than Turks have been in

For and Against Immigrants

Kurdish immigrants in Rome wave the Kurdistan flag and portraits of their historical leader Abdullah Ocalan during Italy's first nationwide "day without immigrants" strike on March 1, 2010 (top). The rally was one of dozens held around Europe in the last year to protest harsh anti-immigrant measures taken by European governments, which some critics say are particularly targeting Muslim immigrants. Anti-Muslim sentiment was evident in Harrow, North London, on Sept. 11, 2009 (bottom), when riot police quelled clashes between Muslims and anti-Islamic extremists protesting outside a London mosque on the anniversary of the 9/11 attacks in the United States.

Germany, where they have no cultural links, argues Bowen, of Washington University. "The very bitterness of France's colonial history channels Muslims toward demanding inclusion in French society," Bowen wrote. "They, or their parents or grandparents, came from former French territories in North or West Africa, where they learned that

they were now part of the grand story of France, albeit in second-class roles."[51]

After World War II, when a devastated Germany needed immigrant labor to help rebuild, Germany's choice of workers would have long-term repercussions. In the mid-1950s, Germany instituted an active immigration policy, first for Italian and Spanish farmworkers.[52] Later, as the economy boomed and industry needed labor, the government turned to North Africa and Turkey for workers, who were expected to stay only two years.

"The German and Austrian governments had recruitment offices in the least-developed rural areas of Anatolia to recruit illiterate Turks because of the false belief that if they can't read, they won't join trade unions and make trouble," explains Viennese demographer Lutz.

But unlike Czech and Ukranian migrants who settled in Austria earlier, Turks did not become absorbed into the society or even learn the language in many cases. "Many Turks didn't think they would stay," Lutz says, "nor did society."

Indeed, most European governments saw the recruitment of immigrant labor as a temporary measure. Temporary "guestworker" programs were initiated in Germany, Belgium and Sweden, recruiting first from Italy and Spain and later from the Mediterranean, North Africa and the Middle East.

Turks made up the largest percentage of German migrants. And the *Gastarbeiter* (guestworker) program was a "hard-currency bonanza" for Turkey, according to author Christopher Caldwell, a columnist for *The Weekly Standard* and *Financial Times* whose book, *Reflections on the Revolution in Europe*, chronicles how Muslims transformed postwar Europe. The Turkish government petitioned hard for inclusion in the program, and the single Turkish men who arrived to work in German mines and steel plants discovered they could make far more money than in Turkey. The number of Turkish guestworkers in Germany burgeoned from 329,000 in 1960 to 2.6 million by 1973, the year the program was discontinued.[53]

But the workers found Germany attractive, and the gap steadily widened between what natives understood the program to mean and what the workers understood. German corporations pressured the government to make the *Gastarbeiter* contracts renewable, to allow workers' families to join them and to permit those that had started families to stay. A "rotation clause" intended to limit a foreign worker's stay in Germany to two years was removed from the German-Turkish guestworker treaty in 1964, partly due to industry pressure.[54]

Europe's acute manpower shortages, however, were not chronic, Caldwell writes. In the 1960s, migrants were manning soon-to-be obsolete linen mills in France and textile mills in England. The jobs would soon be eliminated, creating joblessness among migrants and a growing anti-immigrant reaction.

On April 20, 1968 — two weeks after the assassination of the Rev. Martin Luther King, Jr., triggered riots in Washington, D.C., and other major U.S. cities — Conservative British Parliament member Enoch Powell warned that Britain's growing immigration would lead to similar violent conflicts between immigrants and Britons. Already, he claimed, the native-born English "found themselves made strangers in their own country," and he quoted a constituent's prediction that "in 15 or 20 years' time the black man will have the whip hand over the white man." Citing the poet Virgil, he said, "I seem to see 'the River Tiber foaming with much blood.' "[55]

Powell received enthusiastic letters in response from British natives, and much of the British debate since then has been over whether Powell's "rivers of blood" predictions would prove correct.

'Immigration Stop' Policies

During Germany's 1966-67 recession, many laid-off guestworkers returned home only to find the Turkish economy in crisis. But when the 1973-77 global recession hit, many migrants stayed in their adopted countries, even if they were unemployed — spurring European fears that immigrants would compete for jobs. EU governments between 1973 and 1975 instituted an "immigration stop" policy, aimed at deterring immigration and halting overseas recruitment.[56]

The number of new foreign workers arriving declined, but migration continued — primarily due to extended families joining the original immigrant or new spouses arriving on marriage visas. Today, most immigration into Western Europe involves family migration.

Paradoxically, more immigrants came to Europe during the decades after the "stop" policies were instituted than arrived in the preceding decades, largely because of family immigration. In the Netherlands, the number of first-generation Moroccan and Turkish immigrants increased tenfold in the three decades following the 1974 halt. By 2003, the number of North Africans in France was triple the number from before the government started restricting immigration.[57]

Since then, EU governments have tried repeatedly to discourage immigration. Some, like France, have even offered monetary incentives and continued welfare support to immigrants who return home. Most of the programs ended in failure.[58]

Experts say once an immigration dynamic has been established between countries it is hard to stop. In Belgium, Turkish immigrants from Emirdag settled in Brussels and Ghent, with family and friends living on the same street with their neighbors from back home. Bangladeshis settled in East London, while Pakistanis from Punjab and Kashmir settled in Birmingham and Bradford.[59]

Radical Islam Emerges

During the 1980s some young Muslims, frustrated by job discrimination, turned to their religion as a source of identity. Europe became a target of proselytizing campaigns, helped along by the distribution of Saudi Arabian petrodollars, which financed the construction of new mosques and Islamic schools. Saudi money specifically supported the spread and teaching of the ultra-conservative Wahhabi strand of Islam.[60]

Acts of terrorism in the 1990s and early 2000s fueled fears of radical Islamists. Between 1995 and 1996, radical Algerians exploded bombs on Paris subways and trains, adding to French anti-immigrant sentiment. France and other nations expelled radical Islamists, and members of the French secret services dubbed the British capital "Londonistan" for its role as a refuge for radical Islamist groups.

Then on Feb. 23, 1998, al Qaeda leader Osama bin Laden issued a fatwa stating that all Muslims had a duty to kill Americans and their allies — civilian or military — around the world. Islamic liberation movements worldwide began to shift their emphasis from national revolution to localized, violent terrorism.

The Sept. 11, 2001, attacks on the Pentagon and World Trade Center, in which nearly 3,000 people died, would change forever the way Europeans looked at their Muslim neighbors. Although directed by al Qaeda and carried out by mostly Saudi Arabian jihadists, the attacks had been planned by a group of English-speaking Muslims at a mosque in Hamburg, Germany.

"September 11 turned the spotlight on European Muslims and made people feel insecure; they started looking at Muslims through a security prism," says the European Policy Centre's Shada Islam. Soul-searching about whether Europe was becoming a breeding ground for terrorists intensified after a string of terrorist attacks tied to Muslim extremists: the Madrid subway bombings in 2004; the murder of Dutch filmmaker Theo Van Gogh by a radical Islamist the same year; the "7/7" 2005 London transit bombings that killed 52.

But rather than focus on jobs, education and disaffected youth — the root causes of integration problems — Islam says, the debate about Muslim immigrants was no longer about social disadvantages. Suddenly, "it was as if every Muslim in Europe was a potential terrorist." Islam says the current wave of anti-immigrant, anti-Muslim sentiment would not have "reached this point if September 11 had not happened."

In 2002 far-right Dutch politician Pim Fortuyn (who had criticized Muslims for not assimilating) was murdered by a Dutch man who said he was protecting Muslims. Then in 2004, filmmaker Theo van Gogh, who had made a film critical of the treatment of women by Muslims, was murdered in broad daylight on an Amsterdam street by a Dutch-born son of Moroccan immigrants. As Dutch *Financial Times* columnist Simon Kuper puts it, "violence associated with Muslims suddenly entered the public debate. Nowhere else in Europe has the far right done so well out of 9/11" as in the Netherlands.[61]

In Britain, young Muslims said 9/11 — and the London transit suicide-bomb attacks on July 7, 2005, by radical British Muslims — made them identify as Muslims more than they had before. In 2007, Muslim doctors from India and the Middle East working in Britain tried to blow up the airport in Glasgow, Scotland, and authorities foiled Muslim plots to blow up a U.S. military base in Frankfurt, Germany, and a bomb attack by Muslims in Copenhagen.[62] Polls by the Pew Research Center found that Muslims in France, Spain and Britain were twice as likely as U.S. Muslims to say suicide bombs can be justified.[63]

In 2004, the EU admitted 10 new countries: the Czech Republic, Estonia, Hungary, Latvia, Lithuania, Poland, Slovakia, Slovenia, Cyprus and Malta. Under EU rules, citizens of those countries were free to move to any member country to work, and thousands of Eastern Europeans poured into Western Europe. In 2007, Bulgaria and Romania were admitted, but citizens of those countries do not have full working rights in most EU-15 countries.[64]

While the EU was opening its eastern borders, impoverished West Africans continued to risk their lives to enter Europe from the south. During the early 2000s, scores of Africans drowned when their over-packed small boats capsized en route to Spanish territory. And in 2005, an estimated 11,000 would-be migrants tried to enter Spain by scaling a 10-foot wall surrounding Melilla — a tiny coastal Spanish enclave on Morocco's northern coast. Three immigrants died in the attempts. And in one brazen, pre-dawn incident, about 500 Africans stormed the barrier, using 270 ladders crafted from tree branches. About 100 migrants made it into the Spanish territory before being detained by police.[65]

Examining Multiculturalism

As fear of Muslim extremism and terrorism spread after 9/11, Europeans began to question whether terrorism was caused by a failure to integrate immigrants into society. In their soul-searching, many became increasingly critical of multicultural policies — which sometimes meant government funding of religious and ethnic groups or taking a hands-off attitude toward cultural traditions that may conflict with European laws.

For example, some critics blamed laissez-faire multiculturalism for the failure to prevent up to a dozen suspected "honor killings" every year among Britain's Muslim communities. In these cases, the women were murdered by fathers and brothers, presumably for having "dishonored" the family, such as by dating men outside their ethnic group. One such case particularly spurred outrage: A 20-year-old Kurdish woman, who repeatedly sought help from police, was killed in 2006 by her father and uncle, prompting an investigation into police handling of the case. The Independent Police Complaints Commission found in 2008 that officers had failed to follow up promptly on murder victim Banaz Mahmod's assault allegations, and the Commission recommended "reinforcing" police officers' knowledge about honor-based violence.[66]

Police "may be worried that they will be seen as racist if they interfere in another culture," Diana Sammi, director of the Iranian and Kurdish Women's Rights organization, said at the time.[67]

Globalization Fosters Identity Crisis

"People don't feel at home anymore in their own country."

In the Netherlands, where the same meat-and-potatoes dinner traditionally is eaten night after night, people often "feel threatened" by the mosques and kebab shops proliferating in their neighborhoods, says Floris Vermeulen, who teaches political science at the University of Amsterdam. "Their country is changing, their neighborhoods are changing" and "they don't feel at home anymore in their own country."

Many European countries are experiencing similar national identity crises, as their once monocultural societies — with everyone sharing the same values, ethnicity and food — seem at risk due to the globalization of human migration. That helps explain why Europeans are disturbed at the thought of immigrants living next door who resist interacting with their neighbors. Vermeulen observes wryly, "In many countries this is not considered a problem if they're not killing each other."

But in monocultural societies like Germany or the Netherlands, mainstream politicians want "a new society where everyone has contact and feels the same about all the norms and values." When it comes to a religion like Islam, Vermeulen says, "this is not considered a Dutch, German or northern European value; this is something they have to change. That becomes problematic because how [could] a government . . . change the religious beliefs of a certain people?"

Muslims have been able to resist assimilation with the rest of the society, experts say, partly by importing wives — often illiterate — from their family's village of origin, a custom that has continued into the second and third generation in Germany and the Netherlands. To combat this, European countries have toughened visa requirements for marriage partners. Both the Netherlands and Germany now require spouses to have a basic grasp of the new country's language and pass exams testing their knowledge of the society before they can legally enter. Britain's new

Dominik Wasilewski poses proudly on April 1, 2008, outside the Polish delicatessen where he works in Crewe, England, home to one of Britain's largest Polish communities. Many Europeans feel their once monocultural societies are endangered by the cultural changes caused by increased migration.

Conservative-led government is introducing a pre-entry English test for arriving spouses.

While Ruud Koopmans, director of migration at the Social Science Research Center in Berlin, sees these measures as "very good for integration," economically and socially, others condemn them as discriminatory, aimed mainly at stopping immigrants from Muslim countries. Americans would probably find such pre-entry requirements unduly burdensome, since many of their grandparents entered the country without knowing English.

But Koopmans argues that in Europe's generous welfare societies, where taxpayers bear a heavy burden to support unemployed immigrants, governments have the right to require newcomers to have the necessary tools for employment before entering the country.

— Sarah Glazer

After Sept. 11 and the Fortuyn and Van Gogh murders, even the Netherlands, long considered the leading proponent of multiculturalism, adopted more restrictive immigration policies. Other countries followed suit, including those in Scandinavia, which attempted to limit arranged marriages from abroad. Since then, women's rights advocates have supported legislation to protect women from forced marriages, which they see as often being linked to honor killings. In Norway, participation in a forced marriage brings up to six years in prison;

German Chancellor Angela Merkel (right) arrives with delegates from immigrant groups for the fourth summit on the integration of foreigners in Germany on Nov. 3, 2010, in Berlin. The summit followed recent heated public debates on immigration policy and the integration of Muslims in Germany, punctuated by Merkel's uncharacteristically blunt October remark that Germany's "multicultural" experiment has "utterly failed" — widely interpreted as a criticism of the nation's 4 million Muslims.

Denmark requires that a spouse brought into the country be at least 24 years old — as must the resident spouse.

Defending these laws, Unni Wikan, a professor of social anthropology at the University of Oslo, said Scandinavian countries felt their values — including the belief in gender equality — were being threatened by Muslim communities that failed to integrate. She said several governments were considering such laws because "we're afraid we're leading toward a society that's breaking up into ethnic tribes."[68]

Islam, of the European Policy Centre, agrees forced marriages and honor killings should be treated as crimes: "Let's not let people off the hook by saying this is tribal tradition." But she adds, "You can do it confrontationally or through a process of consultation; let's not assume every single Muslim believes in these crimes or commits them." For example, grassroots Muslim organizations in Belgium have launched school campaigns to warn young African women returning to their home countries for summer holidays that they could be forced into marriages there.

In the Netherlands, the 90-year-old policy of "pillarization," which permits each faith to set up its own government-funded religious schools and organizations, became increasingly unpopular in the 1990s and 2000s because it was seen as further segregating Muslims from society.

Statistics showed that only one-third of non-EU foreigners in the Netherlands were gainfully employed; the rest were either not in the labor market or depended on social benefits. Welfare-dependency rates among foreigners were 10 times that of the native Dutch, and high-school dropout and residential segregation rates were high as well.[69] In 2004, a Dutch parliamentary inquiry into government policy toward ethnic minorities between 1970 and 2000 came to the damning conclusion that if some migrants succeeded it was "in spite of" government policy.[70]

Because of a long tradition in which the state paid for Catholic and Protestant schools, Dutch sociologist Duyvendak says, "We're struggling: On the one hand, we don't want Muslim schools, but we want to protect our privileges — the state paying for our Catholic and Protestant schools," which are considered academically superior to secular public schools.

In reaction to what it saw as alien Muslim values, the Netherlands demanded that immigrants adopt Dutch progressive values. A new policy of civic integration, starting with its 1998 Newcomer Integration Law, required most non-EU immigrants to participate in a 12-month integration course, including Dutch language and civic education.

The 2002 murder of Fortuyn, who had criticized Muslims for not adopting the country's tolerant attitudes towards homosexuals, helped to turn the Dutch government in an even more draconian direction.[71] After March 2006, applicants for family reunification were required to take an integration test at a Dutch embassy abroad to receive even temporary residence. The policy quickly became a model for the rest of Europe, and variations have been adopted by Finland, Denmark, Austria, Germany, France, Belgium, Portugal and Spain.[72]

The policies generally require newcomers to enroll in civic and language courses, either before or after entering the country. Noncompliance could result in financial penalties or the denial of permanent legal residence. Eventually, the policy morphed into a tool to restrict migration, especially of unskilled migrants or relatives from traditional backgrounds.

For example, in May 2006, after intense debates about honor killings in the Turkish immigrant community and ethnic violence in a Berlin public school, German authorities made attendance at a civic integration course a requirement for naturalization. This reversed a previous trend towards liberalization — most notably, Germany's efforts to make it easier for Turkish guestworkers to become citizens, which began in 2000.[73]

France has been spared a major Muslim terrorist attack since the mid-1990s, leading some French experts to conclude that France does a better job of culturally integrating its Muslim immigrants, who mostly come from francophone Africa. But riots in the poor, largely African suburbs of Paris in 2005 and Grenoble in 2010 — both plagued with high unemployment — presented striking evidence that many of France's Muslims feel economically left behind.

Still, Floris Vermeulen, a Dutch expert on radicalization who teaches political science at the University of Amsterdam, says religious radicalism is much less prevalent in France than elsewhere in Europe. Some immigration experts, including anthropologist Bowen, maintain that the French riots of 2005, spurred by joblessness and discrimination, were driven more by a desire to be part of France, rather than a separatist Muslim movement.

For instance, When French Muslims took to the streets in 2004 to protest the proposed ban on headscarves in French schools, their chant was Francophile: "First, Second, Third-Generation: We don't give a damn: Our home is here!"[74]

CURRENT SITUATION

Rise of Extremists

Anti-immigrant parties are surging in popularity among voters in the Netherlands, Sweden and Austria. Although these remain minority parties, the governing coalitions often need their votes to pass legislation.

"The fall of parliamentary seats into extremist hands represents the biggest shake-up in European politics since the disappearance of communism," Denis MacShane, a Labour member of the British Parliament, recently wrote.[75]

Experts say Europe's progressive social democratic regimes and Britain's liberal Labour government have been defeated because they failed to control immigration.[76]

In the Netherlands, the coalition that emerged from this fall's election joined two center-right parties and did not invite Wilders' anti-immigrant Freedom Party into the coalition. But holding only 52 of the parliament's 150 seats, the coalition needs the support of the Freedom Party's 24 members to pass legislation, making Wilders a kingmaker. In exchange for his party's support, Wilders extracted policy concessions, including consideration of a ban on the Islamic face veil and halving immigration from non-Western (read Muslim) countries. The government also agreed to consider making family reunification and marriage immigration more difficult and to make it harder for people from places like Iraq and Somalia to obtain asylum.

But it's unclear whether international agreements will allow the government to implement all these measures, such as refusing to grant asylum to people from certain countries. "That's problematic for the European Declaration of Human Rights," points out Vermeulen, of the University of Amsterdam. As for cutting immigration, he says, "It's already very difficult to immigrate to the Netherlands. We can't do much more."

In Sweden, the nationalist Swedish Democrats won enough votes in September to gain representation in parliament for the first time. Their campaign had included a controversial TV ad showing an elderly, white Swedish woman in a race for pension/welfare benefits beaten by a stampede of burqa-wearing women pushing strollers. The party's leader, Jimmie Akesson, campaigned for a 90-percent reduction in immigration and described Muslim population growth as the greatest foreign threat to Sweden since World War II. Center-right Prime Minister Fredrik Reinfeldt pledged not to work with the Swedish Democrats even though he failed to achieve a majority.[77]

In Austria, the Freedom Party won enough votes in provincial elections to raise speculation it could have a major impact on Austria's national elections in three years. Formerly led by Nazi-sympathizer Jörg Haider, the party won 17.5 percent of the national vote in 2008.[78]

In Germany, a far-right party has not breached the 5 percent threshold for obtaining representation in the national parliament since World War II, usually attributed to the political elite's fear of a Nazi party re-emerging.[79] But recent surveys suggest up to one-fifth of today's electorate would vote for a party to the right of Merkel's Christian Democrats if it were on the ballot today.[80]

In Britain's May elections, many say the deciding moment came when Labour Prime Minister Gordon Brown was caught on tape privately calling a voter who

Is the French ban on headscarves in schools a good idea?

YES
Rémy Schwartz
Member, French Council of State and Former rapporteur, Stasi Commission on Secularism

From "World on Trial," a series of mock International human rights trials created by Pennsylvania State University's Dickinson School of Law, to be Webcast and broadcast on public television stations worldwide in 2011.

France has always welcomed people from all over the world . . . and everyone can worship as they wish here. We've had many Muslims in our country for a long time; the Mosque of Paris was founded in 1920. Islam is the second religion of France. We have Europe's largest mosque and more mosques than any other European country. . . . We didn't wake up one morning in 2004 and say, "Now we're going to discriminate against Muslims."

It's very rare in France to have unanimous decisions between the Left and the Right . . . but after a 15-year discussion, we said we need to stop what the "older brothers" are doing. Young girls came to us and said, "Protect us, we want to be free — free to wear skirts, free to wear pants and not to be forced to wear headscarves. . . . We want to be able to go to school in tranquility." . . .

It was appropriate to protect young children without forcing them to attend private schools or take correspondence courses. . . . We do not wear religious symbols in schools. We did not set out to discriminate against Muslims. The European Court of Human Rights ruled that we did not discriminate.

And where are the victims? Forty-four students were sent [home] from school out of millions of children, and there hasn't been one single incident for the last couple of years. French laws are always being challenged, and yet this law is one of the few that has unanimous consent throughout the country. Even among the Muslim immigrant population, surveys have shown that 70 percent of French Muslims approve of the law. . . . The French Council of Muslim Faith, which represents 6 million French Muslims, accepted this law.

The law is a victory of democratic French Islam against fundamentalists, who want to impose their vision on others. It's also a victory for these young girls. Go onto the Internet and read what the Stasi Commission did. The hearings were recorded, and young women and girls supported this law, and these immigrant women wanted the protection by the state. The women and girls came to us and said, "Thank you for allowing us to be free."

NO
John R. Bowen
Dunbar-Van Cleve Professor of Arts and Sciences, Washington University, St. Louis; Author of Why the French Don't Like Headscarves (Princeton, 2007) and Can Islam Be French? (Princeton 2009)

Written for *CQ Global Researcher*, December 2010

The headscarf ban is not a good idea. Before the 2004 law, France's highest court had consistently held that Muslim girls or women had a constitutional and a human right to wear headscarves. Since then, France has escaped legal sanctions by saying that the law was enacted to protect Muslim school girls who wanted protection against social pressure to wear a scarf, i.e. that it was not about Islam.

Whatever the merits of this argument, it does not reflect the wide range of claims made by French politicians in favor of the ban. France's leaders on the Right and the Left claimed that headscarves led to the oppression of women, that they favored the entry of political Islam onto French soil and that they were responsible for disorder in the public schools. Quite a lot of trouble to pin on the heads of a few hundred girls seeking to practice their faith! At the same time, sociologists and others who had studied reasons why some Muslim girls wear scarves were ignored.

These wild claims kept politicians from having to tackle real social problems, such as social exclusion, high unemployment and police harassment.

But this easy fix came at a price: It stigmatized Muslims who were exercising their religious freedom. Although many Muslims do not wear headscarves, and many agreed with the law, this is hardly a justification for denying others their religious rights.

It is hard to say to what degree the ban has contributed to a sense among some Muslims that France will never accept their right to be publicly Muslim. The ban started France down a "slippery slope" of attacks on people who may be French but who look or act differently. This past year Parliament enacted a ban on women wearing full face-coverings on the street, a practice that some Muslims consider part of their religion. A minister became so enraged when a woman in face-covering and her husband dared to speak out against a traffic ticket that he tried to deprive the man of his French citizenship.

The president brought down European Union criticism for expelling Roma EU citizens rather than ensure their access to decent housing. Once one denies religious rights, whatever the social justification, it becomes easier to erode them just a bit further the next time.

asked him about Eastern European immigrants "a bigoted woman." Party leaders and critics alike said the comment cost him votes among British workers and helped bring the Conservatives to power.[81]

When it came to confronting immigration, politicians like Brown, who had cut their political teeth on anti-racism and anti-apartheid campaigns in the 1970s and '80s, suffered from a "psychological failure," says Tim Finch, head of migration for the Institute for Public Policy Research, a center-left British think tank. "Labour saw migration and race as two sides of the same coin: Anything about immigration control they found instinctively very difficult," he says. But for Labour's working-class base, "immigration was a proxy for economic insecurity and pressure on public services" like public housing, he says. "Race was not a big element of it."

Britain's two right-wing anti-immigrant parties, the British National Party and the UK Independence Party, captured only 5 percent of the vote, but that was enough to cost the Conservatives a clear majority, according to analyst William Galston at the Brookings Institution in Washington, who attributed their growing percentage to anti-immigration sentiment.[82]

Shortly after the election, Conservative Prime Minister Cameron temporarily reduced non-EU immigration by 5 percent, with a permanent cap to be set next April. But in September the business secretary, Liberal Democrat Vince Cable, complained the cap was "very damaging" to industry and that some companies were relocating abroad.[83] Business leaders said the cap would prevent the hiring of IT specialists from India, investment bankers from the United States and other highly skilled workers from outside Europe.[84]

Because EU agreements require Britain to accept workers from all 27 EU countries, the cap only covers non-EU immigrants, who under Britain's newly restrictive point system are skilled and high-skilled workers. "It's insane economically to chop huge numbers out of that; those are people the economy needs," says Finch.

A parliamentary committee recently reported that — given how few migrants can be capped under international agreements — the proposed cap will cover fewer than 20 percent of long-term migrants. So, while barely affecting Britain's overall migration, the cap could do serious damage to Britain's "knowledge economy," the report said.[85]

Under pressure from business leaders, Prime Minister Cameron was expected to increase the number of non-EU migrants allowed under the cap next year — from about 2,600 a month to 4,000 — the British press reported Nov. 16.[86] The government was expected to shift its attention to limiting the entry of "bogus" students and those getting low-level degrees. After the government effectively barred unskilled workers from outside the EU, "student visas rocketed by 30 per cent to a record 304,000 in just one year, as some applicants used it as an alternative work route," Home Secretary Theresa May said in a speech Nov. 5, adding that students now constitute the majority of non-EU immigrants to the U.K.[87]

In September, the independent Joint Council for the Welfare of Immigrants challenged the cap in court, arguing the government sidestepped parliamentary procedures when it introduced the cap.[88]

Like other European governments, Britain is still struggling to find a magic recipe to promote integration while preventing religious radicalism and, ultimately, terrorism among Muslim youth. In November, May announced that the new government was dismantling the previous Labour government's "Prevent" program, an effort to prevent radicalization of Muslim youth by working in their communities.

"Prevent muddled up work on counterterrorism with the normal work that needs to be done to promote community cohesion and participation," May said on Nov. 3. "Counterterrorism became the dominant way in which government and some communities came to interact. That was wrong; no wonder it alienated so many."[89]

Roma Dispute

In July President Sarkozy sparked an international firestorm when he announced he would dismantle 300 illegal Roma camps in France within three months. Sarkozy's office said the camps were "sources of illegal trafficking, of profoundly shocking living standards, of exploitation of children for begging, prostitution and crime."[90] By October, dozens of camps had been emptied and more than 1,000 inhabitants sent home to Romania and Bulgaria.[91] Last year, 10,000 Roma were returned to the two countries.

EU Justice Commissioner Vivian Reding called the deportations a "disgrace." Citing a leaked memo showing that the French had singled out the Roma for deportation,

AFP/Getty Images/Robert Utrecht

Getty Images/Keyston/Hulton Archive

Anti-immigrant Sentiment Returns

Politicians blaming immigrants for economic hardship — such as Dutch anti-immigrant leader Geert Wilders (top), whose Freedom Party made surprising gains in June parliamentary elections in the Netherlands — are not new. Conservative British Parliament member Enoch Powell railed against immigrants in the late 1960s and early '70s, triggering demonstrations such as the August 1972 march on the Home Office by meat porters bearing a petition demanding an end to all immigration into Britain (bottom). Between 1973 and 1975, several European governments instituted "immigration stop" policies, aimed at deterring immigration and halting overseas recruitment.

she told the European Parliament: "This is a situation I had thought Europe would not have to witness again after the Second World War."[92]

Initially, the European Commission announced it was investigating France with an eye towards taking it to court for violating EU free movement rules and for discriminating against an ethnic minority in violation of the Charter of Fundamental Rights. But the commission suspended its disciplinary action on Oct. 19, saying the French government had promised to enact legislation by next spring to align French law with EU anti-discrimination principles.[93]

The Open Society Institute's Grabbe called the action "a P.R. disaster, making the commission look weak and France look vindicated."[94]

Rob Kushen, executive director of the European Roma Rights Centre in Budapest, says "France could . . . amend its legislation and still act in a discriminatory way against Roma." The event highlighted the lack of EU enforcement power on immigration issues. "Ultimately, the only serious sanction that carries weight is the threat of expulsion from the EU, and that's such an extraordinary threat that I don't think it's a credible deterrent."

The EU's freedom of movement directive allows member nations to deport immigrants from EU countries after three months if the migrants cannot show they have sufficient employment or resources to support themselves. However, the directive also requires a case-by-case decision before the person can be expelled.

"France in our view is clearly in violation of all those guarantees," says Kushen, because they have been expelling people without individual determinations of immigration status. Even if an immigrant is convicted of a crime, they cannot be deported without an individual investigation, he notes. "The Roma have been accused as an ethnic group of begging, illegally squatting on land," a clear example of ethnic discrimination, says Kushen.

Roma from Bulgaria and Romania are in a catch-22 situation when working abroad, because under a political compromise struck when the two countries were admitted into the EU in 2007, European governments were allowed to limit Bulgarian and Romanian immigrants' rights to work in their countries for up to seven years.[95] Member nations were "horrified at the thought that Bulgaria and Romania would empty out, and every able-bodied citizen would go to Western Europe looking for work," Kushen explains.

Advocates for the Roma agree with France on one thing: Romania and Bulgaria are to blame for discriminating against the Roma in the first place, keeping them impoverished. "As long as unemployment rates are reaching 80 to 90 percent in Roma communities in Romania, people are going to move, try to go somewhere else where life is better," Kushen says.

Migration Slowdown

Ironically, anti-immigrant fervor in Europe is occurring just as the global recession has brought the rapid growth of foreign-born populations in developed countries to "a virtual halt," according to a report released in October by the Migration Policy Institute in Washington, D.C.[96]

Between 2008 and 2009, immigration to Ireland from new EU member states dropped 60 percent while overall EU migration to Spain plummeted by two-thirds. The number of foreign workers caught trying to enter the EU illegally at maritime borders fell by more than 40 percent during the same period and continues to decline.

Skyrocketing unemployment rates mean immigrants no longer see the EU as the land of promise. In 2009, unemployment among foreign-born youth reached 41 percent in Spain and 37 percent in Sweden. And substantial numbers of young, native-born men are leaving countries like Ireland and Greece to look abroad for work.[97]

If immigration is dropping so drastically, why is anti-immigration sentiment running so high in Europe? There's still a sizable immigrant population in Europe, "and the vast majority of those people will not go home as a result of the crisis," says Madeleine Sumption, co-author of the institute's report. "When there are fewer jobs around, it's natural for people to get more anxious about economic security — and immigration is one aspect of that."

OUTLOOK

'Temporary Blip?'

Europe's big unknown is whether the dramatic recent drops in immigration spell the end of an era or are just a temporary blip, according to the Migration Policy Institute report.

"My own view is that immigration levels, at least in the U.K., will not return to the levels of 2005 or 2006 at least for some time," says Sumption, who wrote the chapter on Britain. "In part, this is because the number of workers coming from Eastern Europe was a function of it being a new opportunity for those workers: There was pent up demand combined with a strong economic boom. I don't see those kinds of conditions returning in the next few years."

Increasingly, experts say, fast-growing developing nations like Brazil and China — not the industrialized countries — will drive most of the future worldwide immigration. And traditional immigrant-exporting countries like India and China, with higher projected economic growth than Europe, are expected to attract their highly skilled diaspora back from abroad, according to Sumption.

Press reports have emphasized both the growing anti-immigrant sentiment and government policies pushed by right-wing parties. But some experts, including those at the Migration Policy Institute, expected even harsher restrictions on immigrants in the wake of the global recession.

"Immigrant-receiving countries have not resorted to the protectionism that many initially feared," says the institute's report. For example, while a few governments have offered to pay immigrants to return home, immigrants have been reluctant to accept these offers, so only a few countries adopted such measures.[98]

And legal protections, like the EU's free-movement agreements, will likely hamper efforts to cut the numbers as drastically as right-wing politicians in the Netherlands, Sweden and Britain have pledged to do. At the same time, economic insecurity tends to stir fears about immigrants taking jobs and living off welfare, with much of the resentment aimed at the foreigners already living in their countries.

The European Policy Centre's Islam, a Belgian citizen born in Pakistan, says the biggest problem for Muslims in Europe is, "We're looking at European Muslims not as Europeans but as exotic foreigners who should really not be at home in Europe — which is absolutely the wrong approach to take if you're going to get serious about integration." If Europe's 20 million Muslims are viewed as legal residents who contribute to the mainstream culture, politics and economy, that would change the conversation, she suggests. "Instead, all these diktats are coming up" — about banning burqas and adopting European values —"and Muslims in Europe are feeling very estranged," she says. "It's a suicidal approach."

Meanwhile, as cash-strapped governments prepare to slash welfare benefits — drastically in the case of Britain's new Conservative-led coalition government — some think that Europe's famous social "solidarity" will turn against immigrants, including second- and third-generation populations who may be as European as the natives.

If the immigration debate is truly about what constitutes national identity, Europeans may need to view their countries as places that embrace their Turkish, Polish, Pakistani and African communities in the same way that ethnic street markets, music and restaurants have become part of the accepted fabric and pleasure of European living.

NOTES

1. "FPÖ Behind Muezzin-Shooter Game," *Austrian-Times*, Sept. 1, 2010, www.austriantimes.at/news/General_News/2010-09-01/26447/FP%D6_behind_muezzin-shooter_game. Austria has hundreds of Muslim houses of prayer and community centers but only three mosques with minarets — in Vienna, Bad Voslau and Telfs. The muezzin is the person at a mosque chosen to broadcast the call to prayer from the mosque's minaret for Friday services and five times daily.

2. *Ibid.* The Freedom Party was forced to drop out of the Styrian parliament in 2005 after suffering election losses. See "SPO-FPO Deal Possible," *Austrian Independent*, Sept. 27, 2010, http://austrianindependent.com/news/Politics/2010-09-27/4708/SP%D6-FP%D6_deal_possible_in_Styria. Also see, "Right-wing Triumph in Vienna Shocks Federal Coalition Partners, Oct.11, 2010, www.austriantimes.at/news/General_News/2010-10-11/27371/Right-wing_triumph_in_Vienna_shocks_federal_coalition_partners.

3. Christopher Bickerton, "Dutch Culture Wars," *The New York Times*, Oct. 22, 2010, www.nytimes.com/2010/10/23/opinion/23iht-edbickerton.html?_r=2&scp=3&sq=Christopher%20Bickerton&st=cse.

4. James Carroll, "The Rising Tides of Xenophobia," *Boston Globe*, Oct. 25, 2010, www.boston.com/bostonglobe/editorial_opinion/oped/articles/2010/10/25/the_rising_tides_of_xenophobia/.

5. "Anti-Establishment Rage is Fueling Populism Everywhere," *Spiegelonline International*, Sept. 29, 2010, www.spiegel.de/international/europe/0,1518,720275,00.html. Also see Ian Traynor, "Dutch Far-Right Party Wins Pledge on Burqa Ban," *The Guardian*, Oct. 1, 2010, www.guardian.co.uk/world/2010/oct/01/dutch-far-right-burqa-ban.

6. "Swiss vote to ban minarets showcases new populism," *The Christian Science Monitor*, Nov. 29, 2009, www.csmonitor.com/World/Europe/2009/1129/p06s05-woeu.html. Also see "Swiss Want to Ban Burka," News24, May 23, 2010, www.news24.com/World/News/Swiss-want-to-ban-burqa-20100523.

7. Anthony Faiola, "Anti-Muslim Feelings Propel Right Wing," *The Washington Post*, Oct. 26, 2010, www.washingtonpost.com/wp-dyn/content/article/2010/10/25/AR2010102505374.html?sid=ST2010102600369.

8. *Ibid.*

9. Stephan Faris, "The Roma's Struggle to Find a Home," *Time*, Sept. 23, 2010, www.time.com/time/world/article/0,8599,2021016,00.html#ixzz13SmqGHDl.

10. James Blitz, "Britons Lead on Hostility to Migrants," *Financial Times*, Sept. 6, 2010, www.ft.com/cms/s/0/231ffb5e-b9fa-11df-8804-00144feabdc0.html#axzz15SUbSd2d.

11. "Migration and Immigrants Two Years after the Financial Collapse," Migration Policy Institute, October 2010, p. 1, www.migrationpolicy.org/news/2010_10_07.php. German migration is negative. "Germany's Population by 2060," Federal Statistical Office, 2009, www.destatis.de/jetspeed/portal/cms/Sites/destatis/Internet/EN/Content/Publikationen/SpecializedPublications/Population/GermanyPopulation2060.psml.

12. About 261,000 people sought asylum in the EU-27 countries in 2009, but only 78,800 were granted legal protection by EU member governments. See "EU Member states granted protection to 78,800 asylum seekers in 2009," Eurostat press release, June 18, 2010, http://epp.eurostat.ec.europa.eu/portal/page/portal/product_results/search_results?mo=containsall&ms=asylum+seekers+&saa=&p_action=SUBMIT&l=us&co=equal&ci=,&po=equal&pi=,.

13. Charles Hawley, "Letter from Berlin: Searching for Facts in Germany's Integration Debate," *Spiegelonline*, Oct. 12, 2010, www.spiegel.de/international/germany/0,1518,722716,00.html.

14. Katya Vasileva, "Foreigners Living in the EU Are Diverse and Largely Younger than the Nationals of the EU Member States," *Eurostat Statistics in Focus*, no.

45, Sept. 7, 2010, p. 5, http://epp.eurostat.ec.europa .eu/cache/ITY_OFFPUB/KS-SF-10-045/EN/KS-SF-10-045-EN.PDF.

15. For background, see Sarah Glazer, "Social Welfare in Europe," *CQ Global Researcher*, Aug. 1, 2010, pp. 185-210.

16. Michael Slackman, "With Film Afghan-German is a Foreigner at Home," *The New York Times*, Oct. 17, 2010, www.nytimes.com/2010/10/18/world/europe/ 18germany.html.

17. Tony Barber, "European Countries Cannot Have it Both Ways on Immigration," *The Financial Times*, Sept. 3, 2010, www.ft.com/cms/s/0/dab74570-b788-11df-8ef6-00144feabdc0.html.

18. Hawley, *op. cit.*

19. Matthew Clark, "Angela Merkel: Multi-culturalism has 'utterly failed,'" *The Christian Science Monitor*, Oct. 17, 2010, www.csmonitor.com/World/Global-News/2010/1017/Germany-s-Angela-Merkel-Multiculturalism-has-utterly-failed/%28page% 29/2.

20. Slackman, *op. cit.*

21. Reiner Klingholz, "Immigration Debate: Germany Needs More Foreigners," *Spiegelonline*, Aug. 30, 2010. See accompanying graphic "A Change of Direction," www.spiegel.de/international/zeitgeist/ 0,1518,714534,00.html. According to *Der Spiegel*, about 10,000 fewer people emigrated to Germany from Turkey in 2009 than left the country for Turkey.

22. Barber, *op. cit.*

23. Klingholz, *op. cit.*

24. Among Germans the fertility rate has fallen from 2.5 children born to each woman in the 1960s to only 1.4 children — far below the 2.1 rate needed to replace the population.

25. Vasileva, *op. cit.*

26. Migration will compensate for natural population shrinkage in more than half the European regions that are expected to grow, according to Eurostat. See "Regional Population Projections," Eurostat, last modified Oct. 12, 2010, http://epp.eurostat.ec .europa.eu/statistics_explained/index.php/Regional_ population_projections.

27. "Economy: Migration Key to Long-Term Economic Growth, Says OECD," Press Release, Organisation for Economic Co-operation and Development, July 12, 2010, www.oecd.org/document/26/0,3343, en_2649_37415_45623194_1_1_1_1,00.html. Also see "International Migration Outlook 2010," OECD, 2010, www.oecd.org/els/migration/imo.

28. John P. Martin, "Editorial: Ensuring that Migrants Are Onboard the Recovery Train," in *ibid.*, pp. 15-17, www.oecd.org/dataoecd/27/0/45593548.pdf.

29. OECD, "International Migration Outlook 2010," *op. cit.* This OECD report finds unemployment for immigrants running about twice the rate for native-born in many countries.

30. Christian Dustmann, *et al.*, "Assessing the Fiscal Costs and Benefits of A8 Migration to the UK," Center for Research and Analysis of Migration, University College London, July 2009, www.econ .ucl.ac.uk/cream/pages/Press_release_A8fiscalimpact .pdf.

31. According to U.N. projections, the share of Europe's population over age 80 will rise from 3.8 percent to 9.5 percent by 2050. Philippe Legrain, "How Immigration Can Help Defuse Europe's Demographic Timebomb," speech delivered in Helsinki, October 2010.

32. Carroll, *op. cit.*

33. "International Migration Outlook 2010," *op. cit.*, p. 206. The new law shortened the time an adult must live legally in Germany before gaining citizenship from 15 years to 8. Under the law, babies born to foreign parents in Germany are considered both German citizens and citizens of their parents' country of origin until age 23. They must reject their parents' citizenship by age 23 or forfeit their German citizenship.

34. "Mesut Özil: Auswärtsspiel in der Heimat," Spiegel TV, Oct. 11, 2010, http://video.spiegel.de/flash/ 1088559_iphone.mp4. Also see, "Turkish President Criticizes Özil Jeers," *Times Live*, Oct. 16, 2010, www.timeslive.co.za/sport/soccer/article710604.ece/ Turkish-president-criticises-Ozil-jeers.

35. Christian Joppke, "Beyond National Models: Civic Integration Policies for Immigrants in Western Europe," *West European Politics*, January 2007,

pp. 1-22, http://dx.doi.org/10.1080/0140238060 1019613.

36. Ines Michalowski, "Citizenship Tests in Five Countries — An Expression of Political Liberalism?" Social Science Research Center Berlin, October 2009, pp. 17, 24, www.wzb.eu/zkd/mit/pdf/dp_sp_iv_2009-702.pdfA.

37. Joppke, *op. cit.*, p. 8.

38. Ruud Koopmans, "Trade-Offs between Equality and Difference: Immigrant Integration, Multiculturalism and the Welfare State in Cross-National Perspective," *Journal of Ethnic and Migration Studies*, January 2010, pp. 1-26, http://193.174.6.11/zkd/mit/projects/projects_Trade_offs.en.htm.

39. "Are Women's Rights Really the Issue?" *Spiegelonline*, June 24, 2010, www.spiegel.de/international/europe/0,1518,702668,00.html.

40. Karima Bennoune, "Secularism and Human Rights: A Contextual Analysis of Headscarves, Religious Expression, and Women's Equality under International Law," *Columbia Journal of Transnational Law*, vol. 45, no. 2, April 11, 2007, pp. 367-426.

41. *Ibid.*, p. 415.

42. "Are Women's Rights Really the Issue?" *op. cit.*

43. *Ibid.*

44. Bennoune, *op. cit.*, p. 421.

45. Patrick Weil, "Why the French Laïcité is Liberal," *Cardozo Law Review*, vol. 30:6, pp. 2699-2714, www.cardozolawreview.com/content/30-6/WEIL.30-6.pdf.

46. "French Senate Bans Burka," CBC News, Sept. 14, 2009, www.cbc.ca/world/story/2010/09/14/france-burka-ban.html#ixzz1496l9Pri.

47. *Ibid.*

48. Bennoune, *op. cit.*, p. 371.

49. However, a majority supported banning veils in airport security checks. "Survey Finds Support for Veil Ban," BBC News, Nov. 29, 2006, http://news.bbc.co.uk/1/hi/uk/6194032.stm.

50. "Straw's Veil Comment Sparks Anger," BBC News, Oct. 5, 2006, http://news.bbc.co.uk/1/hi/5410472.stm.

51. John R. Bowen, "On Building a Multi-Religious Society," *San Francisco Chronicle*, Feb. 5, 2007, http://articles.sfgate.com/2007-02-05/opinion/17231341_1_french-muslims-head-scarves-french-people.

52. Leticia Delgado Godoy, "Immigration in Europe: Realities and Policies," Unidad de Politicas Comparadas, Working Paper 02-18. See Christopher Caldwell, *Reflections on the Revolution in Europe: Immigration, Islam, and the West* (2010), p. 25.

53. Caldwell, *op. cit.*, p. 26.

54. Matthew Bartsch, *et al.*, "A Sorry History of Self-Deception and Wasted Opportunities," *Der Spiegel*, Sept. 7, 2010, www.spiegel.de/international/germany/0,1518,716067,00.html.

55. Caldwell, *op. cit.*, pp. 4-5.

56. Esther Ben-David, "Europe's Shifting Immigration Dynamic," *Middle East Quarterly*, Spring 2009, pp. 15-24, www.meforum.org/2107/europe-shifting-immigration-dynamic.

57. *Ibid.*

58. *Ibid.*

59. *Ibid.*

60. See Sarah Glazer, "Radical Islam in Europe," *CQ Global Researcher*, Nov. 1, 2007, pp. 265-294.

61. Simon Kuper, "Where is the Netherlands that I Knew?" *Financial Times*, Oct. 16/17, 2010, *Life & Arts*, p. 2, www.ft.com/cms/s/2/badfda56-d672-11df-81f0-00144feabdc0.html#axzz15VNBajlD.

62. Glazer, *op. cit.*, p. 267.

63. Pew Research Center, "Muslim Americans: Middle Class and Mostly Mainstream," 2007, http://pewresearch.org/assets/pdf/muslim-americans.pdf.

64. For background, see Brian Beary, "The New Europe," *CQ Global Researcher*, Aug. 1, 2007, pp. 181-210.

65. Daniel Howden, "Desperate Migrants Lay Siege to Spain's African Border," *The Independent*, Sept. 28, 2005, www.independent.co.uk/news/world/europe/desperate-migrants-lay-siege-to-spains-african-border-508674.html.

66. "IPCC Concludes Investigation into MPS and West Midlands Police dealings with Banaz Mahmod," Independent Police Complaints Commission, April

2, 2008, www.ipcc.gov.uk/news/pr_020408_banaz_mahmod.htm.

67. Emine Saner, "Dishonorable Acts," *The Guardian*, June 13, 2007, p. 18.

68. Glazer, *op. cit.*, pp. 277-278.

69. Joppke, *op. cit.*, pp. 1, 6.

70. *Ibid.*

71. "Fortuyn Killed to Protect Muslims," *The Telegraph*, March 28, 2003, www.telegraph.co.uk/news/world-news/europe/netherlands/1425944/Fortuyn-killed-to-protect-Muslims.html.

72. Joppke, *op. cit.*, p. 9.

73. *Ibid.*, p. 14.

74. Glazer, *op. cit.*

75. Quoted from Newsweek in James Kirchik, "Europe the Intolerant," *The Wall Street Journal*, Oct. 12, 2010, http://online.wsj.com/article/SB1000142405 2748704696304575537950006608746.html.

76. Matthew Campbell, "Left's Long Silence on Migration Turns EU to the Right," *The Sunday Times*, Sept. 19, 2010, www.thesundaytimes.co.uk/sto/news/world_news/Europe/article397964.ece.

77. Stephen Castle, "Political Earthquake Shakes Up Sweden," *International Herald Tribune*, Sept. 21, 2010, p. 3.

78. Kirchik, *op. cit.*

79. Michael Slackman, "Germany Hearing Louder Voices from the Far Right," *International Herald Tribune*, Sept. 23, 2010, p. 3.

80. Hawley, *op. cit.*

81. "Gordon Brown 'bigoted woman' comment caught on tape," BBC News, April 28, 2010, http://news.bbc.co.uk/1/hi/8649012.stm.

82. William Galston, "The British Election Was All about Immigration," *The New Republic*, May 11, 2010, www.tnr.com/blog/william-galston/the-british-election-was-all-about-immigration.

83. "Vince Cable: Migrant Cap is Hurting Economy," *The Guardian*, Sept. 17, 2010, www.guardian.co.uk/politics/2010/sep/17/vince-cable-migrant-cap-economy.

84. "Plans to Cap Number of Skilled Workers Under Scrutiny," *Guardian*, Sept. 7, 2010, www.guardian.co.uk/uk/2010/sep/07/plans-cap-migrants-under-scrutiny.

85. Alan Travis, "Immigration Cap Not the Answer to Cutting Net Immigration Figure, Say MPs," *Guardian*, Nov. 3, 2010, www.guardian.co.uk/uk/2010/nov/03/immigration-cap-net-migration-figure.

86. Robert Winnett, *et al.*, "David Cameron Will Bow to Business and Relax Immigration Cap," Nov. 16, 2010, *Daily Telegraph*, 2010, www.telegraph.co.uk/news/newstopics/politics/david-cameron/8132543/David-Cameron-will-bow-to-business-and-relax-immigration-cap.html.

87. "The Home Secretary's Immigration Speech," Office of the Home Secretary, Nov. 5, 2010. www.homeoffice.gov.uk/media-centre/speeches/immigration-speech.

88. Wesley Johnson, "Legal Challenge to Immigration Cap," *The Independent*, Sept. 24, 2010, www.independent.co.uk/news/uk/legal-challenge-to-immigration-cap-2088649.html.

89. Theresa May, "Our Response to the Terrorist Threat," Office of the Home Secretary, Nov. 3, 2010, www.homeoffice.gov.uk/media-centre/speeches/terrorist-response. Also see, Alan Travis, "Theresa May Promises 'Significant' Reform of Counter-Terror Law," *Guardian*, Nov. 4, 2010, p. 20, www.guardian.co.uk/politics/2010/nov/03/theresa-may-counter-terrorism-reform.

90. "Q&A: France Roma Expulsions," BBC News Europe, Sept. 30, 2010, www.bbc.co.uk/news/world-europe-11027288.

91. Matthew Saltmarsh, "EU Panel Suspends Case against France over Roma," *The New York Times*, Oct. 19, 2010, www.nytimes.com/2010/10/20/world/europe/20roma.html?_r=1&scp=2&sq=Matthew%20Saltmarsh&st=cse.

92. "Q&A: France Roma Expulsions," *op. cit.*

93. Saltmarsh, *op. cit.*

94. *Ibid.*

95. For the different rules of EU countries governing Bulgarian and Romanian workers, see European Commission, "Enlargement: Transitional Provisions," http://ec.europa.eu/social/main.jsp?catId=466&langId

=en. For example in the U.K., immigrants generally cannot work unless self-employed, and the restrictions extend to Dec. 31, 2011, but could be extended.

96. "Migration and Immigrants Two Years after the Financial Collapse," *op. cit.*, p. 1.

97. *Ibid.*

98. *Ibid.*, p. 3.

BIBLIOGRAPHY

Books

Bowen, John R., *Why the French Don't Like Headscarves: Islam, the State, and Public Spaces,* **Princeton University Press, 2007.**
In analyzing why the French banned headscarves in schools in 2004, an American anthropologist cites fears — of radical Islam and alien values — and asks how much newcomers must give up to become part of French society.

Caldwell, Christopher, *Reflections on the Revolution in Europe: Immigration, Islam and the West,* **Penguin Books, 2010.**
A columnist for the *Financial Times* and *Weekly Standard* says Muslim immigration is producing "an undesirable cultural alteration" of Europe, which most Europeans don't want and is not economically necessary.

Legrain, Philippe, *Immigrants: Your Country Needs Them,* **Abacus, 2007.**
An economics journalist argues that demand for migrants will rise in aging societies that need a young, cheap work force to do the work that Europeans dislike, such as elder-care, cleaning and child care.

Articles

Barber, Tony, "European Countries cannot have it both ways on immigration," *Financial Times,* **Sept. 3, 2010, www.ft.com/cms/s/0/dab74570-b788-11 df-8ef6-00144feabdc0.html#axzz14xtymjdq. (Subscription required)**
A former *Financial Times* Brussels bureau chief says aging Europe cannot maintain its expensive social welfare states without immigration.

Batsch, Matthew, "A Sorry History of Self-Deception and Wasted Opportunities," *Spiegelonline,* **Sept. 7,**
2010, www.spiegel.de/international/germany/0,1518, 716067,00.html.
Germany recruited Turkish workers in the 1960s, tried to send them home in the 1980s and has struggled with what to do with them ever since.

Bennoune, Karima, "Secularism and Human Rights: A Contextual Analysis of Headscarves, Religious Expression, and Women's Equality under International Law," *Columbia Journal of Transnational Law,* **Vol. 45. No.2, posted May 2007, http://papers .ssrn.com/sol3/papers.cfm?abstract_id=989066.**
A Rutgers University law professor favors the 2004 French ban on headscarves and describes the major legal cases that preceded it.

Klingholz, Reiner, "Germany Needs More Foreigners," *Spiegelonline,* **Aug. 30, 2010, www .spiegel.de/international/zeitgeist/0,1518,druck-71.**
A German population expert says Germany needs more immigrants, not fewer, if it is to maintain a strong economy, attract skilled workers and populate a country that suffers from a declining birth rate.

Koopmans, Ruud, "Trade-Offs between Equality and Difference: Immigrant Integration, Multiculturalism and the Welfare State in Cross-National Perspective," *Journal of Ethnic and Migration Studies,* **January 2010, pp. 1-26, http://dx.doi.org/10.1080/13691830903250881.**
A sociologist finds that immigrants in countries that require them to integrate have higher employment rates than those in other countries.

Weil, Patrick, "Why the French Laïcité is Liberal," *Cardozo Law Review,* **Vol. 30:6, 2009, pp. 2699-2714, www.cardozolawreview.com/index.php?option=com_ content&view=article&id=116%3Atable-on-contents-30-6&Itemid=14.**
A French immigration historian who advised the French government to institute the headscarf ban says the law is not an attack on liberty.

Reports and Studies

"Foreigners Living in the EU are Diverse and Largely Younger than the Nationals of the EU Member States," *Eurostat,* **Sept. 7, 2010, http://epp.eurostat .ec.europa.eu/portal/page/portal/product_details/ publication?p_product_code=KS-SF-10-045.**

The statistical arm of the European Commission finds that foreign immigrants are younger than European natives.

"International Migration Outlook 2010," *Organisation for Economic Co-operation and Development,* **2010, www.oecd.org/document/41/0,3343,en_ 2649_33931_45591593_1_1_1_1,00.html.**
The report says migration is the key to long-term economic growth in aging Western countries, and governments should open their citizenship laws and unemployment benefits to migrants to help them weather the recession.

"Migration and Immigrants Two Years after the Financial Collapse: Where Do We Stand?" *Migration Policy Institute,* **Oct. 7, 2010, www.migrationpolicy .org/news/2010_10_07.php.**
A Washington think tank says migration is slowing to a virtual halt in parts of the European Union, that Ireland has once again become a country of out-migration, and immigrants in Spain and Sweden are suffering high rates of unemployment.

For More Information

European Policy Centre, Résidence Palace, 155 rue de la Loi, B-1040 Brussels, Belgium; (32) (0) 2 231 0340; www .epc.eu. A think tank that focuses on immigration and integration in the European Union.

European Roma Rights Center, Naphegy tér 8, H-1016 Budapest, Hungary; (36) 1 4132200; www.errc.org. Advocates for the legal rights of Roma in Europe.

Eurostat, for English-language inquiries: (44) 20 300 63103; http://epp.eurostat.ec.europa.eu/portal/page/portal/eurostat/ home. The statistical office of the European Union; issues migration statistics for the 27 EU countries.

Institute for Public Policy Research, 4th Floor, 13-14 Buckingham St., London WC2N 6DF, United Kingdom; (44) (0) 20 7470 6100; www.ippr.org.uk. A progressive think tank that has a generally positive perspective on immigration to Britain.

Migration Watch, P.O. Box 765, Guildford, GU2 4XN, United Kingdom; (44) (0) 1869 337007; www.migra- tionwatchuk.com. A think tank that advocates limiting immigration into the U.K.

Open Society Institute-Brussels, Rue d'dalie 9-13, Brussels 1050, Belgium; (32) 2 505.46.46; www.soros.org/initiatives/ brussels. In alliance with the Soros Foundation, promotes tolerant democracies and outspokenly supports Roma migrants' rights.

Organisation for Economic Co-operation and Development, 2, rue André Pascal, 75775 Paris, Cedex 16, France; (33) 1 45.24.82.00; www.oecd.org. Represents 33 developed countries; issues frequent reports about migration.

WZB, Social Science Research Center Berlin, Reichpietschufer 50, D-10785 Berlin-Tiergarten, Germany; (49) 30 25491 0; www.wzb.eu/default.en.asp. Conducts research on immigration and integration in Europe.

Voices From Abroad:

PETER TRAPP

Domestic Policy Analyst
Christian Democrats Party, Germany

Give immigrants intelligence tests
"We have to establish criteria for immigration that really benefit our country. In addition to adequate education and job qualifications, one benchmark should be intelligence. I am in favor of intelligence tests for immigrants. We cannot continue to make this issue taboo."

Accra (Ghana) Mail, June 2010

VINCENT GEISSER

Islamic Scholar, French National Center for Scientific Research

Fear of Islam abounds
"Today in Europe the fear of Islam crystallizes all other fears. In Switzerland, it's minarets. In France, it's the veil, the burqa and the beard."

The New York Times December 2009

MARIE BIDET

Former Interior Ministry Officer, France

The new Gypsies
"These Gypsies created an organization with spokesmen. . . . They speak with [the] authorities, something new in France. They are serious, respectable; they vote, they don't want to burn cars, they want everyone living in peace. That's opposite from the traditional image. . . . [I]t can be underlined that they succeed in their approach."

The Christian Science Monitor September 2010

PIERGUIDO VANALLI

Member of Parliament, Italy

Catholic Church has limited vision of immigration
"The Catholic Church does its job. . . . Ours is a different vision. We have to temper the needs of the people

I'M CLEANING UP FRANCE... WHY DO YOU ASK?

ROMANIA

ROMANI

Sweden/Olle Johansson

who live in Italy with the problems that excessive immigration brings with it. The church sees only one aspect, whereas we have a broader vision."

Los Angeles Times, July 2010

GUIDO WESTERWELLE

Vice Chancellor, Germany

Also address emigration
"Germany is not a country of immigration but of emigration. The question of what we can do against this emigration is just as important as the question of what immigration policy we want."

Spiegel Online (Germany) October 2010

ROBERTO MALINI

Representative EveryOne NGO, Italy

A cruel strategy on the Roma
"The strategy is clear and simple: Rather than forcing someone on the airplane, authorities keep demolishing Gypsy camps so that eventually Roma people have no place to go and leave the country."

The Christian Science Monitor October 2010

RICCARDO DE CORATO

Vice Mayor, Milan, Italy

The zero solution

"These are dark-skinned people [Roma], not Europeans like you and me. Our final goal is to have zero Gypsy camps in Milan."

The Boston Globe, October 2010

KADRI ECVET TEZCAN

Turkish Ambassador to Austria

Leave the ministry out

"Integration is a cultural and social problem. But in Austria . . . the Ministry for Interior . . . is responsible for integration. That is incredible. The ministry for interior can be in charge of asylum or visas and many security problems. But the minister for interior should stop intervening in the integration process."

Die Presse (Austria) November 2010

THERESA MAY

Home Secretary United Kingdom

No more cheap labor

"We will bring net migration down to the tens of thousands. Our economy will remain open to the best and the brightest in the world, but it's time to stop importing foreign labour on the cheap."

Daily Telegraph (England) October 2010

SILVIO BERLUSCONI

Prime Minister, Italy

A potential new Africa

"Europe runs the risk of turning black from illegal immigration, it could turn into Africa. We need support from the European Union to stop this army trying to get across from Libya, which is their entry point."

The Express (England) September 2010

12

Crime in Latin America

Eliza Barclay

Members of the Mara Salvatrucha-18 gang are arrested in Mixco, Guatemala, in September 2005 after fighting between rival gangs in a juvenile prison near Guatemala City left at least 17 inmates dead. Conflicts between gangs in Central America, as well as in Mexico, are a major cause of violence.

AFP/Getty Images/Orlando Sierra

From *CQ Researcher*, September 2010

In April, Julio Scherer García, founder and editor of *Proceso*, a respected Mexican magazine, received an extraordinary invitation: Ismael "El Mayo" Zambada, co-leader of the violent Sinaloa Federation — arguably Mexico's most powerful drug-trafficking cartel — was offering the veteran journalist an interview. The author of several books on organized crime traveled deep into the northern mountains to the hideout of the feared recluse with a $2-million bounty on his head.[1]

In a telling exchange, Scherer asked Zambada whether the Mexican government might ever win the war against the cartels, a fight that has grown increasingly savage in recent years. "The problem with the narco business is that it involves millions" of dollars, Zambada responded. "How do you dominate that? As for the bosses, locked up, dead or extradited, their replacements are already standing by."[2]

Zambada's retort echoed the grim perception of many observers who have watched as crime rates in Mexico and Latin America have swelled to staggering new heights in recent years.[3] Organized crime groups have unprecedented influence, reach and firepower, making criminality look more and more like an unbeatable cancer that cannot be stamped out because it simply re-sprouts and spreads. Yet, while crime in many countries in the region indeed seems to be out of control, others countries have made remarkable progress beating back criminal groups and establishing the rule of law.

A December 2009 report from the Inter-American Commission on Human Rights showed that for the first time in decades crime replaced unemployment as the region's top worry. With an average of 25.6 homicides per 100,000 people, Latin America's rate dwarfs

Europe's rate of 8.9 per 100,000.[4] Other polls have demonstrated a similar rising concern about crime. In the 2009 Latinobarómetro poll of 18 countries in Latin America, published annually by *The Economist*, citizens in seven countries cited crime as the main concern.[5]

The current regional crime wave probably started in the 1980s, according to Marcelo Bergman, a professor in the department of legal studies at the Center for Economic Research and Education, or CIDE, in Mexico City. Since then, crime has expanded into a complex range of activities, from pirated DVD sales to highly sophisticated money laundering and human trafficking.

As recently as Aug. 25, the bullet-pocked bodies of 72 people were found by Mexican authorities on a ranch in Tamaulipas State, in northeast Mexico. Officials believe they were migrants heading to the United States who were killed by a drug gang after resisting demands for money.[6]

"The nature of the threats we face here, and throughout the world, has become both extremely localized and highly globalized," Ronald K. Noble, Secretary General of Interpol, the international police agency, said in Chile in 2009. "And market forces — or market opportunities — have motivated criminals that used to specialize to diversify into new areas of activity."[7]

Most organized crime groups in the region — from Argentina to Mexico — are now involved not only with drugs, money laundering and human trafficking but also arms, smuggling, robbery, kidnapping, extortion, assassinations and counterfeiting. Many experts have noted the evolution of criminal groups in Latin America into

Violent-Crime Levels Highest in Four Nations

Among countries in Latin America, Mexico and three countries in Central America — El Salvador, Guatemala and Honduras — have the highest levels of violent crime, according to the Global Peace Index established by the Australia-based Institute for Economics and Peace. Nicaragua, Chile and Uruguay have the lowest levels of violent crime. The index rates 149 nations on 23 indicators of safety and security.

Level of Violent Crime in Latin America (1 = lowest, 5 = highest)

Source: "Global Peace Index," Institute for Economics and Peace, 2010, www.visionofhumanity.org/wp-content/uploads/PDF/2010/2010%20GPI%20Results%20Report.pdf

Illegal handguns cover a square in Caracas, Venezuela, as Interior and Justice Minister Tareck El Aissami on June 23, 2009, displays hundreds of seized weapons to be destroyed by the government. Venezuela has the region's highest homicide rate; nearly 44,000 people were killed in the country since 2007, or 50 percent more than in Mexico during the same period.

transnational enterprises that conduct business across several continents. Zambada's Sinaloa Federation, for example, may buy chemicals from China to produce methamphetamines, manufacture the drugs in Mexico and then ship them to the United States or Europe. A separate division in the same organization may be responsible for moving cocaine from Colombia to Venezuela to West Africa to Europe.[8] Other crime groups maintain tight and fierce control of vast urban territories: Most of Rio de Janeiro's 1,000-odd slums, or *favelas*, for example, are still more or less within the grip of three drug-trafficking gangs, and the police enter only reluctantly.[9]

The human cost of the groups' expansion and territorial disputes is shocking. In Mexico, more than 28,000 people have been killed in drug-related violence since President Felipe Calderón took on the drug cartels in December 2006.[10] Until recently, Brazil and Colombia also had absurdly high death tolls, with gangs, police and military factions battling in the streets, but now the highest murder rates in the region from drug-related violence belong to Guatemala, Honduras and El Salvador.

Astonishingly, however, the highest overall homicide rate in the region belongs to Venezuela, with more than

16,000 people killed in 2009, or 50 percent more than in Mexico during the same period.[11] Crime's impact on ordinary people is also measured through victimization surveys, which ask whether a family member was the victim of crime in the last 12 months. Recent surveys show victimization rates rising significantly across the region in the last 15 years. Interestingly, the biggest increases are in personal theft, not violent crime.[12]

Feminicide is another horrifying problem in the region. In Ciudad Juárez, near the Texas border, more than 370 Mexican women have been murdered in a spate of killings since 1993.[13] The majority were working-class women, the most vulnerable sector of the border population, according to Kathleen Staudt, a professor of political science at the University of Texas at El Paso. One in three was a young teen who was killed and sexually tortured. The overwhelmed Juárez authorities rarely investigated the murders.

Guatemala has similarly high rates. Between 2001 and 2006, the country's female homicide rate increased by 117 percent while the population only increased by 8 percent, according to a 2007 U.N. study.[14]

The regional predilection for crime is typically explained by three factors: high economic inequality, a ballooning population of youth without viable economic opportunities and weak police forces and law enforcement institutions. With few exceptions — notably Uruguay and Costa Rica — Latin America has the highest levels of income inequality in the world. Unemployment in the region is at 21 percent, according to the annual Latinobarómetro public opinion poll. And the poor often have only two options for steady work: the informal economies or organized crime. "There are thousands of candidates in [Ciudad Juárez] for recruitment [into drug cartels], because of their level of social exclusion," Teresa Almada, director of the CASA youth development center in Ciudad Juárez, says. "They're young and poor and disposable."[15]

To make matters worse, law enforcement is often weak or corrupt. Because of the lack of transparency and efficiency in the criminal justice system in Mexico, for example, fewer than 25 percent of the crimes are reported and just 1 or 2 percent result in a jail sentence, according to a 2010 report by the Trans-Border Institute at the University of San Diego.[16] In most countries (with a few exceptions like Chile and Costa Rica), military and law enforcement agencies accommodate drug traffickers and organized crime, making corruption one of the region's most intractable problems.

Thus, Colombia, Mexico and Guatemala have been forced to turn to the military for crime fighting. Yet the military is often linked to human rights abuses. In its pursuit of drug traffickers Mexico's army has been linked to forced disappearances, acts of torture and illegal raids. Mexico's National Human Rights Commission has received almost 4,000 complaints of army abuses since 2006.[17]

Not surprisingly, crime has become a hot political issue in the region, consistently ranking high among voters' concerns. In recent presidential elections in Guatemala and Colombia, candidates campaigned on "tough on crime" platforms. But "iron fist" or *mano dura* policies in Central America in particular largely have failed to crush the gangs, succeeding only in alienating local communities.[18]

The emergence of Mara Salvatrucha (MS-13) and other violent Central American gangs has become a high-priority regional security issue. The major gang in Central America, MS-13 was formed during the 1980s by Salvadorans in Los Angeles, reportedly for self-protection from other gangs. In time, both the MS-13 and its Los Angeles rival Mara Salvatrucha 18 (M-18) would expand within Central America and beyond. Yet many experts feel that Central American gangs also make an easy scapegoat for governments unwilling to address the root causes of the violence: poverty, easily available firearms and the social fragmentation that comes with high emigration rates.

Of course, the U.S. appetite for drugs remains a central factor in Latin America's crime problem. At the same time, the U.S. role in crime fighting in the region has changed dramatically in recent years. In the 1980s, the United States covertly funneled money and arms directly

Drug Cartels Operate Throughout Mexico

Seven drug cartels control vast swaths of Mexico, including several areas along the U.S.-Mexican border. Violence in Mexico has reached unprecedented levels as a result of both government efforts to confront the cartels using military force and territorial infighting among the cartels. Since President Felipe Calderón launched his challenge to the cartels in December 2006, more than 28,000 people have been killed. Most are involved in drug trafficking, but an increasing number are civilians and military troops. In recent years, several cartels have expanded southward, into Central America.

Areas of Cartel Influence in Mexico

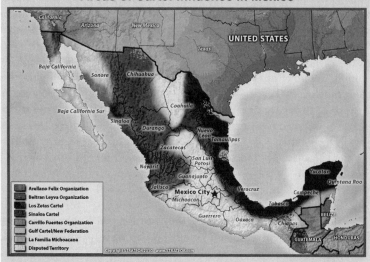

Source: This graphic is republished with the express permission of Stratfor; Dec. 16, 2009

to right-wing militias in Central America to fight leftist guerrilla movements. Arms still flow freely over the border to Mexican cartels, but the U.S. government now has dedicated significant funds to combating crime.

The Bush administration's Mérida Initiative committed $1.4 billion to help Mexico fight drug cartel violence. The Obama administration is currently working to extend Mérida to Central America. And over the last decade the United States has delivered an estimated $7 billion in military and development aid to help Colombia fight drugs and terrorism, while the U.S. military presence in Colombia has slowly decreased.[19]

Yet, as the Inter-American Dialogue think tank said in a 2009 report on regional relations, "after years of disappointment with the United States, Latin American governments are distrustful of Washington and ambivalent about the U.S. role in the region." Helping to fight crime is one area where the United States still has an opportunity to improve its standing.[20]

As Latin Americans grapple with drug cartels and rising crime — and Americans along the Mexican border look on with increasing concern — here are some of the key issues being discussed:

Can Latin American organized crime groups be controlled?

Though independent, small- and medium-sized organized crime groups are operating in every country in the region, the Mexican cartels now dominate the trade in drugs and other goods and form alliances with smaller groups. The Mexicans manage complex supply chains running from the coca or marijuana field all the way to the consumer.

Today, there are seven main Mexican cartels: the Sinaloa Federation, the Gulf Cartel, the Beltrán-Leyva Organization, La Familia Michoacán, the Carillo Fuentes Organization, Los Zetas and the Arellano Felix Organization.[21]

Market savvy and prosperous enough to buy off officials throughout the supply chain, the cartels are more powerful and better at what they do than the Colombian mega cartels of the 1980s and '90s ever were, many crime experts say. And even with billions of dollars spent, the authorities have not fared well against them.

John Bailey, director of the Mexico Project in the Department of Government at Georgetown University, says the crime syndicates have a relatively easy time recruiting new members — or replacing members who are killed or arrested — and solidifying their presence in a community or country. "The growth of prisons, the overcrowding of prisons and the impunity for committing crimes creates incentives for people inside of prisons to return to the world of crime in which the costs of engaging in crime are fairly light," he says.

The celebratory culture and mystique that have blossomed around cartel leaders may add to the difficulty of dismantling their organizations. Mexico's most wanted criminal, Joaquín "El Chapo" Guzmán, who leads the Sinaloa Federation with Zambada, is a legend in some Mexican regions where the federation does its recruiting. When Guy Lawson, a reporter from *Rolling Stone*, visited El Chapo's home state of Sinaloa in 2008, he found a community that both revered — and feared — El Chapo.

"In the imagination of Sinaloa, he is like a god from an ancient world: kind, humble, rich, generous, mysterious," Lawson writes. "Tales of his exploits abound — his fearlessness, his taste in women, his generosity. The area has even given birth to an entire genre of popular songs known as *narcocorridos*, which glorify the triumphs and travails of Chapo and his rivals."[22]

The glorification of El Chapo's exploits has been difficult for the authorities to counter, even when Sinaloans and other Mexicans are confronted with indisputable, and frequent, evidence of his brutality and the heavy toll of infighting between crime groups.

But while the cartels' reach and sway are daunting, some observers believe they may not be impossible to break. Adam Isacson, a senior associate in the regional security policy program at the Washington Office on Latin America, says that Colombia's success in vanquishing its cartels offers some clues as to what may work. "First, we know that you need a government in all territories, including the jungle, the border zones, the slums, all of the places that have traditionally been ungoverned," says Isacson. "And you have to have a justice system that's present."

On August 30, in fact, federal officials said they had captured Edgar Valdez Villarreal, one of Mexico's most ruthless drug lords. Indeed, the arrest was seen as especially significant because the U.S.-born Valdez (nicknamed La Barbie because of his blond hair and blue eyes) had been battling to control the Beltrán-Leyva gang, causing widespread bloodshed.

Valdez is the third major Mexican drug figure to have been captured or killed recently. In December Navy special forces officers killed Arturo Beltrán-Leyva in a dramatic firefight. And in July Mexican army troops killed Ignacio "Nacho" Coronel, the so-called King of Crystal, said to have shipped many tons of crystal methamphetamine across the border.

On the same day Valdez was arrested, federal police announced that 3,200 officers — 10 percent of the force — had been dismissed this year after undergoing lie detector tests and other procedures to uncover corruption.[23]

Isacson emphasizes the importance of intelligence and witness-protection programs, in which countries like Mexico and Guatemala have not invested enough. "In areas that have had success against organized crime, what seems to matter most is not superior firepower, or the police or military, but a very well-funded and trained investigative intelligence unit that is not used for political purposes," Isacson notes.

Colombia's intelligence unit played a key role in dismantling the Medellín and Calí drug cartels in the 1990s. With sufficient investment and political will, Mexico could achieve similar successes, Isacson says.

Costa Rica has also been able to keep organized crime groups at bay with a strong national police unit. "It's not easy for the drug cartels to operate in Costa Rica," says Isacson, though they are making short stops along the coast en route from Colombia north.

Author Sam Logan, the founder of Southern Pulse Networked Intelligence, an open source network on security issues in Latin America, thinks the cartels are vulnerable. Logan, who is writing a book about Mexico's Los Zetas cartel, believes that the Mérida Initiative and the newfound political will and cooperation between American and Mexican intelligence officials may prove formidable over time.

"I don't know that we can beat them entirely, but I predict that in about eight years we may be able to get to a place where these guys can be hit harder and faster," Logan says.

"In Colombia now we see dozens of baby cartels instead of big ones. They are much easier to deal with, and maybe Mexico can get there, too."

Meanwhile, law enforcement agencies are getting better at hitting cartels where it hurts most — their wallets — according to Andrew Tammaro, an officer with the U.S. Immigration and Customs Enforcement's Bulk Cash Smuggling Center. Tammaro, who recently helped recover $41 million in Latin American drug money hidden in cargo containers, said law enforcement agencies are more readily coordinating and sharing intelligence across borders, "offering greater potential for individual jurisdictions to find relevance in seemingly unconnected events. This increased capacity can effectively disrupt

and ultimately dismantle . . . criminal organizations or the illicit systems they employ," Tammaro wrote.[24]

Can police corruption in Latin America be curtailed?

Police corruption is widespread in Latin America, enabling criminals to buy off authorities when caught red-handed with illicit goods and making criminals' well-being a higher priority for police than protecting the citizenry. According to the polling firm Mitofsky International, police agencies are among the least respected of Mexican institutions, with just one in 10 Mexicans saying they respect the police.[25]

Police in much of Latin America receive low pay, which makes them vulnerable to bribes. The United Nations Special Rapporteur on extrajudicial executions, Philip Alston, recommended raising police salaries in a report at the end of his mission in Brazil in 2007. "Low pay for police leads to a lack of professional pride and encourages police to engage in corruption, to take second jobs, and to form 'extermination groups,' 'death squads,' 'militias' and other vigilante groups to supplement their pay," he wrote.[26]

Edgardo Buscaglia, director of the International Law and Economic Development Center at the University of Virginia School of Law and currently a visiting professor at Mexico's ITAM University, thinks anti-corruption measures that have the teeth to prosecute politicians are essential to police reforms. "Police corruption is like the grandson of political corruption," says Buscaglia.

He believes that only two countries, Colombia and Chile, have been able to move forward with anti-corruption measures and political reforms at all levels. "In Colombia 32 percent of national legislators were judicially charged with organized crime," says Buscaglia. "That had a lot to do with hampering police corruption in Colombia."

So police reform cannot happen until political parties agree to put a stop to corruption, he says, which hasn't yet happened in Mexico and many other countries in the region.

Unfortunately, police work is becoming less and less attractive for educated men and women since the cartels have ramped up their attacks on police officers and commanders. Since 2006, more than 1,100 of Mexico's tens

Amid the Chaos, an Island of Calm

Chile has a lot going for it, including a solid economy.

While organized crime groups are terrorizing many Latin American countries, Chile remains an island of relative tranquility. Victimization surveys show crime rates rising throughout the region in the last decade, but in Chile they have not grown markedly. For example, 37.8 percent of 12,000 Chileans surveyed recently had been the victims of a robbery or attempted robbery in the last six months, according to the Citizen Peace Foundation's most recent annual survey, released last October. The figure was slightly lower than the 2008 rate, though 7 percent higher than the 2000 rate. [1] By comparison, Argentina in 2005 had a victimization rate of 47 percent, while Mexico had a rate of 63 percent, according to the Latinobarómetro poll. [2]

What's Chile's secret? Some say it's the *Carabineros* — Chile's national police force, an arm of the Ministry of National Defense. Widely considered to be the most professional police force in Latin America, the *Carabineros* spend more time on crime prevention and civic education than their counterparts in other countries. They are also considered to be among the least corrupt, especially when compared to the scandal-prone forces in Central America and Brazil.

Some also argue that Chile's swift economic growth in recent years, thanks in part to a strong export sector for products such as fruit and salmon, has created a larger, better-educated middle class than its neighbors, making crime a less appealing, and less necessary, path to riches. The World Economic Forum's Global Competitiveness Report for 2009-2010 ranked Chile as the 30th most competitive country in the world and the most competitive in Latin America, with crime scarcely a problem for doing business there. [3]

Chile's geography and ecology may also have insulated it from the reach of the drug cartels. It has no Andean soil suitable for growing coca, nor is it along any trafficking routes. Michael Shifter, president of the Inter-American Dialogue think tank, also cites several cultural factors that may keep crime at bay in Chile.

"Chile is a very institutional, structured society, much more so than its neighbors," Shifter says. "A sense of control has been historically important, and governments of the last

20 years have made a number of reforms to the police that have yielded positive results."

Reforms include the expansion of the forces, the development of community policing and a Block Watch Plan, similar to Neighborhood Watch in the United States.

Drugs are also shunned in Chile, more so than its economic counterparts in South America — Brazil and Argentina — which have both seen escalating ecstasy and cocaine use among the middle and upper classes in recent years. [4]

"Chile is a little like the U.S. about the drug issue; drugs are somehow seen as a moral failing," Shifter says. "A social conservatism makes them very cautious about the spreading of drugs because it could upset the order. Chileans are very concerned about what would upset order."

Indeed, even if crime rates remain relatively low, there is a perception among Chileans that it is a serious problem, perhaps in part because the media tend to sensationalize crime cases and frighten the public.

"Victimization surveys suggest crime has been steady for the last five years or so," said Andres Baytelman, executive director of the Citizen Peace Foundation. "But at the same time, it is certainly true that fear of crime has consistently grown." [5]

Yet experts say they're not particularly concerned about crime in Chile spiraling out of control. If anything, continued economic growth and social vigilance may help push rates even further down over time.

— Eliza Barclay

[1] "Entregan resultados de Índice Paz Ciudadana-Adimark," Citizen Peace Foundation press release, Oct. 22, 2009, www.pazciudadana.cl/prensa_interior.php?idPub=55.

[2] *Ibid.*

[3] "The Global Competitiveness Report 2009-2010," www.weforum.org/en/initiatives/gcp/Global%20Competitiveness%20Report/index.htm.

[4] Alexei Barrionuevo, "Ecstasy Ensnares Upper-Class Teenagers in Brazil," *The New York Times*, Feb. 14, 2009, www.nytimes.com/2009/02/15/world/americas/15ecstasy.html.

[5] Gideon Long, "Is Chile Imagining a Crime Wave?" *Time*, Oct. 22, 2008, www.time.com/time/world/article/0,8599,1852730,00.html#ixzz0sr5rnsTj.

of thousands of drug-related deaths were soldiers, police officers and officials, according to President Calderón.[27]

"I believe that the number of attacks [on police] has increased, and now they are more selective attacks, on command centers, and the most obvious reason is they are trying to intimidate those leaders who try to combat organized crime and also to frighten the rank and file so they don't act," said José Luis Piñeyro, a professor at the National Autonomous University of Mexico.[28]

Others are not so pessimistic about Mexico. In a recent article, three Mexico experts — Andrew Selee, director of the Mexico Institute at the Woodrow Wilson International Center for Scholars; David Shirk, a fellow at the center and an associate professor at the University of San Diego; and Eric Olson, a senior adviser at the center — argued that the government has been sending a stronger signal that corruption will not be tolerated.

"Recent arrests and prosecutions have brought down the head of Mexico's Interpol office, senior officials in the attorney general's office, three state public security chiefs, hundreds of state and local police officers and a few mayors and local police commanders," they wrote. "Meanwhile, Mexico is slowly cultivating a culture of lawfulness, thanks to courageous journalists and new civic organizations calling for greater accountability. Far more can be done, but this is a good start."[29]

Other countries with serious police corruption also are making headway. Brazil's two biggest cities, in particular, are starting to see some positive changes after decades of corruption. São Paulo reformed its police force in the 1990s. And in many *favelas* (slums) in Rio de Janeiro, intelligence units known as UPPs (for Pacifying Police Units) have been established by José Beltrame, the security secretary in the state government and a former federal police chief. Beltrame plans to install 40 UPPs — newly recruited and specially trained to resist corruption -- covering 500,000 residents over the next four years.[30]

Los Angeles Police Chief William Bratton wrote recently that heavy investments in law enforcement and various reforms can enable Latin America to achieve the same significant drops in crime and police corruption seen in Los Angeles and New York.[31]

Bratton and co-author William Andrews acknowledge that Latin America's crime problem is far worse than what the United States encountered in the most challenging era

of the late 1980s and early '90s. "Crime grows unchecked in Latin America for the same reason it grew in the United States," they wrote. "The institutional response from the police and the criminal justice system has been wholly inadequate and uncoordinated."[32]

Bratton and Andrews make a number of specific recommendations for Latin America, starting with the decentralization and reorganization of command structures to improve policing at the local level. Districts should be downsized to 150,000 people or fewer, they say. (Many police districts in Latin American cities cover communities of more than 300,000 people.) With decentralization, "community members begin to recognize that the police are helping, not hurting, their neighborhoods," they write. They also say police departments must generate better crime data through better crime reporting.[33]

But they note that "a decentralized police department must still be centrally controlled to guard against corruption, incompetence and indifference," primarily through record-keeping systems that closely monitor police officers. Police districts also need "quality control units," or units to hold negligent or corrupt cops accountable, and well-staffed and well-equipped internal affairs and corruption-investigation squadrons.[34]

Do Latin American politicians have the political will to curtail crime?

Public security, corruption and crime have roiled the careers of many a politician in Latin America — and destroyed the careers of some. For instance, Manuel Noriega, Panama's former military dictator, served several years in prison in the United States (and is now in prison in France) on drug trafficking, racketeering and money laundering charges.

Today several leaders remain questionably committed to tackling crime in a serious way, according to experts, most notably in Venezuela and Guatemala. In Caracas, Venezuela's capital, there are 200 homicides per 100,000 population, one of the five highest rates in the world, according to the nonprofit organization Venezuelan Violence Observatory (OVV). And the Venezuelan National Counter Kidnapping Commission reports a frightening increase in kidnappings throughout the country since 2006; kidnappings from 2008 to 2009 increased between 40 and 60 percent alone.[35]

Slum Clearance

With Rio de Janeiro, Brazil, set to host the 2016 Summer Olympics, police are focusing new attention on the city's hundreds of crime-ridden favelas, or slums, including Santa Marta (top), nestled in the shadow of Rio's high rises. In an effort to reduce the favelas' high murder rates and stop shoot-outs with drug gangs, police are attempting to institute less confrontational community policing techniques. In the Cantagalo favela, in the famed Ipanema suburb, a young man is questioned by a Special Police Operations officer (bottom) seeking drugs and guns.

President Hugo Chávez has acknowledged that crime, insecurity and violence are "becoming a threat for the [social] revolution." In one of his lengthy speeches on his Sunday television program, Chávez vowed "to defeat the enemy of the revolution that is crime: from the little punk . . . to those much better organized that rob banks, kidnap people, commit homicides and the paramilitary."[36]

Chávez is acknowledging that accelerating crime is a problem because he knows that it makes him vulnerable politically, says Michael Shifter, president of the Inter-American Dialogue.

"Crime has gotten a lot worse under Chávez in the last 10 years, and he is beginning to respond," says Shifter. "The problem is that these efforts are generally pretty improvised, and inefficient. This is a product of the way he has governed the country: He makes all decisions and has politicized everything."

Shifter adds that Chávez may be hinting at the need to develop a professional police force, but that "it's very hard for responses to be effective" because every government institution has become weak under his ironclad grip.

Guatemala is led by a president with a similarly dubious commitment to fighting crime and corruption. Under Álvaro Colóm, drug and gang-related violence seems to be spiraling out of control. Last year, a prominent lawyer was assassinated after accusing Colóm of colluding in the murder of a businessman who had fallen into ill favor with the government. The public responded angrily, with many demanding that Colóm temporarily step down in the face of apparent corruption affecting the highest levels of government; Colóm, however, refused to stand aside. As a publication for mayors noted, "the national press has described the government [of Guatemala] as presiding over the weakest and most inefficient judicial system of all time, which among other things has been infiltrated by organized crime."[37]

In nearby Colombia, however, things are looking considerably rosier. Daniel Mejía, a faculty member of the Economic Development Research Center at the University of the Andes in Bogotá, says newly elected president Juan Manuel Santos has made security a crucial part of his political platform and will build on the success of his predecessor, Alvaro Uribe.

"Santos is very close to the general chief of police [Gen. Oscar Naranjo] who is probably the best director of police we have ever had," said Mejía. "Naranjo knows very well what is going on and has identified the local gangs in Medellín and Calí, is negotiating with them, and is breaking small cartels that are operating to prevent them from growing."

But Kevin Casas-Zamora, a senior fellow at the Brookings Institution think tank and a former vice president of Costa Rica, says it may be premature for Colombia's political class to pat itself on the back. Casas-Zamora notes that drug lords have been buying protection from political parties and candidates in Mexico and Colombia since the 1970s.

"Since then," he writes, "there are reasons to think that the drug-politics link has grown deeper in the region." He notes that in February Mexico's National Action Party, or PAN, shelved all primaries in the border state of Tamaulipas because of the looming threat of drug cartel influence.[38]

BACKGROUND

Cold War Legacy

Petty criminals and criminal groups have been fixtures in Latin America for at least a century. But the ongoing crime wave in many countries in the region has ties to a culture of violence and lawlessness left over from the Cold War conflicts of the second half of the 20th century. In particular in Central America, violence is often seen as an acceptable means of resolving conflict, in part because of the limited and sometimes wanton justice meted out by the government. Each country's story is different, but the criminal gangs in Central America, Colombia and to some extent Peru often have benefited in some way from their expertise in guerrilla warfare and the arms they acquired.

The 1960s saw the rise of the Revolutionary Armed Forces of Colombia, a Marxist guerrilla organization known as FARC (Fuerzas Armadas Revolucionarios de Colombia) and the paramilitary National Liberation Army (ELN). Both groups battled the government in a ruthless civil war that only subsided in recent years under former President Uribe. But today the FARC and paramilitary groups remain entrenched in the drug trade because they are "tenacious, skilled at logistical organization and also heavily armed (with money acquired by growing and selling coca leaf and opium poppies)," writes Alma Guillermoprieto, a respected Mexican-American journalist and author.[39]

In Nicaragua, El Salvador and Guatemala, conflicts between the state and left-wing rebel groups simmered for decades, exacting a traumatic toll: hundreds of thousands of deaths, disappearances, refugees and internally displaced people. Many have argued that the weapons

and veterans left behind from those conflicts have fed directly into the current drug violence, as former soldiers join gangs or train new recruits.

Even though it is not technically at war, Guatemala remains among the world's least peaceful nations, ranking 112 out of 149 in a recent Global Peace Index. Nicaragua ranked 64, far behind more peaceful Costa Rica, which ranked 26. However, four other Latin American nations were rated as even more violent than Guatemala: Haiti, Venezuela, Honduras and Colombia.[40] Members of the former Guatemalan special forces, known as *Kabiles*, also have ties to Los Zetas, whose members include former Mexican special forces officers, according to author Logan of Southern Pulse.

In Guatemala, thousands of women have been the victims of sexual violence, torture and assassination. This culture of violence towards women is partly rooted in the legacy of the civil war, when the government trained its soldiers and other mercenaries to rape and attack women, according the Commission for Historical Clarification. Today, more than 3,800 women and girls have been murdered in Guatemala since 2000, and in 2008 feminicide was recognized as a punishable crime.

But Victoria Sanford, an anthropologist at the City University of New York and author of *Buried Secrets: Truth and Human Rights in Guatemala*, says that the fact that the state never prosecuted the killers and rapists of the 1980s violence leaves little hope that the murderers in today's wave of feminicide will be pursued.[41] "We should be able to find out who is implicated, who gave the orders, but all of these cases are just sitting in court somewhere," says Sanford. "And today the impunity rate is 98 percent, so people who may be tempted to do these crimes know they probably will not go to jail if they do."

Impact of U.S. Policies

U.S. efforts to aid Latin America have often backfired, helping to strengthen the regional networks of organized crime groups and sparking large-scale immigration waves to the United States. In El Salvador alone, hundreds of thousands of people during the 1980s civil war were given asylum status and resettled in Los Angeles, Houston and Washington, among other cities.

As young men fresh from a brutal civil war found their footing in the United States, some were sucked into gang culture. The MS-13, or Mara Salvatrucha, a major

Central American gang, was formed during the 1980s by Salvadorans in Los Angeles. In time, both the MS-13 and its rival MS-18 would expand within Central America and beyond, thanks in part to a U.S. decision to deport gang members to their countries of origin. Between 2000 and 2004, an estimated 20,000 criminals were sent back to Central America.[42]

U.S. drug policy also has had a major influence in the reshaping of cartel networks and power. In the 1980s and early '90s, cocaine transport routes that ran through the Caribbean and South Florida were eventually shut down by American law enforcement. Yet the demand was too great and the profits too high to abandon trafficking. In time, cocaine and other drugs started flowing through Mexico and across the border in trucks, carried by human "mules" through the desert and by air and sea. In 1990, half the cocaine smuggled into the United States passed through Mexico; today it is 90 percent, according to the Council on Foreign Relations.[43]

Relocation of shipment routes from the Caribbean to Mexico helped small Mexican drug operators morph into big drug lords who began producing more marijuana, poppies and methamphetamine themselves and using extreme violence to protect their franchises.

In the beginning the Colombian cartels paid the Mexican cartels in cash for their transportation services, but toward the end of the 1980s the Colombians began instead to offer percentages of cocaine from the shipments. "This arrangement provided a means for the Mexican organizations to actively distribute cocaine, resulting in the formation of formidable trafficking organizations in their own right," writes Customs official Tammaro.[44]

Latin American leaders have grown increasingly critical of U.S. drug policy and its influence on crime. According to Ethan Nadelmann, director of the New York-based Drug Policy Alliance, which seeks to end the war on drugs, the "prohibitionist approach" to drug control has "wreaked havoc throughout the region, generating crime, violence and corruption on a scale that far exceeds what the United States experienced during alcohol prohibition in the 1920s."

Nadelmann's comment is part of a February 2009 report by a distinguished regional group, the Commission on Drug Use and Democracy. Made up of journalists, academics and politicians, including three former

presidents — César Gaviria of Colombia, Ernesto Zedillo of Mexico and Fernando Henrique Cardoso of Brazil — the commission said the U.S. "war on drugs" had "failed."[45]

Shannon O'Neil, a fellow in Latin American studies at the Council on Foreign Relations, also blames U.S. policy for the drug trade's move from Colombia to Mexico. "After four decades and billions of dollars, the U.S. 'war on drugs' has pushed the epicenter of these illegal criminal networks closer to the U.S. border," she wrote.[46]

U.S. firearms policy — specifically the 2004 repeal of the U.S. ban on sales of assault-style weapons — also is seen as aiding Mexican cartels. According to the Mexican government, American arms smuggled across the border account for 90 percent of the confiscated arms in Mexico, which, ironically, has some of the toughest gun-control laws in the world.[47]

Transition to Democracy

Political factors within Latin America also have boosted organized crime groups. In Mexico, the powerful PRI Party, or Institutional Revolutionary Party (Partido Revolucionario Institucional), controlled the presidency for 70 years until 2000 and is widely thought to have protected drug traffickers as they cemented relationships with the Colombians in the 1980s and '90s.

In his new book on narco-trafficking, George Grayson, a professor of government at the College of William & Mary and an expert on Mexico, writes that during the PRI era, "drug dealers behaved discreetly, showed deference to public figures, spurned kidnapping, appeared with governors at their children's weddings, and although often allergic to politics, helped the hegemonic PRI discredit its opponents by linking them to drug-trafficking."[48]

But Vicente Fox and his National Action Party (PAN) upended those relationships when they defeated the PRI in 2000. Fox and his successor, Calderón, have made crime-fighting a top priority, exposing deeply entrenched corruption and a legal system unprepared to handle the complexities of organized crime. Historically, Mexican law enforcement agencies were an extension of the PRI's autocratic system and could impose order, but they were also tools of "patronage and political coercion," according to the Trans-Border Institute at the University of San Diego.[49]

CHRONOLOGY

1970s *President Richard M. Nixon launches "war on drugs," setting the stage for crime-fighting policy in Latin America.*

1980s-1990s *Central American nations confront severe armed conflicts with little resolution; Colombian cartels rise and fall.*

1980 Civil war breaks out in El Salvador; the 12-year conflict leads thousands of Salvadorans to seek asylum in the United States, including youths who form the Mara Salvatrucha (MS-13) gang in Los Angeles.

1982 Guatemala's Gen. Romeo Lucas Garcia, the last in a succession of repressive military leaders that oversaw a 36-year civil war, is overthrown.

1989 Pablo Escobar's Medellín Cartel murders leading Colombian presidential candidate Luis Carlos Galán and declares "total and absolute war" against the government.

1992 U.S. Drug Enforcement Administration's Kingpin strategy focuses investigative and enforcement efforts on specific drug trafficking organizations. . . . Brazilian military police storm Carandiru prison to put down a riot, leading to the massacre of 111 prisoners by police and other inmates.

1993 Escobar is killed in rooftop shootout with Colombian National Police.

1994 North American Free Trade Agreement (NAFTA) lowers trade barriers between United States, Mexico and Canada, eventually squeezing millions of Mexican farmers out of the market and stimulating migration to U.S.

1997 Latin American gang members arrested in sweeps by Los Angeles Police Department are deported, fueling the spread of gangs in Central America.

1998 Family organizations in Ciudad Juárez pressure Mexican government to investigate first of some 400 unsolved cases of murdered women. . . . Hugo Chávez is elected president of Venezuela; crime rates will quadruple in the next 11 years.

2000s *Mexican cartels take control of drug supply chain; U.S. commits unprecedented funds to fighting crime in region; some police and judicial reforms are introduced; violence in Mexico escalates. . . . U.S. Congress approves controversial Plan Colombia to fight drug trafficking and reduce the presence of cocaine in American communities.*

2001 Sinaloa Federation leader Joaquín "El Chapo" Guzmán escapes from Mexican prison. . . . Stricter immigration policies enacted after 9/11 attacks create new opportunities for human trafficking across U.S.-Mexico border.

2003 Film "City of God" poignantly illuminates Brazil's severe gang, arms and violence problems. . . . The Revolutionary Armed Forces of Colombia rebel group (FARC) is classified as a major drug trafficking organization. . . . Mexican Defense Department describes Los Zetas cartel as the most formidable organized crime death squad in Mexican history.

2004 FBI creates MS-13 National Gang Task Force.

2006 Felipe Calderón wins Mexican presidency and vows to curb crime and drug trafficking.

2007 State Department reports that 90 percent of cocaine flowing into the U.S. now comes through Mexico, up from 50 percent in 2000.

2008 U.S. Congress enacts Mérida Initiative providing Mexico and Central American countries with $1.4 billion over three years to fight crime and drugs. . . . Mexican Congress enacts criminal justice reforms, including oral trials where lawyers present a case in front of a judge instead of using entirely written procedures.

2009 President Mauricio Funes of El Salvador announces progressive national security plan targeting gang violence and crime. . . . Obama administration discontinues use of term "War on Drugs." . . . *Forbes* ranks "El Chapo" Guzmán as 41st among the 67 most powerful people in the world.

2010 Peru replaces Colombia as world's leading coca grower. . . . In June, 85 people are executed in a single day in Mexico, the deadliest day since President Calderón took office in 2006.

Cracking Down on Central American Gangs

Does the "iron fist" approach work?

Central American gangs, known as *maras*, have evolved into potent security threats in the region, stymieing law enforcement and terrorizing local communities. With shaved heads and intricate tattoos that brand their allegiance across their faces and bodies, machete-wielding mara members have achieved notoriety for their brutality and fearlessness.

With increasingly sophisticated transnational networks and links with better-organized and wealthy drug cartels, some groups, such as the Mara Salvatrucha (MS-13) and Mara 18, have grown from small-time street gangs focused on extortion into full-fledged crime syndicates. Their numbers, especially in Guatemala, El Salvador and Honduras, are staggering. The anti-mara division of the Honduran Community Police, for example, reported in 2007 there were about 70,000 Mara members in the country, including 800 leaders, 20,000 active members, 15,000 aspiring members or sympathizers, and 30,000 others who were either family members, collaborators or employers.[1]

Law enforcement authorities have been aware of the maras' growing ranks and barbarity, but there has been much disagreement on whether to focus on crackdowns or softer approaches like prevention and rehabilitation. The prevention argument seems to be gaining more traction as harsher policies — known as *mano dura* (iron fist) — like stiff jail sentences for gang members and youths with tattoos are increasingly seen as failing.

In 2006, the U.S. Agency for International Development suggested that law enforcement and prevention programs should receive equal emphasis and funding.[2] And an exhaustive 2007 report on gangs in the United States, many also operating in Central America, showed that social services to at-risk youth are far more effective than the law enforcement approach.[3]

In Los Angeles, for example, law enforcement agencies reported there are now six times as many gangs and at least double the number of gang members in the region since 1985, when the problem fully emerged, even after billions of dollars were spent on enforcement and deportation of members.

The research shows that when gang members have the opportunity to leave gangs early — such as by going back to school or finding a job — there is a lower risk of lasting repercussions later in life. Yet current hard-nosed policies, which typically involve arresting and imprisoning gang members, make it more difficult for them to quit. Prisons serve as "gangland finishing schools" and aggravate the problem, according to investigative journalist Ana Arana.[4]

In recent years, Congress has taken a greater interest in anti-gang efforts in Central America, appropriating roughly $7.9 million in 2008 and $5 million in 2009 to the cause,

Casas-Zamora, the Brookings fellow and former Costa Rican vice president, argues that Latin America's ongoing transition to democracy also has created new opportunities for criminals to influence policy.[50] As elections throughout the region have become more open and competitive and campaign spending has increased, criminals have seized opportunities to invest in politicians supportive of their interests, Casas-Zamora said. Weak enforcement of the few campaign finance laws also helps drug traffickers and their allies stay above the law.[51]

Colombia's shift to democracy stands as a counterpoint to the region's troubles. Aided by the U.S.-funded Plan Colombia, the government has relatively swiftly instituted wide-ranging reforms to the police and criminal justice systems. In time, all of the major Colombian drug lords of the 1980s were eliminated, including the Rodriguez Orijuela family in Calí, Jose Gonzalo Rodriguez Gacha in the central highlands and in Medellín the Ochoa family and Pablo Escobar.

Economic Woes

By the 1990s, most countries in Latin America were facing astronomical foreign debt and hyper-inflation. The new technocrats who replaced the previous authoritarian governments sought advice from the World Bank and the International Monetary Fund, which pushed free-market reforms like privatization of state-run businesses, free trade and foreign investment.

according to Clare Ribando Seelke, a specialist in Latin American Affairs at the Congressional Research Service who has written extensively on the Central American gang issue. [5] Maras have also blipped brighter on Washington radar because of potential ties to terrorist groups.

Maras have been reported to be in contact with al Qaeda, according to Interpol, the international, police agency, and are heavily involved in the human-smuggling business between Central America and the United States. [6]

A few small nongovernmental organizations (NGOs) in Central America have had some success preventing youths from joining gangs and rehabilitating gang members, such as, Jovenes Hondureños Adelante Juntos, or Young Honduras Going Forward Together. Jovel, a member of the group, is now is working to document extrajudicial killings of gang members, an ugly part of *mano dura* policies in Honduras. [7]

Yet the government's own programs have been less than exemplary. "Government-sponsored gang prevention programs have tended, with some exceptions, to be small-scale, ad-hoc, and underfunded," says Ribando Seelke. "Governments have been even less involved in sponsoring rehabilitation programs for individuals seeking to leave gangs, with most reintegration programs funded by church groups or NGOs."

With few places to turn, some gang members have sought asylum in the United States, with varying degrees of success. In an especially memorable case in 2008, the U.S. Board of Immigration Appeals rejected the plight of three Salvadoran teenagers trying to flee the MS-13. [8] More recently, other former Central American gang members have failed to convince American judges to grant them asylum.

"There are gangs everywhere here," said Nelson Benítez Ramos, a Salvadoran and former MS-13 member who has also been unable to win asylum. "When you leave the gangs, even your best friend will murder you." [9]

— *Eliza Barclay*

[1] "Honduras: The presence and activities of the gangs, Mara Salvatrucha (MS) and Mara 18 in Honduras, including their structure, the role of women, and the effectiveness of anti-Mara government measures (2007-January 2010)," Immigration and Refugee Board of Canada, Jan. 28, 2010, www.unhcr.org/refworld/publisher,IRBC,,HND,4b8631d919,0.html.

[2] "Central America and Mexico Gang Assessment," U.S. Agency for International Development, Bureau for Latin America and Caribbean Affairs, April 2006, www.usaid.gov/gt/docs/gangs_assessment.pdf.

[3] "Gang Wars: The Failure of Enforcement Tactics and the Need for Effective Public Safety Strategies," Justice Policy Institute, July 17, 2007, www.justicepolicy.org/content-hmID=1811&smID=1581&ssmID=22.htm.

[4] Ana Arana, "How the Street Gangs Took Central America," *Foreign Affairs*, May/June 2005, www.foreignaffairs.com/articles/60803/ana-arana/how-the-street-gangs-took-central-america.

[5] Clare Ribando Seelke, "Gangs in Central America," Congressional Research Service, Dec. 4, 2009, www.fas.org/sgp/crs/row/RL34112.pdf.

[6] Ronald Noble, "Opening remarks at Interpol's 20th Americas Regional Conference," April 1, 2009, www.interpol.int/public/ICPO/speeches/2009/20090401SG_ARC20.asp.

[7] "San Pedro Sula, Honduras — Jovel, 27, a worker of JHA-JA," Jovenes Hondureños Adelante Juntos Avancemos, http://estria.net/media/docs/3894_massacre_mural.pdf.

[8] Julia Preston, "Losing Asylum, Then His Life," *The New York Times*, June 28, 2010, www.nytimes.com/2010/06/29/us/29asylum.html.

[9] Quoted in *ibid*.

But in hindsight, some development experts argue that these neoliberal reforms did significant damage, pushing even more people into poverty. As public funds were channeled away from social programs, safety nets eroded. And as free trade subjected small farmers — Honduran coffee growers and Mexican corn planters, for example — to the brutally competitive global market, millions of rural people, unable to compete with heavily subsidized U.S. agricultural products flowing into their countries, migrated to the cities or to the United States.

Indeed, globalization has increased inequality and exacerbated poverty in some ways in Latin America, according to a 2010 study by the United Nations University.[52] And as a well-known 2002 study in the *Journal of Law and Economics* showed, income inequality and reduced economic activity are significantly related to growing crime rates.[53]

The theory goes like this: a poor economy in the short-run reduces opportunities for citizens to take part in the legal economy, increasing the attractiveness of criminal behavior. Meanwhile, the wealthy fraction of the population becomes a potential criminal target, while another, larger fraction remains very low income and sees little downside in engaging in criminal activities.[54]

The theory largely was proven in Argentina, where a rapidly widening gap between rich and poor paralleled a jump in crime. After Argentina's peso crisis in 2001, the number of people in extreme poverty doubled, while criminologists also began to see a rising number of minors with guns, according to Marcelo Saín, a professor of political science at the National University of Quilmes in Buenos Aires. Saín sees a link between crime, robberies and high urban poverty.

Drug traffickers also fill a key economic and social role in impoverished communities.

"If you were sick and had no money, they'd take you to the hospital and pay for medicine. If you couldn't afford tortillas, they'd buy some for you," said Veronica Medina, a successful businesswoman from Michoacán, a Mexican state where the La Familia Michoacán cartel operates.[55]

Meanwhile, as the recession has battered the region, gang recruitment has become increasingly easy in Mexico and Central America. Mexico's economy, which is heavily reliant on tourism, remittances and exports, has been hit harder than the United States, as remittances from family members in the United States have tumbled. Immigration, which has long provided lucrative opportunities for many young Latin Americans, is also no longer an option for many. Fewer jobs are available in the United States, and increased border security has made illegal entry more expensive and dangerous.

"The number of uneducated youth is increasing, while the jobs for them are decreasing, which opens the opportunity to enter the criminal workforce," says author Logan. "Now you have these deportees in urban centers who are increasingly involved in sub-contract work for the cartels, driving trucks full of cocaine, for example."

Youth Explosion

High fertility rates and poor access to contraception in the overwhelmingly Roman Catholic region during the 1980s meant the birth of many unwanted children in the 1970s and '80s. Such children, psychologists and sociologists have long argued, are often raised without love and are likely to drift into crime. In Latin America, a sexist, macho culture limits women's empowerment and tolerates men's irresponsibility, limiting the use of contraception.

In recent years, though, experts have begun to promote family planning as a poverty- and crime-alleviation tool. Norman Loayza, lead economist in the research

department of the World Bank, has argued that women need to be empowered to use contraceptives, but that men also need to take more responsibility for the children they father. "More than a particular form of birth control, it's responsible parenthood which holds the key for crime prevention," Loayza, a Peruvian, wrote in *ReVista*, the *Harvard Review of Latin America.*[56]

Nonetheless, many of the children, wanted or not, born in Latin America in recent years have been born into poverty. Almost 63 percent of Latin American and Caribbean children and adolescents suffer some level of poverty, according to a joint report this summer from several United Nations agencies.[57] "Even when children [are] in a situation of 'moderate poverty,' and not so exposed in their living conditions, their future opportunities are seriously curtailed," authors Ernesto Espíndola and María Nieves Rico said in a statement.

Another U.N. report, from UNICEF, showed that from the early 1990s until the beginning of the current decade, child poverty increased in 13 of 17 Latin American countries. The increases were at least 3 percent in Argentina, Brazil, El Salvador, Panama, Costa Rica, Uruguay and Venezuela. Poverty levels only improved in four countries: Nicaragua, Peru, Paraguay and Chile.[58]

Youth unemployment, meanwhile, remains three times higher than for adults, according to the International Labor Organization (ILO). A 2007 ILO study found that 20 percent of youths ages 15 to 24 do nothing during the day, while 34 percent are in school and nearly the same number work. "Some 30 million young people work in the informal economy, mostly under bad working conditions," the report said, while "some 22 million youth neither work nor study due to lack of opportunities or frustration, making them a social risk."[59]

As writer Guillermoprieto recently noted, "We failed to realize that these young people, the *no-futuros*, would become the workforce and the cannon fodder for a phenomenon that is undermining the social stability of one country after another: the worldwide traffic in illegal narcotics."

Guillermoprieto also laments that the young people who are lured into the drug trade can be the most intelligent youths in the community, who are willing to risk their lives for trendy shoes or cars.[60]

CURRENT SITUATION

Violence in Mexico

As the violence in Mexico persists seemingly unabated, the country remains a focal point in the region. The deadliest day in Mexico since Calderón took office was June 11, with 85 drug-related murders. Among the killings that day were the execution-style shootings of 19 people in a drug rehabilitation center.[61] With more than 28,000 people — including civilians, police and drug traffickers killed since Calderón became president — his anti-crime strategies are increasingly seen as failing.[62] "[Calderón] has lost the reins of the country, not partially but totally," the influential journalist and columnist Lydia Cacho wrote recently.[63]

But Calderón is aware that the image of his administration and party is suffering, and he is fighting back with both a renewed commitment to end the violence and a public relations campaign to woo back investors and tourists. In a two-page column in mid-June in papers across the country, Calderón blamed the drug violence on American hunger for drugs and the cartels' easy access to arms coming across the border, along with a lack of opportunities for education and employment. He also defended his policies, noting that the violence is linked to the weakening and splintering of criminal groups, as his police forces have put cartel leaders on the defensive.[64] "If the government were to stop fighting the criminals, there are those who think this would end the violence. I doubt it," Calderón said in remarks on Aug. 4.[65]

Indeed, Logan of Southern Pulse says some leaders of the Zetas and Sinaloa Federation have retreated into Guatemala, where local law enforcement poses little threat, and Mexican law enforcement cannot reach them. "But Guatemala is also a strategic move for these groups because the local criminal groups are not that strong, or well-organized, so they're easy to topple," says Logan.

Organized crime experts also applaud the Mexican government's recent efforts to attack money laundering, which they see as an under-exploited weak spot of the cartels. Mexican banks receive more than $10 billion a year in cash from shady sources, the Finance Ministry says. (U.S. analysts estimate the value of drug-related funds flowing to Mexico at $29 billion.) In June the Finance Ministry announced new rules aimed at cartels that limit bank deposits of U.S. cash to no more than $7,000 a month.[66]

With the $1.4 billion Mérida Initiative slowly moving forward, cooperation between U.S. and Mexican law enforcement agencies also seems to be improving. In 2009, Mexico extradited 107 people to the United States on drug trafficking and other charges. Mexico also warmly received the U.S. government's decision to send 1,200 troops to the border and share intelligence with police in violence-ravaged Ciudad Juárez.[67]

Yet some experts believe these measures will be insufficient. "The U.S. government has spent over a decade taking similar measures, placing the National Guard at the border and building a wall, but there is no significant impact on the flow of drugs or undocumented workers," said Jorge Chabat, a political science professor at Mexico City's Center for Economic Research and Education.[68]

As part of its crime crackdown, Mexico is implementing widespread judicial reforms. With only about 5 percent of Mexican criminal cases ending up in a sentence, criminal justice experts say the reforms are sorely needed. The Mexican Congress enacted the sweeping measures in March 2008, taking aim at three areas: alternative sentencing; greater emphasis on the rights of the accused, such as a presumption of innocence and receiving an adequate legal defense; and changes to police agencies and their role in criminal investigations. As of May, however, the judicial reforms had been implemented in only 13 of Mexico's 31 states, according to the Trans-Border Institute.[69]

Guatemala, meanwhile, is confronting widespread, high-level corruption with few remedies in sight. Carlos Castresana, a Spanish judge, resigned in June as head of the U.N.'s International Commission Against Impunity in Guatemala, saying it was impossible to work with government counterparts who protect criminals.

"There is criminal activity including drug trafficking, murders, contraband, people-trafficking and [authorities who] enable criminal activity by guaranteeing impunity," said Castresana. "The country's institutions are infiltrated." Indeed, Castresana said there was widespread corruption in the judiciary, the interior ministry and the attorney general's office, including the recently appointed attorney general himself.[70]

Drug Trade Spreading

Drug trafficking appears to be spreading to new areas of Latin America. Southern Pulse Networked Intelligence sources show an uptick in drug trafficking activity in

Six police officers allegedly working for a drug cartel are accused of the Aug. 16 kidnapping and murder of Mayor Edelmiro Cavazos of Santiago, an affluent city near the Mexican-U.S. border previously considered immune from cartel violence. Police said seven SUVs rolled up to Cavazos' palatial home and that men in police uniforms abducted the U.S-educated mayor. His body was found on a nearby road, shot in the head.

Honduras and Nicaragua, which have historically played relatively minor roles as transit points for cocaine. Authorities in both countries have recently discovered clandestine airfields used by drug traffickers.[71]

Peru, which has long been overshadowed by Colombia in drug trafficking and violence, has earned a new, unwelcome distinction. The annual report by the U.N. Office on Drugs and Crime (UNODC), released in June, found that coca leaf production — used to make cocaine — in Colombia dropped from 2008 to 2009, and that Peru is now the world's leading coca grower.[72] Some 45 percent of the world's coca now comes from Peru, compared with 39 percent from Colombia and 15 percent in Bolivia, according to UNODC.

UNODC Executive Director Antonio Maria Costa said that despite the crime rise in Peru, overall coca acreage in Columbia, Peru and Bolivia dropped by 5 percent in 2009, due to the large decline in Colombia. Cocaine production there also fell from 672 tons in 2007 to 460 tons in 2009.[73]

Experts say the progress is largely due to Columbia's tougher drug control policy — combining security and development. "If the current trend continues, Peru will soon overtake Colombia as the world's biggest coca producer — a notorious status that it has not had since the mid-1990s," Costa said in a statement. However, Peru's

UNODC representative, Humberto Chirinos, says it is likely that Colombia still produces more coca than Peru.[74]

Members of the Shining Path guerrilla group, which terrorized Peru in the 1980s and '90s, today work as hired guns for drug traffickers, authorities say. And a recent U.N. report suggests members have split into two factions fighting to be the mercenaries of choice for the Mexican and Colombian cartels.[75] Meanwhile, Venezuela has become the principal exporter of cocaine to Europe and the origin of "all clandestine air deliveries detected in Western Africa" and of cargoes destined for clandestine air strips in Honduras, the report said.

Brazil seems to be turning a corner in fighting crime, most notably in Rio de Janeiro. In 2008 there were 29 murders in the infamous Cidade de Deus favela, where the "City of God" documentary was filmed, while this year there has been just one, and it did not involve a firearm, says Rio security chief José Beltrame. Other crime has fallen, too. "It was horror before," Jeanne Barbosa, a favela resident, told *The Economist*. "Bodies would be thrown out of passing cars, and there were kids with revolvers. Now the children can play in the street."[76]

But while Rio's outsized murder rate may be plunging, its drug consumption — along with drug use in São Paolo and Buenos Aires — is rising, especially among the middle and upper classes. Ecstasy has become especially popular in the nightlife scene; Brazil's federal police said they seized 211,000 Ecstasy pills in 2007, 17 times as many as the year before. However, the seizures declined to about 133,000 pills in 2008, possibly reflecting stiffer trafficking penalties.[77]

In 2006, the minimum penalty for drug trafficking was raised to 8 to 20 years, with no minimum quantity of drugs to constitute "dealing."[78]

As arrests increase, some countries are beginning to explore drug decriminalization to deal with their own drug problems, as well as prison overcrowding, organized crime and violence. In 2009, Mexico decriminalized possession of small amounts of heroin, cocaine and other drugs, although critics say that so far its impact has been greater on policy discussions than on Mexican streets.[79] Argentina's Supreme Court ruled the arrest of five young people holding a small quantity of marijuana was unconstitutional. And Brazil is also considering using education instead of jail sentences for small drug offenses.

Did Latin America's transition to democracy lead to rising crime?

YES

Luis Astorga
*Researcher, Institute of Social Research,
National Autonomous University of Mexico;
coordinator, UNESCO Chair on Economic
and Social Transformations Connected with the International
Drug Problem*

Writtin for *CQ Global Researcher*, August 2010

The state created after the Mexican Revolution built security institutions with extralegal power that allowed the state to do two things: protect and contain drug trafficking. Drug trafficking was born under political control, and it maintained this status throughout the rule of the Partido Revolucionario Instutitional (PRI).

But this dynamic began to shift just as the PRI's party system was weakening and fracturing. The world market for illegal drugs was booming, and traffickers' economic capacity for corruption and access to more serious firearms meant their destructive power was greater. At the same time the state's controls were disappearing, and the country was transitioning toward democracy.

Security and the challenges posed by the powerful trafficking organizations weren't a priority for the political class in the first years of the transition, after Vicente Fox of the Partido Accion Nacional (PAN) beat the PRI candidate in 2000 and became president. The political parties were more interested in new opportunities to gain more and better positions of power. But in the scramble for power they forgot to build the institutions of security and justice accordingly for the new era. The result was a fragmentation of the state and the development of a major weakness in confronting defiant criminal groups who went from subordination to politicians to directly confronting them and testing the authority of security institutions.

Some criminal organizations developed a new strategy of territorial expansion and diversified their revenue sources to include, for example, extortion, kidnapping, human trafficking and the sale of pirated goods. The lack of substantive political agreements during the Fox administration and the difficult and polemic circumstances of Calderón's arrival in office ensured the continuation of political strife that would not permit the government in the short term to reach the necessary agreements to reform and consolidate the security and justice agencies.

The unsuccessful use of the military has also made the enemy more tenacious than was expected. The traffickers have become more aggressive not only toward each other but also toward the police, military and other security figures and civil society. Under these conditions the traffickers may continue escalating their use of violence, either in the traditional or terrorist sense, until one group or coalition gains hegemony or the democratic state can impose authority and assert the rules of the game.

NO

Marcelo Bergman
*Professor, Department of Legal Studies,
Center for Economic Research and Education,
Mexico City*

Written for *CQ Global Researcher*, August 2010

Crime has been rising steadily throughout Latin America. Far from being a local problem for a few countries, the high level of criminality is a genuine regional phenomenon.

Most people in the region have been victimized over the last five years, and public outcry has increased due to the states' disappointing performance in fighting public insecurity.

Some theories have claimed that the transition to democracy ushered in unintended consequences. For example, some say the problem was police forces whose hands were tied after new democratic ideals enabled delinquents to feel less threatened, generating higher criminality. But the political factor is just one explanation, and not the only one.

Crime rose in response to a massive economic transformation in the region, including:

- New waves of foreign and local investment;
- New policies promoting consumption, and
- New optimism, which translated into lower and middle classes with higher levels of consumption.

These factors led to the emergence of groups willing to meet a new market demand. In short, conditions were ripe for the emergence of organized crime that posed a challenge to both legal markets and formal authorities. The rise in criminality is largely due to the organization of markets of illegal goods.

Organized crime usually is associated with the Mafia or drug cartels. These are, of course, well-developed and established criminal organizations. However, the emergence of organized crime in Latin America is closely related to the development of markets of small- and medium-sized organizations that developed to supply illicit goods.

Starting in the 1980s and particularly in the '90s, new economic conditions led entrepreneurs in the region to supply goods and services for the growing demand of new consumer groups. The impoverished but nonetheless voracious new consumers demanded products at a very low price that only illegal activities could deliver. And these low prices were possible because the likelihood of detection and punishment of criminals was very low.

In short, the rise in crime is explained greatly by the growth of organized crime. The two main variables that contributed to its explosive growth are the rapid increase in demand for cheap goods and services and the fragmentation of deterrence that yielded poor law-enforcement agency performance.

In February, however, the Vienna-based International Narcotics Control Board (INCB) expressed anxiety over Latin America's "growing movement to decriminalize the possession of controlled drugs, in particular cannabis." The board worried "the movement . . . will undermine national and international efforts to combat the abuse of and illicit trafficking in narcotic drugs and . . . poses a threat to the coherence and effectiveness of the international drug control system."[80]

OUTLOOK

Signs of Optimism

Given the deep roots of the region's crime problem and the need for systemic reforms that can't be implemented overnight, the immediate future looks rather grim to many analysts. But with time, some countries may be able to control organized crime, though it may have to get worse before it gets better. Other countries have brighter near-term prospects of building on recent reforms and increasing security for their citizens.

Buscaglia of ITAM University sees Mexico's drug-related violence worsening as organized crime groups expand their turf. But more strife is the only thing that will force the government to make crucial reforms to the criminal justice system and punish guilty parties at the highest levels, he says. He sees the escalation of violence in Colombia in the 1990s and the subsequent comprehensive response by the government as a useful, if ominous, roadmap for Mexico.

"The kidnappings, extortions and killings have to collectively reach the business and political elite in the realm of hundreds of cases a week," Buscaglia says. "There comes a point, where the political and business elite will start to demand drastic changes as they did in Colombia."

Among other things, members of the country's powerful oligarchy must push legislators to pass tougher laws to hamper the economic power of organized crime, Buscaglia says. In a worst-case scenario, he says Calderón could end up like President Hamid Karzai of Afghanistan, with little control over outlying provinces and their warlords.

But such predictions seem too pessimistic to the authors of "Five Myths about Mexico's Drug War," who say "violence is not as widespread or as random as it may appear" and that "organized crime is not threatening to take over the federal government. . . . Mexico is not turning into a failed state."[81]

Colombia, though, even with its new president also committed to fighting drug trafficking and crime, may be on a collision course with Venezuela over its alleged harboring of drug-trafficking FARC leaders in its wild western region.

"Venezuela is providing a safe haven for the FARC, and that's a big problem for Colombia," says Mejía at the University of the Andes. "Venezuela is not going to cooperate, and that makes it hard to catch the top command of FARC and extradite them to the United States." Mejía adds that this dynamic will be among the biggest diplomatic and security challenges of President Santos' fledgling administration.

In Central America, Logan of Southern Pulse Networked Intelligence says President Mauricio Funes of El Salvador has sent an encouraging signal to the region in the form of a new national security plan aimed at the root causes of crime and violence. Funes has allocated funds for community centers, roads and soccer fields, targeting the listless, impoverished youth who might otherwise be sucked into gangs.

"He had something entirely new with a robust prevention element, so it's not just a *mano dura* [iron fist] approach," said Logan. "This is a very progressive and forward thinking way to get at national security that may, if successful, become a model for security policy in the region."

Poverty also seems to be decreasing throughout the region and is expected to continue to decline, which bodes well for some of the economic factors behind the crime wave. Between 2002 and 2008, the percentage of people living in extreme poverty dropped from 19 percent of the population to 12 percent, according to the Economic Commission for Latin America and the Caribbean (CEPAL). Brazil, Peru and Chile all made notable progress, though CEPAL has cautioned that the global recession may slow the battle against extreme poverty.[82]

At the same time, U.S. and Latin American authorities are confident their countries will continue honing their ability to find and arrest criminals. Cooperation is especially key in an age of transnational crime, where cartel and gang leaders conduct business across multiple borders. Tammaro, of U.S. Immigration and Customs Enforcement, believes that the highly successful joint operation with Colombian and Mexican law enforcement that netted cargo containers filled with cash may have signaled a new era of intelligence sharing.

"To challenge the adaptability of transnational crime, the law enforcement community needs to share its raw material: information," Tammaro writes. "Building a capability that emphasizes coordinated intelligence collection and analysis brings the community closer to this goal."[83]

NOTES

1. Julio Scherer García, "Proceso en la guarida de 'El Mayo' Zambada," *Proceso*, April 3, 2010, www.proceso.com.mx/rv/modHome/detalleExclusiva/78067.

2. *Ibid.* See also Tracy Wilkinson, "Mexican drug lord Ismael Zambada, in a rare interview, says his death wouldn't hurt drug trade," *Los Angeles Times*, April 5, 2010, http://articles.latimes.com/2010/apr/05/world/la-fg-mexico-zambada5-2010apr05.

3. For background see Peter Katel, "Mexico's Drug War," *CQ Researcher*, Dec. 12, 2008, pp. 1009-1032, and Roland Flamini, "The New Latin America," *CQ Global Researcher*, March 2008, pp. 57-84.

4. "Report on Citizen Security and Human Rights," Inter-America Commission on Human Rights, Dec. 31, 2009, http://cidh.org/countryrep/Seguridad.eng/citizensecurity.toc.htm.

5. "A slow maturing of democracy," *The Economist Latinobarómetro* poll, Dec. 10, 2009, www.economist.com/world/americas/displaystory.cfm?story_id=E1_TVDRDVPV.

6. Randal C. Archibold, "72 Migrants Found Dead On a Ranch in Mexico," *The New York Times*, Aug. 26, 2010, p. A4.

7. Ronald Noble, "Opening remarks at Interpol's 20th Americas Regional Conference," April 1, 2009, www.interpol.int/public/ICPO/speeches/2009/20090401SG_ARC20.asp.

8. Mark Townsend, "How Liverpool docks became a hub of Europe's deadly cocaine trade," *The Guardian*, May 16, 2010, www.guardian.co.uk/world/2010/may/16/liverpool-cocaine-mexico-cartels.

9. Jon Lee Anderson, "Gangland," *The New Yorker*, Oct. 5, 2009, www.newyorker.com/reporting/2009/10/05/091005fa_fact_anderson.

10. Tracy Wilkinson and Ken Ellingwood, "Mexico drug cartels thrive despite Calderon offensive," *Los Angeles Times*, Aug. 8, 2010, http://articles.latimes.com/2010/aug/08/world/la-fg-mexico-cartels-20100808.

11. Simon Romero, "More Killings in Venezuela Than in Iraq," *The New York Times*, Aug. 23, 2010, p. A1, www.nytimes.com/2010/08/23/world/americas/23venez.html.

12. Marcelo Bergman, "The Integration of Common Crime and Organized Crime in Latin America, Woodrow Wilson International Center for Scholars, May 19, 2010, www.wilsoncenter.org/index.cfm?fuseaction=events.event_summary&event_id=607885.

13. "Mexico: Killings and abductions of women in Ciudad Juarez and the City of Chihuahua — the struggle for justice goes on," Amnesty International Public Statement, Feb. 20, 2006, www.amnestyusa.org/document.php?id=engamr410122006&lang=e.

14. Victoria Sanford, "A Daily Threat," *ReVista: Harvard Review of Latin America*, winter 2008, www.drclas.harvard.edu/revista/articles/view/1035.

15. John Burnett, "Mexican Cartels Recruiting Young Men, Boys," NPR, March 24, 2009, www.npr.org/templates/story/story.php?storyId=102249839.

16. Matt Ingram and David A. Shirk, "Judicial Reform in Mexico: Toward a New Criminal Justice System," Trans-Border Institute, University of San Diego, May 2010, www.justiceinmexico.org/resources/pdf/judicial_reform.pdf.

17. Steve Fainaru and William Booth, "Mexico Accused of Torture in Drug War," *The Washington Post*, July 9, 2009, www.washingtonpost.com/wp-dyn/content/article/2009/07/08/AR2009070804197_pf.html.

18. "Report on Citizen Security and Human Rights," *op. cit.*

19. Michael Shifter, "A Decade of Plan Colombia: Time for a New Approach," *Política Exterior*, June 21, 2010, www.thedialogue.org/page.cfm?pageID=32&pubID=2407&s=.

20. "Inter-American Dialogue Offers Obama 10-point pragmatic Agenda for Latin America & Caribbean," www.thedialogue.org/page.cfm?pageID=435.

21. Samuel Logan, "Trafficking's Family Ties: Mexico," *Americas Quarterly*, spring 2010, p. 76, www.americasquarterly.org/charticle_spring2010.html.

22. Guy Lawson, "The War Next Door," *Rolling Stone*, Nov. 13, 2008, p. 75, http://guylawson.com/pdf/rollingstone/HowCartelsWork.pdf.

23. See Randal C. Archibold, "Mexican Police Arrest Man Believed to Be Drug Kingpin," *The New York Times*, Aug. 31, 2010, p. A6, and Nicholas Casey and Jose de Cordoba, "Alleged Drug Kingpin Is Arrested in Mexico," *The Wall Street Journal*, Aug. 31, 2010, p. A10.

24. Andrew Tammaro, "U.S. Immigration and Customs Enforcement: Combating Bulk Cash Smuggling," *The Police Chief*, March 2010, p. 28, http://policechiefmagazine.org/magazine/index.cfm?fuseaction=display&article_id=2036&issue_id=32010.

25. Ingram and Shirk, *op. cit.*

26. Philip Alston, "Statement at End of Brazil Mission," United Nations, Nov. 14, 2007, www.unhchr.ch/huricane/huricane.nsf/view01/7F0F08340A31AC6FC1257394003B5D47?opendocument.

27. William Booth, "Mexico's crime syndicates increasingly target authorities in drug war's new phase," *The Washington Post*, May 2, 2010, www.washingtonpost.com/wp-dyn/content/article/2010/05/01/AR2010050102869.html.

28. *Ibid.*

29. Andrew Selee, David Shirk and Eric Olson, "Five Myths about Mexico's Drug War," *The Washington Post*, March 28, 2010, p. B03, www.washingtonpost.com/wp-dyn/content/article/2010/03/26/AR2010032602226_pf.html.

30. "A magic moment for the City of God," *The Economist*, June 12, 2010, www.economist.com/node/16326428.

31. William Bratton and William Andrews, "Eight Steps to Reduce Crime," *Americas Quarterly*, spring 2010, p. 95, www.americasquarterly.org/node/1500.

32. *Ibid.*

33. *Ibid.*

34. *Ibid.*

35. See Romero, *op. cit.*, and "Venezuela Country Specific Information," U.S. State Department, travel.state.gov, http://travel.state.gov/travel/cis_pa_tw/cis/cis_1059.html#crime.

36. "Venezuela tackles crime, 20% of which committed by the police force," MercoPress, Dec. 8, 2009, http://en.mercopress.com/2009/12/07/venezuela-tackles-crime-20-of-which-committed-by-the-police-force.

37. Vanessa Plihal, "President accused of corruption while gangs reign in Guatemala," City Mayors Society, May 27, 2009, www.citymayors.com/society/guatemala-murders.html.

38. Kevin Casas-Zamora, "Dirty Money," *Americas Quarterly*, spring 2010, p. 57, www.americasquarterly.org/casas-zamora.

39. Alma Guillermoprieto, "Crime's Breeding Ground," *Americas Quarterly*, spring 2010, p. 50, www.americasquarterly.org/guillermoprieto.

40. "2010 Global Peace Index," Institute for Economics & Peace, www.visionofhumanity.org/.

41. Sanford, *op. cit.*

42. Clare Ribando Seelke, "Gangs in Central America," Congressional Research Service, Dec. 4, 2009, www.fas.org/sgp/crs/row/RL34112.pdf.

43. Shannon O'Neill, "Mexico-U.S. Relations: What's Next?" *Americas Quarterly*, spring 2010, p. 68, www.americasquarterly.org/node/1505.

44. Tammaro, *op. cit.*

45. Alexei Barrionuevo, "Latin America Weighs Less Punitive Path to Curb Drug Use," *The New York Times*, Aug. 26, 2009, www.nytimes.com/2009/08/27/world/americas/27latin.html. For background see Peter Katel, "War on Drugs," *CQ Researcher*, June 2, 2006, pp. 481-504.

46. O'Neill, *op. cit.*

47. Chris Hawley, "Mexico: Gun controls undermined by U.S.," *USA Today*, April 1, 2009, www.usatoday.com/news/world/2009-03-31-mexicoguns_N.htm.

48. George Grayson, *Mexico: Narco-Violence and a Failed State?* (2010), p. 29.

49. Ingram and Shirk, *op. cit.*

50. For background see Peter Katel, "Change in Latin America," *CQ Researcher*, July 21, 2006, pp. 601-624, and Kenneth Jost, "Democracy in Latin America," *CQ Researcher*, Nov. 3, 2000, pp. 881-904.

51. Casas-Zamora, *op. cit.*

52. Machiko Nissanke and Erik Thorbecke, "Globalization, Poverty, and Inequality in Latin America: Findings from Case Studies," *World Development*, Vol. 38, No. 6, p. 797-802, http://website1.wider.unu.edu/lib/pdfs/WD-38-6-10-1-Nissanke.pdf.

53. Pablo Fajnzylber, Daniel Lederman and Norman Loayza, "Inequality and Violent Crime," *Journal of Law and Economics*, April 2002, http://siteresources.worldbank.org/DEC/Resources/Crime&Inequality.pdf.

54. *Ibid.*

55. William Finnegan, "Silver or Lead," *The New Yorker*, May 31, 2010, p. 39, www.newyorker.com/reporting/2010/05/31/100531fa_fact_finnegan#ixzz0t41Pj DR5.

56. Norman Loayza, "Preventing Violence: Long-Run Crime Prevention Policies," *ReVista: Harvard Review of Latin America*, winter 2008, p. 9, www.drclas.harvard.edu/revista/articles/view/1032.

57. "Almost 63% of Children and Adolescents Suffer some Type of Poverty," Economic Commission for Latin America and the Caribbean, press release, June 22, 2010, www.eclac.cl/cgi-bin/getProd.asp?xml=/prensa/noticias/comunicados/1/39951/P39951.xml&xsl=/prensa/tpl-i/p6f.xsl&base=/tpl/top-bottom.xslt.

58. "Child Poverty in Latin America," *UNICEF Challenges Newsletter*, September 2005, www.unicef.org/lac/Desafios_1_ing(5).pdf.

59. "Unemployment, informality and inactivity menace young people in Latin America and the Caribbean," International Labor Organization, press release, Sept. 4, 2007, www.ilo.org/global/About_the_ILO/Media_and_public_information/I-News/lang-en/WCMS_083989/index.htm.

60. Guillermoprieto, *op. cit.*

61. Thomas Black, "Mexico Has 85 Organized-Crime Deaths, Bloodiest Day of Calderon Presidency," Bloomberg, June 11, 2010, www.bloomberg.com/news/2010-06-12/mexico-has-85-organized-crime-deaths-bloodiest-day-of-calderon-presidency.html.

62. Wilkinson and Ellingwood, *op. cit.*

63. Lydia Cacho, "PLAN B: Se acabó el sexenio, que sigue?" *Día Siete*, June 14, 2010, www.diasiete.com/14-06-2010/plan-b-se-acabo-el-sexenio-%C2%BFque-sigue.

64. Sara Miller Llana, "Mexico Drug War: Has Felipe Calderon lost control?" *The Christian Science Monitor*, June 16, 2010, www.csmonitor.com/World/Americas/2010/0616/Mexico-drug-war-Has-Felipe-Calderon-lost-control.

65. William Booth, "Mexican president calls for nation's help to curb defiant, violent criminals," *The Washington Post*, Aug. 8, 2010, www.washingtonpost.com/wp-dyn/content/article/2010/08/07/AR2010080702604.html.

66. Ken Parks and José de Córdoba, "Mexico Targets Cartels' Finances," *The Wall Street Journal*, June 16, 2010, http://online.wsj.com/article/SB10001424052748703280004575308730570231438.html?mod=WSJ_hpp_MIDDLENexttoWhatsNewsSecond.

67. Nacha Cattan, "Why Mexico Welcomes Obama's Plan to send 1,200 troops to the border," *The Christian Science Monitor*, May 26, 2010, www.csmonitor.com/World/Europe/2010/0526/Why-Mexico-welcomes-Obama-s-plan-to-send-1-200-US-troops-to-border.

68. *Ibid.*

69. Ingram and Shirk, *op. cit.*

70. Sarah Grainger, "Corruption deep in Guatemala's justice system," Reuters, June 14, 2010, www.alertnet.org/thenews/newsdesk/N14165292.htm.

71. "Nicaragua: More clandestine airfields discovered," Southern Pulse Networked Intelligence, June 21, 2010, www.alertnet.org/thenews/newsdesk/N14165292.htm, cited in *ibid.*

72. "Divergent coca crop cultivation trends in the Andean countries," United Nations Office on Drugs and Crime, press release, June 22, 2010, www.unodc.org/unodc/en/frontpage/2010/June/divergent-coca-cultivation-trends-in-the-andean-countries.html.

73. *Ibid.*

74. Kirsten Begg, "Peruvian president slams UN report," *Colombia Reports*, June 23, 2010, http://colombiareports.com/colombia-news/news/10436-peruvian-president-slams-un-coca-report.html.

75. Simon Romero, "Coca Production Makes a Comeback in Peru," *The New York Times*, June 13, 2010, www

.nytimes.com/2010/06/14/world/americas/14peru
.html.

76. "A magic moment for the City of God," *op. cit.*

77. Alexei Barrionuevo, "Ecstasy Ensnares Upper-Class Teenagers in Brazil," *The New York Times*, Feb. 14, 2009, www.nytimes.com/2009/02/15/world/americas/15ecstasy.html.

78. *Ibid.*

79. Dennis Wagner, "Drug law changes little for life in Mexico," *Arizona Republic*, Jan. 10, 2010, azcentral.com, www.azcentral.com/news/articles/2010/01/10/20100110mex-drugs.html#ixzz0wmbLvFfc.

80. Sara Miller Llana, "UN: Latin America undermining drug war by decriminalizing drugs," *The Christian Science Monitor*, Feb. 24, 2010, www.csmonitor.com/World/2010/0224/UN-Latin-America-undermining-drug-war-by-decriminalizing-drugs.

81. Selee, Shirk and Olson, *op. cit.*

82. Simon Romero, "Economies in Latin America Race Ahead," *The New York Times*, June 30, 2010, www.nytimes.com/2010/07/01/world/americas/01peru.html.

83. Tammaro, *op. cit.*

BIBLIOGRAPHY

Books

Bowden, Charles, *Murder City: Ciudad Juarez and the Global Economy's New Killing Fields, Nation Books*, 2010.
A Tucson-based investigative reporter explores the border town of Ciudad Juárez and its disintegration into crime and violence.

Bowden, Mark, *Killing Pablo: The Hunt for the World's Greatest Outlaw, Atlantic Monthly Press*, 2001.
The *Atlantic Monthly* writer tells the compelling story of the rise and fall of Pablo Escobar, the notorious Colombian cartel kingpin who became one of the drug trade's first billionaires.

Garzón, Juan Carlos, *Mafia & Co: The Criminal Networks in Mexico, Brazil, and Colombia, Planeta*, 2008.
A Colombian political scientist analyzes the inner workings and expansion of organized crime cartels in Latin America.

Rosenberg, Tina, *Children of Cain: Violence and the Violent in Latin America, Penguin*, 1992.
Though nearly 20 years old, this powerful work by a Pulitzer Prize-winning journalist continues to be relevant as an investigation into the question: Why is violence so endemic to the region?

Articles

"Narco-trafficking and Transnational Crime," *Americas Quarterly*, spring 2010, www.americasquarterly.org/current.
This issue is dedicated to drug trafficking and crime, with a wealth of informative articles on topics ranging from crime and politics to U.S.-Mexico relations to policing.

Anderson, Jon Lee, "Gangland," *The New Yorker*, Oct. 5, 2009, www.newyorker.com/reporting/2009/10/05/091005fa_fact_anderson.
Anderson takes a comprehensive look at the criminal gangs of Rio de Janeiro, Brazil, with a focus on Fernandinho — one of the most-wanted criminals in Rio — who lives openly in the city.

Corchado, Alfredo, "Two more arrests made in Juarez," *Dallas Morning News*, Aug. 17, 2006, www.amigosdemujeres.org/twomore.pdf.
The arrest by U.S. authorities of Mexican men believed to be part of a gang that raped and killed at least 10 women in Ciudad Juarez is hailed as a significant breakthrough in the slaying of hundreds of women in this area since 1993.

Finnegan, William, "Silver or Lead," *The New Yorker*, May 31, 2010, p. 39, www.newyorker.com/reporting/2010/05/31/100531fa_fact_finnegan#ixzz0t41PjDR5.
Finnegan investigates Mexico's La Familia Michoacán cartel and considers the widespread power of the country's drug traffickers.

Lawson, Guy, "The War Next Door," *Rolling Stone*, Nov. 13 2008, p. 75, www.rollingstone.com.
Lawson's look at the rise of criminal drug lords in Mexico focuses on the Sinaloa Federation and "El Chapo" Guzmán.

Scherer, Julio, "Proceso en la guarida de 'El Mayo' Zambada," *Proceso*, April 3, 2010, www.proceso.com.mx/rv/modHome/detalleExclusiva/78067.
The editor of a leading Mexican investigative magazine interviews El Mayo Zambada, the co-head of Mexico's most notorious drug trafficking organization, the Sinaloa Federation.

Reports and Studies

"Central America and Mexico Gang Assessment," *USAID Bureau for Latin America and Caribbean Affairs*, April 2006, www.usaid.gov/gt/docs/gangs_assessment.pdf.
The report explores the gang problem in Mexico and Central America, including the causes and costs.

"Crime and Development in Central America: Caught in the Crossfire," *United Nations Office on Drugs and Crime*, May 2007, www.unodc.org/pdf/research/Central_America_Study_2007.pdf.
The report looks at why Central America is vulnerable to crime and how crime is hurting development.

Ingram, Matt, and David A. Shirk, "Judicial Reform in Mexico: Towards a New Criminal Justice System," *Trans-Border Institute, University of San Diego*, May 2010, www.justiceinmexico.org/resources/pdf/judicial_reform.pdf.
The report describes the much-needed reforms approved in 2008 for Mexico's criminal justice system and the challenges and prospects for implementing them.

Fajnzylber, Pablo, Daniel Lederman and Norman Loayza, "Inequality and Violent Crime," *Journal of Law and Economics*, April 2002, http:// siteresources.worldbank.org/DEC/Resources/Crime&Inequality.pdf.
A key study of the link between income inequality and violent crime, with a focus on Latin America, concludes that income inequality has a significant effect on the incidence of crime.

Ribando Seelke, Clare, "Gangs in Central America," *Congressional Research Service*, Dec. 4, 2009, www.fas.org/sgp/crs/row/RL34112.pdf.
The report provides background on gangs and addresses anti-gang efforts at the country level and examines alternative approaches and responses to the problem.

For More Information

Americas Society/Council of the Americas, 680 Park Ave., New York, NY 10065; (212) 628-3200. The Society is a forum dedicated to education, debate and dialogue in the Americas; the Council is an international business organization for the hemisphere. The two jointly publish *Americas Quarterly* and co-host many events.

Fundación Paz Ciudadana (Citizen Peace Foundation), Valenzuela Castillo 1881, Providencia, Santiago, Chile; +56 363 3800. Dedicated to reducing crime in Chile.

Open Society Institute, 400 West 59th St., New York, NY 10019; (212) 548-0600. Works to build vibrant and tolerant democracies in Latin America.

Southern Pulse Networked Intelligence, www.southernpulse.com. An open-source, Web-based network on security, politics, energy and business in Latin America.

United Nations Office on Drugs and Crime, regional offices throughout Latin America; www.unodc.org. Develops multilateral partnerships to combat "problems without borders" including drugs, crime and terrorism.

Washington Office on Latin America, 1666 Connecticut Ave., N.W., Suite 400, Washington, DC 20009; (202) 797-2171. Promotes human rights, democracy and social and economic justice in Latin America and the Caribbean.

Woodrow Wilson International Center for Scholars, Ronald Reagan Building and International Trade Center, One Woodrow Wilson Plaza, 1300 Pennsylvania Ave., N.W., Washington, DC 20004-3027; (202) 691-4000; http:// wilsoncenter.org. Provides a nonpartisan forum through its Latin American Program.

Voices From Abroad:

LAURA CHINCHILLA

President, Costa Rica

Violence has several causes

"Lack of access to opportunities, inequalities, and the increase in drug trafficking, as well as organized crime have combined to create a highly explosive environment in Latin America on the issue of violence."

Prensa Libre (Costa Rica) May 2010

FELIPE CALDERÓN

President, Mexico

The problem is crime

"My goal is to free the citizenry from the oppression of criminals and not to eliminate drugs because that is simply impossible."

EFE news service (Spain) November 2009

NEIL MCKEGANEY

Professor of Drug Misuse Research, University of Glasgow, Scotland

Drugs cause political change

"The political change of heart in Latin America is a result of the devastating impact of the drugs trade in those countries — where multiple murder is a daily occurrence and where drug gangs have more weapons than the national army."

The Guardian (England) September 2009

CARLOS PASCUAL

U.S. Ambassador to Mexico

Crime drives up business costs

"We have already frozen the accounts of the Gulf cartel and Los Zetas, crippling their ability to use the financial system

Cagle Cartoons/El Universal, Mexico City/Angel Boligan

and move money for their operations. The cost of doing business is increasing due to the violence generated by criminal organizations."

EFE news service (Spain) April 2010

FERNANDO HENRIQUE CARDOSO

Former President, Brazil

Addressing the problem differently

"The status of addicts must change from that of drug buyers in the illegal market to that of patients cared for in the public health system. Police activities can then be better focused on the fight against the drug lords and organised crime."

The Observer (England)

JOSÉ SERRA

Presidential Candidate, Brazilian Social Democracy Party

Bolivia is weak

"I hate cocaine because it is a disgrace to mankind, to Bolivia, to Latin America, and to Brazil. I believe the Bolivian Government is weak in terms of fighting cocaine."

La Razon (Bolivia), August 2010

CHRIS BRYANT

Foreign Affairs Minister, United Kingdom

Stemming the tide

"The drugs trade in Latin America is a big and violent business. Cartels battle for local control, and ordinary members of the public are mown down in the crossfire. That is why we must continue working with Latin American governments to tackle the corruption and stop the violence."

The Independent (England) October 2009

GEOVANY DOMINGUEZ

Senior Editor, El Tiempo, Honduras

Intimidating reporters

"You get the impression that the government wants you in terror so you don't know what to report. At the end you don't report anything that will make powerful people uncomfortable."

EFE news service (Spain) July 2010

13

Democracy in Southeast Asia

Barbara Mantel

A grieving woman fondly touches a banner honoring former Philippines President Corazon ("Cory") Aquino, who died last August. Aquino is revered for leading the nonviolent People Power movement in 1986 that toppled dictator Ferdinand Marcos and restored democracy. Her son Benigno ("Noynoy") was elected president on May 10, vowing to end widespread government corruption.

From *CQ Researcher*, June 2010.

I t was a bizarre, unsettling scene and, inevitably, it turned ugly. For months, thousands of red-shirted anti-government protesters demanding new elections had camped amid the shimmering skyscrapers of downtown Bangkok, one of Southeast Asia's most modern urban centers. In recent weeks, however, the protests exploded into some of the worst political violence in Thailand's modern history. The clashes erupted on May 13, after a sniper shot a renegade Thai general as he stood talking with a *New York Times* reporter.

The next day troops blockaded the area and "fired tear gas and bullets at protesters, who responded with stones, slingshots and homemade rockets, turning parts of downtown Bangkok into a battlefield," a reporter wrote.[1] After nearly a week of violent street fighting, the military reclaimed the city and arrested several protest leaders. Nearly 100 people were killed and more than 1,000 injured during the nine weeks of demonstrations.[2]

After protest leaders surrendered on May 19, restaurant owner Wanpamas Boonpun, 39, tried to explain why some of the demonstrators felt let down by protest leaders. "We want democracy," she said. "True democracy, free democracy. Why is it so hard? Why?"[3]

Drawn mostly from the country's rural and urban poor, the red shirts support former Prime Minister Thaksin Shinawatra, a billionaire businessman elected in 2001 after promising services to the country's poor. He was ousted five years later in a military coup and eventually fled abroad to avoid arrest for a corruption conviction.

Indonesians Are Freest in Southeast Asia

Indonesia is Southeast Asia's freest country, according to the latest annual survey of global political rights and civil liberties published by Freedom House, a U.S.-based human rights organization. The 2009 survey found that Cambodia, Laos, Myanmar (formerly Burma) and Vietnam were the least free, and the Philippines, Malaysia, Thailand and Singapore were partly free.

Levels of Freedom in Southeast Asia

Source: "Freedom in the World," Freedom House, 2010

He has denied government accusations that he masterminded the protests.

The violence exposed a deep rift in Thai society. The protesters argue that political power in Thailand "has long been dominated by the elite in Bangkok who have . . . neglected the voice of the majority poor in the rural north and northeast regions," says Pavin Chachavalpongpun, a fellow at the Institute of Southeast Asian Studies in Singapore. On the other hand, says Thongchai Winichakul, professor of history at the University of Wisconsin-Madison, Thailand's elites — including government bureaucrats, military leaders, the intelligentsia and members of the royal family — don't trust rural voters and think democracy "is a sophisticated set of systems that needs to be taught."

Indeed, elites hold tight to the reins of power across a diverse swath of Southeast Asia, from the military junta in brutally authoritarian Myanmar (formerly Burma) to the family dynasties who compete, often violently, for power in the chaotic elections of the Philippines. Both Laos and Vietnam are legally one-party states, while Cambodia and Singapore, despite elections, are effectively so. Malaysia holds competitive elections, but the media and freedom of assembly are so restricted the opposition cannot win at the national level. "I call that competitive authoritarianism," says Larry Diamond, a senior fellow at Stanford University's Freeman Spogli Institute for International Studies.

"The next rung up the ladder is electoral democracy," says Diamond. Indonesia and East Timor are the only electoral democracies in Southeast Asia, according to Freedom House, an independent watchdog organization that advocates for democracy and human rights. The Philippines and Thailand were considered electoral democracies until campaign violence in the former and the military coup in the latter caused Freedom House to change their status a few years ago.

Freedom House defines an electoral democracy as a state with:

- a competitive multiparty political system,
- universal adult suffrage for all citizens,
- regular elections with secret and secure ballots,
- absence of massive voter fraud,
- significant access of major political parties to the electorate through the media and open political campaigning.[4]

"But this designation of electoral democracy is in essence the minimum standard for democracy," says Christopher Walker, Freedom House's Director of Studies. "It does not suggest a full, consolidated democracy with all the checks and balances one would look for."

To determine which countries meet that higher standard, Freedom House analyzes political rights, which include the electoral process, government operations and political pluralism and participation. It also analyzes civil liberties, which include freedom of expression and belief, associational and organizational rights, the rule of law and personal autonomy and individual rights. It then determines whether a country is considered "free," "partly free," or "not free."[5] At the moment Indonesia is Southeast Asia's only "free" country.

Southeast Asian countries can rise in the rankings depending on how each faces its particular challenges. For instance, "for a repressive regime like Vietnam," says Walker, the challenge "is whether economic growth will translate into meaningful political liberalization or reform. The evidence to date suggests that it is not." Vietnam's gross domestic product (GDP) grew by an average of 7 percent a year during the past decade, until the 2009 global economic slowdown. Economic growth has occurred even faster in Cambodia, but it is not rising in the rankings; opposition parties are increasingly weak and elections far from fair.[6]

Problems with corruption and the rule of law confront the "free" and "partly free" countries, says Walker. "In Indonesia there have been efforts by senior law enforcement to hamper the work of anti-corruption bodies," says Walker, and several other countries "have had some tragedies and horrors," like the massacre in the Philippines last November when a powerful political family allegedly slaughtered 57 people, nearly half of them journalists, and the rest relatives and supporters of a political rival.[7]

Democratization depends on the public's support and desire for change. According to Diamond, pollsters have found that the public generally supports democracy in five of the region's "free" and "partly free" countries — Indonesia, the Philippines, Thailand, Singapore and Malaysia — with the highest levels of support, perhaps not surprisingly, in Indonesia.[8]

But what do respondents understand democracy to mean? The pollsters asked a series of questions to assess that, and the results vary markedly. For example, Indonesians have a high level of support for liberal values, like freedom of the press and judicial independence, according to Diamond.

However, in Thailand, "The data suggest there is a lot of support for democracy, but it is shallow," Diamond said in late April. "There is not a lot of commitment to democratic values like tolerance of opposition and freedom of the press and of association," he says, "and I think that is perfectly exhibited on the streets of the country now."

With democracy in most of Southeast Asia in distress, scholars, opposition parties, human rights activists and democracy advocates are asking these questions:

Should political parties boycott unfair elections?

In Southeast Asia, only Indonesia and East Timor are seen by international observers as holding free and fair elections.

Malaysia restricts press freedom and compresses campaigning into a two-week period that favors the ruling party; Singapore bankrupts opponents with defamation lawsuits and restricts freedom of assembly and the press. In the Philippines — where elections last month were marred by politically motivated murders — elections historically have been "corrupt and rife with rigging," says Bob Templer, director of the Asia Program at the International Crisis Group, a Brussels-based nonprofit that works to prevent and resolve deadly conflicts.

Myanmar's elections are perhaps drawing the most international scrutiny at the moment. The repressive military junta is expected to hold its first election in 20 years in October. In the last election — in 1990 — the regime lost in a landslide to the opposition National League for Democracy (NLD), but the junta refused to cede power and jailed dozens of NLD members, including party leader Daw Aung San Suu Kyi, who has spent 14 of the past 20 years under house arrest.[9]

But unlike the 1990 elections, which were considered to be free and fair, the upcoming polls are being condemned both inside and outside Myanmar as "a sham"[10] and "an insult to democracy."[11] The country's two-year-old constitution reserves 25 percent of parliamentary seats for the military, allows for the declaration of martial law and preserves draconian laws prohibiting freedom of speech, association and assembly. Three-month-old election rules bar candidates with criminal convictions, effectively eliminating Aung San Suu Kyi and any of the estimated 2,100 political prisoners from running for legislative office.[12]

The rules also require political parties to register with the state or be declared illegal, putting the opposition in the difficult position of having to decide whether to participate in elections it considers political theater or to boycott and become politically inconsequential.[13] In late March, the NLD leadership announced its controversial decision: It would boycott.

"Would political parties in the United States or other truly democratic states participate in an election that has laws that are so absurdly skewed in favor of one party?" asks Roshan Jason, executive director of the ASEAN Inter-Parliamentary Myanmar Caucus,* based in Kuala Lumpur, Malaysia. Caucus members — from parliaments across the region — press for democratic reform in Myanmar. "The NLD was left without a choice really."

"The NLD has only one [source of] leverage with the junta and that is depriving the generals of credibility and

---

Defining Freedom

Each year, Freedom House ranks countries as Free, Partly Free and Not Free. The group assigns each country a ranking of between 1 and 7. Nations with scores of between 1 and 2.5 are designated as "free" and considered electoral and liberal democracies. Countries between 3 and 5 are "partly free;" some may actually be electoral democracies, like Timor-Leste. Those with scores between 5.5 and 7 are "not free."[1]

Here are the three categories:

A *Free* country allows open political competition, a climate of respect for civil liberties, significant independent civic life and an independent media.

A *Partly Free* country has limited respect for political rights and civil liberties and often a high rate of corruption, weak rule of law, ethnic and religious strife and a dominant political party despite the façade of pluralism.

A *Not Free* country allows no basic political rights, and basic civil liberties are widely and systematically denied.

Source: "Freedom in the World, 2010," Freedom House

1 "Freedom in the World 2009, Methodology," Freedom House, 2009

---

* The caucus is a separate organization from ASEAN — the Association of Southeast Asian Nations — which was founded in 1967 to promote economic cooperation in the region. ASEAN now has 10 members: Indonesia, Malaysia, the Philippines, Singapore and Thailand, Brunei, Myanmar (Burma), Cambodia, Laos and Vietnam.

legitimacy in the eyes of the international community," says Muang Zarni, a research fellow at the London School of Economics and a visiting fellow at Chulalongkorn University in Bangkok. "In that sense, the boycott is the right thing to do."

But Templer disagrees. "There was very little internal democracy within the NLD when it came to this decision. It may well doom the NLD to political irrelevance," he says. In fact, when the party did not register by the May 7 deadline, it was officially dissolved, left to transform itself into a nonpolitical social service group. A day later, a senior NLD member formed a splinter group to run in the elections, joining other small opposition parties seeking a place at the polls.[14]

Participating in the elections with a clear statement of regret at their limitations would have allowed the NLD to get into Parliament, "where they might have a more public political voice in the future," Templer says. "Parliaments can evolve into much more representative bodies."

But Zarni replies, "The army is the state. Even with an elected Parliament, you would still have the military in control of the bureaucracy. Every single top position in every single field is occupied either by a military officer or an ex-officer."

Between 1975 and 2006, about 7 percent of multiparty elections in developing nations experienced major boycotts, according to Emily Beaulieu, a professor of political science at the University of Kentucky, who has studied election boycotts around the world. They don't all produce results, she says, but where they "motivate active support from the domestic electorate, beyond simply staying home on election day, and/or lead influential international actors like the U.S. or the European Union to press the government for democratic reform, they seem to work to further democratization in the countries where they occur."

Beaulieu cites the Philippines as an example of a successful boycott. In 1981, the main opposition party boycotted elections on the grounds that it had not been given enough time to campaign and had not had equal access to the media. The Catholic Church lent its support, and "domestic pressure proved strong enough to press [President Ferdinand] Marcos to enact several electoral reforms," says Beaulieu, which eventually helped pave the way for his 1986 downfall.

If a boycott were to succeed in Myanmar, says Beaulieu, it would have to motivate such a massive domestic protest that a government crackdown would not be a viable option. "But I suspect that any partial mobilization of the population would just invite government repression," she says.

Opposition parties also face untenable choices in Cambodia, where they threatened to boycott elections in the late 1990s but eventually participated, according to Beaulieu. Since then the opposition has continued to fragment. "If the opposition can pull itself together before the 2011 elections [for Senate], a boycott there may not be out of the question," says Beaulieu.

But a boycott might not get much popular support. Prime Minister Hun Sen dominates national politics through his Cambodian People's Party (CPP), which has ruled the country since 1979 and has quashed any challenges to its authority "with lawsuits, prosecutions, or extralegal actions," according to a Freedom House report. "Opposition figures, journalists, and democracy advocates were given criminal sentences or faced violent attacks by unknown assailants in public spaces."[15]

While many Cambodians in the capital of Phnom Penh oppose the CPP, "Many of the settled rural areas, which make up about 70 percent of the electorate, have been brought into the CPP system," says Duncan McCargo, a professor of Southeast Asian politics at the University of Leeds in the United Kingdom. It's a very simple patronage system, he says: "If your village elects somebody from the CPP to run the local village council, then your village gets roads built and electricity. If you support the opposition Sam Rainsy Party, then your village doesn't get those benefits." In 2008, the CPP won 90 of 123 national assembly seats.

McCargo says a boycott in 2011 would probably just play into Hun Sen's hands, leaving the opposition to pin its hopes on socioeconomic change. "I suppose the opposition's other hope is that as education levels rise and people in settled villages become more middle class, more educated and gain access to a wider range of information," he says, "they might change their political allegiance."

Can Singapore and Malaysia become liberal democracies?

Democracy-promotion experts today disagree over whether, as societies grow richer, citizens joining the educated middle class demand democratic governments — a premise once considered conventional wisdom.

Erik Kuhonta, a Southeast Asia specialist at McGill University in Montreal, Canada, is doubtful. "It is not clear to me that as economic development proceeds and you get a middle class, that the middle class will be a force for democracy," he says. While the middle class has at times challenged authoritarian regimes, as in Indonesia after the Asian financial crisis in 1997-1998, one can't assume that it always will, he says, citing Singapore as a case in point.

"If the state provides certain public goods, such as economic development, political stability, some degree of accountability and especially rule of law, this will satisfy, for the most part, the interests of the middle class, whether the state is democratic or authoritarian," says Kuhonta.

Singapore has the largest middle class as a percent of its population in Southeast Asia. Its thriving free market economy is built on exports, particularly consumer electronics, information technology products and pharmaceuticals, and on a growing financial services sector.[16]

The People's Action Party (PAP), led by Lee Kuan Yew, has ruled this city-state since 1959 and is responsible for its economic transformation. Lee served as prime minister for 30 years and is now "minister mentor" to his son Lee Hsien Loong, who became prime minister in 2004. The PAP holds 82 of the 84 seats in Parliament.

With newspapers, radio stations and television channels owned by government-linked companies, a limited nine-day campaign period and defamation lawsuits hampering opposition candidates, the 2006 polls "resembled past elections in serving more as a referendum on the prime minister's popularity than as an actual contest of power," according to Freedom House.[17]

While the opposition Singapore Democratic Party acknowledges that pocket-book issues drive elections, Chee Siok Chin, a party leader, says most Singaporeans don't protest the lack of civil liberties because they "have very little idea of what it means to have rights." The PAP tells them they have democracy, and they believe it, she says.

According to Ori Sasson, chair of the PAP Policy Forum Committee, "The essence of democracy is not the number of parties represented in Parliament, or the number of seats held by opposition parties, but rather how the

AFP/Getty Images

Bank worker Prita Mulyasari (right) reacts gleefully to the news that an Indonesian court threw out a criminal defamation case against her for e-mailing her friends complaining about an erroneous diagnosis at a local hospital. The court erupted with applause as the judges dismissed Omni International Hospital's complaint. Indonesians were outraged by the case, which was brought under a roundly criticized new law that imposes penalties of up to six years' imprisonment and a $106,000 fine on anyone who communicates defamatory statements over the Internet.

actions of a country's government impacts on the daily lives of the people."[18]

Many seats in Parliament go uncontested, and Chee attributes that to a climate of fear. Chee, her brother Chee Soon Juan and other party leaders have served multiple prison terms this year on charges of unlawful assembly for peaceful protests confined to no more than half a dozen people. "Our party had a team member whose wife threatened to commit suicide should he stand as a candidate in elections," says Chee.

In addition, the government and former prime ministers have aggressively sued Chee and her brother for defamation, and what many outside experts say is a pliant judiciary has awarded massive fines that have forced the Chees into bankruptcy, seriously undermining their ability to challenge the PAP. "Bankrupts are not allowed to stand as candidates for elections," says Chee. "We are not even allowed to campaign for our party's candidates in the next elections.

"Singapore is one of the most artfully controlled societies on Earth," says Stanford's Diamond. Punishment of critics can be much subtler than taking someone to court. "You may find that you are not promoted in your government job, you may not get tenure,

Rating Press Freedom in Southeast Asia

Timor-Leste has the freest press in Southeast Asia, according to the democracy-advocacy group Freedom House. The media in Laos, Myanmar (Burma) and Vietnam are the least free in Southeast Asia.

Press Freedom in Southeast Asia, 2010

Country	Freedom House rating*	World ranking**	Freedom status
Timor-Leste	35	78	Partly Free
Philippines	48	97	Partly free
Indonesia	52	107	Partly free
Thailand	58	124	Partly free
Cambodia	61	134	Not free
Malaysia	64	141	Not free
Singapore	68	151	Not free
Brunei	75	163	Not free
Vietnam	82	177	Not free
Laos	84	181	Not free
Burma	95	194	Not free

* The lower the rating the freer the press.

** Out of 196, with 1 being most free

Source: "Freedom the Press 2010," Freedom House, May 2010

stale place, where its very rich and prosperous adult citizens are treated like children," says Diamond. "And if Malaysia makes a transition to democracy, right on Singapore's doorstep, I think psychologically this will have an impact on the Singapore model."

Malaysia is in political crisis at the moment, says Diamond. "Democratic ferment . . . is sweeping the country," he says, "and there is a very good chance of some kind of democratic change, if the regime doesn't use even more extreme authoritarian, abusive measures."

The Barisan Nasional (BN) coalition has governed Malaysia since the multiethnic country gained independence from Britain in 1957. At its core is the United Malays National Organization (UMNO), whose leader, Mahathir bin Mohamad, served as premier from 1981 until retirement in 2003. Mahathir is credited with Malaysia's impressive economic growth, but "the physician-turned-politician never hesitated to assault or undermine any democratic institution that got in his way," according to James Chin and Wong Chin Huat of Monash University in Malaysia. He eventually turned the UMNO-dominated Malaysian state into "something resembling a personal dictatorship."[19]

Elections are free, but not fair. Opposition parties compete at the polls, but they do so during a compressed campaign period, with no free press or freedom of assembly. "You need a police permit before you can get out there and protest," says William Case, director of the Southeast Asia Research Centre at City University of Hong Kong, "and there are a whole slew of draconian amendments to enforce all this." In addition, the judiciary often delivers "arbitrary or politically motivated verdicts," according to Freedom House, "with the most prominent case being the convictions of [opposition leader] Anwar Ibrahim in 1999 and 2000 for corruption and sodomy."[20]

and benefits that flow to other citizens may not flow to you," he says.

While coercion is an important reason for a quiescent middle class, says Kuhonta, it's not enough. As long as middle-class needs are met, he does not expect any kind of revolt. "There is a lot of wishful thinking in terms of Singapore becoming democratic," says Kuhonta. "For that to happen, the state would have to show it could no longer manage the economy."

But Diamond and Chee are more optimistic. Lee Kuan Yew is in his mid 80s. "When Lee Sr. passes on, there will be fissures in the ruling party," says Chee. "The executive will not be as compliant, the legislature less acquiescent, the judiciary more independent. I am confident that Singapore will one day be a 'free' country," she says.

Diamond believes change will come as the next generation matures. "Young people are tired of living in a

But the Malaysian government is more corrupt and less astute at managing the economy than Singapore, and the public has become increasingly frustrated with its political leaders. Disillusionment with the Anwar verdict and with a dishonest police force, rampant corruption, UMNO slurs against Malaysians of Chinese and Indian descent and rising crime and inflation led to a shocking result in the 2008 elections. For the first time since 1969, the BN lost its two-thirds majority in the lower house of Parliament.[21] One major reason for the shift was "the ethnic Indians who had always been staunch supporters of the BN had swung in a big way to the opposition," says Terence Gomez, a professor at the University of Malaya in Kuala Lumpur.

"For about six months after the 2008 election we thought there was a chance that Malaysia would become a two-party democracy," says Case, but he now calls the prognosis for democracy "not good." After the election, opposition parties formed a coalition called the People's Alliance, and Anwar vowed it would capture a parliamentary majority by accepting defectors from the BN and form a new government by September 2008. However, he failed, undermining his credibility. He is now in court fighting new government accusations of sodomy that Diamond says are "completely false."

"People talk about a loss of hope since 2008," says Gomez. "The opposition has to get its act together and show that it has the capacity to govern."

Does democracy mean greater accountability and less corruption?

Democracy advocates once thought that democracy automatically led to greater government accountability and less corruption. Today, many are much more pessimistic. And few are surprised by the level of corruption in authoritarian regimes such as those in Cambodia and Myanmar.

"You basically have a predatory government in Cambodia," says Philip Robertson, deputy director of Human Rights Watch's Asia Division. "If I'm a minister who wants to obtain a piece of land to build a shopping mall with some friends who are developers, I would just say, 'hey, here's a little bit of money, and if you don't move, we'll move you,'" says Robertson.

Citizens must routinely pay bribes for basic services, and senior state and military personnel demand kickbacks from foreign companies in the petroleum, gas and logging industries.[22] In fact, Cambodia is ranked near the bottom of Transparency International's Corruption Perceptions Index: 158 out 180 countries.[23]

Myanmar is even worse, considered one of the world's most corrupt regimes, ranking 178th. "Every single sector is corrupt," says Maureen Aung-Thwin,

---

Singapore Is Least Corrupt in Southeast Asia

Singapore ranks as the least corrupt country in Southeast Asia, and Malaysia ranks second. Myanmar (Burma) ranks 178th in the world, with only Afghanistan and Somalia being rated more corrupt.

Corruption in Southeast Asia, 2009

Country	Corruption rating*	World ranking**
Singapore	9.2	3
Brunei	5.5	39
Malaysia	4.5	56
Thailand	3.4	84
Indonesia	2.8	111
Vietnam	2.7	120
Philippines	2.4	139
Timor-Leste	2.2	146
Cambodia	2.0	158
Laos	2.0	158
Myanmar (Burma)	1.4	178

* On a 1-10 scale, with 10 being least corrupt.

** Out of 180, with 1 being the least corrupt

Source: "Corruption Perceptions Index 2009," Transparency International, 2009

Social Networking Can Help Boost Democracy

But it must be accompanied by real grassroots action, experts say.

Social media are exploding in parts of Southeast Asia — a trend being hailed by some democracy advocates as a helpful tool for promoting more open government.

"We were the first political party to make use of Twitter in 2008," says Chee Siok Chin, one of the leaders of the opposition Singapore Democratic Party. "We have also been uploading our videos on YouTube, spreading our message via Facebook."

Driven by declining prices for computers, cell phones and access fees, the use of social media such as Twitter [1] and Facebook [2] has seen spectacular growth in Indonesia and the Philippines, although it's still used by only a fraction of the population.

Social networking also is catching on in some of the more closed nations. More than a fifth of Malaysians now use Facebook, [3] and tiny Singapore accounts for nearly 1 percent of all Twitter users worldwide. [4]

While most people use social media primarily for entertainment and networking, political and social activists have begun to harness its power. Internet access has transformed coverage of events in Myanmar, which is ruled by an iron-fisted military junta. Hundreds of young people used Internet blogs to share news with the world about the Saffron Revolution, which began in late August 2007 when Buddhist monks, students and others took to the streets in peaceful protests and ended a month later with the military's brutal crackdown, according to Kyaw Yin Hlaing, a professor at City University of Hong Kong.

"Thanks to these young activists, the international media came to realize the gravity of the situation in Myanmar," wrote Hlaing. [5]

In Malaysia, the Internet strengthened the democratic opposition in 2007, according to James Chin and Wong Chin Huat of Monash University in Malaysia. "Mushrooming political web blogs . . . together with a handful of online news portals, were providing an alternative to the tightly controlled mainstream print and broadcast media," they wrote. By exposing the ruling party's "misdeeds and corruption," bloggers and online news outlets helped drive the middle class and sections of the working class "toward a major change in attitudes and voting behavior." [6] A series of unprecedented street protests took place, and in the 2008 election the ruling party lost its historic two-thirds parliamentary majority.

director of the Burma Project at the Open Society Institute, a New York-based nonprofit that works to build democracies. Top military officers siphon off natural gas revenues, and poorly paid government workers demand petty bribes.

"You have to bribe your teacher to get a good grade; you have to pay a bribe to get a passport for travel; soldiers will stop people to check their registration and ask for a bribe," Aung-Thwin says. "The only way to purge the corruption is regime change."

But regime change elsewhere in Southeast Asia has not necessarily brought more accountability and less corruption. Indonesia and the Philippines, which were once authoritarian like Myanmar and Cambodia, are considered more corrupt than some of their less democratic neighbors.

"If you look at Transparency International's Corruption Perceptions Index, Singapore is high up and not democratic at all, and the Southeast Asia country that performs second best is Malaysia," says Case of the City University of Hong Kong. "They are well ahead of the Philippines, which is sometimes understood to be democratic, and well ahead of Indonesia, which is the only democracy in the region."

There is no correlation between democracy and reduced corruption, says Danang Widoyoko, deputy coordinator of Indonesia Corruption Watch, a nongovernmental organization in Jakarta. "We inherited the corruption problem that was practiced widely and systematically by President Suharto's New Order regime," says Danang. Gen. Suharto controlled Indonesian politics for 32 years in one of Southeast Asia's most repressive

Technology also helped the anti-government demonstrators in Thailand in April and May, drawn mostly from the rural and urban poor. "In the past they were upset, but they weren't cohesive as a force and coherent in their agenda," said Thitinan Pongsudhirak, a leading political scientist in Thailand and visiting scholar at Stanford University. "New technologies have enabled them to unify their disparate voices of dissatisfaction." [7]

But social networking also has significant limits as a democratizing force. First of all, says Preetam Rai, an educator and technology researcher based in Southeast Asia, online activists' reach is limited, especially in countries where Internet penetration is low. And most people use the Internet for entertainment or socializing. "People get interested in serious issues when certain incidents happen, like the Burmese protests in 2007 or the current Thai situation," says Preetam, "but they go back to their regular online consumption pattern when the situation is normal."

Mong Palatino — a Filipino blogger, youth activist and member of parliament — participated in a student uprising that helped to topple the corrupt Estrada regime in 2001. "We sent rally updates through e-mail and e-groups," he recalls. "For the first time, texting became an important tool in organizing protest activities."

But Palatino warned in his blog earlier this year that "cyber-activism becomes a potent force only if it is fused with grassroots activism." Unfortunately, he said, too many young people are seduced into thinking that signing an online petition or adding a cause to Facebook is enough, and in that sense, cyber-activism can actually be counterproductive by keeping young people from becoming active in the real world.

"Activism in the 21st century features new action words like texting, re-tweeting, clicking, chatting and social networking," blogged Palatino. "But 20th-century action words are still more persuasive and powerful — like talking, organizing, marching, pushing and rallying." [8]

— Barbara Mantel

[1] "Twitter Enjoys Major Growth and Excellent Stickiness," *Sysomos*, March 29, 2010, http://blog.sysomos.com/2010/03/29/twitter-enjoys-major-growth-and-excellent-stickiness/.

[2] "Facebook Sees Solid Growth Around the World in 2010," *Inside Facebook*, April 6, 2010, www.insidefacebook.com/2010/04/06/facebook-sees-solid-growth-around-the-world-in-march-2010.

[3] *Ibid.*

[4] "Twitter Enjoys Major Growth and Excellent Stickiness," *op. cit.*

[5] Donald K. Emmerson, ed., *Hard Choices: Security, Democracy, and Regionalism in Southeast Asia* (2008), p. 172.

[6] James Chin and Wong Chin Huat, "Malaysia's Electoral Upheaval," *Journal of Democracy*, July 2009, pp. 79-84.

[7] Thomas Fuller, "Widening Disparity Strains Traditional Bonds of Thai Society," *The New York Times*, April 1, 2010, p. A4.

[8] Mong Palatino, "Online and Offline Activism," *Mong Palatino blog*, Jan. 12, 2010, http://mongpalatino.com/2010/01/online-and-offline-activism/.

dictatorships before it collapsed in 1998 following the Asian financial crisis. [24] "Corruption in Indonesia is a way of life," says Danang.

Since Suharto's rule ended, "the country has been trying to break with its past experience of centralized power vulnerable to oligarchic abuse," reports Transparency International. Political power has been decentralized, and Indonesia now consists of 33 provinces, each with its own legislature and governor. "The responsibility for most public services such as health, education, culture, public works, land management, manufacturing and trading has been transferred to districts, cities and villages." [25]

While decentralization has helped Indonesia become a relatively liberal democracy with fair elections and extensive freedom of the press and association, it has had the perverse effect of increasing corruption opportunities. "With decentralization, . . . there are more people you have to pay off," says Bridget Welsh, a professor of political science at Singapore Management University.

Last year, Indonesia's Corruption Eradication Commission (KPK), formed in 2002, caught on wiretap Gen. Susni Duadji, then chief of detectives in the national police force, asking for a $1 million bribe. Susni was then reported to have tried to frame two of the anti-corruption commissioners. [26] "If you check the KPK's cases, there have been scandals in the election commission, corruption in the Indonesian Central Bank, bribery of prosecutors, and more," says Danang.

Likewise, the Philippines has had its own corruption scandals, starting with former strongman Marcos.

During his 14-year rule from 1972 to 1986, Marcos and his family "are alleged to have stolen between $5-10 billion worth of state assets," reports Transparency International.[27] Even after mass nonviolent street demonstrations known as the People Power revolution restored democracy, corruption remained. In 2001, President Joseph Estrada resigned amid accusations of graft; he was later charged with stealing more than $80 million in state funds. Convicted in 2007, he was pardoned by his successor, Gloria Macapagal-Arroyo, an economist who was elected in hopes of battling corruption, but who has suffered her own scandals during two terms that ended in May.[28]

The Center for People Empowerment in Governance (CenPEG), a watchdog group based in Quezon City, has called the Arroyo government a kleptocracy that specialized "in awarding contracts and civil service posts to allies and friends."[29]

Transparency International reports that "all levels of corruption, from petty bribery to grand corruption, patronage and state capture, exist in the Philippines at a considerable scale and scope."[30]

The problem is not a lack of laws. "The country has many laws and about 17 agencies that fight corruption, and yet it remains near the top of the list of most corrupt countries in the region if not the whole world," says Bobby Tuazon, CenPEG's director of policy studies.

What's needed is a new mass "people power" movement, says Tuazon, to press for a complete overhaul of the bureaucracy and the creation of "a powerful, independent anti-corruption watchdog that has powers to arrest, jail and prosecute suspects, including the powerful." However, he points out, "the use of threats and legal coercion by those in power are a deterrent to this democratic undertaking by the people. In the Philippines, . . . the 'whistle-blowers' . . . get arrested and threatened."

Danang is more hopeful about Indonesia. "I'm quite optimistic that corruption can be curbed in the future," he says, pinning his hopes on the pressure of continued public outrage expressed through a free media. Both Danang and Welsh see the need for campaign-finance reform to reduce reliance on the private donations of businessmen, and civil service reform to raise salaries and increase professionalism. "It just takes time," says Welsh, "and it is not easy."

In fact, a study examining the role of democracy as a check on corruption comes to basically the same conclusion. Its authors argue that democracy helps to minimize corruption eventually, but that it takes time, sometimes several generations. New democracies must establish the necessary campaign-finance reform, accountable executive branches, independent judiciaries and auditors and the free flow of information.[31]

The challenge is to maintain democracy long enough to do the job. "Corruption deprives people of services and facilities, and when these are not delivered, democracy is eroded because people have less access to economic and social rights," says Edna Estifania A. Co, a professor at the National College of Public Administration and Governance at the University of the Philippines Diliman.

BACKGROUND
Corruption and Violence

"Democracies . . . become consolidated only when both significant elites and an overwhelming proportion of ordinary citizens see democracy . . . as 'the only game in town,'" write the authors of *How East Asians View Democracy*.[32] But in Southeast Asia, that prerequisite for legitimacy is extremely fragile.

In Thailand and the Philippines, for instance, "a significant number of citizens harbor professed reservations about democracy and lingering attachments to authoritarianism," according to surveys. Although Freedom House once ranked both countries liberal democracies, it has not done so since 2005, and by 2007 it no longer considered them electoral democracies either, a less stringent category. In all of Southeast Asia, only Indonesia is now viewed as a liberal democracy, and East Timor an electoral democracy.

Yet the Philippines has the longest experience with democracy of any Southeast Asian nation. When the Philippines gained independence from the United States in 1946, it retained an American-style democratic system that had been put in place under colonial rule.

But by the late 1960s "it became apparent that procedural democracy had not generated social justice and equity," according to Philippine political pollster Linda Luz Guerrero and Rollin Tusalem, an assistant political science professor at Arkansas State University. Powerful families held most of the economic and political power, and half the population lived in poverty. A civil war was brewing on the southern island of Mindanao, and communist insurgents on the northern island of Luzon were demanding land reform.

In 1970, demonstrators tried to storm the presidential palace in Manila, and an attempt was made on the life of visiting Pope Paul VI; the following year grenades were thrown at a political rally. In September 1972, President Ferdinand Marcos declared martial law.[33] Throughout the decade, poverty and government corruption increased, and Marcos' "friends and associates monopolized major industries," write Guerrero and Tusalem.

The 1980s marked a turning point for the Philippines. The military's assassination of opposition leader and democratic reformer Benigno "Ninoy" Aquino in August 1983 as he returned to Manila from self-exile in the United States triggered a funeral procession attended by hundreds of thousands of people. Months of massive demonstrations followed, in which protesters demanded Marcos' resignation and the restoration of democracy. The protests continued intermittently over the next three years, until Aquino's widow, the late Corazon Aquino, led the nonviolent "People Power" uprising that finally toppled Marcos in 1986.

The People Power movement inspired similar movements around the world, including people's rallies in South Korea, the pro-democracy demonstration in China's Tiananmen Square in 1989, the Solidarity movement in Poland and the Velvet Revolution in the former Czechoslovakia.

But reform-minded Aquino was unable to turn back the crony capitalism of the Marcos era. Since the return of democracy, the Philippines has struggled with the same "violence, bossism, and corruption" that plagued the country during martial law, writes Stanford's Diamond. A few dozen clans continue to dominate politics and the economy, and many control private armies responsible for election-year violence; corruption pervades all levels of government; organized crime often operates with official collusion; social injustice feeds a communist insurgency in the north; and in the south, Muslim insurgents agitate for autonomy.[34]

Almost every president since Aquino has been accused of corruption. In January 2001 the Supreme Court ended the presidency of former movie actor Joseph Marcelo Estrada, elected in 1998, after he was found to have

Hundreds of thousands of Filipinos pack Manila streets in 1986, demanding that dictator Ferdinand Marcos step down from power. After Marcos fled the country four days later — following 20 years of autocratic rule — the so-called People Power movement became the inspiration for other nonviolent demonstrations around the world, including those that ended several communist dictatorships in Eastern Europe.

taken payoffs from illegal gambling operations. His successor, economist Gloria Macapagal-Arroyo, suffered through her own series of accusations — that she rigged her reelection in 2004; that her husband was involved in illegal gambling, logging and smuggling and that she fabricated her claim of a coup attempt in February 2006 so she could declare a state of emergency to stop anti-government demonstrations.[35]

This May, Corazon Aquino's son Benigno "Noynoy" Aquino was elected to succeed Arroyo on a campaign pledge — made by almost every other Philippine president — to fight corruption and strengthen democracy.

Shaky Democracy

Thailand is the only nation in Southeast Asian never to have been colonized. An absolute monarchy until a palace coup in 1932, Thailand, like the Philippines, has had an uneven experience with democracy.

What followed the coup was not a genuine participatory democracy, write Thailand scholars Robert Albritton and Thawilwadee Bureekul. "Political power was monopolized by an exclusive elite in a one-party state, . . . which promised full electoral democracy only when at least half the population had completed primary education or 10 years had passed."

CHRONOLOGY

1940s-1950s *Independence arrives in Southeast Asia after World War II.*

1960s-1970s *Authoritarian regimes dominate Southeast Asia.*

1962 Gen. Ne Win leads coup in Burma; military takes control; country is renamed Myanmar.

1964 America's military support of South Vietnam escalates when U.S. bombs North Vietnam; U.S. pulls out in 1973; North Vietnam prevails in 1975 to form the Socialist Republic of Vietnam.

1968 Gen. Suharto becomes president of Indonesia, assumes authoritarian control.

1972 Philippine President Ferdinand Marcos declares martial law.

1975 Khmer Rouge seizes power in Cambodia; up to 2 million people are killed or die from disease, overwork, starvation; Vietnam eventually overthrows the regime and installs new communist government in 1979.

1980s-1990s *Democracy returns to some countries in Southeast Asia.*

1983 Philippine democracy advocate and former Sen. Benigno Aquino is assassinated; mass pro-democracy demonstrations ensue.

1986 "People Power" revolution in Philippines topples Marcos; Aquino's widow Corazon is elected president.

1988 Thailand holds democratic elections after decades of authoritarian rule.

1990 National League for Democracy (NLD) wins parliamentary elections in Myanmar but junta rejects results; and places NLD leader Daw Aung San Suu Kyi under house arrest.

1991 Military coup overthrows elected government in Thailand.

1997 Thailand adopts reformist constitution.

1998 Riots erupt in Indonesia after Asian financial crisis; Suharto is forced to resign.

2000-Present *Corruption scandals and election violence hit Philippines; coup roils Thailand.*

2001 Philippine Supreme Court ends corrupt presidency of Joseph Marcelo Estrada; Gloria Macapagal-Arroyo takes power. . . . Billionaire businessman Thaksin Shinawatra becomes Thailand's prime minister.

2002 East Timor gains independence from Indonesia.

2006 Military coup overthrows Thaksin in Thailand amid accusations of corruption.

2008 Courts remove Thaksin allies from power; opposition politician Abhisit Vejjajiva becomes prime minister. . . . Malaysia's Barisan Nasional party loses its majority in parliamentary election.

November 2009 Fifty-seven people — including journalists and relatives and supporters of a political candidate — are massacred in Philippines, reportedly by supporters of a rival candidate.

2010 Myanmar's military junta imposes restrictive rules for upcoming elections; opposition NLD announces election boycott (March 8). . . . Anti-government protesters begin demonstrations in Bangkok, demanding that Thai Prime Minister Abhisit step down and call new elections (March 12); 25 people die and more than 800 are injured when soldiers and police try to disperse the protesters (April 10). . . . NLD disbands in Myanmar after failing to register for upcoming elections (May 7). . . . Sen. Benigno Aquino, son of former president Corazon Aquino, is elected president in country's first computerized election (May 10). . . . Central Bangkok becomes a battleground as soldiers disperse crowds and protesters burn buildings. . . . Thai government imposes curfews, closes opposition media outlets and issues arrest warrant on terrorism charges for self-exiled former prime minister Thaksin Shinawatra (May 14-May 27). In all, 88 people are killed and more than 1,000 injured during the nine weeks of protests.

Albritton and Thawilwadee write that only six of the years leading up to 1985 could be considered truly democratic. Otherwise, a series of military-supported authoritarian regimes governed Thailand, until public disaffection with the "excesses of the authoritarian right again revived the demand for democracy among the Thai public," culminating in "fully democratic elections" in 1988 and the formation of a coalition government.

But three years later a military coup, supported by Thailand's middle class, dismissed the elected government after the media relentlessly criticized it for corruption. Eventually, popular pressure forced the military junta to promise new elections, and Freedom House once again categorized Thailand as an electoral democracy in 1993. Lawmakers passed a new constitution in 1997 that "radically revised the electoral system" and created a Constitutional Court, an Election Commission and the National Anti-Corruption Commission.

Freedom House raised Thailand's status in 1998 from "partly free" to "free," and in 2001 the polarizing billionaire Thaksin Shinawatra, who had made his fortune in telecommunications, was elected prime minister. He had appealed to the majority electorate in rural northern and northeastern Thailand with promises of development programs and health care reform. But while Thaksin improved the conditions of the rural poor, critics accused him and his associates of undercutting the reformist 1997 constitution, abusing power for personal gain, conducting a brutal "war on drugs" that resulted in at least 2,500 deaths in 2003 and responding with a heavy hand to a Muslim insurgency in Thailand's four southernmost provinces.[36]

When the Thaksin family sold its share of Shin Corp. — one of Southeast Asia's most important information technology firms — to the investment arm of the Singapore government in January 2006, a wave of anti-Thaksin protests in the capital — led by the People's Alliance for Democracy (PAD) — resulted. After snap elections, boycotts and street protests, a military coup forced Thaksin from office, and judicial and parliamentary maneuvering eventually led Abhisit Vejjajiva, leader of the opposition Democratic Party, to take over as prime minister.[37]

Ever since, Thaksin's supporters have been demanding that Abhisit step down and call new parliamentary elections, and demonstrations have been a periodic feature of Bangkok life. They turned violent in April and May as soldiers and protestors battled in the capital's streets. The government dispersed the crowds on May 19, arresting protest leaders, imposing curfews and shutting down opposition media outlets. It also issued an arrest warrant on terrorism charges for Thaksin, accusing him of masterminding the March-through-May street protests. Thaksin, who is in self-exile abroad to avoid arrest on a post-coup corruption conviction, denies the charges.

Free But Corrupt

In marked contrast to the Philippines and Thailand, Indonesia, which became an electoral democracy only in 1999, has become "a surprising political success story," according to Diamond.

"Today, Indonesia is not only a reasonably stable democracy . . . but it is even in some respects a relatively liberal democracy, with reasonably fair elections and extensive freedoms of press and association," Diamond writes.[38] In 2005, Freedom House raised its status to "free."

Indonesia won independence from the Dutch in 1949, and the republic's first president, known only as Sukarno, assumed authoritarian powers in 1957. After Gen. Suharto crushed a coup attempt by the Communist Party of Indonesia (PKI) in 1965, "mass acts of violence followed, ostensibly against suspected PKI members, resulting in an estimated 500,000 deaths," according to Freedom House.[39] Suharto became president in 1968.

Under Suharto, Indonesia was an "authoritarian success story," with average annual economic growth of 7 percent. But "three decades of development and sure-handed economic management imploded in just a matter of months under the strain of the 1997 East Asian financial crisis," writes Diamond. Stories began to circulate of "colossal corruption and monopolistic practices" of the president's children and associates, and riots erupted when the government announced cuts in fuel and electricity subsidies.[40] In 1998, Suharto was forced to resign, and the country soon held its first free legislative elections since 1955.

Graft remains endemic, especially in the government bureaucracy, yet new legislation signed into law last September dilutes the authority and independence of the Corruption Eradication Commission and the Anticorruption

Indonesia's Defamation Laws Stifle Democracy

"Truth is not a defense if an official finds the content of your statement 'insulting.' "

Human Rights Watch (HRW) examines Indonesia's harsh defamation laws in a report issued in April, "Turning Critics Into Criminals: The Human Rights Consequences of Criminal Defamation Law in Indonesia." CQ Global Researcher *writer Barbara Mantel discussed the report with Elaine Pearson, deputy director of HRW's Asia Division.*

CQGR: Indonesia has eliminated many of the most pernicious laws that officials once used to silence critics, but criminal defamation and insult laws remain.

EP: Six criminal defamation and "insult" provisions are commonly invoked by powerful people in Indonesia. These include provisions in the Criminal Code on slander or libel, with higher penalties invoked if the person is a public official. There are also specific provisions against insulting a public authority and a particularly harsh provision that punishes the communication of defamatory statements over the Internet, with up to six years' imprisonment and a fine of up to 1 billion rupiah (approximately $106,000).

CQGR: What if the statements are true?

EP: Under Indonesia's "insult" laws, truth is not a defense if an official finds the content of your statement "insulting." Under the other defamation laws, if defendants want to use truth as a defense they have to both prove their claim is true and also that they acted in the "general interest" or out of necessity. And this is risky; if the judge hears a truth defense but is not convinced, the defendant can be found guilty of "calumny," which carries a more severe penalty of up to four years imprisonment.

CQGR: Why is the penalty higher for defamation over the Internet?

EP: One justification is that Internet defamation has the potential to be far more harmful than regular defamation because the Internet can be used to communicate content to an infinite number of people. Human Rights Watch believes that it is precisely because the Internet can dramatically expand the channels for communication and sharing of information that laws on Internet use should not seek to repress the peaceful airing of grievances.

CQGR: How have officials and powerful private citizens used these laws to silence criticism and opposition?

EP: Because the laws contain extremely vague language, powerful people can use criminal defamation laws to retaliate against people who had made allegations of corruption, fraud or misconduct against powerful interests or government officials. These laws are also open to manipulation by individuals with political or financial power who can influence the behavior of investigators. For instance, in some cases the police aggressively pursued the criminal defamation complaint without properly investigating the validity of the underlying complaint of corruption or fraud.

CQGR: Can you give an example of a government official using the laws to silence opposition?

EP: Three activists from the Coalition of Students and People of Tasikmalaya were put on trial in 2009 for criminal defamation on a complaint filed by a local education official after they held an anti-corruption demonstration related to corruption charges they had made against him. Tukijo, a farmer, was convicted of defamation earlier this year. The charges were brought by a local official whom he asked for the results of a land assessment. He had previously argued with the local official.

CQGR: Can you give an example of these laws' use against the media?

EP: Bersihar Lubis, a veteran reporter, was convicted of defaming the attorney general when he criticized his

Court. The rule of law is seriously undermined "by rampant corruption in the judiciary, and politically well-connected elites rarely face consequences of abuses of power," according to Freedom House. According to its most recent report, the security forces and the military abuse human rights with impunity. "In short, corruption, collusion and nepotism continue to constitute the modus operandi of Indonesian politics," Freedom House's Indonesia analyst writes.[41]

Newest Democracy

While predominantly Muslim Indonesia was building its own democracy, its military was brutally suppressing an independence movement in East Timor, a Catholic enclave decision to ban a high school history textbook in an opinion column. Journalist Risang Bima Wijaya was convicted of defamation and served six months in prison after he published unflattering articles about a local media figure in Yogyakarta who had been accused of a crime.

CQGR: What impact do these criminal defamation laws have on democracy in Indonesia?

EP: All those accused of defamation engaged [in conduct] that included holding peaceful demonstrations against officials accused of corruption, publicizing consumer complaints and disputes with businesses, requesting information from the authorities and lodging complaints with them and reporting in the media on subjects of public importance. Democracy requires a vibrant civil society that can monitor the performance of public officials and a free press that shares information about prominent people and events, even when the news is negative. And democracy requires an atmosphere in which people are free to speak their minds and participate in public discourse. But under Indonesia's defamation laws, people who do these things can be found guilty of a crime if they offend the wrong person.

These laws have a chilling effect on free speech in Indonesia. This is harmful to every individual who has something to say but is afraid to do so because they fear imprisonment. Journalists told us how they are afraid to get an exclusive story on sensitive topics because they fear going to jail.

CQGR: What other countries in Southeast Asia have criminal defamation laws?

EP: Many countries — such as Singapore, Malaysia, Cambodia and Thailand — have criminal defamation laws or other "insult" or national security laws that have a similar chilling effect. However from what we have seen in Indonesia, the use of criminal defamation laws is more widespread. Also Indonesia has more criminal defamation offenses than any other country in the region.

CQGR: Human Rights Watch wants to see criminal defamation laws eliminated. Why is there no place for criminal penalties?

Elaine Pearson, deputy director of Human Rights Watch's Asia Division, denounces Indonesia's new defamation laws, saying that they repress peaceful airing of grievances.

EP: Criminal penalties are always disproportionate punishments for reputational harm and should be abolished. International human rights law allows for restrictions on freedom of expression to protect the reputations of others, but such restrictions must be necessary and narrowly drawn. As repeal of criminal defamation laws in an increasing number of countries shows, such laws are not necessary. Civil defamation and criminal incitement laws are sufficient for the purpose of protecting people's reputations and maintaining public order and can be written and implemented in ways that provide appropriate protections for freedom of expression.

— Barbara Mantel

that occupies half an island on the eastern edge of the Indonesian archipelago. In 1999, the people of East Timor voted for independence from Indonesia, which had invaded and annexed the country in 1975 as the Portuguese were relinquishing control. But after the referendum, "the territory descended into chaos as pro-Indonesian militias and the army engaged in a campaign of terror

and brutality, killing supporters of independence, looting and burning buildings and causing thousands to flee their homes."[42]

Indonesia eventually allowed a United Nations peacekeeping force to enter East Timor, and the country slowly transitioned to an electoral democracy, finally becoming independent on May 20, 2002.

Protesting Repression

Demonstrators in Manila display a photograph of Burmese pro-democracy leader Daw Aung San Suu Kyi (top) as they denounce Myanmar's new election law on March 19. Under the new law, Nobel Peace Prize winner Suu Kyi, who has been held under house arrest for 14 years, cannot run in elections expected to be held in October or November. Supporters of slain UNTV journalist Daniel Tiamzon — one of 57 people killed in an election-related massacre in the southern Philippines in November — demonstrate during his funeral (bottom). They are demanding that the killers, allegedly associated with a politically powerful family, be brought to justice.

East Timor's struggle to build a democracy and a functioning state has been punctuated by violence. The country has made significant progress and is considered an electoral democracy, but — as in other Southeast Asian countries — it has experienced "threatening

episodes of armed rebellion, attempted assassination of the president and prime minister, and violent communal conflict," not to mention high-level corruption, according to Freedom House.[43]

CURRENT SITUATION

Thai Violence

Bangkok streets damaged by bloody battles have been scrubbed, the fires from buildings torched by retreating protesters put out, the demonstrators dispersed and their leaders arrested. But the divisions within Thai society that are at the root of this spring's anti-government protests — which left at least 88 people dead and more than 1,000 wounded — remain.

"I am mourning my fellow protesters who were killed by the government like vegetables and fish," said a middle-aged resident of Thailand's rural northeast region, a stronghold of anti-government sentiment. "Watch out," she said. "People are going to go underground and fight with arms. This is the beginning of a very long war."[44]

The protesters, known as red shirts, took over an area of commercial Bangkok in late March, disrupting hotel service, shopping, tourism and, ultimately, the economy. They numbered tens of thousands at their peak, and for the first weeks they were carefully nonviolent; the military was cautious as well. In fact, many Bangkok residents became increasingly critical of the government for not trying to take back control of that crucial part of the capital.

But on April 10, when soldiers finally did try to disperse the crowds, the protesters counterattacked, repulsing the troops. At the end of the day, at least 25 civilians and soldiers were killed and more than 800 wounded in what was, at that point, the worst violence the country had seen in 20 years. Sporadic fighting continued, with grenade attacks in parts of the city, until on May 14th the protests turned bloody as the military once again moved in. Within a week, dozens more were killed and hundreds wounded, and on May 19, many protest leaders surrendered.

The demonstrators were mostly farmers and small business people from rural Thailand, who account for the majority of the electorate, joined by some of Bangkok's poorer residents, students and professionals. Thailand is a constitutional monarchy, and the red shirts want the current prime minister and his government, which they view as illegitimate, to step down and call new elections.

"I used to think we were born poor and that was that," Thanida Paveen, who grew up in rural Thailand and now lives in the capital's outskirts, told a reporter. "I have opened my mind to a new way of thinking: We need to change from the rule of the aristocracy to a real democracy."[45]

The roots of their protest can be traced to 2006, when a military coup ousted then Prime Minister Thaksin Shinawatra, who had introduced universal health care and brought investment to rural areas. But Bangkok's elite, composed of middle class professionals, military leaders, bureaucrats and members of the royal family, long accustomed to controlling politics and the country, accused Thaksin of vote buying, corruption and undermining the rule of law in a deadly anti-drug campaign. Many took to the streets under the banner of the People's Alliance for Democracy (PAD), also known as the "yellow-shirts," setting the stage for the coup that eventually sent Thaksin into self-exile to avoid arrest on a corruption conviction.[46]

New elections were held a year later. But after Thaksin allies won, the PAD returned to the streets, this time incapacitating the government and shutting down Bangkok's airports for a week. Through a series of court rulings and parliamentary moves, Thaksin's allies were forced from power and their party disbanded. Abhisit became prime minister.

Even though the violence in Bankok has ended, Thai society will remain deeply polarized, say analysts. During its street protests in 2008, the PAD called for "a revamping of the democratic system to prevent the rural sector from dictating the outcome of the elections."[47] It advocated an indirect voting system based on occupation.

"The elites have a very low opinion of people who are not highly educated," says Robert Albritton, an expert on Thailand at the University of Mississippi. "They were asking, 'Are we going to let these uneducated people in the rice fields run the government?' " The elites prefer "guided democracy," he says, with a strong government

Economies Grew Rapidly Across Region

Per capita gross national income (GNI) in Southeast Asia grew dramatically between 2005 and 2008, with Timor-Leste posting more than a 200 percent increase. GNI throughout the region grew at least 26 percent during the period, with eight countries growing at 40 percent or more. Experts disagree on whether economic growth in a country leads to democracy in the government.

Per Capita Gross National Income in Southeast Asia, 2005-2008*

Country	2005	2008	% increase
Brunei	$22,770	n/a	n/a
Cambodia	$450	$640	42%
Indonesia	$1,170	$1,880	61%
Laos	$450	$760	69%
Malaysia	$5,210	$7,250	39%
Philippines	$1,260	$1,890	50%
Singapore	$27,670	$34,760	26%
Thailand	$2,580	$3,670	42%
Timor-Leste	$740	$2,460	232%
Vietnam	$620	$890	44%

* Figures not available for Myanmar (Burma)

Source: The World Bank

bureaucracy loyal to the monarchy and a weak, rubber-stamp Parliament.

The Thai bureaucracy often is unaccountable to the prime minister and his appointees, says Thawilwadee Bureekul, director of research and development at King Prajadhipok's Institute in Nonthaburi, which promotes democracy and good governance. For instance, a politically appointed minister of agriculture would have at his side a permanent secretary, who ascended to his position after years of civil service. "Sometimes the minister will have a difficult time enforcing his policies," says Thawilwadee, "because these government officials won't always support him. We need to reform the bureaucracy."

Thaksin tried to reform the bureaucracy by reshuffling ministries, says Thawilwadee. That's one reason "the bureaucracy had grown to hate him," says Albritton. But Thaksin also had a "dark side" and did not tolerate criticism, opposition or the constraints of the rule of law, according to Diamond of Stanford. He intimidated journalists and critical nongovernmental organizations and

Philippine Election Violence Declined

The recent election season in the Philippines was one of the country's least violent, despite a shocking, election-related massacre last Nov. 23, when 57 people — 30 of them journalists — were killed in Maguindanao Province. During the past decade, the bloodiest year for Philippine elections was 2004, when nearly 200 people were killed.

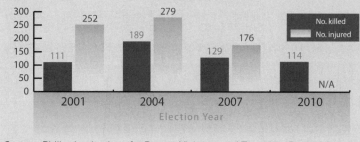

Source: Philippine Institute for Peace, Violence and Terrorism Research

infuriated a nationalist public when he sold his business holdings to a Singaporean firm for nearly $2 billion while paying no tax.[48]

Now the government is accusing Thaksin of terrorism for masterminding the street protests and encouraging violence, charges he has denied. It has issued an arrest warrant and hopes that one of the countries where Thaksin travels in self-exile will extradite him.[49]

Meanwhile Thai authorities have shut down publications linked to the red shirt movement and blocked scores of websites and community radio stations under a state of emergency currently in place in Bangkok and 23 provinces.[50] Yet schools and other buildings continue to be attacked across the country. "The land will go up in flames," said Sa-at, a farmer who participated in the Bangkok protests.[51]

New Philippine President

Opposition Sen. Benigno "Noynoy" Aquino was decisively elected the next president of the Philippines on May 10, delivering a sharp rebuke to outgoing President Gloria Macapagal-Arroyo, who had been embroiled in corruption scandals since taking office in 2001.

Aquino is the son of the late Corazon Aquino, who led the "People Power" uprising that finally toppled Marcos in 1986. Known for her honesty and integrity, Mrs. Aquino promised to clean up the "crony capitalism" that

had riddled the Marcos dictatorship, but she largely failed. Her son campaigned on the slogan "No corruption means no poverty," but his lackluster record in Congress led some analysts to doubt his ability to rid the Philippines of endemic graft. "It simply will take overhauling the entire state bureaucracy, and I don't see him ready to undertake this monumental fight," says Tuazon of CenPEG.

It took only two days for voters to learn that Aquino had likely won, an unprecedented brief time compared to past elections, when it took weeks to tally the votes. Voters used computerized optical scanning machines this time, installed not just to shorten the reporting time but also to prevent the rampant election fraud associated with the pencil and paper ballots of the past. In the 2004 elections, Arroyo was accused of massive vote rigging, later supported by an audiotape that surfaced of a conversation between the president and the head of the Commission on Elections (Comelec).

Many of those who were originally skeptical of the largely untested computerized system and of the tainted Comelec's oversight hailed this year's election as a success. Newspaper columnist Conrado de Quiros wrote, "I was wrong about the automation, I was wrong about the Comelec commissioners . . . and, boy, am I absolutely ecstatic to be so."[52]

But several losing presidential candidates are calling for an audit of the results, claiming that 8 million Filipinos failed to cast their ballots due to technical glitches and long lines on election day.[53] And CenPEG said it had received numerous reports from its field researchers and poll watchers of significant problems, including machine malfunctions and shutdowns, power outages and failed electronic transmission of results, leaving an estimated 15 percent of registered voters unable to vote.

The computerized system could not prevent other ills typically associated with Philippine elections. "Vote buying remains rife," according to a May report from the International Crisis Group. For instance, a candidate in

Should the United States, European Union and Australia maintain sanctions on Myanmar?

YES

Wylie Bradford
Editor, Burma Economic Watch Senior Lecturer, Department of Economics, Macquarie University, Sydney, Australia

Written for *CQ Global Researcher*, May 31, 2010

The most obvious and compelling, yet typically neglected, reason to maintain sanctions against the Burmese regime is simple: morality. The military rulers of Burma are criminals of the most violent and rapacious kind, with decades of murder, torture, rape, oppression and pillage on their records. Common human decency ought to be enough to compel legitimate states to make it as hard as possible for the junta and its cronies to continue to profit from evil.

Sadly, the all-too-common mélange of special pleading, anti-Western propaganda and outright hypocrisy has driven a campaign against sanctions on the grounds that sanctions don't work, impose excessive burdens on the Burmese people and ought to be dropped in favour of greater "engagement" with the regime. The intellectual bankruptcy of these positions is another powerful argument for retaining and extending sanctions.

Nobody argues that limiting trade and financial interaction with Burma will lead in itself to democratisation. Hence any claim that sanctions don't work made on those grounds is no more than a straw man. Sanctions — especially targeted financial sanctions — certainly do work by denying the regime access to our financial systems for the purposes of storing and laundering their blood money.

The claim that sanctions hurt the Burmese population is uninformed at best and dishonest at worst. Five decades of military rule have rendered Burma's economy barely functional, a process of destruction set in motion long before any sanctions were imposed. The extent of regime control over economic activity means there are no sectors immune either to their rapacity or their policy incompetence. The junta is the Burmese people's greatest enemy in every sense.

The pro-engagement case is an exercise in sophistry and distortion. The mechanism through which greater "engagement" will produce change is never spelt out. The fact that flourishing trade with nonsanctioning states has yielded precisely no political gains is elided when arguing for greater Western engagement. The demonstrable ineffectiveness of aid is ignored in favour of unfounded assertions to the contrary, and scholarly access to Burma yields papers that few read and none cite and the indulgence of the *National Geographic* fantasies of tourists seeking cheap holidays masquerade as blows for freedom.

Any and all forms of pressure must be maintained until change occurs. The idea that if we enable the generals' malfeasance long enough they will stop of their own accord can only charitably be regarded as stunningly naïve.

NO

Sreeradha Datta
Fellow, Institute of Defence Studies and Analyses, New Delhi, India

Written for *CQ Global Researcher*, May 31, 2010

Once considered Asia's rice bowl, Myanmar today barely manages economic growth of 3 percent. The ruling junta spends 40 percent of its budget on defense, with marginal spending on sectors that could have stimulated the economy. The lack of economic opportunities has been cited by the junta to argue for removal of the sanctions imposed on Myanmar. Indeed, the lack of development can be attributed to the chronic political instability brought on by the ruling generals and their mismanagement of resources and inept economic decision-making.

The generals, meanwhile, enjoy an envious lifestyle, amassing wealth in several bank accounts — clearly sanitized from the surrounding impoverishment. Arguably, the sanctions have affected the junta's commercial projects, but the biggest hit has been taken by the common masses. The generals, the real targets of the sanctions, are the least affected and continue to hold complete sway, economically and politically. They not only run the country with utter disdain toward any democratic or human rights norms but also continue to isolate political opponents with impunity.

Although the international community exudes a sense of disapproval towards the junta, the sanction regime has found limited appeal. In contrast to the Western nations who have persisted with sanctions for over the last two decades, the regional powers and Myanmar's immediate neighbors have chosen to engage with the generals. Although international sanctions are supported by the opposition groups, sanctions have undermined the reformists' position and reinforced the hardliners within the ruling establishment.

The elections announced for the end of the year likely will be farcical. Not only has the junta engineered the absence of the strongest opposition leaders, but it also has simultaneously planted its own men in several of the political parties contesting the elections. Despite this, the eventual rise of new power centers — even a multiparty system — holds some prospects.

Undoubtedly, Myanmar is in dire need of better governance and pluralism. In the face of splintered opposition the junta's overthrow is not an immediate option. Rather, it needs persuasion towards undertaking some reforms. Concerted peer pressure involving regional players and stakeholders holds greater promise of eliciting a response from the generals. Thus, dialogue is a good beginning, not as a supplement to sanctions but rather as a genuine attempt to engage the ruling elite. The stick failed. How about guided inducement?

Christians in Timor-Leste — Southeast Asia's newest democracy — carry crucifixes during a procession in Dili to mark Palm Sunday on March 16, 2008. The predominantly Roman Catholic country has made significant progress toward democracy since it gained independence from Muslim-dominated Indonesia. Although it is considered an electoral democracy, Timor-Leste — like other Southeast Asian countries — has experienced "threatening episodes of armed rebellion, attempted assassination of the president and prime minister, and violent communal conflict," according to Freedom House.

Maguindanao province described "a system of 'assists,' whereby the heads of families or town mayors would be paid to deliver a certain number of votes."[54]

Violence also marred the campaign season, although there were fewer deaths than in the recent past, surprising some observers. "Our institute forecasted more violence in the May 2010 elections because of the continuing presence of illegally armed groups all over the country," says Rommel Banlaoi, director of the Philippine Institute for Peace, Violence and Terrorism Research. "But we were proven wrong because the police and military seriously prepared themselves in deterring these armed groups." Banlaoi says law enforcement initiated peace covenants between competing politicians and made their presence felt in election hotspots.

But Co of the University of the Philippines disagrees that election violence was reduced. "One should look at the 'quality' of violence, and I thought it was more grim and horrid compared to the past," she says.

The worst case of political violence in the country's recent history occurred last November, when 100 armed men ambushed the wife of a local politician while she traveled with family members, supporters and journalists to file her husband's candidacy for the Maguindanao provincial governorship. A total of 57 people were massacred, their bodies found in graves that appeared to have been dug in advance. "Evidence soon emerged to implicate the Ampatuan clan, which dominated the province's politics and was closely allied with the Arroyo administration," according to Freedom House.[55] More than 60 people were arrested, including the provincial governor, Andal Ampatuan Sr.

"Local polls are essentially an intense competition for political power among the country's political dynasties," says Tuazon, like the Marcoses, the Ampatuan clan and the Cojuangco-Aquinos, the family of the next president, which owns Southeast Asia's biggest sugar plantation.

Many of these families, particularly in the southern Philippines, have their own armies, says Tuazon. "These private armies were mobilized by the government for the counterinsurgency campaigns against the Marxist New People's Army and rebels from the Moro National Liberation Front and Moro Islamic Liberation Front." But families like the Ampatuans have also used their armies to intimidate rival politicians and deliver votes, says Tuazon, who adds that laws meant to disband the armies are "toothless."

"The practice of electoral democracy in the Philippines is still messy, and that implies that our democratic foundation remains fragile," says Banlaoi. "The Philippines is still a young democracy, and we need more time to mature," he says.

OUTLOOK

Pressuring Myanmar

Pressure is mounting for the Association of Southeast Asian Nations (ASEAN) to aggressively push for meaningful change in Myanmar. Last year, U.S. Secretary of State Hillary Rodham Clinton called for the organization to consider expelling Myanmar if it did not release pro-democracy leader Aung San Suu Kyi from house arrest.[56]

In April, 106 lawmakers from across Southeast Asia signed a petition criticizing the Burmese elections expected for October as designed "to do nothing more than firmly entrench the military's role in the future governance of Myanmar." The petitioners demanded that ASEAN suspend Myanmar and impose sanctions against its military government.[57]

The goal is to "force the military to the negotiating table with democracy proponents . . . to ensure fairer and more inclusive elections," says Jason, whose ASEAN Inter-Parliamentary Myanmar Caucus sponsored the petition.

ASEAN was founded in 1967 during the height of the Cold War to reduce the region's "risk of falling victim to global rivalry among the great powers."[58] But economic cooperation, cultural exchange and security between its members were the main objectives; interfering in each other's internal politics was not, and in fact is prohibited in the organization's charter.

Another obstacle to ASEAN sanctioning Myanmar: It would require more than a simple majority. "The problem with any serious sanctions or expulsion is that it requires a full consensus," says Evan Laksmana, a researcher at the Centre for Strategic and International Studies, a think tank in Jakarta. "And that is nearly impossible."

"Unlikely, but not impossible," says Jason. "It will take political will by big ASEAN states such as Thailand, Indonesia, Malaysia, Singapore and Philippines to make this happen."

Ever since ASEAN admitted Myanmar in 1997, the group's leaders have engaged in behind-the-scenes diplomacy with the military junta, and, more recently, have publicly expressed concerns over Myanmar's exclusionary election rules unveiled in March. But the policy of "constructive engagement" and mild public rebuke "has been a failure," says McGill's Kuhonta. "ASEAN leaders had argued that if junta leaders were incorporated into ASEAN, back-room diplomacy would make them less coercive," he says. "But not only did it not have any effect, human rights abuses actually increased."

Both Laksmana and Kuhonta are unsure whether sanctions and expulsion, even if possible, would be wise. "It would not change what's happening in Myanmar," says Laksmana, "because Myanmar can survive without ASEAN" as long as China and India continue to provide economic and military aid and invest in the country. Kuhonta calls expulsion too extreme. "ASEAN would lose all leverage with Myanmar," he says. He thinks perhaps stronger public criticism might be the right path for ASEAN now.

Jason disagrees, arguing that sanctions and expulsion from ASEAN would change things quite a bit. "Can China and India continue to defend Myanmar when its closest allies begin to pull away?" he asks. Jason says Myanmar's political and economic support needs to be broken down "brick by brick."

The election could force ASEAN's hand. "What sort of effort will there be to protest? If the death toll runs into the hundreds and the troops lose their cool, then what will ASEAN do?" asks Donald Emmerson, director of the Southeast Asia Forum at Stanford University.

Emmerson notes that Indonesia, Southeast Asia's only "free" democracy, takes over the leadership of ASEAN next January. "Indonesia may say we cannot tolerate a situation where we look like a club of dictators, and we have to do something about that," he says, adding that he cannot predict what shape that response would take.

NOTES

1. Seth Mydans, "With Guns, Slingshots and Rocks, Thai Troops and Protesters Clash, to Lethal Effect," *The New York Times*, May 15, 2010, p. A4.

2. Eric Talmadge, "Thais up Red Shirt watch: no warrant on ex-PM yet," Associated Press, May 28, 2010, www.google.com/hostednews/ap/article/ALeqM5g3j-vAVG1fg3kEfnogTiH8_4EXvwD9FVOQJ02.

3. Thomas Fuller, Seth Mydans and Kirk Semple, "Violence Spreads in Thailand After Crackdown," *The New York Times*, May 19, 2010, www.nytimes.com/2010/05/20/world/asia/20thai.html?pagewanted=1.

4. Arch Puddington, "Freedom in the World 2010: Erosion of Freedom Intensifies," Freedom House, Jan. 12, 2010, p. 4, www.freedomhouse.org/uploads/fiw10/FIW_2010_Overview_Essay.pdf.

5. "Freedom in the World 2009, Methodology," Freedom House, 2009, www.freedomhouse.org/template.cfm?page=351&ana_page=354&year=2009.

6. "The World Factbook," Central Intelligence Agency, www.cia.gov/library/publications/the-world-factbook/.

7. Mark Tran, "Clan allied to Philippine president suspected of being behind massacre," *The Guardian*, Nov. 25, 2009, www.guardian.co.uk/world/2009/nov/25/death-toll-philippines-massacre-57.

8. Since 2001, pollsters across Southeast Asia have been surveying popular opinion in a project called the Asian Barometer Survey (ABS), based at National Taiwan University, www.asianbarometer.org.

9. "Freedom in the World: Burma," Freedom House, 2010, www.freedomhouse.org.

10. "SPDC Election Laws Set the Stage for Sham Elections," ALTSEAN-Burma, April, 2010, www.altsean.org/Docs/PDF%20Format/Thematic%20Briefers/SPDC%20election%20laws%20set%20the%20stage%20for%20sham%20elections.pdf.

11. "Burmese Election Laws an Insult to Democracy and Rule of Law," International Federation for Human Rights, March 12, 2010, www.fidh.org/Burmese-Election-Laws-an-Insult-to-Democracy-and.

12. "SPDC Election Laws Set the Stage for Sham Elections," *op. cit.*

13. *Ibid.*

14. "Myanmar Opposition to Form New Party," *The Wall Street Journal*, May 8, 2010, http://online.wsj.com/article/SB100014240527487033380045752 29613786634410.html.

15. "Freedom in the World: Cambodia, 2010," Freedom House, www.freedomhouse.org/template.cfm?page=363&year=2010&country=7794.

16. "The World Factbook," Central Intelligence Agency, www.cia.gov/library/publications/the-world-factbook/geos/sn.html.

17. "Freedom in the World: Singapore," Freedom House, 2009, www.freedomhouse.org.

18. "The best system for Singapore is . . .," Ori Sasson, People's Action Party, Sept. 6, 2009, www.pap.org.sg/articleview.php?id=4950&cid=85.

19. "Malaysia's Electoral Upheaval," *Journal of Democracy*, July 2009, Vol. 20, No. 3, pp. 71-85.

20. "Freedom in the World: Malaysia," Freedom House, 2010, www.freedomhouse.org/template.cfm?page=363&year=2009&country=7654.

21. "Malaysia's Electoral Upheaval," *op. cit.*

22. "Countries at the Crossroads: Cambodia," Freedom House, 2010, p. 15, www.freedomhouse.org/uploads/ccr/country-7794-9.pdf.

23. "Corruption Perceptions Index 2009," Transparency International, www.transparency.org/policy_research/surveys_indices/cpi/2009/cpi_2009_table.

24. "Countries at the Crossroads: Indonesia," Freedom House, 2010, www.freedomhouse.org/uploads/ccr/country-7841-9.pdf.

25. "Corruption Challenges at Sub-National Level in Indonesia," U4 Expert Answer, Transparency International, July 21, 2009, www.u4.no/helpdesk/helpdesk/query.cfm?id=210.

26. Norimitsu Onishi, "Exposing Graft, but His Motives Are Murky," *The New York Times*, May 8, 2010, www.nytimes.com/2010/05/08/world/asia/08general.html.

27. "Overview of Corruption and Anti-Corruption in the Philippines," U4 Expert Answer, Transparency International, August 2008, p. 3, www.u4.no/helpdesk/helpdesk/query.cfm?id=212.

28. "Global Integrity Report: Philippines," *Global Integrity*, 2008, http://report.globalintegrity.org/philippines/2008/timeline.

29. "Using corruption for political power and private gain," CenPEG, June 29, 2008.

30. "Overview of Corruption and Anti-Corruption in the Philippines," *op. cit.*, p. 1.

31. Charles H. Blake and Christopher G. Martin, "The Dynamics of Political Corruption: Re-examining the Influence of Democracy," *Democratization*, Feb. 2006, Vol. 13, No. 1, p. 4.

32. Unless otherwise stated, the following material is drawn from Yun-Han Chu, *et al.*, *How East Asians View Democracy* (2010).

33. "Philippines," *The New York Times*, http://topics.nytimes.com/top/news/international/countriesand territories/philippines/index.html.

34. Larry Diamond, *The Spirit of Democracy: The Struggle to Build Free Societies Throughout the World* (2008), p. 221. For background, see Brian Beary, "Separatist Movements," *CQ Global Researcher*, April 2008, pp. 85-114.

35. *Ibid.*, p. 223.

36. "Freedom in the World: Thailand," Freedom House, 2009, www.freedomhouse.org.

37. *Ibid.*

38. Larry Diamond, "Indonesia's Place in Global Democracy," in Edward Aspinall and Marcus Mietzner, eds., *Problems of Democratization in Indonesia: Elections, Institutions and Society*, ISEAS, 2010, pp. 21-49.

39. "Freedom in the World: Indonesia," Freedom House, 2010, www.freedomhouse.org.

40. Diamond, *The Spirit of Democracy*, *op. cit.*, p. 92.

41. "Countries at the Crossroads: Indonesia," *op. cit.*

42. "Indonesia," *The New York Times*, http://topics.nytimes .com/top/news/international/countriesandterritories/ indonesia/index.html.

43. "Countries at the Crossroads: East Timor," Freedom House, 2010, www.freedomhouse.org.

44. Hannah Beech and Khon Kaen, "Raising a Red Flag in Thailand," *Time* in partnership with CNN, June 7, 2010, www.time.com/time/magazine/article/0,9171, 1992244,00.html.

45. Thomas Fuller, "Widening Disparity Strains Traditional Bonds of Thai Society," *The New York Times*, April 1, 2010, p. A4.

46. Erik Kuhonta, "Is the Middle Class a Harbinger of Democracy? Evidence from Southeast Asia," presented at the Annual Meeting of the Association for Asian Studies, March 25-28, 2010, p. 15.

47. *Ibid.*

48. Diamond, *The Spirit of Democracy*, *op. cit.*, pp. 80-81.

49. Eric Talmadge, "Thais up Red Shirt watch; no warrant on ex-PM yet," The Associated Press, May 28, 2010, www.google.com/hostednews/ap/article/ ALeqM5g3j-vAVG1fg3kEfnogTiH8_4EXvwD9FV OQJ02.

50. Martin Petty, "Thailand extends censorship against anti-govt protesters," Reuters, May 27, 2010, http:// uk.reuters.com/article/idUKTRE64Q1VU201 00527.

51. Beech and Kaen, *op. cit.*

52. TJ Burgonio, *et al.*, " 'Eating Humble Pie': Poll automation naysayers 'thrilled to be wrong,' " *Inquirer. net*, May 13, 2010, http://newsinfo.inquirer.net/ inquirerheadlines/nation/view/20100513-269687/ Poll-automation-naysayers-thrilled-to-be-wrong.

53. "Philippine lawmakers to probe poll fraud allegations," Reuters India, May 18, 2010, http://in .reuters.com/article/worldNews/idINIndia-48581 920100518.

54. "Philippines: Pre-Election Tensions in Central Mindanao," International Crisis Group, May 4, 2010, p. 5, www.crisisgroup.org/en/regions/asia/ south-east-asia/philippines.aspx.

55. "Freedom in the World: Philippines," Freedom House, 2010, www.freedomhouse.org.

56. Boonradom Chitradon, "ASEAN rejects Clinton's call to expel Myanmar: Thai PM," Agence France-Presse, July 23, 2009, www.saigon-gpdaily.com.vn/ International/2009/7/72733/.

57. "Petition to ASEAN Leaders attending 16th ASEAN Summit," April 7, 2010, www.aseanmp.org/wp-content/uploads/2008/07/Petition-to-ASEAN-on-Myanmar-2010-election.pdf.

58. Donald K. Emmerson, ed., *Hard Choices: Security, Democracy, and Regionalism in Southeast Asia* (2008), p. 59.

BIBLIOGRAPHY

Books

Chu, Yun-han, *et al.*, ed., *How East Asians View Democracy*, Columbia University Press, 2008.
Contributors dissect polling data from the Asian Barometer Survey, a comparative examination of democratization and values across the region.

Diamond, Larry, *The Spirit of Democracy: The Struggle to Build Free Societies Throughout the World*, Henry Holt, 2008.
With democracy in many parts of the world under pressure, a Stanford University professor examines

why and how it is achieved and what conditions sustain it.

Emmerson, Donald K., ed., *Hard Choices: Security, Democracy, and Regionalism in Southeast Asia,* The Walter H. Shorenstein Asia-Pacific Research Center, 2008.
Contributors debate the role of the Association of Southeast Asian Nations (ASEAN) in ensuring security and encouraging democracy in the region.

Articles

"Myanmar Opposition To Form New Party," *The Wall Street Journal,* May 8, 2010, p. A9.
Myanmar's main opposition movement decides to boycott upcoming elections, and former members launch a splinter group to contest the polls.

"Worsening violence closes Bangkok bank and businesses," *The Guardian,* April 23, 2010, www.guardian .co.uk/world/2010/apr/23/violence-closes-bangkok-banks.
In Thailand's worst violence in 20 years, protesters and soldiers clash, leaving scores dead or wounded.

Boonradom, Chitradon, "ASEAN rejects Clinton's call to expel Myanmar: Thai PM," *Agence France-Presse,* July 23, 2009.
U.S. Secretary of State Hillary Rodham Clinton calls for the Association of Southeast Asian Nations to consider expelling Myanmar if its military junta does not release Nobel laureate and opposition leader Daw Aung San Suu Kyi from house arrest.

Onishi, Norimitsu, "Exposing Graft, but His Motives are Murky," *The New York Times,* May 8, 2010, www.nytimes.com/2010/05/08/world/asia/08general .html.
A former chief of detectives in Indonesia's national police force, accused of soliciting a bribe, threatens to release details of high-level police and government corruption.

Sasson, Ori, "The Best System for Singapore Is . . . ," *People's Action Party,* www.pap.org.sg, Sept. 6, 2009, www.pap.org.sg/articleview.php?id=4950&cid=85.
A member of Singapore's ruling party argues that democracy exists when the dominant party provides for citizens' needs and that a two-party system is not necessary in a democracy.

Reports and Studies

"Freedom in the World: Cambodia," *Freedom House,* 2010, www.freedomhouse.org/template.cfm?page=363&year=2010&country=7794.
Land grabs, official corruption and government harassment of critics worsen in Cambodia as a new law makes defamation a criminal offense.

"Freedom in the World: Singapore," *Freedom House,* 2009, www.freedomhouse.org.
An opposition politician must pay defamation damages to the prime minister and his father, while another opposition politician draws jail time for insulting two judges on his blog.

"SPDC Election Laws Set the Stage for Sham Elections," *ALTSEAN-Burma,* April 2010, www .altsean.org/Reports/2010Electionster.php.
This briefing paper contends that Burma's repressive election laws, along with restraints placed on the media, ensure unfair elections in the fall.

Blake, Charles H., and Christopher G. Martin, "The Dynamics of Political Corruption: Re-examining the Influence of Democracy," *Democratization,* February 2006.
The authors argue that the consolidation of a vital democracy over time exercises a more powerful influence over corruption than past research had indicated.

Buehler, Michael, "Countries at the Crossroads — Indonesia," *Freedom House,* 2010, www.freedom-house.org.
The author reviews how Indonesia has established a liberal democracy since the fall of Gen. Suharto in 1998 but describes how the quality of that democracy remains low.

Chin, James, and Wong Chin Huat, "Malaysia's Electoral Upheaval," *Journal of Democracy,* July 2009, www. journalofdemocracy.org/articles/gratis/Chin-20-3.pdf.
The authors assess what the ruling party's surprising loss of its two-thirds parliamentary majority in the 2008 election means for the future of quasi-democratic Malaysia.

Nawaz, Farzana, "Overview of Corruption and Anti-Corruption in the Philippines," *U4 Expert Answer, Transparency International,* Aug. 17, 2009, www.u4 .no/helpdesk/helpdesk/query.cfm?id=212.
The author describes the endemic corruption that is a significant obstacle to good governance in the Philippines.

For More Information

Asia Society, 725 Park Ave., New York, NY 10021; (212) 288-6400; www.asiasociety.org. A leading global and pan-Asian organization working to strengthen relationships and promote understanding among the people, leaders and institutions of the United States and Asia.

Asian Barometer Survey, Department of Political Science, National Taiwan University, 21 Hsu-Chow Rd., Taipei, Taiwan 100; (886) 2 2357 0427; www.asianbarometer.org. An applied research program on public opinion about political values, democracy and governance in Asia.

Association of Southeast Asian Nations (ASEAN), 70A Jl. Sisingamangaraja, Jakarta 12110, Indonesia; (6221) 7262991; www.aseansec.org. Established in 1967 to accelerate economic growth, social progress and cultural development in the region and to promote regional peace and stability.

Center for People Empowerment in Governance (Cen-PEG), 3/F CSWCD Bldg., Magsaysay St., University of the Philippines Diliman, 1101 Quezon City, Philippines; (632) 929-9526; www.eu-cenpeg.com. A public policy center that monitors elections in the Philippines and advocates for the democratic representation of the poor.

Centre for Strategic and International Studies, The Jakarta Post Bldg., 3rd Floor, Jl. Palmera Barat 142-243, Jakarta 10270, Indonesia; (62-21) 5365 4601; www.csis.or.id. An independent nonprofit organization in Indonesia focusing on policy-oriented studies and dialogue on domestic and international issues.

Freedom House, 1301 Connecticut Ave., N.W., Floor 6, Washington, D.C. 20036; (202) 296-5101; www.freedomhouse.org. An independent watchdog organization that supports democratic change, monitors freedom, and advocates for democracy and human rights.

Global Voices, Atrium, Strawinskylaan 3105, Amsterdam ZX 1077, The Netherlands; http://globalvoicesonline.org. A community of more than 300 bloggers and translators who publicize citizen media from around the world, with emphasis on voices not ordinarily heard in international mainstream media.

Human Rights Watch, 50 Fifth Ave., 34th Floor, New York, NY 10118; (212) 290-4700; www.hrw.org. A leading independent organization dedicated to defending and protecting human rights.

Institute of Southeast Asian Studies, 30 Heng Mui Keng Terrace, Pasir Panjang, Singapore, 119614; (65) 6778 0955; www.iseas.edu.sg. A regional research center dedicated to the study of sociopolitical, security and economic trends and developments in Southeast Asia.

International Crisis Group, 149 Avenue Louise, Level 24, B-1050 Brussels, Belgium; (32) 2 502 90 38; www.crisisgroup.org. An independent, nonprofit, nongovernmental organization committed to preventing and resolving deadly conflict.

Transparency International, Alt-Moabit 96, 10559 Berlin, Germany; (49) 30 3438 20 0; www.transparency.org. A global coalition of more than 90 national offices around the world that fight corruption.

Voices From Abroad:

STEPHEN LILLIE

British Ambassador to the Philippines

A maturing system

"Through their high turnout at the elections, the Filipino people have demonstrated their commitment to the democratic process and their determination to shape their own destiny. This is a good day for politics in the Philippines. . . . This is a welcome sign of the increasing maturity of the Philippine political system."

Philippines News Agency May 2010

IAN STOREY

Senior Fellow, Institute of Southeast Asian Studies, Singapore

A new democratic leader

"It would have been incredible to conceive a few years ago, but this election is showing just how far Indonesia has come. Any hopes about Thailand or Malaysia emerging as democratic voices have fallen away and now Indonesia is the standout."

South China Morning Post July 2009

CHRIS PURANASAMRIDDHI

Construction company manager, Thailand

Embarrassed for my country

"Thailand is the land of smiles, easygoing, and I want it back. The red shirts, they are quite aggressive, and we are not an aggressive country, as everyone knows. For the first time, I am embarrassed for Thailand in front of the world."

The New York Times, April 2010

SOMYOT PRUKSAKASEMSUK

Red Shirt Leader, Thailand

A crisis of faith

"Initially, independent movements of the masses in Bangkok and the regions will begin, then riots will ensue. For

Thailand in the long term, there will be major changes due to the crisis of faith."

The Boston Globe, May 2010

WALDEN BELLO

Senior Analyst, Focus for the Global South Philippines

China's leverage

"ASEAN has not yet managed to consolidate itself as an economic bloc. Yet, here we are launching a free trade area with China that will mean eventually bringing our tariffs down to zero. ASEAN is already noncompetitive with China across a whole range of manufactured goods and agricultural products."

Philippine Daily Inquirer January 2010

RIZAL SUKMA

Executive Director, Centre for Strategic and International Studies, Indonesia

Institutionalize democratic culture

"While the people have once again demonstrated the ability to practice democracy, there is still the challenge of institutionalizing democratic culture, norms and values among the political elite. In the long run, the merit of Indonesia as a full-fledged democracy will also depend on the ability of the elected government to deliver economic prosperity and social justice."

Jakarta (Indonesia) Post July 2009

SHITA LAKSMI

Program Officer, Hivos
Foundation, Netherlands

"Long dear friends"

"It seems that Indonesian people and criminal defamation are long dear friends. It would be difficult to separate them as long as freedom of expression is a dream and the exercise of criticizing or being open to criticism is not a part of our tradition."

Jakarta (Indonesia) Post, January 2010

IRENE KHAN

Secretary General, Amnesty
International, England

A symbol of hope for all

"In those long and often dark years, Daw Aung San Suu Kyi has remained a symbol of hope, courage and the undying defense of human rights, not only to the people of Myanmar but to people around the world."

The New York Times, July 2009

CHARLES CHONG

Member, ASEAN Inter-Parliamentary Myanmar
Caucus, Indonesia

Impatient with Burma

"More and more parliamentarians within ASEAN are beginning to lose their patience with Burma. And, we are calling upon our governments to do more than just expressions of dismay, regret, grave concern and so on, and seriously look at suspending Burma's membership of ASEAN."

Thai Press Reports, May 2009

14

Turmoil in the Arab World

Roland Flamini

An Egyptian citizen smiles proudly after voting in the historic constitutional referendum on March 19. Voters overwhelmingly approved the measures, including one that establishes presidential term limits, one of the major demands of tens of thousands of mostly youthful pro-democracy protesters. Their 18-day demonstration in downtown Cairo earlier in the year led to the Feb. 11 resignation of President Hosni Mubarak, who had ruled for 30 years.

From *CQ Researcher*, May 3, 2011.

Will the current turmoil in the Arab world turn out to be the best of times or the worst of times — the Arab Spring or the Arab Winter?

Not since the collapse of the Soviet Union in 1989 and the turn to democracy of its Central and Eastern European satellite states has an entire region been plunged into such tumultuous change. From the Atlantic to the Persian Gulf, long-entrenched regimes have suddenly faced popular uprisings. Starting in Tunisia in December and spreading to Egypt and a dozen other countries, political unrest has swept across the region like a desert sandstorm, roiling each country differently but with common characteristics: youth-driven demonstrations aided by online social networks and alliances forming across religious, class and tribal lines. So far, two long-entrenched autocratic regimes have been toppled, and others appear to be on shaky ground. At least four have struck back violently to suppress the protesters.

Egyptian historian Khaled Fahmy of the American University in Cairo rates the events as momentous for the region as the collapse of Ottoman control in 1923. The incident that lit the first fuse was the Dec. 17 suicide of a street vendor in Tunisia, unleashing a torrent of pent-up public frustration over government corruption and abuse. Within weeks President Zine El Abidine Ben Ali had quit and left the country, after 23 years in power. Then, following an epic 18 days of mass protests, Egypt's President Hosni Mubarak resigned on Feb. 11, ending his 30-year autocratic rule. From there the protests spread to at least a dozen other countries.

"This was about police brutality, about human rights and personal dignity, equal opportunities and social justice," says Fahmy.

Countries With Unrest Have Youthful Populations

Young demonstrators have played key roles in the recent pro-democracy protests in 14 Middle Eastern and North African countries that so far have toppled two longtime dictators — in Tunisia and Egypt. Throughout the region, nearly half — or more — of the citizens are under age 25. Yemen has the largest "youth bulge," with 65 percent of the population under 25. Although most of the protests have been peaceful, four countries — Libya, Syria, Yemen and Bahrain — have cracked down violently on demonstrators.

Countries With Pro-Democracy Demonstrations
(and percentage of population under age 25)

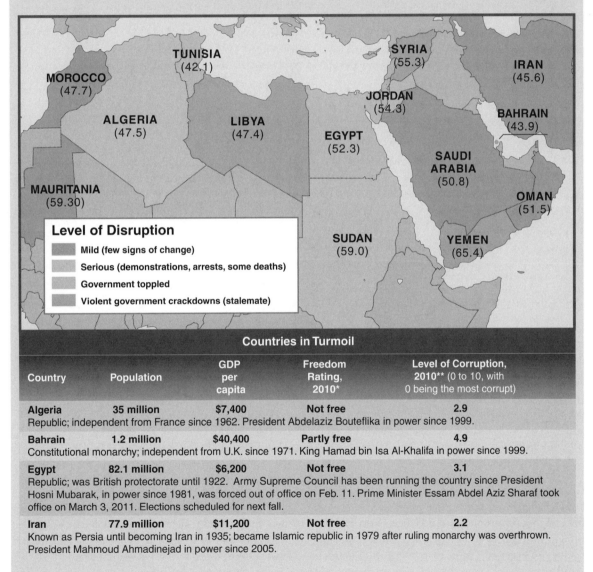

Level of Disruption

- Mild (few signs of change)
- Serious (demonstrations, arrests, some deaths)
- Government toppled
- Violent government crackdowns (stalemate)

Countries in Turmoil

Country	Population	GDP per capita	Freedom Rating, 2010*	Level of Corruption, 2010** (0 to 10, with 0 being the most corrupt)
Algeria	35 million	$7,400	Not free	2.9
Republic; independent from France since 1962. President Abdelaziz Bouteflika in power since 1999.				
Bahrain	1.2 million	$40,400	Partly free	4.9
Constitutional monarchy; independent from U.K. since 1971. King Hamad bin Isa Al-Khalifa in power since 1999.				
Egypt	82.1 million	$6,200	Not free	3.1
Republic; was British protectorate until 1922. Army Supreme Council has been running the country since President Hosni Mubarak, in power since 1981, was forced out of office on Feb. 11. Prime Minister Essam Abdel Aziz Sharaf took office on March 3, 2011. Elections scheduled for next fall.				
Iran	77.9 million	$11,200	Not free	2.2
Known as Persia until becoming Iran in 1935; became Islamic republic in 1979 after ruling monarchy was overthrown. President Mahmoud Ahmadinejad in power since 2005.				

Source: "Mapping the Arab World," The Economist, Feb. 17, 2011,
www.economist.com/blogs/dailychart/2011/02/arab_league_map.

Countries in Turmoil (Cont.)				
Country	Population	GDP per capita	Freedom Rating, 2010*	Level of Corruption, 2010** (0 to 10, with 0 being the most corrupt)
Jordan	6.5 million	$5,300	Not free	4.7
Constitutional monarchy; independent from British mandate since 1946. King Abdallah II in power since 1999.				
Libya	6.6 million	$13,800	Not free	2.2
Dictatorship run by revolutionary leader Moammar Gadhafi since 1969.				
Mauritania	3.3 million	$2,100	Not free	2.3
Military junta; independent from France since 1960. President Mohamed Ould Abdel Aziz in power since 2009.				
Morocco	32 million	$4,999	Partly free	3.4
Constitutional monarchy; independent from France since 1956. King Mohammed VI in power since 1999.				
Oman	3 million	$25,800	Not free	5.3
Monarchy; independent since mid-1700s following Portuguese and Persian rule. Sultan Qaboos bin Said Al-Said in power since 1970.				
Saudi Arabia	26.1 million	$24,200	Not free	4.7
Monarchy; founded in 1932 after several attempts to unify the Arabian Peninsula. King and Prime Minister Abdallah bin Abd al-Aziz Al Saud has been in power since 2005.				
Sudan	45 million	$2,200	Not free	1.6
Independent from U.K. since 1956. Power-sharing government in place since 2005 peace agreement. President Omar al-Bashir has ruled since 1993. Southern part of country will become independent on July 9, 2011, following a referendum in January.				
Syria	22.5 million	$4,800	Not free	2.5
Authoritarian regime; was a French mandate until 1946. President Bashar Assad's family has been in power for 40 years.				
Tunisia	10.6 million	$9,500	Not free	4.3
Republic; independent from France since 1956. Interim President Fouad M'Bazaa took office in January after protests forced Zine El Abidine Ben Ali from office. Next election: October 2014.				
Yemen	24.1 million	$2,600	Not free	2.2
Republic; independent from Ottoman Empire since 1918. South Yemen unified with North Yemen in 1990. President Ali Abdullah Saleh in power since July 1978.				

* According to Freedom House

** Transparency International

Source: "The World Factbook," Central Intelligence Agency, 2011, www.cia.gov/library/publications/the-world-factbook/index.html; "Map of Freedom in the World," Freedom House, 2010, www.freedomhouse.org/template.cfm?page=363&year=2010; "Corruption Perceptions Index Results 2010 Results," Transparency International, October 2010, www.transparency.org/policy_research/surveys_indices/cpi/2010/results.

"What people in [Cairo's] Tahrir Square were chanting was 'dignity, freedom, social justice.'"

But it was also about economics. "The Arab group [of countries] is not a monolithic group . . . but we face the same challenges in terms of employment, in terms of investing in our people," declared Taieb Fassi Fihri, the foreign minister of Morocco, where some minor outbreaks also occurred. "More than 50 percent of our citizens are less than 25 years old, and we have to respond to the legitimate ambitions of our youth."[1]

Although initially peaceful, the demonstrations have not been without violence. At least 872 people died and 6,400 were injured during the nearly three weeks of turmoil in Egypt, largely the result of a government crackdown on the demonstrators, according to a recent fact-finding mission.[2] In Syria and Yemen, more than 635 have been killed in government backlashes, and untold thousands have died in what has devolved into a civil war in Libya.

The unrest has shown that autocracies don't last forever. They are stable — until they are not. But the euphoria generated across the region by the popular uprisings in Tunisia and Egypt quickly turned bleak, as Egyptians grappled with the challenges of rebuilding their nation from the ground up, and entrenched leaders elsewhere fought back against spiraling street demonstrations. With the death toll and arrests mounting daily, there was growing concern in the international community — and, in the case of Libya, a decision by the United Nations and NATO to intervene to protect civilians, which some see as a scenario that could well be repeated elsewhere before the dust settles in the Arab world.

In four countries, security forces and demonstrators have clashed repeatedly. More than 140 demonstrators have died in three months of unrest in Yemen, where protesters are calling for the departure of President Ali Abdullah Saleh (32 years in office).[3] One of the worst incidents occurred on March 18 in Sanaa, the capital, when government snipers firing from rooftops killed at least 45 demonstrators and injured 200.[4] In an effort to halt demonstrations in Syria, President Bashar Assad has promised some reforms, including lifting emergency law, but the unrest continued into late April. In the tiny Gulf kingdom of Bahrain, King Hamad Al Khalifa faces public pressure from a Shiite majority to reform the constitution.[5] In Amman, Jordan, a man was killed when riot police forcibly dismantled a protesters' camp. Demonstrators want King Abdullah II to hasten promised electoral reforms.

But nowhere has the government backlash been as violent as in Libya, where the cost in deaths, injuries and refugees continues to climb, as a rag-tag opposition defies longtime leader Moammar Gadhafi. The fighting has split the oil-rich desert nation, with the rebels in tenuous control of the eastern part, centered in Benghazi. On March 19, urged by the Arab League and armed with a U.N. Security Council resolution, Western nations imposed a no-fly zone over Libya. Initially, U.S. forces destroyed Gadhafi's air operations, and then six NATO countries and one Arab nation — Qatar — began attacking Gadhafi's forces in an effort to protect civilians. The government advance has been stalled, but rebels have been unable to progress. The Obama administration later agreed to send unmanned drones to support the insurrection. Meanwhile, Britain, France and Italy sent advisers to train the fighters.

The international community called on Gadhafi to step down, but the 68-year-old Libyan leader became more defiant daily. The fear, among some experts, is that the Libyan stand-off could encourage other embattled leaders to stay put at all cost, transforming the wave of pro-democracy demonstrations into a series of civil wars.

The Obama administration finds itself caught between old alliances and newly emerging opposition movements. Virtually all the region's dictators — except for Assad in Syria — were U.S. allies, including, most recently, the now demonized Gadhafi. Many of the old regimes cooperated with the United States in the ongoing war against terrorism. But the future shape of the Arab world also has global implications. The Middle East and North Africa provide a third of the 86 million barrels of oil consumed worldwide each day, with 13 million coming from Saudi Arabia and the United Arab Emirates alone.[6] And Egypt and Jordan are key participants in the perennial search for a solution to the Palestinian-Israeli conflict.[7] Although no anti-Israel slogans have been seen in the demonstrations so far, the Arab-Israeli issue has certainly not disappeared from the Arab radar screen.

The new governments in the region "are going to take a fresh look at Arab-Israeli relations," says David Aaron, a former deputy national security adviser and now a Middle East specialist at the RAND Corporation think tank offices in Washington, D.C. "They're going to see that the Israelis had 30 years to do something about implementing the Camp David agreements and — from their perspective — haven't done anything." A new Pew Research Center poll of Egyptians, conducted during the uprising, showed that 54 percent favor canceling the 1979 peace treaty with Israel.[8]

And what can the United States expect from the changes? "What struck me about the Tahrir Square protests was that for the first time the demonstrators didn't burn U.S. flags," comments Gawdat Bahgat, an Egyptian-born professor of political science at the National Defense University in Washington, D.C. "There was no anti-American sentiment." Even so, weeks later, when U.S. Secretary of State Hillary Rodham Clinton visited Tahrir Square, young demonstrators' groups refused to meet with her —"due to her initially negative stance toward the revolution during its inception and the approach of the U.S. administration towards the Middle East region," they said in a statement. On the first day of the uprisings Clinton had called the Egyptian regime "stable."[9]

Women Played Key Roles in Demonstrations

"We went through everything our brothers went through."

I f the upheaval in the Middle East has done nothing else, it has seriously challenged the image of Arab women as second-class citizens in a male-dominated society. In Cairo, Egypt, women joined men in the pro-democracy demonstrations in Tahrir Square, and several female doctors and nurses helped to staff the four field hospitals in the square. Even more striking because of their greater seclusion, young women in Yemen started the protesters' encampment at Sanaa University, in the nation's capital.

In Cairo and Sanaa, as well as in Tunis, Tunisia, and Benghazi, Libya, television coverage showed women wearing blue jeans as well as traditional black, mixing with the men in a collective outburst of yearning for change. "We — the girls — spoke with the media, arranged protests, slept in Tahrir Square," Shehata, a young communications graduate, was quoted as saying. "Some of us got detained. So we went through everything our brothers [went] through." [1]

Says political scientist Alanoud Al-Sharekh, who works in the Chatham House think tank office in Bahrain's capital, Manama, "The traditional view is that Arab women remained in the background; a heavy nationalist movement with women in the fore means that this label can be removed: women have gained legitimacy."

And Gawdat Bahgat, an Egyptian-born professor of political science at the National Defense University in Washington, D.C., says women's role in the demonstrations "begs the question about women in the Arab world. Women demonstrators were not demanding equal rights: They were shouting the same slogans as the men. They were part of the revolution."

Even so, Nadje Al-Ali, a London-based author of studies on Egyptian and Iraqi women, warns against generalizing about the status of Arab women because the situation is different in virtually every country, and even between different social groups within the same country. "Middle-class women in Cairo probably have a better life than middle-class women in New York because they can get more

Women, who have not traditionally been active in Egyptian politics, helped organize and participated in the massive protests in Cairo's Tahrir Square against the regime of President Hosni Mubarak.

AFP/Getty Images/Miguel Medina

domestic help and have more time to follow their own pursuits; it's the working-class women that have more problems," she says.

But can Arab women consolidate their gender gains? The first signs are not encouraging. On March 8, a large gathering of women in Tahrir Square to mark International Women's Day was heckled and taunted by a sea of angry men, who ultimately chased them off the square. "Go home and make mahshy [stuffed vegetables]," the men shouted, to the astonishment of the women. Some of the men even grabbed the placards held by the women — demanding a fair constitution, wide-ranging participation in government and an end to sexual harassment — and tore them to shreds. [2]

Women were particularly disappointed that no females were included in the commission appointed to reform the Egyptian constitution. "Women need to get in there right away because there are some gender-specific issues in the constitution, and women need to be involved in reviewing them," says Al-Ali. Some of the obvious legal inequalities include "getting rid of male guardians [which every Muslim woman must have], and reforming the laws of marriage, divorce and inheritance derived by interpretation of Sharia law," she adds.

Under Sharia family law, for example, a woman's testimony is not acceptable in court. However, a husband can get a unilateral divorce simply by verbally repudiating his wife, but a woman must give justifications. Child custody reverts to the father at a preset age — unless a woman has already lost custody by re-marrying. Sons inherit twice the amount as daughters.

But since 2004 Arab women's-rights activists have been able to point to Morocco, where family-law reforms overturned many discriminatory provisions. The minimum age for Moroccan women to marry was raised from 15 to 18, the same as for men; women are now allowed to marry without approval from a guardian; men can no longer unilaterally divorce their wives, and women were given the right to divorce their husbands. Men can still have multiple wives, but they must first get permission from a judge.

Although female followers of the Egyptian Muslim Brotherhood were among the demonstrators in Cairo, the prospect of the Brotherhood playing what will likely be a significant political role in post-Mubarak Egypt raises fears among some Egyptians that the radical Muslim movement might find a way to impose Sharia law.

Al-Ali concedes that while women historically have taken part in revolutionary movements, "when [the] aims are achieved, women are often pushed aside." Yet she is cautiously optimistic that this time Arab women will make some gains, but not to the same degree in every country. "Women in Saudi Arabia are starting from a different point from women in Egypt," she says.

Laura Guazzone, a Middle East specialist at the Institute of International Affairs and an associate professor of Arab history at Sapienza University in Rome, is equally cautious in her predictions. "The presence of women in the demonstrations was a step forward; I would expect it to translate into a modest amount of liberalization in the national context."

Female Literacy Rates Differ

More than 80 percent of the women in Jordan and Bahrain can read and write — the highest rates among the countries in turmoil in the Middle East and North Africa. Morocco and Yemen have the lowest female literacy rates — below 40 percent. Only about 11 percent of the members of parliament in the region are women, about half the global rate.

Female Literacy Rates in Countries With Unrest*			
Jordan	84.7%	Tunisia	65.3%
Bahrain	83.6%	Algeria	60.1%
Syria	73.6%	Egypt	59.4%
Oman	73.5%	Sudan	50.5%
Libya	72%	Mauritania	43.4%
Saudi Arabia	70.8%	Morocco	39.6%
Iran	70.4%	Yemen	30%

Percentage of Women Serving in Parliament

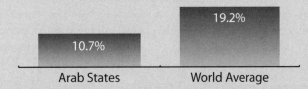

* Based on the most recent post-2000 census available.

Sources: The World Factbook, CIA; Inter-Parliamentary Union, www.ipu.org/wmn-e/world.htm

Even so, in Cairo, prize-winning Egyptian novelist Ahdaf Soueif shrugs off nervousness about the Brotherhood's intentions. "Things can only get better," she says. "This is not a Brotherhood movement, this is an inclusive movement, and when the time comes we'll sort it out."

— Roland Flamini

[1]"Sisters aspire to equality within Egypt's Muslim Brotherhood," *Al Masry Al Youm*, March 16, 2011, www.almasryalyoum.com/en/node/354388.

[2]Hania Sholkamy, "From Tahrir square to my kitchen," *50.50 inclusive democracy*, March 14, 2011, www.opendemocracy.net/5050/hania-sholkamy/from-tahrir-square-to-my-kitchen.

Both activists and Western powers worry the upheaval will open the way for radical Islamists to gain control across the Arab world. But the demonstrations so far have been secular — so secular, in fact, that female demonstrators mixed freely with the men. Still, Bahgat believes, "Post-Mubarak Egypt will be more Islamic, and there will be less cooperation in the war on terrorism," which "is seen by many as war on Islam."

In Egypt, Islamist activism is led by the Muslim Brotherhood, the largest religious-political organization in the region. But Jean-Pierre Filiu, head of Middle East studies at the Political Science Institute in Paris (known as Sciences Po), does not see it as a threat. "There is no [Islamist] bogeyman in Egypt or Tunisia," he says. "I don't see any place where the Brotherhood will win a majority. They will end up part of coalitions."

Fear of rising Islamist influence stems in part from the fact that the regimes under siege had suppressed political opposition for so long that the democratic credentials of protest leaders are unknown and untested. But a more immediate anxiety, says historian Fahmy, is "fear of a counter-revolution, with the old regime coming back under a different guise."

So far, the revolution has raised more questions than it has answered, among them:

Can Western-style democracy take root in Arab countries?

Decades of autocratic government in the region have led to the widely held view that democracy cannot take hold in the Arab world. The familiar arguments include:

- Islam is not a democratic religion;
- There is no Arabic word for "democracy;"
- Abundant oil and gas revenue has meant citizens of some countries do not pay taxes and thus have no expectations of government accountability; and
- Western democracies had reinforced the very autocratic regimes that the protesters are trying to bring down.

Supporting those arguments, Bernard Lewis, a prominent American authority on the Middle East, recently told *The Jerusalem Post* that "the Arab masses are simply not ready for free and fair elections." He recommended that political reform follow traditional regional practices, such as consultative councils between rulers and other officials, with the circle of those consulted gradually expanding.

But Larry Diamond, a senior fellow at Stanford University's conservative Hoover Institution and an expert on democracy, says, "Support for democracy is very broad in the Arab world, and it does not vary by degree of religiosity. Look at the way Iraqis turned out to vote three times in 2005 amid widespread and dire risks to their physical safety, and it is hard to conclude that Arabs do not care about democracy."[10]

Two Middle East scholars — writing in *Survival*, the magazine of the International Institute of Strategic Studies in London — argue that the recent turmoil "has convincingly demonstrated that the Arab world yearns, too, for dignity and better governance. Arab citizens, long thought to be either hopelessly apathetic or uniquely prone to violent political rage, proved to be relentless and, in most cases, peaceful protesters."[11]

And Egyptian historian Fahmy says in recent weeks Egyptians have amply indicated that they understand the essence of democracy. They have consistently demanded "human rights and dignity, social justice, equal opportunities, and the end to police brutality," he says.

But what shape will Arab-style democracy take? "There is no one-size-fits-all, such as U.S.-style democracy," the National Defense University's Bahgat says. "What needs to happen is the start of democratization, which is not the same as democracy; it's the process of getting there — and there will be many bumps along the way."

The Economist doesn't foresee a smooth transition either. "No perfectly formed democracy is about to emerge from the detritus of Mr. Mubarak's regime," the magazine commented recently. "But Egypt, though poor, has a sophisticated elite, a well-educated middle class and a strong sense of national pride." All those factors indicate that "Egyptians can pull order out of this chaos."[12]

Former British Prime Minister Tony Blair, the trouble-shooter for the international Quartet (the U.S., Russia, the U.N., and the EU) responsible for advancing the Palestinian-Israeli peace process, said it was important for the Arabs to understand what constitutes democracy. "It's not just about the freedom to vote," said Blair. "It's about freedom of expression, free markets, freedom of religion, the rule of law and a whole series of things that go to make up a genuine democracy."[13]

Laura Guazzone, an expert on the Middle East at Rome's Sapienza University, says the best outcome would be that some countries will evolve "through a succession of compromises into quasi-democracies, politically much more liberal than the previous regimes but still largely based on the same power structures and orientations in their respective economic and foreign policies." Potential worst-case scenarios range "from a tightening of the existing repression under the same regime (Bahrain, Syria) to secession and Somalia-style fragmentation (Yemen, Libya)."

Is the current upheaval in the best interests of the Western powers and Israel?

Before the current unrest, the status quo in the Middle East and North Africa had served Western strategic interests for decades. Successive American administrations had tacitly supported, and funded, many of the regimes under assault, turning a blind eye to corruption, cronyism and torture.

"Let's face it: Mubarak was a strategic asset to the United States," says Steven A. Cook, a senior fellow at the New York-based Council on Foreign Relations think tank. "He ensured access to the Suez Canal, upheld the Egypt-Israel peace treaty and keptthe Islamists down. . . . The fact that the United States supported this now-discredited government for three decades is not lost on Egyptians."

For decades, "U.S. policy has been to divide the moderate Arabs (Egypt, Jordan, Saudi Arabia) from the extremist Arabs (Syria)," says Bahgat, of the National Defense University.

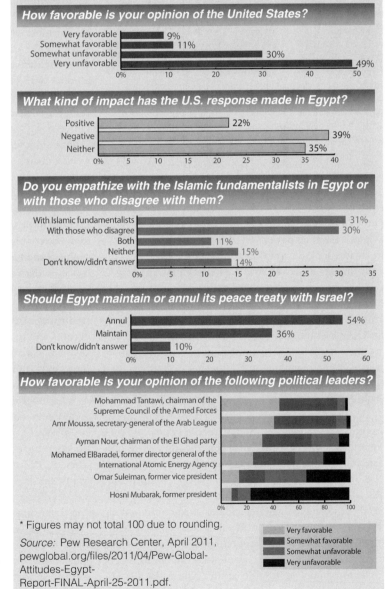

Most Egyptians View U.S. Unfavorably

More than three-quarters of Egyptians say they have an unfavorable view of the United States while the ratio of those who believe the U.S. response to the revolution in Egypt had a negative rather than positive impact is about 2 to 1. Egyptians are about evenly split over Islamic fundamentalists, and more than half believe Egypt should annul its peace treaty with Israel. Among potential political leaders, Mohammad Tantawi and Amr Moussa were clear favorites.

How favorable is your opinion of the United States?

- Very favorable — 9%
- Somewhat favorable — 11%
- Somewhat unfavorable — 30%
- Very unfavorable — 49%

What kind of impact has the U.S. response made in Egypt?

- Positive — 22%
- Negative — 39%
- Neither — 35%

Do you empathize with the Islamic fundamentalists in Egypt or with those who disagree with them?

- With Islamic fundamentalists — 31%
- With those who disagree — 30%
- Both — 11%
- Neither — 15%
- Don't know/didn't answer — 14%

Should Egypt maintain or annul its peace treaty with Israel?

- Annul — 54%
- Maintain — 36%
- Don't know/didn't answer — 10%

How favorable is your opinion of the following political leaders?

- Mohammad Tantawi, chairman of the Supreme Council of the Armed Forces
- Amr Moussa, secretary-general of the Arab League
- Ayman Nour, chairman of the El Ghad party
- Mohamed ElBaradei, former director general of the International Atomic Energy Agency
- Omar Suleiman, former vice president
- Hosni Mubarak, former president

Legend:
- Very favorable
- Somewhat favorable
- Somewhat unfavorable
- Very unfavorable

* Figures may not total 100 due to rounding.

Source: Pew Research Center, April 2011, pewglobal.org/files/2011/04/Pew-Global-Attitudes-Egypt-Report-FINAL-April-25-2011.pdf.

AFP/Getty Images/Mohammed Abed

To show the nondenominational nature of their pro-democracy movement, Coptic Christians and Muslims in Cairo's Tahrir Square raise a cross and the Quran on Feb. 6, the 13th day of protests calling for President Hosni Mubarak to resign. He stepped down five days later. Some "Copts" — an Egyptian Christian sect that predates Islam — fear that they could continue to be persecuted, as they were under the Mubarak regime, if the Islamist Muslim Brotherhood gains power in Egypt.

Now, however, "the moderate camp is collapsing." Whoever assumes power will likely be unknown quantities to Washington and the European capitals.

If the region has become a daunting new challenge, the main issues have remained the same: terrorism, the Arab-Israeli conflict and Iran's nuclear ambitions. The crucial nature of that challenge may account for the Obama administration's initial ambivalence toward the protest movement. *Newsweek* columnist Niall Ferguson called Obama's handling of the situation in Egypt "a foreign policy debacle" by one day urging Mubarak to quit and the next day calling for an "orderly transition."[14]

But the demonstrators in Egypt weren't paying much attention to the United States, recalls Fahmy, of the American University in Cairo. Initially, they were too determined to stay on message; after Mubarak's departure, they were too euphoric. "The 'street' couldn't care less what Obama was saying," he says. "The U.S. had clearly been caught unawares and was ill-equipped to deal with the situation because of Washington's obsession with Islam and terrorism. We kept on saying: There is something else in these societies besides Islam and terrorism."

Washington Post foreign affairs columnist David Ignatius urged Obama to "go to the Middle East and

embrace this moment. I understand his desire to stay out of the limelight, but it's proving to be a mistake. This is a world-historical event, as powerful as the fall of the Berlin Wall."[15]

U.S. Defense Secretary Robert Gates, who had maintained close contact with the Egyptian army throughout the uprising, has visited Cairo and reassured the interim government that U.S. aid ($1.3 billion a year in military support and hundreds of millions in other assistance) will continue.[16]

But most experts say the United States should tread warily. "Regionally, American foreign initiatives are viewed with suspicion, and too ambitious or inconsistent a policy agenda could end up backfiring in a region as volatile as the Arab world," warns Naveed Sheikh, a professor of international politics at Britain's Keele University. Obama is limited by the wars in Iraq and Afghanistan, which Sheikh calls "imperial projects that were neither economically, militarily or morally sustainable."

Though Israel was not a target of the protesters in Tahrir Square, Mubarak's commitment to the Israeli-Palestinian peace process clearly was: Some demonstrators waved placards in Hebrew, claiming the only language the Egyptian president understood was that of Israel's leaders. One of the first acts of Egypt's Supreme Council of the Armed Forces was to reassure Washington and Tel Aviv that it will respect Egypt's international commitments, a reference to the 1978 Camp David Accords and the 1979 Egypt-Israel peace treaty. Experts say the Egyptians probably will not want to return to war with Israel, but will they be prepared to let the peace agreements stand?

"Washington has lost an unconditional ally," wrote Alain Gresh, editor of the French foreign policy journal *Le Monde Diplomatique*. "U.S. regional strategy has relied on Egypt, along with Israel, . . . for the last 30 years. . . . Mubarak was at the forefront of the fight against the 'Iranian threat.' He maintained the illusion of the Middle East 'peace process,' putting pressure on the Palestinian Authority to continue negotiations."[17]

"Egypt under Mubarak participated in the economic blockade of Gaza and helped scuttle all attempts at reconciliation by Hamas and Fatah, even one negotiated by another 'moderate' country, Saudi Arabia [the Mecca accord of 2007]," Gresh continued. "A more representative future government in Egypt . . . will probably be more wary of U.S. attempts to form a common (if undeclared) front between Arab countries and Israel against Iran."[18]

A Cairo-brokered unity pact announced on April 27 between rival Palestinian groups seemed to confirm Gresh's predictions. The announcement that secret reconciliation talks had succeeded between the mainstream West Bank-controlling Fatah and its radical Islamist rival Hamas, which runs Gaza, surprised the international community. The two groups said they had reached an accord in part because of recent large pro-unity demonstrations staged by young Palestinians inspired by events in Egypt. Fatah leader Mahmoud Abbas and his Hamas counterpart Khaled Mashaal agreed to a joint interim government and possible combined elections in December.[19]

However, the deal could alienate Western support for Fatah, since both Israel and the United States call Hamas a terrorist organization and refuse to negotiate with it unless its leaders denounce violence. Nevertheless, analysts say the negotiating role played by Egypt's new government and its recognition of the pro-Hamas Muslim Brotherhood indicate that Egypt's evolving foreign policy could shift the political landscape in the Middle East.

U.S. relations with several other former allies likely will be pricklier as well. For example, Bahrain is immensely important to the United States strategically because it is home to the U.S. Fifth Fleet, which patrols Gulf and Central Asian waters. And Yemen plays a key role in Washington's ongoing anti-terrorism offensive by fighting the supposedly large al-Qaida presence in its rugged hinterlands. But if President Saleh is toppled — as seems likely — will the new regime be so cooperative?

The European Union might have easier relations with the new governments. As soon as Mubarak stepped down, the EU — the second-largest aid donor in the Middle East — immediately promised the interim government $670 million in aid. While the European governments also did business with autocratic Arab regimes, Arabs generally think the EU has tried harder than Washington to reach a solution in the Arab-Israeli conflict and sympathizes more with the Palestinians.

Moreover, "No one has more experience than Europeans do in difficult transitions from dictatorship to democracy," writes *Guardian* newspaper columnist

Timothy Garton Ash. "No region has more instruments at its disposal to affect developments in the Arab Middle East. The U.S. may have special relationships with the Egyptian military and Arab ruling families, but Europe has more trade, gives a lot of aid, and has a thick web of cultural and person-to-person ties across what the Romans called *Mare Nostrum*, our sea." Moreover, he continues, Europe is where most young Arabs "want to come — to visit, to study, to work. Their cousins are here already."[20]

Will the upheaval in the Middle East help Islamic extremists?

For years, most Arab dictators told Washington they were the only bulwarks against an Islamist extremist takeover in the region. Mubarak's bogeyman was the Muslim Brotherhood; Saleh's was al-Qaida, which has also been taken up by Gadhafi — when he isn't blaming youths on hallucinogens.

Three leading Egyptian political figures — Naguib Sawiris, founder and chairman of the giant Egyptian telecom company Orascom, who has just launched his own political party, and presidential candidates Amr Moussa and Mohamed ElBaradei — recently echoed their concern about the Brotherhood. They told *Washington Post* columnist Ignatius they worried that it and other Islamist groups could hijack Egypt's nascent democracy. Sawiris — a Coptic Christian — said he has "a real fear" that "we will get an Iranian type regime here."[21]

"Copts [an Egyptian Christian sect] are definitely concerned about the Brotherhood," affirms historian Fahmy. Egypt's 7 million indigenous Christians were persecuted during the Mubarak regime. Nadje Al-Ali, a gender expert at the School of Oriental and Asian Studies at the University of London, says some Egyptians worry that "the Brotherhood could push for women and Copts not to be able to run for president."

But Sciences Po's Jean-Pierre Filiu says the Brotherhood is not homogeneous, and that internal differences could weaken its influence. "I doubt very much that the Brotherhood will remain unified," he predicts.

Keele University's Sheikh says being in government will make the Brotherhood less militant. "Radical voices flourish if denied public space, legitimacy and responsibility," he explains. "There is a moderating influence in

CHRONOLOGY

1960s-1970s *Egyptian strongman Gamal Abdel Nasser challenges West, strives to unite Arab world under his leadership.*

1952 Military coup led by Lt. Col. Nasser deposes King Farouk II, establishes Egyptian Republic.

1956 Nasser nationalizes Suez Canal in July. . . . In October, Britain, France and Israel attack Egypt in a bid to re-take control of the canal; hostilities cease after United States threatens sanctions against Britain.

1961 Sheikh Isa bin Salman Al Khalifa becomes emir of Bahrain.

1967 Mounting tension between Israel and its Arab neighbors culminates in six days of hostilities: Israel launches surprise air attack on Egypt and then seizes Gaza from Egypt and the Golan Heights from Syria and pushes Jordanian forces out of East Jerusalem and the West Bank.

1970s-1980s *Historic, U.S.-brokered Middle East peace accords halt hostilities between Israel and Egypt.*

1970 Air Force chief Hafez Assad seizes power in Syria. A year later, he is elected president for seven-year term.

1973 In effort to regain territory lost in 1967, Egypt and Syria launch major offensive against Israel on Yom Kippur, the Jewish Day of Atonement. After initial successes, the attack fails.

1975 In Bahrain, emir dissolves National Assembly and rules by decree after Prime Minister Sheikh Khalifah bin Salman Al Khalifah says it is impeding the government's work.

1978 U.S.-led negotiations lead to Camp David Accords between Israel and Egypt. "Framework for Peace" in the Middle East includes limited autonomy for Palestinians.

1981 Egyptian President Anwar al-Sadat is assassinated by jihadist Army officers for his role in signing Camp David Accords. Vice President Hosni Mubarak, wounded during the assassination, becomes president.

1982 Syria's Hafez Assad suppresses Muslim Brotherhood uprising in Hama; tens of thousands of civilians are reported killed.

1987 Tunisian Prime Minister Zine El Abidine Ben Ali takes power after having the aged President Habib Bourguiba declared mentally unfit. Two years later, Ben Ali wins the first of four presidential elections.

1990s-2000s *United States fights two wars against Iraq and opens a new front against al-Qaida after 9/11 jihadist attacks in the United States.*

1990 Iraq invades Kuwait; Syria and Egypt join U.S.-led coalition against Iraq. U.S.-Egyptian relations improve.

1990 Ali Abdullah Saleh, president of North Yemen, proclaims the Unified Republic of Yemen, with himself as president.

1991 Bahrain's port becomes base for U.S. Fifth Fleet.

1992 Aden hotel used by U.S. marines is bombed in first known al-Qaida attack in Yemen. Two Austrian tourists are killed.

2002 Shiite opposition wins 40 percent of Bahrain's parliamentary seats in first election in nearly 30 years. A Shiite is appointed deputy prime minister.

2003 U.S.-led coalition invades Iraq, claiming President Saddam Hussein has stockpiled weapons of mass destruction; none are found.

2009 Saudi and Yemeni al-Qaida branches merge into Al-Qaida in the Arabian Peninsula.

2010 Syria sentences human-rights lawyer Mohannad al-Hassani to three years in jail for "weakening national morale." . . . Former U.N. nuclear chief Mohammed ElBaradei returns to Egypt and forms alliance of activists and opposition politicians for political change; says he might run for president in 2011. . . . Bahrain arrests more than 20 Shiite opposition leaders in broad crackdown for allegedly plotting to overthrow the monarchy.

Dec. 17 A Tunisian vegetable vendor, who had been harassed by police for years, sets himself on fire after a policewoman slaps him. Public frustration over police abuses and lack of jobs erupts into protests that spread across Tunisia. Government cracks down, resulting in more than 60 deaths. Bouazizi dies on Jan. 4.

Jan. 14 Tunisian President Zine El Abidine Ben Ali flees to Saudi Arabia.

Jan. 25 Thousands of Egyptians march to Tahrir Square in Cairo, chanting "Down with Mubarak." Similar protests erupt across the country.

Jan. 27 Thousands of protesters in Sanaa, Yemen's capital, call for end of 32-year regime of autocratic President Ali Abdullah Saleh.

Jan. 31 At least 250,000 demonstrators occupy Tahrir Square, in defiance of military-imposed curfew.

Feb. 11 Demonstrators in Tahrir Square cheer announcement that Mubarak has resigned and handed over power to the army. . . . Protests continue in Yemen; by Feb. 20, seven protesters have been killed in clashes with police.

Feb. 15 Demonstrators break out in Benghazi, Libya. Police break up protest, causing many injuries.

Feb. 19 Benghazi protests degenerate into street fighting, with numerous deaths and injuries. Government officials flee the next day, leaving the city in "rebel" hands.

Feb. 20 Street protests erupt in Libyan capital of Tripoli.

Feb. 22 Libyan leader Moammar Gadhafi blames unrest on Islamists; vows to die as a martyr.

Feb. 26 Mass unrest breaks out in Bahrain, where Shiite majority presses Sunni ruling family for reforms. King Hamad al Khalifa dismisses several ministers, but opposition is not satisfied.

Feb. 26 President Barack Obama says Gadhafi should step down to avoid further bloodshed. Despite aerial bombings, anti-Gadhafi fighters make initial territorial gains, advancing toward Tripoli.

March 7 France and U.K. ask U.N. Security Council to establish a no-fly zone in Libya; Obama administration is hesitant but agrees after Arab League endorses proposal on March 12.

March 10 Well-armed pro-Gadhafi counter-offensive repels rebels.

March 15 Anti-government protests spread in Syria, the first since a state of emergency was issued 48 years ago.

March 18 In Yemen, police snipers kill at least 45 demonstrators near Sanaa University, prompting top military defections.

March 19 U.S. and British ships fire cruise missiles at more than 20 coastal targets in Libya as U.N. no-fly zone goes into effect. . . . Egyptians approve constitutional amendments; one limits presidency to two terms.

April 8 Yemen's Saleh rejects resignation plan brokered by neighboring Gulf States.

April 13 Egypt's Mubarak and his sons are detained after allegations of corruption and abuse of power.

April 17 Eleven killed in Homs, Syria, as unrest continues against regime of President Bashar Assad.

April 20 Pro-Gadhafi forces continue fighting, despite no-fly zone and NATO attacks on troops and armor. U.S., NATO and Qatar agree to fund Libyan revolutionary movement.

April 21 Yemen's Saleh considers second resignation scenario proposed by Gulf States: creation of a national unity government led by the opposition, with Saleh quitting in one month. . . . Assad ends emergency law in Syria, abolishes state security courts and allows citizens to protest peacefully.

April 22 United States decides to use armed drones in Libya.

April 25 Thousands of troops, backed by tanks, confront demonstrators in Syria.

having to compete in the open market place for ideas." In Turkey and Indonesia, for instance, conservative Islamic governments have tended "to focus on 'deliverables' once given a stake in the state," he argues.

Not so, says Ray Takeyh, a senior fellow for Middle Eastern Studies at the Council on Foreign Relations. The theory that the responsibility of governance inevitably moderates Islamic political groups is "a liberal conceit" that denigrates their "commitment to their dogma," he says. Islamist parties can be expected to "menace an inexperienced democratic order" and likely will campaign against women's rights, and their militias "will threaten secular politicians . . . who do not conform to their template."

The danger is not that Islamist tactics would gain them absolute power, Takeyh continues, but that a nervous military would intervene "in the name of stability and order," taking the region's new democracies back to autocratic rule. So the United States and its allies must "strengthen the political center." A massive package of economic assistance to countries such as Tunisia and Egypt could "tether these nations to the United States" — as long as they steer clear of extremism, he suggests.

Meanwhile, the perceived threat level from al-Qaida varies depending on the country. "Al-Qaida will move, will try, will test, will intervene, taking the opportunity of any uncertainties," Moroccan Foreign Minister Fihri warns. "Al-Qaida looks for the space where there is no strong, democratic national power."

That danger could come to fruition in Yemen, where al-Qaida is said to have a firm foothold. "The four provinces where Al-Qaeda is believed to be hiding and strengthening . . . are out of the control of the central government in Sanaa," the *Egyptian Al-Ahram Weekly* reported.[22] The U.S. view is that Al-Qaida in the Arabian Peninsula (AQAP) was behind last fall's attempt to detonate bombs on a Chicago-bound plane and the attempt to blow up a passenger jet over Detroit on Christmas Day 2009. The group also shelters the American-born preacher Anwar al-Awlaki, who has been in Yemen since 2004.

Sapienza University's Guazzone agrees that al-Qaida will try to exploit any vacuum but sees "no structural, long-term way in which al-Qaida networks can reap major political benefits" as a result of the turmoil. The uprisings have been instigated and sustained by "non-ideological, nonviolent" youth movements that are "very concrete in their demands" for freedom, dignity and employment, she points out. "They have no ties nor sympathies with jihadism and its fantasy of restoring a global caliphate through armed struggle."

BACKGROUND

Imperialism and Colonialism

The modern Arab world is, in part, a patchwork of countries carved out of the old Ottoman Empire, the precursor of modern Turkey. At its height in the 17th century, Ottoman power extended from Croatia in the Balkans to Algeria in the western Mediterranean. By 1900, the empire had shrunk dramatically. Then Turkey sided with Germany in World War I, giving the victorious powers the excuse to divide it up into European-controlled "mandates."[23]

Britain controlled the lion's share: Egypt, Transjordan (modern Jordan), Palestine (including modern Israel and the West Bank) and Iraq. France's sphere of influence included Syria and Lebanon (Algeria and Tunisia had been in French hands since the 1830s.) Italy got Cyrenaica — today's Libya. Artificial borders were delineated, compliant dictators and monarchs installed in power and modest political reforms imposed.

However, wrote historian William Cleveland in *A History of the Modern Middle East*, "The same elite that had enjoyed power and prestige before 1914 — the European-educated landed and professional classes in Egypt and the traditional notables in Syria, Lebanon and Palestine — continued to exercise their privileges during the 1920s and 1930s."[24]

The discovery of vast oil deposits in the Arab world in the early 1900s changed the equation. Oil and the machines it powered had proved critical to the world's militaries during World War I. The industrialized Western powers now had a powerful incentive to protect their interests in the region, just as the Arabs began to turn to nationalism and pan-Arabism as political organizing principles.

After World War II, countries in the Arab world, Africa and elsewhere became independent. During the 1950s-1970s, a wave of Arab nationalist leaders and dictators came to power, beginning with Gamal Abdel Nasser in Egypt in 1956, followed later by Moammar Gadhafi (1969) in Libya, Syria's Hafez Assad (1971) and Saddam Hussein in Iraq (1979).

Meanwhile, Western oil companies remained anchored in Saudi Arabia and the other oil-rich Persian Gulf monarchies and in Iran — the latter until the ayatollahs took over in 1979.[25]

Triumph

Today's Arab protesters owe a historic debt to 26-year-old Mohamed Bouazizi, a Tunisian fruit and vegetable seller. Fed up after years of police bullying, Bouazizi set himself ablaze on December 17 to protest abuse from a female police woman who slapped and harassed him in public. The humiliating incident sparked popular frustrations that quickly spun out across the Arab world.[26]

Each Middle East country is different, but Mustapha K. Nabli, the newly appointed governor of the Tunisian Central Bank, says that Arab unrest is rooted in some common grievances. "The first was blatant and increasingly strong corruption that had created a deep sense of unfairness in the population," he says. "Second, the employment-education nexus: Unemployment in the Middle East and North Africa had been high for a long time and we are in a demographic [youth] bulge."

Autocratic Arab regimes also were vulnerable because of "the rapid growth of new communications technologies and social networks," he adds. Without the Internet, "the corruption of [President] Ben Ali and his cronies would not have inflamed the way [it] did, leading to the sudden eruption of outrage following the death of Mohamed Bouazizi." Lucrative government contracts went to the president's cronies, and his supporters and party members got even the lowest government jobs. The family's penchant for building palatial homes was legendary.

In Egypt, Nabli points out, the police murder of Khaled Said, a young blogger who posted a video of two policemen sharing the spoils of a drug bust, became an instant Internet cause célèbre.[27] Before the Internet, Said's death could well have gone unnoticed. "But in the new age, half a million Egyptians joined the We Are All Khaled Said Facebook page, [which] initiated the January 25 revolution," he says.

The discontent that spread across the Middle East, North Africa and the Persian Gulf also bore a common demographic characteristic. Nearly 60 percent of the 360-million-strong Arab population is under 25 — and largely better educated than in the past.[28] Meanwhile, the Arab unemployment rate of 25 percent in the 15-29 age bracket is the highest in the world.[29] In Yemen, about 75 percent of the population is under 30, and the poverty rate exceeds 45 percent; in Egypt, two-thirds of the population is under 30, while 18-22 percent of the country's 82 million citizens lives on less than $2 per day.[30]

Eleven days after President Ben Ali stunned the Arab world on January 14 by stepping down and leaving Tunisia, protests began in Cairo, spurred by online criticism of the Mubarak regime. The president, 82, hadn't announced whether he would run for a sixth term in the spring elections, which would have taken him past 30 years as president, and it seemed likely that he would nominate his 47-year-old son Gamal to run in his stead. Presidential elections in Egypt were widely known to be rigged anyway, so the succession was seen — resentfully — as inevitable.

In hindsight, the elements were there for a showdown. Maha Azzam, a Middle East expert at the London think tank Chatham House, wrote last November, "The government's heavy-handed tactics, such as detention without trial and allegations of police brutality, have become commonplace. Ahead of the elections, there have been new controls." Nilesat, Egypt's leading satellite operator, had been ordered to shut down 12 television channels. "Newspaper editors have been removed from their jobs, bloggers and SMS [text] messaging have been restricted," Azzam reported. Egypt had experienced 1,600 labor protests since 2006, amid growing social and economic discontent.[31]

But early in 2011, when anti-Mubarak demonstrators defied tear gas and armed pro-Mubarak thugs assailed the demonstrators — even charging the crowd in Tahrir Square on camels and horseback — an emboldened Egyptian press joined the campaign.

"Everything that has happened in Egypt points to a dream come true for us," wrote Fahmy Howeidi, a leading Arab columnist, reflecting the general excitement. "A dream that had been stolen from us for several decades, a dream that permits us to speak with one voice as we call for moving away from pharaonic rule to democratic rule."[32]

In the end, 30 years of dictatorship disappeared in 30 seconds. That's how long it took Vice President Omar Suleiman to announce that Mubarak had resigned and that the Supreme Council was taking over as head of state. "The Young People have done it. Mubarak has stepped aside," proclaimed the Pan Arab newspaper

Spotting the Next Generation of Arab Leaders

By crushing opposition, autocratic leaders eliminated likely successors.

Above all else, the autocratic leaders of the Middle East were masters at suppressing opposition. As a result, few obvious leaders are waiting to fill the power vacuums left by regimes collapsing across the region. Still, some names have surfaced among the demonstrators either as influential king makers or as likely presidential candidates themselves.

The lack of a successor is probably most evident in Tunisia, where former President Zine El Abidine Ben Ali kept a tight grip on his country. An interim government is in place, but the powerful labor union UGTT has come into its own, with Ali Ben Romdhane, the union's joint leader, as a spokesman for the reformers.[1]

In March, in advance of the July 24 election for a constituent assembly to reform the constitution, the government legalized the reportedly moderate Islamic organization Ennahdha ("Renaissance"), banned by the Ben Ali regime. The group's leader, Rachid Ghannouchi, who returned from 22 years of exile in London, is considered a presidential contender.[2]

In Egypt, the most widely known politician at Tahrir Square was without question Nobel Peace Prize winner Mohamed ElBaradei, former head of the U.N. International Atomic Energy Agency. He gained world prominence in 2002 and 2003 for being one of the first to challenge the Bush administration's claim that Saddam Hussein had stockpiled weapons of mass destruction. Following his retirement, he returned to his native Cairo in 2010 and was immediately seen as a possible challenger to President Hosni Mubarak in the November 2011 presidential race. ElBaradei, 68, said he would consider running if there were reforms to guarantee a fair election.

A one-time Egyptian national squash champion, ElBaradei has support among the younger generation of demonstrators, but an online poll on the website of

al-Ahram newspaper showed 74-year-old Amr Moussa, departing secretary general of the Arab League and the other declared presidential candidate, as the current front runner.

Both men had distinguished diplomatic careers. As Egyptian foreign minister Moussa occasionally rocked the boat by being quite critical of Israel (much to Washington's annoyance). Mubarak tactfully replaced him after a pop song came out titled, "I hate Israel, and I love Amr Moussa."[3]

The younger generation of Egyptian politicians is represented by Islam Lutfi, 33, and the already legendary Wael Ghonim. Lutfi, a 33-year-old lawyer, heads the youth wing of the Muslim Brotherhood and represents the once-outlawed organization on the recently formed constitutional reform panel. During the demonstrations Lutfi addressed Christian groups in Tahrir Square, saying Egyptians should be united. Under his direction the youth wing of the Brotherhood has pushed the organization's leadership to tackle issues of immediate concern to Egyptians — such as such as corruption and freedom of expression — and, more tentatively, to distance itself from more violent Islamic fundamentalists.

If any one individual launched Egypt's mass protests it was Ghonim, Google's head of marketing for the Middle East. The mild-mannered, 30-year-old father of two moved sideways into politics by designing first ElBaradei's website, which calls for democratic reforms, and then the famous web page memorializing Khaled Said, a young Egyptian who was beaten to death by two Alexandria policemen after he filmed them sharing the proceeds of a drug bust.

Ghonim's Facebook page, "We are all Khaled Said," went viral, making the young man's death a cause célèbre. Ghonim also set the date for the first Tahrir Square demonstration on Jan. 25th — ironically National Police Day. Ghonim himself was arrested in the square and held for 12 days, emerging to find himself a hero of the revolution.

Al-sharq al-Awsat [*The Middle East*], as jubilant crowds in Tahrir Square chanted "Egypt is free!"[33]

On the day Mubarak resigned, Saad Eddin Ibrahim, a leading Egyptian activist who had twice been imprisoned by the regime and was living outside of the country, flew to Cairo and went directly to Tahrir Square. "It was just like the day of judgment," he said later. "The way the day of judgment is described in our scripture, the Quran, you have all of humanity in one place, and nobody recognizes anybody else, just faces, faces."[34]

"This revolution started on Facebook," he said in a recent interview. "I always said, if you want to liberate a society, just give them the Internet."[4]

Ghonim's political future is uncertain. There are "Ghonim for president" websites in Egypt, but he doesn't seem to have political ambitions and wants to get back to his work at Google.

If the Egyptian political landscape is complicated, the scenario in Libya is hopelessly chaotic. A 30-member national council was established in Benghazi headed by former Justice Minister Mustapha Abdul Jalil, described by Western media as a conservative Islamist. The council also includes liberal and left-wing members.

The two international front men for Libya's revolution — who have toured foreign capitals lobbying for support and have met with U.S. Secretary of State Hillary Rodham Clinton, British Prime Minister David Cameron and France's President Nicolas Sarkozy — are Ali al-Essawi, former Libyan ambassador to India, and Mahmoud Jibril, a U.S.-educated former Benghazi university professor.[5]

Adding to the chaos, the rag-tag rebel military has rival commanders — Abdul Fattah Younis, a former interior minister and once a friend of Libyan leader Moammar Gadhafi, and Khalifa Heftar, a former general recently returned to Libya from a long exile in Virginia. Heftar proclaimed himself top army commander and is said to have a following among the fighters.

News reports describe meetings of the opposition leadership as little more than shouting matches between rivals at every level. But that, too, may be part of the revolutionary experience. Nobody ever argued with Gadhafi.

— *Roland Flamini*

AFP/Getty Images/Aris Messinis

Arab League secretary-general Amr Moussa votes in Egypt's constitutional referendum on March 19. He received favorable ratings from 89 percent of the respondents in a recent poll.

[3] "Amr Moussa," *The New York Times*, March 10, 2011, http://topics.nytimes.com/topics/reference/timestopics/people/m/amr_moussa/index.html.

[4] Joyella, Mark, "First Tunisia, now Egypt, What's Next?" *Media ITE*, Feb. 11, 2011, www.mediaite.com/tv/first-tunisia-now-egypt-whats-next-wael-ghonim-says-ask-facebook/.

[5] "Mahmoud Jibril: the international face of Libya's rebels," CBS News, March 30, 2011, www.cbc.ca/news/world/story/2011/03/29/f-libya-jibril.html.

[1] "Tunisie: la nomination de nouveau Premier," Le Pointe.com, Feb. 28, 2011, www.lepoint.fr/monde/tunisie-la-nomination-du-nouveau-premier-ministre-critiquee-sit-in-a-tunis-28-02-2011-1300546_24.php.

[2] "Tunisia to elect constituent team," *Al Jazeera*, Feb. 28, 2011, http://english.al jazeera.net/news/africa/2011/03/20113405133628865.html.

The revolution — like the earlier one in Tunisia — would not have succeeded if the Egyptian army had not been willing to side with the Egyptian people. "The generals were confronted with a serious choice: They could defend Mubarak against the crowd, or defend the crowd against Mubarak," says Professor Fahmy. "The military controls between 5 and 8 percent of the Egyptian economy through weapons manufacturing . . . and other enterprises, and the stand-off was bad for business."

With Mubarak's ouster, Field Marshal Mohamad Hussein Tantawi, chairman of the ruling Supreme Council, became Egypt's fifth consecutive leader to come from the military since a 1952 army coup deposed King Farouk I.*

Almost as soon as Mubarak stepped down, cracks appeared in the protest movement over the nature and pace of reforms and the question of who speaks for the new Egypt. For example, despite the youth movement's demands, the army seemed in no hurry to live up to its promise to lift Egypt's 29-year-old emergency laws. But when the army moved quickly to organize a referendum on March 19 to amend parts of the Egyptian constitution, many of the nascent political groups protested that it was too early. They campaigned to boycott the vote on the grounds that it would only benefit the Muslim Brotherhood, the country's only organized party.

Egyptian voters overwhelmingly approved the referendum. More than 14.1 million people, or 72 percent of those voting, approved the amendments, with 4 million (22.8 percent) opposed. But, partly because of the boycott, only 41 percent of the 45 million eligible voters went to the polls, a disappointment for some commentators but a record for Egypt.[35] The 10 new amendments establish presidential term limits, give the judiciary greater electoral oversight and require a public referendum before a state of emergency can be introduced. The entire constitution is expected to be overhauled next year.

The result reflected a widespread desire for a return to normal life and showed members of the young revolutionary movement that if they wanted to have an impact on reforms they had to be better organized. "The revolutionary dream is now over, and politics must be embraced and welcomed," wrote former Egyptian ambassador Ashraf Surlam. "The battle for the soul and future is on."[36]

Shortly after the referendum, Mubarak and his two sons were detained in connection with allegations of corruption and abuse of power, including — in the former president's case — the killing of demonstrators during the 18 days of unrest.[37] A number of senior regime officials had been detained already for alleged corruption. According to reports, Mubarak was to be moved to the

*The others were Mohammed Neguib, Nasser, Anwar Sadat and Mubarak.

hospital ward of a military prison in Cairo from the hospital in Sharm al-Sheik where he was taken in March after a heart attack. A commission of inquiry into the demonstrations has determined that 846 civilians and 26 members of Egyptian security were killed in the clashes. A commission spokesman said the security forces would have needed Mubarak's permission to use live ammunition.

Contagion

Tahrir Square and Tunisia sent a strong message to other Arabs that "they had the ability to change things if they were prepared to sacrifice themselves for their freedom and if there was unity of purpose," says Ahmed Ibrahim Rizk, who heads the Ibn Khaldun Center, a Cairo research institute. By March anti-government demonstrations had broken out in Jordan, Libya, Bahrain and Syria. Eventually, sporadic protests also were reported in Algeria, Sudan, Morocco, Mauritania, Saudi Arabia, Iran and Oman.

In Bahrain's tiny, oil-rich archipelago the unrest has had sectarian overtones. The minority Sunni-led monarchy is being challenged by the country's Shiite majority, which represents 70 percent of the 1.2 million population. But unlike the protesters in Cairo, who demanded the removal of Mubarak, Bahrain's protesters were not calling for the overthrow of the King Hamad. They wanted better economic conditions, a switch to a constitutional monarchy, curbs on royal power and the ability to replace the prime minister through elections. The king's nephew has occupied the post for 40 years.

"Bahrain remains a very nanny state with free health care, free education and free housing, but there's a perceived distinction in the level of nanny care," explains Alanoud Al Sharekh, a political scientist at the Chatham House office in Bahrain. The Shiite majority feels it doesn't get as much as it's entitled to, she says, so they want "better benefits, and other legitimate demands — not regime change."

But in early March, the mood darkened considerably after clashes between demonstrators and Bahraini security forces resulted in several deaths and injuries. The more militant protesters then began calling for the removal of the royal family and establishment of a Shiite state. "The Sunni-Shia divide is particularly problematic because of the close family connections many Shiites have to Iran," said a London *Daily Telegraph* report. In the past this has led to Iran's Revolutionary Guards establishing terrorist cells in the kingdom, the paper said. Further complicating matters, Iran has long claimed Bahrain as part of its territory.[38]

In Saudi Arabia, an absolute monarchy without an elected parliament, King Abdullah combined stick and carrot to stifle a nascent protest movement. After some demonstrations and cyber calls for reform, the government banned all demonstrations and public meetings. On February 26 at least 330 prominent Saudi professionals and businessmen demanded reforms, and on March 5 the Saudi e-zine *Jadaliyya* published an open letter to the king, "Demands of Saudi Youth for the Future of the Nation," seeking jobs, the release of political prisoners, the introduction of a constitutional monarchy and a top-to-bottom campaign against corruption.[39]

The Saudis, typically, responded to the challenge with cash, promising to add 75,000 government jobs, increase government employees' pay by up to 15 percent, initiate a massive infrastructure program and improve benefits for low-income citizens — essentially Saudi Arabia's restive Shiite minority.

Conflict

In neighboring Yemen — the poorest country in the Middle East — another kind of dynasty was under threat, with a potentially very different outcome. After weeks of violent anti-regime demonstrations, President Saleh, a key U.S. anti-terrorism ally, could be the next domino to topple. For years, the United States has financed and trained elite security and intelligence units that launch counterterrorism operations against al-Qaida camps in Yemen's rugged interior.

Opposition groups repeatedly demonstrated against Saleh's hard-line regime, even building their own Tahrir Square-like tent city at Sanaa University. As in Egypt and Tunisia, the groups demanded that Saleh step down immediately. Saleh was said to be grooming his son as his successor, and the notion of a hereditary presidency had further fueled opposition anger.

Saleh first tried a page out of Mubarak's playbook and said he would remain in office for the remainder of his term, but would not run again in 2013. When that was rejected, he offered to resign at the end of the year and call elections. Amid clashes with security forces, the opposition groups insisted that Saleh leave immediately, just as Mubarak had been quickly forced out.[40]

Resisting Dictators

A rebel fighter near Ajdabiya, in northeastern Libya, celebrates as a rocket barrage streaks toward pro-government troops on April 14, 2011 (top). The North African nation is embroiled in civil war that grew out of demonstrations against the 42-year-long regime of dictator Moammar Gadhafi. In Yemen, a soldier who defected to the opposition joins protesters in the capital Sanaa on March 31, demanding that President Ali Abdullah Saleh resign. Saleh, who has ruled the country for 32 years, is considering a proposal negotiated by representatives of the Gulf States offering him immunity if he will resign, but the opposition is skeptical of the plan.

Then on March 18, at least 45 demonstrators were killed by government snipers stationed on rooftops, and the encampment in the square was bulldozed. Several ministers, diplomats and parliamentarians deserted Saleh in protest, including Brig. Gen. Ali Mohsin al-Ahmar,

Reuters/Wael Hmeden

Tens of thousands of Syrians gather for a pro-government rally under a giant image of President Bashar Assad in downtown Damascus on March 29, 2011. The rally followed nearly two weeks of unprecedented anti-government demonstrations and demands that Assad end his family's 40-year rule of the country. At least 450 people have been killed since the protests began, according to human rights groups. On April 25, troops using tanks and artillery attacked the mostly unarmed protesters in the southern city of Daraa, reportedly killing at least 100 people.

commander of the army's powerful 1st Armored Division and Yemen's top soldier. The general declared his support for the protesters and urged troops to do the same. His defection was seen not just as a major blow to Saleh but also provided a possible candidate to lead an interim government.

After the defection, Saleh in late April was said to be considering a proposal by the foreign ministers of the Gulf Cooperation Council. It would allow him to step down after 30 days in exchange for immunity from prosecution for him, his family and his aides. But by May 1 the deal appeared to have unraveled.[41]

Intervention

In Libya, a unique system of government through local councils had left the aging Gadhafi in effective control, with his Western-educated son Seif al-Islam seemingly destined to succeed him, and other offspring in command of elite forces. To fortify Gadhafi's control, a pervasive security apparatus suppressed all opposition, but the universities had become restless even before the protests began.

The West ended a long period of estrangement when Gadhafi in 1999 allowed the extradition of two Libyans involved in the 1988 bombing of a U.S.-bound airliner

over Lockerbie, Scotland, killing 270 people. But sanctions against Libya were not eased until 2002, when Tripoli paid $1.5 billion in compensation to relatives of Lockerbie victims, and Gadhafi abandoned his nuclear weapons program and pledged to destroy a chemical weapons stockpile. Normal diplomatic relations with the United States were resumed in 2008.

Hemmed in between Egypt and Tunisia, Libya inevitably was infected by the unrest affecting its neighbors. Street demonstrations calling for Gadhafi's ouster quickly met with a tough response, and what started as a protest burgeoned into a rebellion. In Benghazi, Libya's second-largest city and long a hotbed of tribal opposition to Gadhafi, a protest by lawyers swelled into open insurrection. Anti-government demonstrators quickly occupied the eastern coastal area. In a series of bizarre radio broadcasts and television appearances, Gadhafi vowed to re-take his country, claiming the rebels were on drugs and working with al-Qaida.

As opposition casualties mounted, international concerns grew. President Nicolas Sarkozy of France and British Prime Minister David Cameron urged the imposition of a no-fly zone over Libya to ground Gadhafi's air force. EU Commissioner for Competition John Dalli, a former Maltese foreign minister with close Libyan ties, warned, "I know the Libyans, and as much as they believe in forgiveness, they also preach retribution."[42]

On March 3, President Obama called on Gadhafi to quit. "So let me just be very unambiguous about this," Obama declared. "Colonel Gadhafi needs to step down from power and leave."[43]

But Obama, who had already inherited two wars in Iraq and Afghanistan, hesitated to commit America to another seemingly open-ended military action. Then the momentum shifted decisively in favor of the Libyan leader, when a government counteroffensive spearheaded by special forces commanded by Gadhafi's sons pushed back the lightly armed rebellion almost to Benghazi itself, causing many casualties. The uprising seemed close to collapse.

In an unprecedented action against one of its own members, the 22-member League of Arab States asked the U.N. Security Council to authorize a no-fly zone that would effectively ground Libya's air force. On March 17, U.N. Resolution 1973 was passed, asking U.N. members to "take all necessary measures to protect civilians" and extending sanctions on the Gadhafi regime.

Obama agreed to use the U.S. Mediterranean fleet and planes to enforce the no-fly zone, but then handed over operations to a group of NATO countries (Britain, France, Canada, Demark, Italy and Spain) plus Qatar. "The president ordered the best available option," said Secretary of State Clinton. "NATO assuming the responsibility for the entire mission means the United States will move to a supporting role."[44]

"Obama considered that he had two options," Rand's Aaron says. "One was to stand aside and watch the bloodbath and take the criticism for not having done anything, and the other was to get involved, but not too deeply." Later, however, it was revealed that CIA agents had been in Benghazi almost from the start, working with the rebels, and that armed Predator drones were being used against Gadhafi's forces. As Gadhafi continued to defy the international community, the prospect of a costly, long-drawn-out confrontation loomed, and questions were raised whether the limited NATO operation could lead to a resolution.

In Syria, the unrest has larger implications because of the regime's direct involvement in the Arab-Israeli conflict. Protests against Assad's government are unprecedented, and conventional wisdom had suggested that past repression, ethnic-religious diversity and Assad's relative popularity would shield him. As in the early days of the Egyptian unrest, Assad offered concessions every few days — a lifting of the reversal of the ban on the *niqab* (face veil), citizenship for Kurds and ending emergency law.

But much like Mubarak, Assad appears to constantly lag "a step behind the protesters' demands," says Feryal Cherif, a political science assistant professor at the University of California, Riverside. Bottom line, he concludes, "A loyal military and the legacy of limited association rights significantly diminish the prospects of a successful revolution in the country."

CURRENT SITUATION

The Second Act

As a result of the protest movement, millions of Arabs now could have a chance — albeit a precarious one — at democracy.

"Toppling two of the Middle East's tyrants in little more than two months is no mean achievement," opined the *Guardian.* "Initially, that raised hopes extraordinarily high, and the regimes' fight back has injected a dose of realism. It does not mean the revolution is failing or fizzling out, but it does show that many people were expecting too much too soon."[45]

Meanwhile, as several countries face a new beginning, the unanswerable question is: the beginning of what? In Egypt, Mubarak's departure raises questions but few solid answers. And because of Egypt's importance in the region, a successful transition there will serve as a model for other countries.

"How things are going to turn out across the region will depend on how things turn out in Egypt," says Al-Ali, of the Centre for Gender Studies at the School of Oriental and African Studies in London.

When Prime Minister Ahmed Shafiq, a prime target of the Egyptian protest movement, resigned from the Supreme Council of the Armed Forces, the council appointed as his successor Essam A. Sharaf, a former transportation minister and engineering professor at Cairo University. The move was approved in advance by the protesters.

Nevertheless, some hard-core activists continue to press the Supreme Council to speed up the pace of reforms. "The younger generation of activists wants urgent action," says Rizk at the Ibn Khaldun Center. "They feel the army is being too slow in responding to some of the main requests of the revolution, such as corruption trials of former members of the regime and a full reform of the constitution before any elections."

The army recently announced that it had barred Mubarak from leaving the country and has disbanded the hated State Security Investigations Service — a top priority with the protest movement. And, responding to complaints from new groups that more time was needed to organize political parties, the army postponed elections from a tentative date in July to September.

The desire for more time to organize reflected the disarray of the rebellion. "The youth movement, whose amorphous leadership was decisive in its success on the streets, is discovering that it is a weakness when it comes to political deal-making," says Emile Hokayem, a Middle East expert at the London International Institute for Strategic Studies.

Islamist Threat

Shifting the election date also may have been designed to counter suspicions that the army has formed a tacit

AT ISSUE

Is the Arab world changing for the better?

YES
Khaled Fahmy
Chairman, Department of History, The American University in Cairo, and Chairman, Committee on Documenting the Revolution, Egyptian National Library and Archives

Written for *CQ Global Researcher*, April 2011

In my mind, the turmoil is a positive thing and long overdue — by about 50 years. What is happening is a fundamental restructuring of how the Middle East has been run for the past 100 years.

The map of the Middle East was drawn following the collapse of the Ottoman Empire. The borders that were established, the countries that were made up and, later on, the regimes that were put in place did not reflect the forces and demographics of the region in any genuine, natural way. This was all imposed by outside players, mostly by the European victors of the First World War.

Thirty years later reformers attempted to cast off the old political system: That is when Gamal Abdel Nasser in Egypt, and later Moammar Gadhafi in Libya, Hafez Assad in Syria and Saddam Hussein in Iraq all came to power promising a new dawn. But these post-independence states ended up failing. The biggest example of that failure was their defeat by Israel in the Six Day War of 1967.

But it was not only the military failure that signaled the end of the post-independence Arab state. These new states also failed to secure a decent standard of living for their citizens and, in most cases, developed police structures that violated their citizens' basic rights.

Hence, we see the recent attempts to restructure the political landscape, wherein millions of Arabs are struggling to have their voices heard in regard to how their countries are to be run. We have witnessed things in the past weeks that Egypt has not seen in a hundred years. We have brought down two governments and demanded constitutional amendments that will put in place the mechanism leading to a completely new constitution in a year.

For some people the changes are not happening fast enough, but I see this moment as the same in importance as the collapse of the Ottoman Empire.

The discovery of oil allowed these countries to buy some time, and so did the appearance of Israel. Finally, we have seen the largest of the Arab countries rise up against oppression, corruption and mismanagement.

And who knows? Maybe if our revolution succeeds, and there is no setback, it can have a very serious impact on the situation in Syria, Yemen and Saudi Arabia.

NO
David Aaron
Senior Fellow specializing in the Middle East, RAND Corporation; Former White House Deputy National security adviser

Written for *CQ Global Researcher*, April 2011

One can hope the turmoil is a good thing, but it's far too soon to be sanguine. First, the Arab Spring may prove to be as transitory as the European revolutions of 1848, which did not immediately produce functioning democracies. Second, if some measure of democracy does result, the elected governments likely will reflect the popular antipathy that the "Arab street" has for both the United States and Israel.

As a result, the United States could face some unpleasant consequences. Western and American counterterrorism efforts could be undermined. The regimes that are being swept away devoted considerable resources to battling terrorist extremists and collaborated closely with the United States in that effort. Unfortunately, these same security services often were also oppressive. They undoubtedly will be purged, and — given popular hostility to the Bush administration's War on Terror — serious anti-terrorism programs could be reconstituted. Al-Qaida could have far more room to organize, recruit, train and even develop new terrorist weapons to attack the West.

A standoffish regime in Egypt could create many problems for the United States. Denial of automatic overflight rights and priority transit through the Suez Canal could seriously compromise U.S. military flexibility and capability further east. U.S. efforts to turn back the genocide in Sudan's Darfur region have depended heavily on Egyptian cooperation, which always seemed reluctant, but now may prove unavailable.

Most important, a popular government in Cairo is likely to adversely affect relations with Israel. It would be remarkable if politicians do not exploit popular anti-Israel hostility. The Muslim Brotherhood is already a major player in post-Mubarak politics and is on record as wanting to renegotiate the Camp David Accords, which have helped to maintain peace in the region for more than 30 years.

As a harbinger of the future, Egypt is no longer cooperating in Israel's embargo of Gaza. The possibility of war is far from likely, but the Israelis are certain to seek even more material and overt diplomatic support from the United States. This will complicate U.S. efforts to build new relationships of trust with the regimes that emerge from the maelstrom of change sweeping the Arab World.

One can pray that this turmoil will lead to the advance of the values America cherishes — democracy and a better life for all in the Arab world. But celebrations are not yet in order.

alliance with the Muslim Brotherhood, reflecting fear across the Arab world that Islamists are positioning themselves to hijack the "new order."

That is unlikely, says Rizk of the Ibn Khaldun Center. "The transformation of the Arab world today doesn't have a religious orientation. Particularly in Egypt, there are a variety of political currents involved — Islamic, Christian and secular."

Or, as the Cairo journalist Yosri Fouda texted from Tahrir Square during the protests, "This is an Allahu-Akbar-free revolution."[46]*

But will the protests remain Allahu-Akbar-free? Fahmy at the American University of Cairo says, "If this revolution has shown anything it's that the Muslim Brotherhood does not control the street as everybody believed. Within a very short space of time, using the Internet, secular forces managed to do what the Brotherhood couldn't do since 1920. Given some openness in the political system, it [would] represent about 25 percent of the electorate."

As for bin Laden and al-Qaida, Filiu of Sciences Po says with the fall of Arab autocrats the terrorists are losing their best publicists. "These are hard times for al-Qaida," he says. "Consider: peaceful movements managed to topple regimes in Tunisia and Egypt in a few weeks — regimes the jihadis could not destabilize over the past two decades; masses went bravely into the streets to demand democracy, transparency and accountability — concepts alien and even heretical for al-Qaida."

Filiu points out that during the occupation of Tahrir Square, with Egyptian flags flying everywhere, al-Qaida in Iraq warned the protesters against "the putrid idolatry of nationalism." But nobody took any notice.

In Tunisia, Filiu says, "the power is secular. I'm not talking about the army or the government: The unions are very powerful, and they are secular. The moment there is any move to Islamicize, they will react."

Economic Fallout

Economic hardship caused by the political upheavals poses a more immediate challenge. Egypt's mainstay tourist sector,

---

*The common Islamic Arab expression is often translated as "God is the greatest."

A Bahraini woman holds a Quran over her head as she shouts anti-government slogans during a protest on March 25, 2011, in the predominantly Shiite village of Diraz. The Sunni-led government of King Hamad Al Khalifa called in troops from Saudi Arabia — another Sunni-dominated monarchy — to help crush the Shiite-majority-led opposition movement. Bahrain is home to the U.S. Fifth Fleet, which patrols Gulf and Central Asian waters, and a key U.S. strategic partner.

Reuters/Hamad I Mohammed

which accounts for 11 percent of GDP and 10 percent of jobs, has been hardest hit. Tourism dropped by 75 percent during the uprising. "We've had group and individual cancellations up through the winter of 2011," said Laila Nabhan, head of a family-owned tour operation. "Tourists will not return until there is stability in the country."[47]

Each of the 18 days of Egypt's uprising cost the economy $1 billion in lost capital as foreign investors withdrew money from the country, according to the Egyptian stock market. Banks estimate the Egyptian economy lost more than $30 billion overall.[48]

In Tunisia, the banks continued to function, even though 105 branches were looted and burned and 280 ATMs vandalized. Growth has dropped to 2-3 percent — from more than 5 percent — but the financial market was functioning normally. Foreign reserves had fallen somewhat, but the currency has preserved its value.[49]

In Morocco, King Mohammed VI said in a televised speech in March that he was appointing a special committee to work with political parties, civil society groups and trade unions to recommend, by June, amendments to Morocco's constitution that would allow for a multiparty system and an independent judiciary. But the Moroccan Human Rights Association told Al Jazeera in April that it would not cooperate with the committee because it "lacked democratic legitimacy" and "the qualities of a representative body" necessary to draft a new constitution.[50]

In Jordan, as in Bahrain and Oman, the opposition wants more open government and a constitutional monarchy. Reacting to the demonstrators, King Abdullah II sacked the cabinet and asked Marouf Bakhit — a well-regarded ex-general untainted by corruption allegations — to form a new Jordanian cabinet. He also appointed as chief of his court an official experienced in tribal politics. The tribes are the king's biggest supporters and the backbone of the Jordanian security forces and the army.

In Bahrain, negotiations between the protesters and government have failed in part because "the protesters didn't have clear ideas what they wanted," according to Chatham House's Al Sharekh.

But in Yemen, demonstrators know what they want: Saleh's departure. Brig. Gen. al-Ahmar's defection split the army, but some units remained loyal to the beleaguered president. Rival tanks have been deployed in Sanaa, resulting in a stand-off amid rumors that the army was negotiating Saleh's departure. Whether that outcome would satisfy pro-democracy protesters remains to be seen. If the military chooses a successor without substantial reforms, their popular revolution will have been in vain.

OUTLOOK

A Collection of Irans?

Washington's nightmare — as expressed recently by Secretary of State Clinton — would be the transformation of the brave, new Arab world into a collection of Irans. But the 1979 Iranian revolution against Shah Mohammed Reza Pahlavi was mullah-driven from the start, with the formation of an Islamic theocracy under strict clerical control as its undisputed objective. While there is no question that Islamic parties will form part of the new political mix in the region, whether — and where — they will gain dominance is anybody's guess.

Keele University's Sheikh believes, "Iran may benefit from a change in the status quo, but only in the Shia-heavy countries — Bahrain in the Gulf and Lebanon in the Levant. But in general, revolutions, once successful, tend to be nationalist rather than internationalist."

In Egypt, historian Fahmy hopes his country's political course is now clear. "Once we have elected a parliament and a president, then we will have a constitutional assembly, followed by a referendum," he says.

Reforms will need generous financial support from the outside to strengthen ailing economies and create jobs. There are calls for a Western-financed reconstruction program modeled on the Marshall Plan, which enabled Europe to recover from World War II. "The price of democracy is not easy," says Hussein Hassouna, the Arab League's ambassador to the United States. "I would like to see the United States lead the effort to rally support for Egypt's economy."

The United States is being forced to re-think its approach to an entire region. For example, the Obama administration is aiding the Libyan rebels but has yet to officially recognize the temporary government in Benghazi. The same poll that found a majority of Egyptians want to annul the 1979 peace treaty with Israel showed that 79 percent of Egyptians have a somewhat or very unfavorable opinion of the United States, suggesting that the Obama administration faces a major task in repairing a once-close relationship.

Second only in importance to developments in Egypt is the civil unrest in Syria, where Assad has abandoned an earlier carrot-and-stick approach of combining some concessions with tough handling of the demonstrators. In an escalated crackdown, troops backed by tanks began attacking civilians in a week-long assault that began on April 25 in the southern city of Daraa and spread to other cities. Eyewitnesses said they could not retrieve dead bodies lying in the street because of government snipers who were shooting at random. Human-rights groups said soldiers seemed to be firing at random, even entering homes to pursue protesters. Unlike in Egypt, the Syrian military — commanded for the most part by officers from the same Alawite sect as the president — has sided with the government. But witnesses told the Associated Press on April 28 that some soldiers were refusing to shoot civilians and instead were fighting among themselves.[51]

Continued disturbances in Syria — which serves as Iran's channel of communications with Hezbollah in Beirut and Hamas in Gaza — will inevitably affect its neighbors. Historian Patrick Seale, a leading British specialist on Syrian affairs, pointed out, "If the Syrian regime were to be severely weakened . . . Iran's influence in Arab affairs would almost certainly be reduced — in both Lebanon and the Palestinian territories."[52]

The Obama administration's initial response to the bloody clashes in Syria was to consider adding "targeted sanctions" to those already in force.[53] Seale urged Obama to "forget Libya" and pay more attention to Syria. "If there's one country where unrest could truly set the Middle East alight, it's Syria," he wrote.[54]

As with Afghanistan, NATO's role in Libya has sparked internal debate on how far each member state is prepared to go to in assuming a combat role. The larger concern at NATO headquarters in Brussels is that the alliance could be bogged down in Libya for a long time. "A no-fly zone is not an indicator of an early resolution," says Keele University's Sheikh.

The bottom line: No one knows what will happen in the Middle East. Arabs themselves grow up knowing that nothing there is what it seems. Egyptian journalist Tariq Hameed captured this sense of unreality in his February 10 column in the Pan Arab newspaper *Al-Sharq al-Awsat*: "When we look at what is happening in Egypt, do we comprehend it? Egypt isn't in the process of changing; Egypt has changed. We just don't know where it's going.[55]

"There is optimism; there is pessimism," he continued. "We are all clinging to hope; however, what worries us is that our region has yet to grasp that Egypt has changed."

NOTES

1. Taeib Fassi Fihri, "Embracing Reform: A message from King Mohammed VI of Morocco," Minister of Foreign Affairs of Morocco, Brookings Institution, March 23, 2011, www.brookings.edu/events/2011/0323_morocco.aspx.

2. "Events in the Mideast and North Africa," *The New York Times*, April 20, 2011, p. A10.

3. "More protesters slain in Yemen as exit plan is weighed," Reuters, *The Washington Post*, April 26, 2011, p. A8.

4. Laura Kasinof, "In Yemen, Opposition Encourages Protesters," *The New York Times*, March 20, 2011, p. A18.

5. Ethan Bronner, "Bahrain Tears Down Monument as Protesters Seethe," *The New York Times*, March 13, 2011, www.nytimes.com/2011/03/19/world/middleeast/19bahrain.html.

6. "The 2011 Oil Shock," *The Economist*, March 3, 2011, www.economist.com/node/18281774; and "Oil Industry Reassured on Middle East Stability," CNNMoney, March 9, 2011, http://money.cnn.com/2011/03/09/news/international/oil_middle_east/index.htm.

7. For background, see Irwin Arieff, "Middle East Peace Prospects," *CQ Global Researcher*, May 1, 2009, pp. 119-148.

8. "Egyptians Embrace Revolt Leaders, Religious Parties and Military, As Well; U.S. Wins No Friends, End of Treaty With Israel Sought," Pew Research Center, April 25, 2011, http://pewresearch.org/pubs/1971/egypt-poll-democracy-elections-islam-military-muslim-brotherhood-april-6-movement-israel-obama.

9. Mohamed Abdel Salam, "Egypt youth refuse to meet U.S. Sec of State," *Bikyamasr*, March 15, 2011, http://bikyamasr.com/wordpress/?p=30571.

10. Larry Diamond, "Why are there no Arab democracies?" *Journal of Democracy*, January 2010, www.journalofdemocracy.org/articles/gratis/Diamond-21-1.pdf.

11. Elkham Fakhro and Emile Hokayem, "Waking the Arabs," *Survival 2011*, Issue 2, February 2011, www.iiss.org/publications/survival/survival-2011/year-2011-issue-2/waking-the-arabs/.

12. "Egypt rises up; The West should celebrate, not fear, the upheaval in Egypt," *The Economist*, Feb. 3, 2011, www.economist.com/node/18070190.

13. "Interview with Tony Blair," Council on Foreign Relations, CFR Multimedia, April 7, 2011, http://blogs.cfr.org/coleman/2011/04/07/csmd-launch-event-with-tony-blair/.

14. Niall Ferguson, "Wanted: A Grand Strategy for America," *Newsweek*, Feb. 14, 2011, www.newsweek.com/2011/02/13/wanted-a-grand-strategy-for-america.html.

15. David Ignatius, "Obama's fuzzy narrative in the Mideast," *The Washington Post*, March 25, 2011, www.washingtonpost.com/opinions/obamas-fuzzy-narrative-in-the-mideast/2011/03/24/AFt0DRYB_story.html.

16. "Background Note: Egypt," Department of State, Nov. 10, 2010, www.state.gov/r/pa/ei/bgn/5309.htm.

17. Alain Gresh, "Neither with the West, nor against it," *The Morung Express*, www.morungexpress.com/analysis/63756.html.

18. *Ibid.*

19. Ethan Bronner and Isabel Kershner, "Rival Factions of Palestinians Reach an Accord," *The New York Times*, April 28, 2011, p. A1.

20. Timothy Garton Ash, "If this is young Arabs' 1989, Europe must be ready with a bold response," *The Guardian*, Feb. 2, 2011, www.guardian.co.uk/commentisfree/2011/feb/02/egypt-young-arabs-1989-europe-bold.

21. David Ignatius, "Three voices of Egypt's future," *The Washington Post*, April 14, 2011, www.washingtonpost.com/todays_paper/A%20Section/2011-04-14/A/19/18.0.2395308719_epaper.html.

22. Nasser Arrabya, "Saleh stalls as Yemen unravels," *Al-Ahram Weekly* (English version), March 31, http://weekly.ahram.org.eg/2011/1041/re1.htm.

23. For background, see Kenneth Jost and Benton Ives-Halperin, "Democracy in the Arab World," *CQ Researcher*, Jan. 30, 2004, pp. 73-100.

24. William Cleveland, *A History of the Modern Middle East* (2000), p. 170.

25. D. Teter, "Iran between East and West," *Editorial Research Reports*, Jan. 26, 1979, available at *CQ Researcher Plus Archive*.

26. Yasmine Ryan, "The tragic life of a street vendor," *Al-Jazeera*, Jan. 20, 2011, http://english.al jazeera.net/indepth/features/2011/01/201111684242518839.html.

27. Cynthia P. Schneider and Nadia Oweidat, "Why Washington was blindsided by Egypt's cry for freedom,' " CNN, Feb. 10, 2011, http://articles.cnn.com/2011-02-10/opinion/schneider.egypt.us_1_pro-mubarak-egyptian-people-president-hosni-mubarak?_s=PM:OPINION.

28. "Arab Human Development Report 2009: Challenges to Human Security in the Arab Countries," U.N. Development Programme, 2009, pp. 35-36.

29. "Experts raise concern about Middle East youth unemployment," *World Learning*, January 2010, http://worldlearningnow.wordpress.com/2010/01/29/experts-raise-concern-about-mideast-youth-unemployment/.

30. See "Egypt, Arab Rep.," The World Bank, http://data.worldbank.org/country/egypt-arab-republic.

31. Azzam, Maha, "Egypt's Elections: A Challenge to the Regime?" Chatham House, Nov. 25, 2010, www.chathamhouse.org.uk/media/comment/mazzam1110/-/1181/.

32. Fahmy Howeidi, "Egypt: From Pharaonic Rule to Democracy," http://fahmyhoweidy.blogspot.com/2011/02/blog-post.html.

33. "Mubarak Resigns," "Archive for the 'Arabic Press' Category," *Islamic Middle East Blog*, Northfield Mount Herman School, Feb. 11, 2011.

34. Bari Weiss, "A Democrat's Triumphal Return to Cairo," *The Wall Street Journal*, Feb. 26, 2011, http://online.wsj.com/article/SB10001424052748703408604576164482658051692.html.

35. "Egypt Constitutional Referendum — What the Results Mean," VOA News, March 21, 2011, www.voanews.com/english/news/middle-east/Egypt-Constitutional-Referendum--What-the-Results-Mean-118376644.html.

36. Ashraf Swelam, "Egypt's Referendum: Why 'No' lost, and what to do about it," *Ahramonline*, March 26, 2011, http://english.ahram.org.eg/NewsContentPrint/4/0/8622/Opinion/0/Egypt%E2%80%99s-referendum-Why-%E2%80%9CNo%E2%80%9D-lost-and-what-to-do-ne.aspx.

37. "Mubarak to be moved to military hospital," Agence France-Press, April 24, 2011, www.focus-fen.net/index.php?id=n247970.

38. Con Coughlin, "Why the Bahrain rebellion could prove calamitous to the West," *Daily Telegraph*, March 17, 2011, www.telegraph.co.uk/comment/columnists/concoughlin/8389222/Why-the-Bahrain-rebellion-could-prove-calamitous-for-the-West.html.

39. "Demands of Saudi Youth for the Future of the Nation," *Jadaliyya*, March 5, 2011, www.jadaliyya.com/pages/index/818/demands-of-saudi-youth-for-the-future-of-the-nation.

40. "Yemen President Ready to Step Down at End of Year," VOANews.com, March 22, 2011, www

.voanews.com/english/news/Yemen-President-Ready-to-Step-Down-at-End-of-the-Year-118431164.html.

41. "More protesters slain in Yemen as exit plan is weighed," *op. cit.*

42. Kurt Sansone, "Wrong for anyone to tell the Libyans what to do: John Dalli," *TimesofMalta.com*, March 4, 2011, www.timesofmalta.com/articles/view/2011 0304/local/libya-events-amount-to-civil-war-john-dalli.353091.

43. Aamer Madhani, "Obama says Libya's Gadhafi must go," *National Journal*, March 3, 2011, http://national journal.com/obama-says-libya-s-qaddafi-must-go-20110303.

44. " 'This Week' Transcript: Hillary Clinton, Robert Gates and Donald Rumsfeld," ABCNews.com, March 27, 2011, http://abcnews.go.com/ThisWeek/week-transcript-hillary-clinton-robert-gates-donald-rums-feld/story?id=13232096&page=6.

45. Brian Whitaker, "The Arab spring is brighter than ever," *The Guardian*, March 14, 2011, www.guardian .co.uk/commentisfree/2011/mar/14/arab-spring-protest-crackdown-freedom.

46. Ash, *op. cit.*

47. Effat Mostafa, "Europe looks for ways to support Egypt's reforms, boost youth initiatives," Caravan, American University of Cairo, March 23, 1011, http:/ /academic.aucegypt.edu/caravan/story/europe-looks-ways-support-egypt%E2%80%99s-reforms-boost-youth-initiatives.

48. *Ibid.*

49. Economist Intelligence Unit, "Tunisia: Civil unrest damages the economy," March 14, 2011, http:// country.eiu.com/article.aspx?articleid=297893414 &Country=Tunisia&topic=Economy&subtopic= Recent+developments&subsubtopic=Economic+perf ormance%3A+Civil+unrest+damages+the+economy.

50. "Moroccan Human Rights Group Says King's Reform Panel 'Illegitimate,' " BBC Monitoring International Reports, April 10, 2011.

51. Scott Wilson, "Syria escalates lethal crackdown," *The Washington Post*, April 26, 2011, p. A1. See also Elizabeth A. Kennedy and Diaa Hadid, "Activists report clashes between Syrian army units," The Associated Press, April 28, 2011.

52. Patrick Seale, "The Syrian Time Bomb," *Foreign Policy*, March 28, 2011, www.foreignpolicy.com/ articles/2011/03/28/the_syrian_timebomb.

53. David Morgan, "U.S. treads cautiously amid Syria violence," CBS World Watch, April 26, 2011, www .cbsnews.com/8301-503543_162-20057418-5035 43.html.

54. Seale, *op. cit.*

55. Ted Thornton, "Arab Columnist: Where is Egypt Going?" *Islamic Middle East Blog*, Feb. 10, 2010, http:// islamicmiddleeast.nmhblogs.org/2011/02/09/arab-columnist-where-is-egypt-going/.

BIBLIOGRAPHY
Books

Calvert, John, *Sayyid Qutb and the Origins of Radical Islamism, Columbia/Hurst,* **2010.**
A Middle East scholar from Creighton College in Omaha, Neb., argues that one of Egypt's most influential — and most misunderstood — Islamist radicals, had he lived, would not have supported Osama bin Laden.

Clark, Victoria, *Yemen: Dancing on the Heads of Snakes, Yale University Press,* **2010.**
A British journalist examines Yemen's current problems and their daunting complexity.

Gubser, Peter, *Saladin: Empire and Holy War, Gorgias Press,* **2011.**
The late Middle East expert and co-founder of the National Council on U.S.-Arab Relations chronicles the life of the 12th-century Islamic leader who was the architect of Islam's greatest empire.

Lawrence, T. E., *Seven Pillars of Wisdom: A Triumph: The Complete 1922 Text, Wilder Publications,* **2011.**
This re-issued classic, first-person account of the World War I Arab uprising against the Ottoman Empire by the famous British Army officer describes Lawrence's role (and that of the European powers) in creating the new Middle East.

Osman, Tarek, *Egypt on the Brink, Yale University Press,* **2010.**
An Egyptian writer and commentator sets the scene for the current turmoil by describing the political situation

in Egypt and the rift between the cosmopolitan elite and the mass of the younger, underemployed population.

Smith, Lee, *The Strong Horse: Power, Politics, and the Clash of Arab Civilizations, Doubleday*, 2010.
The Middle East correspondent for the conservative *Weekly Standard* contends somewhat tendentiously that the Middle East is not ready for democracy because its populations gravitate instinctively towards autocratic leadership.

St. John, Ronald Bruce, *Libya: Continuity and Change, Routledge*, 2011.
A Middle East scholar from the United States examines the socioeconomic and political development of Libya.

Articles

"Into Libya: The Birth of an Obama Doctrine," Lexington's Notebook blog, *The Economist*, March 28, 2011, www.economist.com/blogs/lexington/2011/03/libya_4.
A columnist finds much to commend in President Obama's speech explaining the U.S. decision to intervene in Libya.

Halimi, Serge, "No Good Choices," *Le Monde Diplomatique* (English Edition), April 2011, http://mondediplo.com/2011/04/01libyawar.
The democratic Arab revolts are redrawing political, diplomatic and ideological boundaries in the Middle East.

Noun, Fady, "Unrest in Muslim Nations: Multinationals, dictators, and the social doctrine of the church," *AsiaNews*, Feb. 8, 2011, www.asianews.it/news-en/Unrest-in-Muslim-nations:-multinationals,-dictators-and-the-social-doctrine-of-the-Church-20715.html.
A prominent Lebanese economist discusses the consequences of the shake-up in the Middle East.

Reports and Studies

Azzam, Maha, *et al.*, "Egypt and the Road Ahead: Era of Change?" *Chatham House*, Feb. 7, 2011.
Current developments in Egypt and their long-term implications are discussed in a symposium held by the London think tank.

Ghallouni, Burham, "Arab Popular Uprisings, Or the Arab incoming to political modernity," *Middle East Studies Online*, Issue 4, Vol. 2, 2011.
A French Middle East scholar at the Sorbonne-Nouvelle University in Paris examines why Arabs have so far failed to build a modern state.

Jerome, Deborah, "Understanding Tunisia's Tremors," *Analysis Brief, Council on Foreign Relations*, Jan. 14, 2011, www.cfr.org/democracy-and-human-rights/understanding-tunisias-tremors/p23798.
The deputy editor of CFR.org, the council's website, examines the Tunisian uprising that triggered the region's current turmoil.

Kumetat, Dennis, "The Arab Region as Part of a Nuclear Renaissance: Outlooks and Alternatives," *Perspectives*, Heinrich Boll Institute, April 2011, www.boell-meo.org/downloads/01_Perspectives_ME_2011-Nuclear_Energy_and_the_Arab_World.pdf.
A German Green Party think tank examines the prospects of nuclear power in the Middle East.

Lindsay, James, "Guest Post: Turmoil in the Middle East and Implications for the Israeli-Palestinian Peace Process," *Council on Foreign Relations*, March 14, 2011, http://blogs.cfr.org/lindsay/2011/03/14/guest-post-turmoil-in-the-middle-east-and-implications-for-israeli-palestinian-peace-process/.
A senior fellow for Middle East and Africa Studies at CFR, offers 10 observations on how the current unrest could affect the Israeli-Palestinian peace process, perhaps the region's most important issue.

For More Information

Al-Ahram Center for Political and Strategic Studies, Al-galaa St., Cairo, Egypt; 20-2-257 86037, http://acpss.ahram. org.eg/eng/index_Eng.asp. A think tank that focuses on broad international and strategic issues, particularly trends between Arab countries and the international community.

Arab-American Institute, 1600 K St., N.W., Suite 601, Washington, DC 20006; (202) 429-9210; www.aaiusa.org. Committed to the civic and political empowerment of Americans of Arab descent. Its founder, James Zogby, is a leading Arab voice in the United States.

Center for Arab Unity Studies, Beit al-Nahda Bldg., Basra St., Hamra, P.O. Box 113-6001 Beirut 2034 2407, Lebanon; 961 1 750088; http://caus.org.lb/Home/index.php?Lang=en. Conducts "independent, scientific research into all aspects of Arab society and Arab unity, free of ties to any government."

Chatham House, The Royal Institute of International Affairs, 10, St. James's Square, London SW1Y4LE, United Kingdom; 44 (207) 7957 5710; www.chathamhouse.org. Leading source of independent analysis on global and domestic issues.

Council on Foreign Relations, The Harold Pratt House, 58 East 68th St., New York, NY 10065; (212) 434-9400; www.cfr.org. An independent think tank that "promotes understanding of foreign policy and America's role in the world."

Emirates Center for Strategic Studies and Research, Abu Dhabi, P.O. Box 4567, United Arab Emirates; 97 12 404 4444, www.ecssr.ac.ae/ECSSR/appmanager/portal/ecssr?_ nfpb=true&_pageLabel=ECSSRPortal_portal_page_1076. An institute dedicated to helping to modernize UAE society.

School of Oriental and African Studies, University of London, Thornhaugh St., Russell Square, London WC1H OXG, United Kingdom; 44 207 637 2388; www.soas.ac .uk. Studies such issues as democracy, development and human rights in Asia, Africa and the Near and Middle East.

Voices From Abroad:

BAN KI-MOON

Secretary General United Nations

Lack of opportunities a root cause

"We have seen the wide[spread] demonstrations, outbursts of demonstrations and voices are now on the streets. That means they have been frustrated enough by the lack of freedom, lack of opportunities. That is the lesson, which the leaders should learn and try to change, as soon as possible, reflecting such strong voices from their own people."

Press Trust of India, February 2011

NZZ am Sonntag/Patrick Chappatte

MOHAMED SAAD KITATNI

Spokesman, Muslim Brotherhood, Egypt

A collective effort

"No single political trend can claim to speak on behalf of the revolution. All segments of the Egyptian public participated in the uprising, and it was this broad-based participation that ensured its success."

Inter Press Service (South Africa) February 2011

SALEH IBRAHIM

President, Graduate Academy, Libya

The people rule in Libya

"But in Egypt, Tunisia or other traditional countries, there is no possibility for change except through the collapse of the ruling party and the coming to power of another party. In Libya, it is the people who rule and can sack people's committees anytime or hold them accountable."

Al Jazeera (Qatar), February 2011

MIKHAIL GORBACHEV

Former President Soviet Union

The people will prevail

"First in Tunisia and now in Egypt, the people have spoken and made clear that they do not want to live under authoritarian rule and are fed up with regimes that hold power for decades. In the end, the voice of the people will be decisive. The Arab elites, Egypt's neighboring countries and the world powers should understand this and take it into account in their political calculations. The events now unfolding will have far-reaching consequences for Egypt itself, for the Middle East and for the Muslim world."

International Herald Tribune February 2011

ALEKA PAPARIGA

General Secretary, Communist Party of Greece

Solutions necessary

"An uprising, in order to have a positive political outlet, first wants to have the people in the street but definitely in order for an outlet to come there have to be political forces, a political force such that they have a real alternative solution. Now the alternative solution being prepared is a succession formation that will not change politics fundamentally."

ANA-MPA news agency (Greece), January 2011

BORHANODDIN RABBANI

Chairman, High Peace Council, Afghanistan

Changes abound

"There is no doubt that these uprisings will not only bring some considerable changes in those countries, but some changes will also emerge in the Arab World, in the Middle East and even there will be considerable changes in those countries' international relations."

Noor (Afghanistan), February 2011

EYAL ZISSER

Chair, Department of Middle East and African Studies, Tel Aviv University, Israel

Storm has hit Syria

"Clearly the storm has arrived in Syria. I don't know whether it will develop to a full storm, but clearly Syria

is not immune. We will have to wait a few more days or weeks to see if it goes on or things calm down."

Xinhua news agency (China) March 2011

SAIF AL-ISLAM GADHAFI

Son of Leader Moammar Gadhafi, Libya

Libya is different

"We will take up arms . . . we will fight to the last bullet. We will destroy seditious elements. If everybody is armed, it is civil war, we will kill each other. . . . Libya is not Egypt, it is not Tunisia."

Press Trust of India, February 2011

15

U.S.-China Relations

Roland Flamini

Bustling Shanghai — with twice the number of high rises as Manhattan — reflects China's phenomenal growth. Some economists worry that China holds nearly $900 billion in U.S. Treasury securities, refuses to fairly value its currency and maintains an annual trade advantage over the U.S. of more than $230 billion.

From *CQ Researcher*,
October 31, 2008. (Updated May 17, 2011)

President Bill Clinton's trip to China in July 1998 was a splashy, 10-day display of America's power and prestige. Clinton arrived in Beijing with an entourage that included his wife, Hillary, and daughter Chelsea, five Cabinet secretaries, more than 500 White House staffers, members of Congress and security personnel, plus a swarm of journalists. His meetings with China's leaders turned into vigorous and lively debates. At Beijing University, Clinton delivered a forthright speech on human rights and answered questions from Chinese students, all of which was televised live nationwide. The authorities released a number of dissidents, and as the American visitors toured China's landmarks large crowds turned out to greet them.[1]

But that was then. President Obama's China visit in November 2009 was a low-key, four-day affair, part of a swing through Southeast Asia. Wife Michelle and daughters Malia and Sasha remained at home in Washington. His one direct contact with the Chinese public, a town meeting with 500 Chinese students in Shanghai, was deemed a local event and not broadcast nationwide. Throughout his stay, Obama made no public statement on human rights — although he did criticize China's Internet censorship, without mentioning China by name. In Beijing, his joint press appearance with his Chinese host, President Hu Jintao, was limited to a statement from each leader, with no press questions taken. Like Clinton, Obama visited the Forbidden City, but only after it was emptied of tourists.

In the years between the two presidential visits, China has emerged as the world's third-largest economy after the United States and Japan, and a force to be reckoned with in global affairs. And

Trigger Points in the East and the west

Cbina shares a western border with pakistan, which buys 36 percent of all Cbina's arms exports –the largest share. Security experts worry that some of those arms may end up in the bands of anti-American insurgents in Afghanistan. In the east, concern focuses on the buildup of China's naval fleets and its bellicose comments about U.S.-supported Taiwan.

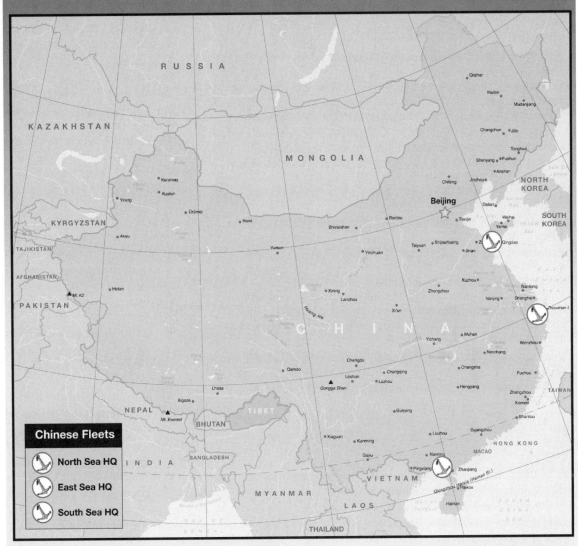

Sources: The World Factbook, *Central Intelligence Agency*

while the United States and Europe continue their uphill struggle to recover from the world recession, China is back on track, posting a phenomenal 11.9 percent growth rate for the first quarter of 2010 — well above the annual 8 percent its leaders consider crucial to keeping unemployment and social unrest at bay.[2]

Last year, China overtook Germany as the world's top exporter. China is now America's second-biggest trading

China at a Glance

Area: 9.6 million sq. km. (slightly smaller than the U.S.)

Population: 1.34 billion (July 2009 est.); U.S.: 308 million

Birth rate: 14 births/1,000 population (2009 est.); United States: 13.82 births/1,000 population (2009 est.)

Ethnic groups: Han Chinese 91.5%; Zhuang, Manchu, Hui, Miao, Uyghur, Tujia, Yi, Mongol, Tibetan, Buyi, Dong, Yao, Korean, and other nationalities 8.5% (2000 census)

Religions: Mainly Daoist (Taoist) and Buddhist; Christian 3%-4%, Muslim 1%-2%

Languages: Standard Chinese or Mandarin (Putonghua, based on the Beijing dialect) about 70%; Yue (Cantonese), Wu (Shanghainese), Minbei (Fuzhou), Minnan (Hokkien-Taiwanese), Xiang, Gan, Hakka dialects, minority languages

Government: Communist state. President and vice president elected by National People's Congress for five-year terms. Unicameral National People's Congress with 2,987 seats; members elected by municipal, regional and provincial people's congresses and People's Liberation Army to five-year terms.

Economy: GDP: $8.8 trillion (2009 est.); United States: $14.43 trillion (2009 est.)

Exports: mining and ore processing, iron, steel, aluminum, other metals, coal; machine building; armaments; textiles and apparel; petroleum; cement; chemicals; fertilizers; consumer products, including footwear, toys, electronics; food processing; transportation equipment, including automobiles, rail cars and locomotives, ships and aircraft; telecommunications equipment, commercial space launch vehicles, satellites.

Unemployment rate: 4.3% (Sept. 2009 est.); United States: 9.3% (2009 est.)

Military expenditures: 4.3% of GDP (2006); United States: 4.06% of GDP (2005 est.)

Sources: The World Factbook, Central Intelligence Agency

partner after Canada, with $62.3 billion in trade to date in 2010 (up from $52.5 billion during the same period in 2009).[3] But China is also the leading trading partner of the European Union, Japan, Brazil and India, reflecting the global reach of its burgeoning commercial activity. It is second only to the United States in energy consumption, has overtaken the U.S. as the biggest producer of greenhouse gasses on the planet and is also the No. 1 market for automobile sales.

The string of accomplishments has tilted the balance of the world's most important bilateral relationship in favor of the Chinese. With America's economy weakened, its military mired in two long and costly wars and its trade imbalance with China heavily in the red (-$238 billion) Obama's trip was fashioned to Beijing's specifications — brief and businesslike. Because China holds more than $877 billion of U.S. Treasury securities, commentators likened the visit to a debtor meeting with his bank manager.

Persuading the Chinese to increase the value of their currency was high on Obama's talks agenda. Concerned American manufacturers and unions say China deliberately keeps the renminbi (also referred to as the yuan) low against the dollar, giving China's goods an unfair advantage in U.S. and other foreign markets. China's refusal to adopt a floating currency system, according to experts, leads to so-called goods "dumping" by Chinese exporters — making their goods cheaper and undercutting foreign manufacturers.

The dispute over pricing has led to a tit-for-tat tariff battle. The United States currently imposes special tariffs and duties on 95 categories of goods imported from China — the highest for any country.[4]

When — shortly before Obama's visit — the United States announced stiff penalties on $3.2 billion in steel pipe from China for use in oil and gas fields, the Ministry of Commerce denounced the move as "protectionist" and said it was looking into whether American sedans and big sport utility vehicles on sale in China were subsidized by the United States government. "By not recognizing China as a market economy, the U.S. is acting in a discriminatory manner," stated ministry spokesman Yao Jian.[5]

Not so, said U.S. Steelworkers Union president Leo Gerard. "We're fed up with [the Chinese] cheating on our trade laws. Penalties for these transgressions are long overdue."[6]

On the foreign-policy front, the Obama administration needs China's help in containing Iran's nuclear ambitions. The next planned step in Washington's high-priority attempt to stymie the ruling ayatollahs' efforts to produce nuclear weapons is tight U.N. sanctions to block Iran from acquiring any more of the technology it still needs. As one of the five veto-wielding, permanent members of the U.N. Security Council, China possesses an indispensable vote needed to pass any U.N. sanctions resolution. (The other members are the United States, Russia, Britain and France.)

But Iran is China's third-largest crude oil supplier, shipping 460,000 barrels a day in 2009 and about the same this year. China's National Petroleum Corp. also has sizable investments in Iranian oil production.[7] In Beijing, the Chinese shared Obama's concern that Iran should become a nuclear power but resisted his pressure to cooperate. Since then they have agreed to help in drafting a U.N. resolution — but have said nothing about voting for it. The president also raised U.S. concern over China's lack of respect for copyright laws and patent rights — a perennial Western complaint. Despite some new legislation to protect intellectual property, the production of knock-offs of famous brand names and the piracy of music, films and electronic game software remains a full-blown industry.[8]

In China's latest copyright scandal, the embarrassed organizers of Shanghai's $40 billion Expo 2010, which opened on May 1, recently withdrew the trade fair's promotional theme song after being deluged with protests that it had been plagiarized from a Japanese pop song.[9]

Such controversies are hardly new, but as China's economy and military have become more robust, so has its belief that it is operating from a position of strength, and the United States from growing weakness. "I think it is a common perception in the region that U.S. influence has been on the decline in the last decade, while Chinese influence has been increasing," Jeffrey Bader, director of Asian affairs at the National Security Council, declared prior to Obama's Asian trip. "And one of the messages that the president will be sending in his visit is that we are an Asia-Pacific nation and we're there for the long haul." Coming from a senior White House adviser the admission was revealing.[10]

In the end there was very little give by the Chinese leadership on either trade or Iran. Obama also made a pitch to the Chinese for what he described as "a positive, constructive and comprehensive relationship that opens the door to partnership on the big global issues of our

A February meeting between the Dalai Lama — Tibet's exiled leader — and President Obama miffed the Chinese government, which maintains that Tibet is an inherent part of China and refuses to recognize Tibetan independence.

time: economic recovery, development of clean air energy, stopping the spread of nuclear weapons and the surge of climate change, the promotion of peace in Asia and around the globe."[11]

Zbigniew Brzezinski, a former U.S. national security adviser who advised the Obama election campaign, described Obama's proposal more succinctly as a Washington-Beijing G-2 partnership. But the Chinese seemed lukewarm to Obama's power-sharing offer. "China fundamentally has not promoted the idea that China and the U.S. will form the two major powers," says Feng Zhongping, the head of the European section of the Beijing-based Chinese Institute of Contemporary International Relations. "China believes that the idea that [China and the United States] could undertake the responsibility of administering the world is incorrect."[12]

As experts try to read the tea leaves on the future of U.S.-China relations, here are some of the questions being asked:

Is a U.S.-China partnership actually possible?

Until the early 1970s, when President Richard M. Nixon made his historic trip to China, the two countries were virtual enemies — militarily and ideologically. Today, as China becomes a global powerhouse and a challenge to U.S. commercial and political interests, the relationship is deeply complex.

China Sells Most Arms to Pakistan

Pakistan purchased more than a third of all Chinese conventional arms from 2003-2007 — by far the largest share. The second-largest buyer was Sudan, followed by Iran, Saudi Arabia and Egypt.

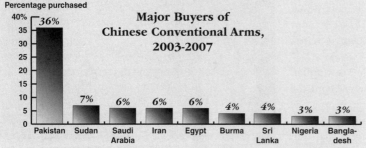

Percentage purchased

Major Buyers of Chinese Conventional Arms, 2003-2007

Source: "Military Power of the People's Republic of China, 2009," Office of the Secretary of Defense

"It may be a cliché, but there are issues on which the United States and China have a common interest, and other issues with divergent interests, and difficulties are going to persist for some time, and occasionally there will be some friction," says China specialist Bonnie Glaser at Washington's Center for Strategic and International Studies. "But China does not want to have an unstable, unhealthy relationship with the United States. It's extremely important to the Chinese to have good relations."

To underline this, Chinese officials pointed out to the author that in Beijing Obama signed 11 bilateral agreements, including those on nuclear proliferation, economic cooperation, climate change, participation in multinational anti-pirate patrols in the Horn of Africa, visits between U.S. and Chinese forces (the U.S. carrier *USS Nimitz* visited Hong Kong in February), plus a joint commitment to strengthen people-to-people exchanges. As part of an enlarged U.S. academic-exchange program, Obama has promised to send 100,000 American students to China — roughly the same number of Chinese currently studying in the United States.[13]

The Chinese leadership's determination to avoid even the impression of giving in to pressure is almost a conditioned reflex because this would mean a dreaded loss of face.

Thus when Obama in Beijing held out the prospect of a closer partnership to tackle the major global issues, the response was noncommittal. Four months later,

President Hu came to Washington to attend the Nuclear Security Summit. In a one-on-one with Obama, according to the official Xinhua news agency, he put forward a five-point proposal "to establish a partnership to jointly deal with common challenges."

Hu's overture covered much the same ground as Obama's, but only up to a point: The second of his five points stressed that each country "would respect the other's core interests and major concerns," a point not specifically made by Obama, and one that left wide latitude for divergence. Two of these interests were Tibet and Taiwan, which "concern China's sovereignty and territorial integrity and its interests," Xinhua stated, and which the United States should "handle with caution."[14]

This balance-of-interests approach by the Chinese is typically — and almost cryptically — expressed by Kaiser Kuo, an associate researcher at Beijing's World Politics Institute. "Sino-American competition and cooperation are increasingly intertwined," Kaiser says. "There is cooperation within competition, and competition within cooperation. There is no absolute cooperation or competition. Therefore, we should not completely reject competition — and we should strengthen cooperation."[15]

In Washington, President Hu also hinted that China might be considering a revaluation of its currency, "based on its own economic and social-development needs." In other words, not because Washington is pressing for it.[16]

Hu also agreed that Beijing should cooperate on the wording of an Iran sanctions resolution. But in Beijing, Chinese Foreign Ministry spokeswoman Jiang Yu repeated China's position that "dialogue and negotiations are the best way."[17]

But some analysts think U.S.-Chinese relations may be less about cooperation and more about an ascendant China challenging the United States in areas once firmly in America's sphere of influence. "Obama and his policy makers are required to face up to a new reality," commented the Seoul-based English-language *Korean Times*, "in which China is jockeying for the world's No. 2

position while the U.S., the world's sole superpower, is waning, especially in the aftermath of the global financial and economic crisis."[18]

Unlike U.S.-Soviet relations during the Cold War, the challenge is not ideological. Still, according to the Congressional Research Service, "China's growing 'soft power' — primarily diplomatic and economic influence in the developing world — has become a concern among many U.S. policy leaders, including members of Congress."[19]

Because of its voracious demand for raw materials, Chinese trade with Latin America — the United States' back yard — grew tenfold between 2002 and 2007. In 2008, Chinese trade with Latin America ($142 billion) was a sixth of U.S. trade with the region — but growing at a faster rate. China's footprint in Africa is even larger in terms of both financial aid and investments.[20] But more significant from Washington's point of view is Beijing's increasing involvement in the Middle East.

In 2009, exports of Saudi Arabian crude to China were higher than to the United States, as Beijing courted the world's largest oil producer — and longtime U.S. ally.

"Saudi Arabia used to be very much an American story, but those days are over," said Brad Bourland, head researcher at Jadwa Investment in Riyadh, Saudi Arabia. The Saudis "now see their relationship with China as very strategic, and very long term."[21]

In a recent interview, Xu Xueguan, director of North American affairs at the Chinese Foreign Ministry's huge headquarters in Beijing, told the author he couldn't understand why China had not been included in the so-called Quartet, the coalition of the United Nations, European Union, United States and Russia that is seeking a peaceful solution to the Israel-Palestine confrontation. When the Quartet was set up eight years ago, China did not yet have the clout to insist on being included. More recently, Beijing has expressed interest in becoming the fifth member of the U.N.-sponsored peace effort, without success — at least so far.

Is a confrontation with China inevitable, as some predict?

The Chinese leadership is "gunning for a paradigm shift in geopolitics. In particular, Beijing has served notice that it won't be shy about playing hardball to safeguard what it claims to be 'core national interests,' " writes Willy Lam, a China specialist at the Washington-based Jamestown Foundation think tank.[22] At the top of those national interests is Taiwan which, *The Economist* magazine said recently, "has been where the simmering distrust between China and America most risks boiling over."[23]

The chance of a war between China and the United States is generally regarded as remote. The Chinese threat to the United States is indirect — for example, if China should decide to use force to annex Taiwan, and America intercedes — as it is committed to do even though the United States does not recognize the island as an independent state.

China hands like Elizabeth Economy, director of Asia Studies at the Council on Foreign Relations think tank in Washington, downplay the new "Red Scare." Economy argues that the West — particularly the United States — has "completely lost perspective on what constitutes reality in China today." Economy concedes that "there is a lot that is incredible about China's economic story, but there is a lot that is not working well on both the political and economic fronts," distorting the real picture.

In other words, China has enough problems without provoking the challenge of an international nemesis. The Chinese leadership appears to worry about a fragile society: A persistent nightmare is that a sudden significant spike in unemployment, officially kept at 4 percent (but possibly higher because of the huge, hard-to-track migrant-worker population) could lead to widespread unrest.[24]

Still, looking at the Chinese as the potential aggressors, does China have the capacity for a military confrontation with the United States?

In the past five years China has spent hundreds of billions of dollars modernizing its armed forces, with special emphasis on the navy. China's 1.7 million Chinese under arms is considerably more than the 1.4 million in the U.S. armed forces, but in 2009 the U.S. defense budget was $738 billion and China's estimated at between $69.5 billion and $150 billion.[25]

The government insists it seeks a peaceful solution to the issue of uniting Taiwan to the mainland, but the Chinese have built up a formidable fleet of submarines and developed anti-ship missiles to counter a possible

U.S. Trade Deficit With China Has Surged

The United States imports far more from China than it exports, causing a significant and growing trade gap. U.S-China trade rose rapidly after the two nations reestablished diplomatic relations and signed a bilateral trade agreement in 1979 and provided mutual most-favored-nation treatment beginning in 1980. In recent years, China has been one of the fast-growing U.S. export markets, and it is expected to grow even further as living standards continue to improve and a sizable Chinese middle class emerges.

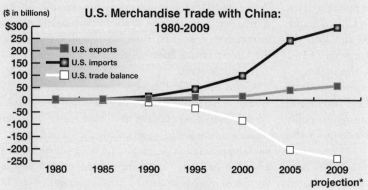

U.S. Merchandise Trade with China: 1980-2009

($ in billions)

* Based on actual data for January-April 2009

Source: Wayne M. Morrison, "China-U.S. Trade Issues," Congressional Research Service, June 23, 2009

U.S. defense of the Taiwan Strait. The Americans will be readyfor them. In its annual report to Congress on China's military power, the Pentagon said it was "maintaining the capacity to defend against Beijing's use of force or coercion against Taiwan."

Beyond the strait, the Pentagon reported, "China's ability to sustain military power . . . remains limited."[26] The Pentagon's annual report is a source of irritation to the Chinese, who routinely denounce it. This year, the Xinhua news agency dismissed the assessment as "a largely subjective report with distorted facts and groundless speculation."[27]

Less hypothetical is the threat to the U.S. government's computer system. The Pentagon's 2009 report said U.S. government computers had been the target of "intrusions that appear to have originated" in China, although not necessarily from the military.[28] And in his annual "Threat Assessment" to the Senate Select Committee on Intelligence, Director of National Intelligence Dennis C. Blair warned in February that "malicious cyber activity is occurring on an unprecedented scale with extraordinary sophistication."

As a result, Blair added, the United States "cannot be certain that our cyberspace infrastructure will remain available and reliable during a time of crisis." Blair did not refer to China directly at that point. However, later in his assessment he called "China's aggressive cyber activities" a major concern.[29]

In January, after Google reported that hackers in China had targeted the computers of more than 30 U.S. corporations, including its own, and that the e-mail accounts of human rights activists had also been hacked, Secretary of State Hillary Rodham Clinton called on the Chinese government to investigate and to make its findings public.[30]

U.S. officials and business executives warn that a trade war could also erupt if the Chinese don't yield to international pressure and raise the aggressive undervaluation of the renminbi, kept artificially low to favor Chinese exports. China's cheap currency is a serious problem for the global economy by undercutting exports throughout the industrial world, including the United States, and contributing to the trade imbalance. (President Obama has contended that if China lets the renminbi appreciate, U.S. exports would increase.)

The Obama administration has so far avoided picking a public fight with China over its currency — even to the extent of postponing indefinitely a Treasury Department report on worldwide currencies originally due out on April 15. Without any movement by Beijing on the currency front, the report could well label China a "currency manipulator." If that happens, Sen. Charles E. Schumer, D-N.Y., is ready with draft legislation that would place more tariffs on Chinese goods.

Chinese Commerce Minister Chen Deming recently told *The Washington Post* that the United States would lose a trade war with China. "If the United States uses the exchange rate to start a new trade war," he said, "China will be hurt. But the American people and U.S. companies will be hurt even more."[31]

One way for America to increase its exports, said Chen, would be to remove the restrictions on high-tech goods with possible military applications, which the United States imposed following Beijing's repressive crackdown on student demonstrations in 1989 in Tiananmen Square — something the Obama administration shows no signs of doing.

Has China's "market authoritarian" model of government emerged as an alternative to Western democracy?

Despite predictions, China's emergence from isolation and its spectacular economic growth have not led to democratization. Instead, China has developed what Stefan Halper, director of the Atlantic Studies Program at Cambridge University, calls "a market authoritarian form of government, in which the free market is allowed to operate, but the government holds a very firm hand on political activity in the country."

In so doing, says Halper, author of the recent book *The Beijing Consensus*, the Chinese have produced an alternative to the Western democratic system that is thought to go hand in hand with a free-market economy. Non-democratic countries around the world like Egypt, Indonesia, Myanmar and Malaysia must find much to envy in a country that has achieved a 9 percent growth rate yet "managed to control its media, the legislature and the dissident voices, and has achieved global prominence," Halper adds.

China's U.S. Holdings Greatly Increased

Since the early 2000s, China's holdings of U.S. securities — including U.S. Treasury securities and corporate stocks and bonds — have risen above $1.2 trillion — an increase of more than 500 percent. While China's U.S. holdings have helped the United States meet its investment needs, some policymakers worry they could give China increased leverage over the U.S. on political and economic issues.

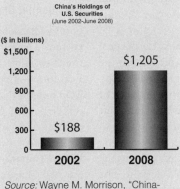

China's Holdings of U.S. Securities
(June 2002-June 2008)

($ in billions)

- 2002: $188
- 2008: $1,205

Source: Wayne M. Morrison, "China-U.S. Trade Issues," Congressional Research Service, June 23, 2009

The Chinese system "offers a seductive model that is eagerly taken up by the leaders of countries that have not yet settled on democratic structures," writes Australian China hand Rowan Callick in *The American*, the magazine of the American Enterprise Institute, a conservative Washington think tank. The Chinese model attracts autocrats because "their broader populations become content and probably supportive because their living standards are leaping ahead."[32]

China, however, has no interest in exporting its form of government. Its dealings with the rest of the world are dominated by the single-minded pursuit of one objective: economic development. As a ubiquitous lender and financial aid donor, China finds the door open in developing countries because Beijing's money comes with no strings attached about human rights and democracy — which is hardly the case with financial assistance from either the United States or the European Union.

Chinese money "is made available relatively easily and quickly without the political, economic, social and environmental conditions . . . that U.S. and European donors typically impose," says the Congressional Research Service report on China's foreign trade.[33]

But envious autocratic leaders should take note: Authoritarian capitalism may only work up to a point, writes Thomas P.M. Barnett, author of the recent book *Great Powers: America and the World after Bush*. He argues that when an economy starts to mature and needs to become more efficient, productive and innovative-based —"then we're talking intensive growth . . . something that nobody ever has been able to plan, because it lives and breathes on fierce competition, which only a true free market, accompanied by democracy, can supply."[34]

Moreover, under closer scrutiny, China's economic success has fragile underpinnings, with some doubting its long-term sustainability. For example, for all its progress, China's per capita income is still $6,546, compared to $40,208 in the United States. China's gross domestic product barely reaches $9 trillion, whereas allowing for the recent volatility of exchange rates, U.S. GDP exceeds $14 trillion.

Because China's economic development is export driven, the world recession caused 23 million Chinese workers to be laid off as Chinese exports dropped by 15-18 percent, says Stephen Green, chief economist at the Sun Trust Bank in Shanghai. By the end of 2009, however, 98 percent of those had found other work, as the Chinese economy bounced back quicker than Western economies, boosted by a 4 trillion renminbi ($586 billion) stimulus package. (The U.S. economic stimulus was $874 billion.)

But the lesson to Beijing was that China can't export itself to growth. Though exports have picked up, the Chinese have turned their attention to trying to develop a domestic market. For example, to stimulate sales of domestic appliances in rural areas, the government offered 13 percent rebates to farmers who buy refrigerators, TV sets and even mobile phones. In 2009, Beijing also spent $755 million to push car sales, cutting the purchase tax from around 15 percent to 5 percent. The result was a record 770,000 sales in March alone, a 27 percent jump over the previous month. Banks had instructions to increase mortgage lending, but the government reined them in again when they started granting loans for third homes.[35]

Though officials in China say 250 million Chinese were lifted out of poverty between 1980 and 2005, about 70 percent of China's population of 1.3 billion still lives in rural areas, often in villages with few paved roads and frequent water and power shortages. An ambitious and costly urbanization program is trying to shift people to the cities.

State-controlled media limit reports about unrest, but "bottom-up pressures for change in China are intense, spontaneous and multifaceted," according to a report by Ying Ma, a visiting fellow at the Hoover Institution at Stanford University. "Every day, Chinese leaders worry about the challenge to regime stability, but they have

responded by continuing to exert brutal and sophisticated top-down control."[36]

"Riots take place in China every day," Ying says. The Chinese authorities reported 10,000 protests throughout the country in 1994, and 87,000 in 2005. Mobile phones and the Internet have given protesters and activists effective new weapons, which the regime is battling tooth and nail. Using the new technology the Chinese people clamor for the government to address their grievances on the local level in increasing numbers: 10 million petitions in 2004 jumped to 30 million the following year.[37]

BACKGROUND

Presidential Challenges

Shortly after Mao Zedong's death in 1976, Chinese leaders took a hard look at their country and didn't like what they saw. China was just emerging from the Cultural Revolution, a decade of mob-led extremism started by Mao himself that had kept the country in chaos. China was desperately poor, deliberately isolated from the world economy and aloof from or opposed to nearly every international institution, including — until 1971 — the United Nations. Under Deng Xiaoping, China's leaders reversed course and embraced globalization.

Since then successive U.S. presidents have wrestled with the challenge of how to deal with China's rapid rise. The Clinton administration fashioned a policy of "constructive engagement," calling for close bilateral economic and political cooperation, at the same time urging democratization and human rights.

"Seeking to isolate China is clearly unthinkable," President Bill Clinton declared in July 1998, defending his approach. "We would succeed instead in isolating ourselves and our own policy."[38]

The George W. Bush administration used the catchphrase "responsible stakeholder," pressing China to become a responsible member of the international community and to embrace democracy. Prior to President Obama's November China trip, Deputy Secretary of State James B. Steinberg mapped out a policy of "strategic reassurance" towards Beijing, and the phrase — as intended — has stuck.

C H R O N O L O G Y

1970s-1980s *After Mao's death Deng institutes sweeping reforms, including relations with the United States.*

1972 President Richard M. Nixon makes historic trip to China, meets Mao Zedong and signs Shanghai Joint Communiqué declaring Taiwan part of mainland China.

1975 President Gerald R. Ford visits China, meets the ailing Mao, who dies the next year.

1978 Deng Xiaoping emerges as new leader, launches economic and social reforms.

1979 U.S. and China establish diplomatic relations. . . . Congress passes Taiwan Relations Act pledging to continue to supply Taiwan with weapons. . . . Deng visits United States.

1982 In joint U.S.-Chinese communiqué, United States pledges to gradually reduce arms sales to Taiwan.

1984 President Ronald Reagan visits China and meets Deng, who says that Taiwan remains a crucial problem in bilateral relations.

1989 President George H. W. Bush visits Beijing, invites dissidents to dinner. . . . People's Liberation Army crushes student-led pro-democracy demonstration in Beijing's Tiananmen Square, killing hundreds of protesters. . . . White House National Security Adviser Brent Scowcroft holds secret meeting in Beijing with Chinese leaders following the Tiananmen Square massacre.

1990s-2000s *China's economy welcomes Western investors; U.S.-China relations continue to warm.*

1992 Reversing a decade of U.S. policy, President George H. W. Bush decides to sell Taiwan F-16 combat planes, infuriating the Chinese.

1993 Newly elected President Bill Clinton establishes policy of "constructive engagement" with China, meets President Jiang Zemin in Seattle.

1996 China tests missiles off Taiwan to discourage vote for separatist Lee Teng-hui in the presidential election;

U.S. sends two aircraft carrier battle groups to area to support Taiwan.

1997 Britain hands Hong Kong back to China after 156 years. . . . Clinton is first U.S. president to visit China in a decade; criticizes Tiananmen massacre but strengthens U.S. commitment not to support Taiwan independence.

2000 U.S. Senate passes Permanent Normal Trade Relations bill (PNTR) giving China the same low-tariff access to the American market as other trading partners.

2001 China seizes U.S. spy plane after midair collision with Chinese fighter, hands over 24 American crewmembers after President George W. Bush apologizes for the Chinese pilot's death. . . . Bush makes first trip to China. . . . China joins World Trade Organization.

2002 Bush makes second visit to China to mark the 30th anniversary of Nixon's historic trip. . . . Future leader Hu Jintao visits White House for talks. . . . President Jiang Zemin visits Bush at his Texas ranch; they agree to cooperate on crisis following North Korea's announcement that it has nuclear weapons.

2003 With U.S. participation, Beijing hosts six-party talks on a unified approach to North Korea's nuclear weapons program.

2006 China's Great Firewall, or Golden Shield, Internet censorship system goes into service.

2008 China closes down Twitter, YouTube to block discussion on 20th anniversary of Tiananmen massacre.

2009 President Obama visits Shanghai and Beijing, makes no headway in persuading Chinese to raise value of their currency or to back sanctions against Iran.

2010 President Hu attends summit on nuclear security in Washington, despite tense U.S.-China relations over Iran sanctions, currency issues and imminent American weapons sale to Taiwan. . . . Expo 2010 opens in Shanghai. . . . Annual "strategic dialogue" between U.S. and China set for late May. . . . U.S. and China to attend G20 summit in Seoul, South Korea, in late June.

2010

Jan. 6 — President Barack Obama approves $6.4 billion in weapon sales to Taiwan despite strong protests from Beijing. Deal includes missiles, ships and helicopters.

Jan. 26 — In retaliation for the U.S. arms deal with Taiwan, China suspends military contact with the United States, imposes sanctions on companies selling weapons to Taiwan.

Feb. 17 — President Obama receives exiled Tibetan spiritual leader, the Dalai Lama. China "resolutely opposes" the meeting.

May 24 — Secretary of State Hillary Rodham Clinton and Treasury Secretary Timothy F. Geithner hold talks with their counterparts in China. Topping the agenda is a discussion of tensions created when North Korea torpedoed a South Korean navy ship in March, killing 46 sailors.

Aug. 16 — Pentagon reports that Chinese military is increasing spending on long-range missiles, submarines, aircraft carriers and cyber warfare. The activities could alter East Asian military balances and enable China to conduct a range of military operations in Asia well beyond Taiwan.

Sept. 24 — President Obama and China's Prime Minister Wen Jiabao hold two-hour meeting on the sidelines of the U.N. General Assembly in New York. Obama urges China to speed up the revaluation of the *renminbi,* complaining that the slow pace of China's proposed currency reforms was affecting both the global and U.S. economies.

2011

Jan. 18 — Chinese President Hu Jintao, visiting Washington, acknowledges for first time that "a lot still needs to be done" with regard to human rights in China.

April 6 — Chinese authorities suppress nascent Jasmine Revolution, inspired by the Arab Spring, arrest many activists.

May 9-10 — Third meeting of U.S.-China Strategic and Economic Dialogue is held in Washington, D.C.

"Just as we are prepared to accept China's arrival as a prosperous and successful power," Steinberg explained, the Chinese must "reassure the rest of the world that its development and growing global role will not come at the expense of the security and well-being of others."[39]

Whatever the label, the fundamental underpinning of American policy toward China has been economic engagement. In 2000, for example, Congress granted China permanent normal trade relations (PNTR) with the United States. In 2001, the United States backed China's entry into the World Trade Organization, thus placing the Chinese under international business rules, which was reassuring for would-be foreign investors.

All Business

In his inaugural address last year, Obama echoed Clinton's 1997 statement that communist China stood "on the wrong side of history." The conventional wisdom about China was that the market forces unleashed by global trade and investment would inevitably give more people a stake in the economy and open up China politically, leading to the creation of political parties and more democracy and respect for human rights.

Only it hasn't happened. In China, the party's far from over. China calls its authoritarian capitalism a "socialist market system," and the ruling Chinese Communist Party (CPC) appears more entrenched than ever — helped by a large, efficient and pervasive police organization.

In 2009, the party celebrated its 60th anniversary, and the state-controlled media took care to trumpet the regime's economic and political achievements.

Yet how much is left of communist ideology is open to question: As the author discovered during a reporting trip to China last November, the huge portrait of Mao still looks out over Tiananmen Square, and Marxist theory is still taught at the party school for senior officials. But the old party slogans praising the proletariat class and condemning capitalism have disappeared from the walls and factories.

The party has opened membership to entrepreneurs and business people, and the state-held shares of the country's 1,300 companies, many of which are listed on the Beijing stock exchange, are publicly traded.

Challenged to explain exactly how Marxism-Leninism fits into the "socialist market system," Chinese officials quote Deng Xiaoping's famous observation that it doesn't matter whether the cat is black or white as long as it kills the mouse.

Officials today will even quote Confucius without first cautiously looking over their shoulder. The great Chinese sage has had his ups and downs. In the Cultural Revolution he was reviled as an imperial lackey because of his position as adviser to the emperor.

But Confucius has been rehabilitated as a symbol of China's glorious past. The Chinese have set up hundreds of Confucius institutes worldwide, including 25 in the United States. The institutes promote Chinese language and culture, just as the Goethe institutes promote German culture, and the Dante Alighieri institutes do the same for Italy.

Even so, "China did not take a missionary approach to world affairs, seeking to spread an ideology or a system of government," writes Robert D. Kaplan, a senior fellow at the Center for a New American Security. "Moral progress in international affairs is an American goal, not a Chinese one. China's actions abroad are propelled by its need to secure energy, metals and strategic materials in order to support the living standards of its immense population."

In Kaplan's view, Beijing "cares little about the type of regime with which it is engaged. It requires stability, not virtue as the West conceives it."[40]

As early as 2005, when China for the first time was included in the annual economic survey of the Organization for Economic Cooperation and Development (OECD), it noted, "Well over half of China's GDP is produced by privately controlled enterprises."[41] But while the trend has continued, communications, transport, infrastructure, banking and energy remain under tight state supervision.

In late November 2009, Xu Kuangdi, a senior adviser to the Chinese Communist Party, told this reporter and other visiting U.S. journalists that it would be dangerous to hold free elections because China was "not ready," and some demagogue might win by promising to take the money from the new rich and give it to the poor! "The ultimate goal is common prosperity," he said, "but we have to let a group of people get rich first."

In 2003, looking for places to put its growing export revenue, China began buying U.S. Treasury bills on a large scale. By 2005, China had acquired $243 billion worth of the U.S. debt, second only to Japan. In 2006, China overtook Japan when its holdings climbed to $618 billion. In 2009, possibly fearing that the global recession would undermine the dollar, China sold some $34 billion of its Treasuries — but was soon back on a buying spree. By February 2010, China held a whopping $877.5 billion in Treasuries.[42] Meanwhile, a well-heeled middle class has emerged in China. Cars create traffic jams in Chinese cities, and the once ubiquitous bicycles are now kept by many Chinese for week-end country excursions.

In Beijing, a five-star hotel is flanked by two glass-fronted dealerships, one for Maseratis, the other for Lamborghinis. Four years ago, the China branch of HSBC Bank launched a credit card: It now boasts 11 million cardholders, said D.G. "Dicky" Yip, of the Bank of Communications in Shanghai last November.

China's new rich have acquired a taste for art as well as luxury cars. First it was contemporary art by artists who a decade earlier had been suppressed or even jailed because of their avant garde works. More recently, classic traditional paintings and Chinese calligraphy have been sold at auction for millions of RMB. In a crowded auction hall in Beijing filled with Chinese bidders in November, a scroll painting by the Ming Dynasty landscape master Wu Bin sold for the equivalent of $24.7 million to a Chinese bidder.

The bad news for the government has been the widening gap between the urban prosperous and the rural impoverished. China's poor are a restive majority running into the hundreds of millions. In 2008, the average income of a rural worker was $690, compared to a city average of $2,290 — and higher in Shanghai and Beijing.[43] But the annual salary of a chief executive in China is around $100,000, a fraction of corporate salaries in the United States but still astronomical in Chinese terms.

Is China Less Welcoming to U.S. Investors?

As Chinese know-how grows, opportunities diminish for foreigners.

It's one of the ironies of the U.S. trade deficit with China that a sizable portion of the goods exported to America are made by Chinese workers for U.S. firms. Earlier this year, the state-run Xinhua news agency reported that of the 200 top exporting firms last year, 153 were "foreign funded firms" — up from 141 in 2008.[1]

It's estimated that at least a third of those companies are U.S.-owned. For example, Shanghai alone has about 3,600 American expatriate business executives — although it was around 4,000 before the 2008 economic downturn. Chongqinq, China's largest city, with a population of 32 million, lists 41 foreign firms operating there, including Lear, Du Pont, Delphi Packard and Pepsi. General Motors, the largest auto maker in China, expects to sell 3 million vehicles in the Asian market by 2015 from its Chinese plants. In 2009, the 665,000 foreign firms in China accounted for 28 percent of the nation's industrial output, 56 percent of its exports and 45 million of its workers. In the first quarter of this year, foreign investment rose 12.1 percent, to $9.4 billion, according to *Business Week*.[2]

Even so, Google's recent difficulties with hackers in China may be an indication that as the Chinese economy matures the investment climate may no longer be as welcoming as it once was. One American executive doing business in Beijing says industrial espionage is rife and that the Chinese are experts at copying products. A foreign firm has at most a two-year window to establish itself on the Chinese market before it is challenged by an emerging local competitor.

As Chinese industrial know-how grows, the opportunities for foreign investors continue to diminish, according to business executives in Shanghai and Beijing. Recently, the Chinese authorities issued a directive encouraging government agencies to buy Chinese goods.

In a country where the state is still a major customer, this is a disturbing measure. But investors remain attracted by China, argues writer Zachary Karabell, author of the 2009 book Superfusion: *How China and America Became One Economy and Why the World's Prosperity Depends on It*. Says Karabell, "There's really nowhere else to go where you have 10 percent growth, 300-600 million emerging middle class Chinese who want to buy stuff and an environment where the rule of law is increasingly at least adequate in enforcement of contracts and getting your investments out of the country."

Google quit China after its servers were hacked, adds Karabell, partly because it wasn't doing very well in the Chinese market, and because it could afford not to do business with China.

The continued uncertain global environment has focused the Chinese government's attention on generating a domestic consumer market, so far with mixed results. Parting older-generation Chinese with their money means reversing a culture of saving, but the younger generations

To make matters worse for the poor, the government has been slow to reform a social system that cuts off the medical and other benefits of China's millions of internal migrant workers once they quit their hometowns. As things now stand many immigrants are left to fend for themselves — even when they find employment.

The social system also needs to catch up with the aging Chinese population, which is getting older faster than in the United States. The problem is exacerbated by a relatively high life expectancy — about 73 — versus 77 in the United States. By 2040 demographers say that each Chinese worker will be forced to support two parents and four grandparents.

An 'Edgy' Game

With the economic boom unfolding against a background of frequent unrest, "The No. 1 challenge for China is to maintain domestic stability and at the same time sustainable economic development," says Yang Jiemian, director of the Shanghai Institute of International Studies.

are avid shoppers. In the modern high rise that houses the Standard Chartered Bank in Shanghai — one of the thousands that crowd the city's skyline — Stephen Green, head of research, says older Chinese stubbornly stick to the "rainy day" syndrome — but "anyone born after 1980 behaves like an American."

In the past decade, for example, Starbucks has opened more than 350 coffee shops in China, where it is flourishing at the same time its U.S. business has been hammered by recession. Starbucks' success is puzzling because the Chinese really don't drink coffee; China produces about 30,000 tons of beans a year but exports most of it.

Caren Li, Starbucks' spokeswoman at the company's downtown Chinese headquarters in Shanghai, says Green Tea Frappuccino is a predictably steady seller, but "we're promoting a coffee culture, offering the Chinese more choices besides tea." Even so, it's not really about coffee: The coffee houses with the round green logo have become trendy meeting venues (there's even one in Beijing's Forbidden City), the chic place to be seen.

In 2009, a former Starbucks executive in China, Eden Woon, launched Toys R Us in China (locally called Toy LiFung), and today the American retailer has 15 stores in the country. China may be the world's leading toy manufacturer, but its citizens buy mainly for very young children. "There's no toy culture in China because parents think toys distract children from their studies," Woon says over breakfast in a bustling hotel restaurant offering acres of dishes ranging from American pancakes and waffles to wonton soup. So Woon launched a campaign in this nation of overachievers with the message: "Toys are an important part of growing up."

Chinese flock to the 350 Starbucks coffee shops in China, including this one in Shanghai, but customers come for tea, not coffee, and because Starbucks is considered cool.

Mary Kay Inc., the Texas-based home-sales cosmetics firm, began operating in China in 1995. Headquartered in Shanghai, it marshals about 200,000 independent beauty "consultants," thanks to a skin-care line tailored to the local market, including a four-week "whitening cream" treatment that sells for the equivalent of $120.

— Roland Flamini

[1] Xinhua news agency, http://news.xinhuanet.com/english2010/business/2010-04/20/c_13260044.htm.

[2] "Foreign Investment in China Jumped in First Quarter," Business Week/Bloomberg, April 14, 2010, www.businessweek.com/news/2010 04-14/foreign-investment-in-china-jumps-in-first-quarter-update1 .html.

The Internet, which has gone from 620,000 users in China in 1997 to 370 million users today — more people than the entire U.S. population — has become a forum for online dissent. The authorities crack down on the deluge of cyber-dissent using a (patchy at best) online censorship, ironically known as the Great Firewall of China — which also tries to block pornographic sites. Persistent blogging about subjects deemed subversive can lead to imprisonment. (There are 20 million bloggers in China.) For example, Chinese writer Liu Xiaobo was jailed for 11 years on Dec. 25 after co-drafting and posting

"Charter '09," a lengthy manifesto calling on the government to introduce democratic reforms.

The regime's biggest nightmare remains large-scale unemployment. To keep it at the current 4 percent level China needs to ensure continued growth generating 24 million new jobs every year.[44] Hence the need to buttress its current dependence on exports by boosting consumer demand at home. But the Chinese are not only great savers but also traditionally have an aversion to being in debt. For example, no doubt to the chagrin of HSBC officials, 80 percent of the bank's credit card holders

'Harmonizing' the Internet in China

China's love affair with the Net is increasing along with censorship.

When a website is censored in China, the screen usually doesn't reveal that the government has blocked it. Instead, either a fake error message appears or an announcement about the site being unavailable, with an invitation to "Please try again."

By now, most of China's estimated 384 million "netizens" (nearly a quarter of the world's Internet users) are not taken in: They know the site has been "harmonized."[1]

In China, Internet censorship is often ironically called "harmonizing" because "harmony" — the absence of public dissent — is a key phrase in the government's propaganda. So as China's love affair with the Internet increases so does the Communist regime's censorship effort intensify — possibly because there is so much more material online for the government to worry about.

"China's blocking of overseas websites — including Facebook, Twitter and thousands of other sites is more extensive and technically more sophisticated than ever," Rebecca MacKinnon, a Hong Kong-based university journalism professor and China Internet expert, tells me via e-mail from Princeton's Center for Information Technology Policy, where she is currently a visiting fellow. "Controls over domestic content have also been tightening."

The Chinese authorities use a filtering system nicknamed The Great Firewall of China, but officially referred to as Golden Shield, to scan Internet content for specific key words and then block, or try to block, Web pages in which such words are used.

A list of blacklisted terms compiled by ConceptDoppler, a tool developed for the purpose by the universities of California, Davis, and New Mexico includes triggers such as "eighty-nine" and "June 4", the year and date of the Tiananmen Square protests, "massacre," "political dissident," "Voice of America," "Playboy magazine" and "Xinjiang independence" — a reference to the restive, predominantly Muslim province in northwestern China. Any one of these terms sends a series of three reset commands to both the source and the destination, effectively breaking the connection, says Jed Crandall, a professor of computer science at the University of New Mexico and one of the developers of ConceptDoppler, in an e-mail message.

A more recent addition to the list is "Charter 08," a lengthy manifesto calling on the Communist regime to relinquish its monopoly of power and introduce democratic reforms. Originally, Charter 08 was signed by 300 intellectuals and activists. After the document appeared briefly on the Internet — and before Chinese censors banned it — some 10,000 other signatures were added.

U.S. computer giants like Google entered the market knowing that they would have to comply with the regime's policy and exercise content censorship. Ultimately, Google found the controls too constricting to live with and earlier this year shifted its operations to less restrictive Hong Kong, at the same time complaining of Chinese hacking into the e-mail accounts of human rights activists and U.S. corporations.

Other U.S. Internet companies still operating in China, including Microsoft and Yahoo!, now face even tougher censorship restrictions. A new law, adopted on April 29 and set to take effect Oct. 1, requires them to stop the transmission of "state secrets" over the Internet, if they "discover" them — effectively requiring them to act as police informers.[2]

Some analysts maintain that while flowers were placed outside Google's Beijing office by users sorry to see it go, the impact of Google's departure is limited because the majority of China's netizens prefer to use homegrown Internet servers that exercise self-censorship rather than jeopardize their access.

Besides, the analysts point out, even with the constraints that grow daily the Internet has given Chinese citizens an unprecedented voice in the country's affairs.

"We should measure protest in China not by protests on the streets or availability of news on protests, but by the involvement of the Chinese citizens in policy decisions," says Yasheng Huang, a China expert at MIT's Sloan School.

"By the latter yardstick, China had made huge progress, thanks largely to the Internet."[3]

In recent years, Internet-based campaigns have pressured the Chinese government to release political prisoners, launch investigations into scandals, such as kidnapping boys for slave labor in mines, and convict corrupt officials.[4] China's version of Facebook, called Douban, and YouTube, called YouKu, as well as thousands of Internet bulletin boards teem with debate on current events.

Still, the censorship is not well-defined, and some well-known dissident bloggers don't know when they have crossed the line until there is a knock at the door.

But mainly, it works by suggestion: "Many Internet users only have access to public computers at Internet cafes or universities, and just the existence of censorship might cause them to avoid topics they know they're not supposed to access, changing their online behavior," says Crandall.

The government maintains that censorship is partly a security measure and partly a responsibility to protect the public from what it sees as the negative side of the Internet's rapid growth.

Qian Xiaoqian, vice minister at the Chinese State Council information office, whose functions include deciding what gets blocked, says that while the government intervenes when a site is seen as plotting to overthrow the state, on another level it is also responding to public worry about the addictive nature of the Net.

"There is a discussion going on in this country about the potential negative influences of the Internet," Qian said last December over cups of tea, invariably served to visitors to any Chinese office. "Chinese parents are worried about the pornography; but not just the pornography." The government blames "Internet addiction" for youthful alienation.

A recently published survey by the Chinese National People's Congress found that 10 percent of Chinese youth were addicted to the Internet, Qian says. Many Chinese parents are sending their children to "boot camp" to cure them of "internetitis" — a solution which the government first encouraged but later seemed to back away from, warning against too much brutality in rehab methods.[5]

Critics of Chinese Internet censorship, including MacKinnon, say the regime uses such arguments to justify tightening control over the Net.

Mounting concerns over security and censorship by the government led Google to leave mainland China in March and relocate in Hong Kong.

But Qian claims "the Chinese government assumes a very important responsibility in managing the Internet. America is a mature society. At this stage Chinese society is still not — and besides, different people have different interpretations of freedom."

For those who prefer the Internet censor-free, the United States is leading the effort to produce circumvention software that connects to blocked websites via proxy computers outside the country. Programs like Psiphon, Tor and the Global Internet Freedom Consortium have been increasingly successful at breaching the wall.[6]

— Roland Flamini

[1] David Talbot, "China's Internet Paradox," *MIT Technology Review,* May/June 2010, www.technologyreview.com/web/25032/page1/.

[2] Mike Elgan, "New Chinese law may force Microsoft, Yahoo, to follow Google," *IT World,* April 29, 2010, www.itworld.com/internet/106191/new-chinese-law-may-force-microsoft-yahoo-follow-google-out, and Jonathan Ansfield, "Amendment Tightens Law on State Secrets in China," *The New York Times,* April 30, 2010, p. A9.

[3] Quoted in Talbot, *op. cit.*

[4] *Ibid.*

[5] The information is from a Chinese television news "magazine" show, with a translation provided to the author.

[6] For example, www.FreeGate.com, the Freedom Consortium's software developed by a group of Chinese expatriates in the United States.

More than 150 nations and 50 international organizations have registered for the Shanghai World Expo, and 70 million visitors are anticipated, making the six-month-long world's fair the largest ever. The Expo's theme — "Better City — Better Life" — is intended to showcase Shanghai as the next great world city in the 21st century.

avoid interest charges by paying their whole bill every month — compared to the national U.S. average of 20 percent.

Commenting on the government's combination of a market economy and tight control, Halper at Cambridge University says, "This is an edgy game, and things could go seriously wrong. Just trying to control the Internet is really tough work. The glue that holds the whole thing together is a ferociously powerful security service."

CURRENT SITUATION

Tense Beginning

This is a period of waiting for the other shoe to drop in U.S.-China relations following a tense first quarter of 2010.

There is unresolved business on the currency front, on Iran sanctions, on the issue of U.S. weapons sales to Taiwan and on the broader question of how the two countries should engage in the future.

The Obama administration has put a lot of effort into trying to convince the Chinese government that it is in both sides' interest to move toward what Obama calls "a more market-oriented exchange rate" for the renminbi. Following a meeting between President Obama and President Hu Jintao in Washington in April, during the Nuclear Security Summit, it seemed clear that the Chinese had not budged on revaluing their currency. Any change would not come from U.S. pressure, Hu said.[45]

In New York, the five permanent members of the U.N. Security Council are working on an Iran-sanctions resolution. "The Chinese were very clear they share our concern about the Iranian nuclear program," said Bader at the National Security Council.[46] Still, the Chinese government has not said that it will vote for a U.N. resolution and still insists publicly that diplomacy and negotiation are the way to go.

Cooperation on climate control seems at a stalemate after Hu told the December Copenhagen summit that China's own emissions control program would not be subject to U.N. supervision. For its part, the United States rejected a Chinese request that developing countries should be compensated for cutting carbon emissions.

Yu Qintgou, the official responsible for climate change at China's Ministry of Foreign Affairs, explained the familiar Chinese position in an interview in Beijing on Dec. 1. Simply put, Yu said, the world's climate change problem was not the making of China or India but of the developed countries. The United States and the other industrialized nations should "acknowledge their historic responsibility" as emitters of greenhouse gases and not put so great a burden on the emerging nations that it would set back their development, he said.

The latest tension had its origins in November, when Obama's Chinese hosts insisted on a low-key visit that minimized his contact with the public.

"It's a mystery," David Shamburgh, a professor of Chinese studies at Georgetown University, told *The Wall Street Journal* during the presidential visit. "[Obama is] a populist politician, but he's not getting any interaction with Chinese people."[47] It's not such a mystery, perhaps, when one considers Obama's popularity worldwide, in contrast to a Chinese leadership with limited contact with its own people.

Indeed, on the morning following Obama's arrival in Shanghai, the city's government-controlled English-language paper carried a large front-page photo of Hu with the prime minister of Canada, who was in China at the time. A one-column photo of Obama appeared

Is today's China a communist country?

YES Xu Kuangdi
President, Chinese Academy of Engineering in Beijing, former Shanghai mayor

NO Stefan Halper
Director, Atlantic Studies Program, Cambridge University'
Author, The Beijing Consensus: How China's Authoritarian Model Will Dominate the Twenty-First Century

Written for *CQ Researcher*, May 2010

Written for *CQ Researcher*, April 2010

The Chinese Communist Party (CPC) has never done things by the book. In the early days, some party members, following the lead of the Soviet Union, launched the workers' movement in the cities. But the party shifted its focus to the rural areas where government control was relatively weak. We mobilized the peasants; we developed land reform.

Today, we don't do things according to what Karl Marx wrote or Vladimir Lenin said 80 years ago. We're doing things to advance the development of productive forces, and we are doing things to serve the interests of the vast majority of people.

Marx is still widely respected by the party. He is a great mind and a very great thinker on the development of civilization. His theories on capitalism inspired us on how to overcome the current financial crisis. But Marx lived 100 years ago; he couldn't predict how science and technology would develop. That is why our new ideology is to keep pace with the times. That doesn't mean we have forgotten Marx. Marxism is still our long-term goal.

The CPC is committed to building a society in which property and well-being can be enjoyed by all, a society of harmony between rich and poor. Today, we have a problem of a widening gap between rich and poor, which we are trying our best to narrow. But it will not be solved by dividing the property of the rich among the poor.

Our previous lessons showed us that the division of property is not the answer. Nor is Western democracy the answer. If we introduced Western democracy, we may have turbulence in the society.

A Western friend told me that he would only go to church three times in his lifetime. The first time is to be baptized, the second for his marriage and the third for his funeral. It doesn't follow that he doesn't have God in his heart. It's the same for us with Communism.

To live up to our beliefs we sometimes have to take different paths. As [former CPC leader] Deng Xiaoping has put it: The ultimate goal is common prosperity, but we have to let some people get rich first.

There's a wonderful comment by the legendary U.S. diplomat and Russia expert George F. Kennan, who said, "Let's not ask what communism has done to Russia, but rather what Russia has done to communism." Much the same didactic is applicable to today's China.

Mao and Stalin would be spinning in their graves if they saw what was happening in China in the name of communism. China has shed any remnants of Marxist ideology, even to the point of directly addressing the question of who owns the land, a serious point of contention in the recent People's Congress. It is now accepted that land can be privately owned and houses built on it.

China is not expansionist, it does not seek to undermine the Western system: instead, its market-authoritarian system provides an example for the world beyond the West where growing numbers of leaders admire China, see China as a Third World nation at the pinnacle of world power and wish to emulate China's progress.

So while China may continue to call itself communist, it certainly isn't communism as we know it, but more of a form of state capitalism; the role of state is market authoritarian, not Marxist-Leninism. A Marxist economy is the polar opposite of the dynamic market economy China is developing today.

The Chinese leadership is highly practical, opportunistic and focused on economic growth and stability. The only remnants of communism are the single party rule of the party, a general embrace of socialist principles and the various structures that the party employs to govern the country: a politburo, a people's congress and a central committee.

Of course, it still calls itself communist, but it's just as much a corporatist state, even a form of fascism in its classical, Mussolini-type form, which is to say a process that coordinates the interest of the state and large corporations. Put another way, the business of China is business.

below the fold. In a country where much importance is attached to not losing face, such signals matter.

The tension had escalated two months later when Obama made two moves calculated to anger the Chinese. First, in February the president received Tibet's exiled spiritual leader, the Dalai Lama, after Beijing had expressly asked him not to do so.

The meeting drew a protest from Beijing even though the White House kept the visit private and carefully avoided showing pictures of Obama and the Dalai Lama together.

In a second affront, Obama approved a long-delayed $6.4 billion weapons sale to Taiwan, which China continues to threaten with hundreds of missiles while at the same time insisting that it wants a peaceful solution to the island's claims of independence. The package includes 114 Patriot missiles worth $2.2 billion, and 60 Blackhawk helicopters worth $3.1 billion.

Beijing promptly ratcheted up its rhetoric, and U.S.-Chinese relations took "a nosedive," *The Washington Post* said.[48] A senior Chinese Defense Ministry official, Huang Xueping, said China was resolved to punish the United States if the weapons were delivered and that the U.S. could expect even greater consequences if Washington added advanced F-16 jet fighters to the sale.[49]

The Chinese went still further. Beijing threatened to sanction U.S. firms involved in the deal. And then it showed off its military prowess by successfully testing — without warning — an advanced missile interception system. The timing also seemed a further demonstration of Beijing's ire. "The people who tied the knot should untie the knot," said Chinese Foreign Ministry spokesman Qin Gang.[50]

Commentators attributed China's new tough and uncompromising attitude to more than one factor. They said China's seemingly quick recovery from the global financial crisis while the West continues to struggle has vindicated the Chinese development model in Chinese eyes and the weakness of the less-disciplined Western approach.

A second explanation, though, was the jostling for position in the leadership in advance of the 2012 Communist Party Congress, an event that spurs aspiring candidates to display their nationalist credentials. Behind the united front China's leadership shows to the world, deep divisions exist between the hard-line "realists" and those who favor openness in China's international dealings

— and the hard-liners currently have the upper hand. According to another explanation, the regime's aggressiveness toward the outside world stems from the government's desire to find a distraction from socioeconomic problems at home.

After all, this is the Year of the Tiger — always turbulent and often unpredictable.[51]

OUTLOOK

The Taiwan Question

It remains to be seen how the Chinese will react, if or when the United States begins delivery of the weapons sold to Taiwan.

Analysts say the recently proposed (but not finalized) additional sale of F-16s would raise the level of China's objections even further. Although the original weapons deal drew protests, it had initially been negotiated by the Bush administration and was well-known to the Chinese. But Jean-Pierre Cabestan, a professor of international studies at Hong Kong Baptist University, predicts that "if an F-16 sale moves forward, we can expect another wave of difficulties between the U.S. and China."

The outlook is hard to forecast with any accuracy because of the ongoing cooperation-competition dance between China and the U.S. For example, despite its protests over Taiwan, Beijing at the same time is committed to working with Washington and other governments in securing vital sea lanes and enforcing regional stability. Early in 2010, China agreed to take a lead role in anti-piracy patrols off Somalia. Chinese navy units had not strayed outside Chinese waters for centuries, but today 80 percent of China's oil imports are shipped through the narrow Straits of Malacca that connect the Indian Ocean and the South China Sea.

There is no indication that China would actually support sanctions against Iran. In the past, China had signed on to three previous U.N. sanctions resolutions — and the Chinese eventually delayed and weakened every one of them, said Iran expert Flynt Leverett, a senior fellow at the centrist New America Foundation think tank.[52]

Also casting a shadow over the next few months is the thorny question of China's undervalued renminbi. Foreign-policy issues are rarely prominent in U.S. elections, but at a time of high unemployment and economic uncertainty, some analysts believe China's currency seems set to become

> *Despite its protests over Taiwan, Beijing at the same time is committed to working with Washington and other governments in securing vital sea lanes and enforcing regional stability.*

China spends more than 4 percent of its gross domestic product (GDP) on its military, about the same ratio as the United States. The country's rising military spending, including the beefing up of key naval bases near Taiwan, has caused concern in Washington.

AFP/Getty Images/Liu Jin

a thorny question in November's mid-term elections, possibly creating anti-Chinese public sentiment.

Given the upcoming elections, some analysts say a slight currency revaluation designed to take the dispute out of the campaign is in the offing. But, says Glaser at the Center for Strategic and International Studies, "The Chinese are not going to revalue their currency because we tell them to. They will choose their own time."

One reason: Chinese leaders cannot afford seeming to act in response to pressure from the "foreign devils" (*qwai lo*) — which to the Chinese is just about everybody including the United States — without serious loss of face in the eyes of their own people.

The United States has a risky card of sorts to play in the shape of the annual U.S. Treasury analysis (mandated by the 1988 Omnibus Trade and Competitiveness Act) of the currencies of foreign countries to determine whether they are manipulating the currency to gain unfair trade advantage. To Congress' exasperation, the Treasury has so far not labeled China a "currency manipulator."

If and when it does, New York's Sen. Schumer has a draft bill waiting that would impose stiff penalties on countries that manipulate their currencies, including possible tariffs. "China's currency manipulation would be unacceptable even in good economic times," Schumer said in a recent statement. "At a time of 10 percent unemployment, we simply will not stand for it."

There is an obvious political edge to Schumer's bill: The senator is up for re-election. But others also feel the time has come to confront the Chinese. The Obama administration "needs to draw a line in the sand, and say to the Chinese: 'You're exporting unemployment by undervaluing your currency by 20 percent to 40 percent,'" says Cambridge University's Halper. If the Chinese don't revalue, "we should impose similar tariffs."

It was out of consideration for Hu's visit in April that Treasury Secretary Timothy Geithner postponed publication of the Treasury report, which is normally released on April 15. No new date has been announced,

but analysts say the delay is strategic, giving the Chinese more time for further reflection.

Two important dates are coming up for possible further discussion — the U.S.-China yearly "strategic dialogue" in late May, and the broader forum of the G20 summit in Seoul, South Korea, in late June.

The Chinese, however, are focused on another event they hope will boost their prestige, much as the 2008 Summer Olympics had done: The Shanghai Expo 2010, which the city expects will attract over 70 million visitors. Its theme reflects China's hopes and aspirations — "Better city, better life."

UPDATE

In early May, the Chinese embassy in Washington opened the doors of its vast I. M. Pei-designed building to more than 800 prominent diplomats, officials and Washingtonians for the annual Opera Ball, one of the capital's premier social and fund-raising events. The embassy's large public rooms were lavishly transformed for the occasion. The main auditorium became an ancient tea house for dancing (to a Western orchestra); another room was turned into "The Peking Duck Gallery," where 10 chefs served China's national dish. And hundreds of red Chinese lanterns were hung for good luck.

Getty Images/Alex Wong

Chinese and American officials meeting in Washington in May for the Strategic and Economic Dialogue at the State Department include, from left: Vice Premier Wang Qishan, State Councilor Dai Bingguo, Secretary of State Hillary Rodham Clinton, Treasury Secretary Timothy Geithner and Defense Secretary Robert Gates.

Hosting this year's event was a significant first for China's once-reclusive diplomats, and another sign of China's growing global confidence.

A week later, a bilateral meeting in Washington between top U.S. and Chinese officials presented a less frivolous symbol of the priority both sides place on their sometimes bumpy relationship.

Hundreds of Chinese officials, generals and businessmen came to Washington for the two-day Strategic and Economic Dialogue. The meeting — the third in two years — was not expected to produce any major decisions but did end with agreement on some key economic issues, which could represent "very promising shifts in the direction of China's economic policy," according to U.S. Treasury Secretary Timothy F. Geithner. Cui Tiankai, China's vice minister of foreign affairs, put it more poetically: "As we say in China, spiritual things can be turned into material ones."

Currency Concerns

The Obama administration worked from an agenda that seemed frozen in time — protecting human rights, curbing Chinese cyber attacks on corporations, raising the value of China's renminbi currency against the U.S. dollar, dealing with North Korea. The administration agreed, for example, to look into easing tariffs on Chinese

goods and easing the ban on selling China high-tech items with potential defense uses. The Chinese government agreed to eliminate the preferential treatment it gives to Chinese companies on government contracts. China also would allow U.S. financial institutions better access to China's state-controlled financial markets.

The longstanding issue over the undervalued *renminbi* (also known as the *yuan*) was less contentious than in the past because the Chinese have allowed their currency to rise about 5 percent against the dollar since June 2010 — double that when adjusted for inflation. While this has helped reduce the price advantage of Chinese exports in U.S. and other foreign markets, concerned members of Congress and U.S. manufacturers still consider China's currency greatly undervalued.

Focus on Human Rights

The strategic dialogue was held against the background of a tough crackdown on Chinese activists who had tried to organize a nonviolent pro-democracy Jasmine Revolution in China, inspired by the so-called Arab Spring in the Middle East. [53] Human-rights groups said the government's reaction was the most severely repressive in a decade. [54] When online calls went out for demonstrations, Chinese security officers quickly locked down the proposed venues and arrested dozens of activists, even those with only a loose connection to the unrest. Florists were even discouraged from selling jasmine, because of its link to the planned dissent.

In the past, the Obama administration has taken a low-key approach to Chinese human rights violations. But as he opened the bilateral conference on May 9, Vice President Joseph R. Biden publicly expressed American "concern" over the recent crackdown in China, including attacks, arrests and the "disappearance of journalists, lawyers, bloggers and artists." Biden said he recognized that "some in China see our advocacy as an intrusion and Lord only knows what else. But President Obama and I believe strongly in protecting fundamental rights and freedom." [55]

Secretary of State Hillary Rodham Clinton has been tougher still. In an interview in *The Atlantic*, she called China's human rights record "deplorable" and said the regime was living on borrowed time. Ultimately, she said, China's communist leadership faced the same destiny as the Arab world's dictators. "They're worried and they are trying to stop history, which is a fool's errand," she told the magazine. "They cannot do it." [56]

With more than 450 million Chinese accessing the Internet, 230 million bloggers and 120 million micro-bloggers (Twitterers), the web has become what China expert Elizabeth Economy, director of Asia studies at the Council on Foreign Relations think tank in New York City, calls China's "virtual political system."[57] A new, homegrown Twitter-like service called QQ has more than 90 million users. [58] News of government corruption and cover-ups goes viral in a matter of minutes, and the regime is forced to react with uncharacteristic speed.

Nevertheless, China has become increasingly sophisticated at censoring undesirable websites. In February, "jasmine" was added to the list of proscribed key words that trigger a blockage. Others include "Hillary Clinton" and "Dalai Lama." The U.S. State Department has undertaken a $19 million program to develop software to circumvent Chinese censorship of websites and searches using terms the government deems subversive. The software will be made available free to anyone in the world wanting to download it.

Given the uptick in China's diplomatic and military assertiveness, the United States must manage an increasingly complex and challenging relationship. For the first time, at U.S. insistence, representatives of the Chinese military (the People's Liberation Army, or PLA) participated in the two-day talks in Washington, and both sides agreed to resume regular military contacts, broken off last year after the Obama administration agreed to sell $6.4 billion in arms — including missiles and 60 Black Hawk helicopters — to Taiwan, over Beijing's strong objections. Despite its enormous size and rapid technical development, the PLA remains inferior to U.S. forces in equipment and capability, even though the United States contends the PLA needs to be closely watched.

'Welcome Air of Reality'

For Jeffrey Bader, a former Obama security adviser on Asian affairs and now a visiting scholar at the centrist Brookings Institution think tank in Washington, the two sides "have developed reasonable expectations about both the possibilities and limits of cooperation, which will reduce the chances of future miscalculation."

Economy says when it comes to relations with China, "a welcome air of reality is blowing through Washington these days."

As a rule, the Chinese cooperate with Washington when it is not against their interests to do so. For example, China was persuaded not to veto the recent U.N. Security Council resolution on Libya, even though it did not favor NATO intervention. But it has been less helpful with sanctions against Iran, where it has sizeable commercial interests.

In Washington, the Chinese lectured administration officials on reducing the U.S. deficit, reflecting Beijing's concern that the United States might run into problems meeting its debt obligations. China is the largest foreign holder of U.S. debt — some $1.7 trillion, according to economists testifying recently before the bipartisan U.S.-China Economic and Security Review Commission. [59] In 2010, the United States imported $365 billion worth of goods from China but exported only $92 billion worth. [60]

As the talks proceeded, Beijing drove home the point of its growing accumulation of U.S. dollars by publishing export data for April showing its worldwide exports exceeded imports by $11.43 billion, primarily in trade with the European Union, United States and Japan. [61]

Normally, the United States responds by pressing the Chinese to enlarge their domestic consumer base, thereby reducing their heavy dependence on exports, and grant foreign manufacturers more access to the Chinese market. In fact, the Beijing government began boosting domestic consumption in 2008, when the global financial meltdown first hit China's exports. China's rapidly growing middle class is expected to reach 700 million people by 2020, or 48 percent of the population. [62] The country aims to increase domestic spending from today's 36 percent of GDP to 42-45 percent by 2015. [63] But first the regime must transform the Chinese — by long tradition a nation of savers — into a nation of spenders.

NOTES

1. "Clinton in China," BBC Special Report, July 3, 1998, http://news.bbc.co.uk/2/hi/special_report/1998/06/98/clinton_in_china/118430.stm.

Also Lin Kim, "Sino-American Relations: a new stage?" *New Zealand International Review*, Vol. 23, 1998, www.questia.com/googleScholar.qst; jsessionid=LY2JTpnRvl29qyD1ByfHwVQxJtmVQQ7bcyJ6RW47LJJnw6WmnYwg!555708061!-1331918248?docId=5001372599.

2. "China's economy grew 11.9 pct y/y in Q1 — sources," *The Guardian*, April 14, 2010. www.guardian.co.uk/business/feedarticle/9031081.

3. U.S. Census Bureau, www.census.gov/foreign-trade/balance/c5700.html#2010.

4. Howard Schneider, "U.S. sets tariff of up to 90 percent on imports of Chinese oilfield pipes," *The Washington Post*, April 10, 2010.

5. Wang Yanlin and Jin Jing, "Trade dispute heats up while Obama visit nears," *ShanghaiDaily.com*, Nov. 7, 2009, www.shanghaidaily.com/sp/article/2009/200911/20091107/article_418781.htm.

6. Schneider, *op. cit.*

7. "China, India, Japan Iran's Top Partners in Crude Oil Trade," Moinews.com, April 14, 2010, www.mojnews.com/en/Miscellaneous/ViewContents.aspx?Contract=cms_Contents_I_News&r=485205.

8. For background see Alan Greenblatt, "Attacking Piracy," *CQ Global Researcher*, August 2009, pp. 205-232.

9. "China Must Protect Intellectual Property," *Korea Herald*, April 22, 2010, www.koreaherald.co.kr/national/Detail.jsp?newsMLId=20100422000363.

10. White House transcript, Nov. 9. 2009, www.whitehouse.gov/the-press-office/briefing-conference-call-presidents-trip-asia.

11. "Commentary: China, U.S. sail in one boat amid global issues," Xinhua news service, Nov. 16, 2009; http://news.xinhuanet.com/english/2009-11/16/content_12463881.htm.

12. Martin Walker, "Walker's World: Haiku Herman's G2," United Press International, Dec 7, 2009, www.spacewar.com/reports/Walkers_World_Haiku_Hermans_G2_999.html.

13. U.S.-China Joint Statement, U.S. Embassy, Beijing, http://beijing.usembassy-china.org.cn/111709.html.

14. "Hu presents 5-point proposal for boosting China-U.S. ties," Xinhua, April 13, 2010, http://english.cctv.com/20100413/102277.shtml.

15. Kaiser Kuo, "The Intertwining of Sino-American Cooperation and Competition," China Geeks Translation and Analysis of Modern China, February 2010, http://chinageeks.org/2010/02/the-intertwining-of-sino-american-competition-and-coopera tion/.

16. Edwin Chen and Rob Delaney, "Hu Tells Obama China Will Follow Its Own Path on Yuan," Bloomberg, April 13, 2010, www.bloomberg.com/apps/news?pid=20601070&sid=a07psM9uKD6g.

17. "China-U.S. agreement sends warning to Iran," *The National*, April 13, 2010, www.thenational.ae/apps/pbcs.dll/article?AID=/20100413/FOREIGN/704139996/1014.

18. "Obama's Asia Visit," editorial, *Korea Times*, Nov. 10, 2009, www.koreatimes.co.kr/www/news/opinon/2010/04/202_55210.html.

19. Thomas Lunn, *et al.*, China's Foreign Aid Activities in Africa, Latin America, and Southeast Asia, Feb. 25, 2009, www.fas.org/sgp/crs/row/R40361.pdf. Report is based largely on research by New York University's Robert F. Wagner Graduate School of Public Service.

20. *Ibid.*

21. Jad Mouawad, "China's Growth Shifts the Geopolitics of Oil," *The New York Times*, March 19, 2010, www.nytimes.com/2010/03/20/business/energy-environment/20saudi.html.

22. Willy Lam, "Beijing Seeks Paradigm Shift in Geopolitics, "The Jamestown Foundation, March 5, 2010, www.jamestown.org/programs/chinabrief/single/?tx_ttnews%5Btt_news%5D=36120&tx_ttnews%5BbackPid%5D=25&cHash=a9b9a1117e.

23. "Facing up to China," *The Economist*, Feb. 4, 2010, www.economist.com/PrinterFriendly.cfm?story_id=15452821.

24. Nicholas D. Kristof, "China, Concubines, and Google," *The New York Times*, March 31, 2010, www.nytimes.com/2010/04/01/opinion/01kristof.html.

25. Drew Thompson, "Think Again: China's Military," *Foreign Policy*, March/April 2010, www.foreign policy.com/articles/2010/02/22/think_again_ chinas_military.

26. "Annual Report to Congress: Military Power of the People's Republic of China, 2009," Department of Defense, www.defense.gov/pubs/pdfs/China_ Military_Power_Report_2009.pdf.

27. "Pentagon issues annual report on China's military power," Xinhuanet, March 26, 2009, www.news .xinhuanet.com/english/2009-08/26/content_ 11079173.htm.

28. Pentagon report to Congress, *op. cit.*

29. Dennis Blair, "Annual Threat Assessment of the U.S. Intelligence Community for the Senate Select Committee on Intelligence," February 2010, www .dni.gov/testimonies/20100202_testimony.pdf.

30. Cecilia Kang, "Hillary Clinton calls for Web freedom, demands China investigate Google attack," *The Washington Post*, Jan. 22, 2010, www.washing tonpost.com/wp-dyn/content/article/2010/01/21/ AR2010012101699.html.

31. John Pomfret, "China's Commerce Minister: U.S. has most to lose in a trade war," *The Washington Post*, March 22, 2010, www.washingtonpost.com/wp-dyn/ content/article/2010/03/21/AR2010032101111 .html.

32. Rowan Callick, "The China Model," *The American*, November/December 2007, www.american.com/ archive/2007/november-december-magazine-contents/the-china-model.

33. Lunn, *et al.*, *op. cit.*

34. Thomas P.M. Barnett, "The New Rules: Why China Will Not Bury America," *World Politics Review*, Feb. 1, 2010, www.worldpoliticsreview.com/articles/5031/ the-new-rules-why-china-will-not-bury-america.

35. Wieland Wagne, "How China is battling global economic crisis," *San Francisco Sentinel*, May 23, 2009, www.sanfranciscosentinel.com/?p=28287.

36. Ma Ying, "China's Stubborn Anti-Democracy," Hoover Institution Policy Review, February/March 2007, www.hoover.org/publications/policyreview/ 5513661.html.

37. *Ibid.*

38. Brian Knowlton, "Citing 'Constructive Engagement,' He Acts to Counter Critics in Congress: Clinton Widens Defense of China Visit," *The New York Times*, July 12, 1998, www.nytimes.com/1998/06/12/ news/12iht-prexy.t.html?pagewanted=1.

39. Evan Osnos, "Despatches from Evan Osnos: Strategic Reassurance," *The New Yorker Online*, Oct 6, 2009, www.newyorker.com/online/blogs/evanosnos/ 2009/10/strategic-reassurance.html.

40. Robert D. Kaplan, "The Geography of Chinese Power," *Foreign Affairs*, May/June 2010.

41. "China could become World's largest exporter by 2010," Organization for Economic Cooperation and Development, Sept. 16, 2005, www.oecd.org/ document/29/0,3343,en_2649_201185_ 35363023_1_1_1_1,00.html.

42. U.S. Department of Treasury, www.ustreas.gov/tic/ mfh.txt.

43. http://news.bbc.co.uk/2/hi/asia-pacific/7833779 .stm.

44. Li Beodong, head of China's delegation to the United Nations in Geneva, official transcript of speech in 2009.

45. The Associated Press, "China's Hu rebuffs Obama on yuan," *Minneapolis Star Tribune*, April 13, 2010, www.startribune.com/business/90728804.html.

46. Transcript of White House press briefing, April 12, 2010, www.whitehouse.gov/the-press-office/press-briefing-jeff-bader-nsc-senior-director-asian-affairs.

47. Ian Johnson and Jonathan Wiseman, "Beijing limits Obama's exposure," *The Wall Street Journal* Online, Nov. 17, 2009, http://online.wsj.com/article/ SB125835068967050099.html.

48. John Pomfret and Jon Cohen, "Many Americans see U.S. influence waning as that of China grows," *The Washington Post*, Feb. 25, 2010, p. A11.

49. Andrew Jacobs, "China Warns U.S. Against Selling F-16s to Taiwan,"

50. *Ibid.*

51. David Shambaugh, "The Year China Showed its Claws," *Financial Times*, Feb. 16, 2010, www.ft .com/cms/s/0/7503a600-1b30-11df-953f-00144 feab49a.html.

52. Corey Flintoff, "Will China Help Sanction Iran's Nuke Program?" NPR, April 14, 2010, www.npr .org/templates/story/story.php?storyId=125991589 &ft=1&f=1004.

53. For background, see Roland Flamini, "Turmoil in the Arab World," *CQ Global Researcher*, May 3, 2011, pp. 209-236.

54. Jamil Anderlini and Richard McGregor, "China elite faces curbs on US visas," *FT.com*, April 26, 2011, www.ft.com/cms/s/0/02bfc8cc-702e-11e0-bea 7-00144feabdc0.html#axzz1LzE8BL9v.

55. Cornelius Lundsgaard, "US Criticizes China Again for Poor Human Rights Record," *The Tibet Post*, May 10, 2011, www.thetibetpost.com/en/news/ international/1680-us-criticizes-china-again-for- poor-human-rights-record.

56. Jeffrey Goldberg, "Hillary Clinton — Chinese System Is Doomed, Leaders on a 'Fool's Errand,' " *The Atlantic*, May 10 2011, www.theatlantic.com/ international/archive/2011/05/hillary-clinton- chinese-system-is-doomed-leaders-on-a-fools- errand/238591/.

57. "450 million Chinese use internet," *Xinhuanet*, Dec. 31, 2010, http--//news.xinhuanet.com/english2010/ china/2010-12/31/c_13671684.htm. See also "Human Rights lecture not needed," statement by Embassy of China in London in *China Daily*, April 29, 2011, www.chinadaily.com.cn/opinion/ 2011-04/29/content_12418153.htm.

58. Michal Kan, "Chinese Top Microblog Hits Over 90 Million Active Users," *PCWorld*, May 11, 2011, www .pcworld.com/article/227608/chinese_top_micro- blog_hits_over_90_million_active_users.html.

59. "China holds more U.S. debt than indicated," *The Washington Times*, March 2, 2010, www.washing- tontimes.com/news/2010/mar/02/chinas-debt-to- us-treasury-more-than-indicated/.

60. "US-China Trade Statistics and China's World Trade Statistics," U.S.-China Business Council, www .uschina.org/statistics/tradetable.html.

61. "China Exports Hit Record in April," *Finance Business News*, May 10, 2011, www.financebusiness- news.net/chinese-exports-hit-record-for-april/.

62. Malbritt Christiansen, "Open Seminar on the Chinese Consumer Market," *Renmin Shimbin*, March 27, 2011, http--//news.asianstudies.dk/ 2011/03/open-seminar-on-the-chinese-consumer- market/.

63. Alan Wheatley, "Analysis — For China, new plan is a question of balance," Reuters, March 14, 2011, http--//uk.reuters.com/article/2011/03/14/us- china-economy-rebalancing-idUKTRE72D4JF 20110314.

BIBLIOGRAPHY

Books

Halper, Stefan, *The Beijing Consensus*, Basic Books, 2010.
A Cambridge University professor analyzes the economic and strategic sides of U.S.-China relations.

Jacques, Martin, *When China Rules the World: The Rise of the Middle Kingdom and the End of the Western World*, Penguin, 2010.
A British commentator predicts that history is about to restore China to its ancient position of global power.

Karabell, Zachary, *Superfusion: How China and America Became One Economy and Why the World's Prosperity Depends on It*, Simon & Schuster, 2009.
An economist and historian writes that despite an increasingly less hospitable business environment, foreign investors keep flocking to China.

Mann, James, *The China Fantasy: How Our Leaders Explain Away Chinese Repression*, Viking, 2007.
A veteran China reporter files a passionate complaint that U.S. elites are misleading the American public to boost trade with a hostile regime.

Shirk, Susan, *China: Fragile Superpower: How China's Internal Politics Could Derail Its Peaceful Rise*, Oxford University Press, 2007.
A former top State Department official says understanding the fears that drive China's leadership is essential to managing the U.S.-China relationship without military confrontation.

Tyler, Patrick, *A Great Wall: Six Presidents and China*, Public Affairs, 1999.
An investigative reporter describes the struggles of six presidential administrations in shaping a sustainable China policy.

Articles

Mufson, Stephen, and John Pomfret, "There's a New Red Scare, but is China Really So Scary?" *The Washington Post*, Feb. 28, 2010, www.washingtonpost.com/wp-dyn/content/article/2010/02/26/AR2010022602601.html.
Two *Post* correspondents argue that America's reading of China is an insight into America's collective psyche.

Talbot, David, "China's Internet Paradox," *MIT Technology Review*, May-June 2010, www.technology-review.com/web/25032/.
China's Internet usage is not as restricted as the regime would wish despite intense censorship efforts.

Wong, Edward, "Chinese Military to Extend its Naval Power," *The New York Times*, April 23, 2010, www.nytimes.com/2010/04/24/world/asia/24navy.html.
The Chinese military is building a deepwater navy to protect its oil tankers.

Xue, Litai, and Jiang Wenran, "Debate Sino-U.S. Ties," *China Daily*, April 20, 2010, www.chinadaily.net/opinion/2010-04/26/content_9772895_2.htm.
Two U.S.-based Chinese scholars debate the state of the U.S.-China relationship.

Ying, Ma, "China's Stubborn Anti-Democracy," *Hoover Institution Policy Review*, February-March 2007, www.hoover.org/publications/policyreview/5513661.html.
An American Enterprise Institute fellow examines why China's economic development hasn't led to democratization.

Reports and Studies

"Annual Report to Congress: Military Power of the People's Republic of China — 2009," Office of the Secretary of Defense, 2009, www.defense.gov/pubs/pdfs/China_Military_Power_Report_2009.pdf.
The Pentagon's annual assessment of the People's Liberation Army invariably draws criticism from Beijing.

Godement, Francois, *et al.*, "No Rush to Marriage: China's Response to the G2," China Analysis, European Council on Foreign Relations and the Asia Center of the Sciences Po, June 2009, ecfr.3cdn.net/d40ce525f765f638c4_bfm6ivg3l.pdf.
An East Asian historian and analyst says that while Europeans worry about an emerging U.S.-Chinese global duopoly, the Chinese are still examining their options.

Green, Michael J., "U.S.-China Relations Under President Obama," July 14-15, 2009, Brookings Institution, iir.nccu.edu.tw/attachments/news/modify/Green.pdf.
A scholar at the centrist think tank examines whether the administration's cooperative China policy will work.

Huang, Ping, *et al.*, "China-U.S. Relations Tending Towards Maturity," Institute of American Studies, Chinese Academy of Social Sciences, June 2009, ias.cass.cn/en/show_project_ls.asp?id=1012.
Four analysts offer a Chinese perspective on relations between the United States and their country.

Lunn, Thomas, "Human Rights in China: Trends and Policy Implications," Congressional Research Service, Jan. 25, 2010, www.fas.org/sgp/crs/row/RL34729.pdf.
The nonpartisan research agency offers the most current periodic report to Congress on human rights in China.

For More Information

American Enterprise Institute, 1150 17th St., N.W., Washington, DC 20036; (202) 862-5800; www.aei.org. A nonpartisan think tank dedicated to research and education on government, politics, economics and social welfare.

Brookings Institution, 1775 Massachusetts Ave., N.W., Washington, DC 20036; (202) 797-6000; www.brookings .edu. Non-profit public policy institution working for a more cooperative international system.

Center for a New American Security, 1301 Pennsylvania Ave., N.W., Suite 403, Washington, DC 20004; (202) 457-9400; www.snas.org. An independent, nonpartisan think tank established in 2007 dedicated to developing strong, pragmatic and principled national security and defense policies that promote and protect American interests and values.

Center for Strategic and International Studies, 1800 K St., N.W., Washington, DC 20006; (202) 887-0200; www .csis.org. A nonpartisan think tank that provides strategic insights and policy solutions to decision-makers in government, international institutions, the private sector and civil society.

Center for U.S.-China Relations, Tsinghua University, Beijing, China 100084; (86-10) 62794360; www.chinausa .org.cn. First research institute specializing in U.S.-China relations established by a Chinese institute of higher education.

China Institute, 125 E. 65th St., New York, NY 10065; (212) 744-8181; www.chinainstitute.org. Promoting a better understanding of China through programs in education, culture and business.

China Institute of International Studies, 3 Toutiao, Taijichang, Beijing, China 100005; (86-10) 85119547; www

.ciis.org.cn. Think tank and research institution arm of the Chinese Ministry of Foreign Affairs.

China-United States Exchange Foundation, 15/f Shun Ho Tower, 24-30 Ice House Street, Hong Kong; (852) 25232083; www.cusf.hk. Fostering dialogue between Chinese and U.S. individuals from the media, academic, think tank and business environments.

Confucius Institute, 0134 Holzapfel Hall, University of Maryland, College Park, MD 20742; (301) 405-0213; www .international.umd.edu/cim. One of more than 60 Chinese cultural institutes established on U.S. campuses by the Chinese government, offering language courses and cultural programs.

National Security Council, www.whitehouse.gov/administra tion/eop/nsc. The NSC is the president's principal forum for considering national security and foreign policy matters with his senior national security advisors and Cabinet officials.

Nottingham University China Policy Institute, International House, Jubilee Campus, Nottingham NG8 1B8, England, United Kingdom; (44-115) 8467769; www.not tingham.ac.uk/cpi. Think tank aimed at expanding knowledge and understanding of contemporary China.

Shanghai Institute for International Studies, 195-15 Tianlin Rd., Shanghai, China 200233; (86-21) 54614900; www.siis.org.cn. Research organization focusing on international politics, economy, security strategy and China's international relations.

U.S.-China Policy Foundation, 316 Pennsylvania Ave., S.E., Suites 201-203, Washington, DC 20003; (202) 547-8615; www.uscpf.org. Works to broaden awareness of China and U.S.-China relations within the Washington policy community.

16

Afghanistan Dilemma

Thomas J. Billitteri and Alex Kingsbury

An Afghan security officer guards two tons of burning heroin, opium and hashish near Kabul, Afghanistan's capital, on March 18, 2009. Nearly eight years after U.S.-led forces first entered Afghanistan, many challenges still confront the U.S., Afghan and coalition forces seeking to stabilize the country: fanatical Taliban and al Qaeda fighters, rampant police corruption, shortages of Afghan troops and a multibillion-dollar opium economy that supports the insurgents.

From *CQ Researcher*,
August 7, 2009. (Updated May 23, 2011)

O n the outskirts of Now Zad, a Taliban stronghold in southern Afghanistan's violent Helmand Province, the past, present and future of the war in Afghanistan came together this summer.

The past: After the U.S.-led invasion of Afghanistan in 2001, Now Zad and its surrounding poppy fields and stout compounds were largely tranquil, thanks in part to the clinics and wells that Western money helped to build in the area. But three years ago, when the war in Iraq intensified and the Bush administration shifted attention from Afghanistan to Iraq, insurgents moved in, driving out most of Now Zad's 35,000 residents and foreign aid workers.

The present: This summer U.S. Marines engaged in withering firefights with Taliban militants dug in on the northern fringes of the town and in nearby fields and orchards.

The future: The situation in Now Zad and the surrounding war-torn region of southern Afghanistan is a microcosm of what confronts the Obama administration as it tries to smash the Taliban, defang al Qaeda and stabilize governance in Afghanistan. "In many ways," wrote an Associated Press reporter following the fighting, Now Zad "symbolizes what went wrong in Afghanistan and the enormous challenges facing the United States."[1]

Nearly eight years after U.S.-led forces first entered Afghanistan to pursue al Qaeda and its Taliban allies in the wake of the Sept. 11, 2001, terrorist attacks, the country remains in chaos, and President Barack Obama faces what many consider his biggest foreign-policy challenge: bringing stability and security to Afghanistan and denying Islamist militants a permanent foothold there and in neighboring nuclear-armed Pakistan.

An Unstable Nation in a Volatile Neighborhood

Almost as large as Texas, Afghanistan faces Texas-size problems, including desperate poverty, an economy dominated by illicit drugs and an unstable central government beset by Taliban militants. Afghanistan's instability is compounded by longstanding tensions between neighboring Pakistan and India, both armed with nuclear weapons. Many Western experts also say Pakistan has failed, despite promises, to rein in Taliban and other Islamist extremists.

The challenge is heightened by the war's growing casualty figures. July was the deadliest month in Afghanistan for U.S. soldiers since the 2001 invasion began, with 43 killed.[2] Twenty-two British troops also died last month, including eight in a 24-hour period. In nearly eight years of war in Afghanistan, 767 U.S. troops have died there, along with 520 coalition forces, according to the Web site iCasualties.org. Thousands of Afghan civilians also have died.

The Afghanistan-Pakistan conflict —"Af-Pak" in diplomatic parlance — poses a witch's brew of challenges: fanatical Taliban and al Qaeda fighters, rampant corruption within Afghanistan's homegrown police force and other institutions, not enough Afghan National Army forces to help with the fighting and a multibillion-dollar opium economy that supplies revenue to the insurgents.

But those problems pale in comparison with what foreign-policy experts call the ultimate nightmare: Pakistan's nuclear weapons falling into the hands of jihadists and terrorists, a scenario that has become more credible this summer as suicide bombers and Taliban fighters have stepped up attacks in Pakistani cities and rural areas,

using Pakistan's lawless western border region as a sanctuary.[3]

"The fact that Pakistan has nuclear weapons and the question of the security of those weapons presses very hard on the minds of American defense planners and on the mind of the president," says Bruce Riedel, who led a 60-day strategic policy review of Afghanistan and Pakistan for the Obama administration. "If you didn't have that angle," adds Riedel, who has since returned to his post as a Brookings Institution senior fellow, "I think this would all be notched down one level of concern."

Pakistan is important to the Afghan conflict for reasons that go beyond its nuclear arsenal. Pakistan has been a breeding ground for much of the radical ideology that has taken root in Afghanistan. A failure of governance in Afghanistan would leave a void that Islamist militants on either side of the border could wind up filling, further destabilizing the entire region.

In March Obama announced what he called a "comprehensive, new strategy" for Afghanistan and Pakistan that rests on a "clear and focused goal" for the region: "to disrupt, dismantle and defeat al Qaeda in Pakistan and Afghanistan, and to prevent their return to either country in the future."[4]

Key to the strategy is winning over the local Afghan population by protecting it from insurgent violence and improving governance, security and economic development.[5]

The effort includes new troop deployments — a total of 21,000 additional U.S. soldiers to fight the insurgency in Afghanistan and train Afghan security forces, plus other strategic resources. By year's end, U.S. troop levels are expected to reach about 68,000. NATO countries and other allies currently are supplying another 32,000 or so, though many are engaged in development and relief work but not offensive combat operations.[6]

An immediate goal is to heighten security in Afghanistan in the run-up to a high-profile presidential election on

Aug. 20. None of Afghan President Hamid Karzai's main challengers are expected to beat him flat out, *The Washington Post* noted, but some observers said other candidates could "do well enough as a group to force a second round of polling, partly because of recent blunders by Karzai and partly because many Afghans are looking for alternative leadership at a time of sustained insurgent violence, economic stagnation and political drift."[7]

Observers say Obama's approach to the Af-Pak conflict represents a middle path between counterterrorism and counterinsurgency — protecting civilians, relying on them for information on the enemy and providing aid to build up a country's social and physical infrastructure and democratic institutions.[8]

Among the most notable features of the new approach is a vow among military officials — beginning with Gen. Stanley A. McChrystal, the newly appointed commander of U.S. and NATO forces in Afghanistan — to avoid civilian casualties. McChrystal pledged to follow a "holistic" approach in which protecting civilians takes precedence over killing militants.[9]

"I expect stiff fighting ahead," McChrystal told the Senate Armed Services Committee at his confirmation hearing. But "the measure of effectiveness will not be the number of enemy killed," he added, "it will be the number of Afghans shielded from violence."[10]

The United Nations said that 1,013 civilians died in the first six months of 2009, up from 818 during the same period last year. The U.N. said 310 deaths were attributed to pro-government forces, with about two-thirds caused by U.S. air strikes.[11]

As part of his strategy, Obama called for a "dramatic" increase in the number of agricultural specialists, educators, engineers and lawyers dispatched to "help the Afghan government serve its people and develop an economy that isn't dominated by illicit drugs." He also

Gates Warns About Civilian Deaths

The number of civilians killed in Afghanistan more than doubled from 2006 to 2008, but based on the toll for the first six months of 2009, the rate may be somewhat lower in 2009 (graph at left). In 2008 nearly half of the civilian deaths were caused by executions or suicide and IED (improvised explosive device) attacks by the Taliban and other anti-government groups (graph at right). Concern over civilian deaths prompted Defense Secretary Robert Gates to call such casualties "one of our greatest strategic vulnerabilities."

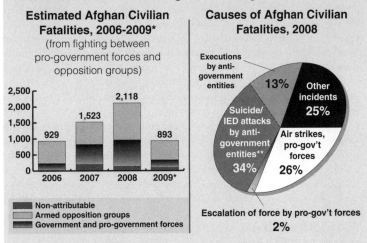

Estimated Afghan Civilian Fatalities, 2006-2009*
(from fighting between pro-government forces and opposition groups)

- Non-attributable
- Armed opposition groups
- Government and pro-government forces

Causes of Afghan Civilian Fatalities, 2008

* Through June; the total is 1,013, according to the U.N.

** Includes Taliban and other insurgents

Source: "Afghan Index: Tracking Variables of Reconstruction and Security in Post-9/11 Afghanistan," Brookings Institution, July 15, 2009

supports economic-development aid to Pakistan, including legislation to provide $1.5 billion annually over the next five years. But Obama's approach on Pakistan also reflects long-held Western concerns that the Pakistani government has been at best negligent — and perhaps downright obstructionist — in bringing Taliban and other Islamist extremists to heel. Pakistan, whose situation is complicated by long-standing tensions with nearby India, will get no free pass in exchange for the aid, Obama vowed. "We will not, and cannot, provide a blank check," he said, because Pakistan had shown "years of mixed results" in rooting out terrorism.[12]

As Obama goes after the insurgency, his Af-Pak policy is under the microscope here at home.

Some have demanded that the administration describe its plans for ending military operations in Afghanistan.

Opium Trade Funds Taliban, Official Corruption

"It's clear that drug money is paying for the Taliban's operational costs."

In the crowded Afghan capital of Kabul, opulent marble homes sit behind guard houses and razor wire. "Most are owned by Afghan officials or people connected to them, men who make a few hundred dollars a month as government employees but are driven around in small convoys of armored SUVs that cost tens of thousands of dollars," reporter Tom Lasseter noted recently. "[M]any of the houses were built with profits harvested from opium poppy fields in the southern provinces of Helmand and Kandahar." [1]

The so-called "poppy palaces" are outward signs of a cancer eating Afghanistan to its core: illicit drugs and narcoterrorism, aided by official corruption.

According to the United Nations Office on Drugs and Crime, Afghanistan grows more than 90 percent of the world's opium, which is used to produce heroin and morphine. [2] Total opium production for 2008 was estimated at 7,700 metric tons, more than double the 2002 level. [3]

In her new book, *Seeds of Terror: How Heroin Is Bankrolling the Taliban and Al Qaeda*, journalist Gretchen Peters says militant groups are raising hundreds of millions of dollars a year from the opium trade.

"It's clear that drug money is paying for the Taliban's operational costs within Afghanistan," she told *Time* magazine. "That means that every time a U.S. soldier is killed in an IED attack or a shootout with militants, drug money helped pay for that bomb or paid the militants who placed it. . . . The Taliban have now thrown off their old masters and are a full-fledged criminal force on both sides of the [Afghan-Pakistan] border." [4]

The biggest challenge to curbing the drug trade, Peters said, is corruption. "As much money as the insurgents are earning off the drug trade, corrupt officials in Afghanistan and Pakistan are earning even more," she said. "It's going to be very complex for the U.S. and for the international community, for NATO, to find reliable and trustworthy partners to work with. I don't think that it is widely understood how high up the corruption goes within the Pakistani government, particularly within their military and intelligence forces."

In recent weeks, the Obama administration has shifted U.S. drug policy in Afghanistan from trying to eradicate poppy fields to seizing drugs and related supplies and helping farmers grow alternative crops. [5]

"The Western policies against the opium crop, the poppy crop, have been a failure," Richard C. Holbrooke, the administration's special representative for Afghanistan and Pakistan, said. "They did not result in any damage to the Taliban, but they put farmers out of work and they alienated people and drove people into the arms of the Taliban." [6]

The Bush administration had advocated intense efforts to eradicate poppy fields, but some experts have said the approach is counterproductive.

"The United States should de-emphasize opium eradication efforts," Air Force Lt. Col. John A. Glaze wrote in a 2007 report for the U.S. Army War College. It recommended a multi-pronged strategy including higher troop levels, more economic aid for Afghanistan, pursuit of drug lords and corrupt officials and development of alternative

A measure proposed by Rep. Jim McGovern, D-Mass., requiring a report from the Obama administration by the end of the year on its exit strategy, drew significant support from Democrats but was defeated in the House this summer amid heavy Republican opposition.

And some critics question the validity of Obama's rationale for the fighting in Afghanistan, particularly the assumption that if the Taliban were victorious they would invite al Qaeda to return to Afghanistan and use it as a base for its global jihad. John Mueller, a political science professor at Ohio State University and author of *Overblown: How Politicians and the Terrorism Industry Inflate National Security Threats, and Why We Believe*

Them, contends that al Qaeda does not need Afghanistan as a base. The 2001 terrorist attacks were orchestrated mostly from Hamburg, Germany, he points out.

What's more, he argues, "distinct tensions" exist between al Qaeda and the Taliban. Even if the Taliban were to prevail in Afghanistan, he says, "they would not particularly want al Qaeda back." Nor, he says, is it clear that al Qaeda would again view Afghanistan as a safe haven. [13]

But administration officials disagree. The Taliban are "the frontrunners for al Qaeda," said Richard Holbrooke, Obama's special envoy to Pakistan and Afghanistan. "If they succeed in Afghanistan, without any shadow of a livelihoods for Afghans, plus exploration of the possibility of participating in the market for legal opiates used for morphine and other medicines.

"U.S.-backed eradication efforts have been ineffective and have resulted in turning Afghans against U.S. and NATO forces . . . ," Glaze wrote. "While the process of eradication lends itself well to the use of flashy metrics such as 'acres eradicated,' eradication without provision for long-term alternative livelihoods is devastating Afghan's poor farmers without addressing root causes."[7]

Brookings Institution scholar Vanda Felbab-Brown, an expert on Afghanistan's opium-poppy economy, says rural development, not poppy eradication, is the best way to attack the drug economy. "Any massive eradication right now . . . , we would lose Afghanistan," she says. "In the absence of resources available to farmers, any eradication would just prompt massive destabilization and invite the Taliban in."

Felbab-Brown says the development of new crops is key, but that such crops must be "high-labor-intensive, high-value crops" that offer more than subsistence income.

"People don't have to become rich, but they cannot continue existing in excruciating poverty. Many people will be willing and motivated to switch to a legal crop," she says, but "it needs to offer some chance of advancement."

Vegetable, fruit and horticultural crops are better options, Felbab-Brown says. Wheat, on the other hand, "has no traction" because the prices are low, people in vast parts of the country don't have enough land to make the crop pay, and wheat is much less labor-intensive than poppy growing, affording fewer opportunities for employment, she says.

For rural development to offer an alternative to illicit poppy production, it must include not only access to land,

legal microcredit and other features, but security for Afghan farmers, Felbab-Brown stresses.

"The lack of security in many ways is the key structural driver of illicit crop cultivation, because the risks of cultivating legal crops in insecure settings are just tremendous," she says.

Rural development, for example, "needs to involve roads, and not just their physical presence but also security on the roads," Felbab-Brown says. Roads are now insecure due to both the insurgents and the Afghan National Police.

"In much of the south, travel on the road is three times as expensive as travel in the north because of the number of bribes that one needs to pay at check stops. For many people, simply to take crops from Laskar Gah to Kandahar, by the time they pay the bribes that they need to pay, they will have lost all profit."

[1] Tom Lasseter, "Western Military Looked Other Way as the Afghan Drug Trade Boomed," *Charlotte Observer*, May 10, 2009, p. 13A.

[2] "World Drug Report 2009 Highlights Links Between Drugs and Crime," United Nations Office on Drugs and Crime, June 2009, www.unodc.org/unodc/en/press/releases/2009/june/world-drug-report-2009-highlights-links-between-drugs-and-crime.html.

[3] "World Drug Report 2009," United Nations Office on Drugs and Crime, www.unodc.org/documents/wdr/WDR_2009/WDR2009_eng_web.pdf.

[4] Bobby Ghosh, "Q&A: Fighting the New Narcoterrorism Syndicates," *Time*, July 17, 2009, www.time.com/time/nation/article/0,8599,1910935,00.html.

[5] Rachel Donadio, "New Course for Antidrug Efforts in Afghanistan," *The New York Times*, June 28, 2009, www.nytimes.com/2009/06/28/world/asia/28holbrooke.html?scp=1&sq=holbrooke+drug%20policy+afghanistan+rome&st=cse.

[6] Quoted in *ibid.*

[7] John A. Glaze, "Opium and Afghanistan: Reassessing U.S. Counternarcotics Strategy," U.S. Army War College, www.strategicstudiesinstitute.army.mil/Pubs/Display.Cfm?pubID=804.

doubt al Qaeda would move back into Afghanistan, set up a larger presence, recruit more people and pursue its objectives against the United States even more aggressively."[14]

As the war in Afghanistan continues, here are some of the questions people are asking:

Is the Obama administration pursuing the right course in Afghanistan?

Early in July, thousands of U.S. Marines began a massive assault in Afghanistan's Helmand River valley, the biggest American offensive of the Obama presidency and a key test of his new strategy in the region.

The operation included 4,000 troops from the 2nd Marine Expeditionary Brigade, who poured into the area in helicopters and armored vehicles. The Marines have run into stiff opposition, but the ultimate goal remains intact: protect local Afghans from insurgent violence and strengthen Afghanistan's legal, judicial and security institutions.

"Our focus must be on getting this [Afghan] government back up on its feet," Brig. Gen. Lawrence D. Nicholson, commander of the brigade, told his officers.[15]

But the mission is fraught with huge risks and challenges, and skepticism about it runs deep, even among some of Obama's fellow Democrats.

Social Conditions Worsened in Many Areas

Living conditions deteriorated between 2007 and 2008 in areas such as education, water quality and availability of electricity, according to surveys of Afghan citizens.

Condition of Infrastructure in Localities, 2007 and 2008

	Very/Quite Good (%) 2007	2008	Quite/Very Bad (%) 2007	2008
Availability of clean drinking water	63%	62%	36%	38%
Availability of water for irrigation	59	47	40	49
Availability of jobs	30	21	69	78
Supply of electricity	31	25	68	74
Security situation	66	No data	33	No data
Availability of medical care	56	49	44	50
Availability of education for children	72	70	28	29
Freedom of movement	72	No data	28	No data

Source: "Afghan Index: Tracking Variables of Reconstruction and Security in Post-9/11 Afghanistan," Brookings Institution, July 15, 2009

army" — one that would have to be financially subsidized by outside powers, says Stephen Walt, a professor of international affairs at Harvard University's Kennedy School of Government. Such an army "would have to be drawn from all these groups and imbued with central loyalty to the state. And there's never been a strong central state. Politics [in Afghanistan is defined by] factional alignments." And, he adds, the challenge is "compounded by levels of corruption and lack of institutions."

"We're sort of trying to impart a Western model of how the Afghan state should be created — with a central government, ministries, defense and so on. That's not the way Afghanistan has been run for centuries. The idea that we know how to do that, especially in the short term," Walt says, is "far-fetched."

Malou Innocent, a foreign-policy analyst at the conservative Cato Institute think tank, says America faces the prospect of an "ambiguous victory" because it is caught amid long-simmering tensions between Pakistan and India, a dynamic, she argues, that the Obama administration has failed to adequately take into account.

Pakistan has long feared an alliance between Afghanistan and India. To hedge its bets, Pakistan aids the insurgency in Afghanistan by providing shelter to the Taliban and other militants, Innocent says. At the same time, she says, Pakistan has accused India of funneling weapons through Afghanistan to separatists in Pakistan's unstable Balochistan province.[19] The ongoing India-Pakistan dispute over Kashmir also remains a cause of friction in the region.

"The regional dynamics are too intractable," Innocent says. "The countries in the region have an incentive to foment and maintain Afghanistan's instability. So we should be looking to get out of Afghanistan within a reasonable time frame — say at least in the next five years."

Innocent sees a U.S. role in training Afghanistan's own security forces and says covert operations against specific insurgent targets could make sense. But the Taliban threat centered along the Afghanistan-Pakistan

In May, House Appropriations Chairman David Obey, D-Wis., suggested that if the White House doesn't demonstrate progress by next year, funding for the war could slow. Asked if he could see Congress halting funding completely, Obey said, "If it becomes a fool's errand, I would hope so," according to *The Hill* newspaper. The success or failure of the Afghan policy is not in the hands of the president or Congress, Obey said, but "in the hands of the practicing politicians in Pakistan and Afghanistan. And I'm dubious about those hands."[16]

Much of the American public is similarly dubious. A June *New York Times*-CBS News poll found that 55 percent of respondents believed the war in Afghanistan was going somewhat or very badly for the United States, an increase of two points since April. Only 2 percent said the war was going "very well."[17]

Critics question the prospect of success in a country long divided by ethnic rivalries, a resistance to central governance and rampant graft that ranges from demands for petty bribes to drug corruption in high levels of government.[18]

"To pacify the place in the absence of reconciliation of the main tribes,* you'd need a very large national

---

* The main ethnic groups are the Pashtun (42%), Tajik (27%), Hazara (9%), Uzbek (9%), Aimak (4%), Turkmen (3%) and Baloch (2%).

border cannot be definitively eradicated, she argues. "We can contain the militancy" and weaken it, she says, "but we can't believe we can have a victory with a capital V."

But Peter Bergen, a counterterrorism analyst and senior fellow at the New America Foundation, is more sanguine about the war's prospects in Afghanistan. In a *Washington Monthly* article, he challenged those who say Afghanistan is an unconquerable and ungovernable "graveyard of empires" where foreign armies have come to ignominious ends.

One telling fact, in Bergen's view, is that "the Afghan people themselves, the center of gravity in a counterinsurgency, are rooting for us to win." He cited BBC/ABC polling data indicating that 58 percent of Afghans named the Taliban — viewed favorably by only 7 percent of Afghans — as the biggest threat to their country, while only 8 percent named the United States.

"[T]he growing skepticism about Obama's chances for success in Afghanistan is largely based on deep misreadings of both the country's history and the views of its people, which are often compounded by facile comparisons to the United States' misadventures of past decades in Southeast Asia and the Middle East," wrote Bergen. "Afghanistan will not be Obama's Vietnam, nor will it be his Iraq. Rather, the renewed and better-resourced American effort in Afghanistan will, in time, produce a relatively stable and prosperous Central Asian state." [20]

Stephen Biddle, a senior fellow at the Council on Foreign Relations, a think tank in New York City, said victory in Afghanistan is possible but only if steps are taken to strengthen Afghanistan's governance. "I do think it's possible to succeed," Biddle said in late July after spending a month as part of a group helping McChrystal formulate a strategic assessment report on the war, due this month. But, he added, "there are two very different requirements for success.

"One is providing security, [and] the other is providing enough of an improvement in Afghan governance to enable the country to function without us. We can keep the patient on life support by providing security assistance indefinitely, but if you don't get an improvement in governance, you'll never be able to take the patient off the ventilator. Of those two challenges, providing security we know how to do. It's expensive, it's hard, it takes a long time, but if we invest the resources there's a substantial probability that we can provide security through our assistance. Governance improvement is a more uncertain undertaking. There are a lot of things we can do that we have not yet done to improve governance, but ultimately the more uncertain of the two requirements is the governance part." [21]

Another member of McChrystal's strategic assessment group, Anthony Cordesman, a scholar with the Center for Strategic and International Studies, also believes the war is winnable, but that the United States and its allies must "act quickly and decisively" in a number of ways, including "giving the Afghan government the necessary legitimacy and capacity" at national, regional and local levels, reducing official corruption and "creating a level of actual governance that can ensure security and stability." [22]

Afghanistan Ranks Low in Developing World

Afghanistan ranked as the second-weakest state in the developing world, after Somalia, in 2008, according to the Brookings Institution* (left). It consistently ranks near the bottom among countries rated for corruption by Transparency International (right).

Afghanistan's Rank					
Index of State Weakness in Developing World, 2008			Corruption Perceptions Index		
Rank	Country	Overall Score	Year	Rank	No. of Countries Surveyed
1	Somalia	0.52	2008	176	180
2	Afghanistan	1.65	2007	172	180
3	Dem. Rep. Congo	1.67	2006	No data	163
4	Iraq	3.11	2005	117	159
5	Burundi	3.21			

* Brookings surveyed 141 nations, allocating a score of 0-10 points for each of four categories: economic, political, security and social welfare. Benin had the median score, 6.36; the Slovak Republic was the least weak, with a score of 9.41.

Source: "Afghan Index: Tracking Variables of Reconstruction and Security in Post-9/11 Afghanistan," Brookings Institution, July 15, 2009

CHRONOLOGY

1838-1930s *Afghanistan gains independence, but ethnic and religious conflicts persist.*

1838-42; 1878 Afghan forces defeat Britain in two wars, but Britain retains control of Afghanistan's foreign affairs under 1879 treaty.

1893 British draw Afghan-Pakistan border, split Pashtun ethnic group.

1919 Afghanistan gains independence after Third Anglo-Afghan War.

1934 Diplomatic relations between United States and Afghanistan established.

1950s-1980s *Political chaos wracks Afghanistan during Cold War.*

1950s-1960s Soviets and Americans funnel aid to Afghanistan.

1953 Gen. Mohammed Daoud becomes prime minister, seeks aid from Soviets, institutes reforms.

1964 New constitution establishes constitutional monarchy.

1973 Daoud overthrows king, is killed in Marxist coup in 1978.

1979-1989 Civil war rages between communist-backed government and U.S.-backed Mujahedeen. Soviets withdraw in 1989, 10 years after they invaded.

1990-2001 *Taliban emerges amid postwar chaos; al Qaeda forges ties with Afghan militants.*

1992 Burhanuddin Rabbani, an ethnic Tajik, rises to power, declares Afghanistan an Islamic state.

1994 Taliban emerges; the militant Islamist group is mainly Pashtun.

1996 Taliban gains control of Kabul.

1996 Taliban leader Mullah Omar invites al Qaeda leader Osama bin Laden to live with him in Kandahar.

1997 Osama bin Laden declares war on U.S. in interview with CNN.

2001 U.S. and coalition forces invade Afghanistan on Oct. 7 after Sept. 11 terrorist attacks; Taliban retreats.

2002-Present *U.S.-led invasion of Iraq shifts focus off Afghanistan; Taliban resurges.*

2002 Hamid Karzai elected head of Afghan Transitional Authority; International Security Assistance Force deployed in Kabul; international donors pledge $4.5 billion for reconstruction.

2003 U.S.-led invasion of Iraq begins, leading to charges Bush administration shifted focus and resources away from Afghanistan; commission drafts new Afghan constitution.

2004 Draft constitution approved; Karzai elected president; Pakistani nuclear scientist A. Q. Khan admits international nuclear-weapons trading; President Pervez Musharraf pardons him.

2005 Afghanistan holds its first parliamentary elections in some three decades.

2006 NATO takes over Afghan security; donors pledge $10.5 billion more.

2007 Musharraf and Karzai agree to coordinate efforts to fight Taliban, al Qaeda; allied troops kill Taliban leader Mullah Dadullah.

2008 More than 50 die in suicide bombing of Indian Embassy in Kabul in July. . . . More than 160 die in November terror attacks in Mumbai, India; India accuses Pakistani militants of carrying out the attacks; in July 2009 a young Pakistani admits to taking part in the attacks as a soldier for Lashkar-e-Taiba, a Pakistan-based Islamic group.

2009 Obama announces new strategy "to disrupt, dismantle and defeat al Qaeda in Pakistan and Afghanistan"; Gen. Stanley McChrystal replaces Gen. David McKiernan as top U.S. commander in Afghanistan; Marines attack Taliban in southern Helmand Province; July is bloodiest month for U.S. and foreign troops in Afghanistan, with 43 Americans killed. . . . Concern grows over security surrounding Aug. 20 presidential election.

2009

July — U.S. and NATO forces launch major offensive against the Taliban in Afghanistan's southern Helmand province; more than 4,000 Marines take part, along with a smaller contingent of Afghan forces.

August — Numerous Taliban attacks mark presidential and provincial elections, which are largely seen as fraudulent by outside observers.

November — Hamid Karzai is sworn in as Afghan president, despite concerns about election fraud.

December — After months of consideration, President Obama opts to send 30,000 additional troops to Afghanistan; at the same time, he announces that U.S. forces will begin a partial withdrawal in 2011. . . . In one of the deadliest days for the CIA in decades, a CIA base in Khost, Afghanistan, is attacked by a double agent turned suicide bomber, killing seven CIA officers.

2010

July — WikiLeaks begins publishing thousands of formerly classified documents detailing the Pakistani security service's backing of the Taliban. . . . Gen. David Petraeus takes command of U.S. forces in Afghanistan after Gen. Stanley McChrystal resigns over comments published in Rolling Stone.

August — Dutch troops end Afghan mission.

2011

May 1 — Al-Qaida leader Osama bin Laden is killed in a U.S. raid; he apparently had been hiding in the same house in Abbottabad, Pakistan, for more than five years, according to U.S. intelligence officials. The raid also netted dozens of computer drives and other materials that the CIA hopes will reveal terrorist planning strategies and show who helped bin Laden remain hidden over the past decade.

Are troop levels in Afghanistan adequate?

When the Marine assault in Helmand Province got under way this summer, only about 400 effective Afghan fighters had joined the American force of nearly 4,000, according to *The New York Times*, citing information from Gen. Nicholson. [23]

Commanders expressed concern that not enough homegrown forces were available to fight the insurgency and build ties with the local population. Gen. Nicholson said, "I'm not going to sugarcoat it. The fact of the matter is, we don't have enough Afghan forces. And I'd like more." [24] Capt. Brian Huysman, a Marine company commander, said the lack of Afghan forces "is absolutely our Achilles' heel." [25]

"We've seen a shift over the past few years to put a lot more resources, including money and attention, toward building Afghan national security forces, army and police forces," Seth Jones, a political scientist at the RAND Corporation, told the "NewsHour" on PBS. "I think the problem that we're running into on the ground in Afghanistan, though: There are not enough Afghan national security forces and coalition forces to do what Gen. McChrystal and others want, and that is to protect the local population." [26]

Worries about the size of the Afghan force have been accompanied by concerns over whether U.S. forces are adequate to overcome the Taliban threat and secure local areas long enough to ensure security and build governance capabilities.

According to a report this summer by veteran *Washington Post* reporter Bob Woodward, National Security Adviser James L. Jones told U.S. commanders in Afghanistan the Obama administration wants to keep troop levels steady for now. Gen. Nicholson, though, told Jones that he was "a little light," suggesting he could use more troops, and that "we don't have enough force to go everywhere," Woodward reported. [27]

"The question of the force level for Afghanistan . . . is not settled and will probably be hotly debated over the next year," Woodward wrote. "One senior military officer said privately that the United States would have to deploy a force of more than 100,000 to execute the counterinsurgency strategy of holding areas and towns after clearing out the Taliban insurgents. That is at least 32,000 more than the 68,000 currently authorized." [28]

The Many Faces of the Taliban

Adherents include violent warlords and Islamist extremists.

When President Barack Obama announced his administration's new Afghanistan strategy in March, he declared that if the Afghan government were to fall to the Taliban, the country would "again be a base for terrorists who want to kill as many of our people as they possibly can."[1]

But defining "the Taliban" is tricky. Far from a monolithic organization, the Taliban is a many-headed hydra, and a shadowy one at that. It is a mélange of insurgents and militants, ranging from high-profile Islamist extremists and violent warlords to local villagers fighting for cash or glory. Western military strategists hope to kill or capture the most fanatical elements of the Taliban while persuading others to abandon their arms and work within Afghanistan's political system.

"You have a whole spectrum of bad guys that sort of get lumped into this catch-all term of Taliban . . . because they're launching bullets at us," a senior Defense official told *The Boston Globe*. "There are many of the groups that can probably be peeled off."

The Defense official quoted by *The Globe* was among "hundreds of intelligence operatives and analysts" in the United States and abroad involved in a broad study of tribes tied to the Taliban, the newspaper said. The aim is to figure out whether diplomatic or economic efforts can persuade some to break away, according to the paper. The examination "is expected to culminate later this year in a detailed, highly classified analysis of the different factions of the Taliban and other groups," *The Globe* said.[2]

Many experts break down the Taliban into four main groups:

• **The Early Taliban** — Insurgents emerged under Mullah Omar and other leaders during the civil war that wracked Afghanistan in the mid-1990s, following the end of the Soviet occupation of the country. Early members were a mix of fighters who battled the Soviets in the 1980s and Pashtuns who attended religious schools in Pakistan, where they were aided by the Pakistani Inter-Services Intelligence agency.[3]

• **The Pakistani Taliban** emerged under a separate organizational structure in 2002, when Pakistani forces entered the country's tribal region in the northwest to pursue Islamist militants.[4]

"At the time of the U.S.-led military campaign in Afghanistan in late 2001, allies and sympathizers of the Taliban in Pakistan were not identified as 'Taliban' themselves," wrote Hassan Abbas, a research fellow at Harvard's Belfer Center for Science and International Affairs. "That reality is now a distant memory. Today, Pakistan's indigenous Taliban are an effective fighting force and are engaging the Pakistani military on one side and NATO forces on the other."[5]

• **Hizb-e-Islami** — Formed by the brutal warlord Gulbuddin Hekmatyar, the group is "a prominent ally under the Taliban umbrella," says *Christian Science Monitor* journalist Anand Gopal.[6]

Hizb-e-Islami ("Islamic Party") was allied with the United States and Pakistan during the decade-long Soviet war, Gopal wrote, but after the 2001 U.S. invasion of Afghanistan a segment led by Hekmatyar joined the insurgency. *The New York Times* has described Hekmatyar as having "a record of extreme brutality."[7]

Hizb-e-Islami fighters have for years "had a reputation for being more educated and worldly than their Taliban

Adm. Mike Mullen, chairman of the Joint Chiefs of Staff, said on CBS News' "Face the Nation" on July 5 that in southern Afghanistan, where the toughest fighting is expected, "we have enough forces now not just to clear an area but to hold it so we can build after. And that's really the strategy." He noted that Gen. McChrystal was due to produce his 60-day assessment of the war this

summer, adding "we're all committed to getting this right and resourcing it properly."[29]

But senior military officials told *The Washington Post* later that week that McChrystal had concluded Afghan security forces must be greatly expanded if the war is to be won. According to officials, the *Post* said, "such an expansion would require spending billions counterparts, who are often illiterate farmers," Gopal wrote last year. In the 1970s, Hekmatyar studied engineering at Kabul University, "where he made a name for himself by hurling acid in the faces of unveiled women."[8]

Today the group has a "strong presence in the provinces near Kabul and in Pashtun pockets in the country's north and northeast," Gopal wrote. In 2008 Hizb-e-Islami participated in an assassination attempt on President Hamid Karzai and was behind a 2008 ambush that killed 10 NATO soldiers, according to Gopal.

"Its guerrillas fight under the Taliban banner, although independently and with a separate command structure," Gopal wrote. "Like the Taliban, its leaders see their task as restoring Afghan sovereignty as well as establishing an Islamic state in Afghanistan."

• **The Haqqani network** — Some of the most notorious terrorist actions in recent months have been linked to the network, including the kidnapping of a *New York Times* reporter and the abduction of a U.S. soldier. Haqqani is "not traditional Taliban, they're more strongly associated with al Qaeda," said Haroun Mir, director of Afghanistan's Center for Research and Policy Studies in Kabul.[9]

Thought to control major parts of eastern Afghanistan, the network in recent years "has emerged . . . as a powerful antagonist to U.S. efforts to stabilize that country and root out insurgent havens in the lawless tribal areas of Pakistan," according to *The Washington Post.*[10]

The network is controlled by Jalaluddin Haqqani and his son, Sirajuddin, the *Post* said. Analysts call the son a "terrorist mastermind," according to *The Christian Science Monitor.*[11]

New York Times reporter David Rohde, who was abducted in Logar Province in Afghanistan and taken across the Pakistani border to North Waziristan, was held by the Haqqani network until he escaped in June after seven months in captivity.[12]

The network also is suspected of the suicide bombing of the Indian Embassy in Kabul in July 2008 that left more than 50 dead, *The Post* said.[13]

According to Gopal, "The Haqqanis command the lion's share of foreign fighters operating in [Afghanistan] and tend to be even more extreme than their Taliban counterparts. Unlike most of the Taliban and Hizb-e-Islami, elements of the Haqqani network cooperate closely with al Qaeda."[14]

---

[1] "Remarks by the President on a New Strategy for Afghanistan and Pakistan," The White House, March 27, 2009, www.whitehouse.gov.

[2] Bryan Bender, "U.S. probes divisions within Taliban," *The Boston Globe*, May 24, 2009, p. 1.

[3] See Eben Kaplan and Greg Bruno, "The Taliban in Afghanistan," Council on Foreign Relations, July 2, 2008, www.cfr.org/publication/10551/tali ban_in_afghanistan.html.

[4] *Ibid.*

[5] Hassan Abbas, "A Profile of Tehrik-i-Taliban Pakistan," *CTC Sentinel*, Vol. 1, Issue 2, pp. 1-4, www.ctc.usma.edu/sentinel/CTCSentinel-Vol1Iss2.pdf.

[6] Anand Gopal, "Briefing: Who Are the Taliban?" *The Christian Science Monitor*, April 16, 2009, http://anandgopal.com/briefing-who-are-the-taliban/.

[7] Dexter Filkins, "Taliban said to be in talks with intermediaries about peace; U.S. withdrawal is called a focus," *The New York Times*, May 21, 2009, p. 4.

[8] Anand Gopal, "Who Are the Taliban?" *The Nation*, Dec. 22, 2008, www.thenation.com/doc/20081222/gopal.

[9] Quoted in Issam Ahmed, "Captured U.S. soldier in Taliban video: Held by Haqqani network?" *The Christian Science Monitor*, Global News blog, July 19, 2009, http://features.csmonitor.com/globalnews/2009/07/19/captured-us-soldier-in-taliban-video-held-by-haqqani-network/.

[10] Keith B. Richburg, "Reporters Escape Taliban Captors," *The Washington Post*, June 21, 2009, p. A1.

[11] Ahmed, *op. cit.*

[12] *Ibid.*

[13] Richburg, *op. cit.*

[14] Gopal, *The Nation, op. cit.*

---

more than the $7.5 billion the administration has budgeted annually to build up the Afghan army and police over the next several years, and the likely deployment of thousands more U.S. troops as trainers and advisers."[30]

As combat has intensified this spring and summer and more troops entered the war zone, commanders focused on one of the most pernicious threats to the

U.S.-led counterinsurgency strategy: the potential for civilian casualties, which can undermine efforts to build trust and cooperation with the local population. Concern over civilian deaths rose sharply in May, when a high-profile U.S. air strike in western Farah province killed at least 26 civilians, according to American investigators.[31] This spring commanders instituted strict new combat rules aimed at minimizing civilian deaths, and Defense Secretary Robert M. Gates has called such casualties "one of our greatest strategic vulnerabilities." [32]

While some fear that the deployment of more troops to Afghanistan could heighten civilian casualties, others say the opposite is true.

"In fact, the presence of more boots on the ground is likely to *reduce* civilian casualties, because historically it has been the over-reliance on American air strikes — as a result of too few ground forces — which has been the key cause of civilian deaths," wrote Bergen of the New America Foundation. [33]

Should the United States negotiate with the Taliban?

In early March, shortly before announcing his new strategy for Afghanistan and Pakistan, *The New York Times* reported that Obama, in an interview aboard Air Force One, "opened the door to a reconciliation process in which the American military would reach out to moderate elements of the Taliban." [34]

In broaching the idea of negotiating with the Taliban, the president cited successes in Iraq in separating moderate insurgents from the more extreme factions of al Qaeda. Still, he was cautious about reconciliation prospects in Afghanistan.

"The situation in Afghanistan is, if anything, more complex" than the one in Iraq, he said. "You have a less governed region, a history of fierce independence among tribes. Those tribes are multiple and sometimes operate at cross-purposes, and so figuring all that out is going to be much more of a challenge." [35]

Nevertheless, the notion of seeking some sort of reconciliation with elements of the Afghan Taliban has received fresh attention recently.

Opponents of the idea argue that it could project an image of weakness and embolden the insurgency and that Taliban leaders cannot be trusted to uphold any deals they may make.

But proponents argue the Taliban is not a unified bloc, but rather an amalgam that includes those who joined the insurgency out of frustration at the lack of security in their villages or because they were forcibly drafted, among other reasons.

"If you look at a security map of Afghanistan between, say, 2003 and today, you have this creep of the insurgency

sort of moving up from the south and east into other parts of the country," J. Alexander Thier, senior rule of law adviser with the United States Institute of Peace. That trend, he says, suggests many local communities and commanders that may have once supported the Afghan government have turned neutral or are actively supporting the Taliban. "There's real room in there to deal with their grievances and concerns about security and justice and the rule of law so as to change that tide."

Thier says he's not talking about seeking a "grand bargain" with the Taliban leadership now ensconced in Pakistan. "If what you're envisioning is [Afghan President] Karzai and [Taliban leader] Mullah Omar sitting on the deck of an aircraft carrier signing an armistice, I don't think that's feasible or realistic," he says. What is feasible are "micro level" negotiations.

"There is an enormous opportunity to work on what I would call mid- and low-level insurgents who, for a variety of reasons, were likely not engaged in the insurgency just a few years ago and were either pro-government or at least neutral. And I think they can and should be brought back to that position."

In an article this summer in *Foreign Affairs*, Fotini Christia, an assistant professor of political science at MIT, and Michael Semple, former deputy to the European Union special representative to Afghanistan, wrote that while "sending more troops is necessary to tip the balance of power against the insurgents, the move will have a lasting impact only if it is accompanied by a political 'surge,' a committed effort to persuade large groups of Taliban fighters to put down their arms and give up the fight." [36]

For reconciliation to work, say Fotini and Semple, Afghans first must feel secure. "The situation on the ground will need to be stabilized, and the Taliban must be reminded that they have no prospect of winning their current military campaign," they wrote. "If the Afghan government offers reconciliation as its carrot, it must also present force as its stick — hence the importance of sending more U.S. troops to Afghanistan, but also, in the long term, the importance of building up Afghanistan's own security forces. Reconciliation needs to be viewed as part of a larger military-political strategy to defeat the insurgency."

Some favor waiting to begin negotiation efforts, while others say they should occur simultaneously with the military campaign. Riedel of Brookings says he sees reason to believe that "a fair number" of Taliban foot soldiers and local commanders are not deeply dedicated to the core extremist cause as espoused by leaders such as Omar. Many rank and file Taliban may be "in this for one reason or another" — perhaps because "their tribe is aligned with the Taliban for local reasons, they're getting paid by the Taliban to do this better than they could be paid by anyone else, or simply because if you're a 17-year-old Pashtun male in Kandahar, fighting is kind of how you get your right of passage," Riedel says.

If the momentum changes on the battlefield "and it's a lot more dangerous to support the Taliban," Riedel continues, "my sense . . . is that these people will either defect or simply go home — they just won't fight."

Still, he says, it's not yet time to begin negotiations. First must come intelligence networks and greater political savvy in each district and province to capitalize on any Taliban inclinations to bend, he argues. "That is primarily an Afghan job, because they're the only people who are going to know the ins and outs of this. That's one of the things the new [U.S.] command arrangement needs to focus on the most. I don't think we're there. This requires really intense local information."

Yet, while the hour for negotiating may not be ripe, "the time is now to do the homework to do that," Riedel says, in order to develop "fine-grained knowledge of what's going on."

But Rajan Menon, a professor of international relations at Lehigh University, says "not coupling" the military campaign against the Taliban "with an olive branch is probably not effective."

Because huge challenges face the military operation — from the threat of civilian casualties to the weakness of the country's central government — the prospect of a long and costly war looms, he says. To avoid that, Menon says, the military effort should be occurring simultaneously with one aimed at encouraging "pragmatic" elements of the Taliban to buy into a process in which they "have to sell [their] ideas in the political marketplace."

The Taliban pragmatists, he says, would be offered a choice: either a long, open-ended war with heavy insurgent casualties or the opportunity to enter the political process as a group seeking victory through the ballot box.

"The question is, can you fracture the [insurgency] movement by laying down terms that are pretty stringent

and test their will," Menon says. Nobody knows if the arms-and-olive branch approach would work, he says, but "you lose nothing by trying."

BACKGROUND
'Graveyard of Empires'

Afghanistan has long been known as the "crossroads of Central Asia," an apt name given the long list of outsiders who have ventured across its borders. It also is known as the "graveyard of empires," reflecting the difficulty faced by would-be conquerors of its remote terrain and disparate peoples.

The list is long. It includes the Persian king Darius I in the 6th century B.C. and the Macedonian conqueror Alexander the Great in 328 B.C., followed by the Scythians, White Huns, Turks, Arabs (who brought Islam in the 7th century A.D.), and the Mongol warrior Genghis Khan in 1219 A.D. [37]

Afghanistan's more recent history is a story of struggle against foreign domination, internal wrangling between reformists and traditionalists, coups, assassinations and war.

Modern Afghanistan began to take shape in the late 19th century, after a bitter fight for influence in Central Asia between the burgeoning British Empire and czarist Russia in what is known as "the Great Game." The contest led to Anglo-Afghan wars in 1839 and 1878. In the first, Afghan warriors forced the British into a deadly retreat from Kabul. The Afghans also had the upper hand over the British in the second war, which resulted in a treaty guaranteeing internal autonomy to Afghanistan while the British had control of its foreign affairs.

In 1880 Amir Abdur Rahman rose to the throne, reigning until 1901. Known as the "Iron Amir," he sought to institute reforms and weaken Pashtun resistance to centralized power but used methods, later emulated by the Taliban, to bring Uzbeks, Hazaras and Tajiks under Kabul's authority. [38] During his reign, Britain drew the so-called Durand Line separating Afghanistan from what was then India and later became Pakistan.

Rahman's son succeeded him but was assassinated in 1919. Under his successor, Amanullah — Rahman's grandson — Afghanistan gained full independence as a result of the Third Anglo War. Amanullah brought reforms that included ties with other countries and coeducational

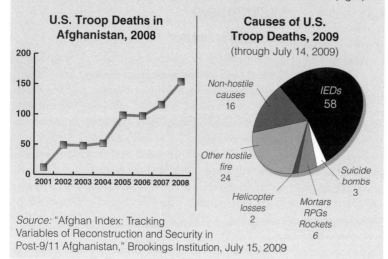

U.S. Troop Deaths Rose Steadily

U.S. troop fatalities have risen steadily since the United States entered Afghanistan in 2001 (graph at left). So far this year, IEDs (improvised explosive devices) caused slightly more than half the deaths (right).

U.S. Troop Deaths in Afghanistan, 2008

Causes of U.S. Troop Deaths, 2009
(through July 14, 2009)

Non-hostile causes 16

IEDs 58

Other hostile fire 24

Helicopter losses 2

Mortars RPGs Rockets 6

Suicide bombs 3

Source: "Afghan Index: Tracking Variables of Reconstruction and Security in Post-9/11 Afghanistan," Brookings Institution, July 15, 2009

Between 1956 and 1978, according to Pakistani journalist Ahmed Rashid, Afghanistan received some $533 million in economic aid from the United States and $2.5 billion in both economic and military aid from the Soviets. [39]

In the 1960s Zahir introduced a constitutional monarchy and pressed for political freedoms that included new rights for women in voting, schooling and employment. "These changes, in a deeply traditional Islamic society, were not popular with everyone," the *Times* noted in a 2007 obituary of Zahir. "But his years were characterized by a rare long period of peace. This tranquility is recalled now with immense nostalgia. On the other hand, peace was not accompanied by prosperity, and the king was faulted for not developing the economy." [40]

schools. But the moves alienated traditionalists, and Amanullah was forced to abdicate in 1929. His successor and cousin, Nadir Shah, was assassinated in 1933.

His death led to the 40-year reign of Crown Prince Mohammad Zahir Shah, Nadir Shah's son, who assumed power at 19.

Chaos and War

Under Zahir, Afghanistan sought to liberalize its political system. But the effort collapsed in the 1970s, and the country became a battleground between communist-backed leftists and a U.S.-backed Islamist resistance movement.

Afghanistan had tilted toward the Soviets in the Cold War era of the 1950s, partly because of U.S. ties to Pakistan, a country created by the partition of India in 1947. Afghan leaders wanted independence or at least autonomy for the Pashtun-dominated areas beyond the Durand Line.

Border tensions led Kabul to seek help from the Soviets, who responded with development loans and other aid in 1950. The United States sought to counter the Soviet Union's influence, and in the 1960s both countries were helping to build up Afghanistan's infrastructure.

Zahir's "experiment in democracy" did not lead to many lasting reforms, but "it permitted the growth of unofficial extremist parties on both the left and the right," including the communist People's Democratic Party of Afghanistan that was ideologically aligned with the Soviets, the U.S. State Department noted. The party split into rival groups in 1967 in a rift that "reflected ethnic, class and ideological divisions within Afghan society." [41]

In 1973 Zahir was ousted while in Europe for medical treatment. His cousin, former Prime Minister Sardar Mohammad Daoud Khan, whom Zahir had forced out in the 1960s, seized power in a bloodless coup. Daoud tried to institute reforms, but political unrest persisted. He aligned closely with the Soviets, but his efforts to build his own political party and forge some links with the United States alienated communist radicals. In 1978, the People's Democratic Party overthrew Daoud, killing him and most of his family.

Soviet Invasion

More upheaval followed. The new leader, Nur Moham-mad Taraki, imposed Marxist reforms that angered Islamic traditionalists and ethnic leaders, sparking revolts. Taraki was ousted and killed, and his successor, Hafizullah Amin, who resisted Soviet pressure to moderate his policies, was himself executed in 1979 by the Soviets.

Shortly before Amin's killing, the Soviets mounted a massive invasion of Afghanistan, starting a decade-long war that would permanently alter Afghanistan's profile in world affairs. In Amin's place, the Soviets installed Babrak Karmal. With Soviet military aid, he tried to impose authority throughout Afghanistan but ran into stiff opposition, especially in rural regions. An Islamist resistance movement called the Mujahedeen began receiving weapons and training from the United States and other countries in 1984, and soon the Soviet invasion was on the ropes.

In 1986 Karmal was replaced by Muhammad Najibullah, former head of the Afghan secret police, but the war continued to sour for the Soviets, who also were dealing with powerful political opposition at home. In 1988 Moscow signed agreements, along with the United States, Pakistan and Afghanistan, calling for an end to foreign intervention in Afghanistan. The Soviets withdrew early the following year, and in 1991 the USSR collapsed.

The Soviet invasion affirmed the idea of Afghanistan as a "graveyard" for invaders. Between 1979 and the Soviet withdrawal in 1989, some 14,500 Soviets died. [42] For the Afghan people, however, the war was a bloodbath that all but destroyed the economy and educational system and uprooted much of the population. The U.S. State Department estimates a million died. [43] Some estimates are higher.

Yet the end of the Soviet invasion brought no peace, but rather more chaos. After the Soviets departed, President George H. W. Bush withdrew support from Afghanistan, setting the stage for the conflict engulfing Afghanistan today. "Having won the Cold War," journalist Rashid wrote, "Washington had no further interest in Afghanistan or the region. This left a critical power vacuum for which the United States would pay an enormously high price a decade later." [44]

When the Soviet Union collapsed and the United States disengaged from Afghanistan, they left a country "that had become a cockpit for regional competition, a shattered state with no functioning security forces or civilian political process, a highly mobilized and armed population increasingly dependent on international organizations and cash for livelihood (including through the

Afghan President Hamid Karzai may face a runoff after the presidential election on Aug. 20, partly because many Afghans are looking for alternative leadership in the face of sustained insurgent violence, economic stagnation and political drift.

drug trade), and a multiplicity of armed groups linked transnationally to both state and non-state patrons," wrote Barnett Rubin, director of studies at the Center on International Cooperation at New York University, where he directs a program on Afghan reconstruction. [45]

The Mujahedeen were not a party to the accord leading to Soviet withdrawal, and through the early 1990s they continued fighting the Najibullah regime. In 1992 his government fell, and Burhanuddin Rabbani, an ethnic Tajik, became president. He declared Afghanistan an "Islamic state" but failed to ensure order.

By 1994 Afghanistan "was fast disintegrating," Rashid wrote. "Warlord fiefdoms ruled vast swathes of countryside. President Rabbani . . . governed only Kabul and the northeast of the country, while the west, centered on Herat, was under the control of warlord Ismael Khan. Six provinces in the north were ruled by the Uzbek general Rashid Dostum, and central Afghanistan was in the hands of the Hazaras. In the Pashtun south and east there was even greater fragmentation. . . . Warlords seized people's homes and farms for no reason, raped their daughters, abused and robbed the population and taxed travelers at will. Instead of refugees returning to Afghanistan, more began to leave the south for Pakistan." [46]

In 1994 a militant Islamist group — known as the Taliban and made up mainly of Pashtuns — sprang up in the south to oppose Rabbani. Their rise stemmed directly from the chaos wracking Afghanistan, Rashid wrote. "Frustrated young men who had fought against the Soviets and then returned to madrassas in Pakistan to resume their religious studies or to their villages in Afghanistan gathered around their elders demanding action." [47]

The Taliban took over Kabul in 1996, and by the early 2000s Rabbani's anti-Taliban Northern Alliance was limited to a slice of northern territory. "The Taliban instituted a repressive version of sharia law that outlawed music, banned women from working or going to school and prohibited freedom of the press," wrote Jones, the RAND political scientist. "While it was a detestable regime that committed gross human rights violations, the Taliban succeeded in establishing law and order throughout most of the country." [48]

At the same time, the Taliban was forging links to al Qaeda. In 1996 Taliban leader Mullah Omar invited Osama bin Laden to stay with him in Kandahar, and even though "the CIA already considered bin Laden a threat . . ., he was left alone to ingratiate himself with Omar by providing money, fighters and ideological advice to the Taliban," Rashid wrote. "Bin Laden gathered the Arabs left behind in Afghanistan and Pakistan from the war against the Soviets, enlisted more militants from Arab countries, and established a new global terrorist infrastructure." [49]

The al Qaeda threat reached full force with the Sept. 11, 2001, attacks on the United States. In October President George W. Bush responded with a military assault called Operation Enduring Freedom. The Taliban promptly collapsed, and its leadership, along with that of al Qaeda, fled, in the view of many analysts, to Pakistan.

Yet still more trouble was to follow.

A Weakening Government

"The collapse of the Taliban government . . . created a condition of emerging anarchy," Jones wrote. In late 2001 a United Nations-sponsored conference in Bonn, Germany, laid down a process to rebuild Afghanistan's political system. With the Bonn agreement, "on paper, Afghanistan looked like it had a central government," Jones wrote. But "in practice . . ., Afghanistan had a fragile government that became weaker over time." [50]

The new government couldn't provide essential services, especially in rural areas, and a 2005 World Bank study found that "the urban elite" were the main beneficiaries of help, Jones wrote. [51] Meanwhile, the Afghan government had various problems, including the inability to provide security outside of Kabul, in large measure due to "the inability of the U.S. government to build competent Afghan security forces, especially the police." [52]

American force levels were low, too, with "the number of U.S. troops per capita in Afghanistan . . . significantly less than in almost every state-building effort since World War II," Jones wrote. [53] Moreover, the United States gave "significant assistance to local warlords, further undermining governance and weakening the ability of the Afghan state to establish law and order." [54]

The Taliban rebounded, aided by what critics have called a lack of focus by the Bush administration after its decision to invade Iraq in 2003. In Afghanistan, reconstruction and security issues were left unattended, critics say, leaving an opening for the Taliban — along with criminals, warlords, drug traffickers and others — to assert brutal control. Afghan opium production soared, al Qaeda sanctuaries in the border region of Pakistan festered and once again the region threatened to unleash a new wave of global terrorism.

The threat came not only from Afghanistan, but Pakistan, too.

In an article last year on the emboldened Taliban and al Qaeda forces in the Pakistani border region, celebrated *New York Times* war correspondent Dexter Filkins noted that Islamist militants continued to be backed by Pakistani military and intelligence services. Then, in 1994, came Pakistan's "most fateful move," he wrote. Concerned about the mayhem that swept through Afghanistan after the Soviet withdrawal, Pakistani Prime Minister Benazir Bhutto and her administration intervened on behalf of the Taliban, Filkins wrote.

"We created the Taliban," Bhutto's interior minister, Nasrullah Babar, told Filkins. "Mrs. Bhutto had a vision: that through a peaceful Afghanistan, Pakistan could extend its influence into the resource-rich territories of Central Asia." Her dream didn't materialize — the Taliban's conquest of Afghanistan fell short, and Bhutto was assassinated in late 2007. But as Filkins noted, the Taliban training camps, sometimes supported by Pakistani intelligence officials, "were beacons to Islamic militants from around the world." [55]

Concerns persist about Pakistan's intentions and security capabilities. In recent weeks, as militants threatened Islamabad and other Pakistani cities, Pakistan has gone after insurgents in the Swat Valley and elsewhere. But Pakistani officials also have criticized U.S. attacks on insurgent strongholds using unmanned drone planes.

The big question, as posed by Filkins and others, is whether Pakistan is willing — or able — to control the radical forces within its border region. "This was not supposed to be a major worry," Filkins wrote, noting that after the Sept. 11 attacks Pakistani President Pervez Musharraf backed the United States, helped find al Qaeda suspects, attacked militants in Pakistan's remote tribal areas and vowed to fight terrorism — all in return for $10 billion in U.S. aid since 2001.

But Pakistani military and civilian leaders have survived by playing a "double game," Filkins wrote, promising the United States they were cracking down on militants, and sometimes doing so, while also allowing, and even helping, the same militants.

One reason for the "double game" is Pakistan's long-standing tension with India, especially over the disputed border region of Kashmir. "You can't address Pakistan without dealing with India," says Riedel, the Brookings scholar.

Some experts say Pakistan views its support of the Taliban as a hedge against an India-friendly government coming to power in Afghanistan.

"The Pakistanis have convinced themselves that India's objective is a friendly Afghanistan that can pose a second front against Pakistan," says Riedel. "They see the Afghan Taliban, in particular, as a very useful asset. It keeps Afghanistan from becoming an Indian client state, and their conviction is that . . . it's only a matter of time" until the United States leaves Afghanistan. The Pakistanis believe that "if they wait it out, their client will be the dominant power at least in southern and eastern Afghanistan."

The Cato Institute's Innocent says the Obama administration has made a "profound strategic miscalculation" by not recognizing how much Pakistani leaders fear a non-Pashtun, India-leaning government assuming power in Kabul.

India has used its influence in Afghanistan, she says, to funnel weapons to a separatist movement in southwest Pakistan's sprawling Baluchistan region — a movement that some say could pose an existential threat to Pakistan. That, in turn, has given Pakistan an incentive to keep Afghanistan from growing closer to India.

Says Innocent, "This rivalry between [Pakistan and India] is the biggest impediment to stabilizing Afghanistan."

CURRENT SITUATION
Measurable Metrics

In the weeks leading up to this summer's Helmand River operation, Defense Secretary Gates expressed optimism about the war in Afghanistan, but acknowledged that the American public's patience with its progress could be limited.

"I think what the people in the United States want to see is the momentum shifting to see that the strategies that we're following are working," he said on CBS' "60 Minutes." "And that's why I've said in nine months to a year, we need to evaluate how we're doing." [56]

Part of that evaluation will be done through "metrics," statistical measurements on everything from civilian casualties to the strength of the Afghan National Army. The approach is part of the Obama strategy.

"Going forward, we will not blindly stay the course," Obama said, but rather "we will set clear metrics to measure progress and hold ourselves accountable. We'll consistently assess our efforts to train Afghan security forces and our progress in combating insurgents. We will measure the growth of Afghanistan's economy and its illicit narcotics production. And we will review whether we are using the right tools and tactics to make progress towards accomplishing our goals." [57]

One measure attracting rising attention in recent weeks is that of troop levels. Michael E. O'Hanlon, a senior fellow at Brookings, wrote this summer in the *Washington Examiner* that "for all its virtues," the Obama administration's Afghan strategy "may still lowball requirements for the Afghanistan mission to succeed."

"The administration's decisions in March to increase U.S. troop numbers to 68,000 (making for about 100,000 foreign troops in all), and Afghan army and police to about 215,000 will leave combined coalition forces at only half the levels in Iraq during the surge," O'Hanlon wrote, "and Afghanistan is slightly larger and more populous."

Should the president announce an Afghanistan exit strategy?

YES

Malou Innocent
Foreign Policy Analyst
Cato Institute

Written for *CQ Researcher*, July 2009

No strategic, political or economic gains could outweigh the costs of America maintaining an indefinite military presence in Afghanistan. Washington can continue to disrupt terrorist havens by monitoring the region with unmanned aerial vehicles, retaining advisers for training Afghan forces and using covert operatives against specific targets.

Many policy makers and prominent opinion leaders are pushing for a large-scale, long-term military presence in Afghanistan. But none of their rationales for such a heavy presence withstands close scrutiny.

Al Qaeda poses a manageable security problem, not an existential threat to America. Washington's response, with an open-ended mission in Afghanistan, is both unnecessary and unsustainable.

Policy makers also tend to conflate al Qaeda with indigenous Pashtun-dominated militias, such as the Taliban. America's security, however, will not necessarily be at risk even if an oppressive regime takes over a contiguous fraction of Afghan territory.

Additionally, the argument that America has a moral obligation to prevent the reemergence of reprehensible groups like the Taliban seems instead a justification for the perpetuation of American empire. After all, America never made a substantive policy shift toward or against the Taliban's misogynistic, oppressive and militant Islamic regime when it controlled Afghanistan in the 1990s. Thus, the present moral outrage against the group can be interpreted as opportunistic.

Some policy makers claim the war is worth waging because terrorists flourish in failed states. But that cannot account for terrorists who thrive in states with the sovereignty to reject external interference. That is one reason why militants find sanctuary in Pakistan. In fact, attempts to stabilize Afghanistan destabilize Pakistan. Amassing troops in Afghanistan feeds the perception of a foreign occupation, spawning more terrorist recruits for Pakistani militias and thus placing undue stress on an already-weakened, nuclear-armed nation.

It's also important to recognize that Afghanistan's land-locked position in Central Asia will forever render it vulnerable to meddling from surrounding states. This factor will make sealing the country's borders from terrorists impossible.

Finally, Americans should not fear appearing "weak" after withdrawal. The United States accounts for almost half of the world's military spending, wields one of the planet's largest nuclear arsenals and can project its power around the globe. Remaining in Afghanistan is more likely to weaken the United States militarily and economically than would withdrawal.

NO

Ilan Berman
Vice President for Policy
American Foreign Policy Council

Written for *CQ Researcher*, July 2009

It has been called the "graveyard of empires," a place that for thousands of years has stymied invading armies. Today, Afghanistan remains one of the West's most vexing international security conundrums — and a pressing foreign policy challenge for the Obama administration.

Indeed, for almost as long as Obama has been in office, critics have counseled the new U.S. president to set a date certain for an American exit from Afghanistan. To his credit, Mr. Obama has done no such thing. To the contrary, through the "Af-Pak" strategy unveiled in March, the White House has effectively doubled down on the American investment in Afghanistan's security. It has done so for two principal reasons.

The first has to do with Afghanistan's importance to the overall struggle against radical Islam. In the years before Sept. 11, Afghanistan became an incubator of international terrorism. And the sinister synergy created there between al Qaeda and the ruling Taliban movement was directly responsible for the most devastating terrorist attack in American history. Preventing a repeat occurrence remains an overriding priority, which is why Washington has committed to propping up the fragile government of Afghan President Hamid Karzai with the troops and training necessary to hold its ground.

The second is an understanding that Afghanistan is essentially a derivative problem. Much of the instability that exists there today is a function of radicalism nurtured next door, in Pakistan. The Taliban, after all, was an invention of Pakistan's Inter-Services Intelligence back in the mid-1990s, and Islamabad's intelligence czars (as well as their military counterparts) remain heavily invested in its future. Today, the Taliban poses perhaps a greater threat to Pakistan's own stability than to that of Afghanistan. But a retraction of U.S. and allied forces from the latter is sure to create a political vacuum that Islamic radicals will be all too eager to exploit.

These realities have defined the Obama administration's approach. Unlike previous foreign powers that have gotten involved in Afghanistan, the United States today is interested simply in what the military calls "area denial." The goal is not to conquer and claim, but to deny the Taliban the necessary breathing room to regroup and re-entrench.

Setting a firm date for an American withdrawal would fundamentally undermine that objective. It would also serve to provide regional radicals with far greater certainty that the U.S. investment in Afghanistan's stability is both limited and reversible.

O'Hanlon cautioned against closing the door on adding more troops and pointed to "troubling signs that the Obama administration may be digging in against any future troop requirements." While "we may or may not have enough forces in Afghanistan" to accomplish the mission's full range of goals, he concluded, "let's not close off the conversation until we learn a little bit more." [58]

NATO's Cold Shoulder

Among the thorniest of the troop-level issues is the role of NATO forces in Afghanistan. As of June, countries participating in the NATO-led International Security Assistance Forces (ISAF), a mission mandated by the U.N. under the 2001 Bonn agreement, have committed about 32,000 troops to Afghanistan, not counting those from the United States, according to the Brookings Institution. The top three were the United Kingdom, which had committed 8,300 troops, Germany (3,380) and Canada (2,830). Several countries, including the U.K. and Germany, were expected to send a small number of additional troops to provide security for the Aug. 20 election.

The Obama administration has been largely unsuccessful in prodding European nations to send more troops to Afghanistan. In April, in what the online edition of the *Times* of London billed as a "charm offensive" by Obama on his "debut international tour," leaders on the European continent "turned their backs" on the president, with British Prime Minister Gordon Brown "the only one to offer substantial help." Brown offered to send several hundred extra troops to provide election security, the *Times* noted, "but even that fell short of the thousands of combat troops that the U.S. was hoping to [gain] from the prime minister." [59]

Nonetheless, Obama has mustered some recent support for his Afghan policy. In late July Spain's prime minister, José Luís Rodriguez Zapatero, said his country was willing to increase its force on long-term deployment to Afghanistan, *The New York Times* reported. [60]

Early this month, NATO approved a reorganized command structure for Afghanistan, agreeing to set up a New Intermediate Joint Headquarters in Kabul under U.S. Lt. General David M. Rodriquez, who will manage the war on a day-to-day basis and report to McChrystal. NATO made the move at the first meeting of its governing body, the North Atlantic Council, under new NATO Secretary General Anders Fogh Rasmussen, former Danish prime minister. [61] Rasmussen, in his first comments as secretary general, called on the United Nations and European Union to help defeat the Taliban. "NATO will do its part, but it cannot do it alone," he said. "This needs to be an international effort, both military and civilian." [62]

The effectiveness of having more NATO troops in Afghanistan has been a matter of debate. At a forum in June, Brookings scholar Jeremy Shapiro, recently back from a visit to southern Afghanistan, suggested U.S. commanders have had little faith in the NATO command structure.

"Each of the main countries there is really running its own provincial war," Shapiro said. "The overall problem is that there really is no unity of command in Afghanistan so we're unable . . . to prioritize and to shift resources to deal with the most important problems. . . . It's related to the fact that for every NATO force in Afghanistan including the Americans, there are two chains of command, one up through the NATO commander who is an American, and one to the national capital, and in case of conflict, the national capital command always takes priority.

"The result is that each of the lead countries in the south, the Canadians in Kandahar, the British in Helmand, the Dutch in Uruzgan, are focused on their own priorities, on improving specific indicators in their piece of the war in their own province or district without a great deal of attention to the impact of that measure on the overall fight."

In impoverished Uruzgan Province, for example, the Dutch are doing "impressive things" with development efforts, but Uruzgan "is to a large degree serving as a sanctuary for insurgents to rest and refit and plan and to engage in the struggle in Kandahar and Helmand" province, Shapiro said.

The Canadians and British "would argue . . . that the priority for Afghanistan is not Uruzgan, it is Kandahar and Helmand and [if] the development of Uruzgan comes at the cost of strengthening the insurgency in other provinces, it's perhaps not the best use of resources."

Shapiro said he believes that as the number of U.S. troops has increased, especially in southern Afghanistan, "the focus for the U.S. military command is on . . . assigning roles to coalition partners that don't require intense coordination. . . . What that presages is an Americanization of the war, including in the south." By next year, Shapiro said, NATO will remain in command, "but I would be very dubious that we'll be truly fighting a NATO war at that point." [63]

Americanizing the War

Such predictions of an Americanized war are at odds with the administration's perception of the Afghan mission. Obama told *Sky News*, a British news outlet, that British contributions to the war effort are "critical" and that "this is not an American mission. The mission in Afghanistan is one that the Europeans have as much if not more of a stake in what we do. . . . The likelihood of a terrorist attack in London is at least as high, if not higher, than it is in the United States." [64]

Any further Americanization of the war will doubtlessly fuel scrutiny of the Afghan strategy in Congress and bolster demands for the Obama administration to set forth an exit strategy.

This summer, the U.S. House of Representatives strongly rejected an amendment calling on the defense secretary to submit a report no later than Dec. 31 outlining an exit strategy for U.S. forces in Afghanistan.

"Every military mission has a beginning, a middle, a time of transition and an end," said Rep. McGovern, the Massachusetts Democrat who sponsored the measure. "But I have yet to see that vision articulated in any document, speech or briefing. We're not asking for an immediate withdrawal. We're sure not talking about cutting or running or retreating, just a plan. If there is no military solution for Afghanistan, then please just tell us how we will know when our military contribution to the political solution has ended." [65]

But "focusing on an exit versus a strategy is irresponsible and fails to recognize that our efforts in Afghanistan are vital to preventing future terrorist attacks on the American people and our allies," argued Rep. Howard McKeon, R-Calif. [66]

The amendment's defeat did nothing to allay scrutiny of the war. Sen. John F. Kerry, D-Mass., chairman of the Senate Foreign Relations Committee, told *GlobalPost*, an online international-news site, that he planned to hold oversight hearings on U.S. involvement in Afghanistan. [67]

"End of summer, early fall," Kerry said, "we are going to take a hard look at Afghanistan."

OUTLOOK

More Violence

Military strategists say the Afghan war is likely to get more violent in coming months as U.S. and NATO forces battle the insurgency.

One immediate concern is whether the Taliban will make good on threats to disrupt this month's presidential election. While additional troops are being deployed to guard against attacks, officials have said ensuring the security of all 28,000 polling places is impossible. [68]

Meanwhile, tensions are likely to remain between those calling for a strict timetable for de-escalating the war and those arguing in favor of staying the course.

"I certainly do not think it would be a wise idea to impose a timeline on ourselves," says Riedel of Brookings, although he points to "political realities" that include the idea "that some measure of improvement in the security situation on the ground needs to be apparent over the course of the next 18 to 24 months."

Riedel expresses confidence that will occur. Once all scheduled troop deployments are in place, he says, "it's reasonable to expect that you can see some impact from [those deployments] in 18 to 24 months. Not victory, not the surrender of [Taliban leader] Mullah Omar, but some measurable decline in the pace of Taliban activity, some increase in the number of districts and provinces which are regarded as safe enough for [non-governmental organizations] to work in."

Beyond demands for on-the-ground progress in Afghanistan, the Obama administration faces other pressures as it struggles to get a grip on the Afghanistan and Pakistan region. One is helping U.S. allies maintain support for the war. In Britain, Prime Minister Brown has faced an uproar over growing British casualties that critics say stem from an underfunded defense budget that led to inadequate troop levels and equipment. [69] At home, as the financial crisis, health-care reform and other issues put pressure on the federal budget, Obama is likely to face opposition in Congress over additional war funding.

And Obama also is under pressure to address incendiary issues left over from the Bush administration. In July, a *New York Times* report detailed how the Bush administration repeatedly sought to discourage an investigation of charges that forces under U.S.-backed warlord Gen. Abdul Rashid Dostum massacred hundreds or even thousands of Taliban prisoners of war during the 2001 invasion of Afghanistan.[70]

In an editorial, the *Times* said Obama has directed aides to study the issue and that the administration is pressing Afghan President Karzai not to return Dostum to power. But, it added, Obama "needs to order a full investigation into the massacre."[71]

In the long run, one of the biggest challenges facing the Obama administration is its effort to instill sound governance in a country saturated with graft.

Afghanistan's corruption "reveals the magnitude of the task," says Walt, the Harvard international affairs professor. "Fixing corrupt public institutions is really hard once a pattern of behavior has been established, where money is flowing in non-regular ways. It's very difficult for outsiders to re-engineer those social and political practices, even if we were committed to staying five or 10 years."

Walt says he hopes he's wrong — "that the injection of the right kind of American power will create space for some kind of political reconciliation." But he's not optimistic. "I believe several years from now, [Afghanistan] will look like a sinkhole."

Defense Secretary Robert Gates and Afghan President Hamid Karzai arrive at a joint press conference in Kabul on March 7, 2011. Karzai's weak, U.S.-backed government is widely viewed as corrupt and dysfunctional, and many Afghans see it as illegitimate.

UPDATE

The dramatic Navy Seal commando raid that killed al-Qaida leader Osama bin Laden on May 1 undoubtedly will affect U.S. anti-terrorism efforts, including the war in Afghanistan. How much remains to be seen.

But even before members of elite Seal Team 6 swooped into Abbottabad, Pakistan, the Obama administration planned to shrink the number of U.S. and NATO soldiers in Afghanistan. Reportedly the reduction would amount to about 5,000 troops out of more than 100,000 currently deployed, not to mention an even larger force of private security contractors.[72] The conflict is now in its 10th year, and analysts predict that 2011 will be its most violent. Many see the conflict as one in which neither side can defeat the other. Nic Lee, director of the Afghanistan NGO Safety Office, a group that advises nongovernmental organizations about security

in Afghanistan, describes it as a "perpetually escalating stalemate."[73]

Moreover, in the decade since the terrorist attacks of Sept. 11, 2001, critics of the conflict, including Richard Haass, president of the Council on Foreign Relations, and former Republican National Committee Chairman Michael Steele say it has gone from a war of necessity to one of choice.[74]

Many argue that Afghanistan is no longer a significant global terrorist threat, a view underscored in May, when bin Laden — the *raison d'etre* behind the conflict — was discovered living in Pakistan, a scant hour's drive from the capital, Islamabad. It appears that he had sheltered there for many years, even as U.S. forces blasted away with bombs and missiles at suspected terrorists and other militants believed to be living in the remote tribal regions between Afghanistan and Pakistan.

U.S intelligence officials — with the aid of materials captured in the bin Laden raid — are now racing to rewrite the history of al-Qaida, in light of bin Laden's decade on the lam. The results will clearly have major implications for the larger conflict between the West and the radical Islamist terrorist organization and others.

It had long been thought that bin Laden was living in a cave, in limited contact with the outside world and not coordinating terrorist attacks worldwide. Those assumptions are now being reconsidered after his lair was discovered just yards from the top Pakistani military academy, and his walled compound yielded a vast trove of al-Qaida information stored on computer hard drives and thumb drives, including plans to attack the United States on the 10th anniversary of 9/11.

Meanwhile, the scheduled drawdown of U.S. forces in Afghanistan, slated to begin in July, will be an important indicator of Washington's long-term plans for the war. The size and nature of the drawdown have yet to be announced.

Even the authorization of military force against perpetrators of the 9/11 attacks and those who harbored them, passed three days after the attacks, is up for consideration. The authorization legally underpins the war effort in Afghanistan and detention of terror suspects at Guantánamo Bay, Cuba. But with the death of bin Laden and capture of others responsible for the 9/11 attacks, experts say the war resolution will need congressional updating. That process will allow lawmakers to craft a long-term framework for any continued military and counterterrorism actions. [75]

Changes on the Ground

There are only a few dozen al-Qaida operatives, at most, in Afghanistan, according to the CIA. [76] But numbers are only one measure of al-Qaida's strength: There were only 200 sworn members of the group when key operatives met in the German city of Hamburg to plan the 2001 attacks on the World Trade Center and Pentagon.

Most troubling for Washington is the weak, U.S.-backed government of President Hamid Karzai in Kabul. It is widely viewed as corrupt and dysfunctional, and many Afghans see it as illegitimate. [77] "The Vietnam War showed us that we shouldn't prop up corrupt governments, and that's what we've got in Afghanistan," said former Democratic National Committee Chairman. Howard Dean. [78]

Dean, who rallied Democratic support as an anti-war presidential candidate in 2004, initially had supported the Obama administration's surge last year of 30,000 additional troops in Afghanistan, but no longer. Republicans, too, are questioning the continued

importance of the war. Rep. Jason Chaffetz, a freshman Republican from Utah, bucked his party and twice voted in the House to force the Obama administration to detail a withdrawal plan. "I believe that it is time to bring our troops home," Chaffetz proclaimed on his website. [79]

Sen. Richard Lugar, R-Ind., the senior Republican on the influential Foreign Relations Committee, is even blunter in his criticism of the war effort. "Nearly a decade later, with al-Qaida largely displaced from the country but franchised in other locations, Afghanistan does not carry a strategic value that justifies 100,000 American troops and a $100 billion a year cost, especially given current fiscal restraints in the United States," Lugar said in May. [80]

Just days after the raid on bin Laden's compound, a bipartisan group of House members wrote a letter to Obama urging that the Afghan mission be recalibrated. "We believe it is no longer the best way to defend America against terror attacks, and we urge you to withdraw all troops from Afghanistan that are not crucial to the immediate national security objective of combating al-Qaida," the lawmakers said. [81]

But other members of Congress have said it would be reasonable to stay the course well into 2014. "A precipitous withdrawal from Afghanistan would be a mistake, and I, for one, would take that option off the table," Democratic Sen. John Kerry, chairman of the Foreign Relations Committee, said in mid-May. [82]

End Game

Many Americans outside Washington are calling for a new direction in Afghanistan. In a *Washington Post/ABC News* poll conducted in March, 64 percent of respondents said the war was no longer worth the cost, though there was nearly an even split on the question of how well things were going. [83]

"For a decade, this country has expended an inordinate amount of its resources, not to mention the more than 1,500 soldiers killed, to fight a war in Afghanistan that never promised to yield comparable strategic results," argued an editorial in the *Philadelphia Inquirer* days after the Navy Seals' raid. "With bin Laden's death, this nation has an opportunity to take emotionalism and politics out of the equation and make some rational decisions about U.S. strategic interests in South Asia, and how best to achieve them." [84]

For the U.S. military, which bears the brunt of the burden in the Afghan War, 10 years of combat in the region have taken an emotional toll as well. The latest survey of military morale found it to be the lowest in five years, even as the intensity of the fighting has spiked to levels comparable to combat in Iraq in 2006-07. Many soldiers have served three or more deployments, and half of the respondents said they had killed enemy fighters, a crucial psychological event for a combat veteran. [85] And the costs are not limited to members of the military and their families: The $110 billion price for the war consumes $1 of every $7 the nation spends on defense. [86]

One of NATO's primary goals in Afghanistan has been to bolster the Afghan national army, seen as crucial for lasting stability and a prerequisite for U.S. troop withdrawal. The Afghan army is on track to meet its growth target of 171,000 troops by October 2011. It's currently short of that goal by about 10,000 soldiers. But desertion rates are high, and there is a severe shortage of officers. What's more, 86 percent of enlisted men are illiterate, and drug abuse is rampant. [87]

Combat Continues

Since the surge in U.S. forces into Afghanistan last year, the strategy has involved both repositioning soldiers to better protect population centers and drastically boosting aerial bombardment, often using the CIA's unmanned aerial drones to target enemy fighters. The two-pronged approach was developed by Gen. David Petraeus, the commander of U.S. Forces in Afghanistan, who is expected to take over as CIA chief in September. [88]

The drone campaign has been crucial in "taking the fight to the enemy," as military officials like to say. Bill Roggio, a military analyst and editor of *The Long War Journal* who has studied the secretive campaign, has kept a running tally of drone strikes, which rose to 117 in 2010, compared with 35 in 2008. There have been 22 reported strikes during the first four months of 2011. In May, on the eve of the summer battle season, NATO announced that the Taliban and other insurgents in Kabul had been "weakened" by both the increase in the number of troops on the ground and an uptick in airstrikes.

But because the drone campaign is classified, no full public accounting has been provided of the targets and success rates for the strikes, including how many civilians have been killed and the number and nature of militants' deaths. Roggio argues that international fighters and terrorist leaders are targeted, but Gilles Dorronsoro, a visiting scholar at the Carnegie Endowment for International Peace, says the drone campaign is problematic. "Now, we're seeing drone airstrikes against low-level foot soldiers and more civilian casualties," he says. "Is it working to use drones to break the back of the Taliban? No."

Airstrikes in the tribal regions alone have not forced the Taliban to the negotiating table, nor have they broken their will to fight on. Moreover, the high number of civilian casualties has made the U.S. war against terrorist groups wildly unpopular in Pakistan. But the death of Osama bin Laden might be the break that many people have been hoping for. Afghanistan's ambassador to Washington said that the demise of the world's most wanted terrorist "created the hope for leadership of the Taliban to join the reconciliation and reintegration process." [89]

In addition, Pakistani security officials announced a new operation to sweep through Quetta, long thought to be the home of the Taliban's government in exile, to make sure that one-eyed Taliban chief Mullah Mohammed Omar and Ayman al-Zawahiri, formerly bin Laden's second in command, aren't also hiding in Pakistan.

NOTES

1. Chris Brummitt, "Afghan firefight shows challenge for U.S. troops," The Associated Press, June 21, 2009, http://news.yahoo.com/s/ap/20090621/ap_on_re_as/as_afghan_taking_on_the_taliban.

2. Laura King, "6 U.S. troops killed in Afghanistan," *Los Angeles Times*, Aug. 3, 2009, www.latimes.com/news/nationworld/world/la-fg-afghan-deaths3-2009aug03,0,3594308.story.

3. For background, see Robert Kiener, "Crisis in Pakistan," *CQ Global Researcher*, December 2008, pp. 321-348, and Roland Flamini, "Afghanistan on the Brink," *CQ Global Researcher*, June 2007, pp. 125-150.

4. "Remarks by the President on a New Strategy for Afghanistan and Pakistan," White House, March 27, 2009, www.whitehouse.gov.

5. See www.boston.com/news/nation/washington/articles/2009/07/23/obama_victory_not_right_word_for_afghanistan/.

6. For background, see Roland Flamini, "Future of NATO," *CQ Global Researcher*, January 2009, pp. 1-26.

7. Pamela Constable, "For Karzai, Stumbles On Road To Election," *The Washington Post*, July 13, 2009, www.washingtonpost.com/wp-dyn/content/article/2009/07/12/AR2009071202426.html.

8. See, for example, Fred Kaplan, "Counterinsur gen-terrorism," *Slate*, March 27, 2009, www.slate.com/id/2214726/.

9. Ann Scott Tyson, "New Approach to Afghanistan Likely," *The Washington Post*, June 3, 2009, www.washingtonpost.com/wp-dyn/content/article/2009/06/02/AR2009060203828.html.

10. *Ibid.*

11. Sharon Otterman, "Civilian death toll rises in Afghanistan," *The New York Times*, Aug. 1, 2009, www.nytimes.com/2009/08/01/world/asia/01afghan.html?scp=1&sq=civilian%20death%20toll%20rises&st=cse.

12. White House, *op. cit.*

13. See also John Mueller, "How Dangerous Are the Taliban?" *foreignaffairs.com*, April 15, 2009, www.foreignaffairs.com/articles/64932/john-mueller/how-dangerous-are-the-taliban.

14. Matthew Kaminski, "Holbrooke of South Asia," *The Wall Street Journal*, April 11, 2009.

15. Quoted in Rajiv Chandrasekaran, "Marines Deploy on Major Mission," *The Washington Post*, July 2, 2009, www.washingtonpost.com/wp-dyn/content/article/2009/07/01/AR2009070103202.html.

16. Jared Allen and Roxana Tiron, "Obey warns Afghanistan funding may slow unless significant progress made," *The Hill*, May 4, 2009, http://thehill.com/leading-the-news/obey-warns-afghanistan-funding-may-slow-unless-significant-progress-made-2009-05-04.html.

17. *The New York Times*/CBS News Poll, June 12-16, 2009, http://graphics8.nytimes.com/packages/images/nytint/docs/latest-new-york-times-cbs-news-poll/original.pdf.

18. See Dexter Filkins, "Afghan corruption: Everything for Sale," *The New York Times*, Jan. 2, 2009, www.nytimes.com/2009/01/02/world/asia/02iht-corrupt.1.19050534html?scp=2&sq=everything%20for%20sale&st=cse.

19. See Malou Innocent, "Obama's Mumbai problem," *The Guardian*, Jan. 27, 2009, www.guardian.co.uk/commentisfree/cifamerica/2009/jan/27/obama-india-pakistan-relations.

20. Peter Bergen, "Winning the Good War," *Washington Monthly*, July/August 2009, www.washington-monthly.com/features/2009/0907.bergen.html#Byline.

21. Greg Bruno, "U.S. Needs a Stronger Commitment to Improving Afghan Governance," Council on Foreign Relations, July 30, 2009, www.cfr.org/publication/19936/us_needs_a_stronger_commitment_to_improving_afghan_governance.html?breadcrumb=%2Fpublication%2Fpublication_list%3Ftype%3D interview.

22. Anthony H. Cordesman, "The Afghanistan Campaign: Can We Win?" Center for Strategic and International Studies, July 22, 2009. Cordesman expands on his ideas in a paper available at http://csis.org/files/publication/090722_CanWeAchieveMission.pdf.

23. Richard A. Oppel Jr., "Allied Officers Concerned by Lack of Afghan Forces," *The New York Times*, July 8, 2009, www.nytimes.com/2009/07/08/world/asia/08afghan.html?ref=world.

24. Quoted in Associated Press, "Marines: More Afghan Soldiers Needed in Helmand," CBS News, July 8, 2009, www.cbsnews.com/stories/2009/07/08/ap/politics/main5145174.shtml.

25. Quoted in Oppel, *op. cit.*

26. Transcript, "Death Toll Mounts as Coalition Forces Confront Taliban," "The NewsHour with Jim Lehrer," PBS, July 15, 2009, www.pbs.org/newshour/bb/military/july-dec09/afghancas_07-15.html.

27. Bob Woodward, "Key in Afghanistan: Economy, Not Military," *The Washington Post*, July 1, 2009, www.washingtonpost.com/wp-dyn/content/article/2009/06/30/AR2009063002811.html.

28. *Ibid.*

29. "Face the Nation," CBS News, July 5, 2009.

30. Greg Jaffe and Karen De Young, "U.S. General Sees Afghan Army, Police Insufficient," *The Washington Post*, July 11, 2009, www.washingtonpost.com/wp-dyn/content/article/2009/07/10/AR20090710 02975 .html.

31. Greg Jaffe, "U.S. Troops Erred in Airstrikes on Civilians," *The Washington Post*, June 20, 2009, www.washingtonpost.com/wp-dyn/content/article/2009/06/19/AR2009061903359.html.

32. Quoted in Robert Burns, "Analysis: reducing Afghan civilian deaths key goal," The Associated Press, June 13, 2009, www.google.com/hostednews/ap/article/eqM5hyNJNBigtMGe2M12B2s3w6OCoAbQD98 Q2VP80.

33. Bergen, *op. cit.*

34. Helene Cooper and Sheryl Gay Stolberg, "Obama Ponders Outreach to Elements of Taliban," *The New York Times*, March 8, 2009, www.nytimes .com/2009/03/08/us/politics/08obama.html?scp= 1&sq=obama %20ponders%20outreach%20to%20 elements%20of%20taliban&st=cse.

35. Quoted in *ibid.*

36. Fotini Christia and Michael Semple, "Flipping the Taliban: How to Win in Afghanistan," *Foreign Affairs*, July/August 2009, p. 34, www.foreignaffairs .com/articles/65151/fotini-christia-and-michael-semple/flipping-the-taliban. Co-author Semple, who has significant background in holding dialogues with the Taliban, was expelled from Afghanistan in 2007 by the Karzai government amid accusations he and another diplomat held unauthorized talks with the Taliban.

37. See, "Background Note: Afghanistan," U.S. Department of State, November 2008, www.state.gov/r/pa/ei/bgn/5380.htm; also, *Grolier Encyclopedia of Knowledge*, Vol. 1, 1991. See also Kenneth Jost, "Rebuilding Afghanistan," *CQ Researcher*, Dec. 21, 2001, pp. 1041-1064.

38. Ahmed Rashid, *Descent into Chaos* (2008), p. 8.

39. *Ibid.*

40. Barry Bearak, "Mohammad Zahir Shah, Last Afghan King, Dies at 92," *The New York Times*, July 24, 2007, www.nytimes.com/2007/07/24/world/asia/24 shah.html.

41. U.S. State Department, *op. cit.*

42. *Ibid.*

43. *Ibid.*

44. Rashid, *op. cit.*, p. 11.

45. Barnett R. Rubin, "The Transformation of the Afghan State," in J. Alexander Thier, ed., *The Future of Afghanistan* (2009), p. 15.

46. Rashid, *op. cit.*, pp. 12-13.

47. *Ibid.*, p. 13.

48. Seth G. Jones, "The Rise of Afghanistan's Insurgency," *International Security*, Vol. 32, No. 4, spring 2008, p. 19.

49. Rashid, *op. cit.*, p. 15.

50. Jones, *op. cit.*, p. 20.

51. *Ibid.* The reference to "the urban elite" comes from "Afghanistan: State Building, Sustaining Growth, and Reducing Poverty," World Bank Report No. 29551-AF, 2005, p. xxvi.

52. *Ibid.*, pp. 20, 22.

53. *Ibid.*, p. 24.

54. *Ibid.*, p. 25.

55. Dexter Filkins, "Right at the Edge," *The New York Times*, Sept. 7, 2008, www.nytimes.com/2008/09/07/magazine/07pakistan-t.html.

56. "Bob Gates, America's Secretary of War," "60 Minutes," May 17, 2009, www.cbsnews.com/stories/2009/05/14/60minutes/main5014588.shtml.

57. White House, *op. cit.*

58. Michael O'Hanlon, "We Might still Need More Troops In Afghanistan," *Washington Examiner*, July 7, 2009, www.washingtonexaminer.com/politics/50044002 .html.

59. Michael Evans and David Charter, "Barack Obama fails to win NATO troops he wants for Afghanistan," *Timesonline*, April 4, 2009, www.timesonline.co.uk/tol/news/world/us_and_americas/article6032342 .ece.

60. Victoria Burnett and Rachel Donadio, "Spain Is Open to Bolstering Forces in Afghanistan," *The New York Times*, July 30, 2009, www.nytimes .com/2009/ 07/30/world/europe/30zapatero.html ?ref=world.

61. Steven Erlanger, "NATO Reorganizes Afghan Command Structure," *The New York Times*, Aug. 4, 2009, www.nytimes.com/2009/08/05/world/05nato .html.

62. Thomas Harding, "New NATO head calls for 'international effort' in Afghanistan," *Telegraph*, Aug. 3, 2009, www.telegraph.co.uk/news/worldnews/asia/ afghanistan/5967377/New-Nato-head-calls-for-international-effort-in-Afghanistan.html.

63. "Afghanistan and Pakistan: A Status Report," Brookings Institution, June 8, 2009, www.brook ings.edu/~/media/Files/events/2009/0608_afghani stan_pakistan/20090608_afghanistan_pakistan .pdf.

64. "Taliban pushed back, long way to go: Obama," Reuters, July 12, 2009, www.reuters.com/article/ topNews/idUSTRE56A2Q420090712?feedType=R SS&feedName=topNews&rpc=22&sp=true.

65. Quoted in Dan Robinson, "U.S. Lawmakers Reject Amendment Calling for an Exit Strategy from Afghanistan," VOA News, June 26, 2009, www .voanews.com/english/2009-06-26-voa1.cfm.

66. Quoted in *ibid*.

67. John Aloysius Farrell, "Kerry: 'We are going to take a hard look at Afghanistan,' " *GlobalPost*, updated July 10, 2009, www.globalpost.com.

68. Pamela Constable, "Karzai's Challengers Face Daunting Odds," *The Washington Post*, July 6, 2009, p. 7A.

69. John F. Burns, "Criticism of Afghan War Is on the Rise in Britain," *The New York Times*, July 12, 2009, www .nytimes.com/2009/07/12/world/europe/12britain .html?scp=1&sq=criticism%20of%20afghan%20 war%20is%20on%20the%20rise&st=cse.

70. James Risen, "U.S. Inaction Seen After Taliban P.O.W.'s Died," *The New York Times*, July 11, 2009, www.nytimes.com/2009/07/11/world/asia/11afghan .html?scp=1&sq=U.S.%20Inaction%20Seen%20 After%20Taliban&st=cse.

71. "The Truth About Dasht-i-Leili," *The New York Times*, July 14, 2009, www.nytimes.com/2009/ 07/14/opinion/14tue2html?scp=5&sq=U.S.% 20Inaction%20Seen%20After%20Taliban&st=cse.

72. Julian Barnes and Adam Entous, "Military Draws Up Afghan Exit Plan," *The Wall Street Journal*, May 10, 2011.

73. "Glimmers of hope; it's been a long slog, but Afghanistan may at last be able to contemplate more stable government," *The Economist*, May 12, 2011.

74. Statement of Richard Haass before the Senate Committee on Foreign Relations, May 3, 2011, http://i.cfr.org/content/publications/attachments/ Testimony.Haass.SFRC.5.3.2011.pdf.

75. Josh Gerstein, "GOP seeks to redefine the war on terror," *Politico*, May 10, 2011.

76. Felicia Sonmez, "Panetta: Maybe 50 to 100 al Qaeda left in Afghanistan," *The Washington Post*, June 27, 2010.

77. Larry Goodson and Thomas H. Johnson, "Parallels With Past: How Soviets Lost In Afghanistan, How US Is Losing — Analysis," *Eurasia Review*, April 26, 2011.

78. McKay Coppins, "Howard Dean to Obama: Get Out of Afghanistan!" *The Daily Beast*, May 18, 2011, www.thedailybeast.com/blogs-and-stories/ 2011-04-18/howard-dean-to-president-obama-get-our-troops-out-of-afghanistan/?cid=hp:beastorigina lsC1.

79. http://chaffetz.house.gov/legislation/strong-national-defense.shtml.

80. "Indiana Senator calling for troop withdrawal from Afghanistan," FOX News, May 3, 2011, www.fox 59.com/news/wxin-richard-lugar-indiana-sena tor-calling-for-troop-withdrawal-from-afghani stan-20110503,0,3670876.story.

81. Letter to President Obama, http://welch.house.gov/ index.php?option=com_content&view=article &id=1466:welch-and-chaffetz-lead-bipartisan-house-group-urging-obama-to-pull-out-of-afghani-stan-and-recalibrate-anti-terrorismstrategy&ca tid=39:2011-press-releases&Itemid=32.

82. "Key US senators warn against hasty Afghan pull-out," Agence France-Presse, May 10, 2011.

83. "Washington Post-ABC News Poll," March 13, 2011, www.washingtonpost.com/wp-srv/politics/polls/post-poll_03142011.html.

84. "Rethink Afghanistan," *Philadelphia Inquirer*, May 9, 2011, www.philly.com/philly/opinion/121482579 .html.

85. Gregg Zoroya, "Strain on forces in the field at a five-year high," *USA Today*, May 8, 2011.

86. "Prepared Statement of Richard Haass," *op. cit.*

87. C. J. Radin, "Afghan National Army Update May 2011," *The Long War Journal*, May 9, 2011, www .longwarjournal.org/archives/2011/05/afghan_ national_army_4.php.

88. Yochi Dreazen, "National Security Reshuffle has Implications for Afghan War," *National Journal*, April 27, 2011.

89. Ashish Kumar Sen, "Without bin Laden, Taliban may talk peace," *The Washington Times*, May 8, 2011.

BIBLIOGRAPHY

Books

Coll, Steve, *Ghost Wars*, Penguin Press, 2004.
The former *Washington Post* managing editor, now president of the New America Foundation think tank, traces the CIA's involvement in Afghanistan since the Soviet invasion in the 1970s.

Kilcullen, David, *The Accidental Guerrilla*, Oxford University Press, 2009.
A former Australian Army officer and counterterrorism adviser argues that strategists have tended to conflate small insurgencies and broader terror movements.

Peters, Gretchen, *Seeds of Terror*, Thomas Dunne Books, 2009.
A journalist examines the role of Afghanistan's illegal narcotics industry in fueling the activities of the Taliban and al Qaeda.

Rashid, Ahmed, *Descent into Chaos*, Viking, 2008.
A Pakistani journalist argues that "the U.S.-led war on terrorism has left in its wake a far more unstable world than existed on" Sept. 11, 2001.

Wright, Lawrence, *The Looming Tower*, Knopf, 2006.
In a Pulitzer Prize-winning volume that remains a must-read for students of the wars in Afghanistan and Iraq, a *New Yorker* staff writer charts the spread of Islamic fundamentalism and emergence of al Qaeda that gave rise to the Sept. 11 attacks.

Articles

Bergen, Peter, "Winning the Good War," *Washington Monthly*, July/August 2009, www.washingtonmonthly .com/features/2009/0907.bergen.html.
A senior fellow at the New America Foundation argues that skepticism about the Obama administration's chances of victory in Afghanistan are based on a misreading of that nation's history and people.

Christia, Fotini, and Michael Semple, "Flipping the Taliban," *Foreign Affairs*, July/August 2009.
A political scientist (Christia) and a specialist on Afghanistan and Pakistan who has talked with the Taliban argue that while more troops are necessary, "the move will have a lasting impact only if it is accompanied by a political 'surge'" aimed at persuading large groups of Taliban fighters to lay down arms.

Hogan, Michael, "Milt Bearden: Afghanistan Is 'Obama's War,'" *Vanityfair.com*, Feb. 5, 2009, www.vanityfair .com/online/politics/2009/02/milt-bearden-afghani stan-is-obamas-war.html.
Bearden, the former CIA field officer in Afghanistan when U.S. covert action helped expel the Soviet Union, says in this Q&A that "the only thing that is absolutely certain about this war is that it's going to be Obama's war, just as Iraq will be Bush's war."

Jones, Seth G., "The Rise of Afghanistan's Insurgency," *International Security*, Vol. 32, No. 4, spring 2008, http://belfercenter.ksg.harvard.edu/files/IS3204_ pp007-040_Jones.pdf.
A RAND Corporation political scientist analyzes the reasons a violent insurgency began to develop in Afghanistan earlier this decade.

Mueller, John, "How Dangerous Are the Taliban?" *Foreignaffairs.com*, April 15, 2009, www.foreignaffairs. com/articles/64932/john-mueller/how-dangerous-are-the-taliban.
An Ohio State University political science professor questions whether the Taliban and al Qaeda are a big

enough menace to the United States to make a long war in Afghanistan worth the cost.

Riedel, Bruce, "Comparing the U.S. and Soviet Experiences in Afghanistan," *CTC Sentinel*, **Combating Terrorism Center, May 2009, www.brookings.edu/~/ media/Files/rc/articles/2009/05_afghanistan_riedel/05_ afghanistan_riedel.pdf.**
A Brookings Institution scholar and former senior adviser to President Barack Obama examines the "fundamental differences" between the Soviet and U.S. experiences in the region.

Rosenberg, Matthew, and Zahid Hussain, "Pakistan Taps Tribes' Anger with Taliban," *The Wall Street Journal*, **June 6-7, 2009, p. A14.**
Pakistani anger at the Taliban in tribal regions bordering Afghanistan is growing, and Pakistan's military leaders hope to capitalize on that anger as they mount a grueling campaign against insurgents in North and South Waziristan.

Reports and Studies

Campbell, Jason, Michael O'Hanlon and Jeremy Shapiro, "Assessing Counterinsurgency and Stabilization Missions," Brookings Institution, Policy Paper No. 14, May 2009, www.brookings.edu/~/media/Files/rc/ papers/2009/05_counterinsurgency_ohanlon/05_coun terinsurgency_ohanlon.pdf.
Brookings scholars examine the status of change in Afghanistan and Iraq and explain why "2009 is expected by many to be a pivotal year in Afghanistan."

Tellis, Ashley J., "Reconciling With the Taliban?" Carnegie Endowment for International Peace, 2009, www.carnegieendowment.org/files/reconciling_with_ taliban.pdf.
Efforts at reconciliation today would undermine American credibility and jeopardize the success of the U.S.-led mission in Afghanistan, argues a senior associate at the endowment.

For More Information

American Foreign Policy Council, 509 C St., N.E., Washington, DC 20002; (202) 543-1006; www.afpc.org. Provides analysis on foreign-policy issues.

Brookings Institution, 1775 Massachusetts Ave., N.W., Washington, DC 20036; (202) 797-6000; www.brookings .edu. Liberal-oriented think tank that provides research, data and other resources on security and political conditions in Afghanistan and Pakistan and global counterterrorism.

Cato Institute, 1000 Massachusetts Ave., N.W., Washington, DC 20001; (202) 842-0200; www.cato.org. Libertarian-oriented think tank that provides analysis on U.S. policy toward Afghanistan and Pakistan.

RAND Corp., 1776 Main St., Santa Monica, CA 90401; (310) 393-0411; www.rand.org. Research organization that studies domestic and international policy issues.

United Nations Office on Drugs and Crime, U.N. Headquarters, DC1 Building, Room 613, One United Nations Plaza, New York, NY 10017; (212) 963-5698; www.unodc .org. Helps member states fight illicit drugs, crime and terrorism; compiles data on opium poppy production.

United States Institute of Peace, 1200 17th St., N.W., Washington, DC 20036; (202) 457-1700; www.usip.org. Provides analysis, training and other resources to prevent and end conflicts.